More Praise for *Fundamentals of Performance Improvement*

"Succeeding today requires constant adaptation to the changing environment as well as the ability to identify and remove the barriers that confront our best employees. Van Tiem, Moseley, and Dessinger have assembled a comprehensive, easy-to-read, step-by-step guide with fantastic case studies, tools, and references to help everyone succeed in this challenging environment. A must have for everyone's professional library!"

Matthew Peters, CPT, Vice Deputy Director for Human Capital,
Defense Intelligence Agency

"This is more than a third edition, it is a new book and it is simply the most complete and comprehensive resource available . . . a 'tour de force.'"

Roger Kaufman, CPT, Ph.D., Professor Emeritus, Florida State University,
Distinguished Research Professor, Sonora (Mexico) Institute of Technology

"*Fundamentals of Performance Improvement* is destined to become THE desk reference for all performance improvement professionals. The case studies provided link the detailed content directly to the four principles of the Performance Technology Standards from the International Society for Performance Improvement."

Guy W. Wallace, CPT, President, EPPIC, Inc.

"You can classify books into a 2 × 2 matrix. There are thousands of examples of books of low practicality and low scholarship, high practicality and low scholarship, low practicality and high scholarship. *Fundamentals of Performance Improvement* is a rare example that falls into combination of high practicality and high scholarship. What makes the book unique is that it explains universal principles to an international audience."

Sivasailam "Thiagi" Thiagarajan, Ph.D., The Thiagi Group

"The third edition of *Fundamentals of Performance Improvement* equips the manager or performance improvement professional with the knowledge and tools necessary to improve workplace performance. It is truly a major upgrade from the first two editions with greatly enhanced models and forty new interventions."

Roger Chevalier, Ph.D., CPT, *A Manager's Guide to Improving Workplace Performance*

"A critical issue for institutional capacity-building in transitioning societies is finding ways to promote sustainable improved performance. USAID has promoted the use of human performance technology in support of improved institutional results for over a decade. This text is extremely valuable laying out a comprehensive framework for applying the principles and techniques across a wide spectrum of organizations."

Lawrence Held, Acting Mission Director, USAID Kyrgyzstan

"HPT has come into its own as a profession, with an emphasis on a framework of systematic and systemic thinking that frames and coordinates relevant models and interventions. This book is a fully contemporary synthesis of this framework. The detailed discussions of major models, coupled with the illustrative case studies, add valuable depth to the discussion. The examination of future directions will stimulate thought and discussion. This volume merits a prominent position on every HPT professional's bookshelf. Experienced practitioners will find the book to be useful in organizing and updating their knowledge of HPT. Those new to the field will use the book as an excellent starting point in their development of professional expertise."

Rob Foshay, Ph.D., CPT, The Foshay Group

"This book is a highly valuable resource about the theory and practice of performance improvement and its results in a wide array of organizations, industries, and levels—from individual to organizational to societal performance. Researchers, performance consultants, managers, and entrepreneurs will find in it ideas and methods tested by experience."

Mariano Bernardez, Ph.D., CPT, Director, Performance Improvement Institute

"*Fundamentals of Performance Improvement* is a comprehensive handbook with useful tools for performance improvement. It allows educators to work with stakeholders to apply a positive, systemic approach to school reform and transformation necessary to meet 21st century skills."

Dr. Phyllis Edwards, Superintendent,
City Schools of Decatur, Georgia

"Improvement of performance is a great priority of firms in Central Europe. The traditional human resource function is slowly transitioning into a real performance partner for the innovative executive. This book provides a superb reference for any professional seeking to build a strong foundation for improved company results based on high-quality performance of employees."

Jake Slegers, Executive Director, American
Chamber of Commerce in Slovakia

"I recommend this book to anyone who is interested in improving people, process, and results. It provides a comprehensive coverage of the entire performance technology field and will appeal to those who are new to the field, as well as experienced practitioners, through its clear explanation of performance technology concepts and models, the inclusion of helpful tools and techniques, and excellent case studies that illustrate performance technology in action. Its international flavor, with practitioner comments and examples drawn from across the world, enhances its appeal, as more and more professionals operate in an increasingly global context."

Daljit Singh, Asia Pacific Director of Talent Management,
Baker & McKenzie, Sydney, Australia

FUNDAMENTALS OF PERFORMANCE IMPROVEMENT

About Pfeiffer

Pfeiffer serves the professional development and hands-on resource needs of training and human resource practitioners and gives them products to do their jobs better. We deliver proven ideas and solutions from experts in HR development and HR management, and we offer effective and customizable tools to improve workplace performance. From novice to seasoned professional, Pfeiffer is the source you can trust to make yourself and your organization more successful.

Essential Knowledge Pfeiffer produces insightful, practical, and comprehensive materials on topics that matter the most to training and HR professionals. Our Essential Knowledge resources translate the expertise of seasoned professionals into practical, how-to guidance on critical workplace issues and problems. These resources are supported by case studies, worksheets, and job aids and are frequently supplemented with CD-ROMs, websites, and other means of making the content easier to read, understand, and use.

Essential Tools Pfeiffer's Essential Tools resources save time and expense by offering proven, ready-to-use materials—including exercises, activities, games, instruments, and assessments—for use during a training or team-learning event. These resources are frequently offered in looseleaf or CD-ROM format to facilitate copying and customization of the material.

Pfeiffer also recognizes the remarkable power of new technologies in expanding the reach and effectiveness of training. While e-hype has often created whizbang solutions in search of a problem, we are dedicated to bringing convenience and enhancements to proven training solutions. All our e-tools comply with rigorous functionality standards. The most appropriate technology wrapped around essential content yields the perfect solution for today's on-the-go trainers and human resource professionals.

Pfeiffer
www.pfeiffer.com

Essential resources for training and HR professionals

About ISPI

The International Society for Performance Improvement (ISPI) is dedicated to improving individual, organizational, and societal performance. Founded in 1962, ISPI is the leading international association dedicated to improving productivity and performance in the workplace. ISPI represents more than 10,000 international and chapter members throughout the United States, Canada, and forty other countries. The society reaches out to more than 20,000 performance improvement professionals through publications and educational programs.

ISPI's mission is to develop and recognize the proficiency of our members and advocate the use of Human Performance Technology. This systematic approach to improving productivity and competence uses a set of methods and procedures and a strategy for solving problems for realizing opportunities related to the performance of people. It is a systematic combination of performance analysis, cause analysis, intervention design and development, implementation, and evaluation that can be applied to individuals, small groups, and large organizations.

Website: www.ispi.org
Mail: International Society for Performance Improvement
1400 Spring Street, Suite 260
Silver Spring, Maryland 20910 USA
Phone: 1.301.587.8570
Fax: 1.301.587.8573
E-mail: info@ispi.org

International Society for Performance Improvement

WHERE KNOWLEDGE
BECOMES KNOW-HOW

With deep appreciation, we dedicate this book to those who have already contributed to our field and the emerging professionals who are innovating and providing new insights.

Our field is unique because it is possible to pinpoint the date and time of its origin. We fundamentally began in New Orleans in the early 1960s. Our origin was composed of those committed to applied behavioral science and programmed instruction. Our field advanced to performance improvement when programmed instruction and behavioral approaches alone did not resolve educational and workplace issues. Many scholar/practitioners have contributed their powers of observation, reflection, research, and practice to advance the field.

We also dedicate this book to experts beyond the performance improvement field because resolving workplace problems includes theory and practice from related fields such as instructional design, psychology, communications, industrial engineering, ergonomics, quality, communications, and finance to name a few.

To the International Society of Performance Improvement and to my students and graduates at the University of Michigan–Dearborn and Capella University. Our world is better because of them.
—*Darlene M. Van Tiem*

To my graduate students in performance improvement and evaluation for professional success and career happiness.
James L. Moseley

To our readers—you are the ones who will make performance improvement happen.
Joan Conway Dessinger

FUNDAMENTALS OF PERFORMANCE IMPROVEMENT

Optimizing Results Through People, Process, and Organizations

THIRD EDITION

Interventions, Performance Support Tools, Case Studies

Darlene M. Van Tiem
James L. Moseley
Joan C. Dessinger

Pfeiffer
A Wiley Imprint
www.pfeiffer.com

Library of Congress and CIP data
Van Tiem, Darlene M.
    Fundamentals of performance improvement : optimizing results through people, process, and organizations / Darlene Van Tiem, James L. Moseley, Joan C. Dessinger.—Third edition.
        pages cm
    "The third edition of Fundamentals of Performance Improvement began as a project to revise Fundamentals of Performance Technology and Performance Improvement Interventions and combine them into one book. However, performance improvement is advancing rapidly and our task . . . became updating the contents of both books"—Acknowledgments.
    Includes bibliographical references and indexes.
    ISBN 978-1-118-02524-6 (pbk.); ISBN 978-1-118-22204-1 (ebk.); ISBN 978-1-118-23574-4 (ebk.);
    ISBN 978-1-118-26071-5 (ebk.)
    1. Performance technology. 2. Performance. 3. Personnel management. I. Moseley, James L. (James Lee), 1942– II. Dessinger, Joan Conway. III. Van Tiem, Darlene M. Fundamentals of performance technology. IV. Van Tiem, Darlene M. Performance improvement interventions. V. Title.
HF5549.5.P37V35   2012
658.3'128—dc23

2012000871

Acquiring Editor:	Matthew Davis
Editorial Assistant:	Michael Zelenko
Director of Development:	Kathleen Dolan Davies
Developmental Editor:	Susan Rachmeler
Production Editor:	Michael Kay
Editor:	Rebecca Taff
Manufacturing Supervisor:	Becky Morgan
Cover Design:	Charlotte Martin and Jeff Puda

THIRD EDITION
Printing   10 9 8 7 6 5 4 3 2 1

Contents

List of Figures

List of Tables

List of Exhibits

List of Case Studies

List of Performance Support Tools

Acknowledgments

"Writing a book is an adventure; to begin with, it is a toy and an amusement, then it becomes a master, and then it becomes a tyrant; and the last phase is just as you are about to be reconciled to your servitude—you kill the monster and fling it—to the public."

Sir Winston Churchill

The third edition of *Fundamentals of Performance Improvement* began as a project to revise *Fundamentals of Performance Technology* and *Performance Improvement Interventions* and combine them into one book. However, performance improvement is advancing rapidly and our task—a daunting one—became rewriting the contents of both books.

Our field has shifted from focusing on people and processes within the workplace and military to including organizations and society. In this new book, we have moved well beyond the traditional settings to educational institutions, governmental agencies, healthcare, under-developed countries, non-profits, small businesses, and many more. Another change is the use of new and more business- and organization-oriented terminology in this edition. Since our practice is increasingly global, this edition also includes case studies, practitioner comments, and extensive examples from the Slovak Republic, Saudi Arabia, England, Ghana, Canada, Turkey, and the United States of America.

We were only able to accomplish this with a lot of help from our friends and colleagues. The lists of Case Studies and Exhibits acknowledge many individual contributors from the field. However, several colleagues made multiple content contributions, and we want to give them a special acknowledgement.

The colleagues who field tested the updated model included three ISPI international board members—Judith Hale, ibstpi Fellow and 2011–2012 ISPI president; Steven J. Kelly, partner, KNO Worldwide, Bratislava and Prague, Europe, and ISPI board of directors; and Lisa Toenniges, chief executive officer, Innovative Learning Group, Michigan, ISPI treasurer, and recently elected ISPI president-elect—plus Mary Jo Bastuba, senior national field manager, Nintendo/NMi, California; and Eileen Banchoff, president, Banchoff Associates, Michigan. Steven Kelly and Lisa Toenniges also provided examples and a case study.

Judith also field tested the model, wrote a foreword, and was the subject-matter expert on certified performance technology, certified school improvement specialist, and code of ethics. Roger Addison, performance architect, Addison Consulting, California, furnished considerable detail about the origins of performance improvement. Roger Kaufman, professor emeritus, Florida State University, and distinguished research professor, Sonora (Mexico) Institute of Technology, provided us with his latest organizational elements model (OEM) and an international case study. Robert Mager supplied us with an interview and updated performance analysis flowchart model. Bonnie Beresford, vice president of client services at Capital Analytics, Michigan, contributed a case study and helped us navigate the use of predictive analytics for evaluating impact. Ann Chow, instructional technology administrator, Alexandria Community Schools Corporation, Indiana; Karen E. Hicks, doctoral applicant, Wayne State University; and the graduate students from Wayne State University's Instructional Technology 7320 class, Spring 2011, provided content expertise.

Humor often conveys insight that is not possible from words alone. Cartoons contributed by Jed Vier and his partner Buck Jones were originally published as a daily feature on the American Greetings website (www.americangreeetings.com).

A book is content presented to align with reader interests. In addition, a book is produced by the hard work of editors, computer experts, and publishing professionals. Not only was Joan Dessinger a co-author, she also was our internal editor. Joy Wilkins created most of the tables, figures, and graphics with patience and persistence; she was creative and has an eye for the value of the visual. In addition, Anne M. Blake, director of strategic planning, The Blake Company, Michigan, and Branden Mack, master's applicant, Wayne State University, assisted in manuscript preparation and computer expertise. William Scott Pitts, director, State and Federal Grants, Chippewa Valley Schools, Michigan, furnished editorial expertise.

In addition, books are dependent upon publishers. We are particularly grateful for the confidence expressed by April Syring Davis, executive director of the International Society of Performance Improvement and by Matthew C. Davis, acquisitions editor of Pfeiffer. As the field advanced, they recognized the value of connecting fresh thinking with new professional applications. We also appreciate the support of John Chen, ISPI's past publications/project manager. Michael Kay, senior production editor, Rebecca Taff, editor, and Michael Zelenko, Pfeiffer editorial assistant, added their magic touches, making everything pleasant to read and artful, even though this book may be classified as "technical scientific professional literature."

A sincere thanks to all the others who offered suggestions or advice, wrote comments, and in any other way contributed to this book and the well-being of the authors as they wrote the book. And last, but not least, we acknowledge the comments and recommendations of readers of previous editions regarding new ideas to include and new processes or procedures to describe. We hope when you read this book you recognize that we were listening!

Darlene Van Tiem, Jim Moseley,
and Joan Dessinger

Foreword—The Practice of Performance Improvement

Fundamentals of Performance Improvement captures the full scope of the profession of performance improvement. The book has been a long time in coming and will be a valuable resource to both academic programs and practitioners.

The practice of performance improvement has finally reached a level of maturity where it can be described in a way that others can understand it as a profession, not just an assembly of interventions and models. It has also matured to the point at which practitioners are less predisposed to advocating single or simplistic solutions, such as training, performance support, process reengineering, or hardware and software systems to solve complex social economic organizational problems. Previous attempts at describing the essence of performance improvement have struggled with the tension between the technical demands required to adequately analyze the workplace to identify specific interventions, the conceptual demands required to fully comprehend the complex combination of variables that contribute to organizations' under-performance or poor performance, and the bias that comes with a predisposition of focus on people or jobs instead of the workplace as a whole. Previous books have also struggled with how to describe performance improvement as a practice that embraces organizations as dynamic systems that are constantly in response to external economic and internal political, social, and technological pressures. Van Tiem, Moseley, and Dessinger have successfully overcome these challenges.

What is especially laudable about *Fundamentals of Performance Improvement* is that it captures the systemic and systematic aspects of the practice. The authors do not attack the subject through the lens of interventions, models, or inputs-outputs, but have put forth a framework of performance improvement that is a representation of a process that is both elegant and dynamic. They have captured the elements that make up the body of knowledge on which the profession is based and they have explained the research and rationale behind each element.

Fundamentals of Performance Improvement will contribute to the advancement of the profession and the professionalism of its practitioners. It will serve as an excellent textbook for academic programs and a practical reference to those wanting to help organizations be more competitive and socially responsible.

Judith A. Hale, Ph.D., CPT
Ibstpi Fellow
President of Hale Associates

Foreword—Fundamentals of Performance Technology

What are the fundamentals? Fundamentals are the concepts and tools necessary for understanding how to improve workplace performance? Why do some people perform well and others poorly in the workplace? This book provides the answer: People do what they do because that is what they have learned in the workplace!

- If people loaf on the job, they have been taught to do so. How? Perhaps by supervisors or managers making confusing or contradictory demands, discouraging people who are diligently trying to do a good job. Perhaps by learning that doing a good job is ignored, whereas loafing is fun until the boss comes by and screams (and then goes away again). Or perhaps by learning that it is more fun to loaf with peers than to be punished by peers for working hard.
- If people "don't think" on the job, they have been taught not to. How? Perhaps by having their ideas and suggestions ignored. Perhaps by being punished for showing initiative, or asking tough but important questions, or for doing things better (but differently) than the boss wanted.
- If people engage in highly productive teamwork, they have been taught to do so. How? Perhaps by learning how to do work that has been designed for a team. Perhaps by taking part in on-the-job problem-solving teams. Perhaps by being trained in teamwork behaviors that are then supported on the job.

What is performance technology? This book provides an answer: It is "the systematic process of linking business goals and strategies with the workforce responsible for achieving the goals." (The workforce includes everyone: a salesperson, a third-shift setup mechanic, the chief executive officer, the chief financial officer, the receptionist in the human resources department, and everyone else.) Performance technology is a technology for linking people to organizations in mutually beneficial ways. Performance technology is about supporting people's effort to:

- Learn how to perform competently.
- Perform competently.
- Learn how to perform even more competently in the future.

Performance technology is about making sure that the people side of the business works. What makes the financial side of the business work? People. What makes the technical side of the business work? People. Performance technology is about making organizations work by helping people work. Performance technology is about helping people work by creating organizations that support high levels of performance. Performance technology is about installing instructional systems and performance support systems. Performance technology is about establishing win-win relationships between organizations and people.

That's a lot. What is performance technology not about? It is not about a specific type of intervention (such as training, incentive systems, quality improvement, reengineering, cost reduction, or right sizing, and so forth). Performance technology is about improving human performance in the workplace; it is not about specific techniques for improving performance. Performance technology is about making systems work; it is not about making parts of systems work better (whether or not doing so actually helps the organization work better). Performance technology is about wholes, not parts.

The mission of the International Society for Performance Improvement (ISPI) states it clearly: "Improving human performance in systematic and reproducible ways." Performance technology is not about changing light bulbs and hoping performance improves; it is about improving performance in a systematic and reproducible approach.

What is the performance technology approach? This book provides an answer: Practitioners of the field select the right tools for the job and evaluate progress to assure that the tools are doing the job. This book is organized around the flow of performance technology in action. The performance technology flow chart, as shown in many International Society for Performance Improvement publications, was generated a few years ago by Bill Deterline and Marc Rosenberg. It shows that one begins with a performance analysis to find gaps between what is happening now and what should be happening now or in the future. Cause analysis identifies the causes of deficient performance and, at the same time, what is necessary to achieve high levels of performance. After specifying desired performance and identifying the variables that support performance, the next step is to select and design an intervention that will enable people (and organizations) to perform at the levels specified. The next step is the one that takes the most time, resources, and ingenuity: implementing the intervention. Evaluation is the final step only in the flow chart—it is integrated competently. In other words, it shows people how to do performance improvement projects in systematic and reproducible ways! I wish a book like this had been written years ago.

Does the book enable readers to learn everything that they must learn to be highly competent performance technology professionals? No. Readers who use this book well will be the ones who already know a lot about human behavior in the workplace. Perhaps they are managers who have heard about and want to understand and use performance technology. Perhaps they are total quality management professionals looking for new ways to make total quality initiatives succeed a little more often. Perhaps they are human resource development professionals who want to get out of the training box. Perhaps they are graduate students in instructional design who want to make sure their designs add value. The book will be most valuable to people who know a lot about related matters, for example, some of the many interventions used in performance technology.

Does the book provide something that those new to performance technology would benefit by knowing? Yes. It is a handbook for doing performance technology. Stolovitch and Keeps' *Handbook of Human Performance Technology* (2nd ed., 1999) is a handbook about the field that is rich in material for doing. Darlene Van Tiem, James Moseley, and Joan Conway Dessinger have produced a handbook for doing performance technology. I think of them as companion volumes, each valuable in different ways.

Does this book provide anything for experienced professionals? Yes. It is the only book available that takes the reader through the whole performance technology process. It is a journey that experienced professionals take often and, with the help of this book, one they might travel more competently the next time out. It, like Langdon, Whiteside, and McKenna's *Intervention Resource Guide: 50 Performance Improvement Tools* (1999), shows many different interventions performance technology professionals can use. Even experienced professional tend to be competent in using only a few of the interventions and would benefit from learning more about the interventions to be used.

Is this book flawed in any way? Of course. It is flawed in the same way that Deterline and Rosenberg's marvelously useful flow chart is flawed. It shows a systematic process, but it doesn't show the performance technology practitioner how to think systematically. Does that flaw diminish the book's value? Not really. If a practitioner has learned to think systematically, the flow chart is an added tool. If the practitioner hasn't learned to think systematically, the flow chart, used often, will enable her or him to add value while learning why systemic thinking is so important.

Dale Brethower
Professor Emeritus, Psychology, Western Michigan University
Author of *Performance Analysis and Performance-Based Instruction*

Foreword—Performance Improvement Interventions

Performance Improvement Interventions: Enhancing People, Processes, and Organizations Through Performance Technology may just be the only book you will ever need about putting a human performance technology (HPT) organization into action. It covers just about everything. It not only tells in great detail what to do, but it also explains how to do it, then goes on to provide the tools to accomplish it.

The first thing that has to impress you when you begin to delve into this book is the amazing synthesis of information. The authors list all of the sources they used to develop their concept of the HPT Model—from B.F Skinner's theory of human behavior to Douglas McGregor's Theory X and Theory Y. I'm quite certain that when most of these writers contributed to their disciplines, they never imagined that one day they would be adding to the field of HPT.

I was gratified to see that Darlene, Jim, and Joan took the time to explain how all of their sources contributed to HPT theory! Not many books take the time to fully explain the grounding of the discipline. Some of the theories included in their model include human resources, training, organization development, career development, psychology, quality management, ergonomics, and financial systems. A lot of readers will skip over the theory sections of most books because they are "too esoteric." They just want "the facts." Most publishers won't publish books with "too much theory" for fear readers will not buy them. I congratulate both the authors and ISPI for being so perceptive. As W. Edwards Deming, one of the listed theorists, said, "You must understand theory. It is the only thing that allows you to ask the right questions." Not understanding theory is the reason, in my estimation, that HPT efforts often fall short of expectations. Practitioners often miss asking that one important question that leads to a deeper level of understanding of the business issue. Understanding theory would have intuitively led then to ask that question.

The authors draw attention to the fact that the HPT Model is a return to the craftsman era when businessmen were experts in their fields, took pride in their work, and maintained quality by limiting the number of people who entered the craft. A silversmith and apprentice of the 1700s in America would never have had to take a course in customer service. It was hammered into the silver with the pride of having produced it. Why did corporations ever desert that model? Oh, yes, the Industrial Revolution! Assembly line mass production has probably had the greatest impact on the deterioration in workmanship in products and deterioration of customer service. I think of the factory worker in a major automobile assembly plant who, upon retirement, was asked what was the first thing he was going to do after retirement. He responded, "I'm going to walk down to the other end of this assembly line and see what comes out the other end."

This book is important because most of the world is no longer in a manufacturing environment where lack of knowledge of the part-to-whole relationship is acceptable. Only one hundred years ago, 80 percent of all work was mechanical and 20 percent intellectual. Today, the opposite is true. That means employees cannot work in isolation. They have to have a broader picture of what is happening in their organizations and how what they do impacts everyone else. As organizations become more complex, so is the task of making certain everyone knows and appreciates the organizational goals of the company.

The complexity of engineering worthy performance should come through the pages, along with the realization that an organization will probably never find the "superman" who embodies all of these areas of specialized knowledge. Moving from a training department to an HPT function sounds the death knell for the one-person training department. This book will help organizations determine the areas of expertise they need to find and/or develop.

The book also addresses why HPT is complex. With training all you have to think about are the "activities." HPT requires thinking "systematically." The HPT professional must be integrated at the strategic level of a corporation, not just be an "order taker" serving up management decisions.

The HPT Model from analysis through evaluation forms the foundation of the book, but what's in between is filled with such topics as the importance of communication, the structure of the HPT organization, knowledge management, employee selection, financial systems, recognition, and technology. You can expect this book to help readers recognize the impact of almost any workplace activity, and it is designed to be a "desk reference" of performance solution opportunities, even containing discussions of such topics as hiring, retirement, compensation, and the cost of turnover.

The treatment of knowledge management is very impressive and comprehensive. It is good to have this valuable resource companies lose when experienced employees leave. The coverage of technology as the receptacle and delivery mechanism for knowledge, information, and communication is very pointed and contains a lot of common sense.

The numerous case studies interspersed throughout the book demonstrate how the various tools can be used within each phase of the process. They show the practical application of the concepts that the authors put forth.

William W. Lee
Director of Performance Technology
American Airlines Corporation Flagship University, Texas

Introduction

"We've got problems—right here in our workplace." "Advertisements just aren't catching shoppers' attention." "Too many phones are ringing to be answered promptly." "Parts are being produced with flaws." "Customers just won't buy the latest product improvement." "Schoolchildren with special needs require professional support that is costly." "Hospitals are challenged to contain costs while providing a vast array of services."

Every organization offers challenges, and many situations seem unsolvable. Workers and managers hold meetings, write plans, and pledge new energy and resolve. Sometimes the new ideas work, sometimes nothing changes or matters get worse. It often seems difficult to systemically and systematically control a situation and confidently improve workplace problems. Why do problems persist? Why do people resist new ideas? Why do managers seem so "bossy" and insensitive?

It is not enough to create successful performance improvement and beneficial change; the efforts need to be feasible, sustainable, and realistic in terms of scope and resources. Otherwise, situations will eventually revert to the way they were. Or worse yet, the improvement efforts might actually establish unintended situations that make matters worse. To be effective, performance improvement experts need to plan carefully and wisely so that the new situations they create are realistic, sustainable, and add value. In addition, it is essential that performance improvement processes be reliable and repeatable so that performance improvement practitioners can consistently accomplish successful results.

Performance improvement promotes opportunity, offers the structure to engage in new services, products, or methods; and is future-focused. Considering feasibility and sustainability as integral to performance improvement connects with executives and sponsors of new ideas. Careful implementation and maintenance built on multifaceted evaluation leads to enduring impact and often to culture shift.

Performance Improvement/HPT Model: The Challenge

A performance improvement mindset challenges consultants and practitioners to be thoughtful, observant, knowledgeable, systemic and systematic, hopeful, comprehensive, and scientific. Performance improvement includes theories of systems, quality, communications, learning, human resources, organizational design and development, and more. This book applies the Performance Improvement/HPT Model to illustrate performance improvement processes and procedures. Performance improvement practitioners can adapt this process model to the unique requirements of their own situations.

The performance support tools (PST) or job aids in the book are designated as "permission granted for unlimited duplication for non-commercial use." As a result, it is possible to use them for meetings or internal courses, but not for commercial training or fee-based consulting. Performance improvement practitioners typically adapt the Performance Improvement/HPT Model and performance support tools to the mission, strategic direction, and culture of each organization.

What to Expect in This Book

Fundamentals of Performance Improvement is an easy-to-understand guide to a proven, successful approach for workplace improvement. Designed as a "how to" book, *Fundamentals of Performance Improvement* is grounded in evidence and research to practice, as documented by the extensive citations and references at the end of each chapter.

Purpose

There are several purposes for the book. One intention is that the reader can go to an initial performance improvement planning meeting and use the job aids and performance support tools to effectively begin the project. After the initial meetings, more detailed and precise activities may be necessary, probably based on specialized resources.

For those new in the field, the overall objective is to provide a step-by-step guide. For seasoned professionals, the objective is to explain why performance improvement projects work so it is possible to predict successful outcomes for future projects. The book can serve as a comprehensive desk reference or be read sequentially to receive the full benefit.

Fundamentals is an overview for project teams to understand the approach and work effectively in collaboration. For champions, sponsors, and those who support an improvement effort, the book provides the context and encouragement needed to successfully complete the intervention project.

Fundamentals of Performance Improvement explains how to apply the Performance Improvement/ HPT Model in the workplace and society. The Performance Improvement/HPT Model represents systemic and systematic methods, processes, and procedures used for performance improvement under any name—performance improvement (PI), human performance improvement (HPI, human performance technology (HPT), or performance technology (PT). In addition, the model is generic and applicable to the full range of performance issues in fields as broad as communication, organization development, industrial engineering, quality, change management, financial consulting, and others, in a broad array of industries including service, armed forces, health care, education, religious institutions, manufacturing, government, power plants, fossil fuels, agriculture, and many more.

Goal and Objectives

The goal of this book is to enable readers to strengthen their existing performance improvement practice or begin applying performance improvement concepts wherever there is a need for change or an opportunity for advancement, such as a new product or service. Using this book, performance improvement practitioners will be able to:

1. Analyze the current situation, determine the desired situation, and describe the cause of the performance challenge.
2. Determine options to improve the situation, select, design, and develop suitable interventions to alleviate need or promote opportunity.
3. Create a business case using an iterative approach enabling senior leaders and the organization to finance and manage the effort effectively.
4. Put into practice, monitor, and establish lasting change.
5. Evaluate intermediate steps, determine immediate response to initiative, and verify that desired change occurs and is sustained.

Audience

Performance improvement requires a comprehensive approach; thus the book is designed for many audiences.

1. Anyone interested in making change within a work group, an organization or society, as principles of performance improvement can be broadly applied.
2. Performance improvement practitioners desiring to enhance their efforts by expanding their options and trying new intervention ideas.
3. Professionals from related fields who will integrate their expertise with performance improvement concepts, such as psychology, communications, industrial engineering, education, quality, business, and many more.
4. People from all workplaces, industries, cultures, and societies including military, finance, government, manufacturing service, education, agriculture, and others too numerous to mention.

Benefits of Applying the Book

Fundamentals of Performance Improvement contains a compendium of interventions. It is also designed as a desk reference of improvement processes and performance solution opportunities. Like an IKEA, Sears, or J.C. Penney's catalog, there is something for almost any need and nearly every situation. The intent is to identify and explain common improvement interventions or solutions. Each intervention is defined, its scope is briefly discussed, and its implementation is described. In addition there is at least one performance support tool or job aid per intervention category to assist readers in applying the intervention. There is also at least one case study for each section that demonstrates the interrelationships within the performance improvement process.

Another benefit of this book is to help readers recognize and anticipate the impact of any performance intervention. Some interventions may be common concepts, but unfamiliar as interventions, such as, strategic planning, globalization, profit versus cost centers, or security management. At times, intervention activities are carried out or innovations are adopted without thinking through the impact on the organizational culture, group dynamics, or workers' behavior. For example, once senior officers complete a strategic plan they typically convey this vision to executives. On the other hand, if the strategic plan is communicated throughout the workforce, it can affect job performance and decisions within the entire organization.

Finally, the book also contains an intervention selection process and tool enabling the reader to choose the most appropriate intervention or interventions. Due to the enormity of intervention options and the complexity of interfaces between the interventions, the intervention selection process includes individual and group considerations. Successful intervention implementation requires consensus among at least the leaders and representatives of affected parties.

Overview of Book Sections and Chapters

Fundamentals of Performance Improvement is organized based on the Performance Improvement/ HPT Model.

Section One: Performance Improvement and the Performance Improvement/HPT Model provides the context and background to understand major performance improvement concepts and practices. Becoming familiar with the evolution of performance improvement thinking provides context enabling readers to look ahead at new directions for the performance improvement field. Performance improvement processes and considerations are represented by the comprehensive Performance Improvement/Human Performance Technology (HPT) Model. Change management is foundational for performance improvement because change is the desired result of all improvement efforts.

Section Two: Performance Analysis focuses on understanding the opportunity or challenge, including the current situation and definition of future expectations that sets the stage for successful outcomes. Defining organizational expectations leads to the definition of desired performance. Environmental analysis results in a comprehensive understanding of the actual performance. The process of comparing the difference between desired and actual is known as gap analysis. It is not enough to understand the opportunity or need gap; it is essential to consider causes that lead to the gap, for example, a medical doctor may determine that the actual symptoms are fever, rash, and runny nose and the desired state is energy and enthusiasm. The physician then decides that the cause of the symptoms is allergy and the interventions could be an antihistamine and avoiding pollen. Likewise, performance analysis leads to consideration of interventions or resolutions of challenges.

Section Three: Intervention Selection, Design, and Development provides a wealth of information about over one hundred interventions within seven categories—what they are, the scope of their usage and workplace implementation, suggestions for designing and classifying them, elements of successful interventions, and practical guidelines based on consulting experiences. For certain interventions, practitioners who have used them in their consulting practices added commentary in The Practitioner's Voice. Section Three contains the Intervention Selection Process and an Intervention Selector Tool. Business case development, including feasibility and sustainability, provides the context and conveys financial and leadership expectations promoting informed decision making.

Section Four: Intervention Implementation and Maintenance is the most active phase. Through collaboration with all stakeholders, it is possible to minimize resistance and promote positive adapting as the implementation unfolds. Communication and employee development lead to a clear understanding of the improvement effort and potential benefit. Project management provides the structure for comprehensive thinking and doing.

Section Five: Evaluation is often an under-valued aspect of performance improvement; it is the checks and balances enabling confidence as the effort progresses. Formative evaluation focuses particularly upon preparation prior to roll-out. Summative evaluation considers immediate changes and application. Confirmative evaluation examines the sustainability of the effort and long-term value. Meta evaluation promotes improvements to the evaluation process.

Case Studies

Case studies are presented at the end of each section. The headings within the case studies cover the four principles from the International Society for Performance Improvement (ISPI) Performance Technology Standards and the phases of the Performance Improvement/HPT Model. Although each case study is designed to illustrate a particular topic, the case studies all illustrate that the model applies broadly.

Conclusion

This comprehensive book should be considered a desk reference and not a book to master. It requires years in the field of performance improvement to master the concepts. It takes broad experiences to encounter most of the intervention options. As a result, performance improvement practitioners prize their networks; they collaborate with colleagues who focus on results and outcomes.

SECTION 1
PERFORMANCE IMPROVEMENT AND THE PERFORMANCE IMPROVEMENT/HPT MODEL

"MAYBE I DON'T WANT TO FETCH A PAIL OF WATER."

Overview of Performance Improvement

"America is a nation where creative approaches yield real solutions to our problems. . . . It's clear to me that performance technology is just such an approach."

President George Bush[1]

Society, work, and the workplace have changed dramatically. As the Industrial Era emerged from agriculture and craft orientation, people began working in large groups and living in large communities. Gone were the isolation and independence of farming or as craftspersons in small towns supported by and supporting agriculture. Industry brought large-scale machinery operated by large workforces. The industrial workplace emphasized work design and quality.

With the Information Era, the workplace began to focus on information and the people who add value to information. Just as industrial machinery was automated to improve its functionality, much has been done to automate information through software, hardware, and internet innovation. The Information Era brought increasing recognition of the value of people as integrators and users of information. Leaders of progressive organizations successfully envision and promote people and people issues. Although there is considerable emphasis on information, there is an ongoing need for manufacturing, medicine, service, military, government, and many other organizations. There remains more need to coordinate and collaborate because there is great interdependence.

Performance Improvement: Precursors

Performance improvement as a field of study has gradually evolved as the world has evolved. Craftsmanship established standards; work design improved efficiency; quality focused on customer expectations; the ever-widening distribution of information enabled a global economy, and the people became more valuable to their organizations.

Craftsmen and Artisans

Through much of recent history, agriculture provided sufficient productivity to support artisans and craftspeople and to request their services. Architectural masterpieces, such as religious edifices, jewelry, household goods, and so forth were made according to expectations and often based on scientific standards.

Work Design

Work, work processes, and job design took on great importance as people began working together in factories. Efficiency was the goal. The ability to coordinate and control hundreds of employees in one location led to product dominance and business success. Frederick Taylor was a leader in scientific management, also known as *Taylorism,* based on time and motion studies.[2] For example, many small companies could build automobiles, but only Henry Ford, with his assembly line and upgraded labor pay scale, could create vehicles that were affordable by the common man. Maximizing the capability of a larger workforce was a significant competitive advantage.

Quality

As time went on, the ability to coordinate and control workers was not enough. Competitive advantage now moved to the quality of the product. Value was measured by the ability to provide customers with timely, innovative, defect-free, and cost reasonable merchandise. The quality movement flourished and helped unify work practices globally. An American, W. Edwards Deming, over thirty years, helped Japan improve their product quality, spearheading efforts to produce items with little variation and extraordinary reliability.[3]

Information

Optimizing information became the next competitive edge. Data became readily available for analysis, problem solving, and decision making. Software was written to integrate work, thereby increasing accuracy, reducing time and cost, and extending predictions and planning. For example, Thomas Watson at IBM envisioned the value of computers and helped incorporate them universally in organizations. Bill Gates enabled information to be readily available and usable throughout the world.[4]

Peter Drucker discussed the origin of the information age:

> "Whether this transformation began with the emergence of the first non-Western country, Japan, as a great economic power or with the first computer—that is, with information—is moot. My own candidate would be the GI Bill of Rights, which gave every American soldier returning from World War II the money to attend a university, something that would have made absolutely no sense only thirty years earlier at the end of World War I. The GI Bill of Rights and the enthusiastic response to it on the part of America's veterans signaled the shift to a knowledge society."[5]

People

Over the years, truly great organizations have realized the value of people and worked to maximize their potential.[6] All the efficient machinery operation, quality control, and information access in the world does not make an organization outstanding. People, with their skills, knowledge, motivation, values, and dreams, make organizations thrive and prosper. For instance, Jack

Welsh, CEO of GE, harnessed the value of people to make a world renowned, competitive, innovative, energized organization.[7]

Just as work design, quality, and information require continuous commitment to achieving maximum competitiveness, people-related performance issues need unwavering attention as well. Thomas Gilbert, the founder of performance technology,[8] described people's behavior in terms of "worthy" or worthwhile performance. In his Behavior Engineering Model, which focused on environmental support and employees' repertory of behavior,[9] he established the framework for performance improvement outcomes and performance technology.

Performance Improvement: Definition and Scope

Performance improvement (PI), also known as performance technology (PT), human performance technology (HPT), or human performance improvement (HPI), is the science and art of improving people, process, performance, organizations, and ultimately society. Sanders and Ruggles[10] use the analogy of alphabet soup and make the case that there are not too many letters in the performance improvement soup. Each letter, expert contributor, or discipline adds flavor or nutritional value to the performance improvement soup pot. (See Tables 1.1, 1.2, and 1.3 later in this chapter.)

PI, PT, HPT, and HPI are different in nuance; however, they are often used interchangeably. *Human* performance technology (HPT) and *human* performance improvement (HPI) imply a focus on improving people/worker performance; performance *technology* (PT) implies a focus on using a set of methods and procedures to improve the work, worker, workplace, and/or world. However, no matter what it is called, performance improvement is a systemic process that links organizational and business goals and strategies with the workforce responsible for achieving the goals.

Performance improvement is a science and an art. It is a science because analytical processes and methods are the bases for selecting and implementing solutions, known as performance improvement interventions. It is also an art because it requires intuition and creativity due to the interconnectedness and complexity or performance challenges, including issues of people with all of their values, emotions, idiosyncrasies, and variability.

PI, HPI, PT, and HPT practitioners use a common methodology to understand, inspire, and improve people; they systematically analyze performance problems and their underlying causes and describe exemplary performance and success indicators. Practitioners also select, design, develop, implement, and maintain performance improvement interventions to alleviate problems or take advantage of opportunities.

Human performance technology by any name has two major drivers: evaluation and change:

> "Largely, HPT is evaluation—and change-driven. At each stage of the performance improvement process, activities and outputs are evaluated and focus on the ultimate target of organizational results. Solving problems, improving organizations, and actualizing opportunities by their very nature mean change."[11]

PI, PT, HPI, and HPT all use widely accepted, common practices, including quantitative and qualitative analytical methods for evaluation and decision making.[12] Practitioners should evaluate inputs, processes, and outputs throughout the performance improvement cycle and remain focused on change management throughout the life of the intervention. (See the Performance Improvement/HPT Model in Chapter 2.)

Performance Improvement: Key Terms

The most important performance improvement terms are those used to accomplish performance improvement and successful outcomes. Rosenberg[13] suggests three key terms: performance improvement, performance consulting, and performance technology. We have added a fourth term—*performance improvement interventions.*

Performance Improvement

Performance improvement or human performance improvement is both the process of making performance better and the actual positive result of the performance improvement process. Performance improvement is the outcome. Performance improvement is measured by success indicators and comparison of current or baseline situations to desired outcomes looking for the gap or movement toward the desired or ideal situation as a result of the effort.

Performance Consultant

The performance consultant is the practitioner who actually leads and conducts the improvement effort. Performance consultants apply the principles, processes, tools, and techniques of performance improvement. In this book, the words performance improvement or performance technology practitioner or performance consultant will be used interchangeably.

Performance Technology

Performance technology or human performance technology is the process, tools, and techniques used to accomplish the improvement. The Performance Improvement/HPT Model illustrates the phases and steps in the improvement process. Professionals with substantial experience often refer to this as "HPT." HPT may be used in this book as a synonym for performance improvement.

Performance Improvement Interventions

Performance improvement interventions are the processes, methods, and/or plans selected, designed, developed, and implemented to improve performance, after performance analysis is completed. Interventions are also known as solutions. Because every workplace or situation is unique, the range of possible interventions that can be used for performance improvement is infinite. This book discusses more than one hundred potential interventions and contains an intervention selection tool, but there are many more. Just as society, organizations, and workplaces are ever changing, so new interventions are developed and used to optimize the changed dynamics.

Performance Improvement: Key Concepts

There are also important concepts or beliefs associated with improvement efforts and improvement principles. Performance improvement is eclectic and comprehensive; it draws from many related fields, such as organization development, business, psychology, communications, industrial engineering, analysis, evaluation, problem solving, engineering, and many more. The following pages discuss some of the key concepts that have been influenced by other fields.

People-Oriented

Performance improvement or human performance technology is *people-oriented* and, as a result, practitioners typically share a set of common beliefs:

- People are important;
- Appropriate performance improvement solutions are beneficial for the present situation and are also future-oriented;
- Approaches to analysis, design and development, implementation and maintenance, and evaluation need to be multidimensional; and
- Performance improvement professionals work in a manner that is team-oriented and interdependent.

Performance improvement professionals are committed to people—their capabilities and their potential. People are part of the core energy of organizations. Equipment and financial reserves are important, but people are the heart and soul of organizations. People purchase, operate, and maintain the equipment; budget, account for, and report the financial status; plan, engineer, design, and implement. People are behind everything that happens.

Clearly, the trend toward valuing people and knowledge requires a paradigm shift. PI provides such a methodology. PI can be sustained because people and their knowledge truly are the organization's most valuable resources. While performance improvement also involves work, workplace, and world, interventions are selected, planned, developed, implemented, and maintained by people and people drive the change that makes performance improvement happen.

Positive and Future-Oriented

Performance improvement professionals have a positive outlook and are oriented to the future. They believe it is possible to improve situations and design solutions that are beneficial for people, no matter how complex the problem, how great the hurdle to overcome, or how discouraging the current situation is. They believe the solutions should be sustainable over time.

Multidimensional Approaches

Performance improvement professionals are committed to adopting comprehensive interventions or solutions that include or alleviate many of the major factors identified in cause analysis. Rather than rushing in with interventions based on gap analysis or the difference between what is desired and what is currently present, practitioners first consider causes. Reducing performance gaps prior to determining causes often provides only temporary relief, but eliminating causes can fix real problems. Performance resolutions without considering causes are like band aids. Fixing problems based on causes are like curing the disease.

Commitment

Equally important to solving problems is gaining commitment from senior management and other stakeholders or champions to support and sustain the interventions. Performance improvement practitioners help gain commitment by conducting feasibility studies, establishing sustainable frameworks so that the improvements are lasting, and developing business cases that provide a strong rationale for improvement. Through partnering, networking, communication, and alliance building, performance improvement practitioners systematically implement effective and value added interventions based on strategic planning and results-oriented feedback.

Team-Oriented

Performance improvement professionals accomplish performance improvement and change through groups or teams. Sustaining improvement requires senior management to articulate organizational needs, support analysis, and sponsor interventions and follow-up evaluation. Comprehensive intervention designs usually contain many specialized factors, such as work environment, motivation, and skill development. Specialists in areas such as production processes, client services, staff selection, or job design need to work together with human performance technologists to craft communication plans, intervention timelines, and follow-up strategies so that desired changes are accomplished and sustained.

Sports Analogy. The sports arena provides an appropriate analogy to performance improvement. Most sports teams have a long tradition of strategically selecting players and planning competitive plays. Football players, for example, study the strengths and weaknesses of opponents and practice their assignments accordingly. Coaches motivate players to win by giving feedback and encouraging team playing. As Casey Stengel, the legendary manager of baseball's New York Yankees, often remarked, "Finding good players is easy; getting them to play together is the hardest part."[14]

Business Analogy. Businesses and other organizations, like sports teams, need to recognize the strengths, weaknesses, and interdependencies of their workforce to ensure that workers "play together" effectively in support of business objectives. Today's knowledge era organizations are creating team cultures that are dependent on contributions by all team members. Fisher and Fisher predict that most future work will be mental and team based.[15] Individuals will bring their specialized knowledge and skills to teams. Teams will often be virtual, and their membership will be constantly shifting as team members accomplish their tasks and move on to another assignment. Team members may never physically meet their co-workers.

In this knowledge era, organizations need to value and reward the sharing of information. Intensely competitive or territorial organizations, in which personnel tend to hoard all information, will achieve less success than those companies in which top management encourages an open, cooperative workplace.[16] Organizations need to encourage information exchange and ensure that employees do not lose power when they share knowledge.

Not Just a Bandwagon

People are the most important resource for the knowledge era; people are the fundamental determinants of economic growth and productivity.[17] But performance improvement is a relatively new and dynamic approach for putting this concept into practice. Human resources and training and development survey results indicate that more and more senior managers are committed to people as their most important resource.[18]

However, there is skepticism regarding people issues in the business sector. Frequently, people-oriented initiatives are viewed as passing bandwagons. They are colorfully and convincingly presented to workers and enthusiastically supported by senior management. Then they are hastily replaced by a different bandwagon initiative when workplace improvements are not quickly achieved. Performance improvement is a systemic, comprehensive, systematic, and analytical approach. It links many factors together to generate solutions and is well-suited for the people-oriented, team-based, knowledge era. Will PI become a passing bandwagon, like the bandwagons that came to town and left with the circus? Can PI maintain its enthusiastic supporters? Does PI stand up to application in the workplace?

Performance Improvement: Foundations

Performance improvement is a comprehensive approach. It assimilates and integrates ideas and theories from many disciplines. Table 1.1 illustrates the disciplines that are most influential to performance improvement and performance technology.

Performance Improvement: Leading Contributors

Many experts have shaped the field of performance improvement and performance technology. Although each expert focused and refined a particular knowledge area, PI practitioners need to integrate their contributions in order to provide a background to the field. Performance improvement applies the knowledge and models of many experts by fitting their ideas, as subsets, into the Performance Improvement /HPT Model. Although Table 1.2 is extensive, it is only a selected list of the contributions of experts.

Table 1.1 and Table 1.2 illustrate the origins of performance improvement by describing the complexity and comprehensiveness of the theory base and the major contributors. In addition to the individuals mentioned in this chapter, many, many other men and women have made significant contributions to our field of performance improvement. While it is not possible to list them

TABLE 1.1. Theoretical Foundations of Performance Improvement

Discipline	Focus	Contribution
Behaviorism	Predicting behavior	Small steps of instruction and feedback
		Learn to manipulate and control the environment by the individual's responses to it
Diagnostic and Analytical Systems	Data as basis for understanding behavior	Practitioners use comprehensive analytical tools
		Diagnosis is based on gap (difference between desired and actual situation)
		Causes of situation are defined before intervention is selected and implemented
Instructional Systems Design and Organizational Learning	ADDIE (analysis, design, development, implementation, and evaluation) model, forerunner of the Performance Improvement/HPT Model	Developed in 1940s and 1950s, responding to need to train thousands of military personnel during World War II
		Various instructional methods were found to be valuable, such as role play, video, case study, and lecture
Organization Design (OD) and Change Management	Changing performance at organizational and individual levels	OD interventions improve culture, group dynamics, and structure of organization
		Change management helps individuals and groups adapt to change through timely information, appropriate resources, and strategies to minimize resistance and turmoil that accompanies change
		Theoretical basis includes systems dynamics, human motivation, group and team dynamics, competency modeling, organizational learning systems, and feedback systems
Evaluation	Determining value and impact of interventions	Produces credibility that practitioners need
		Real costs against real savings attained by organization, return on investment (ROI)
Management Sciences	Dividing "thinkers" and "doers" and analyzing and describing jobs and tasks	Theories led to standardized production system, such as Henry Ford's assembly line
		Emphasis evolved to physical and psychological issues, such as motivation, job satisfaction, professional growth, and empowerment

Source: Adapted from Sanders and Ruggles, 2000, pp, 27–36. Used with permission.

here, the reader is encouraged to check the authors who appear in editions 1 through 3 of the *Handbook of Human Performance Technology*[19] as well as the authors who appear in Volumes 1 through 3 of the *Handbook of Improving Performance in the Workplace.*[20] The stellar work of those people has collectively advanced our field and forever changed our performance landscape.

Performance Improvement: Prominent Early Leaders

Current efforts in performance improvement were built upon the work of those who have paved the way and gone before us. They have raised the questions, done the research, applied their

TABLE 1.2. Leading Contributors to Performance Improvement and Performance Technology

Leader	Field	Focus	Contribution
Chris Argyris	Action Science	Reflection and inquiry on the reasoning that underlies people's actions	Developed concepts of learning organization, double loop learning, and feedback systems
			"Coined the term *skilled incompetence* to explain how defensive behavior and the fear of collective inquiry by management may protect us from threat or embarrassment but also may block learning" (p. 31)
			Pioneered team building with upper management
Benjamin Bloom	Educational Technology	Hierarchical taxonomy of intellectual or cognitive objectives based on what learners are supposed to do	Vary instruction according to learning requirements and difficulty of cognitive domain level
			Revealed that instructional efforts were largely aimed at the bottom levels of the cognitive hierarchy
W. Edwards Deming	Total Quality Management (TQM)	Emphasized quality rather than production targets	"14 points" model of quality
			Statistician who helped turn around Japanese economy after World War II
Peter Drucker	Management Sciences	Businesses are human centers as well as economic centers; work must have social meaning	Developed concepts of decentralized large organizations, management by objectives, and role of the knowledge worker
		Coined phrase "Self-governing plant community," proposing that many managerial responsibilities should be undertaken by individual employees or work teams	
Robert Gagne'	Instructional Systems Design	Task analysis and sequencing tasks	Created Information Processing Model and Nine Events of Instruction
			"Learners need to receive feedback on individualized tasks in order to correct isolated problems" (p. 32)
			HPT needs to deal with multiple rather than serial objectives
			Five types of learning: (1) Psychomotor skills; (2) Verbal information; (3) Intellectual skills; (4) Cognitive strategies; and (5) Attitudes
Thomas Gilbert	Behavioral Engineering	Founded the field of Human Performance Technology	Behavioral Engineering Model focuses on changing work environment aspects such as information resources, incentives, knowledge, capacity, and motives to improve performance
			"Absence of performance support (not skills and knowledge) is the greatest block to exemplary work performance" (p. 32)
Joe Harless	Front End Analysis	Diagnose problems early because problem cause often dictates solution	Coined phrase "front end analysis" to describe the rigorous diagnostic framework applied prior to addressing solutions
			HPI tools can reduce training expense considerably (p. 33)

(Continued)

TABLE 1.2.   (Continued)

Leader	Field	Focus	Contribution
Roger Kaufman	Strategic Planning	Addresses mega (societal), macro (organizational), and micro (individual) levels	Emphasized that performance improvement work impacts society and should impact society and that performance improvement should be planned astutely.
Donald Kirkpatrick	Evaluation	Four levels of evaluation criteria (reaction, learning, behavior, and results)	Clarified role of evaluation relative to performance improvement and training
Malcolm Knowles	Andragogy	Adult learning needs to be lifelong and ideally should involve learning contracts	Adults need to (1) Self-direct their own learning; (2) Know the purpose of what they are learning; (3) Apply their relevant experiences to learning; and (4) Apply a problem-solving approach
Kurt Lewin	Force Field Analysis	Force field assesses human behavior in terms of opposing forces (driving and restraining) that motivate action	Performance improvement occurs when restraining forces are reduced
			Participative management linked Taylor's scientific thinking with democratic values
			Three-stage organizational change: (1) Unfreezing old behavior; (2) Moving to new level of behavior; (3) Refreezing new behavior
Robert Mager	Instructional Objectives	Instructional objectives should describe what learners will be able to do and represent improved performance	Described objectives to accomplish desired instructional results using a branching format of programmed instruction.
			Created performance analysis flowchart with Peter Pipe
Douglas McGregor	Theory X and Theory Y	X management style is repressive, authoritarian, fearful Y management style is optimistic, creative, and interdependent	Metaphors for master and servant polarity Pioneered industrial relations
Susan Markle	Programmed Instruction	Developed concept of programmed instruction following experiments with Skinner's teaching machine	Three types of learning necessary for programmed instruction: discriminations, generalizations, and chains
			Programmed Learning Model combines operant conditioning, cognitive learning, with information gathering (developed with Phillip Tiemann)
Geary Rummler	Three Levels of Organizational Performance	Organizational, Process, and Individual Job or Performer	Emphasized the importance of improved organizational processes, which he called the "white space"
Peter Senge	Learning Organization	Five critical practices for creating a learning organization: (1) Personal Mastery; (2) Mental Models; (3) Shared Vision; (4) Team Learning; and (5) Systems Thinking	Pioneered systems oriented approach to achieving high performance
B.F. Skinner	Behaviorism	Small step instruction, followed by extensive feedback, enhances learning	Behavioral theories fundamental to performance improvement and instructional design.
			Invented linear programming methodology
Frederick Taylor	Scientific Management	Integration of methods, policies, planning, and people	Scientific management principles include: authority based on knowledge instead of position; the first wage incentive system; breaking down tasks into smaller components; creation of a productivity expert Laid the foundation for the modern assembly line

TABLE 1.2.   (Continued)

Leader	Field	Focus	Contribution
Sivasaliam (Thiagi) Thiagarajan	Games and Playfulness	Integrated playfulness, person-to-person interaction, and experiential learning	Elevated serious play, games, and fun as performance interventions
Donald Tosti	Feedback	Critical characteristics of feedback are tied to who gives it, the content, where and when it is given	Specialized in applying human performance technology and performance improvement to organizational change culture
Marvin Weisbord	Six Boxes	Organizational diagnostic framework composed of six critical areas: purpose, structure, leadership, relationships, rewards, helpful mechanisms	Widely used in organization development

Source: Adapted from Sanders and Ruggles, 2000, pp. 27–36. Used with permission.

knowledge, evaluated, and revised their thinking again and again. They have challenged each other, learned from each other, and taught our field their lessons learned.[21] Today, our great thinkers and our many practitioners are refining their thinking and applying their concepts in new ways.

The basis of the field of performance improvement started in early days of the National Society for Programmed Instruction (NSPI), now the International Society for Performance Improvement (ISPI). The first NSPI conference was in San Antonio, Texas, in 1962. Robert Mager provided the first banquet speech. Some of the first to be involved were Gabriel Ofiesh, Robert Mager, Lloyd Homme, Susan Markle, Thomas Gilbert, Don Tosti, Roger Kaufman, Dale Brethower, Jim Evens, Geary Rummler, George Geis, and others.[22] In a personal communication Mager[23] wrote:

> "Many of us joined because of our interest in understanding and implementing this new format of instruction. Over the years the focus shifted away from instructional improvement, to several other areas, and the performance improvement field now has many techniques allowing it to create instruction *only* when it will, in fact, solve the performance problem at hand; and in those relatively rare instances when instruction *is* indicated, to guarantee that the instruction developed will lead students to competence."

Four of the leading early performance improvement experts are highlighted below and in Table 1.3 to provide perspective regarding the science and the art of performance improvement. The experts and their contributions provide examples of the foundations and evolution of performance improvement and human performance technology.

Thomas Gilbert

Gilbert[24] established much of the conceptual framework for performance improvement. He studied behavioral psychology under B.F. Skinner for one year at Harvard University and, as a result, much of Gilbert's work is detailed, creative, and behavioristic.[25]

TABLE 1.3. Early Leaders

Early Leader	Performance Improvement Aspect
Thomas Gilbert	Worthy Performance
Geary Rummler	Components of Performance
Roger Kaufman	Societal and Organizational Effectiveness
Robert Mager	Objectives and Analysis

TABLE 1.4. Thomas Gilbert's Behavior Engineering Model

	Information	Instrumentation	Motivation
Environmental Support	Data	Instruments	Incentives
Repertory of Behavior	Knowledge	Capacity	Motives

Source: Adapted from Gilbert, 1978. Used with permission.

Gilbert identified *worthy performance* as behavior valued for its accomplishment. Worth is determined by dividing value by cost (W = V/C). This was the first conceptualization of return on investment. Gilbert believed it unwise to define change in terms of desired behavior; rather change should be described in terms of performance outcomes or results.

Gilbert created one of the earliest models for performance improvement. "The Behavior Engineering Model (BEM), developed by Gilbert and presented in his landmark book, *Human Competence: Engineering Worthy Performance,*[26] provides us with a way to systematically and systemically identify barriers to individual and organizational performance."[27] According to Gilbert, "The behavioral engineering model serves one purpose only: It helps us to observe behavior in an orderly fashion and to ask the 'obvious' questions (the ones we so often forget to ask) toward the single end of improving human competence."[28] Gilbert describes individual characteristics as repertory of behaviors, meaning the entire stock of individual behaviors resulting from knowledge, motivation, and abilities. (See Table 1.4.)

Gilbert's Behavior Engineering Model (BEM) consists of six basic aspects of human behavior that impact performance improvement: three are related to the environment and three are related to the individual:

- Environmental Supports—data such as production standards, instruments, or equipment—and incentives or rewards provided by the environment; and
- A Person's Repertory of Behavior—knowledge or the know how to perform, capacity or physical and intellectual ability, and motives or willingness to work for the incentives collected and stored by the individual.

Gilbert further identified two attributes of the six basic aspects of the BEM model: cost and impact.

Gilbert asserted that data or information has the highest impact and the lowest cost, and resources have the next highest impact and the next lowest cost. Knowledge has the highest cost with the lowest impact. To assess cost versus impact, begin at the left top and go across the top set of cells to the right and then drop to the lower set of cells and go from right to left. Many are surprised to realize that training and acquiring knowledge can be the most costly solution and the one with the least impact.

The BEM has been applied as a cause analysis model, helping to identify what causes the gap or problem or a description of what needs to be improved[29] and represents cause analysis in the Performance Improvement/HPT Model. Chapter 8 has more information on Gilbert's Behavior Engineering Model.

Geary Rummler

It is difficult to overestimate the impact of Rummler's work on performance improvement. "[Rummler's] work fundamentally changed our work, our way of thinking, and the way we behave as professionals."[30]

Rummler[31] defined the five components of performance systems. His work helped performance improvement practitioners view the components of individual performance as much more than behavior and outcomes. Rummler stressed the interrelationship of employees, the organization, and many other factors, believing an organization is only as good as its processes. He stated that performance systems have five components:

1. *Job situation*—the occasion of the performance
2. *Performer*—the worker
3. *Response*—the action or decision that occurs
4. *Consequence*—a reward, punishment, or non-existent consequences
5. *Feedback*—information about whether the response was adequate or inadequate

Later, Rummler and Brache[32] described the accumulative, collective impact of performance variables based on *Level:* Organization, Process, or Job/Performer and *Performance Needs:* Goals, Design, and Management. They emphasized the importance of managing the interrelationships between departments and processes; what they called the *white space on the organizational chart*. They stressed that it is critical to create harmony and reduce tension in order to create departments that are "centers of excellence."[33]

The white space is often the area of greatest potential for improvement or the greatest area for problems because it is the area between functions and it is a challenge to determine responsibility. That is why cross-functional teams have potential for resolving organizational challenges.[34]

Rummler also made a major contribution when he described the relationships between aspects of performance[35] Figure 1.1 illustrates the impacts and interconnections between performance variables associated with individuals, processes, organizations, and societies. The three acronyms

TABLE 1.5.   Rummler's Nine Performance Variables Matrix

	Goals and Measures	Organizational Design and Implementation	Organizational Management
Organizational Level	Organizational goals and measures of organizational success	Organizational design and implementation	Organizational management
Process Level	Process goals and measures of process success	Process design and implementation	Process management
Activity or Performance Level	Activity goals and measures of activity success	Activity design and implementation	Activity management

Source: Rummler and Brache, 1995. Used with permission.

in the model apply to critical issues that impact every performance improvement project: critical business issues (CBI), critical process issues (CPI), and critical job issues (CJI).

Roger Kaufman

Roger Kaufman sounded a clarion call for a very long time, urging performance improvement practitioners to also impact society. It is not sufficient to improve the worker, the workplace, and the organization. We must also improve society; it is our ethical social responsibility.[36] As those around Roger have heard for many years, "If we are not contributing to society, we are taking away from it." At this point, his message of "mega' has been accepted by many; it connects, particularly with those committed to earth's sustainability and eliminating the world's challenges.[37]

Kaufman developed the Organizational Elements Model (OEM) to provide a practical framework for planning, assessing needs, and evaluating. The model enables performance improvement practitioners to think through how their improvement projects impact society as well as the more traditional impacts on the organization, processes, products, and inputs.[38] (Too often, a proposed project will resolve an immediate dilemma, but it will actually be harmful in the long run.)

For example, a manager may come to a training department asking for a listening course because employees are just not "getting it" when he tells them what to do. Actually, the manager may need coaching and feedback in supervision and management. If we agree to provide training in listening, we are using people and monetary resources for the training, even though we may suspect that very little will be accomplished. In fact, a negative consequence may be that the manager says "bad things" about the training department's inability to meet expectations. Kaufman's OEM (Table 1.6) illustrates that, when we focus on processes and inputs, we are conducting "quasi needs assessments." When we focus on products, outputs, and outcomes, we are looking at the value adds.

Kaufman is also committed to a high level of expectations and attainment for mega thinking and planning. He developed a table listing examples of planning elements and type of result for each level. (See Table 1.7.)

FIGURE 1.1.   Anatomy of Performance

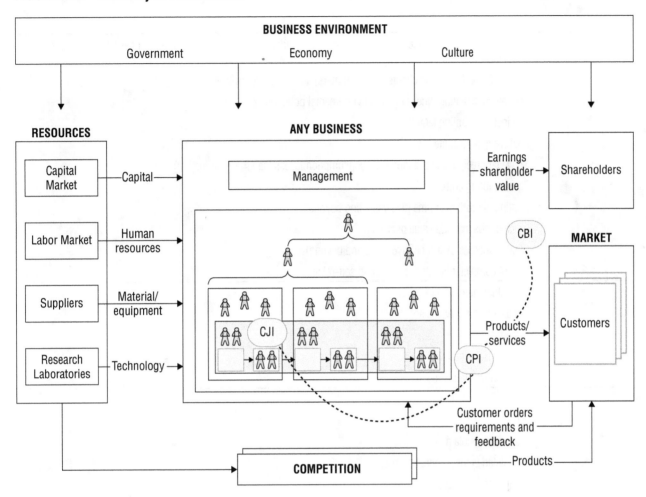

Source: Brethower, 2009, p. 21. Used with permission.

TABLE 1.6.   The Organizational Elements, Related Results, and Definitions

Element	Level of Planning and Focus	Brief Description
Outcomes	Mega	Results and their consequences for external client and society
Outputs	Macro	The results an organization can or does deliver outside of itself
Products	Micro	The building-block results that are produced within the organization
Processes	Process	The ways, means, activities, procedures, and methods used internally.
Inputs	Input	The human, physical, and financial resources an organization can and does use

Source: Moore, Ellsworth, and Kaufman, 2011, 15–24. Used with permission.

TABLE 1.7.   Examples for Each of the Organizational Elements

Element	Example
Mega	All persons are self-sufficient and self-reliant—not under the care, custody, or control of another person, agency, or substance
	Organizations (including clients and customers) are successful over time
	Eliminated disabling illness due to environmental pollution
	Eliminated disabling fatalities
	Positive quality of life
	No welfare recipients (and thus their consumption is less than their production)
	Zero disabling crime
	Continued profit over time (five years and beyond)
	Created jobs that add value over time
	Clients' success over time (five years and beyond)
	School completer is self-sufficient and self-reliant
Macro	Assembled automobiles
	Goods and /or services sold
	System delivered
	Patient discharged
	High school graduate
Micro	Tire
	Fender
	Production quota met
	Completed carpet production batch
	Completed training manuals
	Competent worker
	Course completed
	Operation completed
	Test or course passed
Processes	Organization development
	Management techniques
	Operating production line
	360-degree feedback
	Training
	Six Sigma
	Curriculum
	Examining a patient
	Strategic (or tactical or operational) planning
	Assessing needs
	Course development

TABLE 1.7.   (Continued)

Element	Example
Inputs	Money
	People
	Equipment
	Facilities
	Existing goals
	Existing policies
	Time
	Resources
	Individual values
	Laws
	Current economic conditions
	Regulations
	History
	Organizational culture
	Current problems
	Existing materials
	Current staff and their skills, knowledge, attitudes, and abilities
	Characteristics of current and potential clients
	Predicted client desires and requirements

Source: Adapted from Kaufman, 2011, pp. 24–25. Used with permission.

Robert Mager

Robert Mager played an important role in the methods for the instruction and performance improvement. He provided the concept of objectives as a consistent framework for describing desired outcomes. Objectives are statements that are precise and clear descriptions of *performance* or what the learner or worker is to be able to do; *conditions* or important circumstances under which the performance is expected to occur; and *criterion* or the quality or level of performance that will be considered acceptable. Mager helped human performance technologists define desired performance using common terminology. For example:

> "Given a DC motor of ten horsepower or less that contains a single malfunction, and given a kit of tools and references, be able to repair the motor. The motor must be repaired within forty-five minutes and must operate to within 5 percent of factory specifications."[39]

Mager wrote *Preparing Instructional Objectives* in the branching format of programmed instruction, invented and developed by Norman Crowder. The book explains the importance of clarifying intended outcomes before attempting to design instruction that can be guaranteed to accomplish those outcomes.

In *Analyzing Performance Problems*, Mager covers the steps in solving a problem, from identifying the gap to selecting and implementing a solution. The reader often discovers why training and education of any sort may not be relevant to solving the problem. This revelation alone has been worth many thousands of dollars in savings to its users.[40]

Mager and Pipe developed a flow diagram (Figure 1.2) designed to take the "mystery" out of performance problems. Their system was designed to:

- "Identify the causes of the problems.
- Decide which problems are worth solving
- Describe solutions which will help you solve the problems, and
- Decide which solutions will be both practical and economically feasible."[41]

An important aspect of Mager and Pipe's thinking was the consideration of practicality and feasibility. All too often, interventions make sense for the immediate situation but are not designed to be sustainable in the future.

Multidisciplinary Collaboration

Performance improvement is clearly a complex and comprehensive field based on combining the ideas and research of many fields as needed to resolve particular problems or opportunities. Performance improvement practitioners draw from many models and theories as appropriate to accomplish the desired change and the anticipated outcomes.

Mariano Bernardez mapped the scope and depth of the field, illustrating the multiple human performance technology and non–human performance technology frameworks used in performance improvement based on the fishbone diagram format seen in Figure 1.3. The diagram is based on external (strategic), internal (tactical/operational), and conceptual (foundations) and reflects the disciplines contributing to transforming performance into measurable value added to customers, employees, shareholders, communities, and environment. Performance improvement impacts and adds value at many levels, including micro or job task, macro or organizational, and mega or society and external clients. Bernardez (2011) includes *theories* based on scientific method, systems theory, and experimental psychology; *external strategic considerations* such as cultural models strategic performance models business and economic models; and *internal tactical/operational considerations*, such as individual performance models, learning and technology models, process and organizational performance models, and management and organizational models. "In the real world, most performance problems have multilevel causes and consequences and require the collaboration of multiple specialists as multidisciplinary teams" (p. 42).

FIGURE 1.2.   Mager's Performance Analysis Flowchart

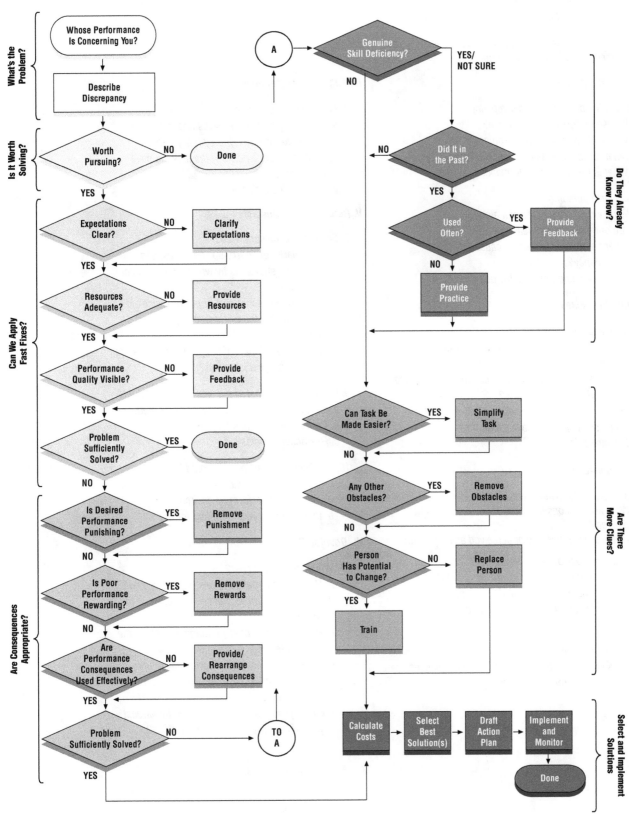

Source: Adapted from Mager and Pipe, 1997. Used with permission.

FIGURE 1.2. (Continued)

Quick Reference Guide

Use the following guide as a way to help others see why they "really oughta wanna" re-evaluate solutions they have already decided upon.

I. Describe the problem

1. What is the performance discrepancy?
   a. Whose performance is at issue?
   b. Why is there said to be a problem?
   c. What is the actual performance at issue?
   d. What is the desired performance?

2. Is is worth pursuing?
   a. What would happen if I let it alone?
   b. Are our expectations reasonable?
   c. What are the consequences caused by the discrepancy?
   d. Is that cost enough to justify going on?

II. Explore Fast Fixes

3. Can we apply fast fixes?
   a. Do those concerned know what is expected of them?
   b. Can those concerned describe desired performance? Expected accomplishments?
   c. Are there obvious obstacles to performance?
   d. Do these people get feedback on how they are doing?

III. Check Consequences

4. Is desired performance punishing?
   a. What are the consequences of performing as desired?
   b. Is it actually punishing or perceived as punishing?

5. Is undesired performance rewarding?
   a. What rewards, prestige, status, or comfort support the present way of doing things?
   b. Does misbehaving get more attention than doing it right?

6. Are there any consequences at all?
   a. Does desired performance lead to consequences that the performer sees as favorable?

IV. Enhance Competence

7. Is it a skill deficiency?
   a. Could they do it if their lives depended on it, i.e., could they do it if they really had to?
   b. Could they once perform the task but have forgotten how?
   c. Is the skill used often?

V. Remove Other Obstacles

8. Can the task be simplified?
   a. Particularly for "hurry up" demands, can I reduce the standards by which performance is judged?
   b. Can I provide some sort of performance aid?
   c. Can I redesign the workplace or provide other physical help?
   d. Can I parcel off part of the job to someone else or arrange a job swap?

9. Does something get in the way of doing it right?
   a. Lack of knowledge about what's expected?
   b. Conflicting demands?
   c. Restrictive policies?

10. Is it likely that this person could learn to do the job?
    a. Does this person lack the physical or mental potential to perform as desired?
    b. Is this person over-qualified for this job?

VI. Develop Solutions

11. Which solution is best?
    a. Have all potential solutions been identified?
    b. Does each address one or more parts of the problem(s)?
    c. Have estimates of any intangible costs of the problem(s) been included?
    d. What is the cost of each potential solution?
    e. Which solution(s) are most practical, feasible, and economical?
    f. Which yields most value, solving the largest part of the problem(s) for least effort?

FIGURE 1.3. Beyond HPT: Factors and Contributors to Performance Improvement and Value Creation

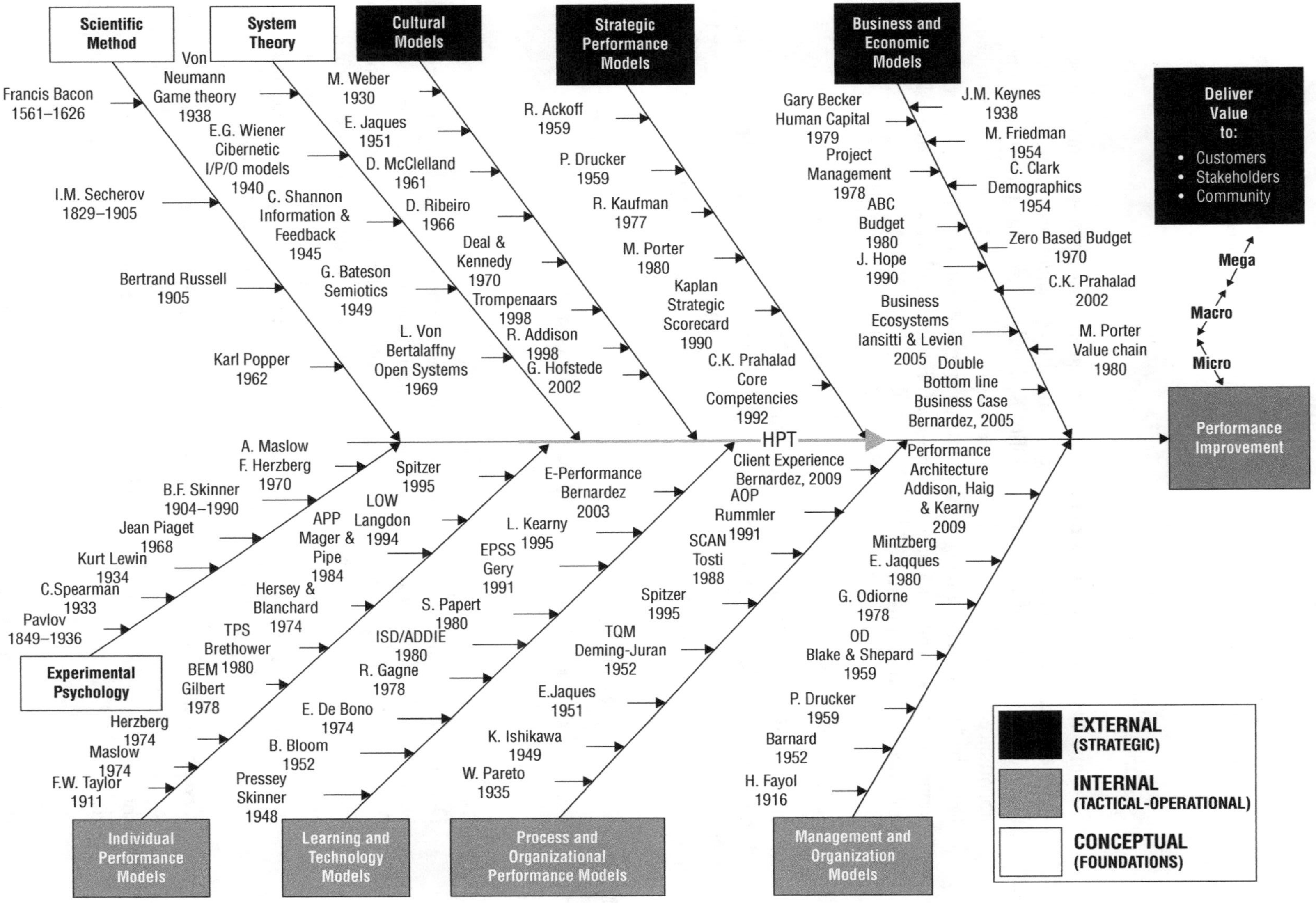

Source: Bernardez, 2011, p. 42. Used with permission.

Performance Improvement: Emerging Trends

Three emerging trends are highlighted here: sustainability, appreciative inquiry, and positive psychology, plus the emergence of performance improvement processes in primary and secondary education. These trends are not here today and gone tomorrow; they are in themselves sustainable.

Sustainability Trend

Sustainability will be an important trend for performance improvement because the opportunities are great, the solutions are innovative, and the consequences of not focusing on sustainability are becoming more apparent. Sustainability is already increasing and will continue to increase in importance. One of the principal benefits of sustainability is improved company or brand image; followed by "cost savings; competitive advantage; employee satisfaction, morale, or retention; product, service, or market innovation; new sources of revenue or cash flow; effective risk management; and enhanced stakeholder relations."[42]

EXHIBIT 1.1. THE PRACTITIONER'S VOICE: SUSTAINABILITY

"In my humble opinion, sustainability is the single biggest advancement in thinking in the performance improvement field that I have seen. Our job is not to design, develop, and implement correct interventions. . . . It is to create lasting organizational improvement. Learning how to build sustainable change is at least as important as the process of *what* to change!"

Jeff McElyea, M.A., M.S., Lucid Business Strategies

www.lucidbusiness.com, Michigan, USA

Definition. The most widely respected early definition of sustainability is part of the United Nations World Commission on Environment and Development's report, Our Common Future in 1987. The definition asserts that sustainability "refers to forms of progress that meet the needs of the present without compromising the ability of future generations to meet their needs." While presenting the commission's report to the United Nations in Kenya, G.H. Brundtland stated that sustainability "requires fair access to knowledge and resources and a more equitable distribution within and among nations. It requires broad participation in decision-making."[43]

Key Challenges. The report covered common challenges: population and human resources; food security: sustaining the potential; species and ecosystems: resources for development; energy: choices for environment and development; industry: producing more with less; and the urban challenge.[44] The key challenges covered here are population increases, global economics, and communications.

Population Increases. From the beginning of human existence on the Earth, there have been gradual adaptations due to lifestyle change from hunters and gatherers to agricultural cultures. Famines, wars, catastrophes, and epidemics kept population growth in check. However, beginning in the late 1700s, human population began to increase due to agricultural improvements. By the end of the 1800s, improvements in medicine and sanitation began to swell the number of people.[45] Medical advances and agricultural productivity have led to extraordinary population growth.[46]

Population growth requires increases in food. Agricultural research resulted in a "Green Revolution" relying on genetically engineered foods enhanced by petroleum-based fertilizers and pesticides and reliable sources of water. Globally, people are going to need employability skills and an economic system that fosters their well-being. Performance improvement professionals are needed to assist underdeveloped countries establish and sustain economic, civic, and educational structures to advance their citizens' lifestyles. Developed countries will need to adapt to the rapid changes throughout the world.

Global Economics. Our world economic situation will be adapting due to changes in economic, military, and political realities. Military organizations are becoming nation builders as well as armed forces. Political situations are becoming more inclusive and broad. Economies are developing new social mechanisms, such as micro-banks and free markets, to distribute goods and services more broadly and provide employment more widely.

"The world's economic balance of power is rapidly shifting and world trade is being transformed. Developing countries in Asia and Latin America will join traditional Western powers as the world's largest economies. Rapid labor force growth, high rates of investment, and the continued absorption of technology in emerging markets will make this growth possible."[47] As a result, there will need to be a greater global understanding of finance, economics, and politics.

These changes will provide opportunities for greater social responsibility. Ethics and accountability will increase due to expectations of increased transparency and common good. Greater interdependence will lead to increased respect for intellectual property rights.[48] International banking and monetary policies will adapt, as they were established in the 1940s and need updating.[49] Performance improvement professionals will support development of social institutions as well as the development of skills, knowledge, and abilities throughout the world.

Communication. Improvements in communication have changed the expectations of people throughout the world. Instant news coverage leads to immediate knowledge of events and builds an expectation that change makes an important difference. Newscasts include segments from social media investigating what is behind the major stories, providing a more balanced insight. Distance education brings information, knowledge, job skills, and so forth, enabling people in remote locations to understand the significance of issues. Communication has improved health by educating regarding human immunodeficiency virus (HIV), malaria, tuberculosis, and other common diseases resulting in healthier and energetic individuals. People are aware of possibilities and potential for themselves, their environment, their government, and their life style, plus they have increased desire to accomplish and sustain a better life.[50]

Eco-Efficiency. One of the early pioneers in eco-efficiency or doing more with less was Henry Ford, the automobile industrialist and founder of Ford Motor Company. Ford was committed to lean and clean policies, saving money by recycling and reusing materials, reducing the use of natural resources, and established the time-saving assembly line. Ford stated: "You must get the most out of the power, out of the materials, and out of the time."[51]

Ford Motor Company continues the tradition of sustainability under the leadership of Henry's great-grandson, William Clay Ford, Jr. In 2002, Ford Motor Company adopted the Ford Business Principles as part of the way forward relative to accountability, community, environment, safety, products and customers, financial health, and quality of relationships.[52] An example of Ford's commitment to sustainable design in collaboration with McDonough and Braungart was the stunning transformation of the Ford Dearborn Model T plant on the Rouge River into a modern truck plant that is a model of eco-efficiency. The plant site was littered with industrial waste, mounds of debris, and abandoned buildings from the early 1900s. The new manufacturing plant has roofs made of plants to absorb and filter rain water and porous parking lots to capture storm run-off, taking three days for storm water to seep to the river. This new approach transformed a dark, unpleasant factory into an enjoyable, people-friendly, sky lit workplace.[53]

Business Issues. Sustainability is a timely consideration because, at this point, "A small number of companies . . . are acting aggressively on sustainability—and reap substantial rewards. Once companies begin to pursue sustainability initiatives in earnest, they tend to unearth opportunities to reduce costs, create new revenue streams, and develop more innovative business models. The early movers' approaches have several key characteristics in common: they incorporate a comprehensive set of data into a robust business case, which they then integrate throughout all relevant aspects of their operations to deliver measurable financial results."[54] Embedded sustainability means the incorporation of environmental, health, and social value into core business activities with no tradeoff in price or quality.[55]

Elkington, an early leader in corporate sustainability and corporate social responsibility, coined the term "triple bottom line," which refers to people, planet, and profit. He focuses on the three aspects of sustainability: environmental, social, and economic, in relation to seven revolutions: markets, values, transparency, life-cycle technology, partnership, time, and corporate governance. People refers to fair and beneficial consequences for people, such as working conditions, agricultural practices, or community enrichment. Planet pertains to environmental practices, such as energy, renewable products, waste, and conservation issues. Profit means real economic value not short term corporate impact.[56]

Complex Issues. Sustainability is a complex concept because so many entities need to be considered. Insurers consider the potential for lawsuits from environmental impact. Lenders and investors think about the need for expensive solutions, such as scrubbers for exhaust released into the atmosphere. Governments validate that environmental laws are complied with. Customers are interested that labor laws and fair practices are adhered to. Media look for good stories about sustainable success. Other important issues are resource depletion and climate change.

For example, in the late 19th century, a Yorkshire, England, textile company began making products with asbestos. They began experiencing lawsuits filed by former workers and others affected by the asbestos. In the late 20th century, Federal Mogul Corporation, a Detroit, Michigan-based auto supplier, having done careful due diligence, purchased the Yorkshire company. Their lawyers determined that the asbestos litigation would be an acceptable liability. A few years later, Federal Mogul filed for bankruptcy protection and went through very tough times financially because they underestimated the impact of asbestos litigation.[57] With many other harmful ecological situations worldwide, it is likely that there will be increasing liability issues.

Establishing successful business synergies is challenging. "There are many reasons why companies have difficulty tackling sustainability more decisively. First, companies often lack the right information upon which to base decisions. Second, companies struggle to define the business case for value creation. Third, when companies do act, their execution is often flawed."[58]

Opportunity and Challenge. Sustainability provides an increasing opportunity and challenge for performance improvement professionals. Performance improvement and performance technology concepts and practices are critical for effective, feasible, and sustainable change. Our field is diverse and very interdependent. As a result, performance improvement approaches are extraordinarily inclusive and comprehensive involving many fields such as engineering, psychology, communications, quality, education, and others.

Appreciative Inquiry/Positive Psychology Trend

Another emerging trend for performance improvement is appreciative inquiry and positive psychology.[60] Workplaces improve through positive thinking. People are most productive when they are encouraged to contribute through their strengths. World famous and highly respected Peter Drucker observed that "only strength produces results" while "only weaknesses produce headaches". Drucker said about executives, "In every area of effectiveness within an organization, *one feeds the opportunities and starves the problems*. Nowhere is this more important than in respect to people."[61]

EXHIBIT 1.2. SUSTAINABILITY IN ACTION

Using the principles of performance improvement and mega planning, Mariano Bernardez, Roger Kaufman, Adam Krivatsy, and Carmen Arias created a plan to transform Colon City, Panama, from a deteriorating city to a thriving city. Deteriorating cities experience "crime and insecurity, pollution, traffic jams, sanitary and waste management problems, air and water damage, and loss of property, property value, broken schools, ailing infrastructure, high taxes for poor quality services and quality of life in a seemingly endless sequence of calamities."[59]

Following performance improvement principles and processes as illustrated in Figure 1.4, Bernardez and Kaufman's team intends to make a very big difference through the following outcomes:

1. Increased security
2. Job creation and employment
3. Recovery of real estate values
4. Improved health and sanitation

Details are available in M. L. Bernardez, C.M. Arias, A. Krivatsy, and R. Kaufman. (2012). City doctors: A systemic approach to transform Colon City, Panama. *Performance Improvement Quarterly, 24*(4), 43–62.

FIGURE 1.4.   Framework for Colon Panama's Transformation

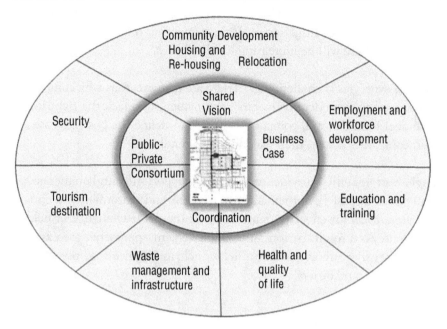

Source: M. L. Bernardez, C.M. Arias, A. Krivatsy, and R. Kaufman. (2012). City doctors: A systemic approach to transform Colon City, Panama. *Performance Improvement Quarterly, 24*(4), 43–62. Used with permission.

Definitions. Positive psychology and appreciative inquiry are emerging concepts that have enormous potential for change management and the entire performance improvement practice. The University of Pennsylvania's Martin Seligman is the leader of the positive psychology approach, while David Cooperrider of Case Western Reserve University is the founder of appreciative inquiry.

Positive psychology focuses on health and opportunities of individuals and organizations, rather than problems and hindrances.[62] Currently, psychology predominantly focused on diseases, such as depression, bipolarism, and autism in clinical psychology; biases, illusions, or foibles in social psychology; or considered selfishness in economic psychology; and many more. Positive psychology, on the other hand, is committed to human potential, motives, and capacities.[63] "Positive psychology is the scientific study of optimal human functioning. It aims to discover and promote the factors that allow individuals and communities to thrive. The positive psychology movement represents a new commitment on the part of research psychologists to focus attention upon the sources of psychological health, thereby going beyond prior emphasis on disease and disorder."[64]

"Appreciative Inquiry is about the coevolutionary search for the best in people, their organizations, and the relevant world around them. In its broadest focus, it involves systematic discovery of what gives 'life' to a living system when it is most alive, most effective, and most constructively capable in economic, ecological, and human terms. AI involves, in a central way, the art and practice of asking questions that strengthen a system's capacity to apprehend, anticipate, and heighten positive potential. It centrally involves the mobilization of inquiry through the crafting of the 'unconditional positive question' often involving hundreds or sometimes thousands of people."[65]

Leaders in the Discipline. Any discipline builds on the shoulders of previous thinkers; positive psychology began in earnest with Carl Jung's work regarding searching for the meaning of life. After World War II, the Veterans Administration encouraged psychology to focus on mental illness. Gradually, humanistic psychologists, such as Abraham Maslow and Carl Rogers, changed people's thinking about potential and buffers against mental illness, such as courage, future mindedness, optimism, interpersonal skills, faith, work ethic, hope, honesty, perseverance, and insight. At the present time, Martin Seligman at The University of Pennsylvania is the leader in positive psychology.[66]

Appreciative inquiry, recognized as positive change management, had a very definite beginning. The development of appreciative inquiry was straightforward and part of dissertation research. David Cooperrider conducted his dissertation research titled "Appreciative Inquiry: Toward a Methodology for Understanding and Enhancing Organizational Innovation" at Case Western Reserve University under the guidance of his dissertation advisor, Suresh Srivastva. The study focused totally on the factors contributing to the high functioning of an organization and totally ignored everything else.[67]

Performance Improvement and Appreciative Inquiry. Concepts and practices of performance improvement can be aligned with appreciative inquiry and provide an alternative approach to organizational change. Performance improvement is often based on needs or problems and opportunities. Frequently, practitioners focus on solving problems based on defining and resolving gaps. Appreciative inquiry is committed to enhancing the good of the individual or in the organization or culture.[68] This does not mean using an approach that glosses over problems. It means finding what is good in an individual or organization and then strengthening the "goodness." Appreciative inquiry "is gaining ground as a relevant force in organizational, community, and even national transformation."[69]

Focusing on what is good captures a natural way we think. Consider a teen trying to decide the best sport to play in high school or post-secondary school. The teen is quite good at track, moderate at soccer, and particularly challenged with baseball. The choice probably seems obvious, participate in track. In other words, the student could struggle and gradually get better in baseball or work hard to be a second-rate soccer player, or be on the primary or varsity team in track. People often naturally gravitate to choices that will enhance their strengths.

However, in organizations, we often focus on our greatest challenges or biggest problem areas. Through positive approaches, while we are enhancing what is going well, we can resolve our problem areas as a result. We can ask our customers who continue to use our products and services why they remain loyal or ask our former customers why they left. It is easier to retain a customer than to secure a new one, so we should consider what is important to our current customers and enhance that experience. As we strengthen our best features, we will automatically eliminate factors that do not enhance our products or services.

The challenge to overcome problems and sustain changes may be limited by resistance of employees or suppliers. Resistance saps energy from the effort. Appreciative inquiry envisions what might be and then determines what could and should be. In the end, is the glass half full or half empty? Is the situation half full or an opportunity that could be enhanced or is the situation half deficient and requires the problems to be resolved?[70]

Appreciative Inquiry Four-D Cycle. The process used for appreciative inquiry involves extensive group involvement. The first stage is based on including everyone or extensive interviewing of others using positive provocative questions to determine what is going well in an organization and exploring optimum ways to enhance positive situations for organizational and business advantage. There are four steps: discovery, dream, design, and destiny, shown in Figure 1.5.

Discovery means posing positive questions to determine effective processes and results, factors that have proven successful and do not promote defeat and resistance. The dream phase enables organizations to determine what would be needed for the future that would draw from past successes. Design determines how to bring successes forward to shape new products, services, organizational structures, and so forth. Destiny emphasizes successful practices that will be carried forward and stresses the need for research in order to accomplish desired new outcomes.[71]

Appreciative inquiry is based on the following beliefs and assumptions:[72] Within every society, organization, or group something works well. What is focused on becomes reality. There are multiple realities. The act of asking questions changes the situation or group in some way. People are more confident carrying the successes of the past into the future. What is brought forward into the future should be the best of the past. It is important to value differences. The language used creates reality. Performance Support Tool 1.1 provides guidelines for discussing assumptions about appreciative inquiry. The items may be adapted to guide a discussion of assumptions related to other topics as well.

School Improvement Trends. The final emerging trend in performance improvement is primary and secondary school improvement.[73] An important global performance improvement

FIGURE 1.5.   The Four-D Model

Source: Cooperrider and Whitney, 2005. Used with permission.

challenge is schooling and educating. Education is a critical aspect of economic wellbeing both individually and for society. The highly respected Organisation for Economic Co-operation and Development, based in Paris, France, is a leader in tracking factors that impact economies. OECD Deputy Secretary-General Aart de Geus presented the following *Education at a Glance 2007* indicators, confirming the positive value of education:

- "The estimated long-term effect of one additional year of education equals between 3 and 6 percent of the Gross Domestic Product (GDP) in OECD countries.
- Employment rates rise with educational attainment in most Organisation for Economic Cooperation and Development (OECD) countries.
- The employment rate for graduates of tertiary education [colleges and universities] is significantly higher than those of upper secondary graduates [high schools]; at the same time, unemployment rates fall with higher educational attainment.
- On the personal level, those who have attained upper secondary, post secondary or tertiary education face substantial earnings advantages."[74]

Education is an asset and should be targeted for performance optimization for the greatest impact. Performance improvement philosophy, processes, procedures, and certifications enhance school improvement efforts because they are systematic, add value, and focus on outcomes or results.

Behavioral-Oriented Learning Improvements. Early educational efforts in the performance improvement field were associated with applied behavioral analysis; the science of controlling and predicting behavior, in this case, leading to efficient and effective learning, particularly through programmed instruction. Beginning in the 1960s, colleagues of B.F. Skinner, such as Susan Markle, Dale Brethower, Lloyd Homme, Lt. Col. Gabriel Ofiesh, and Thomas Gilbert studied how to provide reinforcements and motivation, as well as how to analyze and present information using an auto instructional approach, also known as programmed instruction.[75] Joe Harless, Claude Lineberry, Don Tosti, Geary Rummler, Robert Mager, and Roger Kaufman were also engaged in analysis. For instance, in 1962, Robert Mager convinced educators that educational objectives were essential, publishing *Preparing Instructional Objectives* and *Analyzing Performance Problems* with Peter Pipe in 1970. Educational objectives impact most educational efforts even today.

Joe Harless remains active in improving education; he published two books on primary and secondary education (preschool to high school): *The Eden Conspiracy* in 1998 and *Turning Kids On and Off* with Claude Lineberry in 1971.[76] While this work was exciting and had substantial impact, particularly Mager's work, school improvement also involves many other factors, such as curriculum and instruction, teacher preparation and ongoing education, appropriate resources (such as textbooks and supplies), incentives, societal expectations, and many more that combined to foster school performance improvement.

Ogden Lindsley developed precision teaching based on B.F. Skinner's operant conditioning and Carl Binder continues to work on direct instruction and precision teaching.[77] Educators, learning scientists, and instructional designers advance behavioral analysis in the United States,

PERFORMANCE SUPPORT TOOL 1.1. APPRECIATIVE INQUIRY DISCUSSION GUIDE

Directions: Concepts and assumptions apply whether oriented to problem solving or a positive approach. As a group, read each assumption associated with appreciative inquiry and its description. Discuss each concept, looking for a consensus opinion. Briefly write down consensus opinions.

Assumption 1: Finding What Works. Even the most troubled organizations have people, processes, or practices that work. Identifying and uncovering these assets offers insight and a foundation for progress.

Assumption 2: Choosing the Right Focus. What we focus on grows. Appreciative inquiry therefore suggests that framing our challenges and opportunities using an affirmative view of the situation we face is critical.

Assumption 3: Creating Reality. Reality is a function of the world we live in as well as the insights and experiences we bring to it. Reality is unique for each of us, and many realities can coexist.

Assumption 4: Asking the Right Questions. If we believe that what we focus on grows, then the questions we ask become the starting point for our future. As David Cooperrider says, "Change starts with the first question."

Assumption 5: Carrying the Past Forward. The journey of change becomes less threatening when we bring with us the comfort of ideas and practices we know and trust.

Assumption 6: Carrying the Best of the Past. Following the affirmative thread, if we're going to retain parts of the past as we journey into the future, it makes sense to keep those that represent our greatest strengths.

Assumption 7: Valuing Differences. Our differences, represented by our unique realities, offer innovation and many possibilities for building the future we most desire.

Assumption 8: Using Positive Language. Language drives our thoughts and action. It is therefore important to consider the words we choose, particularly the framing of the questions we ask.

Adapted from Hammond, 1996. Used with permission.

South Africa, and other parts of the world.[78] Precision teaching and behavioral analysis proponents consider that (1) quality schooling should help students learn more rapidly than they would on their own; (2) what students learn should benefit the individual learner and society; and (3) learning should employ positive rather than coercive or punitive methods.

Education for All. Lack of education is closely associated with poverty, poor health, and the inability to compete economically. "As global citizens of the world it is our responsibility to critically think about these issues and attempt to come up with solutions to the problems plaguing education."[79] "In 2007, there were approximately 775 million illiterate people in the world, of whom two-thirds lived in the Asia-Pacific region, and more than 60 percent were women.[80] That means one-fifth of adults above age fifteen and a quarter of adult women above age fifteen lack minimum literacy skills. To receive an education is a human right and an opportunity to improve one's life. Literacy is at the heart of basic education for all, and essential for eradicating poverty."[81]

Education for All is a global movement of the United Nations Educational, Scientific and Cultural Organization (UNESCO) focused on learning needs of children, youth, and adults designed to eliminate illiteracy.[82] The movement officially began in Jomtien, Thailand, in 1990 at the World Conference on Education for All, stressing education as a fundamental universal human right. Ten years later, the World Education Forum in Dakar, Senegal, established six measurable goals:

1. Expanding and improving comprehensive early childhood care and education, especially for the most vulnerable and disadvantaged children;
2. Ensuring that by 2015 all children, particularly girls, children in difficult circumstances, and those belonging to ethnic minorities, have access to and complete free and compulsory primary education of good quality;
3. Ensuring that the learning needs of all young people and adults are met through equitable access to appropriate learning and life-skills programs;
4. Achieving a 50 percent improvement in levels of adult literacy by 2015, especially for women, and equitable access to basic and continuing education for all adults;
5. Eliminating gender disparities in primary and secondary education by 2005, and achieving gender equality in education by 2015, with a focus on ensuring girls full and equal access to and achievement in basic education of good quality;
6. Improving all aspects of the quality of education and ensuring excellence of all so that recognized and measurable learning outcomes are achieved by all, especially in literacy, numeracy, and essential life skills.[83]

Clearly, there are many opportunities for performance improvement in schools, using performance improvement methods discussed in this book and improvements methods associated with the standards. In addition, many performance improvement professionals, particularly Carl Binder with Precision Teaching, has vast experience with curriculum and course development.

Certified School Improvement Specialist. The ultimate role of education is to prepare citizens to lead productive and meaningful lives and enhance society.[84] Universal education is a relatively new concept, beginning with the 20th century and the Industrial Revolution. Schools are adapting to meet the needs of so many, such as increasing use of technology, benchmarking, and increasingly sophisticated techniques for accountability.[85] The future role of the educator will include many new aspects, such as individualized and customizing learning, virtual and physical learning, nonlinear and collaborative, problem-based learning, discovery learning that engages the whole mind, and more emphasis on multimedia and technology.[86] Establishing and maintaining quality education is optimized by substantial understanding of performance improvement.

Recently, Deb Page and Judy Hale researched successful schools in the state of Georgia in the United States. They focused on school improvement specialists who had sustained improvements for at least three years to determine what factors led to good schools.[87] The goal was to create a proficiency-based certification unique to school improvement. It was necessary to document competencies required to successfully improve schools and to maintain high quality education for the 21st century.[88] The resulting school improvement competency domains are

1. Analyze and apply critical judgment.
2. Facilitate meaning and engagement.
3. Focus on systemic factors.
4. Plan and record.
5. Organize and manage efforts and resources.
6. Guide and focus collaborative improvement.
7. Monitor accountability and adoption.
8. Demonstrate organizational sensitivity.
9. Build capacity.
10. Implement for sustainability.

This school improvement certification is available through the International Society for Performance Improvement and can be found at ISPI.org, under the tab "Certification." The certification indicates that the school specialist has accomplished sustained school improvement and is a recognized school leader. (See Appendix B.)

Citations

1. Deterline & Rosenberg, 1992, p. 3
2. Gramsci, 2000; Blake & Moseley, 2010
3. Deming, 1986
4. Stewart, Taylor, Petre, & Schlender, 1999
5. Drucker, 1995, pp. 75–76
6. Gerson, 1999
7. Stewart, Taylor, Petre, & Schlender, 1999
8. Dean, 1992, p. 83; Sanders & Ruggles, 2000
9. Gilbert, 1978
10. Sanders & Ruggles, 2000

11. Pershing, 2006, p. 28

12. Beish, 2011

13. Rosenberg, 1998

14. Millman, 1997

15. Fisher & Fisher, 1998

16. Millman, 1997

17. Drucker, 1993; Carnevale, 1993

18. AON Consulting, 1997; ASTD 1998, 1999.

19. Stolovitch & Keeps, 1992, 1999; Pershing, 2006

20. Silber & Foshay, 2010; Watkins & Leigh, 2010; Moseley & Dessinger, 2010

21. Tosti & Kaufman, 2007

22. Addison, Personal Communication, August 9, 2011

23. Mager, Personal Communication, August 5, 2011

24. Gilbert, 1978

25. Dean, 1992, p. 83; Dean & Ripley, 1997; Lindsley, 1996, p. 11; Tosti & Kaufman, 2007

26. Gilbert, 1978

27. Chevalier, 2003, p. 8

28. Gilbert, 1978, p. 95

29. Chevalier, 2003; Marker, 2007

30. Bloem & Vermei, 2009, p. 42.

31. Rummler & Brache, 1995

32. Rummler & Brache, 1995

33. Rummler & Brache, 1995, p. 169

34. Ramias & Rummler, 2009

35. Rummler, 1986

36. Moore, 2010

37. Kaufman, 2003, pp. 35–39, Kaufman, 2004

38. Singh & Narahara, 2001

39. Mager, 1962, p. 63

40. Mager, 2011

41. Mager & Pipe, 1984, p. 4

42. Berns, Townend, Khayat, Balagopal, Reeves, Hopkins, & Kruschwitz, 2009, p. 11.

43. Brundtland, 1987, pp. 4–5

44. The World Commission on Environment and Development, 1987

45. Population Reference Bureau, 2011

46. World Bank, n.d.

47. Carnegie Endowment for International Peace, 2010, p. 1

48. Donaldio & Goodstein, 2009

49. Elliott, 2009

50. The World Bank Group, 2011; Madden & Weisbrod, 2008

51. Ford, 1926, as cited in McDonough & Braungart, 1998, p. 2

52. Letter from Bill Ford, 2003, as cited in Shaffer & Schmidt, 2006

53. McDonough & Braungart, 2002, pp. 157–165

54. Berns, Townend, Khayat, Balagopal, Reeves, Hopkins, & Kruschwitz, 2009, p. 14

55. Laszio & Zhexembayeva, 2011

56. Elkington, 1999

57. British Asbestos Newsletter, 2006; Armley Asbestos Disaster: T N Response, 2010

58. Berns, Townend, Khayat, Balagopal, Reeves, Hopkins, & Kruschwitz, 2009, p. 5

59. Bernardez, Arias, Krivatsy, & Kaufman, 2012, p. 43

60. Fauvre, Rosenzweig, & Van Tiem, 2010

61. Drucker, 1966, p. 98

62. Cameron, Dutton, & Quinn, 2003

63. Sheldon & King, 2001

64. Akumal Manifesto, 2000

65. Cooperrider & Whitney, 2005

66. Seligman, 2000

67. Watkins & Mohr, 2001, p. 15

68. Srivastva & Cooperrider, 1998; Whitney, Trosten-Bloom, & Rader, 2010

69. Conkright, 2011, p. 31

70. Lewis & Van Tiem, 2004; Van Tiem & Lewis, 2006

71. Cooperrider & Whitney, 2005

72. Hammond, 1998, pp. 20–21, in Rosenzweig & Van Tiem, 2007

73. Gerson & Gerson, 2008

74. Organisation of Economic Co-operation and Development, 2008, p. 4

75. Huglin, 2010

76. Harless, 1998; Harless & Lineberry, 1971

77. Lindsley, 1991; Binder & Watkins, 1990

78. Leon, Ford, Shimizu, Stretz, Thompson, Sota, Twyman, & Layng, 2011; Robbins, Weisenburgh-Snyder, Damons, Van Rooyen, & Ismail, 2011

79. Binder, 2007, pp. 14–21

80. TakingITGlobal.org, n.d.

81. EFA-Education for All, n.d., p. 60

82. UNESCO.org, n.d.

83. UNESCO, 2000

84. Harless, 1998

85. Tashlik, 2010

86. Jukes, McCain, & Crockett, 2010/2011

87. Hale, 2011

88. Hale, 2011, p. 10

References

Akumal Manifesto. (2000). UPenn Positive Psychology Center. Philadelphia, PA: University of Pennsylvania. Retrieved from www.ppc.sas.upenn.edu/akumailmanifesto.htm.

AON Consulting. (1997). *The 1997 survey of human resource trends*. Detroit, MI: AON Consulting, Human Resource Consulting Group.

ASTD. (1997). *The 1998 national HRD executive survey: Trends in HRD*. Alexandria, VA: American Society for Training and Development.

ASTD (1998). *The 1998 national HRD executive survey: Leadership development*. Alexandria, VA: American Society for Training and Development.

Beish, K. (2011). Using the HPT model to identify and resolve issues for foreign workers in a lean U.S. assembly plant: a case study. (Doctoral dissertation.). Minneapolis, MN: Capella University.

Bernardez, M.L. (2011). Should we have a universal model for HPT? A practical alternative that works. *Performance Improvement, 50*(9) 41–48.

Bernardez, M.L. Arias, C.M., Krivatsy, A., & Kaufman, R. (2012). City doctors: A systemic approach to transform Colon City, Panama. *Performance Improvement Quarterly, 24*(4), 43–62.

Berns, M., Townend, A., Khayat, Z., Balagopal, B., Reeves, M., Hopkins, M., & Kruschwitz, N. (2009, September). *The business of sustainability: Imperatives, advantages, and actions*. Boston, MA: The Boston Consulting Group, Inc.

Bloem, M., & Vermei, A. (2009, November/December). Rummler's swim lanes in a Dutch swimming pool. *Performance Improvement, 48*(10), 41–46.

Brethower, D.M. (2009, November). It isn't magic, it's science. *Performance Improvement, 48*(10), 18–24.

Brundtland, G.H. (1987, June 8). Presentation of the report of the world commission on environmental and development to UNEP's 14th governing council session. Nairobi: Kenya.

Cameron, K.S., Dutton, J.E., & Quinn, R.E. (Eds.). (2003). *Positive organizational scholarship: Foundations of a new discipline*. San Francisco: Berrett-Koehler.

Carnegie Endowment for International Peace. (2010, March 10). The new world economic order: Are capitals ready? Retrieved from www.carnegieendowment.org/events/?fa=eventDetail&id=2833

Chevalier, R. (2003, May/June). Updating the behavior engineering model. *Performance Improvement, 42*(5), 8–15.

Conkright, T.A. (2011, July). Improving performance and organizational value through a virtual appreciative inquiry summit. *Performance Improvement, 50*, 31–37.

Cooperrider, D.L., & Whitney, D. (2005). *A positive revolution in change: Appreciative inquiry*. San Francisco: Berrett-Koehler.

Dean, P.J. (1992). Allow me to introduce . . . Thomas F. Gilbert. *Performance Improvement Quarterly, 5*(3).

Dean, P.J., & Ripley, D. (1997). *Performance improvement pathfinders: Models for organizational learning*. Washington, DC: International Society for Performance Improvement.

Deming, W.E. (1986). *Out of the crisis*. Boston, MA: Massachusetts Institute of Technology, Center for Advanced Engineering Study.

Deterline, W.A., & Rosenberg, M.J. (1992). *Workplace productivity: Performance technology success stories*. Washington, DC: International Society for Performance Improvement.

Donaldio, R., & Goodstein, L.D. (2009, July 8). Pope urges forming new world economic order to work for "common good." *New York Times*. Retrieved from www.nytimes.com/2009/07/08/world/europe/08pope.html.

Drucker, P. (1966). *The effective executive*. New York: HarperCollins.

Drucker, P. (1993). *Managing for the future*. Oxford, UK: Butterworth Heinemann.

Drucker, P. (1995). *Managing in a time of great change*. New York: Truman Talley Books/Plume.

Education for All. (n.d.) Educational Cooperation Programme. Retrieved from www.accu.or.jp/jp/en/activity/education/02–01.html.

Elkington, J. (1999). *Cannibals with forks–The triple bottom line of 21st century business*. Oxford, England: Capstone Publishing.

Elkington, J. (2004). Enter the triple bottom line. In A. Henriques & J. Richardson (Eds.), *The triple bottom line, Does it all add up?: Assessing the sustainability of business and CST* (p. 3). London, England: Earthscan.

Elliott, L. (2009, October 4). World Bank welcomes new economic order from the ashes of crisis. *The Observer*. Retrieved from www.guardian.co.uk/business/2009/oct/04/world-bank-power-shift

Fauvre, M., Rosenzweig, J., & Van Tiem, D.M. (2010). Appreciative inquiry. In R. Watkins & D. Leigh. *Handbook of improving performance in the workplace, volume 2: Selecting and implementing performance interventions*. San Francisco: Pfeiffer.

Fisher, K., & Fisher, M.D. (1998). *The distributed mind: Achieving high performance through the collective intelligence of knowledge work teams*. New York: AMACOM.

Gerson, R.F. (1999, November/December). The people side of performance improvement. *Performance Improvement, 38*(10), 19–22.

Gerson, R.F., & Gerson, R.G. (2008, February). HPT in the classroom: Practical applications, *Performance Improvement, 47*(2), 41–45.

Gilbert, T.F. (1978). *Human competence: Engineering worthy performance*. New York: McGraw-Hill.

Gramsci, A. (2000). *Prospects: The Quarterly Review of Comparative Education*, 1993, 3/4, 597–612. Paris, France: UNESCO: International Bureau of Education. Retrieved from: www.ibe.unesco.org/publications/ThinkersPdf/gramscie.pdf.

Hale, J.A. (2011, April). Competencies for professionals in school improvement. *Performance Improvement, 50*(4), 10–17.

Hammond, S.A. (1996). *The thin book of appreciative inquiry* Bend, OR: Thin Books.

Harless, J.H. (1998). *The Eden conspiracy: Educating for accomplished citizenship*. Wheaton, IL: Guild V Publications.

Harless, J.H., & Lineberry, C.S. (1971). *Turning kids on and off*. Springfield, VA: Guild V Publications.

Huglin, L.M. (2010, April). Research themes in HPT: A content review of the ISPI journals. *Performance Improvement, 49*(4), 9–16.

Jukes, I., McCain, T., & Crockett, L. (2010, December/2011 January). Education and the role of he educator in the future. *Kappan, 92*(4), 15–21.

Kaufman, R. (2003, February). Value, value: Where is the value? *Performance Improvement, 42*(2), 36–38.

Kaufman, R. (2011). *The manager's pocket guide to mega thinking and planning*. Amherst, MA: HRD Press.

Laszio, C., & Zhexembayeva, N. (2011). *Embedded sustainability: The next big competitive advantage*. Palo Alto, CA: Stanford Business Books.

Leon, M., Ford, V., Shimizu, A.H., Stretz, A.H., Thompson, J., Sota, M. Twyman, J.S., & Layng, T.V.J., (2011, April). Comprehension by design: Teaching young learners how to comprehend what they read. *Performance Improvement, 50*(4), 40–47.

Lewis, J., & Van Tiem, D.M. (2004). Appreciative inquiry: A view of a glass half full. *Performance Improvement, 43*(8), 19–24.

Lindsley, O.R. (1991). Precision teaching's unique legacy from B.F. Skinner. *Journal of Behavioral Education, 1*(2), 253–266.

Lindsley, O.R. (1996, Spring). In memoriam: Thomas F. Gilbert 1927–1995. *The Behavior Analyst, 19, 11–18*.

Madden, P., & Weisbrod, I. (2008, April). Connected ICT and sustainable development: Forum for the future. Retrieved from www.forumforthefuture.org.uk.

Mager, R.F. (1962). *Preparing instructional objectives*. Belmont, CA: Fearon.

Mager, R.F., & Pipe, P. (1984). *Analyzing performance problems or 'You really oughta wanna.'* Belmont, CA: Fearon.

Mager, R.F., & Pipe, P. (1997). *Analyzing performance problems or 'You really oughta wanna.'* (3rd ed.). Atlanta, GA: CEP Press.

Marker, A. (2007, January). Synchronized analysis model: Linking Gilbert's behavior engineering model with environmental analysis models. *Performance Improvement, 46*(1), 26–33.

McDonough, W., & Braungart, M. (1998, October). The NEXT industrial revolution. *The Atlantic*. Retrieved from www.theatlantic.com/magazine/print/1998/10/the-next-industrial-revolution/4695/

McDonough, W., & Braungart, M. (2002). *Cradle to cradle: Remaking the way we make things*. New York: North Point Press.

Millman, H. (1997, November 17). The pros and perils of mining intellectual capital. *InfoWorld, 19*(4), 128.

Moore, S.L. (2010). *Ethics by design: Strategic thinking and planning for exemplary performance, responsible results, and societal accountability.* Amherst, MA: HRD Press.

Moore, S.L., Ellsworth, J.B., & Kaufman, R. (2011). Visions and missions: Are they useful? A quick assessment. *Performance Improvement, 50*(6), 15–24.

Organisation for Economic Cooperation and Development. (2008, April 14). *2nd OECD global forum on education: Improving the effectiveness of education systems.* EDU/GF (2008)1 Unclassified. Retrieved from www.oecd.org/document/0/0,3746,en_21571361_39572393_39699147_1_1_1_1,00.html.

Page, D. (2011, April). RSVP in action: Systemic improvement in the city schools of Decatur. *Performance Improvement, 50*(4), 18–25.

Pershing, J.A. (2006). (Ed.). *Handbook of human performance technology: Principles, practices, potential* (3rd ed.). San Francisco: Pfeiffer.

Population Reference Bureau: World Population Growth. (2011). Retrieved from www.prb.org/Educators/TeachersGuides/HumanPopulation/PopulationGrowth.aspx.

Ramais, A.J., & Rummler, R. (2009, November/December). The evolutions of the effective process framework: A model for redesigning business practices. *Performance Improvement, 48*(10), 25–31.

Robbins, J.K., Weisenburg-Snyder, A.B., Damons, B., Van Rooyen, M., & Ismail, C. (2011, April). Partnerships for educational excellence and research: HPT in the townships of South Africa. *Performance Improvement, 50*(4), 31–39.

Rosenberg, M.J. (1998, November/December) Tangled up in terms. *Performance Improvement, 37*(9), 6–8.

Rosenzweig, J., & Van Tiem, D.M. (2007, May/June). An appreciative view of human performance technology. *Performance Improvement, 4*(5), 36–43.

Rummler, G.A. (1986). *Organizational redesign: Introduction to performance technology.* Washington, DC: International Society for Performance Improvement.

Rummler, G.A, & Brache, A.P. (1995). *Improving performance: How to manage the white space on the organization chart* (2nd ed.). San Francisco: Jossey-Bass.

Sanders, E.S., & Ruggles, J.L. (2000, June). HPI soup: Too many cooks haven't spoiled the broth. *Training + Development, 54*(6), 26–36.

Seligman, M.E.P., & Csikszentmihalyi, M. (2000, January). Positive psychology: An introduction. *American Psychologist, 55*(1), 5–14.

Shaffer, S.P., & Schmidt, T.M. (2006). Sustainable development and human performance technology. In J.A. Pershing (Ed.), *Handbook of human performance technology: Principles, practices, potential* (3rd ed.). San Francisco: Pfeiffer.

Sheldon, K.M., & King, L. (2001, March). Why positive psychology is necessary? *American Psychologist, 56*(3), 215–217.

Singh, L., & Narahara, S. (2001, July). Unsung heroes: Allow us to introduce: Roger Kaufman. *Performance Improvement, 40*(6), 16–18.

Srivastva, S., & Cooperrider, D.L. (1998). *Organizational wisdom and executive courage.* San Francisco: New Lexington Press.

Stewart, T.A., Taylor, A., Petre, P., & Schlender, B. (1999, November). Businessman of the century. *Fortune, 140*(10), 108–128.

Stolovitch, H.D., & Keeps, E.J. (1992). (Eds.). *Handbook of human performance technology: A comprehensive guide for analyzing and solving performance problems in organizations* (1st ed.). San Francisco: Jossey-Bass.

Stolovitch, H.D., & Keeps, E.J. (1999). (Eds.). *Handbook of human performance technology: Improving individual and organizational performance worldwide* (2nd ed.). San Francisco: Pfeiffer.

TakingITGlobal.org: Education. Retrieved from http://issues.tigweb.org/education.

Tashlik, P. (2010, March). Changing the national conversation on assessment. *Kappan, 91*(6), 55–59.

Tosti, D.T., & Kaufman, R. (2007, August). Who is the "real" father of HPT? *Performance Improvement, 46*(7), 5–8.

UNESCO.org: World education forum at Dakar, Senegal: Final report. (2000). Retrieved from http://unesdoc.unesco.org/images/0012/001211/121117e.pdf.

UNESCO.org: The EFA movement. (n.d.). Retrieved from www.unesco.org/new/en/education/themes/leading-the-international-agenda/education-for-all/the-efa-movement/

Van Tiem, D.M., & Lewis, J. (2006). Appreciative inquiry: Unraveling the mystery of accentuating the positive. In J.A. Pershing. (Ed.), *Handbook of human performance technology: Principles, practices, potential* (3rd ed.) (pp. 1147–1164). San Francisco: Pfeiffer.

Watkins, J.M., & Mohr, B. (2001). *Appreciative inquiry: Change at the speed of imagination.* San Francisco: Pfeiffer.

Whitney, D., Trosten-Bloom, A., & Rader, K. (2010). *Appreciative leadership: Focus on what works to drive winning performance and build a thriving organization.* New York: McGraw-Hill.

World Bank. (n.d.). Development educational program's DEPweb: Explore sustainable development: World population growth. Retrieved from www.worldbank.org/depweb/beyond/beyondco/beg_03.pdf.

The world bank group: In focus. (2011). Retrieved from http://go.worldbank.org/G4PCUA5AN0.

The World Commission on Environmental and Development. (1987). *Our common future.* Oxford, England: Oxford University Press.

Performance Improvement/HPT Model—An Overview

2

"The world has entered a new economic era characterized by rapid and unprecedented change, with competitiveness and productivity challenges never encountered before. Increasing competitiveness and productivity will not result from more machines, improved computers, or reliance on cost cutting. Greater productivity will be accomplished through one of the world's most critical resources: *people*."[1]

Slywotzky and Morrison, 1997, p. 79

Introduction

Performance improvement is optimized by using evidence-based, thoughtful approaches associated with performance technology, quality, communications, organizational development, project management, business processes, and many more. The Performance Improvement/HPT Model is a diagnostic and strategic tool for improving workplace performance because it is a thoughtful, evidence-based approach. It is the traditional, systems-based model used by many performance improvement practitioners.

Responsive

The Performance Improvement/HPT Model is responsive to the knowledge and models of experts and practitioners in the field. Gilbert's Behavior Engineering Model is integrated into the cause analysis component of Performance Analysis. The 2012 Performance Improvement/ HPT Model stresses the concepts that performance improvement issues may be opportunities as well as problems, emphasizes the role of change management in all phases of successful performance improvement, and includes the concepts of feasibility and sustainability.

Adaptable

The Performance Improvement/HPT Model is also adaptable. It may be used to address a variety of workplace challenges as well as different organizational needs and requirements. For example, the process of preparing a business case has been added during the selection, design, and development phase (see Chapter 19).

Focused on Accountability and Integrity

The Performance Improvement/HPT Model provides performance improvement practitioners, performance technology consultants, human resource specialists, quality leaders, and others interested in improvement with a framework for accountability and integrity. PI practices are based on RSVP—results, systemic, value, partnership—the four essentials for successful performance improvement practices and the first four performance technology standards:

- **Results**—Results-oriented means clarifying the outcomes expected and the measures that will indicate success.
- **Systemic**—Complexity and interconnectedness of situations means it is essential to be inclusive and acknowledge relationships in a system approach; to deal with the situation as a whole system rather than as parts.
- **Value** added—Interventions should increase the worth of the situation for the internal organization or external client.
- **Partnership**—Work with stakeholders, participants, and content experts using collaborative approaches to improve and enhance workplace performance.

The model, shown in Figure 2.1, incorporates each of these essentials throughout its various phases.

Inside the 2012 Model

The 2012 Performance Improvement/HPT Model is still organized in systems-based phases: Performance Analysis, Intervention Selection, Design, Development, Intervention Implementation and Maintenance, and Evaluation. The Implementation and Change Phase has been changed to Implementation and *Maintenance* to emphasize the growing need for sustainable performance improvement interventions. Right from the beginning, considerations include whether the effort can be maintained over the long term based on thorough determination of feasibility and sustainability. Change now surrounds the model because it is an integral part of every phase in the performance improvement process.

The model is still designed to imply both a linear and an iterative progression of events. There are advantages to following the phases sequentially with no phase being omitted. Just as a medical doctor diagnoses a condition and then prescribes treatment based on the patient's symptoms, physical exams, and diagnostic tests, PI practitioners should not prescribe an intervention without first observing and analyzing the situation. In performance improvement, recommendations

FIGURE 2.1.   The Performance Improvement/HPT Model

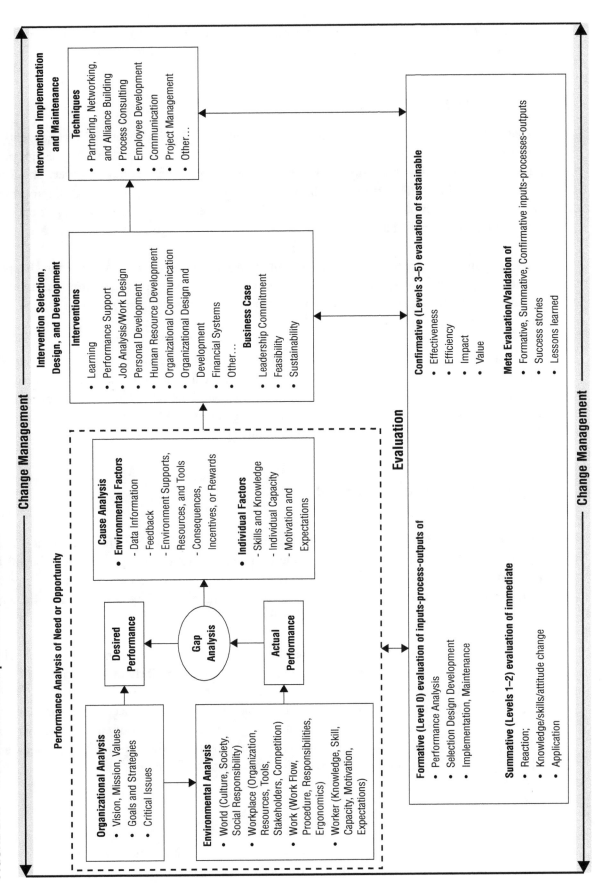

are made after analyzing the current organizational state and determining its ideal situation. Only then can valid interventions be selected. Each of the phases will be discussed later in this chapter.

Change Management

A major change in the 2012 Performance Improvement/HPT Model (Figure 2.1) is change itself. Performance improvement means change. The 2012 model illustrates a systemic process for planning and accomplishing the desired changes. Change management encompasses every phase and each aspect of the entire performance improvement process. As the performance improvement practitioner works through each phase the practitioner considers how the problem or opportunity or intervention will change the world, workplace, work, and worker.

Too often, unwanted change occurs, insufficient change makes matters worse, or change happens in the beginning but then wanes or reverts to the previous situation because of not considering the interdependence of factors, the feasibility of solutions, or not enlisting sufficient support from within the organization.

As a result, change management now surrounds each stage in performance improvement to signify that change occurs and must be accounted for from the first analysis question. It is often said that asking the first question is the beginning of change. Throughout the entire performance improvement process as the organization is developing, adapting, or resisting, we need to prepare the organization for accomplishing and maintaining expectations.[2] (See Chapter 3.)

Performance Analysis Phase

The first phase in the HPT Model (Figure 2.2) is performance analysis. Performance improvement and change are needed when there is a problem to be alleviated and/or there is a need to innovate and create opportunities. Performance improvement practitioners begin by understanding the challenge, need, or opportunity such as a new product, service, or process. "Performance analysis is the process of identifying the organization's performance requirements and comparing them to its objectives and capabilities."[3]

Performance analysis is important because it identifies what is causing problems or what strengths are available for innovation. It is difficult to fix a problem if there is no agreement as to what the problem is; there will be slightly different versions of the situation in everyone's mind and progress will be viewed slightly differently by each individual. It is necessary to first identify the challenge before attempting to remedy it through cause or opportunity analysis. Otherwise, it is easy to focus on something totally unrelated to the problem, thus wasting time, money, and other resources.[4] Performance analysis is discussed at length in Chapter 4.

Organizational Analysis

Organizational analysis looks into the heart of the organization—its vision, mission, values, goals, strategies, and critical issues driving the need for change. (See Chapter 5.)

FIGURE 2.2. Performance Improvement/HPT Model: Performance Analysis Phase

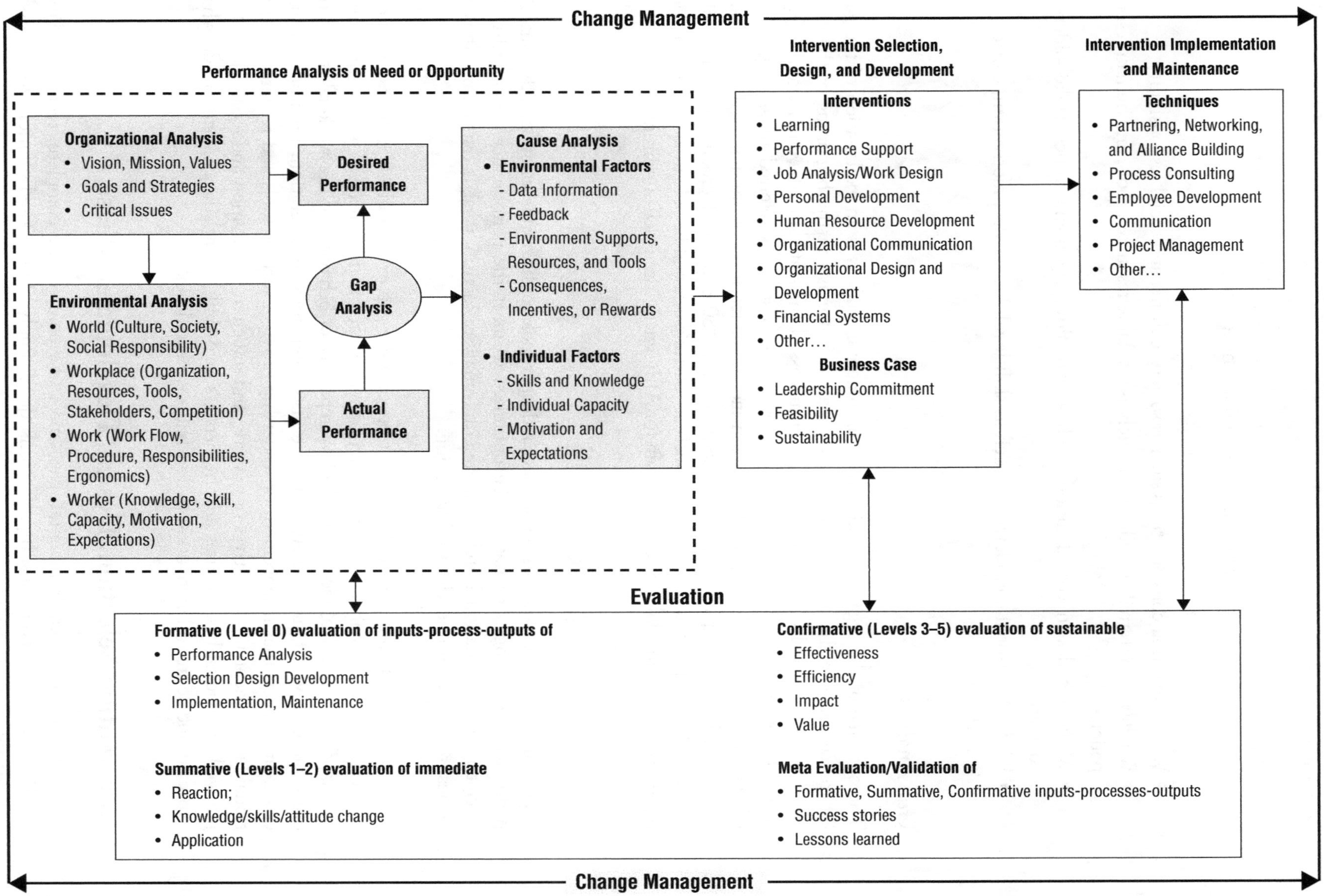

Change Management

Performance Analysis of Need or Opportunity

Organizational Analysis
- Vision, Mission, Values
- Goals and Strategies
- Critical Issues

Environmental Analysis
- World (Culture, Society, Social Responsibility)
- Workplace (Organization, Resources, Tools, Stakeholders, Competition)
- Work (Work Flow, Procedure, Responsibilities, Ergonomics)
- Worker (Knowledge, Skill, Capacity, Motivation, Expectations)

Desired Performance

Gap Analysis

Actual Performance

Cause Analysis
- **Environmental Factors**
  - Data Information
  - Feedback
  - Environment Supports, Resources, and Tools
  - Consequences, Incentives, or Rewards
- **Individual Factors**
  - Skills and Knowledge
  - Individual Capacity
  - Motivation and Expectations

Intervention Selection, Design, and Development

Interventions
- Learning
- Performance Support
- Job Analysis/Work Design
- Personal Development
- Human Resource Development
- Organizational Communication
- Organizational Design and Development
- Financial Systems
- Other...

Business Case
- Leadership Commitment
- Feasibility
- Sustainability

Intervention Implementation and Maintenance

Techniques
- Partnering, Networking, and Alliance Building
- Process Consulting
- Employee Development
- Communication
- Project Management
- Other...

Evaluation

Formative (Level 0) evaluation of inputs-process-outputs of
- Performance Analysis
- Selection Design Development
- Implementation, Maintenance

Summative (Levels 1–2) evaluation of immediate
- Reaction;
- Knowledge/skills/attitude change
- Application

Confirmative (Levels 3–5) evaluation of sustainable
- Effectiveness
- Efficiency
- Impact
- Value

Meta Evaluation/Validation of
- Formative, Summative, Confirmative inputs-processes-outputs
- Success stories
- Lessons learned

Change Management

45

Environmental Analysis

Environmental analysis identifies and prioritizes the realities that support actual performance. (See Chapter 6.) Environmental analysis examines the following:

- *World*—external considerations such as society, culture, and social responsibility
- *Workplace*—internal considerations such as available resources, tools, and human resources policies
- *Work*—job design considerations such as workflow, ergonomic issues, stakeholders and competition
- *Worker*—personal considerations such as skill level, knowledge, motivation, capacity, and expectations.

Gap Analysis

The outcome of the organizational and environmental analysis is an explanation of the gap or difference between the current state, or the reality as it exists in the beginning of the change effort, and the desired state, or the ultimate or successful end state after the change and improvements have occurred. The difference between the two states is referred to as a "gap." (See Chapter 7.) Although this appears to be scientific and exact, it is not unusual for the gap description to include both quantitative statements such as "80 percent of production errors will be eliminated" and qualitative descriptions such as "participants will be able to apply basic accounting skills to make an adult day care program for Alzheimer citizens self-sustaining."

Cause Analysis

The final performance analysis phase takes a deeper look to determine what actually caused the performance challenge or what can be optimized to meet the performance opportunity. (See Chapter 8.) Organizational and environmental analyses identify *what* is happening. It is now critical to also determine *why* it is happening.

Cause analysis determines why the need or opportunity gap exists. Gilbert indicated that probable causes can be attributed to either environmental factors that create a lack of environmental support or individual factors or a lack of repertory of behavior for the worker.[5] In addition, organizational, world, and society issues are also taken into consideration. Environment-based causes are aspects that management or leadership provide, such as tools and resources, motivational factors including incentives or rewards, and sufficient information and feedback to do the job well. Individual-based causes are the person's own skills, knowledge, capacity to do what is expected, and desire and motivation to do what is expected well.

Intervention Selection, Design, Development Phase

After organizational, environmental, gap, and cause analyses are complete, recommendations can be made for interventions. Interventions, quite simply, are proposed solutions to address the gaps identified in an organization.

Intervention Selection

Interventions should be selected based on outcomes or results, impact, value, costs, and benefit to the organization and the situation. Following are many examples of interventions. This book contains a comprehensive coverage of the most common or high-value PI interventions in each category (see Chapters 10 though 17). Chapter 9 also contains an Intervention Selector and Intervention Selection Tool to help performance improvement practitioners select the most appropriate intervention or blend of interventions for a specific situation.

Interventions. The Selection, Design, and Development Phase of the Performance Improvement/HPT Model (see Figure 2.3) contains a list of the major categories of performance improvement interventions and individual chapters in this book discuss common interventions that fall into each category. Table 2.1 describes the intervention categories in the model.

Blending Interventions. There are many possible options and combinations of options. It is usually necessary to have a comprehensive, holistic approach that covers many of the issues or aspects of the challenge or opportunity. That normally means selecting more than one intervention because most situations are complex and require comprehensive solutions.

Criteria for Successful Interventions

Factors that need to be considered if successful interventions are to take place include return on investment, sustainability, and accountability.

Return on Investment. The intervention needs to be cost-effective for the organization. "Although overused, the term 'bottom line' still captures the attention of management. A candid discussion of budgets, including overhead and additional expenses, if related to the expected results, will preclude later rejection of the program."[8] Projects should always provide value, sometimes based on tangible breakeven and future financial benefits and other times based on intangible value such as increased team work, stronger succession plan, more robust culture, or integrated departments.

Sustainability. If the intervention is not one that is easily maintained, then once the performance improvement practitioner leaves the project or the organization shifts to new priorities, the interventions probably will have little support and may be discontinued.

Accountability. An intervention needs a sponsor or champion, someone who will provide support and encourage its maintenance. Sponsorship means on-going commitment. "It should never be assumed that intervention sponsorship and support will be perpetual. Sponsorship must be nurtured."[6]

Intervention Design and Development

This edition of *Fundamentals* includes separate chapters on designing and developing interventions. Design is the planning part of the intervention selection, design, and development phase. The performance improvement practitioner plans how to "transform the intervention selection decision into reality."[7] The output is a design document that may be used as a guide for

FIGURE 2.3. Performance Improvement/HPT Model: Intervention Selection, Design, and Development Phase

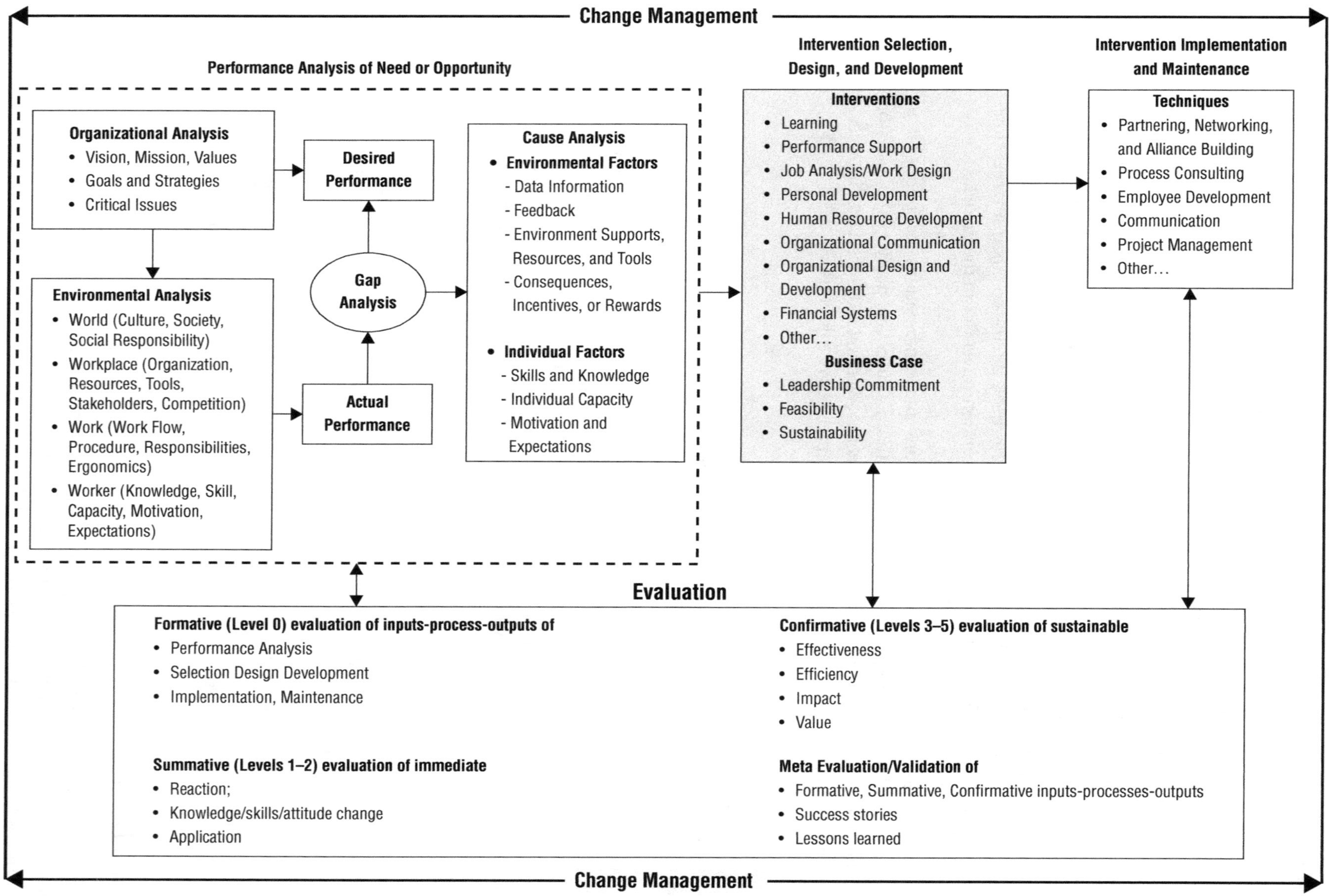

TABLE 2.1. Overview of Intervention Categories

Intervention	Description	Chapter
Learning	Knowledge and skills can be improved through learning interventions such as training, education, learning organizations, and so forth.	10
Performance Support	Job aids or performance support tools, expert systems, and other support interventions expedite the intervention implementation or application.	11
Job Analysis/Work Design	Work processes can be analyzed or jobs can be redesigned to improve productivity and effectiveness, health, wellness, comfort, or ergonomics.	12
Personal Development	Personal development interventions may include coaching, mentoring, career development, effective supervision, and reliable and informative feedback.	13
Human Resource Development	Measurement and metrics help the human resources to staff, compensate, reward, and evaluate employees.	14
Organizational Communication	Communication interventions may include collaboration, knowledge capture for computer referencing, leadership development, and grievance and suggestion systems.	15
Organization Design and Development	Organization development interventions can be selected to improve organizational culture, increase appreciation of diversity, build teams to solve problems, benchmark other organizations, and strategically plan for the future.	16
Financial Systems	Financial system interventions such as forecasting, cash flow analysis, open book management, or careful planning for mergers, acquisitions, or joint ventures can advance the organization as well as the individual.	17

developing and implementing the intervention. Development is "an extension of design. It prepares the design for implementation."[8]

Design and development together determine exactly what will be included in the intervention or intervention project and then produces the materials and/or programs that are required to implement the intervention and support successful results. (See Chapters 18 and 20.) Performance improvement practitioners prepare a design document that lists exactly what will be included. Consideration is made to determine whether the effort should be an internal initiative or whether an external consultant will be hired. This decision making is known as "make vs. buy." Once that is accomplished, it may be necessary for the internal unit to manage and collaborate with an external consultant or organization to produce the products or conduct the processes that will make the intervention "happen." Development may entail creating and rapid prototyping materials, finalizing time lines, conducting pilot tests, and making adjustments to prepare the intervention for implementation.

Business Case. Business cases are written to document the need or opportunity and convey confidence that the change effort will be executed wisely and garner support from senior leadership and a project champion. (See Chapter 19.) Performance improvement and performance technology efforts can get caught up with the enthusiasm of the team members and others committed to change without taking a good hard look at leadership commitment, feasibility, and sustainability plus business issues.

The business case document begins with an executive summary providing a high-level project description, rationale for the change, anticipated performance measures, and major milestones. The project scope section includes goals and objectives, measureable results or outcomes and deliverables, benefits and value added, and financial and resource requirements. The project plan includes risk analysis and contingency planning to alleviate risks, quality and communications planning, timelines, and milestone descriptions.

In addition, business cases need to document stakeholders and stakeholder expectations. All too many performance improvement projects do not include sufficient consideration of the feasibility of the effort, including cultural considerations. Finally, business cases need well-documented discussions on sustainability and how the change effort will leave the organization sufficiently robust to continue the improvements and then also continuously improve as further change is needed.[9]

Intervention Implementation and Maintenance

The next step in the HPT Model (Figure 2.4) is intervention implementation and maintenance. This step requires the actual doing, the putting into motion of the selected intervention or interventions. Performance improvement practitioners need to network, partner, and build alliances with various involved departments, stakeholders, and champions to ensure an accurate understanding of expectations and concerns.

Problem solving or optimizing opportunity may need internal or external consulting to define the details of the effort. Process consulting may be necessary if the improvement involves extensive redesign of processes. Employee development, such as training, learning organizations, job aids, documentation, mentoring, or coaching, are likely so that all involved will be prepared to fully participate. In addition, ongoing employee development enables employees to retain competitiveness and to prepare for the organization's future. Communication is critical to achieving this phase. There is a need to communicate expectations throughout the organization. Performance improvement implementation requires communication of plans and progress.

It is not unusual for the project team to be so focused on the implementation that there is inadequate preparation for long-term maintenance. Most performance improvement efforts are comprehensive and intense. Once this level of effort is expended, it is critical that the successes be sustained, which requires planning to prepare all participants and leadership. Maintenance means securing roles for the aspects needed for the future and ensuring that leadership is ready to endorse the successes and adapt as the initiative evolves.

Careful attention to resistance and fears helps contain problems or enhance new adoptions of ideas.[10] The effort needs to be carefully structured using project management to ensure that aspects are done on time, within budget, and as expected. In order for all of these many factors to integrate and augment each other, performance improvement practitioners must be vigilant and apply the concepts of change management. It is important to ensure that the implementation plans are sufficient to make the change required. (See Chapters 21 and 22.)

Evaluation

Measuring and reporting results are critical for maintaining the confidence of the organization and stakeholders, such as the champion and employees. (See Chapters 23 and 24.) Inputs,

FIGURE 2.4. Performance Improvement/HPT Model: Implementation and Maintenance Phase

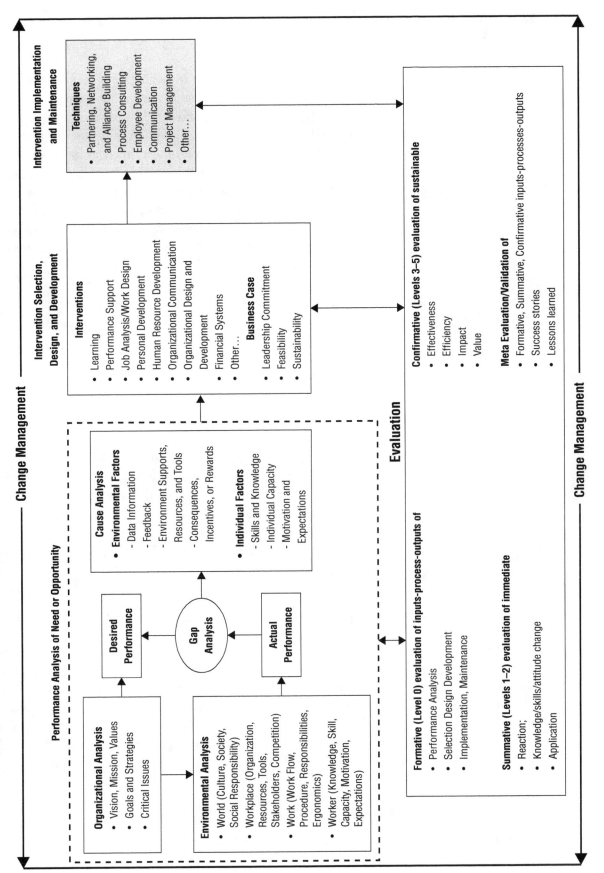

process, and/or outputs should be measured throughout the performance improvement/HPT process. (See Figure 2.5.)

Pre-formative or Level 0 evaluation establishes the baseline throughout the improvement effort to ensure that intended results are occurring. Formative evaluation occurs during performance analysis and intervention selection, design, development, and at the intervention implementation and maintenance stages, as needed. Summative or Level 1 and 2 evaluation determines the immediate reaction; knowledge, skill, and attitude change; plus initial application or adoption of the intervention or interventions. Confirmative evaluation or Level 3 to 5 focuses on sustainable effectiveness, efficiency, impact, and value, including return on investment. Is the value worth the effort? Finally, it is also critical to evaluate the evaluation process, known as meta evaluation, to ensure that optimal information is garnered and considered. By documenting success stories and lessons learned, it is possible to predict future change initiatives and plan effectively for positive outcomes.

Evaluation may use a number of different approaches to establish the value of an input, process, or output. For example, using an appreciative inquiry approach to evaluation focuses on the positive factors associated with the performance improvement effort. Appreciative inquiry looks for what is working well in an organization "instead of analyzing the possible causes and solutions, they envision what it might be like if 'the best of what is' occurred more frequently."[11]

The HPT Model as a Process Model

Many elements within the phases are iterative. For example, sustainability should be considered within each phase because intervention efforts need to continue after the project is integrated into the organization or society and does not receive the attention present in the beginning. Another example of an iterative element is the need to communicate throughout the effort. Senior leadership should be informed and their approval sought and maintained. Communicating to all stakeholders frequently reduces resistance. The HPT Model is a guide, a holistic visualization of how to accomplish success.

Certified Performance Technology Standards and Ethics

For performance improvement practitioners and performance consultants, there is certification that recognizes those who apply the principles of performance improvement and the practices, processes, and methods of performance technology. The certification is based on ten standards reflected in the model. In order to be certified, it is also necessary to sign and follow the Performance Improvement Code of Ethics.[12] The rest of this chapter will summarize the Standards and Code of Ethics. For further information on the standards, Code of Ethics, or the CPT designation, see Appendix A and Appendix C or go to www.ISPI.org and select the "Certification" tab.

Performance Technology Standards

The first four ISPI Performance Technology Standards cover the core principles of performance improvement. The acronym, RSVP, represents results orientation, systemic approach, value

FIGURE 2.5. Performance Improvement/HPT Model: Evaluation Phase

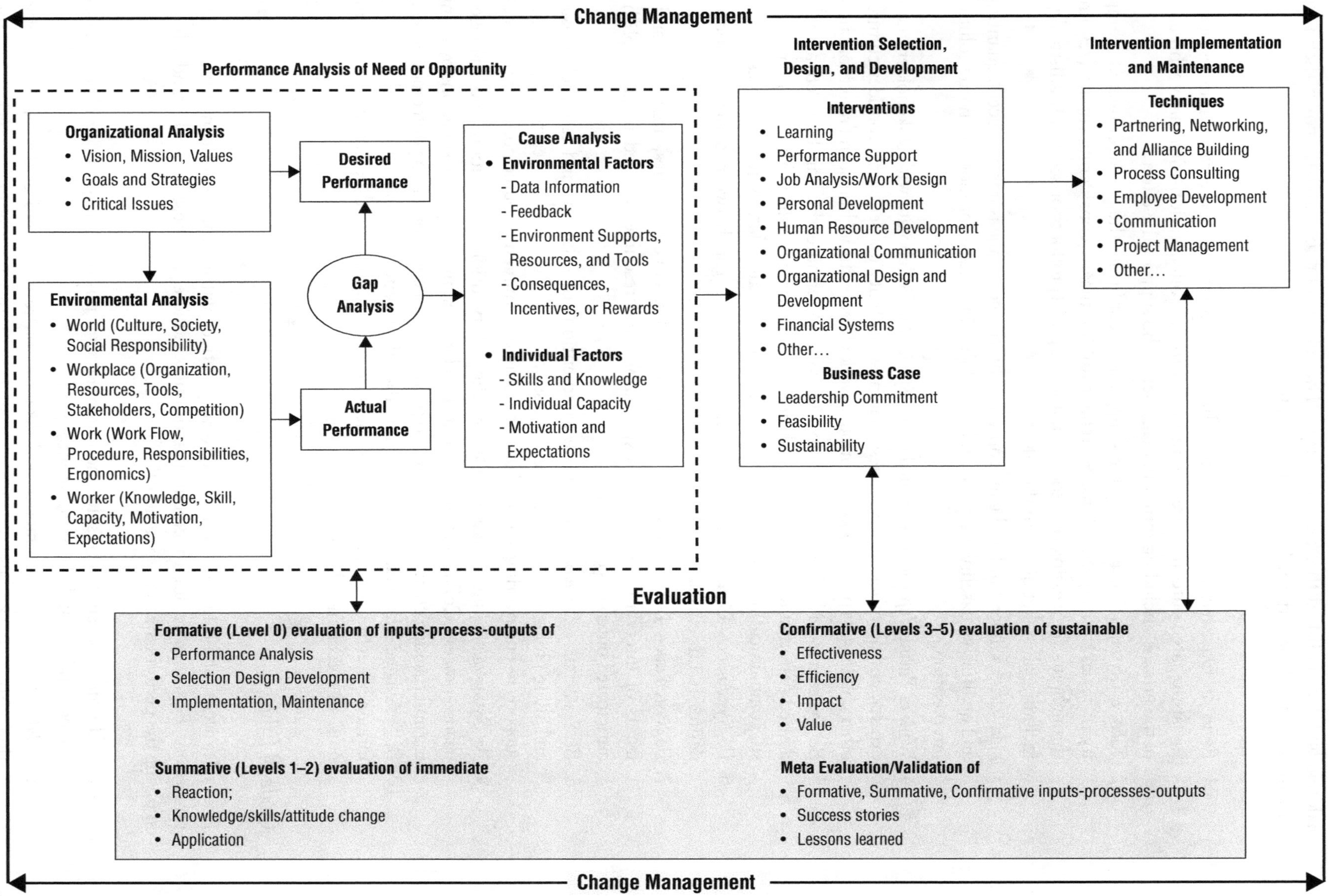

Change Management

Performance Analysis of Need or Opportunity

Organizational Analysis
- Vision, Mission, Values
- Goals and Strategies
- Critical Issues

Environmental Analysis
- World (Culture, Society, Social Responsibility)
- Workplace (Organization, Resources, Tools, Stakeholders, Competition)
- Work (Work Flow, Procedure, Responsibilities, Ergonomics)
- Worker (Knowledge, Skill, Capacity, Motivation, Expectations)

Desired Performance

Gap Analysis

Actual Performance

Cause Analysis
- **Environmental Factors**
  - Data Information
  - Feedback
  - Environment Supports, Resources, and Tools
  - Consequences, Incentives, or Rewards
- **Individual Factors**
  - Skills and Knowledge
  - Individual Capacity
  - Motivation and Expectations

Intervention Selection, Design, and Development

Interventions
- Learning
- Performance Support
- Job Analysis/Work Design
- Personal Development
- Human Resource Development
- Organizational Communication
- Organizational Design and Development
- Financial Systems
- Other...

Business Case
- Leadership Commitment
- Feasibility
- Sustainability

Intervention Implementation and Maintenance

Techniques
- Partnering, Networking, and Alliance Building
- Process Consulting
- Employee Development
- Communication
- Project Management
- Other...

Evaluation

Formative (Level 0) evaluation of inputs-process-outputs of
- Performance Analysis
- Selection Design Development
- Implementation, Maintenance

Summative (Levels 1–2) evaluation of immediate
- Reaction;
- Knowledge/skills/attitude change
- Application

Confirmative (Levels 3–5) evaluation of sustainable
- Effectiveness
- Efficiency
- Impact
- Value

Meta Evaluation/Validation of
- Formative, Summative, Confirmative inputs-processes-outputs
- Success stories
- Lessons learned

Change Management

53

adding, and accomplished through partnering. The subsequent six standards cover the processes and methods used for performance technology efforts.

1. *Focus on Outcomes or Results.* Once the goals, vision, and expectations are established, the anticipated outcomes are determined through collaboration with many who are part of the process, including senior management who support the effort.

2. *Take a Systems View.* A systems approach confirms the interconnected complexity of issues and organizations. Systems thinking means considering inputs (resources), throughputs (processing of resources), and outputs (products or services) holistically and including all stakeholders in the effort.

3. *Add Value.* Understand and gain consensus on the goals, measures of success, quantitative and qualitative baseline metrics, and probability of success for more than one solution or intervention.

4. *Work in Partnership with Clients and Other Specialists.* Collaborate with stakeholders, content experts, and all other vested parties; share responsibility for decisions; consider culture and other challenges (plus resources or inputs, work effort or throughputs, and results or outputs).

5. *Be Systematic—Needs or Opportunity Analysis.* Determine the gap between actual and desired performance using job or task analysis, process analysis, work environment analysis, communication systems analysis, market analysis, and data systems analysis.

6. *Be Systematic—Cause Analysis.* Determine why the gap between actual situation and desired results exists.

7. *Be Systematic—Design.* Describe a design plan that covers features, attributes, and elements of interventions and the expectations and resources needed to accomplish the anticipated outcomes or results.

8. *Be Systematic—Development.* Create interventions or solutions and test their feasibility and their probability of sustained success, whether they involve learning, performance support, re-engineering a workplace, or changing a human resource policy or practice.

9. *Be Systematic—Implementation.* Deploy the intervention or solution and manage the change process. Collaborate with clients to adopt and maintain new situations by monitoring and tracking change, responding to problems, and communicating outcomes or results.

10. *Be Systematic—Evaluation.* Determining the effectiveness and efficiency of the effort, performance technology practitioners measure and capture data, determine success measures, and recommend next steps.

Code of Ethics

Principles were established to promote ethical practices within the performance improvement profession. Performance improvement practitioners adhere to these ethical standards while applying the performance improvement/HPT model.

1. *Add value.* Focusing on results and outcomes that positively impact the client, their customers, and the global environment.

2. *Validated practice.* Base practice and decisions on research and evidence. Share information with clients and use practices that are consistent with literature, research, and theory.

3. *Collaboration.* Plan for a win-win outcome by integrating the client and social responsibility needs into each project. Based on PI principles, anticipate client issues and prepare positive outcomes.

4. *Continuous improvement.* Investigate new ideas and creatively apply new concepts, tools, strategies, and technologies to benefit the client.

5. *Integrity.* Honesty and truthfulness are essential with colleagues, clients, and others while practicing performance improvement. Accept only engagements where qualifications meet needs and expectations.

6. *Uphold confidentiality.* Respect trade secrets and intellectual property of clients. Withhold disclosing that is not appropriate for communication. Be selective and express data in a honest format. Never knowingly mislead a client, colleague, or the profession.

Other Performance Improvement Process Models

The Performance Improvement/HPT Model is not the only model that has been developed to represent performance improvement processes or concepts. Two other models are presented here: Pershing's Performance Improvement Process Model (Figure 2.6) and the Performance

FIGURE 2.6.   Pershing's Performance Improvement Process Model

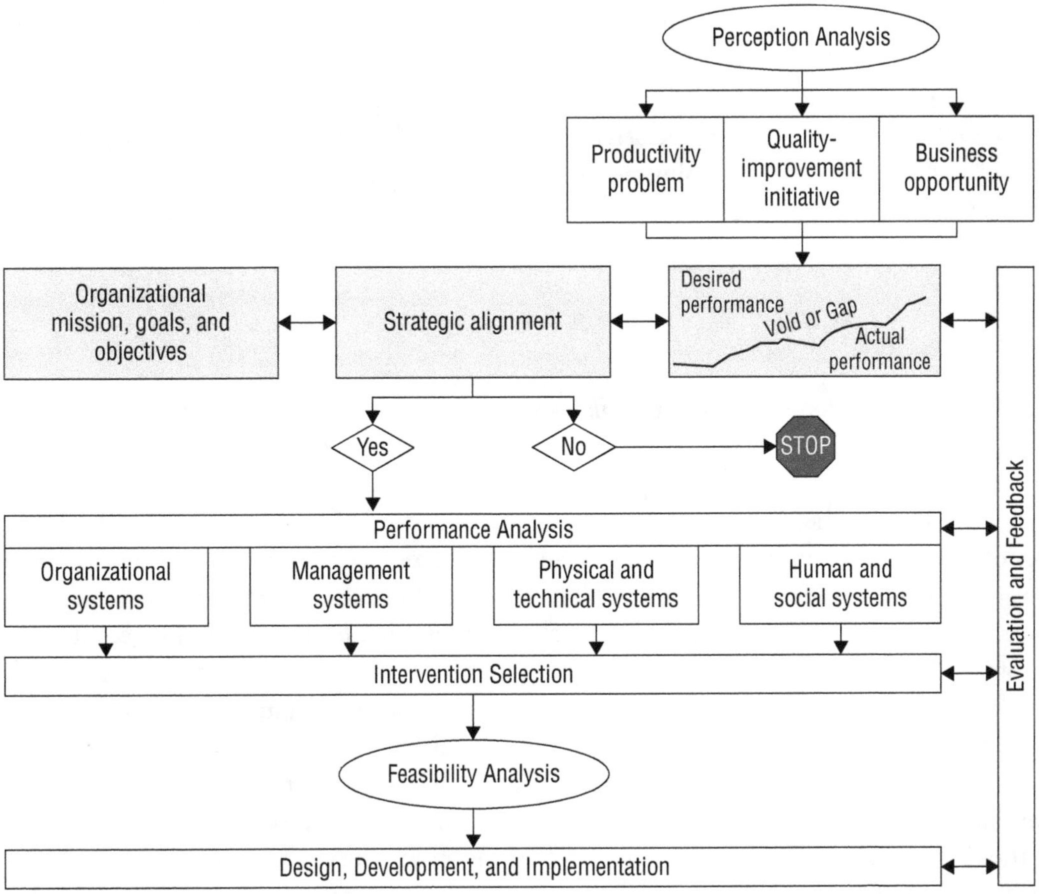

Source: Pershing, 2006, p. 15. Used with permission.

Improvement/HPT Model: Appreciative Inquiry Approach Model by Rosenzweig and Van Tiem (Figure 2.7).

Pershing's model highlights important issues. It begins with perception of an important issue to the organization. It may be a productivity problem, such as employee turnover or waste, or customer complaints. It may be a quality challenge, such as return on investment or cost reduction, or a business opportunity, such as an acquisition or expansion of a product line. At this point, there seems to be a void or gap between desire and actual. If an issue is in alignment with the strategic direction of the organization, then proceed. If there is not adequate alignment, then the effort should stop. Performance analysis is conducted from the organizational, to management, to physical and technical, to human and social systems. Once a number of intervention options are considered, it is critical to determine the feasibility of the effort or the likelihood of success. Most intervention plans include a number of interventions or an intervention set. The feasibility of each single intervention as well as the combined set should be determined. Pershing's feasibility decision matrix[13] includes return on investment, strength of support, organizational change impact, barriers to implementation, available resources, urgency, and more. Evaluation and feedback include formative and summative considerations used to determine the worth or value of the performance improvement effort.

The HPT Model/Appreciative Inquiry Approach in Figure 2.7 applies change management and the principles of performance improvement to positive approaches. It focuses entirely on positive, enhancing considerations, usually based on summits or substantial input from a wide variety of stakeholders. It is important to maintain the position that what is said, the questions asked, the models developed, and plans and implementation of the plans need to be entirely focused on success. The appreciative inquiry model blends the positive concepts with performance improvement by combining discover, dream, design, and destiny with the stages of the Performance Improvement/HPT Model. (See Chapter 1 for a full discussion of appreciative inquiry.)

And the Dialog Goes On . . .

In October 2011, the *Performance Improvement Journal* published a special issue titled Exploring a Universal Model for HPT: Notes from the Field.

The issue addressed by the contributors to that publication was: Does the field require different types of models to define the field and inform and guide practitioners, or should there be a universal performance improvement model? There was a flood of responses to the request for submissions to this issue and, at the time this article was submitted to the editor, the commentaries had spread out into the January and February 2012 issues of PIJ. Binder[14] offered these words of advice: "evolutionary consequences will select models based on their value to users" and "I recommend that we get these basic conceptual distinctions clear [outcomes and results] before we try building a universal model of performance." Dierkes asked whether the field should reduce the total number of models to four or five in order to "eliminate confusion and repetition, and provide the shared understanding, credibility, and return on investment of time and effort."[15] At this time there is no full consensus from the contributors; however, the dialog is continuing.

FIGURE 2.7. HPT Model: Appreciative Inquiry Approach

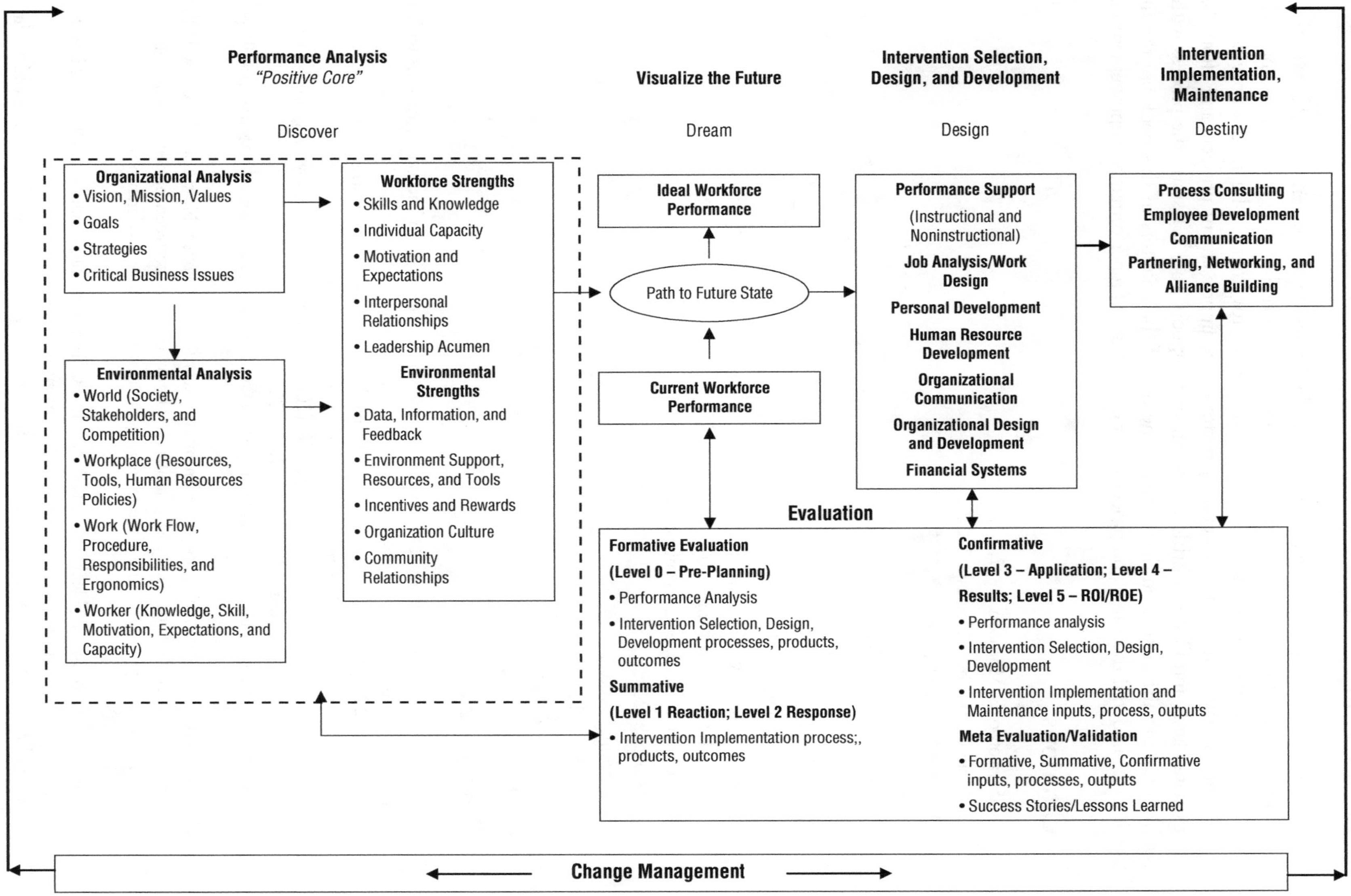

Performance Analysis
"Positive Core"

Discover

Organizational Analysis
- Vision, Mission, Values
- Goals
- Strategies
- Critical Business Issues

Environmental Analysis
- World (Society, Stakeholders, and Competition)
- Workplace (Resources, Tools, Human Resources Policies)
- Work (Work Flow, Procedure, Responsibilities, and Ergonomics)
- Worker (Knowledge, Skill, Motivation, Expectations, and Capacity)

Workforce Strengths
- Skills and Knowledge
- Individual Capacity
- Motivation and Expectations
- Interpersonal Relationships
- Leadership Acumen

Environmental Strengths
- Data, Information, and Feedback
- Environment Support, Resources, and Tools
- Incentives and Rewards
- Organization Culture
- Community Relationships

Visualize the Future

Dream

Ideal Workforce Performance

Path to Future State

Current Workforce Performance

Intervention Selection, Design, and Development

Design

Performance Support
(Instructional and Noninstructional)

Job Analysis/Work Design

Personal Development

Human Resource Development

Organizational Communication

Organizational Design and Development

Financial Systems

Intervention Implementation, Maintenance

Destiny

Process Consulting

Employee Development

Communication

Partnering, Networking, and Alliance Building

Evaluation

Formative Evaluation
(Level 0 – Pre-Planning)
- Performance Analysis
- Intervention Selection, Design, Development processes, products, outcomes

Summative
(Level 1 Reaction; Level 2 Response)
- Intervention Implementation process;; products, outcomes

Confirmative
(Level 3 – Application; Level 4 – Results; Level 5 – ROI/ROE)
- Performance analysis
- Intervention Selection, Design, Development
- Intervention Implementation and Maintenance inputs, process, outputs

Meta Evaluation/Validation
- Formative, Summative, Confirmative inputs, processes, outputs
- Success Stories/Lessons Learned

Change Management

Source: Rosenzweig and Van Tiem, 2007. Used with permission.

Conclusion

This chapter provided an overview of the Performance Improvement/HPT Model and the Standards of Performance Technology that were established to designate professionals who practice the concepts and principles of performance improvement. The model provides an effective and reliable process for structuring performance improvement projects and efforts based on the Standards and Code of Ethics. Performance Support Tool 2.1 starts the process with guidelines for an initial situation description. The rest of the chapters in this book use the model to describe in detail the value and processes for each phase of a performance improvement effort.

Citations

1. Slywotzky & Morrison, 1997, p. 79
2. Mourier, Smith, & HeeKap, 2002
3. Rosenberg, 1996, p. 6
4. Castle, 2002
5. Gilbert, 1978, p. 88
6. Spitzer, 1992, p. 121
7. Rothwell, 2000, p. 71
8. Spitzer 1999, p. 164
9. Silber & Kearny, 2006
10. Griffith-Cooper & King, 2007
11. Coghlan, Preskill, & Catsambas, 2003, p. 5
12. *Standards*, 2011
13. Pershing, 2006
14. Binder, 2012
15. Dierkes, 2012

References

Binder, C. (2012). Commentary: Do not confuse the flow of behavior and accomplishments with the variables that influence it. *Performance Improvement, 51*(2), 6–7.

Castle, D.K. (2002, October). Physician, heal thyself: A case study demonstrating dramatic outcomes by using performance analysis. *Performance Improvement, 44*(9), 14–26.

Coghlan, A.T., Preskill, H., & Catsambas, T.T. (2003, Winter). An overview of appreciative inquiry in evaluation. *New Directions in Evaluation, 10*(5), 22.

Dierkes, S.V. (2012). Commentary: Human performance technology—Not a "one-size-fits-all" profession. *Performance Improvement, 51*(2), 8–9.

Gilbert, T.E. (1978). *Human competence: Engineering worthy performance.* New York: McGraw-Hill.

Griffith-Cooper, B., & King, K. (2007, January). The partnership between project management and organizational change: Integrating change management with change leadership. *Performance Improvement, 46*(1) 14–20.

Mourier, P., Smith, M., & HeeKap, L. (2002, July). Conquering organizational change: How to succeed where most companies fail. *Performance Improvement, 41*(6) 44–47.

Pershing, J.A. (2006). Human performance technology fundamentals. In J.S. Pershing (Ed.), *Handbook of human performance technology* (3rd ed.). San Francisco: Pfeiffer.

Rosenberg, M.J. (1996). Human performance technology: Foundations for human performance improvement. In W.J. Rothwell (Ed.), *ASTD models for human performance improvement: Roles, competencies, and outputs* (pp. 5–10). Alexandria, VA: American Society for Training and Development.

Rosenzweig, J., & Van Tiem, D.M. (2007, May/June). An appreciative view of human performance technology. *Performance Improvement, 45*(5), 36–43.

Rothwell, W.J. (2000). *The intervention selector designer & developer implementor: A self-guided job aid with assessments based on ASTD models for workplace learning and performance.* Alexandria, VA: American Society for Training & Development.

Silber, K.H., & Kearny, L. (2006). Business perspectives for performance technologists. In J.A. Pershing (Ed.), *Handbook of human performance technology: Principles, practices, and potential* (3rd ed., pp. 55–92). San Francisco: Pfeiffer.

Slywotsky, A.J., & Morrison, D.J. (1997). *The profit zone: How strategic business design will lead you to tomorrow's profits.* New York: Random House.

Spitzer, D.R. (1992). The design and development of effective interventions. In H.P. Stolovitch & E.J. Keeps (Eds.), *Handbook of human performance technology: A complete guide for analyzing and solving performance problems in organizations* (1st ed., pp. 114–129). San Francisco: Jossey-Bass.

Spitzer, D. (1999). The design and development of high impact interventions. In H.D. Stolovitch & E.J. Keeps (Eds.), *Handbook of human performance technology: Improving individual and organizational performance worldwide* (2nd ed., pp. 163–184). San Francisco: Pfeiffer.

Standards for the Certified Performance Technologist Designation. (2012). Silver Spring, MD: International Society for Performance Improvement. Retrieved from www.ispi.org/content.aspx?id=418.

Van Tiem, D.M. (2000). Course pack for EDT514: Application of Instructional Design. Dearborn, MI: University of Michigan–Dearborn.

Van Tiem, D.M., Moseley, J.L., & Dessinger, J.C. (2012). *Fundamentals of performance improvement: Optimizing results through people, process, and organizations.* San Francisco: Pfeiffer.

PERFORMANCE SUPPORT TOOL 2.1. INITIAL PRE-PROJECT SITUATION DESCRIPTION

PURPOSE

Performance improvement begins with agreement on the overall critical factors for the effort. The performance improvement practitioner and the requesting organization should discuss and agree on the following topics prior to beginning the Selection, Design, and Development Phase. The practitioner should also monitor these aspects of the situation throughout all the phases to make sure that the situation does not change in a way that could also change the "goodness" of the performance improvement intervention or process.

Statement of the Need or Opportunity: Describe challenge or option.

Work Environment: Overview and define culture, department responsibilities, processes, and inputs/outputs. Describe all major factors that may influence performance.

Target Audience: Describe improvement participants involved by roles, current performance level, and desired performance level.

Resources Required: Estimate financial, material and equipment, labor, intellectual capital, and other factors necessary for this project.

Sponsor: Describe champion, who is the senior-level person committed to the performance improvement effort and will stand behind the effort if a setback or problem arises. (Determine whether there is strong enough commitment and whether sponsor is at the appropriate level.)

Performance Improvement Goal: Write overall *anticipated benefit.*

Measures of Success: Write *anticipated changes to employees, processes, organization, or society.*

Anticipated Roadblocks or Difficulties: What might happen to hinder accomplishment of the goals.

Change Management

Overarching the entire performance improvement/human performance technology effort is *change*. Change management is "a process whereby organizations and individuals proactively plan for and adapt to change."[1] The purpose of an improvement effort is to change, whether it is developing and implementing a new service or product or reinvigorating and rescuing a lagging product or service.[2] In other words, change is the heart of the effort. In the Performance Improvement/HPT Model shown in Figure 3.1, change management encompasses the entire effort and begins with the first question during the first discussion of what should be done.[3]

Definitions

Change means to alter the course or to transform the direction of an activity, process, organization, or situation. Change has been going on since the beginning of time, as long as humans have been adapting to climate and environmental challenges. As the world has increased in sophistication, ideas about change have changed also and become more codified.

Change as it relates to performance improvement includes the worker, work, workplace, and world. Change can make a radical difference or it can be gradual. Radical or transformational change may engender greater resistance, while gradual or incremental change may be easier to accept and support. However, that is not always the case. Sometimes, when it is obvious that change is necessary, even radical change can be welcomed.

In any case, change requires communication of the importance, the value, the anticipated outcomes, and the benefits of converting to a new process, product, or situation. Change requires the support of stakeholders, whether executive leadership, government officials, media and press, community supporters, early adopters, and the informal culture among those affected.

Change management is "a process whereby organizations and individuals proactively plan for and adapt to change." It is "any action or process taken to smoothly transition an individual or group from the current state to a future desired state of being."[4] In effect, organizations have to be proactive in thinking about and executing change. It is not something that is separate and distinct from their policies, procedures, practices, and everything else they do. "Change management must be an internal—and external—capability, present within the company at every moment. Organizations now have to be "change capable" all the time."[5]

FIGURE 3.1. Performance Improvement/HPT Model

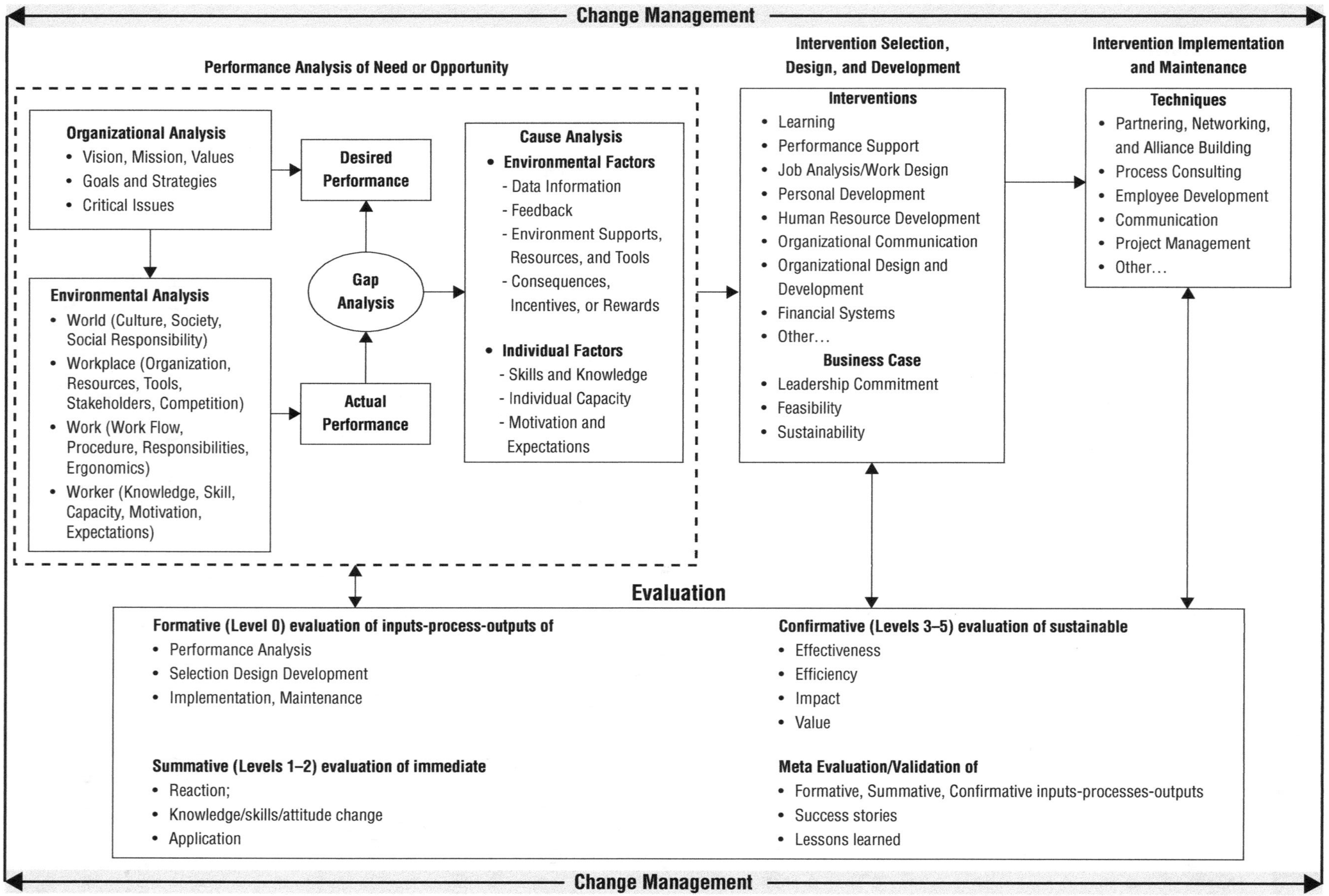

Change Management

Performance Analysis of Need or Opportunity

Organizational Analysis
- Vision, Mission, Values
- Goals and Strategies
- Critical Issues

Environmental Analysis
- World (Culture, Society, Social Responsibility)
- Workplace (Organization, Resources, Tools, Stakeholders, Competition)
- Work (Work Flow, Procedure, Responsibilities, Ergonomics)
- Worker (Knowledge, Skill, Capacity, Motivation, Expectations)

Desired Performance

Gap Analysis

Actual Performance

Cause Analysis
- **Environmental Factors**
  - Data Information
  - Feedback
  - Environment Supports, Resources, and Tools
  - Consequences, Incentives, or Rewards
- **Individual Factors**
  - Skills and Knowledge
  - Individual Capacity
  - Motivation and Expectations

Intervention Selection, Design, and Development

Interventions
- Learning
- Performance Support
- Job Analysis/Work Design
- Personal Development
- Human Resource Development
- Organizational Communication
- Organizational Design and Development
- Financial Systems
- Other…

Business Case
- Leadership Commitment
- Feasibility
- Sustainability

Intervention Implementation and Maintenance

Techniques
- Partnering, Networking, and Alliance Building
- Process Consulting
- Employee Development
- Communication
- Project Management
- Other…

Evaluation

Formative (Level 0) evaluation of inputs-process-outputs of
- Performance Analysis
- Selection Design Development
- Implementation, Maintenance

Summative (Levels 1–2) evaluation of immediate
- Reaction;
- Knowledge/skills/attitude change
- Application

Confirmative (Levels 3–5) evaluation of sustainable
- Effectiveness
- Efficiency
- Impact
- Value

Meta Evaluation/Validation of
- Formative, Summative, Confirmative inputs-processes-outputs
- Success stories
- Lessons learned

Change Management

Change Management Models

Performance improvement is based on evidence from experts and those who have done research. The experts have developed many organizational and individual change management models. Experts provide the framework for understanding the interrelationships and interdependence associated with change.

Process Models

Kotter's eight-step model for change focuses on people and their feelings toward change. It is a business model for organizational change.[6] Lewin's three-step process entails unfreezing from the current state, transitioning to a future state, and refreezing in the new state, which anchors new behaviors into daily routines and culture of the organization.[7] Prosci's ADKAR model addresses awareness, desire, knowledge, ability, and reinforcement as foundations for change.[8] These models and others provide the theoretical framework and guidance for implementing and institutionalizing interventions in the workplace.

Conceptual Models

There are many aspects of change management to think about throughout the entire process. The major change management concepts and theories outlined in Table 3.1 include a breadth of important models for change management. The dates represent the first publication of each model. The following descriptions include the thinking and clarification of these key change management leaders.

Three Stages of Change. Kurt Lewin was an early leader in focusing on resistance to change, which is a major roadblock. Change can be promoted through three stages of change: unfreeze, transition, and refreeze. Old notions need to be released or unfrozen, then new actions and thinking need to be tried and developed, and finally the new methods and processes can be refrozen into a new focus.[9] *Unfreezing* recognizes the conditions that would benefit by changing, such as industry regulations, new customer preferences or fads, new features in customer products of services, and the opportunity to introduce a radically different product or service. Changing focuses on modifying elements such as technology, structure, tasks, or culture. *Refreezing* means creating a new normal and sustaining the changes. Refreezing benefits from executive support, social networks within the organization, clear expectations and understanding of expectations, and preparations that are feasible and recognized as of value.[10]

McKinsey 7S Framework. McKinsey covers seven major aspects of change: strategy, structure, systems, staff, style, skills, and shared values. These seven organizational internal, interrelated factors need to be in alignment to improve performance.[11] The model was developed by Tom Peters and Robert Waterman while at the McKinsey and Company consulting firm. Peters and Waterman, based on research, identified excellent companies, such as IBM, Hewlett-Packard, Wal-Mart, and General Electric. They determined that excellent companies had important characteristics in common. They were committed to customers, supported their employees, and had a bias for action. Executives managed the values of the company. Excellent companies focus on

TABLE 3.1.   Change Management Theory Models

Models	Principles	Focus
Three Stages of Change		
Lewin, 1951	Unfreeze, transition, refreeze.	Mitigation of workforce resistance to change.
McKinsey 7-S Framework		
Waterman, Peters, & Phillips, 1980	Strategy, structure, systems, shared values, style, staff, skills.	Seven elements align for change in organizations to be effective.
Total Quality Management		
Deming, 1986	Integrates quality, processes, cures, and ownership.	Targets incremental quality control changes geared toward stability.
Leadership Culture-Change Actions		
Schein, 1986	Attention, reaction to crises, role modeling, allocation of rewards, and criteria for selection and dismissal.	The way an organization approaches its functions dictates how leadership can change the culture.
Kaizen		
Imai, 1986	Aligns strategy and vision for process improvement, innovation, and sustainable systems.	Change management is a continuous improvement endeavor.
Business Process Re-Engineering		
Davenport, 1992	Seeks efficiency and modernization of workforce and processes.	Top-down approach for rethinking and redesign of competitive advantage.
8-Step Model to Organizational Change		
Kotter, 1996	Urgency, coalition, vision, communicate vision, remove obstacles, create wins, build on change, anchor change in culture.	Leadership must lead by example for change initiative to be successful.
ADKAR		
Hiatt, 2006	Awareness, desire, knowledge, ability, and reinforcement.	Goal-orientated model for organizational awareness.

From Fireside, 2011, p. 26. Used with permission.

what they are good at. They are able to have control while empowering their employees.[12] Later, Peters stated that there are not excellent companies but companies doing excellent things, since some of the companies cited in their McKinsey research later floundered.[13]

Total Quality Management (TQM). The famed leader of TQM is W. Edwards Deming, a University of Michigan professor who became well known for his work in Japan, reforming their manufacturing to produce quality products. Later, Deming's fourteen points were the basis of transforming American industry.[14] The fourteen points highlighted constant commitment to purpose; management leading by adopting a new philosophy; eliminating fear in the workplace; producing correctly the first time rather than inspect to find errors; eliminating purchasing based on cost without considerations such as quality; continuously improving; instituting training, education, and self-development; breaking down barriers between departments and others; and including everyone in the transformation. Deming asserted that management was responsible for about 80 percent of the quality problems and the workforce about 20 percent. It was the major responsibility of management to create a quality focused organization.

"It is not enough that top management commit themselves for life to quality and productivity. They must know what it is that they are committed to—that is, what they must do. These obligations can not be delegated. Support is not enough, action is required."[15]

Leadership Culture Change Actions. This theory was described by Edgar Schein in *Mechanisms of Change*.[16] Change in behavior or attitudes "tends to be emotionally resisted because even the possibility of change implies that previous behavior and attitudes were somehow wrong or inadequate, a conclusion which the change target would be motivated to reject. If change does occur, therefore, it must be preceded by an alteration of the present stable equilibrium which supports the present behavior and attitudes."[17] It is essential to build positive and hopeful regard for proposed change. Change participants need to view the change as welcomed and essential. The content of the message and the receiver are critical to success. Positive and negative attention to the person can be bolstered through group involvement by realizing and then integrating their reactions to the source of the change information. It is essential to focus on potential resistance and to remove threats or barriers for the group as well as individuals.

Schein first described corporate culture as a pattern of basic assumptions about behaviors, norms, dominant values, rules, procedures and processes, and the feeling or climate conveyed without being described. For successful change, the organizational culture needs to support the planned changes. Organizational change requires a level of consensus regarding the core mission, goals, how to accomplish the goals, means to measure progress, and how to alleviate problems.[18]

Kaizen. Kaizen or continuous improvement was defined by Masaaki Imai in his well-respected book, *Kaizen: The Key to Japan's Competitive Success*.[19] Imai explained that what people know is essential, but their wisdom is gained by doing. He stressed that Western management bases change on knowledge, while Japanese management includes both knowledge and wisdom.

"The difference between knowledge and wisdom are very important to our thinking about total quality management. Knowledge is something we can buy. We can gain knowledge by reading books and attending seminars and classroom lectures. Knowledge remains just knowledge until we put it into action. On the other hand, wisdom is something we can learn by doing. Practice is the best way of learning, and wisdom emerges from practice."[20]

Kaizen represents constant commitment to quality and efficiency in the workplace. Supervisors help "employees who may be having difficulty doing the standardized work. Once the employee can meet the standard, the standard is raised-usually with the employee's input. Kaizen is a simple concept, one that involves constant improvement."[21] While management needs to focus on innovation, all levels need to be committed to Kaizen.[22]

Business Process Reengineering. Davenport[23] stated that a five-step approach for business process reengineering (BPR) involves developing a business vision, identifying processes to be redesigned, understanding measurement of existing business expectations, identifying business design, and building new methods. The BPR approach is particularly helpful when organizations exist in a competitive or fast-changing environment. Reengineering means starting from zero and rebuilding processes or organizations. It does not represent "tinkering with what already exists or making incremental changes that leave basic structures intact."[24]

Reengineering is "the fundamental rethinking and radical redesign of business processes to achieve dramatic improvements in critical, contemporary measures of performance, such as cost, quality, service, and speed."[25] Key ideas are dramatic, radical, and fundamental.[26] It is important to make decisions and take action based on knowledge. However, situations are not neat and often knowledge deals with complexity. "Although it is tempting to look for simple answers to complex problems and deal with uncertainties by pretending they don't exist, knowing more usually leads to better decisions than knowing less, even if the 'less' seems clearer and more definite."[27]

Few businesses succeed without a competent workforce. "Many reengineering projects fail because only average performers are assigned to them. Companies that make this mistake often figure that top talent cannot be spared to work on the redesign project and instead staff it with undistinguished performers."[28] For example, less competent, less motivated, and less experienced workers require more supervision. It is difficult for them to be empowered because they need more attention.[29]

Eight-Step Model of Organizational Change. In 1996, John Kotter wrote *Leading Change* to transform by "the adoption of new technologies, major strategic shifts, process reengineering, mergers and acquisitions, restructuring into different sorts of business units, attempts to significantly improve innovation, and cultural change."[30] "People change what they do less because they are given *analysis* that shift their *thinking* than because they are *shown* a truth that influences their *feelings*."[31]

Change involves a gradual and planned dynamic. "Successful large-scale change is a complex affair that happens in *eight stages*. The flow is this: push urgency up, put together a guiding team, create the vision and strategies, effectively communicate the vision and strategies, remove barriers to action, accomplish short-term wins, keep pushing for wave after wave of change until the work is done, and, finally, create a new culture to make new behavior stick."[32]

ADKAR. "The awareness, desire, knowledge, ability, and reinforcement model (ADKAR) of organization change was created by a leading change management firm Prosci, to create multifunctional project teams considerate of the human and technical side of a change initiative. ADKAR supports the people side of change by utilizing readiness assessments, coaching, communication, and resistance management."[33] ADKAR is flexible and focuses on desired outcomes that are adapted to each situation.

Levels, Modes, and Control of Change

Performance improvement practitioners need to take into consideration the level of change that will be occurring, the mode of change, and the control of change.[34]

Level of Change

The level of change can be *transformational* or *incremental*. *Transformational* change makes a radical difference and can be caused by change of leadership, changes in society and the world, changes in competition or supplies, changes in politics, and so on. Transformational change is infrequent, requires an extensive effort of analysis, planning, determined execution, and intentions of sustainability. *Incremental* change can be informal, gradual, and frequent adaptation to changing conditions within the workplace, competition, or desires of customers and clients. The degree of planning and care will vary considerably between transformational and incremental change.

Mode of Change

The mode of change can be *proactive* or *reactive*. In many instances, the performance improvement effort will be looking to the future and will involve *proactive* planning for new needs, expectations, availability of supplies, or changing conditions. For example, it is relatively easy for retail establishments to plan for seasons and holidays, or hospital emergency rooms to plan for frostbite in winter or sunburns in summer. On the other hand, *reactionary* situations like the impact of extreme weather, such as hurricanes and typhoons or earthquakes and tsunamis, can be lessened by preplanning through building codes, going to places of safety, or practice drills.

Control of Change

Control of change can be planned or unplanned. Societies can prepare for hurricanes with hurricane-resistant windows and strong glass, or *plan* for changes in government through elections. *Unplanned* change results in unanticipated costs and outcomes and can be the result of fire, accident, or disease. Spontaneous situations benefit from resilience and robustness. For example, evacuation and community safety plans, hospital emergency procedures practice, or adequate supply chain collaboration can ease even the most unexpected occurrences. Most performance improvement efforts focus on planned change; however, performance improvement may also be dealing with the aftermath of unplanned change.

Planning Change

Change benefits from complex planning to minimize risk, resistance, and uncertainty.[35] (See Figure 3.2.)

Change management involves planning, implementing, and sustaining change. Malopinsky and Osman[36] illustrate the actual change process evolution, while the Performance Improvement/ HPT Model is more holistic and considers a full spectrum of aspects that go into any change or performance improvement effort. Throughout planning the change process, it is essential to visualize how the change will affect the people, culture, performance, technology, structure, workday, and processes of the organization.[37] Financial considerations include budgets; project plans include task lists, timelines, contingency plans, and schedules; communications plans include "elevator speeches," feedback mechanisms, training schedules, and observations.[38]

Change Management Roles

Change management roles are adapting as organizational interdependence and collaboration increase. It is important to realize that collaboration leads to more flexibility and greater options.

FIGURE 3.2.   Managing the Change Process

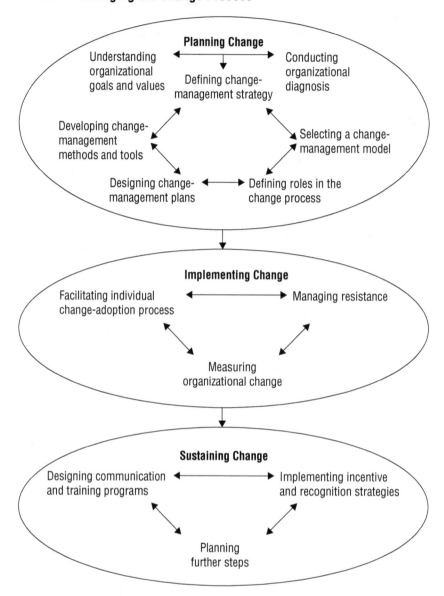

Source: Malopinsky and Osman, 2006, p. 269. Used with permission.

Change Agent

The change agent is generally one person who leads the change effort. That person can be the performance improvement consultant, practitioner, or specialist or an internal leader supported by a performance improvement department, or a quality or organization development expert. The change agent makes sure that there are appropriate plans and execution for analysis, intervention selection, design, development, implementation, and evaluation. Change agents need to focus on results and outcomes, ensure the effort of value add, think systemically, and partner and form alliances to minimize resistance and encourage enthusiasm for the effort. Performance improvement practitioners need to be careful to establish confidence of the organization and shared vision among stakeholders.[39]

Change Manager

No implementation process is successful without a change manager who develops, leads, and supports the change effort. The change manager may well be the performance improvement practitioner. The role of the change manager has evolved from controlling to facilitating the change process.

In the past, changes were decreed by executives. Today, change efforts require worker involvement to maximize each person's contributions. Change managers were once responsible for planning, commanding, and coordinating the effort. Today, change managers consult, communicate, collaborate, and mediate to minimize resistance or fear.[40] They need to be effective negotiators and equitable resource allocators to maintain confidence.

In addition, change managers need to be effective communicators to alleviate foot-dragging. Change managers build support for change. Support is "readiness for change backed by the resources necessary for acting appropriately . . . also connotes the willingness of others to cooperate with change."[41]

Leadership Supporter/Champion

Probably the most crucial aspect of any change management effort is strong and consistent leadership engagement. Champions are the executives who ensure that there are sufficient resources, minimize and eliminate roadblocks, and support sustainability so that the change effort is maintained and prospers after the initial process and outcomes. In addition, sufficient support is needed in upper and middle management so that the change can take hold and flourish.[42]

For employees to "buy into" and adopt change, they need to believe that their immediate boss, the person who has the power to provide or withhold rewards—money, advancement, recognition, approval, and so forth—is in favor of adoption.[43] Although performance improvement practitioners may play such a role, there needs to be a sponsor or champion who makes the change process happen by articulating the vision and showing by example how the interventions are implemented and by guiding the process toward institutionalizing and sustaining the interventions effort. The sponsor is a true advocate and has both the time and authority to make things happen.

Opinion Leaders

Although there are clearly defined job, roles, duties, and responsibilities, much of an organization's culture and influence occur in a less formal and defined manner within the informal organizational structure. Opinion leaders can be at any level; they are influential and can sabotage an effort if they do not believe it is the right thing to do.[44] If opinion leaders believe in and are willing to support the change effort early in the process, the entire process will progress with less effort.

Change Management Functions

The various roles that are involved in successful change management must perform two major functions: managing resistance and promoting readiness for change. In addition, they all have a communication function and some or all of the roles have a learning and support function.

Managing Resistance

One of the greatest stumbling blocks of change is resistance. Positive psychology and appreciative inquiry can minimize resistance by active participation throughout the process, focusing on what is going well and expanding on the positive aspects of the organization while minimizing the challenging situations.[45]

Passive and Overt Resistance. Change agents need to be watchful of passive and overt resistance. Often passive resistance is fostered by previous efforts that were viewed as "flavor of the year" or emphasis of the year. Once the year or certain time frame is over, the organization goes on to another initiative and forgets the last effort. The previous change effort is not sustained. As a result, employees learn to wait and not make substantial changes because the workplace will probably resume the old way when another new emphasis arrives and supersedes the current effort.

Signs of Resistance. Everyone involved in implementing change needs to be aware of the signs of resistance. When people feel threatened or do not believe change is in their best interest, they will resist, which can undermine success.[46] Employees worry that their feelings are not being taken into consideration. Longer-term employees often believe that the good aspects of the previous processes are not adequately preserved. When feeling threatened, employees can dwell on seemingly trivial details instead of visualizing the bigger picture. It is important for PI and PT practitioners to acknowledge the employees' concerns and to explain the reasons behind the changes. In some cases, it may be necessary to agree to disagree in order to move ahead. The key is to acknowledge and respect each individual's reactions.

Suggestions to Minimize Resistance. Five suggestions for minimizing resistance to change and new ideas were proposed by Dormant.[47] The emphasis is on accentuating the positive and defusing the negative in the minds of those targeted to participate in the change. Careful change preparation can have a dramatic impact on results.

1. *Relative Advantage:* Highlight the advantages for the user and present a compensatory advantage for each disadvantage. Use cost-benefit information and focus on quick return.
2. *Simplicity:* Make changes seem doable and valuable through success stories, site visits to similar applications, and peer testimonials. Minimize hurdles through job aids, training, and other performance support.
3. *Compatibility:* Identify similarities in aspects, procedures, and results with current situations, and acknowledge potential problem areas.
4. *Adaptability:* Highlight areas to be changed without loss of functioning. Identify all areas most likely to be changed.
5. *Social Impact:* Identify relationships with key people and key groups. Anticipate how changes will affect them. Use empathy when communicating workable solutions.

Managing Readiness for Change

Change readiness requires the following conditions:

- Focused alignment through clear objectives;
- Solid sponsor who is committed and willing to make tough decisions to make the project happen;
- Stakeholders who understand the effort and value success;
- Organizational infrastructure and process with sufficient governance and priority;
- Resource availability, including the right people to do the right thing at the right time, financial resources, equipment and tools, information, and so forth;
- Innovation with sufficient consideration of risk, including copyright and trade secret issues;
- Organizational sustainability based on feasibility and sufficient resources and leadership support for the long term;
- Implementation risks and readiness, including consequences if the project is no longer part of the strategic direction and consideration of hurdles and contingency plans;
- Budgets approved that have cushion or direction on what to do if the project exceeds the budget, with status communicated regularly; and
- Change leadership and planning to prepare for resistance, determination if policies or procedures need to be changed, and sufficient informal and formal leaders.[48]

Readiness for change varies considerably at the worker, work, workplace, and world levels. Some are eager to move to the future and believe that they are ready to make changes. Others see the obstacles and are concerned about readiness for change. They move more slowly and deliberately.[49] Figure 3.3 shows the speed of adoption for an innovation.

Roles During Adoption Process. Figure 3.3 illustrates the various roles people play during the adoption of innovations. Some people and organizations are open to change. They are comfortable with ambiguity and do not mind taking risks. These people are *innovators*, inquisitive and eager to try new things. Then there are the *early adopters*. Many are highly regarded and respected in the organization. They are influential and generally widely respected leaders in the culture of the organization. Early adopters learn from the innovators and make accommodations from lessons learned.

The *early majority* form a substantial part of the organization. They are often the average people; they like to watch and see the success of the trials before making substantial change. They often constitute about one-third of those who will be part of the change. The *late majority* are also approximately one-third of those involved in the change effort. Initially, they are skeptical and hesitant until most of the challenges and obstacles are resolved. They can now visualize the benefits of the change and are ready to support the effort.

At the end of the curve are the *laggards*, those who are late to adapt and are the major resistors. They have major concerns. Their resistance may be passive. They may say that they are in favor of

FIGURE 3.3.   Adoption Curve

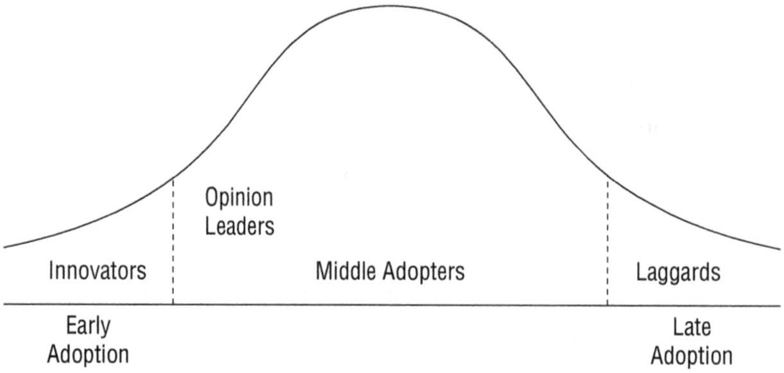

Source: Rogers, 1995, p. 262, as cited in Dormant, 1999, p. 247. Used with permission.

the change, but then resist and avoid acting to support the change. They are often the people who are concerned about one isolated factor and do not see the benefit of the greater good. They often embrace change when it is more difficult to resist change than to go along with the change.

Communication

Clear, consistent, persuasive, well-supported communication is essential for positive change outcomes and is a major function throughout the change management process. Messages need to be conveyed through newsletters, posters, and video clips from high-level management and senior executives. In addition, social media can discuss situations, highlight successes, anticipate next steps, and promote discussion of concerns. Communication also means notifying those involved of awards for progress, rewards for change as it occurs, and also notifying those involved of potential opportunities for future benefits.

Learning and Performance Support

Change efforts typically involve learning new perspectives, new skills, knowledge, or abilities. While formal education may be needed in some instances, the learning organization can provide mutual support and change participants can learn from each other. Since change is often gradual, coaching and mentoring can occur on an informal or formal basis, which minimizes resistance. Often, new initiatives, such as new software, organizational structure, service or product lines, and quality expectations, are difficult for some to achieve. Through ongoing support, it is possible to have advice and documents, such as job aids, to remind and further explain the new processes or procedures.[50]

Change Management and the Performance Improvement Process

While it is important that performance improvement practitioners can apply the concepts of change management, it is essential that change management be integrated within the entire improvement process. Change begins with the first discussion on the first day. Each phase will be supported by early adopters and resisted by laggards. Each phase will require psychological changes, including unfreezing, transition, and refreezing and goal orientation. Each phase will require all levels to be wise and knowledgeable and understand the organizational culture to rethink processes and redesign workforces. Management will need to realize that they have the greatest impact and greatest responsibility for positive and successful change. Each phase will require formative evaluation and continuous improvement.[51] Each phase will integrate strategy, structure, systems, shared values, style, staff, skills, and more.[52] As PI practitioners, we need to be watchful for resistance and for opportunities for positive change.

Address Stages of Concern

Employees' concerns tend to occur according to the following stages: information, personal, implementation, impact, collaboration, and refinement.[53] In the beginning, people want to be informed about the positive and negative details of the change effort. They are worried about the impact change has on each individual, including the benefits, losses, and new skills needed.

It is important to talk about the details of the implementation process, including timeframes and what happens if the change doesn't work out. Impact concerns revolve around results relative to employees and the organization. Collaboration questions focus on how people will cooperate and work together. Finally, employees will often have ideas for making the original changes better and will want to work toward continuous improvement. As employees work through the change process stages, they can come to appreciate the value of the changes.

The performance improvement practitioner has to explain that change is a process, not an event and it is accomplished in five stages; each stage has its corresponding strategy for gaining acceptance.[54]

Stage 1: Awareness—Advertise

Stage 2: Curiosity—Inform

Stage 3: Visualization—Demonstrate

Stage 4: Tryout—Train

Stage 5: Use—Support

It is important to watch for each stage and then apply the strategy recommended to complete the stage.

Take a Positive Approach

While experiencing change, one of the greatest opportunities to remain focused and enthusiastic is through positive approaches.[55] Change can be viewed as an opportunity to make things better. Questions and discussions can be positioned as thinking about how the workplace will be better, how the new situation will be optimized.[56]

As discussed by Schein, Kotter, Lewin, Dormant, and others, people will naturally resist unless there is skillful planning to create and maintain a thoughtful culture. Appreciative inquiry (introduced in Chapters 1 and 2) is organizational change, redesign, or planning that begins with a comprehensive inquiry, analysis, and dialogue based on a positive core, that includes many stakeholders and creates strategic change and positive priorities.[57]

As stated previously, change during performance improvement efforts begins with the first question. Instead of asking, "What can we do to overcome the problems with our operating room intake process?" the positive question can be, "How can we create a welcoming and reassuring environment so that those preparing for surgery can feel confident and calm?" Positioning efforts in the positive engages creativity and innovative thinking and establishes energy in those engaged with the change effort.[58] Language, whether positive and creative or negative and complaining, sets the tone for the workplace and the change effort. It is important to believe in the best change possible.

Positive change occurs when there is a positive organizational culture and an organization based on favorable values. An organization based on values can overcome marketplace stress, technological challenges, competitive uncertainties, or societal changes. Strong positive cultures have values and norms that are admired and respected by organization members; they create a collective identity and commitment and a common vision for the future.[59] Although a positive approach is ideal, it may be difficult to attain quickly. Performance improvement practitioners and change managers will probably need to be patient and use an incremental and gradual process so that the organization's culture eventually becomes a positive workplace.

Monitor After Implementation

Once the interventions are implemented in the workplace, the human performance specialist, along with the change manager if they are not the same person, should diligently monitor the process. Formative evaluation is applied throughout the design and development phases and is critical to adapt and accommodate issues that arise then and during the implementation process.

Focusing on change management, the following evaluation questions should be considered:

- How well is the intervention effort addressing the root cause(s) of human performance gaps?
- What measurable improvement can be observed and documented?
- How much ownership have stakeholders vested in the intervention, and what steps can be taken to improve the ownership leading to sustaining the effort?
- How are changing conditions inside and outside the organization affecting the intervention?
- Is the change effort flexible enough to adapt and continue?[60]

Conclusion

Attention to change management will take effort and attention throughout the process. There is much to be learned from the theories considering psychological dimensions and resistance, process and strategy, participant involvement and leadership, and planning. It is necessary to notice roles, levels, modes, and control of change. Change management focuses on the part of the PT practitioner to think not only of the issues associated with the certain performance improvement/HPT phase, but also the issues that make for successful change. A good place to begin is with the Change Management Planner in Performance Support Tool 3.1 and a good place to continue and end is with the Change Management Evaluator in Performance Support Tool 3.2.

Citations

1. Reynolds, 1993, in Biech, 2006
2. Martin, Hall, Blakely, Gayford, & Gunter, 2009
3. Rosenzweig & Van Tiem, 2007
4. Varkey & Antonio, 2010, p. 268
5. Gossage & Lee, 2011, p. 32
6. Kotter, 1996
7. Robbins & Coulter, 2012, p. 153
8. Hiatt, 2006
9. Harvey & Broyles, 2010, p. 13; Schein, 1969
10. Malopinsky & Osman, 2006, pp. 267–268; Schein, 1969, p. 98
11. Peters & Waterman, 1982, pp. 9–11
12. Peters & Waterman, 1982, pp. 13–17
13. *Business: The Ultimate Resource*, 2002, p. 1036
14. Deming, 1986, pp. 23–24
15. Deming, 1986, p. 21
16. Schein, 1969, pp. 98–107
17. Schein, 1969, pp. 98–99
18. *Business: The Ultimate Resource*, 2002, p. 937
19. Imai, 2002; Womack & Jones, 1996, p. 128
20. Imai, 2002, p. 173
21. Caroselli, 1991, p. 134
22. Caroselli, 1991, p. 197
23. Davenport, as cited in Fireside, 2011, p. 35
24. Hammer & Champy, 1993, p. 31
25. Hammer & Champy, 1993, p. 32
26. Hammer & Champy, 1993, pp. 33–34
27. Davenport & Prusak, 1998, p. 9
28. DuBrin, 1996, p. 29
29. DuBrin, 1996, p. 33
30. Kotter, in Kotter & Cohen, 2002, p. ix
31. Kotter & Cohen, 2002, p. 1
32. Kotter & Cohen, 2002, p. 2
33. Hiatt, 2006, as cited by Fireside, 2011, p. 36

34. Malopinsky & Osman, 2006, pp. 264–266

35. Mourier & Smith, 2002

36. Malopinsky and Osman, 2006, p. 269

37. Varkey & Antonio, 2010, p. 268

38. Varkey & Antonio, 2010, p. 271

39. Alexander & Christoffersen, 2004

40. Felkins, Charkiris, & Charkiris, 1993, p. 26

41. Rothwell, 2005, p. 72

42. Griffith-Cooper & King, 2007

43. Dormant, 1986, p. 252

44. Dormant, 1999, pp. 250–251

45. Rosenzweig & Van Tiem, 2007

46. Jellison, 1993

47. Dormant, 1999, pp. 237–259

48. Griffith-Cooper & King, 2010, pp. 398–405

49. Dormant, 1999, pp. 249–280

50. Lee & Krayer, 2004

51. Imai, 2002

52. Peters & Waterman, 1982

53. Blanchard, Zigarmi, & Zigarmi, 1994, pp. 1–31

54. Dormant, 1999, p. 15

55. Quinn, 2004

56. Whitney & Trosten-Bloom, 2010

57. Cooperrider & Whitney, 2005, p. 12

58. Cooperrider, Sorensen, Whitney, & Yeager, 2000

59. Cameron & Quinn, 1999, p. 4

60. Rothwell, 1996, p. 15

References

Alexander, M., & Christoffersen, J. (2004, April). Politics in organizational change and the human performance technologist. *Performance Improvement, 43*(4), 21–27.

Blanchard, K., Zigarmi, D., & Zigarmi, P. (1994). The organization. *Situational leadership II participant's workbook*. Escondido, CA: Blanchard Training and Development.

Cameron, K.S., & Quinn, R.E. (1999). *Diagnosing and changing organizational culture: Based on the competing values framework*. Reading, MA: Addison-Wesley.

Caroselli, M. (1991). *Total quality transformations: Optimizing missions, methods, and management*. Amherst, MA: Human Resource Development Press.

Cooperrider, D.L., Sorensen, P.F., Whitney, D., & Yeager, T.F. (Eds.) (2000). *Appreciative inquiry: Rethinking human organization toward a positive theory of change*. Champaign, IL: Stipes Publishing.

Cooperrider, D.L., & Whitney, D. (2005). *Appreciative inquiry: A positive revolution in change*. San Francisco: Berrett-Koehler.

Davenport, T.H., & Prusak, L. (1998). *Working knowledge: How organizations manage what they know*. Boston, MA: Harvard Business School Press.

Deming, W.E. (1986). *Out of the crisis*. Cambridge, MA: Massachusetts Institute of Technology Press.

Dormant, D. (1986). The ABCD's of change. In M. Smith (Ed.), *Introduction to performance technology* (pp. 238–254). Washington, DC: International Society for Performance Improvement.

Dormant, D. (1999). Implementing human performance technology in organizations. In H.D. Stolovitch & E.J. Keeps (Eds.), *Handbook of human performance technology: Improving individual and organizational performance worldwide* (2nd ed., pp. 237–259). San Francisco: Pfeiffer.

DuBrin, A.J. (1996). *Reengineering survival guide: Managing and succeeding in the changing workplace*. Cincinnati, OH: Thomson Executive Press.

Felkins, P.K., Charkiris, B.J., & Charkiris, K.N. (1993). *Change management: A model for effective organizational performance*. White Plains, NY: Quality Resources.

Fireside, M. (2011). Change management in a non-profit sector of a for profit industry: A phenomenological study of strategies used by credit union COOs and CEOs. Unpublished dissertation proposal. Minneapolis, MN: Capella University.

Gossage, W., & Lee, D. (2011, March). Are you change capable? *Talent Management, 7*(3), 32–35.

Griffith-Cooper, B., & King, K. (2007, January). The partnership between project management and organizational change: Integrating change management with change leadership. *Performance Improvement, 46*(1) 14–20.

Griffith-Cooper, B., & King, K. (2010). The change readiness rubric. In R. Watkins & D. Leigh (Eds.), *Improving performance in the workplace, volume 2: Selecting and implementing performance interventions*. San Francisco: Pfeiffer, and Washington, DC: International Society of Performance Improvement.

Hammer, M., & Champy, J. (1993). *Reengineering the corporation: A manifesto for business revolution*. New York: HarperBusiness.

Harvey, T.R., & Broyles, E.A. (2010). *Resistance to change: A guide for harnessing it's positive power*. Lanham, MD: Rowan & Littlefield.

Hiatt, J.M. (2006). *ADKAR: A model for change in business, government and our community: How to implement successful change in our personal lives and professional careers*. Loveland, CO: Prosci Research.

Imai, M. (2002). The true total quality. In *Business: The ultimate resource*. Cambridge, MA: Perseus.

Jellison, J.M. (1993). *Overcoming resistance: A practical guide to producing change in the workplace*. New York: Simon & Schuster.

Kotter, J.P. (1996). *Leading change*. Boston, MA: Harvard Business School Press.

Kotter, J., & Cohen, D.S. (2002). *The heart of change: Real-life stories of how people change their organizations*. Boston, MA: Harvard Business School Press.

Lee, W.W., & Krayer, K.J. (2002, August). An integrated model for organizational change. *Performance Improvement, 43*(7), 22–26.

Malopinsky, L.V., & Osman, G. (2006). Dimensions of organizational change. In J.A. Pershing (Ed.), *Handbook of human performance technology: Principles, practices, and potential* (3rd ed.). San Francisco: Pfeiffer.

Martin, F., Hall, H.A., Blakely, A., Gayford, M.C., & Gunter, E. (2009, March). The HPT model applied to a kayak company's registration process. *Performance Improvement, 48*(3), 26–35.

Mourier, P., & Smith, M. (2002). *Conquering organizational change: How to succeed where most companies fail*. Atlanta, GA: CEP Press.

Peters, T.J., & Waterman, R.H. (1982). *In search of excellence: Lessons from America's best-run companies*. New York: Harper & Row.

Quinn, R.E. (2004). *Building the bridge as you walk on it: A guide for leading change*. San Francisco: Jossey-Bass.

Reynolds, R. (2008). In E. Biech (Ed.), *ASTD handbook for workplace learning professionals* (p. 865). Alexandria, VA: ASTD Press.

Robbins, S.P., & Coulter, M. (2012). *Management* (11th ed.). Upper Saddle River, NJ: Prentice Hall.

Rosenzweig, J., & Van Tiem, D.M. (2007, May/June). An appreciative view of human performance technology. *Performance Improvement, 46*(5), 3–43.

Rothwell, W.J. (1996). *ASTD models for human performance improvement: Roles, competencies, and outputs*. Alexandria, VA: American Society for Training and Development.

Rothwell, W.J. (2005). *Beyond training and development* (2nd ed.) New York: AMACOM.

Schein, E.H. (1969). The mechanisms of change. In W.G. Bennis, K.D. Benne, & R. Chin (Eds.), *The planning of change* (2nd ed.). New York: Holt, Rinehart & Winston.

The Editors. (2002). *Business: The ultimate resource*. Cambridge, MA: Perseus Publishing.

Van Tiem, D.M., Moseley, J.L., & Dessinger, J.C. (2012). *Fundamentals of performance improvement: Optimizing results through people, process, and organizations*. San Francisco: Pfeiffer.

Varkey, P., & Antonio, K. (2010, July/August). Change management for effective quality improvement: A primer. *American Journal of Medical Quality, 25*(4), 268–273.

Whitney, D., & Trosten-Bloom, A. (2010). *The power of appreciative inquiry: A practical guide to positive change* (2nd ed.). San Francisco: Berrett-Koehler.

Womack, J.P., & Jones, D.T. (1996). *Lean thinking: Banish waste and create wealth in your corporation*. New York: Simon & Schuster.

PERFORMANCE SUPPORT TOOL 3.1. CHANGE MANAGEMENT PLANNER

Directions: Anticipating and preparing for change is important for performance improvement success. Answer the following questions to consider essential issues relative to change.

What changes are needed to meet customer, client, or stakeholder expectations?

What performance gaps currently exist in meeting the expectations?

How will customer, client, or stakeholder expectations be determined?

How will employees know when customer, client, or stakeholder expectations are met?

PERFORMANCE SUPPORT TOOL 3.2. CHANGE MANAGEMENT EVALUATOR

Directions: Answer the following set of more detailed questions.

Have the change expectations been thoroughly defined?

How will this change disrupt the current organization?

Does the organization have a history of intervention implementation problems? If so, describe them.

Are the sponsors or champions sufficiently committed to the project? If not, would education or replacing the sponsors help?

Does synergy exist between sponsors and change target groups? If not, what can be done to improve relationships?

What resistance is anticipated within the target groups?

Is the planned change consistent with the organizational culture?

Are participants sufficiently ready for the change effort? What would help?

Are the right people, right communication plan, and right success measures in place?

Boutique Marketing Company

Topic: *Appreciative Inquiry*

Jennifer Rosenzweig, Doctor of Professional Studies, CPT, *Dragonfly Organization Resource Group, Birmingham, Michigan, USA*

Background

Boutique Marketing [not its real name] is a strategic marketing services company located in downtown Boston. They have developed a unique and proprietary approach and method for conducting email and Internet marketing campaigns for their clients. Their approach relies on solid analytics that allow them to be efficient and targeted in their promotions. They pride themselves on the quality of their talent, their analytical rigor, their client responsiveness, and their creativity.

Situation

As a ten-year-old company, Boutique Marketing has gone through the struggles of a start-up and is now on solid footing. Their revenues doubled in 2008 during the depth of the recession, and they have seen increases in revenue and profit in subsequent years. Their reputation has attracted brand name clients in the apparel, sports and food and beverage industries, making for an interesting and diverse customer base.

The owners of the firm recognized that a key to their success has been the quality of the talent that they've hired. They have a group of age "twenty- and thirty-something" marketers who enjoy the challenges of leveraging the software to design client-centered solutions. However, as their team has become more proficient and their company's reputation has grown, other competing firms have started to heavily recruit these team members. Wanting to avoid a cycle of high turnover—which they knew would have a negative impact on client satisfaction and ultimately bottom-line performance—they sought an intervention that would engage their employees and identify ways to make staying at the company more attractive to them.

Intervention

To gain insight on how best to tackle their initiative, Boutique Marketing partnered with two consultants, who ultimately recommended that an appreciative approach to performance improvement be deployed. Their goal was to leverage the many strengths of the organization and to engage the entire workforce in imagining improvements to their company that would be both effective and compelling.

The process began with leadership interviews, which included the three owners of Boutique Marketing. They also conducted an initial employee engagement survey to create a baseline and to provide information for the leadership discussions. The results of the survey and ensuing discussions reinforced the desire by leadership to make changes that would allow them to become a greater employer of choice. But they also decided that there were some opportunities to make business improvements that would address some of the growing pains that had emerged through their recent rapid growth. For example, the owners were unhappy with the current organization structure and wanted to identify ways to improve upon it. Their final goals were to (1) retain top talent and (2) identify and enact on business process and structural improvements while still retaining their entrepreneurial spirit.

Strengths Analysis. The first step was to extend the data collection (discovery) process to include the workforce. Everyone participated in an interview cascade in which employees used a survey to have structured conversations about organizational strengths and opportunities for improvement. Key strengths that emerged included admiration for the leadership team; the challenge and responsibility of the work; and the team-based and collegial atmosphere. As they explored potential opportunities, they decided to focus on (1) leadership across the organization (looking beyond the owners); (2) redesigning the organizational structure; and (3) ways to encourage personal growth and development.

Vision ("Dream"). Rather than establish a vision on behalf of the organization and then just announce it to everyone, the owners invited the entire company to a series of meetings in which they jointly imagined the future of the company. Specially, they discussed what leadership meant to the company as a whole, different ways they might organize to better serve their clients and themselves, and opportunities for stretching personal boundaries and growing beyond their current roles. Many exciting and creative ideas were shared, and these became the basis for a series of employee-led projects.

Interventions ("Design"). At the conclusion of the visioning sessions, projects were established to enact the most powerful ideas. These projects included the design of a new on-boarding process for new employees, a mentoring program to encourage cross-training, a new client-centered organizational structure, the establishment of a communications team, and the development of a sustainability charter. This last element stemmed from a single interview comment during the discovery phase in which one employee wondered whether there was a way to look beyond the company needs and have a stronger societal view. This proved to be a captivating idea for the group and became a positive outlet for significant creative energy.

Results. Ultimately, the team accomplished the following:

- *Organizational structure.* A new dynamic structure was designed to be flexible and adaptive, while remaining responsive to client and business demands.
- *Sustainability team.* A rotating group of employees manned a sustainability team that focused on improvements to how the "planet" was cared for (for example, a recycling program was instituted) as well as the "people" (for example, they instituted "Friday fun fests" to communicate current business issues, followed by a social hour).
- *On-boarding program.* Instead of having a randomly implemented orientation, they created a much richer and better organized method for introducing new employees to the "inside story" of Boutique Marketing.
- *Mentoring program.* Employees were asked to identify areas in the company they'd like exposure to, and formal plans were created to cross-train them. In addition, more people were included in the company's sales and marketing efforts, for example, by including them on sales calls; by having them write white papers; by encouraging them to submit proposals to speak at conferences, and so forth.

Critical Business Issue

What is: Employee turnover was increasing at a time in the company's evolution in which it was critical to have a skilled and talented workforce fully prepared to meet client needs. The company was also experiencing some growing pains, which suggested the need to redesign internal processes and structures.

What should be: Employees should have a voice in how best to create an organization that meets the needs of both the talent and the clients. It should be a healthy, productive, and stimulating environment that enriches all those involved.

Focus on Outcomes or Results

The owners had two primary outcomes: (1) retain top talent and (2) identify and enact a business process and structural improvements while still retaining the company's entrepreneurial spirit.

Focus on Systems View

Inputs. Feedback and ideas were elicited from everyone in the company, assuring that a rich, full picture of the entire internal system was captured. Data streams also included company finances, strategic plans, and client feedback.

Process. Meetings were held over several weeks with all employees. Team members worked in small groups as they explored the results of their initial data collection (the cascade interviews) and imagined the world they wanted to live in as part of the Boutique Company.

Output. Several project teams emerged from their discussions. All of them were populated by employee volunteers who had an interest in the project, and each team had a leadership sponsor. The sponsors did not lead the teams, but were a resource for problem solving and support.

Constraints. Employees were encouraged to ignore potential constraints as they worked through the discovery and design processes. Once interventions were identified, constraints fell within the normal concerns of finding the time to add the project to their workload and securing the necessary financing (if needed) from their sponsors.

Focus on Value

Value was generated for everyone involved. There was a lot of energy and excitement as new ideas were formulated and employees considered how they could make business improvements. The owners were both surprised and pleased with the quality of discussion and saw several young leaders emerge through the process. They also anticipated value being generated for the clients, for they would also be beneficiaries of any improvements in how work was done.

Focus on Establishing Partnerships

The entire process was undertaken with a partnership mentality. Each person was considered an equal partner in the effort—no voice, including management's, was greater than anyone else's. Ideas and suggestions were vetted for their practical value and desirability, and not based on "who said it." This opened up the dialogue and allowed even the most reticent individuals to speak out and feel more connected to their colleagues and to the organization.

Be Systematic in Assessment of Need, Opportunity, or Challenge

Attention was given to gaining a clear view of the situation right from the start. First, leadership had a chance to weigh in, but even after they established their own perspective on how best to move forward, the rest of the company was invited in. While this solidified much of what management had concluded, it also reshaped and expanded the goals and added substance to others.

Be Systematic in the Analysis of Work, Worker, Workplace, and Worldview to Identify the Causes or Factors That Limit Performance

Because an appreciative approach was selected for this initiative, a strengths analysis and visioning session were used to identify the future state. The consultants relied on the data generated by all of the employees to guide them and used that to frame the meetings in which the future state was defined. Again, by including every employee in the organization, there was greater assurance that the ultimate solutions would be well targeted and committed to by the company as a whole.

It was also broadening for the group to think about their organization's impact on the world and to capture a societal view as well as a work, worker, and workplace view. Initially, leadership was a bit skeptical about whether there was a place in the dialogue for societal considerations, but as interest in exploring sustainability increased, any hesitations faded away.

Be Systematic in the Design of the Solution

Because employees knew they would be responsible for the design and implementation of the selected solution, they were thoughtful about what they selected and how they designed it. However, they were also encouraged to think big . . . this was a clean sheet of paper so they were welcome to expand their thinking and move in new directions if it suited the circumstances.

Be Systematic in the Development of the Solution

Each project team was given complete latitude to develop their solution. Their sponsors were available to encourage their progress, keep them on track, and identify resources if needed.

In order to keep efforts coordinated overall, teams reported on progress at all-employee meetings. They also identified some small areas of overlap between projects, minimizing potential complications. These meetings also served to keep the entire organization informed about each project, which enhanced how quickly employees were able to adapt to new expectations.

Be Systematic in the Implementation of the Solution

As the various solutions were implemented, attention was given to ensuring that the new changes were self-sustaining. One of the more interesting approaches to this was with the "Friday fun fest" team. They chose to create a Friday "rotation" in which pairs of individuals would take on responsibility for planning the Friday agenda and taking care of refreshments and other details. To track their work, a log was created. The agenda was recorded in the log, as well as high-level details from the meetings. This provided a history that could be used for reference over time.

Be Systematic in the Evaluation of the Process and the Results

The consultants and owners used a mix of quantitative and qualitative means to measure the impact of the various projects.

The first measure of success came with the employee engagement survey, which was conducted approximately one year after the overall initiative began. The results showed a 9 percent improvement in how employees felt about the organization. Their scores were already high, as this was a well-functioning organization, so everyone was pleased with the upward trend.

A qualitative survey and focus groups also yielded a variety of positive results. One outcome was that leadership recognized that the level of creativity had gone up, as individuals understood that they could influence the company and its outcomes more than they realized. As noted by one owner: "Our company is now coming up with new products and solutions that not only help us, but help our clients, too."

Enhanced teamwork was also a byproduct of the effort. While they were already strong in this area and routinely worked on client projects, "It really opened everyone's eyes to the fact that we're one team working together to achieve our shared goals."

There was also a stronger sense of ownership for results overall. None of the projects that the group chose to work on faded away. Each one came into fruition: the new employee orientation; the personal development and learning plans; the sustainability effort. As one employee noted, "The best part was creating project teams and action plans that are actually getting things done."

Finally, the president of the company commented on how much he ended up appreciating the value of the all-company "discovering" and "dreaming" sessions. "I loved the Eureka moments!"

■   ■   ■

Lessons Learned from the Case

- Initially there was some impatience, especially on the part of leadership, as they wanted to move from the early stages of discovery right into implementation. Their belief was that, since they knew what they wanted to do, it was best to simply get on with it. However, by bringing the entire company into the dialogue, they ultimately saw that it allowed them to accelerate implementation (because everyone was clear on the direction) and it increased the quality of the solutions overall.
- The overall project work had the desired effect on employee turnover, but it also prompted some unexpected changes. Voluntary turnover stabilized over the following months (specifically, two employees who received competing job offers chose to stay). But the process also revealed the need to make further changes. It became clear through the many dialogues that two employees were not a good cultural fit for the company. In combination with some questions related to performance, it was decided that they should be laid off. Then, as part of the restructuring, two other individuals were hired, but into different roles that matched the new vision. It should be added that the restructuring created the opportunity to move people into new roles for cross-training purposes, so they were able to do that with 20 percent of the team. (Much more than that would have pushed client service boundaries.) These personnel moves led to improved customer service as well as increased employee satisfaction.
- Several lessons emerged from the dialogue on sustainability. The first was the inclusion of the topic itself to the all-company discovery and dream meetings. The concept first came out of the initial engagement survey as a response to a general open-ended question. Because only one voice shared an interest in it, the leadership initially dismissed the interest in sustainability as a minority view. However, the consultants were aware than many companies that are considered "employers of choice" have a strong connection to society, so they encouraged its inclusion on the agenda. The agreement was that, if there was no further interest, the subject would be dropped. So the first lesson learned was that, even if there isn't a majority voice, that doesn't mean that the view shouldn't be given strong regard.

- The next lesson related to the fact that the topic of sustainability initially "stumped" the team who worked on it. They liked the idea in theory; they just couldn't connect it to their daily business. It took several meetings for them to start to embrace the thought that as an online marketing company, they are environmentally friendly in their paperless approach. It therefore made sense to take a more environmental view to other aspects of their business. The first, simple solution was to start recycling. But they are coming up with other ways they can embrace a "green" approach to business. So the lesson here is to pay attention to "intuition" and to allow difficult topics to incubate over time. You may be very surprised and pleased with what emerges!

Jennifer Rosenzweig, D. Prof, M.S.A., M.S.O.D, CPT, is a partner with Dragonfly Organization Resource Group, where she is a performance consultant who applies appreciative approaches to her practice. She enjoys the challenges that change brings as well as the excitement that emerges from co-creating the future. She can be reached at 248.302.0461 or jrosenzweig@dragonflyorg.com.

Strategic Performance Management in Georgia Education

Topic: School Improvement

Deb Page, B.S., CPT, *Willing Learner, Atlanta, Georgia, USA*

Background

Prior to this intervention, Georgia schools and school systems engaged in strategic planning and performance reporting that focused primarily on lagging indicators of performance, such as state student test data, graduation rates, and other metrics that encouraged a reactive approach to improvement. Accreditation plans, developed every five years, were mainly focused on application of programs to perceived needs. Improvement plan goals were frequently expressed as programs to be implemented rather than appropriate performance metrics and target. Most district leaders' evaluations were not connected to performance metrics, nor was accreditation supported by a system of measurable performance.

Situation

Deb Page was the senior executive director of the Georgia Leadership Institute for School Improvement. The Institute had been formed in 2002 with a large private grant and state funding. With a background as a K–12 educator and more than twenty years of corporate experience in performance improvement, Deb was hired and charged with leading adoption of performance improvement practices commonly used in other sectors to the improvement of schools in the state. The Wallace Foundation provided funding to support the development of a performance culture in education in Georgia and alignment between state and local education agencies.

Critical Issues

School improvement in public schools in the United States is impacted by a complex set of interdependent performance factors and conditions with multiple causes. In 2000 and 2001

Georgia passed education reform laws, followed shortly in 2002 by United States Department of Education's *No Child Left Behind*, a federal mandate that required all students to reach the performance standards for their grade in key subjects each year, as measured by standardized tests, regardless of existing gaps in students' knowledge and skills. At the same time, the accrediting agency for educational institutions was revising its requirements to require data-driven planning and assessment of impact. In order to meet these mandates, education leaders needed to learn to collect and process interim student performance data that would support predictive performance analysis. The results would allow teachers, administrators, and staff to intervene to improve performance. However, a review of state school systems identified only two that were using performance data and result-based planning and evaluation to drive improvement. Interventions were needed in Georgia to close the gap in performance management practices and create alignment of practices from the classroom to the state.

Focus on Outcomes and Results

Page targeted the following performance targets and adoption indicators: (1) strategic performance improvement curriculum and tools developed and delivered to 300+ senior leaders in the 181 school districts in the state; (2) 50 percent of districts, the State Department of Education (DOE) and State School Board Association adopting strategic management tools and processes within five years; (3) alignment of the strategic management tool with a new school superintendents' evaluation developed by the Georgia School Superintendents Association; (4) inclusion of strategic performance management in State School Board standards; and (5) inclusion of data-driven performance management in school and district accreditation requirements.

Balanced scorecards were recognized as an opportunity to train and support education leaders in their use as an action vehicle for creating increased focus on performance indicators, outcomes, and results. Balanced scorecards were an innovation by Drs. Robert Kaplan and David Norton of the Harvard Business School in the early 1990s. The tool is used extensively in business and industry, government, and non-profits to align activities to the vision and strategy of the organization, improve internal and external communication, and monitor performance against strategic goals. The tool provides a more balanced view of performance than just financial metrics so that the drivers of performance are measured and managed. A balanced scorecard transforms a strategic plan into a dynamic document that helps plan what should be done, monitor execution, and measure and communicate performance. Applied in education, a balanced scorecard focuses on student achievement as the "lagging indicator" of performance, just as profit is the "lagging indicator" or bottom line in a for-profit organization. Team learning and growth, student and stakeholder engagement, and organizational effectiveness are "leading" and predictive indicators of student achievement. The tool helps education leaders focus on the causal relationships between the systems of work in the organization and teaching and learning outcomes. For example, data regarding the leading indicator of on-time school bus arrival can be predictors of student achievement because when students miss instructional time they are less likely to master all the curriculum upon which they are assessed. Improving arrival time protects students' time on task in the classroom, which research has confirmed improves learning.

Focus on a Systemic View

Page's approach included achieving grass-roots support and advocacy for the adoption of the tools and new practices from school superintendents and other stakeholders, building capacity in new practices, aligning performance practices, terminology, expectations, and evaluation, and improving perceptions of strategic management practices and tools in order to develop a performance culture in public schools. Balanced scorecard training and related measurement and tracking tools also were action vehicles to ensure education leaders adopted a systemic approach to improving student achievement; organizational effectiveness; student, teacher, and stakeholder engagement, and team learning and growth.

Focus on Adding Value

The project was designed to add value for school and district leaders who would be able to better plan, measure, monitor, and communicate about their performance. The state board would be able to raise standards to support more strategic governance. The State Department of Education adoption would create alignment between the state and local education agencies. Superintendent evaluation would be supported by the strategic tools and practices and the performance data in the balanced scorecards. School systems could access an electronic balanced scorecard so that district and school plans were aligned to each other and to the state's. The accrediting entity could ensure that school systems had access to training and tools to support the increased expectations of data-driven planning and improvement. The Institute would be able to fulfill funders' expectations of development of a performance culture in Georgia schools.

Focus on Establishing Partnerships

A local school superintendent was identified who was already using a balanced scorecard. A small group of high-performing school superintendents were recruited into a learning community, along with the leader of a university MBA program to work with the learning community. One superintendent became an early adopter, creating a demonstration site in his district to model best practices for others. Page then developed and delivered a free statewide training program and offered free training sessions at professional association conferences. She taught superintendents how to use the performance management tools with their evaluation systems.

Later Page directed funding to the School Board Association to embed the new tools, including an electronic balanced scorecard, within their planning software. She trained and assigned a staff member to work directly with the School Board Association and the State Department of Education to create alignment in terminology, tools, and practices. She worked with the accrediting agency to develop a memorandum of understanding for partnership in advancing strategic performance management tools and practices. Finally, she served as a volunteer to help the state board update school board standards to align school governance practices to support strategic performance management.

Be Systematic in Assessing the Need or Opportunity

To assess the situation, the early adopter school superintendents were interviewed and Harvard Business School research was reviewed concerning adoption of the tools and practices in education. Page conducted focus groups, researched strategic performance management adoption in education in other states, and hired a researcher to provide a report on use of strategic management tools in public education. She reviewed goals developed by school superintendents and their accreditation plans to assess their ability to develop effective goals and metrics. She conducted a job-task analysis of the work of school leaders. The analysis process revealed the gaps in current and best practice and confirmed links between successful adoption of the new practices and sustainable school improvement. The study revealed the positive deviants in the state and nation, showed their performance advantages and best practices, and helped identify and determine the key stakeholders who needed to be informed to adopt or advocate for the practices and provide funding for the change.

Be Systematic in Design of the Solution

The analysis pointed to the need for a suite of solutions:

1. *Capacity building to support potential adopters.* Training and job aids were needed for school superintendents, district staff, principals, education agencies, and others who work in schools to support school improvement to master strategic performance management;

2. *Tools to aid adoption and reduce time to competency in new practices.* A template of a balanced scorecard with data types organized by the goal areas of student achievement, organizational effectiveness, student and stakeholder engagement, and team learning and growth was needed to support adoption and make the new work easier to master. Tools, job aids, and performance criteria were needed to guide education leaders through aligning their strategic plan to their balanced scorecard and cascading the tools and processes from the state to school districts to schools.

3. *Motivation of potential users by increasing the ease of adoption, providing evidence of the success of earlier adopters, and rewarding adoption and alignment of current practices, such as strategic planning and evaluation, with the new practices and tools.* Opportunities to showcase the practices and results of early adopters were needed to convince potential adopters that the new ways of planning, measuring, monitoring, and communicating about performance were resulting in improvements in student achievement and were making the work of education leaders easier and more effective.

4. *Alignment between schools and districts, school systems and their local and state governance, professional associates and the state and school districts.* The Wallace Foundation had challenged the state to create alignment between the goals of the state and how results were measured and communicated and those of school districts. Governance and the professional associations that influenced and supported education leaders needed to use and advocate for the use of the performance management tools, practices and measures contained in an education balanced scorecard.

5. *Development of a performance culture.* The new way of planning, measuring, monitoring, and communicating about performance needed to be adopted by a critical mass of education leaders.

Be Systematic in the Development of the Solution

The design was outlined in grant applications and the grants were awarded to support development of:

1. *A demonstration site for the early adopter to model practices.* The superintendent converted a workroom into a data room organized around the goal areas of the district's new balanced scorecard. The superintendent allowed other districts to come to the site for the free training Page provided and participated in delivery of the training.

2. *A balanced scorecard template for education including key metrics.* The early-adopter superintendent and another superintendent who had just retired from the only district in the state that was currently using a balanced scorecard developed a template with all the metrics that schools and the state education agencies could use to plan, measure, monitor, and communicate about school performance.

3. *Training of the targeted adopting entities.* Page and the two superintendents provided training to state education agencies and the Wallace Foundation provided training for the state agency leaders through the Darden Business School at the University of Virginia. Page provided the training to school districts and later transitioned the training to the two superintendents who delivered it to peers.

4. *A terminology guide.* Page charged the two superintendents with development of a terminology guide. They later provided the guide to the state School Board Association to support their development of online strategic planning tools and an online Balanced Scorecard.

5. *Site visits in Georgia and other states by leaders for all the school districts, agencies, professional associations, and the accrediting entity with embedded training and modeling to support transfer to practice, advocacy, proof of effectiveness, and acceptance of the practices and related terminology.* Page and the two superintendents organized a bus tour for education leaders to see strategic performance management practices at work in high-performing school districts and schools in Georgia and Florida. During the trip, training was delivered aboard the bus and at the demonstration sites.

6. *Memorandums of agreements with partners.* Agreements with the accrediting agency were developed to ensure the work Page was leading was aligned with the needs and expectations of the accrediting agency, and that the accrediting agency was encouraging school districts to adopt the new practices and tools to support the data-driven accreditation process.

7. *Consulting support to state agencies.* Page and members of her team volunteered consulting support to the Board of Regents of the University System of Georgia, the Georgia Department of Education, the Department of Early Care and Learning, the Professional Standards Commission, and others to support adoption of the new tools and practices.

Be Systematic in the Implementation of the Solution

Page led the project team to support the diffusion of the innovation and collected data from the State Department of Education concerning the number of school systems that had adopted the scorecard and related performance management tools. Evaluators tracked the number of leaders attending training. Page developed resources to hire two superintendents who had adopted the practices and tools to take over the training program and provide it, along with consulting support to the targeted stakeholders. Tools were published on the Institute's website to support ease of implementation and were revised as users refined their use, transferring ownership to the users and stakeholders. Page transferred management and monitoring to the superintendents hired to sustain the practices through an ongoing executive development program.

Be Systematic in the Evaluation of the Solution

Page engaged university researchers and internal staff in evaluation of the solutions. They found that the suite of interventions had produced the intended results:

- Over five years more than seven hundred leaders were trained.
- Fifty percent of districts reported use of the new practices and tools.
- The Georgia Department of Education evidenced adoption of the practices and tools.
- The School Board Association embedded the tools and terminology in the strategic planning software.
- The superintendent evaluation and the new tools and practices created an aligned, data-driven evaluation process for superintendents.
- Revised school board standards and accreditation standards required use of data-driven strategic management tools and practices.

■ ■ ■

Lessons Learned from the Case
- Systemic adoption of new tools and practices requires performers to see successful adoption by others and have the time and support to master new practices.
- Transferring ownership is key to long-term adoption and diffusion of practices.
- Good tools support faster adoption of new practices, especially when the tools make the work easier and produce tangible results.
- Effectively designed training can be an action vehicle for changes in practices and perceptions,
- Alignment of practices, terms, and tools for performance management and improvement across organizations requires creating value for each organization.
- Focusing attention to successful early adopters and utilizing peer-to-peer networks and training creates motivation for adoption by others.

Deb Page, B.S., CPT, president of Willing Learner, Inc., is a performance consultant who has worked extensively across multiple sectors to improve individual and organizational performance. She earned a bachelor's degree in education. She founded and led the Georgia Leadership Institute for School Improvement and co-manages national delivery of the evidence-base Certified School Improvement Specialist job certification offered by ISPI. She can be reached at Deb.Page@WillingLearner.org or at 678.428.2363.

Reducing Municipal Strife Through Engagement

Topic: Performance Improvement/ HPT Model

Steven J. Kelly, M.A., CPT, *KNO Worldwide, Bratislava, Slovak Republic, Europe*

Background

The client, a municipality of about 250,000, is located in Northwest United States. It has a workforce of just over one thousand employees, with the bulk of them involved with public safety, fire protection, and public works. The city has an elected mayor and city council for governance, which employs a professional city manager as an executive officer to oversee implementation of the council priorities and administer the department citizen services and municipal laws. At this time the city had only recently transitioned into having a city manager. Most long-term department heads had been used to independent action, relying on their political relationships with the elected council for support of budget and initiatives.

Critical Business Issue

At the time of the project engagement, the municipality was involved in a multi-year series of expensive litigations with the labor unions within the city. Although a small workforce, the employees were represented by a number of bargaining units (twelve) representing the employees and management within various departments. Conflict between the city management and several of the larger unions escalated into expensive arbitration and legal battles that were incurring costs of several million dollars annually. These conflicts, especially within the police and fire departments, extended beyond the usually specific issues of complaint. There was a broader challenge to the authority of the city manager's office to oversee the city as an integrated entity addressing a common mission.

At the same time, within the protective service departments, several long-term professionals had been seeking unsuccessfully to obtain funding for an employee assistance program (EAP) to provide counseling support for experienced veterans who were having difficulties with substance abuse or other conditions related to the stress of the job. At the time, the city procedures only allowed for discipline or termination of employees exhibiting these types of job performance issues.

Intervention

An opportunity for a grant from the Federal Mediation and Conciliation Service opened and was successfully applied for by the city Human Resources department with union support. The funding ($165,000) extended over a period of three years, with a primary focus of the grant to improve relations between management and employees through the provision of internal actions (such as Employee Assistance Program and informal dispute resolution) while increasing the level of mutual trust and communications.

This funding acted as a seed mechanism to start a comprehensive new level of engagement among the senior managers in the city and the leaders within the employee unions. In addition to a large reduction in litigation costs over this period, the steering group jointly created a number of initiatives: to recognize employee contributions, develop internal career capacity, and reduce costs during a time of budgetary restraint. Most of these initiatives are still active in the municipality today.

Focus on Outcomes or Results

The primary outcome of this effort was targeted to be increased trust between city management, department heads, and key employee "opinion leaders," who were often active in influencing bargaining unit actions. Increased trust would support more effective communication and allow for informal resolution of developing problems prior to escalation to legal actions. Given the difficulty of measuring ongoing relationship improvements, specific proxy targets were set to measure outcomes:

- Reduction of legal fees (40 percent) spent on formal disputes between city and bargaining units
- Improved scores (+10 percent on trust elements) in a city-wide employee satisfaction survey after three years
- Reduced cost through higher productivity (and less turnover of trained staff) as a result of specific initiatives

Focus on Systems View

In addressing this issue, it was important to address the problem within a very complex system of interactions. Within the city government were twelve separate departments, of which one , the city attorney is an elected official, and another, the city clerk, appointed directly by the council. Two of the departments, police and fire, consisted of over 60 percent of the workforce. To support twenty-four-hour citizen protection, both of these departments used shifts. Also, the workforce was organized into twelve bargaining units. To complicate matters, both in the police and fire departments, middle managers were also represented by several bargaining units (sometimes three or four members) who were both representing management to employees while at the same time bargaining for their own benefits. Facilities for the city employees were distributed across over forty locations throughout the municipality.

Although most of the department heads reported on paper to the city manager, in practice, several of the long-term managers had direct relationships with the elected mayor and council, who approved policy and budgets. Several of the union leaders also provided electoral support for individual candidates and had access to these officials if needed.

The external environment at the time influenced the situation. City receipts were down slightly from recent years and budgets were up for reduction. Luckily, the council was not involved in longstanding controversial issues and was supportive of this initiative to reduce city expenses.

At the time of the initiation of this intervention, the city manager had been appointed for just over a year. Rather than simply take a narrow approach to the opening that the grant funding allowed, he encouraged the consultant to take a broader approach to strengthening communication in the city.

Focus on Value

The scope of the approved federal grant was to focus on building trust by piloting forms of informal dispute resolution, as well as supporting union members (city employees) through the start-up of an employee assistance program for crisis and professional counseling. The consultant, based on an initial assessment, determined that a broader effort would be required to achieve these challenging goals. With the direction and approval of the city manager, the consultant used the grant, with small supplemental contributions from the city, to initiate a wider effort to engage employees to improve internal staff communications and better citizen services. As described further below, this steering committee–supervised program resulted in a wide range of actions to improve communication, recognize and reward commitment, and develop professional skills in support of the city mission.

Focus on Establishing Partnerships

An important challenge for this intervention was the need to build legitimacy for the effort to include stakeholders from throughout the city. Perception (or actual reality) that the initiatives were simply a top-down program to force-feed "trust building" could not work. This was accomplished with several tactics by the consultant/facilitator. The first was the creation of a management and employee steering committee to direct the activities of the grant. The committee of twelve included several department senior managers and members selected by the larger bargaining units to participate. While the city manager, as the chief executive of the organization, needed to approve final recommendations for changes to policy or commitment of funds outside the project, there was a steady respect for the committee work and independence.

A second initiative was the execution, under the direction of the committee, of the first-ever city-wide survey of employee attitudes and views of workplace satisfaction. This was successfully administered (with a 70 percent participation rate) and provided a baseline for evaluating future success. Results of the survey were published, employee briefings held, and data analyzed by the committee to contribute to recommendations for action.

The third initiative was the organization of an off-site retreat, sponsored by the committee, early in the process with all key stakeholders attending. The group, more than forty people, included all department heads, most deputies, and senior members of all the bargaining units. Held in a rustic setting, the climate allowed for both discussions of workplace trust issues as well as strengthening of social bonds. It also provided for a legitimatizing of the work of the steering committee, which came to be seen as the working delegation after the offsite.

A final tactic was to find a neutral workspace, outside the boundaries of the city manager's office space. This allowed for ongoing interviews and ad hoc discussions with employees at all levels outside management territory.

Be Systematic in the Assessment of the Need, Opportunity, or Challenge

As a front end to building the steering committee and initiating activity, the consultant conducted interviews throughout the organization. The approved grant award had documented the critical need to reduce legal battles. However, generally everyone was in agreement that the issue was broader than just contractual violations for litigation. This included department managers, union leaders, and rank-and-file workers. While the department heads were primarily oriented toward finding ways to fulfill citizen service requirements on limited resources, the bargaining unit leadership was focused on maintaining hard-won incremental benefits. Due to historical episodes of intermittent negotiation battles, several union leaders had a strong suspicion of any management initiative to "build trust." However, even these people agreed that efforts to reduce spiraling litigation expense were worth pursuing.

As described previously, further assessment and buy-in were accomplished during the offsite meeting of all key stakeholders.

Be Systematic in the Analysis of Work, Worker, Workplace, and World View to Identify the Causes or Factors That Limit Performance

Under the guidance of the consultant, the steering committee collected and analyzed data developed from the off-site retreat, the employee survey, and follow-up interviews and focus groups. Additionally, research was conducted of best practices from the International City Manager's Association resource base. The analysis identified some of the critical factors that were reducing communication effectiveness leading to trust:

1. Heavily siloed departments; many employees only knew the small circle of people within their work areas and relied on the grapevine for updates.

2. A strong perception that employees were not valued by city management; little recognition for achievements, no systemized employee development or career path (except in protection services).

3. Little visibility of city top management in the workplace.

4. An authoritarian management style by almost all department heads; lack of consist staff meetings in many units.

5. Lack of city-wide information sources, social events.

6. Rotation of city manager and key staff every three or four years; difficult to sustain progress.

Be Systematic in the Design of the Solution

Based on the analysis of the data and the nature of the factors influencing the gap, the steering committee designed a set of parallel sub-interventions to address the issues. The consultant worked closely with working subcommittee teams to design the sub-intervention elements. The designs of specific sub-interventions were based on collected best-practice programs from International City Manager Association sources and the experience of the consultant.

The following sub-interventions were developed and staged over several years:

- A walk-around program by the city manager to visit all departments twice a year.
- Bi-weekly top management meetings chaired by the city manager to update all department heads on key issues; flow-down staff meetings in departments following these.
- An employee recognition awards scheme including time in service awards, suggestion incentives, and quarterly exemplary service recognition (selected by an independent committee).
- A formal performance review and career coaching process for the non-protective service department staff.
- A city-wide professional skills training program (supervisory and administrative), with courses based on an annual needs assessment.
- The employee assistance program with confidential counseling open to employees and families.
- A pilot procedure for an informal dispute resolution process to be used prior to moving into formal arbitration or litigation.
- An integrated citizen resource guide combining previously siloed reference information and contact numbers (later added to website).
- Annual summer employee picnic and winter holiday party.

Be Systematic in the Development of the Solution

The development and implementation of the sub-interventions was done in stages. Most of the development work was done by steering group subcommittee (under the guidance of the consultant) using best-practice models. Cost was reasonable—primary new budgetary costs were time-in-service awards, a part-time training coordinator, and funds for external training instructors and materials. The consultant participated in the drafting of new policies and procedures that were reviewed within the steering committee and by department heads. Other than the

EAP program, which required a larger external contract with a service provider approved by the city council, all other sub-interventions were funded by existing human resource and city manager budgets (along with the federal grant). The performance management, awards recognition, and training programs were passed on to the HR department after the second year of operation.

Be Systematic in the Implementation of the Solution

The implementation of the complex set of sub-interventions was done in waves. The highly visible (and inexpensive) recognition awards, management meetings, and social events were implemented quickly within the first year, along with the EAP. By the second year, the training needs assessment was completed and a pilot training program put in place. The development and review/comment of the performance management system was more involved and was implemented at the end of the second year, with uneven application among the departments.

The challenge of implementing the informal dispute resolution process was the most difficult. Over a period of six months, a procedure was drafted and reviewed by the bargaining units. At the end, several of the larger unions chose to drop out of the process. It was accepted by some of the administrative units and published in the procedures manual. However, during the three years it was never activated in a real case.

The duration of the grant over three years allowed for a continual follow-up of all the initiatives by the consultant (on a part-time basis), and follow-through on the handoff to the HR department.

Be Systematic in the Evaluation of the Process and Results

At the conclusion of the grant period, a formal evaluation and report was completed. In the matter of litigation costs, there had been a reduction of over 70 percent during this time. This was based on several factors besides this intervention, especially the interest of the city manager to build stronger relations with the union leaders. These savings of more than a million dollars from litigation more than paid for the ongoing costs of the other elements. The employee suggestion program in the first two years alone identified five innovations that saved the city over $120,000 in direct costs. The employee survey was administered again thirty months into the project. Coordinated by the HR department, the survey had a lower participation (38 percent) so it was not possible to evaluate its impact reliably.

The consultant was able to follow the progress of the city from afar for some years, and even a decade later the recognition awards, the training program, and the EAP were active. The city manager left the city a year after the conclusion of the grant effort, and it is likely some of the management initiatives suffered from his departure (although the job was taken for a few years by his former deputy who had been involved in all the initiatives). The litigation between the city and labor unions has cycled up and down during the past years, but the level of expense during the years preceding the intervention have not been reached again.

■ ■ ■

Lessons Learned from the Case

- The commitment and action of top management is critical in complex system interventions where old behaviors are set by historical precedent, political intrigue, and lack of belief in change. The top management commitment does not ensure success, but without it, no progress can happen.

- The involvement of opinion leaders in organization change efforts, throughout the structure, is important to ensure comprehensive interpretation of the data during analysis, buy-in for intervention recommendations and execution, and promotion of the changes within the workplace.

- Despite the conflict between the key actors (managers and labor representatives), all were interested in providing the highest service possible for the city's citizens. While there could never be agreement on all aspects of labor contracts, the opportunities for ongoing facilitated dialogue outside the conflict builds good will that transfers beyond the single disagreements.

- Effective change in a complex system of information flow, personal relationships, and geographical dispersion usually requires an integrated set of several parallel interventions that are mutually supportive toward the same goal. Standing alone, none can be effective, but together they can build momentum toward success despite weal elements among them.

Steven J. Kelly, M.A., CPT, has thirty-five years' diversified experience in the performance improvement arena. He is a founder (1979) of KNO Worldwide, headquartered in Central Europe since 1991. In this role, he acts as a consultant to business and government in Central Europe and the former USSR to implement institutional and staff productivity strategies. Steven holds a master's degree in management and human relations from Pacific Lutheran University. He currently serves on the international board of directors of ISPI.

Amway Corporation: Driving Consistent, Strategic Performance of Distributors Globally*

Topic: *Performance Improvement/ HPT Model*

Steven Sniderman, M.A., *Amway Corporation, Ada, Michigan, USA, and*
Valerie Brown, M.A., *Innovative Learning Group, Royal Oak, Michigan, USA*

Background

Amway Corporation is a direct seller of nutrition, beauty, personal care, and home care products. It is a global organization with ten autonomous regions and more than four million active distributorships in more than eighty countries. These distributorships earn money by selling Amway products and also by sponsoring others into their own businesses. Amway's learning organization consists of ten autonomous regional training groups and Global Training and Education, a shared-services function that supports the regions.

---

*This case study was excerpted and/or adapted from the following article: V. Brown & S. Sniderman (2012). Using Performance Modeling to Drive Consistent, Strategic Performance of Amway Distributors Globally. *Performance Improvement Journal,* 51(1), 26–35.

Situation

In March 2007 Amway identified a strategic need to improve its distributors' performance on critical metrics related to retail sales, the number of new distributors, and the retention of existing distributors. Although Amway had considerable anecdotal information about successful distributors, it had no comprehensive understanding of the behaviors critical to effective distributor performance. Further, the existing anecdotal data were inconsistent across regions. Without a complete set of consistent performance data, there was no way to determine how to improve distributor performance.

Amway's ten regions around the world had no comprehensive curricula focused on success-critical performance. Prior to 2009 a number of Amway regions offered primarily product training. Training on how to run a business or how to sell were typically delivered by higher-level distributors, with varying levels of effectiveness. Where the regions had developed training, each region had created its own. This led to different content in similar solutions, duplication of efforts, and inefficient use of resources.

Intervention

Global Training and Education had a clear vision that achieving Amway's goals and improving distributor results required that distributors perform the behaviors critical to those results and goals. To address this need, Global Training and Education launched an intervention to define that set of critical distributor tasks and behaviors for distributors globally.

The intervention consisted of six components, selected specifically to balance global consistency (by driving to the global behaviors) and regional autonomy (by leaving alignment, design, and development to each region). Given the global nature of the organization and the autonomy of the regions, achieving this balance was a fundamental requirement for the intervention's success.

Intervention components include:

Distributor Performance Model. The heart of the intervention, this model details the linkage from Amway's goals to critical distributor results, critical distributor behaviors, the key knowledge, skills, and attitudes that enable performance, and the learning solutions that build the specified skills, knowledge, and attitudes. The model's design was adapted from the "impact map" concept presented by Brinkerhoff and Apking (2001). The purpose of an impact map is to focus performance improvement efforts (and especially learning) on those tasks and behaviors most directly linked to achievement of worthwhile organizational goals (Brinkerhoff & Apking, 2001). Unlike the Brinkerhoff and Apking impact map, however, the Distributor Performance Model was intended to be a deep-dive tool for use in designing and developing performance improvement solutions, including training. Thus, the performance model varies from the typical impact map in that the model includes three levels of detail related to tasks; it is multiple pages in length; and the model identifies the learning objectives and solutions that achieve the critical knowledge, skills, attitudes (Brinkerhoff & Apking, 2001).

The focus in the Distributor Performance Model was on cell four, Knowledge, of Thomas Gilbert's Behavior Engineering Model (Gilbert, 1996). The intervention team also gathered information on non-training factors affecting performance. The team captured these data on a separate worksheet within the performance model, categorized them by the remaining cells of the Behavior Engineering Model (Data, Instruments, Incentives, Capacity, Motives) (Gilbert, 1996), and shared them with the appropriate Amway functions.

Distributor Impact Map. To communicate the performance model purpose and contents to key stakeholders, the intervention team created a one-page Distributor Impact Map. This map distilled the following data from the full performance model: Amway Goals and Measures, Distributor Results, and Critical Behaviors. As with any impact map, the Amway Distributor Impact Map also showed the linkages among its contents (Brinkerhoff & Apking, 2001).

Distributor Curriculum Map. The Distributor Curriculum Map depicts in graphic format learning solutions that enable the critical distributor behaviors. This map shows not only what the learning solutions are, but also their ideal sequence. From this map, each region has regrouped/combined different learning elements to best reflect the needs of their region.

Module Specifications. Module specifications outline a high-level design for the learning solutions identified on the Distributor Curriculum Map. The specifications include prerequisites, objectives, delivery methods, materials, and existing courses to leverage. Instructional designers use these specifications to create detailed learning solution designs aligned with the critical behaviors.

Alignment Mapping. The intervention team worked with several Amway regions to map existing curricula to the performance model. In other cases, the regions did their own alignment mapping and shared the results with Global Training and Education. The purpose of the mapping was to drive to a critical set of consistent behaviors while making appropriate use of as much existing curriculum as possible. The regions retained control of how to address any gaps. Results of the alignment mapping were documented on the Distributor Performance Model.

Learning Solutions. Global Training and Education partnered with several of the regions to develop learning solutions aligned with the performance model. For example, since 2008 Global Training and Education has worked intensively with Amway Latin America to develop courses for the major activities (beginning, selling, business building, and leading an organization) of the distributor business. Typically, web-based and instructor-led versions were created to help ensure that training fits the distributors' available learning time, learning styles, and access to technology. Global versions of each course are available to all regions for localization.

Critical Business Issue

Amway needed to improve the performance of its distributors globally on key metrics related to sales, number of new distributors, and distributor retention. A key factor in being able to achieve this goal was to drive globally to distributor performance of a consistent set of business-critical tasks.

Focus on Outcomes or Results

The intended outcomes of this intervention were the fundamental reason the intervention was developed and implemented; the focus from the start was on improving distributor performance. The Distributor Performance Model was intentionally structured to ensure that the intervention team maintained that focus; the model links critical tasks, behaviors, skills/knowledge/attitudes, and learning solutions back to distributor results and Amway goals. This outcomes focus assured that the skills, knowledge, and attitudes taught in training around the world were those that enabled a consistent set of strategic behaviors.

Focus on Systems View

Global Training and Education knew from the beginning that it needed to take a systems view in order for this intervention to succeed. Factors that drove this systems approach, and their implications, included:

- *Region-specific strategic plans:* Any identified solution needed to be adaptable to each region and contribute to the regions' strategic plans.
- *Deliberately fostered regional autonomy:* Global Training and Education respected regional autonomy and had no desire to *impose* a solution on any region.
- *Amway distributors as independent businesses:* Amway cannot hold distributors accountable for their capability, development, or performance.
- *Huge, global distributor populations:* Distributors represent a wide range of cultures, knowledge, experience, educational levels, access to technology, and amount of time devoted to their Amway businesses. One solution would not fit all.

Keeping in mind the factors the team could influence, the team identified the intervention deliverables and created one at a time. One output became an input to another deliverable: the research data led to the performance model, from which the impact map and curriculum map were created; the curriculum map was an input to the alignment maps and module specifications; and the module specifications were used to design the learning solutions. The deliverables themselves and the processes used to create them formed a system aimed at improving performance.

Focus on Value

It has always been Amway's philosophy that a performance improvement intervention should only be undertaken if it adds value. In this intervention, demonstrating the value was important in order to: show the organization that the intervention had contributed to organizational goals and show the regions the benefits of implementing the intervention for their distributors.

Focus on Establishing Partnerships

The intervention was researched, developed, and implemented by a core team consisting of Global Training and Education performance improvement and instructional design consultants and external consultants, key among which was Innovative Learning Group. Additionally, Global Training and Education recognized early that regional input and buy-in were critical to project success so the core team collaborated throughout with corporate experts, training leaders, instructional designers, and subject-matter experts from the regions, and practicing distributors. Further, the team used the Amway Global Training Conference in 2007 to gain regional training leader input into and acceptance of the intervention. Continuing into 2011, regional validation and localization of the intervention include collaboration among the corporate team, regional stakeholders, and learning experts. Finally, the intervention team works on an ongoing basis with corporate and regional experts in learning, in subject matter, and in current research on distributor best practices. These partnerships have been key factors in the sustainability of the intervention.

Be Systematic in Assessment of Need, Opportunity, or Challenge

Due to the scale of the intervention, the team knew that the analysis phase of the intervention needed to obtain multiple perspectives on the distributor audience, required performance, and training and non-training needs. The team systematically determined the best sources of data; these were identified as best practice literature, market research, and a series of initial interviews with exemplar distributors. The goal was to gather data on the major activities within a distributor's business (beginning, selling, business building, and leading an organization).

Be Systematic in the Analysis of Work, Worker, Workplace, and Worldview to Identify the Causes or Factors That Limit Performance

With the need to analyze data on the distributors, their ideal performance, and training/non-training needs, the team based its analysis on Gilbert's Behavior Engineering Model, which would enable it to identify issues related to worker, work, workplace, and worldview. Since Global Training and Education's main focus was on supporting the development of new/enhanced distributor skills, knowledge, and attitudes, the intervention team captured data related to work (ideal performance) and worker capability within the Distributor Performance Model. Then, non-training barriers to performance were captured on a separate sheet, as mentioned previously. This first phase of analysis, which produced the first full draft of the performance model, took roughly four months to complete.

Amway did not stop its data analysis here. Since the first draft of the performance model, additional distributor interviews (total interviews now number over five hundred) have been conducted to validate and fine-tune the model.

Be Systematic in the Design of the Solution

From project start, the intervention team thought through the solution components that were necessary and the order in which they should be developed. The performance model, an output of the analysis phase, defined the desired performance and non-training barriers to success. From there, the plan for accomplishing the objectives consisted of these key steps:

- Abstract the key data from the performance model into the impact map.
- "Chunk" the model's critical tasks, behaviors, and key knowledge and skills into proposed learning and performance improvement solutions.
- Represent the solutions in recommended sequence on the curriculum map.
- Develop the module specifications.
- Obtain team member and stakeholder feedback throughout the project.
- Provide partnering support as needed to those regions ready to implement the performance model.

This helped ensure that we leveraged all possible learning and efficiency from one component to the next.

Be Systematic in the Development of the Solution

The intervention team has continued systematically in the development of performance improvement solutions. Each learning solution project is led by a Global Training and Education project manager who is part of the intervention team. This helps ensure that each learning solution is developed to maximize achievement of the targeted behaviors. Further, Amway tasked the lead Innovative Learning Group consultant with ensuring that each solution aligns with the performance model and curriculum architecture and that solutions developed concurrently are complementary and not redundant. Finally, the team collects feedback throughout the development process from a wide range of stakeholders to ensure clarity of content and appropriateness of instructional design.

Be Systematic in the Implementation of the Solution

The implementation strategy is designed for sustainable change. Consistent with the collaborative nature of this project, responsibility for managing the change has resided with Global Training and Education, the regions, and key corporate stakeholders. Factors that have supported effective implementation and sustainability have included: communication, leadership support, and region-specific launch strategy and timing.

Ongoing communication to Amway executive leadership, the regions, and other corporate stakeholders has been a critical tool for success. The director of Global Training and Education was intentional in presenting regular updates to Amway's executive leadership, who quickly understood the purpose and potential impact of the intervention.

The launch strategy and timing were region-dependent. However, Amway executive support of the intervention was very effective in getting the regions to begin strategizing development of aligned learning curricula. The critical factors affecting timing were how closely the intervention aligned with current strategic initiatives and how the outcomes of these other initiatives would affect implementation. When a region was ready to implement, the intervention team provided ongoing shared-services support; this was an intentional strategy to assure consistent implementation of the intervention globally while preserving the autonomy of the region.

Be Systematic in the Evaluation of the Process and the Results

To date, Amway has focused impact evaluation on the Amway Latin America region, which had done an extensive implementation of a performance-model-based curriculum. To measure business results, the intervention team and Amway Latin America compared quantitative distributor performance data, one year after implementation in Latin America, on the metrics that this intervention aimed to improve. Global Training and Education intentionally did not attempt to segregate the impact of this intervention, as they worked as partners in each region to enable performance through multiple routes. Quantitative data, however, points to the intervention's learning solutions as critical factors in improved performance.

Evaluation efforts have demonstrated that the intervention is being readily adopted and is producing important, measurable results. Specifically, the intervention shows increased sales and increased sponsoring of new distributors among those who have participated in intervention-aligned training. The intervention is also increasing efficiency and the return on performance improvement investment for Global Training and Education and regional training organizations. The results for Global Training and Education have been achieved because newly created learning solutions are focused on critical tasks and behaviors (only necessary training is developed), and learning solutions are being repurposed across regions and delivery methods.

■ ■ ■

Lessons Learned from the Case

- By defining performance globally but keeping ownership of solution development local, global organizations effectively balance driving for consistency, deploying solutions that fit local needs, and maintaining local autonomy.
- Achieving adoption of global performance standards becomes easier when the local organization sees that they are free to achieve the desired performance in the way that best suits their organization and that they are partners with the corporate learning function.
- It is possible to have a single performance model for a global organization. Amway's validation data shows that on average 85 percent of defined behaviors applied around the world.
- New performance improvement applications for the model continue to emerge; because the focus was on performance (and not simply training), the model's data can be repurposed to other human resource needs.

References

Brinkerhoff, R. O., & Apking, A. M. (2001). *High-impact learning: Strategies for leveraging business results from training*. Cambridge, MA: Perseus.

Gilbert, T. F. (1996). *Human competence: Engineering worthy performance* (Tribute Edition). Amherst, MA: HRD Press.

Valerie Brown is a performance consultant at Innovative Learning Group, Inc. She is the lead external consultant for the Amway performance modeling intervention, which won a 2011 Award of Excellence from the International Society for Performance Improvement (ISPI). Valerie has twenty-five years' experience leading projects focused on improving human performance, including projects involving impact mapping; curriculum architecture design; learning solution design; and evaluation studies. She has a master's degree in human resource development from Western Michigan University and has completed all coursework toward a doctorate in that field. Valerie can be reached at 269.226.9472 or valerie.brown@innovativelg.com.

Steven Sniderman is manager of Learning Solutions, Design & Development within the Global Training and Education team at Amway Corporation in Ada, Michigan. Steve is an experienced instructional designer, facilitator, and project manager, with more than twenty years' experience in designing and developing programs, educational systems, and performance improvement materials. Steve is well-versed in the corporate, retail, and manufacturing segments of industry, where he has worked both as an external training partner and as internal training manager. He holds a master's degree in educational systems development from Michigan State University. Steve can be reached at 616.787.7879 or steve.sniderman@amway.com.

Using Human Performance Technology (HPT) to Select Projects That Yield Results

Topic: *Change Management*

Susan M. Pavelek, B.B.A., CPT, *Internal Consultant, Oxy, Inc., Colleyville, Texas, USA*

Background

During a time when training organizations appeared to be frequently outsourced rather than maintained as an internal department, the training team within a mid-size mortgage company was interested in expanding its capabilities and services by providing non-training solutions to address performance issues. The hope was to develop a process to be used to select internal performance improvement projects that would yield results proving value-added. Furthermore, the team wanted to incorporate human performance improvement best practices to ensure success. The team had recently developed a long-term departmental strategic plan and realized that a gap existed about how incoming projects were selected for involvement by the team. The team engaged department leaders to sponsor the shift from traditional training providers to a more performance-focused group offering a broader set of services.

Critical Business Issue

Historically, when the team was contacted by various department leaders to engage in a project, the request usually came in the form of client-determined training solutions. In addition, the incoming project requests typically surpassed the team's capacity to provide support. The team needed a way to differentiate the projects so that the projects it engaged in would add value to the organization. It also wanted to better balance the workload among team members, as project support was assigned based on individual team member skill in specific topic areas, not on the capacity to take on more work. No collective process existed to track or manage projects; all projects were individually tracked and monitored. Along with the new processes, the team had a desire to infuse a mindset of performance improvement throughout the company's leadership team members.

Intervention

The team prioritized the strategic plan items and selected two for immediate action: (1) the team wanted to ensure its decisions were made using objective data (rather than its existing first-come-first-serve approach.) and (2) it wanted to establish a well-defined method for accepting/dispersing projects (to better balance team workload). The processes essential to enable this transition required design, development, and deployment.

While implementing the new processes for managing incoming projects was iterative and took place over approximately six months, the team collaborated to quickly focus on designing the new processes. The team dedicated Friday mornings to collaborative team work sessions. Weekly work sessions were conducted to not only learn performance improvement methods, but also to design and develop the methods and tools needed to be successful. Through these work sessions, the team designed tools it would use to collect and analyze the customers' request for training (and non-training) services, along with a new approach to managing incoming performance improvement projects on behalf of the collective team.

Focus on Outcomes or Results

The entire new process was designed to focus on outcomes and potential results rather than activities. Expected outcomes were gathered up-front using a new form designed by the team. Once the project was accepted and prioritized by the team, resources were assigned, including a project owner, and while the type of project might differ, consistent tools were used to track and report on project results. Data were collected during the initial customer meeting about cost of the problem, cost of the proposed solution, and estimates for the financial value (or return) the customer expected to gain was determined where possible.

Focus on Systems View

Prior to implementing the new process, input was collected by team members individually using individual team member questions and style. In most cases, follow-up phone calls were required to collect additional information in order to provide the team member the complete situation. The new approach targeted "actual" and "desired" performance and focused on the three areas that must be considered in human performance improvement initiatives: the work, workplace, and worker. The new approach involved implementation of five new methods and or tools. Each of the following tools is explained in more detail in the sections below:

1. *Customer Discovery and Rating Tool.* A consistent form/tool to gather incoming project request data.
2. *Team.* A sub-team used to manage the entire process, track project data, and consistently report results.

3. *Experience/Interest Matrix and Team Availability Log.* A tool used to compare the experience level of all team members, and a process to better balance team capacity and workload.
4. *Statement of Work.* A standard statement of work (SOW) process to serve as an internal customer contract.
5. *Customer Report Card and Lessons Learned Template.* To gather customer feedback and identify recommendations for further improvements.

Focus on Value

The team had already changed many of its training deliverables to focus on performance outcomes rather than simply responding to a request to train a specific topic. To further this effort, the team's adoption of performance-based approaches to managing projects, and the subsequent design of forms/tools established processes to enable it to capture financial data surrounding both the cost of the solution (or project) as well as the resulting value (if the project was selected by the team) of the completed project to both the customer and the company. Team members developed consulting and questioning skills that not only grew the team's collective capabilities, but also helped the customer focus on and articulate the potential value of the project.

Focus on Establishing Partnerships

During the team's transition from training-focused activities to a more performance-based mind-set (focused on outcomes rather than training-prescribed topics), it had already laid the groundwork for partnering with customers to concentrate on value-added results. Frequent requestors became accustomed to the mind-set of how the training might improve the department's performance results (such as improved cycle-time in processing work, improved team relationships, improved percentages of sales, and so forth). The new approach to managing training and non-training projects was well received by key customers throughout the company. The team also partnered with the departmental leadership team to help communicate and market the new performance-focused approach to managing internal projects.

When a team member received an incoming call requesting services, he or she scheduled the initial customer meeting and invited key decision-makers to attend to ensure the interviewing team members gained a clear picture of the request. In addition, the caller was asked to bring any data that might serve as evidence of the problem and/or cause(s) to better describe/support the request. By inviting decision-makers to attend the initial meeting, the team eliminated the need for multiple follow-up phone calls/meetings, thereby avoiding potential project delays. Customers were not accustomed to this approach, but most expressed approval for including the right people in the initial meetings, which helped save time and clarified expectations up-front.

Be Systematic in Assessment of Need, Opportunity, or Challenge

The team designed and implemented a consistent form/tool, the Customer Discovery and Rating Tool, to be used by all team members to collect important, comprehensive customer data surrounding each project request. The tool included a rating/scoring section whereby the same criteria could be applied to all projects, as well as a section to estimate the financial value of the expected project outcomes. The Customer Discovery and Rating Tool was not only used to assess all incoming project requests, but was also used to assess all internally initiated projects (driven by the training department). The tool was used as an agenda during the initial one-hour customer meeting to discuss the project. A sample is shown below.

Be Systematic in the Analysis of Work, Worker, Workplace, and Worldview to Identify the Causes or Factors That Limit Performance

The Customer Discovery and Rating Tool was designed to gather data surrounding the work, worker, and workplace (department-specific) and included questions to explore the project's link to key organizational strategic goals (the larger, strategic focus served as the "worldview"). During the initial customer meeting, the team's interviewers asked the series of performance-based questions (and prompts) in an attempt to gain insight into the problem and possible cause(s) of the problem, as well as what the customer thought about a potential solution. In addition, estimated costs of implementing the proposed solution, along with projected savings, revenue, or productivity gains (financial benefits) were entered into an online template containing pre-formulated, company-specific data. This enabled the team to have the information they needed to make a data-driven decision.

Upon conclusion of the customer meeting (provided complete information was obtained), the interviewing team discussed the project details, and applied the rating criteria portion of the tool. The team began with two qualifying questions that were prerequisites to any project it would agree to accept. Provided the project passed the qualifying questions, the team continued the rating process. The team assigned a numeric rating (0 to 9) to six critical items outlined on the tool. The team discussed to what degree each of the six items applied to the project being rated to determine the appropriate number assignment. Criteria for rating projects included the following:

Once the project was rated and scored, the team would make an accept/decline decision based on the data compared to other projects. The project data were also used to prioritize the newly accepted project with other projects in work and determine the team resources and other project support that would be required.

Be Systematic in the Design of the Solution; Be Systematic in the Development of the Solution

An internal project sub-team was formed (the @Team) charged with managing the new processes on behalf of the department. Team members would rotate on/off of the @Team.

Upon acceptance of the project, the @Team assigned project resources using a team availability log combined with an experience/interest matrix. For the team availability log, all team members (including the leadership team) used a simple spreadsheet to enter the number of hours

CUSTOMER DISCOVERY AND RATING TOOL

SECTION 1: ISSUE IDENTIFICATION

A team description of request as recorded on the incoming project request log.

1. What brings you here today? (Probe for a description of the problem or need.)
2. What evidence is there that this problem exists? (Probe for objective data, descriptions, and/or metrics.)
3. How is the current process/method/condition being done? What are the current results of this process/method/condition?
4. How should the process/method/condition be done? (May be expressed as experienced insight or simply be objective opinion.) What should the results be?

SECTION 2: PERFORMANCE ISSUE CAUSES

The identified performance issue is caused by needs in one or more of the following areas: organization, worker, work environment, or work.

1. How does this type of performance align with (corporate/departmental) key performance indicators (KPIs)?
2. Does this type of performance align with any regulatory compliance requirements?

If yes, the project priority will rate higher.

3. Do the workers know they are expected to do the process/method/task(s)?
4. Do the workers know how to perform the needed process/method/task(s)?
5. Have the workers successfully performed the process/method/tasks in the past—*resulting in desired results being achieved*?
6. What factors in the work environment *negatively* impact performance? (That is, workers know they are expected to perform the process/method/task(s) and are attempting to do the task to the desired proficiency, but do not have the resource(s) needed to do so successfully, such as time/opportunity, rewards, equipment, access codes, or experience unintended negative consequences, and so forth).
7. What factors related to the work itself *negatively* impact performance (for example, workers know they are expected to perform the process/method/task(s) and know how to successfully perform the process/method/task(s), and they have the required resources, but are not completing the task(s)? OR they are completing the task(s), but not to the desired proficiency)?

SECTION 3: PROPOSED SOLUTIONS

1. What other factors will help describe the situation?
2. What has already been done to improve the issue?
3. What is the proposed solution? (May encompass multiple interventions.)
4. What is the timeframe for the proposed solution? How negotiable is it?
5. Does this situation and/or proposed solution impact other departments? If so, which ones?
6. How many people are affected by this situation and/or proposed solution?
7. If completed, what would success "look like"? (Probe for objective descriptions and meaningful metrics.)

CUSTOMER DISCOVERY AND RATING TOOL

Qualifying Questions Yes   No

1. Does the project align with our team mission? *If NO,* ***do not continue*** *rating.*
2. Does the project align with our team's strategic imperatives? *If NO,* ***do not*** *continue rating.*

Item	Criteria	Yes			No
		High = 9—7	Med = 6—4	Low = 3—1	0
1.	Its link to a legal, regulatory, or compliance requirement.				
2.	Its link to a strategic project or organizational focus (may add each corporate key performance indicator for individual rating)				
3.	Its link to job performance				
4.	Its relation to resolving an ongoing or potential performance issue				
5.	Its link to improving the customer experience				
6.	Its importance and/or priority to the client				

Subtotals:

7. List the expected financial return and its justification logic (cost reductions, revenue generation, reduced cycle time, reduced defect rate, increased value, estimated number of people impacted). Ranges should correlate to the projected financial return, for example:

$0—$5,000	0—5
$5,001—$25,000	6—25
$25,001—$50,000	26—50
$50,001—$75,000	51—75
$75,001—$100,000	76—100
over $100,001	Correlate based on estimate, i.e., $120K = 120; $149K = 149

Overall Project Score: _____

(or anticipated hours) already assigned to existing projects, or ongoing operational work. Based on the data added by each team member, the spreadsheet was programmed to reflect the balance of *available work hours* for each individual. The @Team used the log to assign work.

The experience/interest matrix (Pavelek, 2004) was a self-assessment tool used to identify the team's individual proficiency surrounding forty-seven human performance interventions. Over time, the team expressed a concern that projects were being assigned strictly based on experience and that several team members were not being given the opportunity to learn new skills.

Likewise, team members with a high level of skill in a specific area expressed an interest to help others learn the skill in order to expand the overall team's capability (and give themselves a break!). As a result of this feedback, an *interest* component was added to the matrix. In addition to experience, team members self-rated their *interest* in developing each of the forty-seven human performance interventions. Implementing the experience/interest matrix helped the team better balance its capacity and workload, as well as create an atmosphere of continual team development. An example is shown below.

Also upon project acceptance, the @Team implemented a statement of work (SOW) using an internal template (Pavelek, 2004) to serve as an internal customer contract. The @Team would meet with the customer a second time (usually the second meeting was scheduled during the initial meeting) to review the SOW, outline project details, clarify consultant/customer responsibilities, articulate projected outcomes, and set expectations for ongoing communication and partnering. If the project was not accepted, the @Team contacted the customer to advise of the decision and reasoning for turning down the project.

Two other forms/tools designed, developed, and implemented included processes to gather customer feedback *after the project was delivered* and to identify recommendations for further improvements. The customer report card was used to gather information from the customer

Sample Experience/Interest Matrix

Team Experience/Interest	Member 1		Member 2		Member 3		Member 4		Member 5		Member 6		Member 7	
Organization/Team	**E**	**I**	**E**	**I**	**E**	**I**	**E**	**I**	**E**	**I**	**E**	**I**	**E**	**I**
Strategic Planning	3	1	7	2	6	3	4	1	7	2	6	2	8	3
Change Navigation	3	1	8	3	7	3	4	1	7	2	2	2	4	3
Survey Design and Feedback	5	1	7	2	8	3	3	2	5	1	5	3	5	2
Recognition and Reward Systems	7	2	7	3	5	3	6	2	7	2	6	3	4	2
Succession Planning Systems	1	1	7	3	4	3	4	1	8	2	2	2	3	2
Leadership Development Training	3	4	7	2	6	2	6	2	7	2	6	3	6	2
Technical and Professional Training	4	3	8	2	8	2	6	2	9	2	9	2	4	1
Competency Design	3	2	9	3	7	2	2	1	7	1	3	1	5	3
Work Flow Analysis	5	2	5	1	8	2	6	2	7	2	6	2	5	1
Conflict Resolution	6	2	8	3	5	2	5	1	5	2	3	1	5	1
Team Assessment	3	1	6	3	9	3	5	1	7	1	2	2	5	2
Team Skill Development	4	1	8	3	8	3	5	2	8	1	2	2	5	2
Distributed/Virtual Teams	2	2	4	1	6	2	4	2	7	2	1	2	3	1
Life/Career Planning	3	1	8	3	6	3	4	2	6	2	2	2	6	1
Job Aids/Quick Reference Guides	6	3	6	2	9	3	8	2	8	2	9	3	3	1

surrounding his or her experience and satisfaction with the project team and deliverables (Level 1) and included a section on actual financial improvements realized as a result of the project (Level 4.). The lessons learned template was used by the assigned project team to summarize project statistics and recommend changes to help improve future projects of a similar nature.

Be Systematic in the Implementation of the Solution

Once finalized, @Team processes and tools were applied to all projects, and job aids and procedure documents were created to ensure consistency.

Finally, the team implemented a project log to track project-specific details, monitor progress, and document *actual* hours spent on project support. The @Team provided monthly and quarterly presentations to the other team members outlining project summary statistics/ results, customer report card, and lessons learned data for completed projects. The @Team also included recommendations for improvements to team processes and project execution approaches based on the report card and lesson learned feedback.

■ ■ ■

Lessons Learned from the Case
- The new methods resulted in actual financial returns of approximately $3.3 million in the first year.
- The team experienced challenges when attempting to gather accurate and meaningful financial-related data upon project completion. In many cases, the team used a productivity savings formula for valuing time.[1] The team customized the formula to include company-specific information to more accurately reflect improved productivity results.
- Adding the interest component to the experience/interest matrix provided an added bonus and enabled expanded team capability through project support assignments.
- The team integrated technology and automated processes where possible to streamline project management/tracking.
- Although the @Team reported actual results to the other team members, it did not include a process to adequately report actual project results to senior leaders.

Citation

1. Hale, 1998

Reference

Hale, J.A. (1998). *The performance consultant's fieldbook: Tools and techniques for improving organizations and people*. San Francisco: Pfeiffer.

Susan M. Pavelek, B.B.A., CPT, became involved with performance technology mid-career after an extensive background in operations/customer service in the travel and transportation field. She has led global training/organizational development teams to higher levels of performance through application of HPT methods and tools. Susan now serves as an internal consultant at Oxy, Inc., and can be reached at 817.715.5353, or susan.pavelek@yahoo.com.

SECTION 2
PERFORMANCE ANALYSIS

"YOU'RE BLOWING THROUGH THE WRONG END."

Overview of Performance Analysis

4

Performance analysis is the first step in the Performance Improvement/HPT Model (see Figure 4.1). There is no possibility of a chicken-or-egg syndrome when it comes to performance analysis. Without first identifying and clarifying the problem or performance gap it is unsound and certainly unsystematic to state the cause and select or design a solution.

Definition and Scope

Performance analysis is "the process of identifying the organization's performance requirements and comparing them to its objectives and capabilities."[1] According to Rossett, performance analysis "involves partnering with clients and customers to help them define and achieve their goals . . . reaching out for several perspectives on a problem or opportunity . . . determining any and all drivers toward or barriers to successful performance . . . [and] proposing a solution system based on what is learned, not on what is typically done."[2] Table 4.1 explores the scope of Rossett's definition in more detail, and introduces the concept that performance analysis examines performance directions and drivers.

Directions and Drivers. During performance analysis, performance improvement practitioners seek two broad kinds of information. First, they seek directions—the performance and perspectives that the organization and its leaders are trying to put in place, such as vision, mission, values, goals, strategies, and critical business issues of the organization that particularly impact the desired state of performance. They also seek information about performance drivers, the factors that are now blocking or aiding performance or those that might do so in the future, such as organization, competition, work, performer, and social responsibility factors from the internal and external environment that particularly affect the performance state. The quest for directions maps the scope of the effort; the analysis of drivers determines what needs to be done to successfully develop performance, people, and the organization.[3]

Focus for Analysis. In the Performance Improvement/HPT Model, performance analysis focuses on these four areas:

- Desired performance state
- Actual performance state
- The gap between desired and actual performance
- Causes of gaps in performance

FIGURE 4.1. Performance Improvement/HPT Model: Performance Analysis Phase

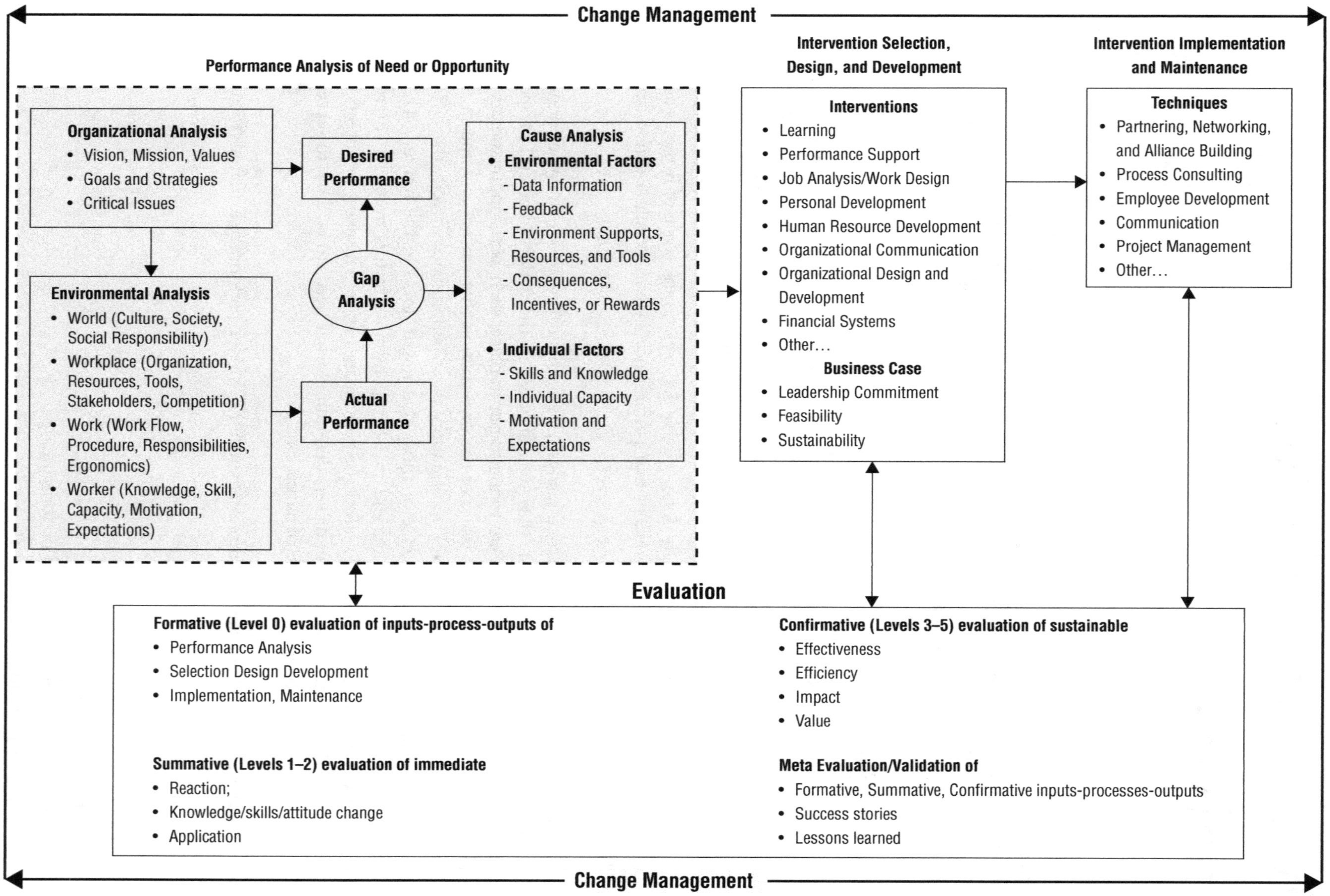

— Change Management —

Performance Analysis of Need or Opportunity

Organizational Analysis
- Vision, Mission, Values
- Goals and Strategies
- Critical Issues

Environmental Analysis
- World (Culture, Society, Social Responsibility)
- Workplace (Organization, Resources, Tools, Stakeholders, Competition)
- Work (Work Flow, Procedure, Responsibilities, Ergonomics)
- Worker (Knowledge, Skill, Capacity, Motivation, Expectations)

Desired Performance

Gap Analysis

Actual Performance

Cause Analysis
- **Environmental Factors**
  - Data Information
  - Feedback
  - Environment Supports, Resources, and Tools
  - Consequences, Incentives, or Rewards
- **Individual Factors**
  - Skills and Knowledge
  - Individual Capacity
  - Motivation and Expectations

Intervention Selection, Design, and Development

Interventions
- Learning
- Performance Support
- Job Analysis/Work Design
- Personal Development
- Human Resource Development
- Organizational Communication
- Organizational Design and Development
- Financial Systems
- Other...

Business Case
- Leadership Commitment
- Feasibility
- Sustainability

Intervention Implementation and Maintenance

Techniques
- Partnering, Networking, and Alliance Building
- Process Consulting
- Employee Development
- Communication
- Project Management
- Other...

Evaluation

Formative (Level 0) evaluation of inputs-process-outputs of
- Performance Analysis
- Selection Design Development
- Implementation, Maintenance

Summative (Levels 1–2) evaluation of immediate
- Reaction;
- Knowledge/skills/attitude change
- Application

Confirmative (Levels 3–5) evaluation of sustainable
- Effectiveness
- Efficiency
- Impact
- Value

Meta Evaluation/Validation of
- Formative, Summative, Confirmative inputs-processes-outputs
- Success stories
- Lessons learned

— Change Management —

TABLE 4.1.   Defining Performance Analysis

Essential Components	Elements
Partnering	Additional resources, expertise, markets Fresh perspectives Buy-in
Goals	Targeted Achievable, specific, worthwhile Set deadlines Evaluate progress
Several Perspectives	Multiple views and visions Data from many sources
Problems and Opportunities	Glitches in job functions, costly errors, waste New business channels, new product development Enhanced customer service
Drivers and Barriers	Triggers that encourage, sustain, impede performance
Solution Systems	Deliberate, conscious attempts to change behavior in an integrated, synergistic manner

Adapted from A. Rossett (2009). *First things fast: A handbook for performance analysis* (2nd ed.), pp. 20–34. Copyright John Wiley & Sons, Inc. Used with permission.

Since performance does not occur in isolation, the organization and the environment have a considerable impact on both the performance and the performer. Organizational directions have a significant impact on the performance standards that are used to determine desired or optimal performance, while environmental drivers significantly affect actual performance.

Anatomy of Performance Analysis

One way to view performance analysis is to picture "the anatomy of performance"[4] (see Chapter 2). Although organizations vary in purpose, function, size, and scope, they all have a common anatomy. In order for them to remain high-performing and function strategically in an ever-changing competitive environment, they have to "plan, design, and manage performance at three levels: organization, process, and job."[5]

The anatomy of performance (see Table 4.2) contains nine performance variables—three levels of performance and three performance needs for each level. The nine variables provide "three critical interdependent levels of performance. The overall performance of an organization (how well it meets the expectations of its customers) is the result of goals, structures and management actions at all three levels of performance"[6]

- Goals—Specific standards that reflect customers' expectations for product and service quality, quantity, timeliness and cost
- Structures—The design of the organization, process, or job to efficiently meet the goals
- Management—Practices that ensure that goals are current and are being achieved[7]

TABLE 4.2. Anatomy of Performance

Three Performance Needs That Determine Overall Performance at Each Performance Level

Performance Levels	Goals	Design	Management
Organization Level	Organization Goals	Organization Design	Organization Management
Process Level	Process Goals	Process Design	Process Management
Job/Performer Level	Job/Performer Goals	Job Design	Job/Performer Management

Adapted from G.A. Rummler and A.P. Brache (1990), p.19. San Francisco: Jossey-Bass. Copyright ISPI. Used with permission.

TABLE 4.3. Principles of Performance Analysis

Guiding Principles . . .	Reflective Points . . .
1. Preparation before action improves quality	Provide clear answers that make sense to client Use data-driven approaches Clarify responses
2. Employ several sources	Triangulate data Use multiple perspectives to tailor solutions Include involvement from those familiar with need/opportunity
3. Gather data from sources	Collect formal and informal data View data as pieces of a jigsaw puzzle Use data to provide clear pictures of the situation
4. Employ a systematic approach to analysis	Focus on purpose, components, data, input, transactions, outputs Use a consistent approach to determine informed decisions for action
5. Employ a systemic approach to solutions	Envision the performance system Conduct systematic analysis Follow systemic approaches to resolve client issues

Adapted from A. Rossett (2009). *First things fast: A handbook for performance analysis* (2nd ed.), pp. 36–47. Copyright John Wiley & Sons, Inc. Used with permission.

Purpose

The purpose of performance analysis is to establish what the *desired* or optimal performance should be, identify what the *actual* performance is, and identify the *gap* between the two. Performance analysis is the root of the whole performance improvement system because it focuses on "systematic and thorough workplace diagnosis and documentation . . . the true basis for improving performance at the organizational, process, and worker levels"[8]

Principles

Five pivotal principles guide a thorough and meaningful performance analysis. They are noted in Table 4.3 with brief points of reflection.

Analysis Techniques and Tools

Performance analysis utilizes techniques from industrial and organizational psychology, industrial engineering, and organizational behavior.[9] A complete performance analysis should include the following five techniques:

- Extant data analysis
- Needs analysis
- Knowledge task analysis
- Procedural task analysis
- Systems task analysis

Extant Data Analysis

Extant data analysis focuses on analyzing accomplishments or performance inputs, processes, outputs, and outcomes that are documented in various company records such as sales reports, customer surveys, safety reports, quality control documentation, and so forth. Analysis of existing data makes it possible to make inferences about the actual performance.

Needs Analysis

Needs analysis is "the systematic effort that we make to gather opinions and ideas from a variety of sources on performance problems."[10] The sources may include performers, stakeholders, customers, management, subject-matter experts, etc. Needs analysis seeks opinions and ideas about what *should* be happening, what *is* happening, how the sources feel about what is or is not happening, and what is *causing* the problem. The resulting data are always subjective; however, they may illuminate why a desired performance is occurring or not occurring and *what* needs to happen in order to reach or maintain the desired performance.

Knowledge Task Analysis

Knowledge task analysis searches for detailed information about what the performer needs to know—the invisible part of performance—in order to successfully complete a specific job or task. The analyst collects and analyzes information from the performance field, subject matter experts, and expert performers to uncover the body of knowledge "which, if mastered, would contribute to or enhance work behavior."[11] Identifying and synthesizing the invisible details of optimal performance insures that the complete performance picture is in place when it comes time to compare the desired performance state with the actual performance state in order to determine whether or not there is a performance gap.

Procedural Task Analysis

Procedural task analysis focuses on the visible details of optimal performance by "documenting people-thing workplace expertise in terms of precisely what people are required to know and be able to do to perform the task."[12] The term "people-thing" refers to the interaction between the performer and the object of the performance. An example of documenting people-thing expertise is a task analysis that examines what performers or people need to know and be able to do to fill out a form or thing. The result of procedural analysis is a document containing "cookbook-style, step-by-step procedures."[13] The limitation of procedural task analysis is that it frequently focuses on tasks conducted under normal conditions and does not take into account what is required for optimal performance under abnormal conditions.

Systems Task Analysis

Systems task analysis picks up where procedural task analysis ends by focusing on the "expertise workers must have to respond effectively to abnormal conditions."[14] Systems task analysis provides a series of snapshots, which, if viewed collectively, provide a composite of the total performance system:

- System overview—description, flow, components, and purpose,
- Process analysis, and
- Troubleshooting analysis.

"Systems analysis can help develop a more accurate picture and understanding of the selected system, the connections among subsystems, and the expertise required of those connections and handoffs from one expert worker to another."[15]

When to Use What

Linking analysis techniques to a particular situation is often difficult and requires knowledge of why the analyst is conducting the analysis. The basic analysis techniques and when to use them are illustrated in Table 4.4. Once purpose and techniques are determined and matched, "It is how the analysis phase is carried out . . . that determines whether performance improvement efforts support major business processes or are simply a series of activities."[16]

TABLE 4.4. Linking Basic Analysis Techniques to Purpose

Use this technique . . .	To find out about . . .			
	Desired State	*Actual State*	*Organization*	*Environment*
Extant Data Analysis		X	X	X
Needs Analysis	X	X	X	X
Knowledge Task Analysis	X	X		
Procedural Task Analysis	X	X		
Systems Task Analysis	X	X		

Analysis Tools

Every performance improvement specialist should have knowledge of and skill in the use of familiar data collection tools: interviews, group processes (brainstorming, focus groups, etc.), observation, and surveys. Plugging the tools into Table 4.5 below turns it into a performance analysis job aid.

Surveys, group processes, and interviews are tools that the performance practitioner can adapt to support all the techniques except extant data analysis, which requires a special set of quantitative and qualitative data analysis tools. Surveys, group processes, and interviews are also well suited to analyzing the desired and actual performance states, the organization and the environment. Observation is best suited to procedural analysis and systems analysis. When to use which tool is determined by organizational climate and the availability of resources such as time, money, and skilled personnel. Specific techniques and tools for organizational, environmental, gap, and causes will be discussed in greater detail in the following chapters.

Typical Performance Analysis Questions

There are numerous questions performance improvement practitioners can conceivably ask a client in order to conduct a thorough performance analysis. The questions may be used for surveys or interviews or even group activities. The reality is, however, that it is impossible to ask questions about everything. Basic questions guide the practitioner in collecting relevant information:

- Who is affected by the performance gap?
- What is the desired situation? The actual situation?
- When and where did the performance first occur?
- How has the gap been affecting the organization?
- How much has the gap been costing the organization? [17]

In addition to these questions, the practitioner asks questions about gap dimensions, focusing on magnitude, value, and urgency.[18] For example, gap-focused questions might include: To what

TABLE 4.5.   When to Use Specific Analysis Techniques and Tools

Purpose	Extant Data Analysis	Needs Analysis	Knowledge Task Analysis	Procedural Task Analysis	Systems Task Analysis
Desired State	NA	Surveys, Group Interviews	Interviews, Survey, Group	Observation, Interviews, Group	Interviews, Observation, Group
Actual State	Qualitative/Quantitative Analysis Tools	Survey, Group Interviews	Interviews, Survey Group	Observation, Interviews, Group	Observation, Interviews, Group
Organization	Qualitative/Quantitative Analysis Tools	Survey, Group Interviews	NA	NA	NA
Environment	Qualitative/ Quantitative Analysis Tools	Survey, Group Interviews	NA	NA	NA

degree does the gap affect organizational goals? To what extent do the stakeholders support closing the gap? Does the gap require immediate action?

Conclusion

Performance analysis assures that the performance improvement effort is focused on reality and not on opinion. It enables those involved in the effort to understand the complexity of the current situation and see the potential for future outcomes, whether the outcomes may be successes or failures.

Citations

1. Rosenberg, 1996, p. 6
2. Rossett, 2009, p. 20
3. Rossett, 1998, pp. 33–34
4. Rummler & Brache, 1995, pp. 17–19
5. Rummler, Ramais, & Rummler, 2010, p. 11
6. Rummler & Brache, 1995, p. 17
7. Rummler & Brache, 1990, p. 19
8. Rossett, 1998, n.p.
9. Abernathy, 2010, pp. 5–17
10. Rossett, 1989, p. 63
11. Swanson, 1994, p. 190
12. Swanson, 1994, p. 123
13. Swanson, 1994, p. 151
14. Swanson, 1994, p. 151
15. Swanson, 1994, p. 187
16. Swanson, 1994, p. ix
17. Rothwell & Dubois, 1998, pp. 2–4
18. Stolovitch & Keeps, 2004, pp. 53–54

References

Abernathy, W.B. (2010, May/June). A comprehensive performance analysis and improvement method. *Performance Improvement, 49*(5), 5–17.

Rosenberg, M.J. (1996). Human performance technology: Foundations for human performance improvement. In W.J. Rothwell, *ASTD models for human performance improvement: Roles, competencies and outputs* (pp. 5–10). Alexandria, VA: American Society for Training & Development.

Rossett, A. (1989). *Training needs assessment.* Englewood Cliffs, NJ: Educational Technology Publications.

Rossett, A. (1998). Responding to customers, experts, personnel. Retrieved from www.josseybass.com/rossett/respond.

Rossett, A. (2009). *First things fast: A handbook for performance analysis* (2nd ed.). San Francisco: Pfeiffer.

Rothwell, W.J., & Dubois, D.D. (Eds.). (1998). *In action: Improving performance in organizations.* Alexandria, VA: American Society for Training & Development.

Rummler, G.A., & Brache, A.P. (1990). *Improving performance: Managing the white space on the organization chart*. San Francisco: Jossey-Bass.

Rummler, G.A., & Brache, A.P. (1995). *Improving performance: Managing the white space on the organization chart* (2nd ed.). San Francisco: Jossey-Bass.

Rummler, G.A., Ramais, A.J., & Rummler, R.A. (2010). *White space revisited: Creating value through process*. San Francisco: Jossey-Bass.

Stolovitch, H.D., & Keeps, E.J. (2004). *Training ain't performance*. Alexandria, VA: American Society for Training & Development.

Swanson, R.A. (1994). *Analysis for improving performance: Tools for diagnosing organizations and documenting workplace expertise*. San Francisco: Berrett-Koehler.

Organizational Analysis

5

Organizational analysis is a first step in the performance analysis process. It looks into the heart of the organization—its vision, mission, values, goals, strategies, and critical issues—because all organizational elements should be strategically aligned. Just as tires need to be aligned for better vehicle operation, an organization's people, processes, and culture benefit from aligning with the organization structure. Figure 5.1 is a high-level summary of the organizational analysis component of the Performance Improvement/HPT Model.

Definition and Scope

Organizational analysis is an examination of the components that strategic plans are made of. This phase of performance analysis analyzes the organization's vision, mission, values, goals, strategies, and critical business issues.

Vision. The vision is the organization's long-term view of its desired end state; it is what the organization wants to be. Vision is a description of the core values and principles that make the organization unique.

Mission. The mission is the organization's reason for being, in effect, why it exists. The mission as expressed in the mission statement gives direction and purpose and is driven by such forces as market needs, production capability, natural resources, regulatory action, technology, methods of distribution, products and services offered, and the like.

Values. Values are enduring core beliefs. Values envision compelling futures and deepen foresight. They have intrinsic value for the organization and they need to make sense in terms of brand, marketing, and financial assessment.

Goals. Goals represent targets for accomplishment. They must be aligned with the organization's vision, mission, and values. They also need to be clearly defined, relevant, understandable, realistic, and reflect the organization's cultural dynamics.

FIGURE 5.1. Performance Improvement/HPT Model: Organizational Analysis Component

ORGANIZATIONAL ANALYSIS
• Vision, Mission, Values • Goals and Strategies • Critical Issues

TABLE 5.1.   Various Strategic Planning Definitions

Term	Respondent	Definition
Vision	1	Overall future direction; like "north" on a compass
	2	Where the organization is heading; the picture of success
	3	Desired destination
Mission	1	Focus, like Saudi Arabia on a world map
	2	Reason for being; purpose
	3	How the organization is going to reach the pictured of success
Goals	1	Instructions on how to get there; directions
	2	Milestones to achieve along the way
	3	Steps to support mission and vision; the to-do list

Strategies. Strategies are the organization's plan for growing the business. Strategies are needed to determine a market position, identify and nurture customers, compete in the global environment, focus on competitive advantage, achieve broad goals and objectives, and so on.

Critical Issues. Critical issues are problems or opportunities that determine an organization's success and may represent a gap in results that must be closed. Some call them critical *business* issues, others call them critical *success* issues, but no matter what they are called they all affect the business in terms of success or failure. Typical examples may include increasing customer satisfaction and, ultimately, employee or customer retention; increasing market share; reducing or eliminating excessive waste; and so on.

Individual members of any organization may vary in how they define the words that the organization has selected. For example, three strategic planners were asked to define *vision*, *mission*, and *goals*.[1] Their responses are listed below in Table 5.1.

Purpose and Timing

The purpose of organizational analysis is to seek directions—"the performance and perspectives that the organization and its leaders are trying to put in place."[2] Directions need to be identified early during the performance analysis because they set the expectations for desired or optimal performance.

The major factors that set the direction for the organization are vision, mission, values, goals, strategies, and critical issues. These factors are found in the organization's strategic plan. The plan represents where the organization should be heading and sets forth an action plan for achieving the goals that have been identified. Heracleous says that "the real purpose of strategic planning is to improve strategic thinking."[3] Both planning and thinking are necessary for successful strategizing; strategic planning refers to a programmatic, analytic thinking process and strategic thinking is creative and divergent. Eckel and Witmer liken a strategic plan to a budget that constantly needs tweaking as the organization's goals and priorities influenced by economic factors change.[4]

As part of an organizational analysis, the performance improvement practitioner examines the customer's current or future needs and expectations. The HPT practitioner analyzes such factors as:

- Organizational structure,
- Centrally controlled systems,
- Corporate strategies.
- Key policies,
- Business values, and
- Corporate culture.[5]

Conducting an Organizational Analysis

The performance improvement practitioner begins an organizational analysis by reviewing existing documents such as the organization's strategic plan, history, by-laws, board meeting minutes, annual reports, new employee orientation material, project management data, payroll reports, benchmarking data, talent management databases, customer satisfaction data, dashboards, and others.[6] Then the performance improvement practitioner gathers feelings and opinions from as many internal and external stakeholders as possible.

For example, one major but often ignored stakeholder is the customer: what the customer thinks, feels, and why the customer keeps coming back. Fitz-enz says that a satisfied customer is "pleasant, content, grateful, satiated, and safe"; whereas, an engaged customer is "passionate, energized, involved, committed, and trusting."[7] These feelings lead to desirable behaviors. Leaders of successful organizations use information on present and future customer requirements and expectations to help them set the course or direction for their organizations. Figure 5.2 illustrates how input from the customer helps to establish the desired performance state as a foundation for performance gap analysis.

FIGURE 5.2.   Grant and Moseley Customer-Focused Performance Analysis Model

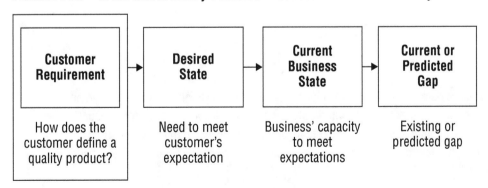

Adapted from D.A. Grant and J.L. Moseley (1999, July). Conducting a customer-focused performance analysis. *Performance Improvement, 36*(10), 25. Copyright ISPI. Used with permission.

Organizational Analysis Tools

Time, cost, the culture of the organization, and the availability of resources are prime considerations when selecting tools for conducting an organizational analysis. Since it is extremely important to gather both facts and perceptions, the major analysis techniques are extant data analysis, interviews, surveys, and group processes. These may be conducted in real time or virtually using online or mobile technologies.

Interviews. Conducting one-on-one or group interviews is probably the most helpful tool for accessing both fact and perception. The following three strategies are particularly appropriate for interviews:

1. Let the flow of the other person's thoughts and ideas lead the conversation so that the interviewer's questions clarify, confirm, and guide.
2. Ask questions about purposes, goals, objectives, priorities, or dreams. Not only does that help define success, but it also uncovers problems that are almost always there, such as conflicting goals and priorities or a lack of consensus or clarity.
3. A useful question is: 'Who else should I talk to? It enables the interviewer to find the key players, the opinion leaders, the technical experts, and the potential saboteurs; ensures that the analysis will be open; and provides the basis for setting up an appointment.[8]

Group Processes. Brainstorming sessions, focus groups, consensus activities, and other group processes are also helpful for generating or prioritizing ideas from stakeholders.[9] Brainstorming is honest group dialogue in which everyone participates equally. Focus groups members are asked about their opinions, perceptions, and attitudes relative to an issue. Consensus activities ask for agreement from participants to reach a common decision.

Surveys. Surveys are more anonymous than interviews. Surveys can generate both facts and perceptions about the directions established by the organization.

Record Critical Behavior. The critical incident technique, case studies, and even storytelling are techniques for observing and reporting on behavior that may have a critical positive or negative impact on an organization. Once the behavior or incident is recorded it may be used to help solve performance problems or take advantage of performance improvement.

EXAMPLE

Vince Araujo, manager of performance delivery at Sprint, developed an Organizational Scan Model that documents improved performance. "At its core, the SCAN is the basic input/output system model complete with dual loops for formative and evaluative feedback. Structured to show the conditions or the three levels of the organization on the left side, and the receivers on the right, the organizational scan provides a snapshot of any aspect of performance at whatever level of detail is required."[10]

Tosti and Jackson also developed a set of questions that provide structure for a thorough organizational scan.[11] Performance Support Tool 5.1 suggests typical questions for planning an organizational scan.

PERFORMANCE SUPPORT TOOL 5.1. TYPICAL QUESTIONS FOR AN ORGANIZATIONAL SCAN

CONDITIONS, ORGANIZATIONAL LEVEL: STRATEGY, STRUCTURE

1. Is the change compatible with the organization's mission and strategic direction? If so, is that clear to people who carry out the change?

2. Will the change help (or at least not hinder) the organization in addressing external business drivers or pressures on the organization?

3. Does the organization's current division into units or functions support the proposed change? Do the functions have outputs of recognized value? Will groups that need to work closely together find it easy to do?

4. Will people have the budget or decision making authority they need to implement the change and meet their goals and responsibilities?

CONDITIONS, PEOPLE LEVEL: CLIMATE, PRACTICES

1. Is the change compatible with current organizational values and with what the organization considers important about the way it conducts business? Are those values generally consistent across organizational groups affected by the change?

2. Is there typically a match between what the organization stated as values and the kind of behavior that is actually recognized and rewarded?

3. Do current management and leadership practices support the change?

4. Do current team norms about work behavior support the change?

5. Is the change compatible with people's beliefs about integrity and ethical behavior?

CONDITIONS, WORK LEVEL: ENVIRONMENT, RESOURCES

1. Does the current physical environment support the change?

2. Do people have the equipment, tools, materials, and information they need to make the change work?

(Continued)

3. Are the support services or personnel necessary to make the change work available?

4. Are the resources people will need to make the change work easily accessible to them?

5. Will the overall workload be manageable, given the change effort?

PROCESS, ORGANIZATION LEVEL: SYSTEMS

1. Are the current systems (information, rewards, etc.) centralized or decentralized in a way that supports the change? Does the degree of consistency or variability of operations from one area to another support the change?

2. Does the degree of consistency or variability of operations from one area to another support the change?

3. Do organizational systems currently have the degree of flexibility required to support the change?

PROCESS, PEOPLE LEVEL: PERFORMANCE REQUIREMENTS

1. Do the people who will make the change happen have the skills, knowledge, and experience to make it work?

2. Are the on-the-job aids available to support the change, if needed?

3. Are the people currently selected for qualities that match the requirements of the roles they will need to fill?

4. Do people have the confidence they need to try the change and make it work?

PROCESS, WORK LEVEL: METHODS

1. Is the current assignment of job functions or tasks appropriate to support the change?

2. Are work procedures or processes currently supportive of the change?

3. Is the current workflow designed to support change efficiently and effectively?

4. Is the work design generally free of duplications of effort or gaps that could interfere with the change?

(Continued)

Outcomes, Organizational Level: Organizational Results

1. Are the goals in units involved in or related to the change consistent and compatible with the change's requirements and the results expected?

2. Are organizational measurements in place that will allow people to determine the success of the change? Are those measurements clearly tied to organizational success?

3. Will the change contribute to increasing or maintaining satisfaction of shareholders, owners, or others who have a stake in the organization's performance?

Outcomes, People Level: Motivation, Feedback

1. Is the way in which people now obtain feedback about their work compatible with the change, frequent enough, timed appropriately, and in usable form?

2. Are people currently rewarded and recognized for behavior that is compatible with or supports the change?

3. Are the current expectations about work and work behavior compatible with what the change will require?

4. Will the change contribute to increasing or maintaining employee satisfaction?

Outcomes, Work Level: Products, Services

1. Are current productivity levels sufficient to meet the requirements of the change?

2. Are work standards or criteria currently compatible with those the change requires?

3. Will the change contribute to increasing or maintaining customer satisfaction?

4. Are current time requirements or allowances for completing work compatible with the change?

5. Is the predictability of the workload compatible with the requirements of change?

(Continued)

PERFORMANCE SUPPORT TOOL 5.2. ORGANIZATIONAL ANALYSIS SURVEY

Directions: Select the terms or sections of this performance support tool that are appropriate for the organization being analyzed. Use the selected sections as a survey instrument or a group discussion guide. The target audience should include all levels of management, workers, and internal or external stakeholders, including competitors or customers. The goal is to identify both facts and perceptions from a broad range of internal and external stakeholders, and to help determine whether the organization's vision, mission, values, goals, strategies or critical issues are aligned with the desired and actual performance state. There are no *wrong* or *right* answers and there is no answer key.

Pick the definition from Column A that *best* matches the term in Column B and write the number in the parentheses next to the term in Column B. Remember that there is no correct or incorrect answer.

Mission/Vision/Goal

Column A Definitions	**Column B: Terms**
1. The reasons for making the plan	A. ( ) Vision
2. Our principles and standards	B. ( ) Mission
3. Our reason for existing	C. ( ) Values
4. What we do	D. ( ) Goals
5. The end state to be achieved	E. ( ) Objectives
6. Our notion of success	F. ( ) Strategies
7. Milestones along the way	G. ( ) Critical Issue(s)
8. The means to be used	H. ( ) Strategic Thinking
9. The path to be taken	
10. Who we are	
11. Increase in products and services	
12. Precedes strategic planning	

Vision

What is the organization's vision?

Is the vision clearly defined?	Yes	No
Is the vision adequately communicated?	Yes	No
Does the vision make sense in terms of internal strengths and weaknesses?	Yes	No
Does the vision make sense in terms of external threats and opportunities?	Yes	No

(Continued)

Mission

What is the organization's mission?

Is the mission clearly defined?	Yes	No
Is the mission adequately communicated?	Yes	No
Does the mission make sense in terms of internal strengths and weaknesses?	Yes	No
Does the mission make sense in terms of external threats and opportunities?	Yes	No

Values

What are the organization's values?

Are the values clearly defined?	Yes	No
Are the values adequately communicated?	Yes	No
Do the values match the mission and vision?	Yes	No
Do the values make sense in terms of internal strengths and weaknesses?	Yes	No
Do the values make sense in terms of external threats and opportunities?	Yes	No

Goals

List the organization's goals for each category:

- Products and services:

- Customers and markets:

- Competitive advantage:

- Product and market priorities:

Is each of the goals clearly defined?	Yes	No
Is each of the goals adequately communicated?	Yes	No
Does each goal match the mission, vision, and values?	Yes	No
Does each goal make sense in terms of internal strengths and weaknesses?	Yes	No
Does each goal make sense in terms of external threats and opportunities?	Yes	No

(Continued)

Strategies

Consider the organization's strategies for meeting its goals in each of the following categories:

- Products and services (What are we going to do?)

- Customer groups or markets: (For whom will we do it?)

- Competitive advantage(s): (Why will the customer buy from us?)

- Product and market priorities: (Where will we place our emphasis?)

Is each of the strategies clearly defined?	Yes	No
Is each of the strategies adequately communicated?	Yes	No
Does each strategy match the mission, vision, values and goals?	Yes	No
Does each strategy make sense in terms of internal strengths and weaknesses?	Yes	No
Does each strategy make sense in terms of external threats and opportunities?	Yes	No

Critical Issues

What is (are) the organization's critical issue(s)?

How have the critical issues been influenced by the organization's history, its traditions and culture, market share, brand?

Is (are) the critical issue(s) clearly articulated? How so?	Yes	No
Does (Do) the critical issue(s) impact the customer? In what ways?	Yes	No
Does (Do) the critical issue(s) impact financial stakeholders? In what ways?	Yes	No

Is (Are) the critical issue(s) aligned with the vision, mission, values, goals, and strategies of the organization?   Yes   No

State the critical issue(s) in simple, clear, declarative sentences.

Adapted from G.A. Rummler and A.P. Brache, 1990. *Improving performance: How to manage the white space on the organization chart*, p. 19. San Francisco: Jossey-Bass and F. Nickols (1996). The mission/vision thing. Retrieved from trdev-1@psuvm.psu.edu and G.A. Rummler (2007). *Serious performance consulting: According to Rummler*, p. 21. San Francisco: Pfeiffer.

Citations

1. Nichols, 1996
2. Heracleous, 1998, p. 482
3. Heracleous, 1998, p. 485
4. Eckel & Witmer, 2010, pp. 32–35
5. Tosti & Jackson, 1997, p. 23
6. Phillips & Phillips, 2007, pp. 51; 218
7. Fitz-enz, 2009, p. 118
8. Brethower, 1997, p. 21
9. Zemke & Kramlinger, 1982, pp. 83–84; 141–142
10. Haig, 2010, pp. 2–3
11. Tosti & Jackson, 1997

References

Brethower, D.M. (1997b). Rapid analysis: Matching solutions to changing situations. *Performance Improvement, 36*(10), 16–21.

Eckel, N., & Witmer, P.N. (2010, September). Strategic planning simplifies. *Training + Development, 64*(9), 32–35.

Fitz-enz, J. (2009). *The ROI of human capital: Measuring the economic value of employee performance* (2nd ed.). New York: AMACOM.

Haig, C. (2010, June). The organizational scan (pp. 2–3). Retrieved from www.performanccexpress.org/

Heracleous, L. (1998). Strategic thinking or strategic planning? *Long Range Planning, 31*(3), 482–485.

Nickols, F. (1996). The mission/vision thing. Retrieved from trdev-1@psuvm.psu.edu.

Phillips, P.P., & Phillips, J.J. (2007). *The values of learning: How organizations capture value and ROI and translate them into support, improvement, and funds.* San Francisco: Pfeiffer.

Rummler, G.A. (2007). *Serious performance consulting: According to Rummler.* San Francisco: Pfeiffer.

Rummler, G.A., & Brache, A.P. (1990). *Improving performance: How to manage the white space on the organization chart.* San Francisco: Jossey-Bass.

Tosti, D., & Jackson, S.D. (1997). The organizational scan. *Performance Improvement, 36*(10), 22–26.

Zemke, R., & Kramlinger, T. (1982). *Figuring things out: A trainer's guide to needs and task analysis.* Reading, MA: Addison-Wesley.

Environmental Analysis

6

Performance does not occur in a vacuum. The performance improvement practitioner "recognizes individual and organizational realities when solving on-the-job performance problems."[1] The world, workplace, work, and worker environments have the potential to sustain actual performance or raise actual performance to the desired or optimal level. (See Figure 6.1.)

Definition and Scope

Environmental analysis is a process used to identify and prioritize the realities that support actual performance. The performance analysis section of the original HPT Model was based on Rothwell's Environments of Human Performance[2] and focused on environmental support from the organizational environment, work environment, work, and worker. Based on evolving discussion and input from the field, the authors enhanced the environmental analysis component of the 2012 Performance Improvement/HPT Model (Figure 6.1) and Rothwell's environments model (Figure 6.2) to include world, workplace, work, and worker. The term "workplace" includes both the organizational environment of stakeholders, and competition and the work environment of resources and tools.

World. This is a mega or extra-large perspective and so it requires mega or extra-large thinking. Analysis of the world environment focuses on global societal realities that impact organizational and human performance and on cultural issues which affect the performance of the workplace, work, and workers. The ultimate purpose of a responsible organization in today's global workplace is to be mindful and vigilant about the greater societal impact and contribute to society by initiating corporate social initiatives and engaging in communities of practice to promote accountability.

FIGURE 6.1.   Performance Improvement/HPT Model: Environmental Analysis Component

ENVIRONMENTAL ANALYSIS

World	Workplace	Work	Workers
• Culture • Society • Stakeholders • Competition	• Organization • Resources • Tools	• Work flow • Procedure • Responsibilities • Ergonomics	• Knowledge • Skill • Capacity • Motivation • Expectations

FIGURE 6.2.   Variations on Rothwell's Environments of Human Performance

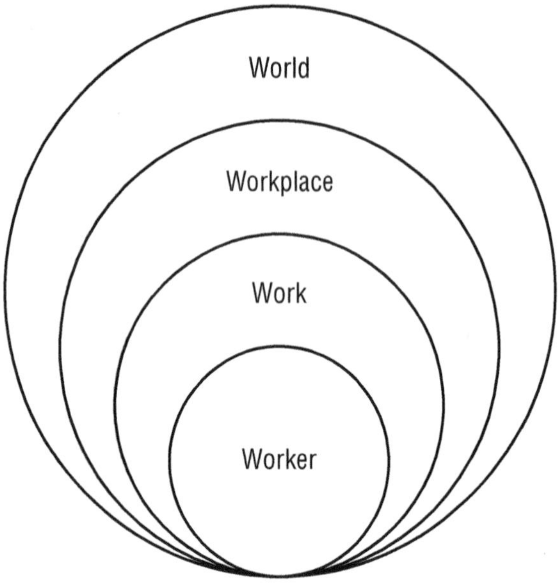

Source: Rothwell, 2005, p. 41. Used with permission.

Organizations and performance improvement professionals should pay attention to the wide range of cultures that comprise the backbone and fabric of the workplace and engage those cultures effectively, respectfully, and confidently. Learning about differences in cultural heritage helps people understand the reason behind a certain behavior, expectation, or belief. It is particularly helpful in developing a sensitivity to nonverbal communication.

Workplace. This analysis focuses on what is happening inside the organization to support performance. Included in environmental analysis are resource allocation, tools, policies for recruiting and hiring, feedback, consequences of performance or nonperformance, retention efforts, and succession planning.

There is another face to the workplace environment—a human face. The Great Place to Work Institute identified five dimensions of great workplaces: *credibility*, including communication, competence, and integrity; *respect*, including support, collaboration, care; *fairness*, including equity, impartiality, justice; *pride*, including personal job, team, company; *camaraderie*; and *intimacy*, including hospitality and community.[3]

Work. This analysis focuses on what is happening at the job design or process level. A robust work-based environmental analysis considers the organization of work, including its implications for personal satisfaction, societal welfare, and social well-being.

Worker. Last, but far from least, analysis of the worker or performer focuses on what is happening with employees, more specifically, their knowledge, skills, capacity, motivation, and expectations. Worker analysis discovers what employees know or don't know, their physical or mental powers to function in a job, their motivation for doing the job, and their expectations about performing the job.

Purpose and Timing

The purpose of environmental analysis is *not* to identify problems, but to assess what is actually happening, both outside and inside the organization, that might help explain why people do what they do.[4] Environmental analysis may take place during or after performance gap analysis. Often it is an integral part of analyzing actual performance. For example, while observing a performer on the job, the performance improvement practitioner may note, at the workplace level, that safety procedures are not clearly posted on the job site or that, at the worker level, the person does not have the necessary skill or knowledge to perform the job.

Analyzing the World Environment

Organizations today function in a global environment. Analyzing the world focuses on commitment—on giving back and taking pride in supporting the communities in which an organization lives and works. It addresses the need for corporate social responsibility, which is accountability rooted in the core values of the organization, and on cultural sensitivity.

Organizations focused on world commitment encourage and foster communities of practice or collaborative teams whose members work interdependently to achieve common goals. They focus on mega results where the primary client and beneficiary is society. Corporate social responsibility is "a commitment to improve community well-being through discretionary business practices and contributions of corporate resources"[5] and corporate social initiatives as "major activities undertaken by a corporation to support social causes and to fulfill commitments to corporate social responsibility."[6]

Analyzing the environment of work at a mega level has myriad benefits for the present and future well-being of an organization, ranging from positive corporate image and the ability to hire and retain personnel to improving brand positioning and increasing market share. Corporate social initiatives have six dimensions, as shown in Table 6.1.

TABLE 6.1.   Corporate Social Initiatives

Initiative	*Description*
Cause Promotions	Organization sponsors and/or supports a social cause
Cause-Related Marketing	Contributing or donating a percentage of revenues to a cause
Corporate Social Marketing	Sponsoring and supporting campaigns which lead to behavior change and accomplishment
Corporate Philanthropy	Making a charitable contribution to support a cause
Community Volunteering	Volunteering time and effort in the community
Socially Responsible Business Practice	Employing business practices that support social causes

Source: Kotler and Lee, 2005, pp. 22–48. Used with permission.

Analyzing the Workplace

Workplace analysis looks within the organization to discover what is happening at the "big picture" level (see also Organizational Analysis) and what is happening at the department, work team, or job level.

Analyzing the Organizational Environment

During an organizational environmental analysis the performance improvement practitioner determines the following: Who are the external stakeholders? Which stakeholders are most critical to the success of the organization? The organization's external stakeholders include customers, suppliers, distributors, stockholders, industry regulators, and so forth.

The performance improvement practitioner then reviews existing documents, such as customer surveys or safety reports, and uses interviews, group processes, or other data collection tools to discover "how well the organization is interacting with its external environment."[7] One strategy is to collect information from within and outside the organization and compare the findings. For example, one manufacturer randomly monitored conversations between product service representatives and customers on a product hot line, then surveyed both the product service representatives and the customers to identify facts and perceptions about what was happening at both ends of the hot line.

Analysis of the constantly changing competitive challenges facing the organization is also part of the organizational environment analysis. This analysis should include an ongoing review of documents that chronicle industry activity, input from customers and knowledgeable employees, or product comparisons. Interviewing or surveying customers, sales staff, and even competitors may provide important insights into the competitive environment.

Analyzing the Work Environment

The people who can provide the answers include representatives from all levels of management, supervision, and the workforce. Seeking input "from groups likely to have unique perspectives, such as temporary workers, recently retired workers, or others who have intimate and recent firsthand knowledge of the organization" broadens the perspective of the analysis.[8] The information that is gathered during this phase of analysis answers the following questions:

- What factors or practices within the workplace have influenced how effectively and efficiently people perform their work?
- What factors or practices within the workplace are most critical to achieving desired performance?

Open-ended questions are the best source of information, so survey data, interviews, or group processes are the analysis tools of choice.

Analyzing Work

Work analysis concentrates on job design and examines whether or not the job is structured to enable the performer to achieve the desired goals through optimal performance. Effective and efficient job design includes the following:

- Allocation of responsibilities among jobs to support rather than hamper the achievement of desired results;
- Logical sequence of job activities or work flow;
- Job policies and procedures that are clearly defined, documented, and accessible to the worker; and
- Ergonomic design of the physical work space to minimize barriers to optimal performance.[9]

The performance improvement practitioner may use interviews, survey data, or group processes to collect information from supervisors and workers. Observation and review of documents such as quality reports, cycle time studies, safety reports, annual reports, and so forth may also provide useful information.

Analyzing the Worker

The worker is the core of performance improvement. Worker analysis zooms in on the performer to identify the individual's actual skills, knowledge, capacity, motivation, and expectations. To discover facts, opinions, or feelings, the performance improvement practitioner reviews personnel documents, observes performers, and uses interviews, survey data, or group processes. Case Study 2.1., The Blake Company/Mutschler Kitchens, focuses on conducting a thorough environmental analysis, including observing and interviewing the workers and other stakeholders. Use Performance Support Tool 6.1 to help you find what's happening in your environment.

Citations

1. Seels & Richey, 1994, p. 89.
2. Rothwell, 2005, p. 41.
3. Burchell & Robin, 2011, p. 4.
4. Rothwell, 2005, pp. 100–101.
5. Kotler & Lee, 2005, p. 3.
6. Kotler & Lee, 2005, p.3.
7. Rothwell, 2005, p. 100.
8. Rothwell, 2005, p. 101.
9. Rummler & Brache, 1995, pp. 68–69.

References

Burchell, M., & Robin, J. (2011). *The great workplace: How to build it, how to keep it, and why it matters*. San Francisco: Jossey-Bass.

Grant, D.A., & Moseley, J.L. (1999, July). Conducting a customer-focused performance analysis. *Performance Improvement, 39*(6), 16.

Kotler, P., & Lee, N. (2005). *Corporate social responsibility: Doing the most good for your company and your cause*. Hoboken, NJ: John Wiley & Sons.

Langdon, D.G. (1995). *The language of work*. Amherst, MA: HRD Press.

Rothwell, W.J. (2005). *Beyond training and development* (2nd ed.). New York: AMACOM.

Rummler, G.A., & Brache, A.P. (1995). *Improving performance: Managing the white space on the organization chart* (2nd ed.). San Francisco: Jossey-Bass.

Seels, B.B., & Richey, R.C. (1994). *Instructional technology: The definition and domain of the field*. Washington, DC: Association for Educational Communications and Technology.

PERFORMANCE SUPPORT TOOL 6.1. WHAT IS HAPPENING?

Directions: Here are some questions that might uncover what is really happening in the performance environment that affects the success or failure of the targeted performance.

Organizational Environment

What is happening when the organization interacts with its external stakeholders and competition?

- Customers
- Suppliers
- Distributors
- Industry regulators
- Stockholders
- Special interest groups
- Professional associations
- Competitors
- Other _____

How does the organization interact with its external stakeholders?

Which interactions are most critical to the success of the organization?

What is the effect of competition on the organization, the work environment, the work, and the worker?

What does the organization need to do to stay competitive?

How do the various stakeholders define a quality product or service?

(Continued)

Workplace Environment

What is happening inside the organization to support optimal performance?

- Resources (time, money, staff, tools, materials, space)
- Information
- Policies and procedures
- Other _____

Does the performer have adequate resources to achieve optimal performance?

Does the performer have the information required to achieve optimal performance?

Do policies for recruiting, hiring, feedback, and consequences support optimal performance?

Work Level

What is happening on the job?

- Job design
- Work flow
- Job responsibilities
- Other _____

Is the job designed for optimal performance?

Does the work flow foster efficient completion of tasks?

Are job responsibilities clearly established?

(Continued)

Worker Level

What is happening with the workers?

- Skills
- Knowledge
- Motivation
- Expectations
- Capacity or ability

Does the performer have the requisite knowledge or skills to achieve success?

Is the performer motivated to achieve?

Do the performer's expectations match the reality of the total performance environment:

Is the performer able to achieve success:

World Commitment Level

What is the organization's commitment to the greater society?

- Corporate social responsibility
- Communities of practice

Are people in the organization committed to being good global citizens?

(Continued)

How are the corporate social initiatives linked to the organization's mission, vision, values, and goals?

How are corporate community engagement and maximizing profit and shareholder value *not* mutually exclusive, but rather mutually reinforcing?

Adapted from D.G. Langdon (1995). *The language of work.* Amherst, MA: HRD Press; W.J. Rothwell (2005). *Beyond training and development* (2nd ed.). New York: AMACOM; G.A. Rummler & A.P. Brache (1995). *Improving performance: How to manage the white space on the organization chart* (2nd ed.). San Francisco: Jossey-Bass; P. Kotler & N. Lee (2005). *Corporate social responsibility: Doing the most good for your company and your cause.* Hoboken, NJ: John Wiley & Sons, Inc; "Conducting a Customer-focused Performance Analysis," by D.A. Grant & J.L. Moseley (1999, July). *Performance Improvement, 39*(6), 16. Used with permission.

Gap Analysis

7

There is an old children's rhyme that goes something like this:

Good, better, best
Never let it rest
'Til your good is better
And your better best.

Analyzing the desired and actual performance states or gap analysis (Figure 7.1) is another step in the performance analysis phase of the Performance Improvement/HPT Model and the first step toward making a poor performance *good* and a good performance *better* or *best*. During this step all the performance pieces come together.

Problem or Opportunity?

Too often the implied focus of human performance improvement is the performance *problem*. "In fact, the technology can and should be used proactively to address new opportunities and to make that which is good even better."[1] For example, appreciative inquiry helps us look at the glass half full—positive aspects focus—rather than half empty—problem focus. Performance gaps should be viewed as performance improvement opportunities that provide a chance to:

FIGURE 7.1. Performance Improvement/HPT Model: Gap Analysis Component

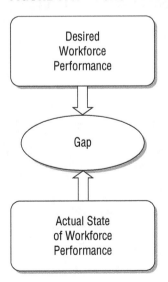

- Improve the actual performance state when it does not measure up to the desired performance state, or
- Enhance or intensify the actual performance state when it is equal to or excels the desired performance state, which may also be called innovation.

Desired State—Reasonable Goals

Revisiting the gap analysis literature provides evidence to support the idea of ensuring that organizations set reasonable goals for reaching the desired state—goals that are both feasible and sustainable:

> "Our starting point for gap analysis is to determine the existing and desired levels of performance, and then set a reasonable goal or milestone for measuring progress in terms of quality, quantity, time, and cost. At the most basic level, a reasonable goal can be set for such areas as productivity, waste, sales, service, and customer service. At an intermediate level, a reasonable goal can be set for such issues as reliability, calls on warranty, customer retention, or customer referrals. At the business outcome level, reasonable goals can be set for profitability and market share. The reasonable goal serves to show progress in closing the performance gap and it also serves to better motivate the people who will do the work to close the performance gap."[2]

A graphic representation of Chevalier's ideas appears in Figure 7.2.

Definition and Scope

Gap analysis identifies the type of performance improvement opportunity that exists and paves the way for cause analysis and intervention selection or design. From the perspective of many leaders in the field, performance gap analysis is very much like needs assessment.

Gap or Needs Assessment? During needs assessment, needs are often viewed as "gaps in results, consequences, or accomplishments" and needs assessment is defined as "a very valuable tool for identifying where you are or the current results and consequences and where you should be or the desired results and consequences"[3] (see Figure 7.3).

FIGURE 7.2.   Performance Gap Analysis with a Reasonable Goal

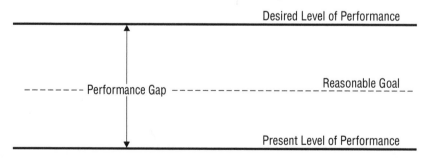

FIGURE 7.3.   Kaufman's Definition of Need

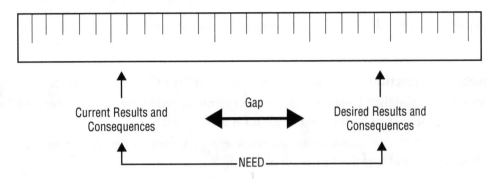

Source: Kaufman, Rojars, and Mayer, 1993. Used with permission.

FIGURE 7.4.   Rothwell's Six-Cell Gap Analysis

	Positive Gaps ⇓	**Neutral Gaps** ⇓	**Negative Gaps** ⇓
Present Gaps ⟶ *(current state of performance)*	actual performance state *exceeds* the desired performance state	actual performance state is *the same as* the desired performance state	actual performance state is *less than* the desired performance state
Future Gaps ⟶ *(what to expect if trends continue)*	actual performance state *will exceed* the desired performance state	actual performance state *will be the same as* the desired performance state	actual performance state *will become less than* the desired performance state
	⇑	⇑	⇑

Performance Enhancement Opportunities

Source: Rothwell, 2005, pp. 126–128. Used with permission.

There are two major differences between needs assessment and performance gap analysis:

- Needs assessment tends to focus on knowledge, skills, and attitude; performance gap analysis "identifies any deficiency or proficiency affecting human performance."
- Needs assessment tends to focus on the past and present while performance analysis also looks to the future.[4]

Six-Cell Gap Analysis. There are six potential gaps in performance: present positive, present neutral, present negative, future positive, future neutral, future negative.[5] Figure 7.4 illustrates the concept of the six gaps in terms of the Performance Improvement/HPT Model.

Opportunities

The HPT practitioner should watch for yellow caution flags regarding positive and neutral gaps:

- Decision-makers and practitioners should not become "complacent" about positive gaps.
- Organizations that experience breakthrough improvements in productivity are sometimes able to distinguish themselves by applying innovation to a neutral gap.
- The greatest opportunity for performance improvement may occur when future neutral gaps exist "because competitors tend to overlook them."[6]

Purpose and Timing

Within the framework of the Performance Improvement/HPT Model and the work cited above, the purpose of performance gap analysis is to identify present and future gaps between the desired performance state and the actual performance state. Along the way the analyst identifies the gaps as positive, neutral, or negative as well as the type of performance improvement opportunity offered by each gap. Then the analyst prioritizes the performance gaps according to how important (criticality) the gap is to meeting the goals of the organization, how difficult (complexity) it will be to resolve the gap, and how often (frequency) the gap occurs.

The proverbial horse-before-the-cart analogy applies here. Performance gap analysis must occur prior to cause analysis that, in turn, must occur before intervention selection and implementation. Performance gap analysis is truly the key to successful performance improvement or enhancement.

Conducting Gap Analyses

The systems approach to analyzing performance gaps includes the sequential steps of:

1. Identifying and analyzing actual and desired performance.
2. Identifying the gaps—present and future; positive, neutral or negative—between the actual and the desired performance state.
3. Prioritizing the gaps.
4. Analyzing the causes.

Actual Performance. The performance improvement practitioner states the current situation as simply and concisely as possible by determining reasons why the current state exists as it does. Then the practitioner assesses the current state from multiple perspectives rather than relying on a single perspective.

In the actual state ask "Is" questions. For example, What *is* the current state of product sales in the region? What *is* a typical technical training encounter like?

Desired Performance. Alignment is the key in the desired workforce performance. Customer needs, organizational goals, primary and support processes, functions, jobs, roles, and the entire human performance system components must be aligned individually, vertically, and horizontally.[7] In the desired state, "Should. . . ?" questions are asked. For example, what *should* be the metrics that need to be in place to measure optimal performance? What *should* a star employee at the Grade 6 level be producing?

Performance Gaps. Identifying performance gaps may be approached by one or a combination of methods.[8] The performance improvement practitioner collects and analyzes information by using familiar data collection techniques. Major tools are surveys, interviews, and group processes such as brainstorming to generate, prioritize, and rank ideas; focus groups to identify needs through planned participation, and so forth (see Chapter 8).[9]

For example, a group of stakeholders, including the practitioner, may collect and analyze documents containing data on the desired and actual performance. They may also use group processes to examine individual and group feelings, opinions, and ideas. In addition, they may include the use of surveys or interviews before, during, or after the life cycle of the group.

Another technique is to conduct a summit or meeting for upper-level leadership. When an organization sends its leadership and managerial teams to a summit, a high level of participation and buy-in result. The performance improvement practitioner may plan and implement activities that encourage participants to focus on desired and actual states and resulting gaps and their relative importance in light of the organization's mission, strategy, and goals. And when stakes are high, a large-scale, short-term change effort is usually the best method for analyzing performance gaps. The purpose is to reach a general consensus among a broad base of stakeholders. Tools include both small group sessions and large-scale (general assembly) sessions using a variety of group processes.

The practitioner may also initiate a Delphi group[10] to gather and validate information, which allows for wider participation, particularly if the Delphi is conducted using email or bulletin boards. A Delphi is useful for forecasting, prioritizing, and gaining consensus. During a Delphi, participants comment on questions or statements. The responses are then analyzed and synthesized and the respondents have another chance to comment or prioritize based on the results of the first round. The process is continued until consensus is reached.

Prioritizing Performance Gaps

Ideally, a group of people, preferably the stakeholders in the performance improvement effort, are involved in prioritizing the performance gaps. It is a crucial part of performance gap analysis because "merely identifying a difference between what people are doing and what you would like them to be doing is not enough reason to take action."[11]

In addition to the Delphi method discussed above, a number of group processes help groups to prioritize items and reach agreement or consensus on the results. As a facilitator, the performance improvement practitioner may provide a list of performance gaps or begin with a brainstorming session.[12] Then the practitioner may use one of the following or a combination of the following sorting tools to prioritize the gaps and gain consensus:

- A typical sorting and prioritizing tools is the "paired comparison analysis." This type of analysis allows participants to compare items on a list with all other items individually, decide which is important, and consolidate results for a prioritized list.
- Grid analysis calls for prioritizing tasks when many different factors need consideration.
- An "action priority matrix" is a diagramming technique for comparing the value of a task against the effort it takes to complete the task. This technique allows the practitioner to see the greatest payback in the shortest timeframe and leads to quick prioritization decisions.[13;] (See a sample in Performance Support Tool 7.1.)

Citations

1. Geis, 1986, p. 6.
2. Chevalier, 2010, p. 5.
3. Kaufman, Rojas, & Mayer, 1993, p. 4.
4. Rothwell, 1996, p. 132.
5. Rothwell, 2005, pp. 126–128.
6. Rothwell, 2005, p. 128.
7. Rummler, 2007, p. 33.
8. Rothwell, 1996.
9. Rothwell & Kazanas, 2008, pp. 72–73
10. Jackson & Schuler, 2006, p. 141.
11. Mager & Pipe, 1984, p. 13
12. Ivancevich, Lorenzi, Skinner, & Crosby, 1997, p. 132.
13. Prioritization, 2011

References

Chevalier, R. (2010, August). Gap analysis revisited. *Performance Improvement, 49*(7) 5–7.

Geis, G.L. (1986). Human performance technology: An overview. In *Introduction to performance technology* (pp. 1–20). Washington, DC: The National Society for Performance and Instruction.

Ivancevich, J.M., Lorenzi, P., Skinner, S.J., & Crosby, P.B. (1997). *Management: Quality and competitiveness* (2nd ed.). Chicago: Irwin.

Jackson, S.E., & Schuler, R.S. (2006). *Managing human resources through strategic partnerships.* Mason, OH: Thomson South-Western.

Kaufman, R., Rojas, A., & Mayer, H. (1993). *Needs assessment: A user's guide.* Englewood Cliffs, NJ: Educational Technology Publications.

Mager, R.F., & Pipe, P. (1984). *Analyzing performance problems or you really oughta wanna* (2nd ed.). Belmont, CA: David S. Lake Publishers.

Prioritization: Making the best of your time and resources. (2011). Online article retrieved from www.mindtools.com/pages/article/newHTE_92.htm.

Rothwell, W.J. (1996). *Beyond training and development: State-of-the-art strategies for enhancing human performance*. New York: AMACOM.

Rothwell, W.J. (2005). *Beyond training and development* (2nd ed.). New York: AMACOM.

Rothwell, W.J., & Kazanas, H.C. (2008). *Mastering the instructional design process: A systematic approach* (4th ed.). San Francisco: Pfeiffer.

Rummler, G.A. (2007). *Serious performance consulting: According to Rummler*. San Francisco: Pfeiffer.

PERFORMANCE SUPPORT TOOL 7.1. SAMPLE PRIORITY MATRIX

Directions: After considerable analysis, we have identified the following performance gaps within our organization. The gaps are listed in the first column. We are asking you to help us determine how critical each gap is to the attainment of our organization's strategic goals. Rank (1 through 10) each gap on the Criticality Scale below, then be prepared to compare and discuss your results with the rest of the group. Together we need to reach consensus on which gaps are the most critical (especially important) and need to be resolved for the organization.

	Low				Criticality Scale					High
Performance Gap	**1**	**2**	**3**	**4**	**5**	**6**	**7**	**8**	**9**	**10**
1.										
2.										
3.										
4.										
5.										

Cause
Analysis

8

Cause analysis is the final step in the Performance Analysis Phase of the Performance Improvement/HPT Model. A cause analysis will determine *why* the performance gap exists leading to the real issues and not the superficial ones. Figure 8.1 shows the cause analysis component of the model.

Definition and Scope

"Cause analysis is the process of determining the root cause(s) of past, present, or future performance gaps. It follows, but is integrally related to, performance analysis."[1] Cause analysis is integral to conducting a thorough performance analysis. While organizational, environmental, and gap analyses yield valuable information, a cause analysis determines why the performance gap exists.

Cause analysis is the "bridge" between performance analysis and the appropriate intervention(s) that will eliminate the performance gap. Using the roots of a tree as an analogy, Rosenberg suggests: "look under the performance gap to discover its roots . . . select intervention(s) . . . to both feed the high performance roots and eliminate the roots that caused the performance gap."[2] Linking training to business needs, cause analysis "provides us with the data to respond to either of these two questions: What is causing an end-result and/or on-the-job performance deficiency? What might prevent newly learned skills from being transferred to the job?"[3]

Various experts have viewed causes from different perspectives. Historically, experts like Robert Mager, Peter Pipe, Thomas Gilbert, Geary Rummler, Alan Brache, and Joe Harless suggest that performance problems are essentially deficiencies of knowledge, skills, training or a host of

FIGURE 8.1. Performance Improvement/HPT Model: Cause Analysis Component

CAUSE ANALYSIS	
Environmental Factors	**Individual Factors**
• Data Information • Feedback • Environment Supports • Resources and Tools • Consequences, Incentives or Rewards	• Skills and Knowledge • Individual Capacity • Motivation and Expectations

management deficiencies.[4] Rossett identified four kinds of drivers, causes, barriers, or obstacles that impact success or failure: lack of skill, knowledge, and information; flawed incentives; flawed environment, tools, and processes; and lack of motivation. Drivers are "everything that it takes to enable performance to 'grow.'"[5]

Robinson and Robinson identified three major causes of performance deficiencies: causes due to the learner, causes due to the manager or boss of the learner, and causes due to the organization.[6] Perhaps the most influential listing of performance causes comes from Gilbert's work on human competence, especially his three *leisurely theorems* and his Behavior Engineering Model (BEM).

Three Leisurely Theorems

Gilbert, affectionately known as the "father of human performance," developed the three leisurely theorems to provide structure to both cause analysis and human performance. They offer guidance and insight and serve as beacons for performance improvement practitioners and their clients.

1. *Value Is in Accomplishment.* Worthy performance is the relationship between valuable accomplishments and costly behavior. "The true value of competence is derived from accomplishment, not from behavior."[7] In simple terms, accomplishment equals value; whereas, behavior equals cost. Gilbert goes on to say that "human competence is found in overt performance, not in hidden behavior."[8]

2. *Measure Against a Standard.* Performance can be measured against a standard, "comparing the very best instance of performance with what is typical."[9] This measure of competence—the ratio of exemplary performance to typical or actual performance—he calls the PIP or the "potential for improving performance." PIP tells us our current state of competence and our opportunities for bettering the situation.

3. *Assess Environmental Versus Individual Causes.* This theorem "identifies where we have to look in order to find the causes of competence and incompetence."[10] Gilbert also refers to this theorem as the "management theorem." Stolovitch, paraphrasing Gilbert, says "Deficiencies in accomplishments are ultimately caused by management system weaknesses."[11] Gilbert's Behavior Engineering Model (BEM), with its emphasis on behavior and environment, is the heart of theorem 3.

Behavior Engineering Model

According to Gilbert, there are three factors that influence performance—information, instrumentation, and motivation. The Behavior Engineering Model (Figure 8.2) illustrates that factors may be either rooted in the environment or in the individual.

The Behavior Engineering Model contains six cells. The data, instrumentation, and incentives cells represent "the system"—environmental factors affecting performance. "If you pit a good performer against a bad system, the system will win almost every time."[12] Knowledge,

FIGURE 8.2.   Gilbert's Behavior Engineering Model

Information	Instrumentation	Motivation
Data	**Instruments**	**Incentives**
• Relevant and frequent feedback • Performance descriptions • Clear and relevant guides to performance	• Tools and materials of work to match human factors	• Financial incentives • Nonmonetary incentives • Career development opportunities

Rooted in the Environment

Knowledge	Capacity	Motives
• Scientifically designed training • Placement	• Flexible scheduling of performance • Prosthesis • Physical shaping • Adaptation • Selection	• Assessment of Motives to work • Recruitment of the right people

Rooted in the Individual

Adapted from Gilbert, 1978. Used with permission.

capacity, and motives represent individual factors affecting performance. The BEM has been adapted to guide the performance improvement practitioner in the search for causes (see Table 8.1).

Chevalier updated the Behavior Engineering Model language to make it more individual, team, and organization-friendly.[13] Another update is offered by Binder in his Six Boxes™ Model. Behavior influences are sorted into six sets similar to Gilbert's; however, the labels used for each cell and some details discussed within each category are different. The Binder cells are Expectations and Feedback, Tools and Resources, Consequences and Incentives, Skills and Knowledge, Capacity or Selection and Assignment, and Motives and Preferences or Attitude.[14]

Conducting Cause Analysis

Too often performance improvement practitioners are overly confident in their diagnostic abilities and they move from performance analysis to intervention selection before thoroughly understanding the causes of the performance gap. Symptoms are often disguised as causes. Without a solid understanding of cause analysis and how it affects work, workers, workplace, and the world perspective, the choice of incentives is flawed. Cause analysis determines *why* the performance

TABLE 8.1.   BEM Adapted to Cause Analysis

Performance Drivers or Causes	Performance Questions	Performance Deficiency Examples
Data, Information, Feedback	How well are people given data, information, and feedback to perform when they are needed?	Information not given on a timely basis Lack of feedback mechanisms Little documentation Performance standards are non-existent Are data tied to performance?
Environment Support, Resources, Tools	How well are people supported with resources, tools, equipment, etc.?	Ergonomic deficiencies Inadequate working conditions Tools unavailable or not optimally arranged Insufficient time to get job done
Consequences, Incentive, Rewards	How well do performers see the results or consequences of what they do? How well are they rewarded or provided with incentives?	Work unrelated to organization's mission and needs. Rewards not performance based Competing incentives Poor performance rewarded
Skills and Knowledge	How well do performers' knowledge and skills match performance requirements?	Lack of knowledge, skills, training, education Unable to maneuver the system
Individual Capacity	How well can people perform?	Lack of aptitude, ability, physical or manual dexterity Inadequate job analysis
Motivation and Expectation	How well are people motivated to perform? Are expectations realistic?	Boring and punishing performance system Payoffs are unrealistic

Sources: Rothwell, 1996, pp. 13–14; Dean, 1997, pp. 45–51. Used with permission.

gap exists and *how* it affects the unique mission, needs, wants, and desires of the organization. Only then can the practitioner choose the appropriate intervention(s).

Steps

The following steps can be used to conduct a cause analysis of a performance gap:

1. Identify the driver or cause of the performance gap;
2. Classify the driver or cause by determining where it originates within the enhanced classification of the environment of human performance—world, workplace, work, or worker;
3. Prioritize the driver or cause according to high or low impact on the performance environment;
4. Generate as many cause examples as possible. This provides an opportunity to look at many sides of the problem. If either skills or knowledge is identified as a cause, then the list may include examples showing that the employee has forgotten how to use the skill; doesn't have adequate information; lacks training in specific processes and procedures; doesn't know the components of the system, and so forth. If consequences are a cause and incentives and rewards are identified, then the list may include examples

that indicate poor performance is rewarded, no management planning exists, competing incentives send mixed messages, and so forth; and

5. Verify causes and corresponding examples with another performance improvement colleague by asking who, what, when, where, and why questions. In addition, stakeholders may shed light on the topic and stakeholder support and buy in are necessary.

Techniques and Tools

There are a variety of techniques and tools for conducting cause analysis, shown in Table 8.2.

TABLE 8.2.   Cause Analysis Tools

Name of Tool	Brief Description
Interview	Structured or unstructured
	Excellent for rapport building and follow-up questions
	Questions can be open-ended or probing
Observation	Captures current skills and knowledge as well as context
	Inferences about work are generated
	Takes time to effectively use
Surveys or Questionnaires	Anonymous
	Large numbers of people can be surveyed
	Require clarity, effective directions, user-friendly questions, and skill in constructing
Focus Groups	Structure opportunities for soliciting information
	Participants must be briefed and debriefed
	Role of facilitator and scribe are crucial
Root Cause Analysis	Trace the causes and effects of accidents or other problems that are past-oriented
	Chronology of events reported and recorded on paper
	Relationship of one event to another becomes clear
	Result is a wall-sized flow chart
	Participants questioned to pinpoint root cause of problem
Fishbone Diagram	Cause-and-effect diagram, used in Total Quality Management (TQM)
	Past-oriented with focus on identifying negative performance gaps
	All causes traced to people, policies/procedures, equipment, climate
	Troubleshooting tool
Portfolio Analysis	Financial management tool with focus on positive performance gaps
	Develop grid
	Make decisions based on likelihood of payoff
	Great for stakeholder involvement

In addition, flow charts, histograms, Pareto charts, and run charts are useful for identifying causes of performance gaps. Computerized programs and systems are also available. TapRoot by System Improvements, Inc., and REASON Root Cause Analysis by Decision Systems, Inc., and PROACT RC Analysis by Info@Reliability.com are useful to shape a cause analysis.[15]

Lack of Environmental Support

Environmental support includes those things that management provides and that the performer needs to perform effectively and efficiently. According to Gilbert, environmental performance support includes the following:

- Information (data, information, and feedback)
- Instrumentation (environment support, resources, and tools)
- Motivation (consequences, incentives, and rewards)

A gap between the available environmental support components, as shown in Table 8.3, and the performance support requirements or needs of the worker usually drive or cause a performance gap.

Data, Information, and Feedback

"A successful performer (person) knows how to do what is expected and when it is appropriate to do it."[16] Part of this knowledge may come from schooling or past experience; however, complete, clear, unambiguous, and up-to-date data on performance expectations and information regarding correct procedures are required for successful on-the-job performance. The data or information must also be available and easily accessible to the performer. Data and information that are vital to successful performance may include organizational policies, job or task procedures, tolerance levels for machinery, customer requirements, or supplier concerns. "Lack of information is not identical to 'lack of timely information.' Instead, it means that performers receive no information and remain in the dark about changes affecting the organization."[17]

Performers also need frequent and timely feedback on the results of their performance:

"Lack of feedback on consequences means that performers are not being given feedback on the results of their work activities. They are performing in a vacuum . . . No timely feedback means that the time lag is excessive between worker performance and feedback received about

TABLE 8.3. Gilbert's Behavior Engineering Model—Environmental Support

	Information	Instrumentation	Motivation
Environmental Support	Data, Information, Feedback	Work Environment Support, Resources, Tools	Consequences, Incentives, Rewards
Repertory of Behaviors	Skills, Knowledge	Individual Capacity	Motivation, Expectations

Adapted from Gilbert, 1978. Used with permission.

that performance. People do not know what they are responsible for doing or what results they should be achieving. Hence they are not accountable for what they do."[18]

Environment Support, Resources, and Tools

Environment support, resources, and tools are those things that management provides to support or assist the performer. *Environment support* may include ergonomic, health, wellness, and safety factors that have an impact on performance. For example, problems with such diverse factors as air quality, workspace, rest areas, lighting, workload, hazardous material handling, work flow design, or workstation construction may cause performance gaps.

Resources refer to the time, money, materials, and personnel allocated to the performance. Resources must be adequate and of sufficient quality to allow for successful accomplishment of the performance. Allocating inadequate resources or substituting poor quality resources may cause performance problems.

Tools are instruments required to complete the job, such as a computer and software for filling out tax forms or the correct equipment to attach a car part on the assembly line. Tools should be available, accessible, efficient, and safe.

Sometimes employees do not have the environment support, resources, and tools they need to do their job—either what they need does not exist because the company has not made the investment or what they need exists, but is not functioning properly. Performing an appendectomy in a hospital operating suite is a fairly routine procedure. The operating room has a sterile, controlled environment, state-of-the-art machinery and instruments, and qualified personnel. Emergency equipment and staff are on hand in case of complications. In contrast, performing an appendectomy in the wilderness without the appropriate facilities, machinery, tools, staff, or emergency backup would not be routine and could cause a gap between desired and actual performance.

Consequences, Incentives, or Rewards

Consequences are events or effects produced by a preceding act. For example, inappropriate lighting may cause eyestrain and prevent an employee from doing a stellar job. *Incentives* are the stimuli that influence or encourage people to do their jobs. Incentives may be internal or external. Working very hard on an assigned task may be sufficient for one employee to earn merit, while another employee may need feedback from a supervisor. On the other hand, *rewards* are items given in return for services. Rewards may be monetary or nonmonetary.

Gilbert lists three types of performance-based incentives: monetary incentives, nonmonetary incentives and career development opportunities.[19] Examples of monetary performance-based incentives include suggestion systems that offer money to employees whose suggestions are adopted, profit sharing, stock options bonuses, business class air travel, and membership in health clubs. Examples of nonmonetary performance-based incentives include time off with pay, gifts, simple recognition awards or programs, special parking places, and popular company logo items. Career development opportunities may be monetary or nonmonetary, depending on whether the opportunities include tuition reimbursement or an increase in pay upon completion of a program. Both monetary and nonmonetary incentives can contribute to increasing productivity and self-esteem.

Assessing consequences, incentives, or rewards helps determine why people do what they do. Most employees perform tasks, react to their environments, and interact with colleagues based on perceptions of rewards for performance and consequences of actions. They maximize positive consequences, incentives, or rewards and minimize negative forces.

Analyzing Environmental Factors That Influence Performance

It is important to acknowledge that the work environment can cause performance problems; it is also important to determine from *where* in the work environment the problem exists. In addition to assessing consequences, incentives, and monetary or nonmonetary rewards, the performance improvement practitioner should also assess whether the organization consciously or unconsciously supports a policy of *disincentives*.

Rossett writes about companies "speaking with two voices" and cites two common examples of disincentives:

- One common problem is ignoring desired performance. When you ask a group of training professionals about the incentives for excellent performance, they'll often laugh. Too frequently, they perceive none. In fact, some contend that there is punishment associated with excellence, with the best people getting the thorniest clients or challenges.
- Another typical problem with incentives is when they conflict, that is, when the organization is rewarding behavior that crowds out the desired performance. This happens to customer service people who are often measured and applauded for the quantity of their contacts but exhorted to deliver high-quality, relationship and loyalty building interactions.[20]

Recognizing that the BEM model was not sufficient in itself to pinpoint the causes of performance gaps within the work environment, Gilbert developed the PROBE (PRO=Profiling BE=Behavior) model.[21] The model provides a series of questions that help performance improvement practitioners probe and assess the work environment for performance gap drivers or causes. (See Performance Support Tool 8.1.)

Lack of Repertory of Behaviors

Another cause of performance problems is people's lack of "repertory of behavior"—an accumulation of knowledge and skills gathered from experience. There are three factors that have an effect on workplace performance and make up an individual's repertory of behavior:

1. Information (skills and knowledge)
2. Instrumentation (individual capacity)
3. Motivation (motivation and expectations)

PERFORMANCE SUPPORT TOOL 8.1. PROBING FOR ENVIRONMENTAL SUPPORT DRIVERS OR CAUSES

Directions: This tool is an adaptation of Gilbert's PROBE Model. Answers to the following questions help to establish the drivers or causes of performance gaps. Some of the answers may be found in documentation for the performance gap analysis. Other answers may require additional input from the actual performer(s).

Category	Questions	Yes	No
Data			
1.	Are there sufficient, accessible data (or signals) to direct an experienced person to perform well?		
2.	Are they accurate?		
3.	Are they free of confusion and stimulus competition that slow performance and invite errors?		
4.	Are directions free of data glut, stripped down to the simplest form, and not buried in extraneous data?		
5.	Are they timely?		
6.	Are good models of behavior available?		
7.	Are clear and measurable performance standards communicated so that people know how well they are supposed to perform?		
8.	Do they accept the standards as reasonable?		
Feedback			
1.	Is work-related feedback provided describing results consistent with the standards and not just behavior?		
2.	Is it immediate and frequent enough to help employees remember what they did?		
3.	Is it selective and specific, limited to a few matters of importance and free of data glut and vague generalities?		
4.	Is it educational, positive, and constructive so that people learn something from it?		
Tools			
1.	Are the necessary implements usually on hand for doing the job?		
2.	Are they reliable and efficient?		
3.	Are they safe?		
Information			
1.	Are procedures efficient and designed to avoid unnecessary steps and wasted motion?		
2.	Are they based on sound methods rather than historical happenstance?		
3.	Are they appropriate to the job and skill level?		
4.	Are they free of boring and tiresome repetition?		

(Continued)

Category	Questions	Yes	No
Resources			
1.	Are adequate materials, supplies, and assistance usually available to do the job well?		
2.	Are they efficiently tailored to the job?		
3.	Do ambient conditions provide comfort and prevent unnecessary interference?		
Incentives			
1.	Is the pay for the job competitive?		
2.	Are there significant bonuses or raises based on good performance?		
3.	Does good performance have any relationship to career advancement?		
4.	Are there meaningful nonmonetary incentives (recognition and so on) for good performance based on results and not behavior?		
5.	Are they scheduled well, neither too frequently (lose meaning) nor too infrequently (becoming useless)		
6.	Is there an absence of punishment for performing well?		
7.	Is there an absence of hidden incentives to perform poorly?		
8.	Is the balance of positive and negative incentive in favor of good performance?		

Based on P.J. Dean and D.E. Ripley (Eds.). (1997). *Performance improvement pathfinders: Models for organizational learning systems,* pp. 57–58. Washington, DC: ISPI. Used with permission.

If a gap exists between desired and actual performance, and the gap is not caused by environmental support problems, the question is: "Could they do it if their lives depended on it?"[22] Do they have the necessary "repertory" of skills, knowledge, capacity, motivation, and expectations?

If the answer is "No," the performance improvement practitioner should focus on determining the skills or knowledge deficiency that interferes with the accomplishment of the desired performance. If the answer is "Yes," the practitioner can rule out a skill or knowledge deficiency and focus on lack of individual capacity, motivation, or expectations (see Table 8.4).

Skills and Knowledge

If people "couldn't do it if their lives depended on it,"[23] the performance improvement practitioner should suspect a skill or knowledge deficiency. People cannot be expected to perform to standards if they lack the required skills or knowledge. "It is not possible for people with the right motivation, performance standards, resource tools, support, capacity, and motive to be successful performers if they don't know how to perform."[24]

Analyzing Skills and Knowledge

Identifying the cause of a performance gap as lack of skills and knowledge is not as simple as it sounds. First, the performance improvement practitioner needs to discover what skills and knowledge are required for the desired performance. Documentation (job or task analysis, performance standards, and other records) from the performance gap analysis should provide this information.

Then the performance improvement practitioner needs to consider the following:[25]

- Did the employee once know how to perform as desired?
- Has the employee forgotten how to perform as desired?

Perhaps the employee possessed the necessary skills and knowledge at an earlier time, but the nature of the job has changed and she or he needs to be updated. Another possibility is to examine whether or not the employee possesses the necessary skills and knowledge, but has not had the opportunity to use them for some time.

There is another perspective on lack of knowledge and skills that requires examination: "[Maybe] there is just too much to know."[26] In today's information age employees are frequently inundated

TABLE 8.4.   Gilbert's Behavior Engineering Model—Repertory of Behavior

	Information	*Instrumentation*	*Motivation*
Environmental Support	Data, Information, Feedback	Work Environment, Support, Resources, Tools	Consequences, Incentives, Rewards
Repertory of Behaviors	Skills, Knowledge	Individual Capacity	Motivation, Expectations

Adapted from Gilbert, 1978. Used with permission.

with documentation or updates until it becomes "disinformation" (sic) or the employees just plain "tune it out."

Finally, the practitioner may want to look at the report from the environmental analysis. The workplace has to support the performer's knowledge and skills. "If you pit a trained employee against an environment that does not value the new skills and knowledge, the environment wins every time."[27]

Individual Capacity

Individual capacity is another component of people's repertory of behavior. Capacity "represents the individual's ability to perform the job. It is represented by a match or mismatch between the employee and the job requirement."[28] Individual capacity helps to match the right person to the right job. A mismatch, or employee selection error, can cause a performance gap.

The lack of ability means that a mistake was made during employee selection. An individual was hired, transferred, or promoted into a job that the person lacked the ability to perform or to learn. In one organization, an employee was promoted to executive secretary, who was unable and unwilling to learn the new company wide project management software.

Employee selection processes also helps to avoid a potential performance gap. An individual was interviewing for a job as a customer service representative. The final question was, "Based on everything you have heard about this job, are there any areas that may be problematic?" Without delay, the person replied, "I really despise people." Needless to say the individual was not hired, although possessing the required skills and knowledge. But the person lacked the capacity or ability to accomplish the desired performance—selling shoes to people.

Analyzing Individual Capacity

To determine whether or not a lack of individual capacity is causing a performance gap, the performance practitioner needs to look at capacity from two perspectives:[29]

- Does the individual lack the capacity (ultimate limits to which an individual develops any function given appropriate training and environment) or ability (physical, mental, or social powers, inherited or acquired by an individual) to perform or learn?
- Do the organizational, workplace, and work environments support the individual's capacity to perform or learn?

First, the performance improvement practitioner needs to review the performance gap analysis to discover what individual capacity or ability is required to meet the desired performance requirement. The following questions may help to identify individual capacity requirements for a specific performance:

- Is it certain and proven that one must have special aptitudes, intelligence scores, verbal skills, manual dexterity, and so on, to perform in an acceptable, if not exemplary, manner?
- Is the proof so sound that there are virtually no exceptions?[30] The performance improvement practitioner then looks at the employee to assess whether or not the individual's physical and mental capacity match the performance requirements. A review of the gap analysis or personnel records, or an interview with the employee, may provide information on the performer's aptitude, intelligence, verbal skills, and so forth.

Finally, the performance improvement practitioner may look at the organizational and environmental analyses to find out whether the organization, workplace, and work environments support the individual's capacity or ability to perform and learn. For example, does either the organization or the environment:

- Offer flexible scheduling to accommodate people when they are at their sharpest?
- Consider the difficulty level and individual capacity when selecting someone to perform a task?
- Provide response aids, for example, large-print job aids for older workers, to determine whether lack of individual capacity is causing a performance gap?[31]

Motivation and Expectations

Motivation comes from within. The performer encourages himself or herself to succeed. Expectation also comes from within the person by expecting or believing that certain conditions or resources are required to accomplish a given task. If the employee is not motivated to perform, or feels that his or her expectations are not met, there is a good chance that there will be a gap between desired and actual performance.

It was Gilbert's contention that motivation, the third factor related to the individual, will be high if all the other five cells, especially if those related to work environment are provided. Thus he believed that evidence of low motivation is a signal to look for deficiencies in information, resources, or incentives. In communicating this concept, he stressed that factors in the work environment will not directly motivate employees. Rather, by dealing with these work environment factors, the organization can create an environment within which the employees' own intrinsic motivation can flourish.[32]

Analyzing Motivation and Expectations

It is difficult at best to determine what motivates an individual to accomplish peak performance. It is almost as difficult to discover a performer's expectations. Perhaps the first step is to ask, "Is the performance system inherently so dull, unrewarding, or punishing that people must have special motives to succeed in it, even when the incentives provided are excellent?"[33] The organizational, environmental, and gap analyses should shine some light on the nature of the performance system in which the performer is functioning. The same documents should uncover what expectations the performer might have given optimal work environment.

The performance improvement practitioner may also want to interview the supervisor, manager, coworkers, and performer or observe the performer in action. However, these methods are less than scientific and rely on self-reporting from the performer) or perceptions from the supervisor, manager, and/or co-workers.

Citations

1. Rothwell, 1996, p. 79
2. Rosenberg, 1996, p. 380
3. Robinson & Robinson, 1989, p. 109
4. Rothwell, 1996, pp. 153–154
5. Rossett, 1999, p. 38
6. Robinson & Robinson, 1989
7. Gilbert, 1996, p. 18
8. Gilbert, 1996, p. 19
9. Gilbert, 1996, p. 30
10. Gilbert, 1996, p. 76
11. Stolovitch, 2010, p. 10
12. Rummler & Brache, 1995, p. 13
13. Chevalier, 2003, pp. 8–14; Chevalier, 2008, pp. 9–18
14. Binder, 2007, pp. 3–4
15. Lauer, 2002, pp. 42–43
16. Rossett, 1999, p. 38
17. Rothwell, 1996, p. 161
18. Rothwell, 1996, pp. 159–160
19. Gilbert, 1996, p. 88
20. Rossett, 1999, p. 43
21. Gilbert, 1982, pp. 21–30
22. Mager & Pipe, 1984, p. 31
23. Mager & Pipe, 1984, p. 31
24. Rosenberg, 1996, p. 375
25. Mager & Pipe, 1984, p. 17
26. Rossett, 1999, p. 45
27. Rummler, 1983, pp. 75–76
28. Dean, 1997, p. 48
29. Gilbert, 1996
30. Dean, 1997, p. 51
31. Gilbert, 1996, pp. 87–88
32. Dean, 1998, pp. 48–49
33. Dean, 1998, p. 51

References

Binder, C. (2007). The six boxes: A descendant of Gilbert's behavior engineering model. Retrieved from www.binder.riha.com/sixboxes.html.

Chevalier, R. (2003), May/June). Updating the behavior engineering model. *Performance Improvement, 42*(5), 8–14.

Chevalier, R. (2008, November/December). The evolution of a performance job aid. *Performance Improvement, 47*(10), 9–18.

Dean, P.J. (1997). Engineering performance improvement with or without training. In P.J. Dean & D.E. Ripley (Eds.), *Performance improvement pathfinders: Models for organizational learning systems* (pp. 45–64). Washington, DC: International Society for Performance Improvement.

Dean, P.J. (1998). Performance improvement interventions: Methods for organizational learning. In P.J. Dean & D.E. Ripley (Eds.), *Performance improvement interventions: Performance technologies in the workplace* (Vol. 3, pp. 2–19). Washington, DC: International Society for Performance Improvement.

Gilbert, T.F. (1982, September). A question of performance, Part I: The PROBE model. *Training and Development Journal, 43*(9), 21–30.

Gilbert, T.F. (1996). *Human competence: Engineering worthy performance* (Tribute Ed.) Amherst, MA: HRD Press/ISPI.

Lauer, M.J. (2002, April). Doing cause analysis. *Performance Improvement, 41*(4), 42–45.

Mager, R.F., & Pipe, P. (1984). *Analyzing performance problems or you really oughta wanna* (2nd ed.). Belmont, CA: David S. Lake Publishers.

Robinson, D.G., & Robinson, J.C. (1989). *Training for impact: How to link training to business needs and measure the results.* San Francisco: Jossey-Bass.

Rosenberg, M.J. (1996). Human performance technology. In R.L. Craig (Ed.), *The ASTD training and development handbook: A guide to human resource development* (4th ed., pp. 370–393). New York: McGraw-Hill.

Rossett, A. (1999). *First things fast: A handbook for performance analysis.* San Francisco: Pfeiffer.

Rothwell, W.J. (1996). *Beyond training and development: State-of-the-art strategies for enhancing human performance.* New York: AMACOM.

Rummler, G.A. (1983). Training skills isn't enough. *Training, 20*(8), 75–76.

Rummler, G.A., & Brache, A.P. (1995). *Improving performance: Managing the white space on the organization chart* (2nd ed.). San Francisco: Jossey-Bass.

Stolovitch, H.D. (2010, June). A leisurely approach to performance. *Talent Management, 6*(6), 10.

PERFORMANCE SUPPORT TOOL 8.2. PROBING FOR PEOPLE'S REPERTORY OF BEHAVIOR DRIVERS OR CAUSES

Directions: This tool is an adaptation of Gilbert's PROBE Model. Answers to the following questions help to establish the drivers or causes of performance gaps. Some of the answers may be found in documentation for the performance gap analysis. Other answers may require additional input from the actual performer(s). Check either Yes or No.

Category	Questions	Yes	No
Knowledge and Training			
1.	Do people understand the consequences of both good and poor performance?		
2.	Do they grasp the essentials of performance? Do they get the big picture?		
3.	Do they have the technical concepts to perform well?		
4.	Do they have sufficient basic skills such as reading?		
5.	Do they have sufficient specialized skills?		
6.	Do they always have the skills after initial training?		
7.	Are good job aids available?		
Capacity			
1.	Do the incumbents have the basic capacity to learn the necessary perceptual discriminations with accuracy and speed?		
2.	Are they free of emotional limitations that would interfere with performance?		
3.	Do they have sufficient strength and dexterity to learn to do the job well?		
Motives			
1.	Do incumbents seem to have the desire to perform well when they enter the job?		
2.	Do their motives endure? Is the turnover low?		

Adapted from P.J. Dean and D.E. Ripley (Eds.). (1997). *Performance improvement pathfinders: Models for organizational learning systems*, pp. 57–58. Washington, DC: ISPI. Used with permission.

The Blake Company/ Mutschler Kitchens

Topic: *Performance Analysis*

Anne M. Blake, **M.A., Ed.S.,** *Director of Operations, The Blake Company,*
Michigan, USA

Background

The Blake Company is a residential building company outside of Detroit, Michigan. Originally the organization focused on purchasing old estates in the upscale suburb of Grosse Pointe, subdividing the property into smaller lots, and building homes on the lots. As the supply of large estates dwindled, the owner of the company branched into major renovations of existing homes. Within this context he frequently worked with a well-established kitchen company in the area, Mutschler Kitchens.

Situation

After several years, the owner of The Blake Company purchased Mutschler Kitchens in an attempt to gain economies of scale in his business. However, shortly after purchasing the business, the new owner realized that there were some serious performance issues within the newly acquired organization. A review of the financial data indicated that the margins were lower than they needed to be for the organization to make a profit. Jobs were not being closed out due to minor details that were not finished in a timely manner. There were rumors in the community that customer satisfaction levels were dropping.

Intervention

Over the course of the next year, the owner embarked on a performance improvement journey. He began by analyzing every aspect of the Mutschler Kitchens organization. He interviewed the employees, the suppliers, the subcontractors, and the customers. He visited successful competitors to see how they did business. He reviewed all of the company's processes, policies, and forms. He analyzed the work flow and the procedures that the kitchen designers followed while they attempted to make a sale. He visited construction sites to watch the process in action.

Based on this review, the owner developed three goals: (1) to increase customer satisfaction, (2) to increase the profit margin for each job, and (3) to decrease the uncertainty and number of crises at the construction sites.

To accomplish these goals, the owner took a close look at the causes of the problems that existed. He determined that the biggest problem for all of the stakeholders was that the kitchen remodeling jobs were being sold with too many undefined issues on the table. The result was that customers did not clearly understand what they were buying, kitchen designers did not understand what they were selling, and subcontractors did not clearly understand what they were building. This caused high levels of on-the-job stress, crises, and frequent job stoppages due to unanticipated shortages and required decisions. Budgets were difficult to create and adhere to, resulting in lower than desired profit margins.

The owner developed the following design and sales process to address this issue:

- The kitchen designer holds a series of selection meetings with the customer to discern their needs.
- The designer develops a preliminary plan that includes a ballpark cost estimate.
- The customer and the designer collaborate to modify the plan until everyone is satisfied with it.
- When the customer is happy with the plan, he/she signs a design agreement and makes a deposit. This allows the organization to get a commitment from the customer before the organization spends a prohibitive amount of time and money doing detailed specifications.
- After the design agreement is signed, the designer works with the customer to plan every detail of the new kitchen. Specifications and working drawings are created.
- Next, the potential subcontractors walk through the job with the detailed specifications. This ensures that the owner can compare bids between competing subcontractors. If the customer wants to make a change to the plans, a change order is created and the plans and specifications are updated. This ensures that the specifications match the construction drawings, which reduces crises at the job site.

Critical Business Issue

What is: Remodeling jobs were being sold with too many undefined issues so that customers did not clearly understand what they were getting, resulting in low levels of customer satisfaction. Designers and subcontractors did not have detailed plans to work from, resulting in high levels of on-the-job stress, crises, and frequent job stoppages due to unanticipated decision points. Budgets were difficult to create and adhere to, resulting in lower than desired profit margins.

What should be: All elements of the job should be defined at the time of the sale, so that the job can be produced on budget with high customer satisfaction rates and low levels of on-the-job crises.

Focus on Outcomes or Results

The owner had three desired outcomes: (1) an increase in customer satisfaction, (2) an increase in profit margins for each job, and (3) a decrease in uncertainty and crisis at the construction sites.

Focus on Systems View

Inputs: The inputs for any construction project include accurate, detailed construction plans, drawings and specifications. In order to create these documents, customers need to make numerous selection decisions, including their choices of cabinets, appliances, tile, light fixtures, floor coverings, as well as the placement of plugs, racks, etc. Based on these selections, the kitchen designers can give customers accurate cost estimates.

Process: Customers participate in a series of design meetings with the kitchen designer. Once a general design plan is agreed upon, but before detailed construction drawings are developed, customers sign a design agreement and make a non-refundable deposit. After the design agreement has been signed, detailed specifications are developed. Potential subcontractors are invited to perform a "walk-through" of the job using the detailed specifications so that they can develop accurate bids.

Output: The output from the process described above is a complete set of job specifications that matches the construction drawings. This reduces uncertainty for all of the stakeholders. For example, the buyer knows what type of faucet they are getting and where the outlets will be placed in the kitchen island. The electricians know where to run the wiring and where to place the light fixtures.

Constraints: This process reduces uncertainty at the point of construction, but requires tremendous effort before the sale is complete. It is often difficult to get customers to make decisions before construction has begun. Construction subcontractors are a notoriously independent group of people, so it is challenging to get them to complete their job bids based on the detailed specifications provided to them. The kitchen designers at the organization had approximately twenty-five years of experience without a structured environment, so they were initially resistant to the development of a design process.

Focus on Value

By implementing this design process, the business owner is trying to bring value to customers in several ways. First, customers will receive a realistic estimate of the cost of the project before they commit to it, so that they can determine whether or not they can afford to do the renovation. Second, the detailed specifications will reduce uncertainty in the construction process and eliminate the need for clients to make decisions on the job site. Third, the specifications will allow the construction team to order cabinets, appliances and fixtures in a timely manner, which eliminates construction delays. Fourth, the project manager can schedule subcontractors efficiently, which will streamline the construction process and get the job done quickly. This is particularly important if the buyer continues to live in the house during the renovation.

Focus on Establishing Partnerships

The process of completing the drawings and specifications helps the kitchen designer discern the clients' needs and wants. As clients are increasingly able to articulate what they are looking for, the kitchen designer is able to focus on a design that is aesthetically pleasing, functional, and affordable.

The owner must also establish partnerships with a group of subcontractors. This relationship has an inherently adversarial element to it because the subcontractor wants to charge as much as possible, while the business owner wants to pay as little as possible.

Be Systematic in Assessment of Need, Opportunity, or Challenge

The owner approached the performance issue from every angle within the organization. He considered the perspective of each stakeholder: the buyer, the designer, the project manager, the suppliers, the construction team, as well as his own interests.

By talking with people in the community, the owner got an understanding of the frustrations that most people have when they deal with a home renovation. It is very disruptive to have a house under construction and to have normal routines disrupted. It became clear that it is important to get a job done quickly and neatly, and to keep the owner informed of the progress on a daily basis.

The owner had a gut feeling that many potential customers came to Mutschler Kitchens to get ideas about a new kitchen design, and then had someone else do the construction for them. The owner saw an opportunity to get more construction jobs by asking customers to sign a design agreement and pay a deposit after they received preliminary drawings. This would have the added benefit of saving him money in terms of the hours that the kitchen designers spent drawing detailed plans and giving them to customers who then failed to return for the construction process.

Under its previous ownership, Mutschler Kitchens had not followed costs on a job-by-job basis. The new owner wanted to know how much each job cost so that he could develop a sense of where costs could be reduced and profits maximized.

Be Systematic in the Analysis of Work, Worker, Workplace and Worldview

The owner asked stakeholders to describe their roles and the challenges faced as part of their jobs. The business owner concluded that the organization needed a comprehensive set of procedures to guide the design and build process. He met with staff members to discuss ideas. Initially, employees were reluctant to give opinions, but the owner found that, as he included people in the planning process, they began to contribute ideas in a meaningful way.

The owner learned from the kitchen designers that they were reluctant to ask potential customers to make selection decisions early in the process.

The owner could also see that potential subcontractors were reluctant to give detailed bids for jobs based on vague construction drawings and specifications.

Be Systematic in the Design of the Solution

The business owner understood that in order to be successful he needed buy-in from the stakeholders within the organization. He engaged employees in the design of the processes that would guide future jobs.

Initially, some of the kitchen designers were understandably resistant to the idea of designing a structured process for sales. It is easier to sell a job if the conversation deals in generalities. It is harder to sell a job if you ask the customer to make detailed decisions early in the process.

The owner also read current trade magazines, talked to other business owners, and shopped at competing kitchen companies. Since the industry publications did not address the design and development of a systematic process, the owner had to rely on his own organizational resources to design the solution.

The owner decided to transfer the Mutschler Kitchens division to the same construction accounting program that he used in the new construction portion of his business. This allowed him to begin to track costs for each job in great detail.

Be Systematic in the Development of the Solution

The owner worked collaboratively with the employees to develop a detailed process manual. In addition, he created a one-page performance support tool to illustrate the sequential steps that employees should follow through the sales process. Over the course of the next year, the manual was edited four or five times as processes were refined. In addition, the owner developed a one-page explanation of the new process that was given to potential customers early in the design process.

Be Systematic in Implementation of the Solution

The implementation of the new processes was challenging for all of the stakeholders. The kitchen designers had been working without written processes for many years and occasionally needed to be reminded to follow the procedures that had been established.

Some of the customers were resistant to making decisions early in the process. The owner worked with the designers to educate the customers about the benefits of the new process. By pointing out to the customers that they would receive a better result at a lower cost and in less time, the owner was able to gain buy-in from the vast majority of customers.

Be Systematic in Evaluation of the Process and the Results

The owner developed a customer satisfaction survey in order to obtain systematic feedback on the new processes. The results have been overwhelmingly positive, with all of the customers in the past five years indicating that they were extremely satisfied with their experience.

The cost accounting program provided the owner with detailed information about profit margins for each job. They were able to accurately predict gross profit within 2 percent.

With the implementation of the design agreement process, the owner saw an immediate decrease in his costs to develop kitchen designs for customers who were not really serious about following through with the process.

The owner immediately began to see a decrease in change orders, which resulted in fewer administrative costs and more certainty for the client, since they did not inadvertently add costs to the project that would result in a decrease in their level of satisfaction when they received the bill.

■   ■   ■

Lessons Learned from the Case
- Involving all internal and external stakeholders provides buy-in, collaboration, and partnership as well as establishing an atmosphere of trust and mutual cooperation.
    - Initially, performance improvement can be a long, tedious, trial and error experience. However, with systematic processes in place, targeted accountability mechanisms identified, and a genuine desire to do the right thing in an ethical manner, an organization will reap the benefits associated with success.
    - Work with vendors to encourage pride in their deliverables. Work with clients by providing value in quality and service.
    - Be patient in implementing planned and systematic change and monitor the process.

Anne M. Blake, M.A., Ed.S., is director of operations for The Blake Company, Grosse Pointe Farms, Michigan. She has an M.A. in adult continuing education from the University of Michigan and an Ed.S. from Wayne State University's Instructional Technology Program, with an emphasis in human performance improvement. She and The Blake Company can be reached at 313.881.6100 or ablake@theblakecompany.net.

Physician Performance Report Accuracy and Timeliness

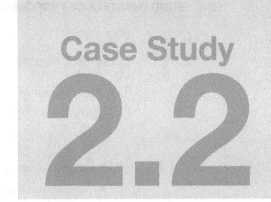

Topic: *Gap and Cause Analysis*

Hillary N. Leigh, M.A., *Senior Consultant with Kaiser Permanente, California, USA*

Background

Allied Health [not its real name] is an HMO located in the Midwestern United States. The mission of a health maintenance organization (HMO) is to provide quality health care focusing on prevention and healthy living. In order to fulfill this mission, national standards and guidelines have been developed that outline steps that ought to be taken by an HMO to provide quality health care. A core component of these guidelines relates to providing physicians with informative reports on various process and outcomes measures.

Situation

In particular, one of the national standards relates to providing primary care physicians (PCPs) with performance data that demonstrate comparisons with the performance of peers. These data should measure individual PCPs' performance on a number of utilization, pharmacy, and quality measures (such as cancer screenings) and provide the PCPs with actionable information to improve their performance in these areas. In order to comply with national standards and guidelines, Allied Health has negotiated contracts that specify expectations for the distribution of performance data reports.

Critical Business Issues

Over the past two years, Allied Health has exceeded contract requirements for timeliness of reporting and has received a number of complaints about the accuracy of these reports.

Focus on Outcomes

The general goal of this project was to improve distribution cycle time and data accuracy on the PCP Profiles (performance reports). The following measures served as indicators of performance:

- Report accuracy
- Turnaround time
- Provider satisfaction with reports
- Changes in provider performance

As will be seen in this case, the first two indicators played an important role in the gap and cause analysis, but the latter two indicators helped to frame the deeper purpose for the project and as "downstream" effects, were considered in the overall evaluation of the interventions over time.

Systems View. These outcomes were selected by taking a systemic view of the critical business issue, using the following questions as a guide: (1) How does the performance problem relate to the mission of the organization? (2) How does the performance problem influence compliance with national guidelines and contract agreements? (3) How does this problem impact key stakeholders?

Value Added. The project adds value to the organization through its close ties to the mission. Instead of concentrating on a particular method or procedure, the project focused on the desired outcomes/results of meeting contract requirements and report accuracy.

Forming Partnerships. Results were achieved through partnering with internal and external stakeholders to carefully consider pressures, expectations, constraints, and consequences. As will be demonstrated in the following sections, external stakeholders were engaged at multiple points through interviews and questionnaires. Internal partnerships also played a key role in the project, especially when identifying current levels of performance. While outside the scope of the case, these partnerships were leveraged again in the identification of interventions. These partnerships were critical to maintaining a focus on outcomes, understanding the critical business issue from a systems perspective, and supporting the adoption of the interventions within the organization.

Gap Analysis. The gap analysis sought to answer questions that are relevant to the gap in performance through the collection of quantitative and qualitative data. The following table demonstrates key questions and methods used:

These questions and data collection methods were used to assess current performance, establish a desired level of performance, and quantify a performance gap for each indicator. Selection of data collection methods was a key decision in this phase, with special consideration of whether the method was likely to provide a credible answer to the key question it targeted. Of course, practical considerations came into play and extant data were used where they existed and were relevant to the questions. This assessment was used to guide cause analysis.

Key Questions	*Data Collection Method*
What is the level of accuracy of the reports?	Review of extant data (provider complaints and supplemental follow-up)
What kinds of complaints about accuracy are being received?	
What level of accuracy is expected?	Review of extant data (previously collected questionnaires and interviews)
What is the performance of similar health plans?	Benchmarking and literature review
What is the current distribution cycle?	Time study
What tasks do people perform during distribution?	
How long do these tasks take?	
What problems do people encounter when performing these tasks?	Job observation/interviews
How satisfied are providers with the current reports?	Review of extant data (provider complaints and previously collected questionnaires)
How are providers performing on the measures that are included in the PCP profile?	Trend analysis

Indicator 1: Report Accuracy

A questionnaire conducted just prior to the beginning of the project was available for the team to review. The results of the questionnaire were that 40 percent of the respondents perceived the reports to be accurate, 26 percent noted that the reports were inaccurate, and 24 percent were uncertain of the reports' accuracy. Respondents noted dissatisfaction with the accuracy of the patient panel reports (these are the reports that are used to identify patients who are due or overdue for services).

A shortcoming of this questionnaire was that an exceedingly small number of the physician providers responded. Therefore, the team sought other information to validate the results. This was accomplished by vigorously investigating individual complaints received from providers in order to determine trends. The process is described further in the section on cause analysis.

Indicator 2: Timeliness of Reporting

The project team assessed the current overall distribution cycle and determined that reports were distributed sporadically. The most recent distribution occurred seventy-three days past the end of the previous quarter, which far exceeds industry standards and stakeholder expectations. Through interviews with senior leaders and their front-line staff, the secretary pool that collates the reports, and a time study/observation, the team observations can be seen at the top of page 188.

Indicator 3: Provider Satisfaction with Reports

Allied Health is required to conduct an annual survey to determine how satisfied its physician providers are with the services provided by the health plan. Therefore, the team was able to assess trends in provider satisfaction with the panel and profile reports. In general, provider satisfaction with these reports appeared to be improving.

Task	Department responsible	Duration of task
Request list of active physician providers	Informatics	14 days
Load claims data	Information Technology	13 days
Develop databases	Informatics/Pharmacy/Quality Measures	13 days
Perform quality check on data	Informatics	9 days
Print reports	Informatics	3 days
Deliver reports to secretarial pool	Informatics	1 day
Prepare reports for mailing	Secretary Pool	32 days
Deliver reports to mailroom	Secretary Pool	1 day

At the time of project initiation, Allied Health did not track provider complaints relating to these reports. Therefore, the team worked to characterize complaints related to accuracy by obtaining copies of the complaints that were recorded. These complaints fell into two categories:

- Inaccurate patient panel reports (incorrect patients)
- Overdue service when that service was already performed

Establishing Desired Performance Level and Qualifying the Gap

In order to determine a desired level of performance for report accuracy, interviews were conducted with key stakeholders, including physicians and senior leaders. The former stakeholders were selected due to their perspectives on the ultimate utility of the reports and competitors' performance, while the latter were chosen for the input related to industry standards and organizational capabilities. These interviews surfaced a limitation in terms of the relative "lag" in reporting. Because data are not reported in real time, there was not an expectation of 100 percent accuracy for both indicators.

For each of the accuracy indicators targets were determined as follows:

Indicator	Desired Performance	Current Performance
Panel accuracy complaints	1	6
Panel accuracy	95 percent	66 percent
Service accuracy	75 percent	56 percent

During the interviews, the team discovered that Allied Health, as well as other health plans, send physicians reports on a quarterly basis; however, these reports generally arrived prior to Allied Health's reports.

In addition to interviewing stakeholders, the team conducted a literature review to determine how other health plans were performing in this area. The search unearthed few specifics in terms of report accuracy and timeliness of distribution, but revealed useful information about physicians' expectations regarding data validity, reliability, and desire for actionable data. The American Academy of Family Physicians (AAFP)[1] and American Medical Association (AMA)[2] both have published policies and guidelines for health plans to use when profiling physicians. A survey conducted by Medstat demonstrated a trend toward quarterly performance reporting to physicians.[3]

The team determined that the current contract requirements for report distribution were aligned with external competitors' practices, and established a desired performance level.

Indicator	Desired Performance	Current Performance
Report distribution cycle frequency	Quarterly	Quarterly-Sporadic
Report distribution cycle duration	≤ 45 days	73 days

Cause Analysis Methods

Before conducting a cause analysis, the team determined whether the gaps in performance were worth the time and resources necessary to continue. There are several factors that demonstrated worthiness to proceed:

1. Performance closely tied to organizational mission and contract arrangements
2. Availability of extant data
3. The cost of "doing nothing" exceeded the cost of analysis

This process only required a small amount of time and resources, yet provided a compelling justification to senior leaders and front-line managers for moving ahead with cause analysis. During this phase, the team investigated what might be likely root causes for these performance deficiencies. The following methods were used to develop hypotheses about why these gaps existed:

	Sub-Indicator	Method(s) of Analysis	Target
Report Accuracy	Panel accuracy complaints	Review of extant data	Provider complaints
	Panel accuracy	Review of extant data	Provider complaints
			Panel reports
		Interview	Data analyst
	Service accuracy	Review of extant data	Provider complaints
			Panel reports
Timeliness of Reporting	Report distribution cycle frequency	Interviews	Senior leaders and front-line staff from each department
	Report distribution cycle duration	Time study/observation	Process cycle
		Interviews	Secretary pool

As a result of what was learned during gap analysis, the consideration of the indicator related to provider satisfaction with reports was collapsed into the others. The team used an updated version of Gilbert's Behavior Engineering Model,[4] in order to propose likely causes for the performance gaps.

Indicator 1: Report Accuracy

The team had already discovered during needs analysis that the bulk of accuracy issues were related to the panel reports. During a review of extant data and interviews with the data analyst who produces the reports, the team discovered the following:

Panel Accuracy: 33 percent of the panel accuracy errors occurred at the end of a physician's report. Each physician's report is organized alphabetically by patient and the data sorting process was not inserting a break at the right place in the report.

- The data analyst was not aware of what aspect of the report query was causing this to happen.

Service Accuracy: Where physicians noted that a service had already been completed (and, therefore, was inaccurate), 51 percent of these services were completed prior to the date that the reports were executed.

- Further analysis of the process demonstrated that the report period was limited to the end of the prior quarter because this is when the database is considered most accurate; however, 40 percent of these services were available in the database when the reports were executed but were excluded from the reports by the data report period constraints.

Panel Accuracy Root Cause	Knowledge, Resources (Process)
Service Accuracy Root Cause	Resources (Process)

Indicator 2: Timeliness of Reporting

The team had already determined that reports were distributed sporadically and that the distribution cycle far exceeded industry standards and stakeholder expectations. Through interviews with senior leaders and their front-line staff, the secretary pool that collates the reports, and a time study/observation, the team observed the following:

- *Distribution Frequency:* Departments that contribute to the quarterly report have a high level of accountability for their individual tasks in the process, but are unaware of the expectations of senior leaders and the recipients of the reports. Furthermore, departments do not communicate during the process, and few participants have even seen the final product that is mailed to physicians. Senior leaders comment that departments ought to experience more accountability.
- *Distribution Cycle:* The primary task that is impacting the duration of the cycle is when the secretary pool prepares reports for mailing (thirty-two days). Upon observation, it

was discovered that this task required rework and reprinting due to errors. Collation is complicated due to special arrangements with individual networks, and the secretary pool is completing these in addition to regular and unrelated tasks.

Summary

As a result of the gap and cause analyses phases, a compendium of interventions was identified and implemented. Many of these interventions focused on process redesign, assignment of tasks, and communication of expected timelines. Due to the scale of change that was required, the team executed a number of balancing interventions to support the management of these changes as well.

■   ■   ■

Lessons Learned from the Case

- The major lessons learned in this project highlight the importance of gap analysis in a successful performance improvement project.
- In this case, the method employed for establishing current performance was also a key aspect of the cause analysis.
- The time study not only documented the current process but also revealed that the bulk of the timeline was devoted to one task, making it a prime opportunity for intervention.
- Moreover, the process stakeholders were engaged in studying the process as it existed, so that when it came time to intervene, they were not only involved in the implementation of interventions, but also in their design.
- Finally, shortcomings of the analysis phase can be leveraged and overcome. For example, the survey of physicians related to report accuracy yielded a fairly low return. Therefore, the team elected to follow up extensively with those who responded and on complaints received about the reports.
- After in-depth review of a few of the inaccuracies, the solution to the problems with report accuracy turned out to be a simple change to the report programming. This helped to illustrate that the rigor of analysis does not always depend on mountains of data, but rather on the thoroughness and suitability of the questions asked.

Citations

1. American Academy of Family Physicians. *Physician Profiling Guiding Principles*, March 1999. Retrieved from www.aafp.org/x6972.xml February 10, 2005.
2. Development and Use of Physician Profiles. Retrieved from www.ama-assn.org/apps/pf_new/pf_online?f_n=browse&doc=policyfiles/HnE/H-406.993.HTM February 10, 2005.
3. HealthLeaders Fact File, "Know Thy Physicians." July 2004. Retrieved from www.medstat.com/healthcare/jul04.pdf February 10, 2005.

4. Chevalier, R. Updating the Behavior Engineering Model. Retrieved from www.pignc-ispi.com/articles/Vol42_05_08.pdf February 28, 2005.

Hillary N. Leigh, M.A., is a senior consultant with Kaiser Permanente. Hillary has a master's degree in performance improvement and instructional design from the University of Michigan–Dearborn. She is a doctoral candidate at Wayne State University's Instructional Technology Program with an emphasis in human performance. She can be reached at 626.405.6237 or Hillary.N.Leigh@kp.org.

SECTION 3
INTERVENTION SELECTION, DESIGN, AND DEVELOPMENT

"USING DYNAMITE AS A BATON HAS DRAMATICALLY IMPROVED THEIR TIME."

Intervention
Selection

9

Intervention selection is an integral part of the performance improvement phase that also includes intervention design, intervention development, and producing a business case. The Performance Improvement/HPT Model (Figure 9.1) illustrates where intervention selection is positioned in the performance improvement process.

Performance improvement is complex because it involves many uncertainties, such as individual human behavior, collective organizational behavior, and the dynamics of the internal and external environment. Almost anything can influence behavior: culture, leadership, workspace design, supervision, communication, financial systems, motivation, strategic and operational planning, or skills, attitudes, and knowledge. In turn, an infinite range of performance improvement interventions exists. Creativity and "out-of-the box" thinking can lead to selecting intervention solutions that match the culture and goals of the organization.

There is an old tale about an operations manager who needed help with a performance problem, and so he brought in a wide range of consultants. The accounting expert recommended an accounting intervention to solve the problem. The product engineering expert recommended product redesign. The process improvement specialist recommended a process change. The performance improvement practitioner, who did not come in with a bias for any particular solution, proposed a structured process, using the Performance Improvement/HPT Model, for validating the problem, determining the root cause, and identifying a range of potential solutions prior to make a selection decision.[1] The performance intervention selection phase as presented in the Performance Improvement/HPT Model (Figure 1.5) and the example above structures and reinforces the performance improvement process and, in turn, depends on collaboration and openness to new ideas for its success.

Definitions and Scope

Before beginning a discussion of how to conduct intervention selection, it is important to make sure the author and the readers are on the same page. Therefore, the terms *interventions* and *intervention selection* both need to be clarified.

Interventions. Interventions are deliberate, conscious acts that facilitate change in performance. They are measures that are planned, selected, and designed to solve workplace problems or address promising opportunities and challenges.

Some interventions are change efforts that are long-term, evolutionary, and progressive.[2] They are targeted to organizations, departments, work groups, and individuals. Interventions are "the kinds

FIGURE 9.1. Performance Improvement/HPT Model: Intervention Selection Component

Performance Improvement/HPT Model: Intervention Selection Component

Change Management

Performance Analysis of Need or Opportunity

Organizational Analysis
- Vision, Mission, Values
- Goals and Strategies
- Critical Issues

Environmental Analysis
- World (Culture, Society, Social Responsibility)
- Workplace (Organization, Resources, Tools, Stakeholders, Competition)
- Work (Work Flow, Procedure, Responsibilities, Ergonomics)
- Worker (Knowledge, Skill, Capacity, Motivation, Expectations)

Desired Performance

Gap Analysis

Actual Performance

Cause Analysis
- **Environmental Factors**
  - Data Information
  - Feedback
  - Environment Supports, Resources, and Tools
  - Consequences, Incentives, or Rewards
- **Individual Factors**
  - Skills and Knowledge
  - Individual Capacity
  - Motivation and Expectations

Intervention Selection, Design, and Development

Interventions
- Learning
- Performance Support
- Job Analysis/Work Design
- Personal Development
- Human Resource Development
- Organizational Communication
- Organizational Design and Development
- Financial Systems
- Other…

Business Case
- Leadership Commitment
- Feasibility
- Sustainability

Intervention Implementation and Maintenance

Techniques
- Partnering, Networking, and Alliance Building
- Process Consulting
- Employee Development
- Communication
- Project Management
- Other…

Evaluation

Formative (Level 0) evaluation of inputs-process-outputs of
- Performance Analysis
- Selection Design Development
- Implementation, Maintenance

Summative (Levels 1–2) evaluation of immediate
- Reaction;
- Knowledge/skills/attitude change
- Application

Confirmative (Levels 3–5) evaluation of sustainable
- Effectiveness
- Efficiency
- Impact
- Value

Meta Evaluation/Validation of
- Formative, Summative, Confirmative inputs-processes-outputs
- Success stories
- Lessons learned

Change Management

196

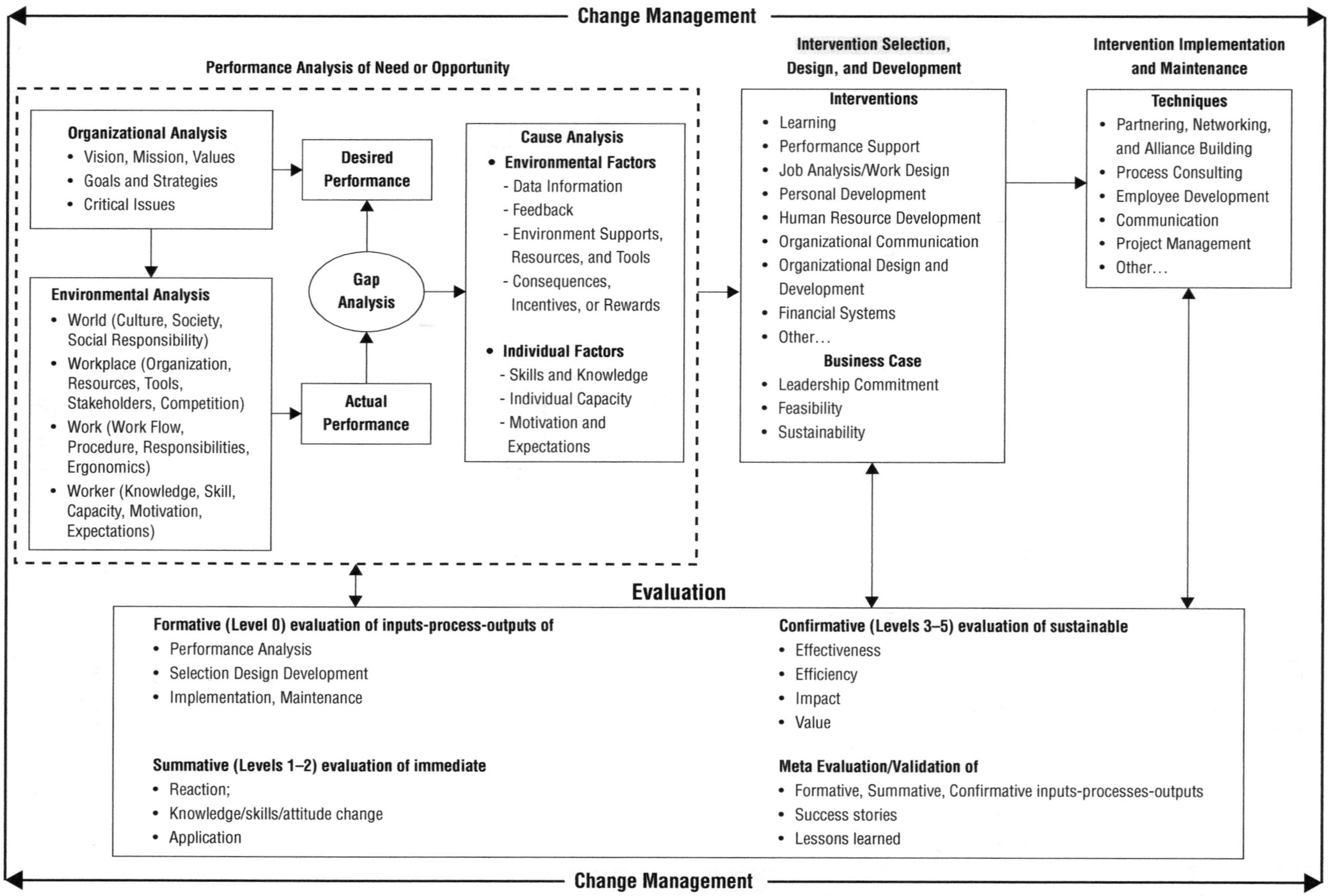

of things you can do to bring about changes in job performance."[3] An intervention is "another name for a solution or set of solutions, usually a combination of tools and techniques that clearly and directly relate to solving a performance gap or implementing an organizational change."[4]

However, they are defined, interventions run the gamut from large-scale organizational change efforts to individual or small group efforts. Large-scale initiatives affect entire organizational systems at local, national, and global levels; more modest interventions include ergonomic changes that provide comfort from repetitive stress syndrome to performance support tools, which remind, aid, or assist workers to evaluate and do work.

Langdon[5] also considers types of performance change that are required prior to intervention selection. There are interventions such as mentoring, modeling, training, and so forth, that establish performance; business planning, coaching, feedback, and other interventions that improve performance; interventions such as compensation, performance standards, work schedules, and so forth that maintain performance; and outsourcing, withholding rewards, withholding information, and other interventions that extinguish performance.

Finally, one single performance problem or gap may require more than one intervention. For example, resistance to using new software can be caused by software glitches, learning time, and memory requirements and require multiple interventions such as continuous improvement of the software, help systems, feedback, rewards, performance support, and coaching. Usually, organizations will choose several interventions to resolve the many aspects of the problem. The interventions are then *blended* or integrated so they work together as a unit. Blended solutions can be phased in at separate times or used concurrently.

Intervention Selection. Intervention selection is the process of identifying and recommending the most appropriate activities to successfully resolve a performance improvement problem, opportunity, or challenge. The intervention selection process helps manage and simplify the selection effort so that interventions may be selected, planned, and implemented carefully.

Usually, there is a formal or informal diagnosis phase to determine and gain consensus regarding the workplace situation. Using sound selection methods is actually more important than simply getting the right "answer." Group involvement and group commitment to the ultimate decision will minimize conflict and resistance later during implementation. Performance improvement practitioners normally facilitate this selection process because they have experience and expertise in performance improvement. The selection team and the practitioner collaborate to identify the best interventions.

There is no easy method for selecting possible interventions or solutions to performance problems or opportunities. The intervention selection process is divided into preliminary, survey, and selection phases to keep tasks manageable. The techniques and tools described in this chapter are designed to simplify and structure the selection tasks. In addition, possible interventions are clustered into categories to demonstrate the relationship between interventions: learning, performance support, job analysis and work design, personal development, human resource development, organizational communication, organizational design and development, and financial systems. Categories and subcategories of interventions will be described later in this section.

Purpose. The major goal or purpose of the intervention selection process is to identify and recommend the most appropriate performance improvement intervention(s) to resolve the problem. Other goals include selecting an intervention(s) that has strong employee and management commitment, is feasible in terms of resource allocation and environmental issues, and is sustainable throughout the cycle of need. People need to believe the selected interventions are likely to solve or alleviate the problems and improve organizational or individual performance.

Collaborative Approach to Selection

The recommended way to select a performance improvement intervention is to use the team approach. The performance improvement practitioner collaborates with the intervention champion(s) and other stakeholders in a team effort to select the most effective and feasible intervention for the given situation.

Practitioner Roles and Competencies

Intervention selection is one of the core capabilities required of successful performance improvement practitioners. Practitioners must be able to go beyond common sense. First, they must know the wide range of possible interventions that are available and/or where to locate experts and resources for more information; second, they must be able to align their recommendation with the results of the performance analysis; third, they must be able to select the intervention(s) that are most feasible and sustainable in the given situation; and fourth, they must be able to communicate their recommendation in a way that builds on and ensures stakeholder commitment.

Hutchison and Stein[6] and Hutchison and Carleton[7] did extensive research on performance improvement practitioner competencies and view the practitioner as "generalists" who must be:

- Expert in fifteen to twenty-five interventions across broad classes,
- Have a working knowledge of forty-five to seventy-five interventions across the classes, and
- Know the basic tenets or principles in more than half the interventions, as well as how to contact the experts or access the resources related to the interventions.

These may appear to be extremely difficult competencies; however, Hutchison and Stein add: "We stand by these numbers because both of us have significantly exceeded them and we do not believe that we are uniquely capable. Many of our colleagues have also exceeded these specifications."[8]

Stakeholder Roles

Successful implementation of performance interventions also depends on strong stakeholder support, carefully appointed team members, good decision making, and determined change-management leadership during both the selection and implementation phases. Collaboration and commitment are especially vital to the success of the selection process.

Champion Roles

Champions are committed to performance improvement. People need to believe the selected interventions are likely to solve or alleviate the problems and improve organizational or individual performance. The support of a champion is essential for creating and sustaining commitment. The champion should have a fairly high level of function, such as a senior executive. Steady, consistent backing of the project is essential. If not, change efforts eventually fizzle and have minimal impact. The role of the champion is to:

- Set direction and establish authority and responsibility,
- Lend credibility and clout,
- Rally senior executives,
- Alleviate concerns and resistance,
- Maintain a high profile commitment to the change effort, and
- Support the team through difficulties.

Team Roles

Teams of stakeholders can offer both commitment to performance improvement and help in determining the most appropriate interventions. Interventions usually have a substantial impact on the affected organization. Therefore, it is essential to have broad acceptance and support for any improvement activity. Creating a team to select potential interventions helps to ensure that there is a broad base of support. In addition, team members can provide different perspectives and ideas that can enrich the group's decisions.

The intervention selection process should be structured so that the ideas of all team members are valued and considered. It is equally important that the teams be cross-functional to ensure a diversity of experiences and ideas needed to harness the creative forces within the organization. Teams should include representatives from the departments involved in the problem. Some representatives should be enthusiastic and energetic supporters of change and some should be more reserved and tend to ask "tough questions." There should also be cross-departmental involvement from areas that provide or receive associated output and may be affected by the interventions.

Timing

When do performance improvement practitioners begin the intervention selection process? They begin after a solid performance analysis. "If you do not accurately and completely define the performance gap, you cannot hope to select all the needed interventions."[9] The performance improvement practitioner needs to identify the gaps in performance and the kinds of performance changes that are indicated by the gaps. "It is critical in intervention selection that you first determine, as part of the performance analysis, what the various changes in performance will be. When the analysis is structured to reveal the various elements of the performance, greater accuracy in the selection of interventions will be ensured for each performance change."[10]

Introduction to the Intervention Selection Process

Selecting the most appropriate performance improvement interventions(s) for an organization requires a systematic approach. The three phases and seven major steps of the performance intervention selection process are mapped in Figure 9.2. The steps in the Preliminary Phase may overlap the Analysis Phase as the performance improvement practitioner and stakeholders determine or confirm the performance gap and its cause(s) and either moves directly to the Survey Phase or prioritizes gaps and causes before beginning the Survey Phase. During the Survey Phase the practitioner and stakeholders identify and prioritize potential interventions and then move on to the Selection Phase to select the most appropriate intervention(s) and plan next steps.

Preliminary Phase

The Preliminary Phase sets the stage for selecting interventions. Intervention selection depends on reliable performance and cause analyses. It is essential to have agreement on what the problems are and what causes the problems. If formal analyses already are completed, the intervention selection team needs to concur that the findings and recommendations are valid. Analysis data are a powerful resource for decision making.

If no formal performance gap and cause analyses were conducted, the team should at least conduct an analysis or facilitate discussion and come to agreement about performance problems,

FIGURE 9.2.   Intervention Selection Process

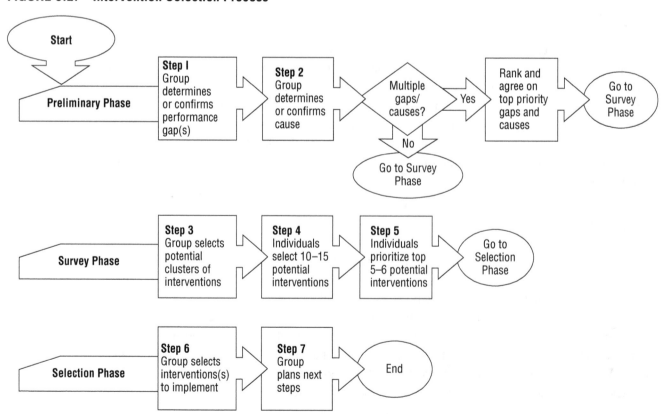

gaps, and causes before the intervention selection process begins. There is a great advantage to conducting a structured analysis of performance including organizational, environmental, gap, and cause analyses prior to selecting interventions. Section 2 in this volume provides information about performance analyses.

If there are multiple problems, it is necessary to rank the problems according to pre-selected criteria; for example: Which problem has the most impact on the bottom line? Which problem can be fixed in the shortest time and for the least expenditure of resources? Usually, the criteria can be developed from the results of the performance analysis, especially the organizational and environmental analyses.

The purpose of the Preliminary Phase is to focus attention on the performance problem(s) and the cause(s), rather than the symptoms. Interventions based on symptoms may temporarily improve a situation, but the underlying problem remains. In order to make headway and to be effective, it is necessary to select interventions that will alleviate or improve causes of poor performance and benefit both the worker and the organization.

Steps 1 and 2: Validate and/or Conduct Performance Gap and Cause Analysis

It is necessary to have a good grasp of the performance gap and its causes before beginning to think about solutions. In fact, Rummler suggests that "performance consultant 'right stuff' includes, among other things, remaining solution-neutral."[11]

Validate Performance Gap and Cause. If the intervention selection team did not participate in the original performance analysis, the team needs to validate the analysis results as Step 1 in the intervention selection process. In the preferred scenario, a performance improvement practitioner facilitates the process of validating the performance gaps, and causes that surfaced during the performance analysis. In other cases, quality teams or performance improvement teams validate the analysis using quality or group process tools to validate the analysis.

Without a clear consensus on the problem and its cause, it is difficult to agree on solutions or their implementation. It is too easy to put energy into efforts that miss the mark. These failed attempts cause discouragement in the workforce and lead to loss of credibility and trust for senior management and the improvement team.

Focus on Causes. A cause is the underlying issue or opportunity that triggers the need for performance improvement. A symptom is the presenting characteristic. When the performance improvement effort eliminates a symptom, another one usually crops up.

When the performance improvement effort focuses on the cause, the underlying problems are usually resolved. A symptom, such as absenteeism, is usually caused by an unsatisfactory culture or an undesirable supervisor, and so forth. Threatening dire consequences for one more absence may alleviate the absenteeism but that does not deal with the undesirable supervisor. In order to make headway and to be effective, it is necessary to focus attention on the most important causes and select interventions that will alleviate or improve causes to benefit workforce performance.

TABLE 9.1.   Summary of Gap and Cause Analysis Conducted *After* Intervention Implementation

Activity	Results
Gap Analysis	Although employees attended training, they resist using new software and prefer the previous or legacy systems.
Cause Analysis	1. There are a few software glitches and employees do not know how to overcome them.
	2. New software system takes longer to use at first (time to proficiency) and managers push for speed.
	3. Employees can't remember all the steps and using the documentation is awkward on their desks.
Intervention Selection	Cause: Glitches in the software
	Interventions:
	• Continuous Improvement–To remove glitches
	• Help System–To communicate glitches and offer solutions
	• Cause: Time to proficiency
	Interventions:
	• Feedback–Managers stress importance of using new software to generate reports and so forth
	• Reward–Token of appreciation for efforts to become proficient in use of new software
	• Cause: Documentation problems
	Interventions:
	• Performance Support–Small spiral notebook containing key steps only
	• Coaching–Readily available resource person to help employees with initial usage

Conduct an Analysis. There are two instances when the intervention selection team may need to *conduct* a performance analysis during the preliminary intervention selection phase:

- A performance analysis has not been conducted prior to intervention selection, or
- The gap and cause were not validated during the preliminary intervention selection phase and/or a *new* performance problem(s) surfaces during design, development, or implementation of the intervention.

Consider the situation of employees who were reluctant to use new customized software *after* they began using it on the job. The software was designed based on a performance analysis to make their jobs easier and to improve accuracy. There is plenty of work, so there is no fear of job loss to technology and automation. Yet, after training, employees still prefer the old system. Whether this problem was caused by failure to validate the original performance analysis prior to selecting the new software or it was a new performance problem, the selection team conducted a new gap and cause analysis and the results are summarized in Table 9.1.

Survey Phase

The Survey Phase of the Intervention Selection Process includes Steps 3 through 5. Each step requires creativity and a willingness to try new strategies. During Step 3, the group, with a team leader or performance improvement practitioner, reads through the possible interventions listed on Performance Support Tool 9.1 and discusses possibilities. During Steps 4 and 5 of the Survey

PERFORMANCE SUPPORT TOOL 9.1. INTERVENTION SELECTOR

Directions: Identify a maximum of ten to fifteen possible interventions and rank or prioritize the following interventions.

LEARNING INTERVENTIONS

- ❏ Knowledge Management
- ❏ Organizational Learning
- ❏ Learning Management System
- ❏ Content Management System
- ❏ Education/Training
- ❏ Self-Directed Learning
- ❏ On-the-Job Learning
- ❏ Just-in-Time Learning
- ❏ Action Learning
- ❏ Blended Learning
- ❏ Technical and Non-Technical Learning
- ❏ Social Learning
- ❏ Interactive Learning Technologies
- ❏ Enterprise Learning
- ❏ Classroom Learning
- ❏ Distance/Distributed Learning
- ❏ Online/e-Learning
- ❏ Wikis, Avatars, and More
- ❏ Games/Simulations

PERFORMANCE SUPPORT INTERVENTIONS

- ❏ Performance Support Tools (PSTs) or Job Aids
- ❏ Electronic Performance Support Systems (EPSS)
- ❏ Documentation and Standards
- ❏ Expert Systems

JOB ANALYSIS/WORK DESIGN INTERVENTIONS

Job Analysis
- ❏ Job Descriptions
- ❏ Job Specifications

(Continued)

Work Design

- ❏ Job Design
- ❏ Job Enlargement
- ❏ Job Rotation
- ❏ Job Enrichment
- ❏ Reengineering, Realignment, Restructuring

Human Factors

- ❏ Ergonomics
- ❏ Safety Engineering
- ❏ Security Management
- ❏ Green Workplace

Quality Improvement

- ❏ Total Quality Management (TQM)
- ❏ Continuous Improvement
- ❏ Preventive Maintenance (PM)
- ❏ Six Sigma
- ❏ Lean Organizations

PERSONAL DEVELOPMENT INTERVENTIONS

- ❏ Feedback
- ❏ Coaching
- ❏ Mentoring
- ❏ Emotional Intelligence
- ❏ Social Intelligence
- ❏ Cultural Intelligence
- ❏ Communities of Professional Practice

HUMAN RESOURCE DEVELOPMENT (HRD) INTERVENTIONS

Talent Management

- ❏ Staffing
- ❏ Employee Development
- ❏ Retention
- ❏ Compensation/Benefits

(Continued)

- ❏ Health and Wellness
- ❏ Retirement Planning
- ❏ Labor Relations

Individual Growth

- ❏ Motivation
- ❏ Performance Management
- ❏ Key Performance Indicators (KPIs)
- ❏ Performance Appraisals
- ❏ 360-Degree Appraisals
- ❏ Competencies
- ❏ Competency Testing

Organizational Growth

- ❏ Succession Planning
- ❏ Career Pathing
- ❏ Leadership Development
- ❏ Executive Development
- ❏ Management Development
- ❏ Supervisory Development

ORGANIZATIONAL COMMUNICATION INTERVENTIONS

- ❏ Communication Networks
- ❏ Information Systems
- ❏ Suggestion Systems
- ❏ Grievance Systems
- ❏ Dispute Resolution
- ❏ Social Media

ORGANIZATIONAL DESIGN AND DEVELOPMENT INTERVENTIONS

Empowerment

- ❏ Team Strategies
- ❏ Virtual Teams
- ❏ Problem Solving

(Continued)

Organizational Pro-Action

- ❏ Strategic Planning
- ❏ Environmental Scanning
- ❏ Appreciative Inquiry
- ❏ Outsourcing
- ❏ Benchmarking
- ❏ Balanced Scorecard
- ❏ Dashboards

Organizational Values

- ❏ Culture
- ❏ Diversity
- ❏ Inclusion Strategies
- ❏ Globalization
- ❏ Localization
- ❏ Social Responsibility
- ❏ Ethics
- ❏ Decision Making

FINANCIAL SYSTEMS INTERVENTIONS

- ❏ Open Book Management
- ❏ Profit Versus Cost Center
- ❏ Financial Forecasting
- ❏ Capital Investment and Spending
- ❏ Cash Flow Analysis
- ❏ Cash Flow Forecast
- ❏ Mergers, Acquisitions, Joint Ventures

Phase, each team member reads the survey descriptors individually and reflects on a maximum of ten to fifteen possible interventions.

Each team member relies on personal experience and judgment to independently select potential interventions and prioritize them according to pre-selected criteria. The Survey Phase should be completed as a facilitated group activity or it may be done privately on an individual basis. In either case, there should not be any external influence on the process beyond the members of the intervention selection team.

Step 3: Group Selects Potential Interventions

With the performance improvement practitioner or team leader, the team may be able to choose the most likely categories (such as financial systems or personal development) to focus on by using Performance Support Tool 9.4. Intervention Selector Tool. When in doubt, it is best not to eliminate any potential categories as an opportunity for performance improvement. Thinking creatively at this point may provide the greatest leverage and opportunity for successful results.

It is impossible to identify a definitive list of interventions that would fit all circumstances. The Intervention Selection Tool records a listing suggested by the authors and other performance improvement experts based on empirical observation and/or experience. The interventions selected for this edition have been refined or restructured from the previous editions of the book or added as new. They reflect what is happening in the field at this moment in time as well as point to what may happen in the future.

Chapters 10 through 17 provide definitions, scope, and workplace implementation suggestions for the interventions listed in the Intervention Selector. Definitions for each intervention are also in the Glossary. After the participants select possible categories, the practitioner makes sure that everyone on the team understands the meaning of each intervention in the category. Some interventions will be familiar and others will be less common.

Step 4: Individuals Select Potential Interventions

Each participant reads the descriptors for the selected categories in the Intervention Selector. Each individual team member selects ten to fifteen potential interventions.

Step 5: Individuals Prioritize Potential Interventions

Finally, participants individually prioritize the possible interventions (see Performance Support Tool 9.2). The outcome of the individual activity is a prioritized list of approximately five to six interventions that the group can work with during Step 6 of the Selection Phase. The activity also clarifies how each person describes the interventions he or she selected.

PERFORMANCE SUPPORT TOOL 9.2. INTERVENTION PRIORITY CHART

Directions: After reflection, select six interventions from the ten to fifteen interventions you checked on the Intervention Selector that you believe to be the *most* feasible solutions for the identified performance gap and cause. Enter the name of the intervention next to the priority number that you would assign to the intervention (6 = highest priority to 1 = lowest priority). If you select fewer than six interventions, you should still begin with six and leave the lower numbers blank. (See the example below.)

After you have prioritized the interventions use Column 3 to briefly describe each intervention in your own words.

Priority (6 to 1)	Intervention	Personal Description of Intervention
6 (Example)	Coaching	Readily available resource person to help employees with initial usage
6		
5		
4		
3		
2		
1		

Selection Phase

The Selection Phase requires group involvement. The Survey Phase was primarily an individual effort; it is now necessary to come together as a group to make a final intervention(s) selection and determine next steps.

Group acceptance and support are necessary in order to make changes in people, processes, or the organization. Group involvement assures that many ideas are included and that any decisions have collaboration and participation from diverse areas and levels of the organization. Diversity is critical for bringing all the potential issues to the discussion table before implementation. In addition, team decisions can serve as communication mechanisms so that the entire affected organization feels a sense of participation.

The team uses brainstorming and multi-voting to select the intervention(s) that best resolves the performance problem or potential opportunities. Then the team participates in an action planning activity to plan next steps.

Step 6: Group Selects Intervention(s) to Implement

During Step 6 team members brainstorm and discuss their own opinions and judgments about prioritizing the possible interventions. Then the group uses multi-voting to reach a consensus.

Brainstorming. The performance improvement practitioner or team leader will facilitate a group discussion of the individual priority lists gathered during the survey phase. Using brainstorming techniques, each team member discusses his or her highest or sixth priority intervention using a round-robin format. All team ideas are recorded.

After the first round, each team member discusses his or her own intervention selection in the fifth position. This continues downward to the lowest. Although there may be substantial redundancy in the interventions discussed, each team member has a unique reason for making the selection. Therefore, each intervention needs to be discussed relative to the reason why each person selected it.

Multi-Voting. Each intervention selection team member should review his or her personal priorities based on the team discussion. The PI practitioner or team leader will establish the multi-voting process.

Multi-voting means that each team member has a few votes so there is no need to choose only one possible intervention. Depending on the size of the team and the number of potential interventions, multi-voting should allow approximately one-third of the possibilities. For example, if there are twelve potential interventions, then each team member would have four votes. Each team member can cast all votes for one choice or spread out their choices over four different interventions. Teams sometimes use sticky dots or felt pens on flip-chart paper. At this point it may be possible to see clear agreements. These should be confirmed through group decisions. If there are not clear indications, the team should discuss the voting results. A second voting may be needed to narrow down the top selections. This second vote should result in clear priorities so that action planning can begin.

Selecting Successful Interventions

Here are some general suggestions for selecting successful interventions:

1. Base decisions on a comprehensive understanding of the situation. This is where previous performance and cause analysis efforts come together.
2. Target the right people, in the right setting, and at the right time.
3. Have a sponsor who will champion the activity.
4. Use a team approach; draw upon expertise from all areas in the company.
5. Include cost and be value sensitive.
6. Meet comprehensive, prioritized requirements, based on what is most important.
7. Investigate a variety of intervention options because a new intervention can be costly to develop.
8. Consider long-term versus short-term effectiveness. Use multiple strategies to effect change. Interventions should be sufficiently powerful.
9. Thought must be given to institutionalizing the intervention over time and engraining it in the organization's culture. Interventions should be sustainable.
10. Keep viability of development and implementation in mind. An intervention needs human resources and organizational support, and it must be cost and value effective.[12]

Step 7: Group Plans Next Steps

The final step in the Selection Phase is to scope out action plans and reasonable timelines for implementation and change management. Exact plans and timelines may be refined later during actual implementation planning. Substantial planning is important because interventions should be scoped out and managed in the same way as projects are scoped and managed.

The performance improvement practitioner or team leader frames a context to support the team in making sound design, development, and implementation decisions. The intervention selection group needs to think about the organizational culture and history of related change efforts. Interventions need to fit into the mission, vision, goals, and strategic thinking and planning of the organization and be planned in context with other initiatives.

It is not sufficient to simply select interventions. The team needs to describe the process for others to hear. Using Performance Support Tool 9.3, the team also needs to provide ideas, steps, and examples for how to actually implement the interventions. This is not the time for complex and detailed planning. It is simply a method for capturing the team's discussions and the reasoning behind the decisions sufficiently so that people assigned to implementation will know the basis for the priorities.

The performance improvement practitioner or team leader frames a context to support the team in making sound decisions. The intervention selection group needs to think about the organizational culture and history of related change efforts. Interventions need to fit into the mission, vision, goals, and strategic thinking and planning of the organization and be planned in context with other initiatives.

In addition, the intervention selection team creates potential timetables that can be used by senior executives for endorsement and sanction. They can also be used to communicate intervention decisions to all employees so that everyone feels part of any change process.

Citations

1. Van Tiem, Moseley, & Dessinger, 2004, p. 2
2. Rothwell, 1996, p. 79
3. Carr, 1994, p. 65
4. Biech, 2008, p. 873
5. Langdon, 1999, p. 22
6. Hutchison & Stein, 1998, pp. 18–19
7. Hutchison & Carleton, 1991
8. Hutchison & Stein, 1998, p. 19
9. Langdon, 1999, p. 15
10. Langdon, 1999, p. 19
11. Rummler, 2007, p. 8
12. Spitzer, 1999

References

Biech, E. (Ed.) (2008). *ASTD handbook for workplace learning professionals*. Alexandria, VA: American Society for Training & Development.

Carr, C. (1994). Invasion of the performance interventions. *Training, 31*(4), 65–66.

Hutchison, C.S., & Carleton, J.R. (1991). Potential strategies and tactics for performance improvement. (Unpublished working document). Conifer, CO: Conifer Consulting.

Hutchison, C.S., & Stein, F.S. (1998). A whole new world of interventions: The performance technologist as integrating generalist. *Performance Improvement, 37*(5), 18–19.

Langdon, D.C. (1999). Selecting interventions. In D.G. Langdon, K.S. Whiteside, & M.M. McKenna (Eds.), *Intervention resource guide: 50 performance improvement tools* (pp. 15–22). San Francisco: Pfeiffer.

Rothwell, W.J. (1996). *ASTD models for human performance improvement: Roles, competencies, and outputs.* Alexandria, VA: American Society for Training & Development.

Rummler, G.A. (2007). *Serious performance consulting: According to Rummler.* San Francisco: Pfeiffer/ISPI.

Spitzer, D.R. (1999). The design and development of high-impact interventions. In H.S. Stolovitch & E.J. Keeps (Eds.), *Handbook of human performance technology* (2nd ed.) (pp. 173–180). San Francisco: Pfeiffer/ISPI.

Van Tiem, D.M., Moseley, J.L., & Dessinger, J.C. (2004). *Fundamentals of performance technology: A guide to improving people, process, and performance* (2nd ed.) Silver Spring, MD: International Society for Performance Improvement.

PERFORMANCE SUPPORT TOOL 9.3. INTERVENTION ACTION PLANNER

Intervention Title: _____   PT Practitioner or Team Leader: _____

Project Sponsor: _____   Preparer: _____

Intervention Purpose and Objectives: _____
_____
_____

Project Stakeholders (Direct and Indirect): _____
_____
_____

Customer Expectations and Deliverables: _____
_____
_____

Possible Timetable and Anticipated Constraints: _____
_____
_____

Reviews and Approvals Required: _____
_____
_____

Estimated Budget Requirements: _____
_____
_____

Lessons Learned (from Successes and Failures) from previous performance improvement efforts: _____
_____
_____
_____
_____
_____
_____
_____

PERFORMANCE SUPPORT TOOL 9.4. INTERVENTION SELECTION TOOL

Purpose: The purpose of this tool is to help groups or individuals select *possible* interventions that meet the needs of their organization and improve performance. For additional information about the complete selection process and each intervention, see Chapters 9 through 17.

Content: All the interventions from the Intervention Selector (Performance Support Tool 9.1) are described in the Selection Tool. Each intervention is described by a *best practice example statement*. Although the statement represents best *common* practice, it does *not* represent the *only possible* best practice.

Below each best practice statement are qualifying descriptions or characteristics that may indicate whether an organization is ready or not ready for successful implementation of the intervention. The qualifiers represent a continuum of factors that may result in good to poor implementation. Again, they are by no means the *only* examples of qualifiers that may affect successful implementation.

Directions: Rate your organization based on your personal opinions, experience, and judgment. Read each best practice statement and the qualifying descriptions. Decide which description best characterizes or represents your organization. Circle the appropriate rating number.

LEARNING INTERVENTIONS

Forward-thinking organizations integrate learning and doing to help obtain the knowledge or skill they need to initiate new performance or improve existing performance. They support the performer on the job and just in time and may replace or enhance training.

Learning helps initiate new performance or change actual performance until that performance is equal to or better than the desired performance.

❏ *Knowledge Management (KM):* Organization systematically identifies, captures, codifies, stores, transforms, disseminates, and shares knowledge and encourages people to use their collective knowledge and experience to foster business innovation (creativity) and competitive advantage.

1	2	3	4	5	6
Organization has no process in place to manage collective knowledge or create and share knowledge.		Organization uses technology to share and integrates existing knowledge to enable individual learning.			Organization recognizes importance of existing knowledge, technology, and learning but focuses on people creating and sharing new knowledge.

(Continued)

❑ ***Organizational Learning:*** Organizations as entities can learn. They function effectively, efficiently, and provide value to customers through the goods and services they offer. Organizational learning focuses on Senge's core disciplines which permit an organization to function as a learning organization.

1	2	3	4	5	6
Limited effort and time spent on how individuals, teams and organizations learn; low tolerance for risk taking		Emphasis on organizations that function effectively, efficiently, and provide value; some emphasis on encouraging employees to strive for and maintain their full potential			Viewed as a continuous process within an organization; learning results when it is tied to the strategic objectives of the organization and is targeted at performance improvement

❑ ***Learning Management System (LMS):*** The organization fully utilizes an LMS to provide information to employees allowing the system and the employee to manage learning and reporting.

1	2	3	4	5	6
The organization has all instructor-led updates and training opportunities, with practice experience coming solely from the job functions		The organization has both LMS and instructor-led training but provides limited practice experience outside job functionality			The organization uses LMS training and updating systems that provide automated, measurable practice experience which can be changed, tracked, managed, and reported

❑ ***Content Management System (CMS):*** The organization actively uses appropriate software to provide management and structure to its data, information, and content.

1	2	3	4	5	6
The organization has no concrete way to manage its content, data, and information		The organization has a CMS but used limitedly (limited employee inclusion, and limited data management)			The organization uses a CMS fully and functionally throughout all levels of the enterprise to store, manage, and widely deliver data, information, and electronic content

❑ ***Education and Training:*** Organization uses education and training to enhance and enable employee learning and development. The use of interactive learning technologies involve the learner and supports just-in-time and just-for-me learning. Emphasis on education and training help organizations achieve goals of employee retention and competitive advantage.

1	2	3	4	5	6
Organization does not value, support, or reward education or training		Organizations sometimes encourages members to obtain education but may not support it, may or may not provide training for members, or does not reward education or training			Organization values, supports, rewards education and training for all members

(Continued)

❑ *Self-Directed Learning:* Learners take initiative to increase their knowledge and skill bases with new information and avenues to advance quality of life.

1	2	3	4	5	6
Learner not inclined to be self-directed; acquires knowledge and skills through formal means		Learner acquires knowledge and/or skills through formal means; little opportunities for diagnosing and formulating learning needs; some evidence of being proactive learner			Learner takes initiative for acquiring and managing knowledge and/or skills; can be informal, for example, reading a magazine article or formal, such as enrolling in a university course

❑ *On-the-Job Learning:* Process for increasing learners' competencies while working; can be formal or informal; can occur consciously or unconsciously. Easy to integrate; saves both time and money.

1	2	3	4	5	6
Learner has to wait for professional development, workshops or training to become competent in daily work related tasks		Limited opportunities provided for on the job learning; learner gains competencies in work-related tasks after occasional evaluation			Learner is able to instantly increase competencies while working with new knowledge and/or skills applied and integrated immediately on the job

❑ *Just-in-Time Learning:* Learning or training that occurs at either precisely the time the worker needs to apply the learning or training or at the time the learning or training are being utilized for reinforcement of the worker's new skill set or knowledge application.

1	2	3	4	5	6
A learn-and-do intervention without management assistance for design and development of necessary learning		Relevant and effective flexible learning and training that reinforce the integration of workplace learning and performance using a systematic approach			Learning or training that is timely and important and reflects "need to know" rather than "nice to know," resulting in "just the right amount of training"

❑ *Action Learning:* The organization uses small groups to solve real, relevant, and challenging organizational problems and encourages learning by doing. Members of the group share, question, experience, reflect, make decisions, and take action on a single project basis or as an open group.

1	2	3	4	5	6
Organization does not accept or does not use action learning to solve problems		Organization does not consistently use action learning to solve problems or does not always accept outcomes of action learning			Organization shows desire, knowledge, and ability to create a shared vision through action learning

(Continued)

❏ *Blended Learning:* Organization uses a mixed model of learning employing many different technologies to deliver learning and educational experiences creating a balanced combination of learning environments. This includes different types of online and face-to-face learning environments.

1	2	3	4	5	6
Organization has some training in using various possible formats, including reference and performance support materials, but does not have an overall system or strategy for performance improvement learning interventions		Organization has one or two different learning strategies or a few different technologies, but does not have an overall plan where all types of learning environments are aligned			Organization has a robust blended learning program that consists of multiple online trainings including real-world scenarios that work in a system with face-to-face learning through mentoring, coaching, role playing, and classroom learning

❏ *Technical and Non-Technical Learning:* The organization identifies the hard (technical) and soft (non-technical) skills needed to meet business goals. Interventions for technical and non-technical learning are varied but the focus is on instruction.

1	2	3	4	5	6
Effort placed on technical learning and training with limited effort on non-technical exposure or adequate support for interpersonal and other generic needs without adequate coverage of job specific preparation		Some effort made to have appropriate delivery methods selected based on learning effectiveness, cost effectiveness, and time allocation			Training and learning support the organization's needs and critical business issues, and they are aligned to the organization's strategies, vision, mission, and goals

❏ *Social Learning:* The organization uses social learning to provide opportunities for continual development through informal interactions among employees which allows learning to take place in the context of the workplace and embedded in actual work processes enabling organizations to become more efficient and cost-effective.

1	2	3	4	5	6
Most learning takes place in formal settings		Social learning takes place on an individual or inconsistent basis			Training and learning support the organization's needs and critical business issues, and they are aligned to the organization's strategies, vision, mission, and goals

(Continued)

❏ *Interactive Learning Technologies:* Used by the organization to encourage and support the active involvement of the learner with the content, the instructor, the technology, other learners, and the learning resources.

1	2	3	4	5	6
Interactive learning is undervalued by the organization as necessary for learning		Interactivity happens but is not planned for by organization or sought by learners			Learning technologies enhance or enable learner interactions with technology content, instructor, and/or other learners or resources

❏ *Enterprise Learning:* Enterprise learning or training is both a driver and client of interactive learning technologies. Enterprise learning is a comprehensive approach throughout the organization.

1	2	3	4	5	6
Enterprise learning or training not at the forefront of the organization's business responsibilities		Some components of a standard enterprise learning platform are in place and are aligned with the business goals of the organization			The technology infrastructure required for a standard enterprise learning platform include: learning management system (LMS), virtual classroom, assessment/e-testing system, database, reporting system, learning content management system, and learning analytics

❏ *Classroom Learning:* Live classroom learning is used for all types of learning and it remains resilient and dominant.

1	2	3	4	5	6
Classroom learning is neither well-planned nor carefully executed		Classroom learning can be stand-alone or part of a blended training strategy; it is always live and real			Classroom learning has three distinguishing features: a live instructor, a group of students, and a location that is separate from the workplace. All features are aligned to produce a dynamic learning environment

(Continued)

❑ *Distance/Distributed Learning:* Online learning can help an organization provide information quickly in a world in which adapting to change in a global marketplace is key to an organization's survival. Training is just-in-time, interactive and engaging, secure, and promotes a climate of improvement through easily accessible materials.

1	2	3	4	5	6
Workplace is not a dynamic environment. Online, computer-based, or individualized learning is not offered. Continuous learning is not promoted		Online, computer-based, or individualized learning is available, but infrastructure is lacking and material is primarily didactic			Online, computer-based or individualized learning is backed by strong infrastructure where a variety of formats are utilized. Content is easily adapted to rapidly changing environment

❑ *Online/e-Learning:* Online/e-learning informs by communicating information and performs by building procedural and strategic skills.

1	2	3	4	5	6
Focus on format alone; little emphasis on strengths and limitations of electronic technology		e-Learning formats are used without consideration of the most frequently occurring e-learning practices			Multiple e-learning formats are used: synchronous (virtual classrooms), asynchronous (self-paced, self-directed), and hybrid (blended)

❑ *Wikis, Avatars, and More:* Wikis, avatars, and other emerging technologies are potential interventions for enhancing learning and instruction in business, industry, healthcare, and other settings. They require careful design, development, implementation, and evaluation.

1	2	3	4	5	6
Emerging technologies are just beginning to appear in organization learning and communication efforts.		Some emphasis on emerging technologies, but not fully integrated within organization			Organization fully committed and engaged in emerging technologies

❑ *Games and Simulations:* The organizational culture supports experiential learning techniques to enhance problem solving and bring near reality into interactive learning.

1	2	3	4	5	6
Learners or owners of training do not accept the use of games or simulations		Games or simulations only used occasionally or are not always accepted by learners or owners of training			Games or simulations are used whenever appropriate for the learning task

(Continued)

PERFORMANCE SUPPORT INTERVENTIONS

Performance support interventions, also called performance support systems, integrate doing with technology, but may inherently or consciously include elements of learning and instruction. These interventions use a variety of technologies—print, computer, video, mobile and others—to provide workers with just-in-time and just enough information to perform a task.

❑ *Performance Support Tools (PSTs) or Job Aids:* Organization uses performance support tools to provide just-in-time, on-the-job, and just-enough information, enabling a worker to perform a task efficiently and successfully without special training or reliance on memory.

1	2	3	4	5	6
Job aids or perform-ance support tools are not used due to lack of knowledge or expertise		Job aids or performance support tools are infrequently used, despite indications they would be useful			Job aids or perform-ance support tools are accepted as an alternative to training, based on task and user analysis

❑ *Electronic Performance Support Systems (EPSS):* Electronic (computer-mediated) technology is used to empower learners, enhance organizational learning, and enable knowledge management. Like a job aid, EPSS supports the concepts of just-in-time, on-the-job, just enough information, and just for me.

1	2	3	4	5	6
Organization does not have resources or expertise or desire to develop EPSS		EPSS resources and expertise available, but not used due to lack of acceptance			EPSS are accepted and used; technology and expertise exist; task and user analyses drive decisions

❑ *Documentation and Standards:* Workers are informed of job expectations through well-designed documents. Outputs, outcomes, and performance are measured using clear, concise standards.

1	2	3	4	5	6
Organization does not see value of documen-tation or standards		Organization's use of documentation is not systematic, not consistent in developing and following standards			Organization has systematic process for developing user-friendly, accessible documentation; uses standards to guide and measure performance, outputs, and outcomes

(Continued)

❏ *Expert Systems:* An expert system can be used as an EPSS for decision making.

1	2	3	4	5	6
The organization has no formal way of incorporating human knowledge, reasoning, and information into software systems		A true expert system that includes the components of a knowledge base, knowledge representation, and knowledge engineering is not yet fully integrated within the organization's infrastructure			The organization makes full use of information systems in which computer programs store facts and rules to replicate the abilities and decisions of true, human experts

JOB ANALYSIS/WORK DESIGN INTERVENTIONS

Job analysis is collecting information about duties, tasks, and responsibilities for specific jobs. Work design is a blueprint of job tasks structured to improve organizational efficiency and employee satisfaction.

Job Analysis Interventions

❏ *Job Descriptions:* The work of the job positions are so well portrayed that the duties are clear. The new employee understands the job if s(he) reads the job description.

1	2	3	4	5	6
Formal job descriptions unavailable or, at best, unspecific and unclear job tasks		Formal job description available, but not very useful; gives incomplete data			Formal job descriptions available, includes what job incumbent does, how to do it, the environment, and conditions of employment

❏ *Job Specifications:* Job descriptions are extended to include human traits and experiences required to perform the job as well as the kind of person to recruit.

1	2	3	4	5	6
Job descriptions are unavailable or non-specific		Job descriptions are available but sketchy and unfocused			Job descriptions are concise and include all traits and experience required in recruiting

(*Continued*)

Work Design Interventions

❑ *Job Design:* This involves duties performed at work, the activities associated with the duties, the responsibilities shared by employers and employees, and the performance outcomes required by the organization.

1	2	3	4	5	6
Jobs occur in the organization without setting the stage for discussing alternatives to designing or redesigning jobs		The organization provides job design training regarding methods. However, job design, work enlargement, rotation, and enrichment efforts are not commonplace			There is a systematic process established in the organization to review how jobs reflect the organizational vision, mission, and workers' interests, capabilities, and aspirations. Job rotation, job enrichment, and job enlargement are commonplace

❑ *Job Enlargement:* Organization encourages enlargement to offset high specialization, tediousness, and boredom associated with narrow job scope.

1	2	3	4	5	6
Breadth is non-existent or seen as a ploy by management to increase productivity while rightsizing		Opportunities exist within organization for additional same-level task activities			Knowledge enlargement added to task enlargement result in more job satisfaction, fewer job errors, and enhanced customer satisfaction

❑ *Job Rotation:* As a lateral transfer process, this intervention exposes employees to a kaleidoscopic view of organizational life.

1	2	3	4	5	6
Little opportunity for workers to move from one job to another		Some opportunity to relieve boredom and burnout by cross-training			Complete re-energizing and recommitting employees to organizational work

❑ *Job Enrichment:* Organizations increase job depth and empower employees to be independent thinkers and responsible workers.

1	2	3	4	5	6
Little opportunity for redesigning jobs		Some opportunity for job redesign by adding tasks and responsibilities			Great opportunities for workers to experience feelings of responsibility, achievement, and growth as tasks and responsibilities equally added

(*Continued*)

❑ *Reengineering, Realigning, Restructuring:* Radical workplace redesigns are used to increase efficiency, implement lessons learned, streamline processes, and create a foundation for positive organizational growth.

1	2	3	4	5	6
Hasty changes, reactionary		Changes not supported fully by executives			Strong champion, sufficient resources, patience, adequate time to succeed

HUMAN FACTORS

This is an interdisciplinary approach to the workplace environment in which machines and employees are consciously and purposefully linked to produce results. Focus is on the processes, tools, and physical and psychological environments that maximize the productivity, health, and safety of all employees.

❑ *Ergonomics:* The organization fashions an appropriate fit between the machine and the work environment.

1	2	3	4	5	6
Little attention paid to creating ergonomically sound workplaces		Some attention paid to ergonomic issues in work practices and workstation design			Organization supports and encourages an appropriate balance between physical ergonomics and cognitive ergonomics

❑ *Safety Engineering:* Organizations establish systematic processes to make the work environment safer and healthier for employees.

1	2	3	4	5	6
Physical and psychological aspects of safety downplayed or ignored		Physical context and psychological context for promoting safety applied sporadically			Organization makes concerted efforts to address safe and healthy work environments for employees; commitment to workers primary

❑ *Security Management:* Security risks can be managed or reduced when managers are aware of all controls available and implement the most effective ones.

1	2	3	4	5	6
Security risks and costs are not carefully explained and acted upon		Recognition of risk assessment and risk analysis to recognize threats and rote system vulnerabilities			Active governance with emphasis on security risk and awareness training to protect the physical and intellectual property of the organization

(Continued)

❑ *Green Workplace:* The entire organization, at all levels, supports and actively contributes to maintaining a green, sustainable environment. Its mission, values, and culture are reflective of a commitment to social responsibility and reducing the environmental impact of business activities.

1	2	3	4	5	6
Little to no value is placed on social responsibility and the impact of business activities on the environment Some value is placed on environmental impact.		Sporadic efforts to reduce waste and conserve energy are made, but not at all levels within the organization			Consistent efforts to reduce waste, conserve energy, and reduce company's carbon footprint are evident at all levels within the organization. Culture is one of social responsibility

QUALITY IMPROVEMENT

These interventions involve conducting business right the first time, every time. They imply commitment to continuous improvement.

❑ *Total Quality Management (TQM):* Organization-wide policies and practices support a strategic management perspective of product, service, and customer quality.

1	2	3	4	5	6
Quality efforts are reactive and only as much as absolutely necessary		Efforts generally paid to TQM concepts, but organization fails to involve all employees in process			Concepts of quality fully ingrained within organizational fabric; frequent use of TQM tools to solve problems

❑ *Continuous Improvement:* Organizations establish strategies for improvement to learn what customers want so their needs can be better served; it has long-range focus and is both internal and external.

1	2	3	4	5	6
Efforts viewed as single, isolated occurrences, not seen as routine component		Quality and continuous improvement emphasized in policies but not in practices			Goals reflect top management commitment, total workforce involvement, and skill and knowledge training; employees held accountable for performance

(Continued)

❑ *Preventive Maintenance (PM):* Organizations establish proactive processes for all systems and subsystems before major problems occur.

1	2	3	4	5	6
No formal preventive maintenance program in place; organization operates in reactive mode		Limited proactive processes in motion; collaborative relationships among personnel diffused			Proactive approaches to preventive maintenance address zero failure, zero trouble, zero waste; benefits justify costs

❑ *Six Sigma:* The organization improves the quality of process outputs by identifying and removing the cause of defects (errors) and minimizing variability in processes. Projects follow a defined sequence of steps with quantified financial targets.

1	2	3	4	5	6
Errors are not identified or monitored		Organization has some quantified measures			Every project follows a system development methodology

❑ *Lean Organizations:* Lean organizations are efficient and effective and employ management principles within a framework of least cost and zero waste.

1	2	3	4	5	6
Some lean techniques are implemented; however, a lean organizational structure incorporating lean management principles is absent		The organization implements a lean structure and realizes value and insight for lean operations, but employees are not fully engaged in the process			The organization strives to streamline processes, eliminate waste, reduce the need for non-essential functions, minimize response time, and maximize flexibility

PERSONAL DEVELOPMENT INTERVENTIONS

Personal development interventions are planned work-related activities that are the employee's personal responsibility. Individuals assume ownership of success or failure. Personal development requires and enables individuals to take control of their own job situation. The organization provides the structure and processes so that employees can make accurate, positive decisions and improve their performance.

❑ *Feedback:* Managers and co-workers freely provide suggestions and advice. Structured feedback, such as 360-degree feedback, is viewed as non-threatening and helpful.

1	2	3	4	5	6
Reluctantly given, threatening		Tolerated, likely to be ignored			Welcomed. valued, and sought

(Continued)

❑ **_Coaching:_** Managers assist employees to improve performance by analyzing problems, offering suggestions, discussing errors and mistakes, and recommending organizational resources (such as training) to overcome problems.

1	2	3	4	5	6
Information only when problem arises		Little regular information about job performance			Suggestions viewed as positive and useful

❑ **_Mentoring:_** Experienced employees help new hires or people with new job assignments to quickly adapt to new job requirements. Following the wise counsel of mentors leads to job advancement or better projects and assignments.

1	2	3	4	5	6
Reluctance due to fear of loss of job		Advice tolerated but viewed as of question-able value			Highly visible, struc-tured program with senior executives participating

❑ **_Emotional Intelligence:_** Self-management skills of self-awareness, self-regulation, motivation, empathy, and social adeptness are encouraged and modeled.

1	2	3	4	5	6
Autocratic, manipula-tive, harsh work envi-ronment		Employee well-being taken for granted			Open, caring culture, self-confident manage-ment, service orienta-tion

❑ **_Social Intelligence:_** This science of success can promote a highly competitive and global world that advances the "social radar" or social self-awareness of people to help them become more aware of the feelings, needs. and interests of others.

1	2	3	4	5	6
Little emphasis is paid to the daily activities of observing, learn-ing, developing, and reflecting on personal awareness		Competence in surveying one's personal life space and environment and responding with socially successful conduct			Emphasis placed on sensitivity to the needs and interests of others; an attitude of generos-ity and consideration, and practical skills for interacting with people in multiple settings

(*Continued*)

❏ *Cultural Intelligence (CQ):* Organization looks at CQ and cross-cultural awareness as an essential piece of its internal and external needs in a market and workplace that are increasingly diverse and multi-cultural. The organization seeks to build CQ through both cognitive and behavioral activities and works to build CQ into each employee's skill sets.

1	2	3	4	5	6
Diversity policy but no formal program or procedure for building cultural intelligence		Organization has some focus on building behavioral CQ but no structured program to build overall CQ			Organization has structured programs focused on building employees' cognitive and behavioral skills through declarative and procedural knowledge exercises; diversity of opinion and diversity of knowledge lead to the best results

❏ *Communities of Professional Practice:* Practitioners and professionals come together around a shared domain of interest. They engage in problem solving, information sharing and experience sharing and enable people to take responsibility for managing the knowledge required to perform their jobs.

1	2	3	4	5	6
There are no communities of professional practice to build capacity and strengthen relationships		Existing communities of professional practice are neither recognized nor supported in the organization			Resources made available to communities of professional practice formed around key strategic initiatives; relationship formed and strengthened

HUMAN RESOURCE DEVELOPMENT INTERVENTIONS

Human resource development interventions are essential to human resource management and are shaped by the organization's mission and its ability to maintain market share.

❏ *Talent Management:* Talent management is a human resource management approach bringing together the functions of recruitment, selection, learning and development, retention, and other key human resource functions. Employees become empowered to think and act in the process. It is a business issue and a societal issue (engaging talented people in organization life). It connects value, strategy, and people.

1	2	3	4	5	6
In theory, organization supports talent management framework; in practice, it coexists with other organizational programs and systems and not used as strategic resource and competitive advantage		Viewed essentially as a string of programs and processes to managing talent; organization working to employ it as a systems approach to thinking about talent			Organization fully supports an integrated set of processes, programs, and cultural norms to attract, develop, deploy, and retain talent

(Continued)

❑ **Staffing:** Organizations and individuals benefit from a carefully conceived staffing process that manages human capital.

1	2	3	4	5	6
Staffing process seen as complete once applicants are hired or promoted		Some attention paid to helping new employees achieve familiarity with policies, procedures, and endeavors			Total orientation of new employees to the organization and unit; efforts seen as ways to retain and maximize human resources

❑ **Employee Development:** Both the organization and the individual play pivotal roles in the employee development process from the time the candidate accepts the offer through the employee's entire tenure.

1	2	3	4	5	6
Little done within the organization to encourage employee development		Some aspects of employee development in place; organization working to develop full spectrum			Organization focuses on a full spectrum of development: employee training, employee development, career development, and organization development

❑ **Retention:** Retention efforts that are related to customer satisfaction, customer loyalty, quality outcomes, and financial performance are prime drivers and indicators of business outcomes.

1	2	3	4	5	6
Limited emphasis placed on retention practices identified by theory research and practice		Organization has interest in retention efforts for all the valid reasons but followthrough is slow and deliberate			Efforts to improve employee retention are carefully planned and aligned with strategic thinking and strategic planning

❑ **Compensation:** Compensation policies and practices reward employees with salary benefits for the job they perform within the organization.

1	2	3	4	5	6
Pay systems perceived as unfair with respect to level of compensation received and mechanisms used to determine pay		Compensation practices partially in place; organization working on establishing a full compensation system			Direct and indirect compensation practices available within the organization; just compensation system is the norm

(Continued)

❑ **Benefits:** The indirect financial and nonfinancial payments employees receive for working are included in the compensation package.

1	2	3	4	5	6
Most full-time employees receive benefits required by law; however, negative comments and resistance		Employees receive benefits required by law; but minimum additional benefits. Not seen as a valuable part of employee satisfaction or retention			Benefits are designed with care and they include (1) pay for time not worked (holidays, sick leave, vacations, maternity leave); (2) insurance benefits (workers' comp, wellness programs, long-term care); (3) retirement benefits (pension plans); (4) services (employee assistance programs, elder care)

❑ **Health and Wellness:** Organizations sponsor initiatives that focus on health promotion, health protection, and health prevention.

1	2	3	4	5	6
No direct attempt to modify or change behavior		Activities designed to educate and instruct; limited attempt to modify, alter, or change behavior			Activities designed to create organizational environment that encourages and helps employees maintain healthy, energized lifestyles

❑ **Retirement Planning:** Organizations assist employees to exit from the labor force. Planning process may be bittersweet.

1	2	3	4	5	6
Very little effort devoted to retirement preparation		Traditional retirement practices influence ongoing retirement planning			Senior well-being influences retirement planning

❑ **Labor Relations:** A proactive approach is used by the organization to build and maintain positive employee-employer relationships. It is a long-term investment of time and resources and is most successful when all individuals in the process are informed of the facts and make good short- and long-term decisions.

1	2	3	4	5	6
Limited communication between workers or union and management prior to a problem		Relationship between workers and management is cordial, with communication occurring but not planned for on a regular basis			Regular and planned communication to discuss potential issues managing unionized and non-unionized labor; worker and collective bargaining issues are integral

(Continued)

INDIVIDUAL GROWTH

This is the part of human resources that focuses on retaining high-performance personnel in an organization. It requires employees to remain energized, engaged, enthusiastic, and committed to job excellence and career development.

❑ *Motivation Systems (Incentives and Rewards):* Employees are enthusiastic and energized to work effectively; organization demonstrates appreciation through rewards and incentives.

1	2	3	4	5	6
Employee efforts ignored		Appreciation minimal and infrequent			Appreciation structured and genuine

❑ *Performance Management:* Performance management is used to monitor employee growth as objectively as possible. Clear guidelines and criteria are the norm, and managers are properly trained in not only assessing employee performance but also in how to best mentor and coach.

1	2	3	4	5	6
Appraisal system is nonexistent or contains biases and subjectivity		Appraisal system is present, limits subjectivity, but provides no avenue to support employee growth			Appraisal system is present, benchmarked, and free from most bias. Appraisers act as good mentors to help workers achieve maximum potential

❑ *Key Performance Indicators (KPIs):* The organization has clear mission, goals, and objectives; identifiable stakeholders make data-driven decisions based on sound data collection relevant to predetermined performance indicators.

1	2	3	4	5	6
No organizational mission or goals outlined. Decisions are made arbitrarily and are not informed by sound data		Some decisions are made based on data relevant to key performance indicators			Clear mission, goals, and objectives outlined; stakeholders and expectations identified; measurable indicators determined and aligned with program or project being evaluated; decisions constantly made based on sound data

❑ *Performance Appraisals:* Performance appraisals are viewed as constructive, containing honest representation of employee efforts and helpful recommendations for improvement.

1	2	3	4	5	6
Create fear and resentment		Annual event to be endured but not beneficial			Healthy dialogue establishing workable objectives and planning for consistent application

(Continued)

❏ *360-Degree Appraisals:* A multi-source feedback approach that allows multiple individuals to rate skills and behaviors of an employee.

1	2	3	4	5	6
Emphasis on 360 degree as a tool, but not as a dynamic and versatile process for organizational growth; seen as a one-time event		360-degree tool is known and used; organizational support systems not in place for change to be sustained			Emphasis on assessing and improving employee performance while enhancing and maximizing organizational and individual development

❏ *Competencies:* Capabilities of an individual that result in successful job performance. They are also organizational capabilities that align employee behavior and action with the organization's strategic plan.

1	2	3	4	5	6
Individuals expected to perform on the job; however, little emphasis is given to capabilities of an individual that result in successful job performance		Organization is beginning to develop competencies of its employees; formal efforts in initial stages of design and development			Emphasis placed on competencies dealing with people, competencies dealing with business, and self-management competencies

❏ *Competency Testing:* Competency testing determines appropriate skill levels and job readiness.

1	2	3	4	5	6
Testing used for discipline or workforce reduction		Testing not related to actual jobs			Testing identifies best candidates

ORGANIZATIONAL GROWTH

A company's organizational growth is strongly enhanced as it invests in talent. Organizations need people who possess the "big picture" mindset within the framework of systems thinking and collaborative understanding.

❏ *Succession Planning:* Systematic processes are used to identify employees for senior management positions.

1	2	3	4	5	6
No formal process in place for preparing high-level personnel		Planning is sporadic, with minimum implementation			Experiential assignments, mentoring, training, and personnel development prepare people for high-level assignments

❏ *Career Pathing:* Organization effectively develops employees through a series of jobs and related assignments.

1	2	3	4	5	6
Systematic planning does not include development of people		Opportunities may be available, but no systematic approach exists			Vertical and horizontal lines of opportunity in place

(Continued)

❏ *Leadership Development:* Organization provides opportunities for individuals to manage human capital by creating vision and aligning people.

1	2	3	4	5	6
Organization does little to encourage and develop specific leadership development		Opportunities exist for individuals to influence followers who think differently, feel passionately, and act responsibly			Formal leadership programs and training opportunities firmly in place; leadership development moves from an event into a process that lasts an entire career

❏ *Executive Development:* Opportunities for high-level strategic development prepare people for value-driven visionary implementation.

1	2	3	4	5	6
Executive development neither linked to vision, values, strategies nor to organization's core capabilities		Some attention given to executive development, but training in real-time interaction with real-life business issues and trends ignored			Prepares leaders to make wise decisions; the primary level that triggers an organization's vision, values, strategies, and business needs

❏ *Management Development:* A variety of formal and on-the-job training opportunities that are organization-specific are linked to the organization's mission, vision, goals, and structure for accomplishing business needs.

1	2	3	4	5	6
Little attention paid to interpersonal, technical, administrative, conceptual, and decision-making skills		Some attention paid to organization's changing needs; individuals reluctant to take control of personal management development			Wide range of management development activities exist incorporating corporate inventories, university-based programs, professional organizations, and in-house programs

❏ *Supervisory Development:* Experienced personnel interface between management and employees in a continuously evolving role based on sensitivity and empathy.

1	2	3	4	5	6
No formal program exists; decisions autocratic and manipulative		Reality-oriented practice and concrete examples used sporadically			Critical competencies that are conceptual, interpersonal, technical, and political in nature are identified; supervisor seen as trainer, adviser, mentor, facilitator

(Continued)

ORGANIZATIONAL COMMUNICATION INTERVENTIONS

Organizational or business communication makes it possible to send and receive messages between different components within an organization, among separate organizations, and between organizations and society. Effective communication is essential for creating, maintaining, or improving the culture and performance of organizations.

❏ *Communication Networks:* Organization supports and encourages a communication system that allows messages to move from sender to receiver, informally and formally, enhancing job performance and job satisfaction.

1	2	3	4	5	6
Organization does not see value of establishing, enabling, enhancing, communication networks		Organization uses formal or informal networks; strategy is not balanced; flow does not empower or enable employees			Organization develops and analyzes networks to enhance and enable communication between and among members and improve performance

❏ *Information Systems:* People, data, and technology work together to retrieve, process, store, and disseminate information, supporting informed decision making and sound organizational management.

1	2	3	4	5	6
Organization does not have a formal information system		Organization has an information system, but not linked to business needs			Information management links people, data, technology, business procedures to current and future business needs

❏ *Suggestion Systems:* Proactive organizations rely on suggestions of employees to improve products, processes, and services.

1	2	3	4	5	6
Organizational fabric neither supports suggestion systems nor provides for feedback and recognition		Suggestion systems loosely structured to match the goals and values of the organization			Organization encourages and supports formal and informal suggestion systems to improve performance

(Continued)

❑ *Grievance Systems:* Organizations set grievance systems in place to investigate complaints about wages, hours, and conditions of employment and/or work practices.

1	2	3	4	5	6
System informally structured; process for resolving employee problems perceived as complex and time-consuming		Moderate efforts expended to work with union and non-union personnel in protecting employees and assisting management in settling conflicts			Formal processes in place for submitting, evaluating, and providing feedback; seen as charter for organizational justice

❑ *Dispute Resolution:* Organizational culture allows individuals or groups to resolve differences of opinion amicably or through negotiation, mediation, or collaboration.

1	2	3	4	5	6
Organization fosters disputes among members (may be called competition)		Organization not consistent in resolving disputes or supporting collaboration			Organization develops and uses sound dispute resolution practices; encourages and rewards collaboration

❑ *Social Media:* Social media as an organizational communication technology is represented in discussion forums, blogs, wikis, podcasts, videos, pictures, and so forth.

1	2	3	4	5	6
File sharing and online collaboration is minimal; little opportunity for public comments and responses		Online collaboration is haphazard; however, people can share their own ideas while expanding others' ideas			An infrastructure for collaboration exists and is both streamlined and regularly utilized to create and exchange content in a virtual environment

ORGANIZATIONAL DESIGN AND DEVELOPMENT INTERVENTIONS

Organizational design and development is a process that examines the operation and management of an organization and facilitates needed changes in an effort to improve efficiency and competitiveness.

Empowerment

Empowerment is an enabling concept allowing people to develop a sense of self-confidence and energizing them to take action. It is key to unlocking the potential of a high-performing and strategically aligned workplace.

(Continued)

❑ *Team Strategies:* Teams are empowered and supported throughout developmental stages by strong sanction and reliable sponsorship.

1	2	3	4	5	6
Teams have responsibility, but inadequate authority		Teams assigned, but outcomes ignored			Teams highly visible, and efforts valued and rewarded

❑ *Virtual Teams:* The virtual connection generates opportunities for efficiency in resources, effectiveness of functions, and team synergy unrealized in traditional team and employee interaction and organizational bonding.

1	2	3	4	5	6
Organization reluctant and non-trusting in supporting virtual teams; not viewed as effective as traditional teams; limited positive team dynamics; no accountability		Organization beginning to support virtual teams with emerging markets in geographic locations and changes in organizational participation			People can work from anywhere at any time with minimal, if any, face-to-face contact; supported by both hardware and software; work day opportunity is 24 vs. 8

❑ *Problem Solving:* Systematic and systemic problem solving is a part of daily work life, as evidenced by encouraging continuous performance improvement.

1	2	3	4	5	6
Problems ignored or solved by crises		Alleviate problems as absolutely necessary			Systematic approach to resolving issues proactively

Organizational Pro-Action

Organizational pro-action is thinking ahead, planning for the future with creativity and commitment, and understanding the economic, political, and social climate sufficiently to inspire employee confidence. It helps employees succeed and it also helps them believe in their own future.

(Continued)

❑ *Strategic Planning:* The organization's strategic plan provides direction, focus, and clear, well-accepted goals and targets.

1	2	3	4	5	6
"Two-faced" public statement, viewed as executive's brainchild, not widely publicized		Plan ignored, organization rudderless			Basis for departmental and individual planning

❑ *Environmental Scanning:* Organization keenly aware of internal and external environmental threats and opportunities through ongoing observations and data collection.

1	2	3	4	5	6
Ignores signs of change, doesn't use opinion polls and data		Too little, too late, "drags feet" acknowledging changing conditions			Continuous monitoring of employees, customers, competition, stakeholders, and markets for possibilities

❑ *Appreciative Inquiry (AI):* The organization seeks to identify the best in people and actively seeks to discover more of what is good through collaborating and working successfully.

1	2	3	4	5	6
Efforts to recognize and employ the dynamics of AI seldom in organizational thinking and planning		Organization believes in the philosophy and process; however, the four phases of AI are not inextricably related			Input, opinions, and creativity are positive and useful, with focus on achievement of the best possible outcomes and practices

❑ *Outsourcing:* The organization enhances productivity, decreases operating costs, and leverages talent by entering into contractual agreements identifying the exchange of labor.

1	2	3	4	5	6
All work performed by internal resources only		Some project teams leverage internal and external resources			Every project is open to consideration of external service providers

(Continued)

❑ *Benchmarking:* Organization systematically compares self to other organizations for purpose of learning better methods and determining best practices.

1	2	3	4	5	6
Committed to "our way" of doing things		Improvements make work easier for employees but do not address opportunities			Keen awareness of competition and expectations of customers and stakeholders

❑ *Balanced Scorecard:* The organization monitors the financial and non-financial measures of performance, keeps track of the execution of activities, monitors consequences of performance, and identifies the measures and targets associated with the activities required to implement corporate strategy.

1	2	3	4	5	6
There is a low accountability culture and limited use by organization of measurement and tracking as a management and strategic planning system		Organization has some tracking measures, but they are not fully aligned with the vision and strategies			Performance is aligned, monitored, and evaluated from four perspectives: learning and growth, business, customer, and financial

❑ *Dashboards:* Graphical representation of performance measurement allows for tracking flow of business processes in the organization.

1	2	3	4	5	6
Specific data points may or may not be captured and reported, but no visual representation of measuring performance		An executive information system user interface is designed for easy reading; reports generated without showing details or trends			Visual representation of all systems in an organization with detailed reports and trends; use of the three main types of digital dashboards: stand-alone software applications, web-browser-based applications, desktop application

ORGANIZATIONAL VALUES

Organizational values are the "stuff we all live by," our organizational energy, the reason for the organization to exist. They create the organization's vision of the world—how people are treated, how employees act, how they function as teams and make decisions, how people respond to mistakes and failure, how they take risks, learn, and grow, and how information is communicated and shared.

(Continued)

❏ ***Culture:*** Organizational culture is aligned with and generally supports the organization's mission, vision, and core values.

1	2	3	4	5	6
Not supportive, passively or openly resistant		Generally supportive with some resistance, but willingness to change if change is viewed as reasonable and helpful			Highly supportive, welcomes and encourages change to adapt and become a leading organization

❏ ***Diversity:*** Organization respects and encourages unusual ideas, various points of view, and other differences, even if they are counter to senior management's views.

1	2	3	4	5	6
Discourages unusual ideas or differences		Tolerates unique ideas and differences, but not seen as important to health of organization			Encourages unique ideas and differences; realizes that diversity leads to better decisions and organizational success; respectful of differences in race, religion, national origin, gender, gender preferences

❏ ***Inclusion Strategies:*** Organizational culture respects and values diversity and is open to anyone who can perform a job. An inclusion strategy is efficient, effective, and sustainable when it is regarded as a business strategy, leading to changes that help organizations achieve their business objectives and bottom-line results.

1	2	3	4	5	6
Lip service paid to diversity and inclusion strategies; differences respected but not viewed as organizational assets; inclusion only minimally reflected in developing and retaining talent		A modicum of effort made to build an inclusive organization, but not reflected in strategic thinking and planning and how it can build productivity, innovation, and creativity			A company's organizational culture and readiness and capacity for change are effective and sustainable. Conscious effort made to create an inclusive work environment through intercultural competence and talent management

(Continued)

❑ *Globalization:* Global strategies include appropriate implementation tools, such as multinational problem solving and collaboration.

1	2	3	4	5	6
Headquarters' "correctness"		Overseas "foreign" mentality			Collaborative partnership uniquely purposed

❑ *Localization:* Adapting a global application already blueprinted for localizability to a specific culture and locale. Localization processes that are successful and lasting in products and services are those developed within the local culture.

1	2	3	4	5	6
Little effort made to include cultural sensitivities and customizing application; minimum effort made to address localization market or geared only to language development		Partial efforts generated in adapting products and services in software, documentation, websites, and applications to local practices and culture. Customizing products and services are new to the organization			Consistent and deliberate effort made to adapt products and services that are sensitive and appropriate to regional conventions and cultural dynamics (language, gender and roles, holidays, rituals and customs)

❑ *Social Responsibility:* The organization, with its employees and stakeholders, is continuing to evolve to a consciousness in which it has a sense of belonging and collective responsibility for one another and for society as a whole.

1	2	3	4	5	6
The organization is focused only on meeting financial benchmarks and doesn't encourage staff to increase their knowledge or contribute to the greater good. Employees don't feel they have the tools to be successful, nor do they feel secure with their employment policies in place for appropriate pay and benefits		Employees have a sense that they are valued in the organization. There are meaningful ways of becoming involved in community activities that are sponsored by the organization and encouraged by management. Employees at the organization sometimes feel that by working on the team they are a part of a bigger community effort			Employees feel deeply interconnected with the successes and failures of the organization and vice versa. Employees are evaluated on their civic activities in the annual evaluation process. The organization has a known philanthropic presence for international issues

(Continued)

❏ *Ethics:* "Doing the right thing" is ingrained in the organizational culture.

1	2	3	4	5	6
Words and actions mismatch		Situation by situation approach			All levels adhere

❏ *Decision Making:* Decision making develops group support through systematic and fair practices.

1	2	3	4	5	6
Judgmental, rushed decisions		Inadequate implementation, often return to "former ways"			Risk taking encouraged, resulting in impressive improvements

FINANCIAL SYSTEMS

Financial systems refer to the monetary affairs (income, reserves, expenses, and dividends) of an organization. They are usually summarized in an annual report that includes an income statement, balance sheet, cash flow statement, and explanatory notes.

❏ *Open Book Management:* Financial information is widely available, enabling employees to focus on helping the organization make money and provide desired and appropriate services which increases productivity and long-term financial performance.

1	2	3	4	5	6
Organization neither open nor aligned; information restricted		Review, discussion, advice, and corrective position of financial information minimal			Complete sharing of financial information; employees make a difference

❏ *Profit- Versus Cost-Center:* The decision to create a profit or cost responsibility center is based on solid business practices.

1	2	3	4	5	6
Responsibility centers viewed as wasteful, ineffective, and non-productive		Solid business practices considered but not implemented with rigor			Centers perceived as lean, efficient, effective, flexible, and highly regarded

(Continued)

❏ *Financial Forecasting:* Planning for the financial future of the organization includes traditional factors such as profits, interest, supply and demand, and non-traditional issues such as innovation, culture, new products and services, competitors, and so forth.

1	2	3	4	5	6
Limited to short-term financial measurables only		Medium range; some attention to demography, economics, marketing social patterns			Prepares organizations for future trends, events outcomes, and customer satisfaction

❏ *Capital Investment and Spending:* Prudent practices are used to identify opportunities and analyze alternatives for acquiring investments of permanent value.

1	2	3	4	5	6
Limited match with the strategic goals and objectives of the organization		Some attention to planning, assessing, deciding, evaluating to align with organizational goals			Processes maximize value and minimize risk

❏ *Cash Flow Analysis:* Systems are in place to anticipate various sources and uses of cash and to make accurate projections.

1	2	3	4	5	6
Negative corrective actions frequent and poorly planned		Positive and negative corrective actions selected but not optimized			Stability and long-term profitability viewed as positive indicators

❏ *Cash Flow Forecast:* This is an essential forecasting tool since organizations must identify their financial cycles to ensure that adequate cash is available; based on economic assumptions and forecasts of sales and production.

1	2	3	4	5	6
Forecast not prepared from audited financial statements; loses accuracy the more futuristic the projection		Forecast provides the organization with a schedule of when financing is required throughout the year, and in what dollar amounts; employees unprepared in managerial accounting and financial management			The organization identifies its financial cycles and ensures that cash is available to support its activities; supports open book management, and improves the ability of employees to understand the significance of data

(Continued)

❏ *Mergers, Acquisitions, and Joint Ventures:* Organizations are well-prepared to address short-term and long-term financial issues as well as organizational change efforts to effectively maintain competitive advantage.

1	2	3	4	5	6
Decisions made in haste leading to financial and organizational problems		Financial aspects are successful but culture issues neglected			Up-front planning permits accommodating differences in culture, financials, products, services, and potential for future growth

Learning Interventions

In the first two editions of *Fundamentals of Performance Technology*, the authors wrote about Performance *Support Systems* (PSS) that integrate learning and doing and technology to help workers obtain the knowledge or skills they need to initiate new performance or improve existing performance in a way that consistently meets the organization's goals, objectives, and strategic initiatives. Performance support system interventions were categorized as instructional or non-instructional.

In this, the third edition, the authors present two separate categories that are not classified as performance support systems but stand on their own. The first category is *learning*. These initiatives are largely information and/or learning-based and may include knowledge management, learning management and content management systems; education and training; and interactive learning technologies. The second category is *performance support*, which refers to interventions that support the performer on the job and just in time and may enhance or

FIGURE 10.1. Learning Interventions

Learning Interventions
• Knowledge Management
• Organizational Learning
• Learning Management Systems
• Content Magagment Systems
• Education/Training
• Self-Directed Learning
• On-the-Job Learning
• Just-in-Time Learning
• Action Learning
• Blended Learning
• Technical and Non-Technical Learning
• Social Learning
• Interactive Learning Technologies
• Enterprise Learning
• Classroom Learning
• Distance/Distributed Learning
• Online/e-Learning
• Wikis, Avatars, and More
• Games/Simulations

replace learning. Performance support is covered in Chapter 11, while this chapter describes the learning interventions outlined in Figure 10.1. Listen carefully—the voice of the practitioner may be heard commenting on a specific intervention.

The performance improvement practitioner selects or designs a learning intervention when a gap exists between the current knowledge, skill, or attitude of a worker or group of workers and the job specifications. Typical categories of performance support interventions include, but are not limited to, knowledge management, learning management and content management systems, education and training, and interactive learning technologies.

Knowledge Management (KM)

Definition. Knowledge management is a systematic and conscious effort to identify, capture, codify, store, transform, disseminate, and share knowledge so that people within an organization can use the organization's collective knowledge and experience to foster business innovation and competitive advantage. Since knowledge management is about "applying knowledge in new, previously unencumbered or novel situations, each organization should define it in terms of its own business objectives."[1]

Scope. In a knowledge economy, workers are paid for their expertise and knowledge. An organization supports explicit and tacit knowledge. Explicit knowledge is recorded and transmitted among people; for example, written policies and procedures, rules and regulations, and so forth. Tacit knowledge is the know-how that is not recorded and is rooted in personal experience, for example, procedures for solving peculiar problems.[2]

A knowledge management system supports people, technology, and content:

- "Knowledge lives in people's heads and is embedded in process through people."[3] The process of knowledge management begins and ends with people who select or design, use, and maintain the technology required to transform and share knowledge.[4]
- "Technology is an enabler, not an answer."[5] A knowledge management system requires the same basic technology as an information system and usually includes an intranet and groupware.
- "The heart of a good knowledge management system is in the content itself. If the knowledge management does not provide users with timely, accurate information, inform them of best practices, and link them to expertise, organizations will not realize the full value of their investment in the system."[6]

Workplace Implementation. The knowledge management construct has been examined and applied in a wide variety of disciplines, including business process reengineering, decision support systems, expert and executive information systems, total quality management, business intelligence, library and information science, information technology, e-learning, learning organizations, computer-supported collaborative work, and document management. The performance improvement practitioner becomes a subject-matter expert (SME) on knowledge management and the various domains and disciplines that support it.

Typical inputs to knowledge management are cognitive science, expert systems, library and information sciences, technical communication, document management, decision support systems, organizational science, among others.[7] In addition, the practitioner needs to be a life-long learner and remain updated on changes in the world of work and how they affect the organization's coping with and managing the knowledge. The practitioner also looks for pockets of organizational strength where employees are involved with knowledge creation and sharing and models and encourages knowledge sharing.[8]

If knowledge management is not active within the organization, the performance improvement practitioner could help design a knowledge management system that is user friendly. User-friendly knowledge management systems, whether off-the-shelf or custom designed, link collection, storage, and retrieval of knowledge to how people will use the knowledge and support people when they capture and share knowledge. During strategic design, the practitioner can help explore how knowledge is used and valued in the organization. The practitioner can also support integration of knowledge management with other strategic initiatives.

Once knowledge management is implemented, the performance improvement practitioner uses his or her consulting skills to "nurture the communities in which knowledge is created and shared."[9] The practitioner can also play a vital role in helping the organization focus the evaluation up front during the strategic planning process since measuring learning is essential to the knowledge management process. This increases chances for successfully evaluating the knowledge management system.

Two performance support tools in this chapter support these efforts. Performance Support Tool 10.1 can help guide the planning of a new or evaluating an existing knowledge management intervention. Performance Support Tool 10.2 is a diagnostic survey that helps an organization determine the effectiveness of its knowledge management practices.

Organizational Learning

Definition. Organizational learning is a conscious and deliberate way to design organizations so that they function effectively, efficiently, and provide value to their customers or clients through the goods and services that they offer. Employees are encouraged to strive for and maintain their full potential and, ultimately, make society a better place in which to live and function.[11] It goes beyond individual and team learning in that "organizations as entities can also learn and in fact must learn in order to survive."[12]

Scope. Organizational learning focuses on Senge's core disciplines or characteristics,[13] which permit an organization to function as a learning organization. The characteristics include:

- *Systems Thinking:* An organizing framework for looking at the world in terms of wholes and seeing patterns and relationships among the parts of the system.
- *Team Learning:* Employees working together with a synergistic commitment of productivity, mutual trust, cooperation, collaboration, and shared vision.

Text continues on page 258

PERFORMANCE SUPPORT TOOL 10.1. A KNOWLEDGE MANAGEMENT PRIMER

Directions: Use the following activities and questions to guide the planning of a new or evaluating an existing knowledge management intervention. Revise the questions as needed to meet existing or emerging organizational needs.

1. Identify knowledge assets (explicit and tacit).
   - Where is the knowledge asset?

   - What does it contain?

   - What is its use?

   - What form is it in?

   - How accessible is it?

2. Analyze how each knowledge asset can add value.
   - What are the opportunities for using the knowledge asset?

   - What would be the effect of its use?

   - What are the current obstacles to its use?

   - What would be its increased value to the company?

(Continued)

3. Specify what actions are necessary to achieve maximum usability and added value for each knowledge asset.
   - How to plan the actions to use the knowledge asset

   - How to enact actions

   - How to monitor actions

4. Review (evaluate) use of each knowledge asset to ensure added value.
   - Did its use produce the desired added value?

   - How can the knowledge asset be maintained for this use?

   - Did the use create new opportunities?

PERFORMANCE SUPPORT TOOL 10.2. KNOWLEDGE MANAGEMENT ASSESSMENT TOOL (KMAT)

BACKGROUND

The Knowledge Management Assessment Tool (KMAT), is primarily intended to generate dialogue, inquiry, and action planning organization-wide. It also can be used to examine the effectiveness of knowledge management practices within or between departments and external clients to help identify "information flow" and knowledge-sharing bottlenecks. The KMAT was derived by Maier and Moseley[10] based on a literature and internet search. They found that five common dimensions of the knowledge management construct appear to be particularly important: identification and creation, collection and capture, storage and organization, sharing and distribution, and application and use. These dimensions, described below, represent an integrated and procedural approach to the knowledge management discipline.

1. *Knowledge Identification and Creation* begins with identifying and creating knowledge—transforming data or isolated facts with no meaning and information or interpreted data with meaning into a value-added, actionable resource. It provides employees with the ability to perform a particular task or identify hidden trends and unusual patterns within data and information for operational and strategic decision making. Identification and creation of knowledge is often accomplished through interviews, observation, brainstorming sessions, focus groups, portfolio analysis, root-cause analysis, and other similar techniques that generate new ideas and knowledge. These are very often led by experts in the particular domain.

2. *Knowledge Collection and Capture* uses either on paper or an electronic format. Organizational intranet portals, knowledge bases, and network servers are the most effective methods. Job analyses, work documentation, organizational audits, and case studies are examples of collection instruments used by organizations. Because an overwhelming amount of knowledge often exists in an organization, it should be prioritized; only that which is critical to the organization's competitive edge and knowledge management goals should be collected and captured. It is also essential that how knowledge moves through an organization or the "information flow" be collected and captured. This aids in the improvement of ineffective processes that hinder the knowledge management initiative.

3. *Knowledge Storage and Organization* avoids the unorganized storage of knowledge which can cause significant losses in employee time, productivity, and customer service quality. It will ultimately "bottleneck" the knowledge management process and render it useless. Because people think about information differently, depending on their positions and needs, it must be organized or categorized in multiple ways to allow quick and easy retrieval. Typical classification schemes for organizing include product line, industry, activity, and department or function.

4. *Knowledge Sharing and Dissemination,* also known as "corporate memory," improves business processes, increases productivity, and fosters innovation, allowing an organization to maintain a competitive edge. Knowledge can be shared and disseminated through many traditional, non-electronic means, such as meetings and memos. Advanced electronic technologies now available offer the best solution for large, often global organizations that contain enormous volumes of knowledge. Such technologies include email, threaded discussion, knowledge bases, groupware and collaboration tools, online whiteboards, search engines and agents, intranet portals, e-business portals, customer relationship management software, learning and document management software, and digital libraries.

5. *Knowledge Application and Use* is expansive because technology such as online analytical processing provides an organization with the ability to analyze information and look for relationships, trends, patterns,

(*Continued*)

exceptions, and other valuable, often "hidden" information. Data-mining tools present in online analytical processing and other business intelligence software allow an organization to make logical inferences and draw conclusions about specific business areas using statistical models and algorithms. Consumer trends, competitive product offerings and pricing, current marketing campaigns, research and development projects, and human and capital asset utilization are examples of these business areas. Organizations that make use of their corporate memory tend to surpass their competition in exploiting collective experiences, meeting customer demands, managing increasing complexity and globalization, and improving the bottom line through strategic and operational decision making.

Each of the five dimensions can be further examined in terms of two perspectives: explicit knowledge and tacit knowledge:

1. *Explicit knowledge* represents *recorded* information, intelligence, and expertise. These include organizational databases and data warehouses, market reports, sales reports and presentations, product specifications and white papers, press releases, news stories, price sheets, training materials, job descriptions, documentation, annual reports, organizational charts, minutes of meetings, strategic plans, and the like.
2. *Tacit knowledge* represents *personal expertise* not formally recorded and, therefore, essentially unofficial. It includes facts that give rise to corporate memory and knowledge, processes, procedures, mechanisms, and strategies. It also includes the prejudices, values, intuitions, biases, and trust that cause employees to think and act. This information, sometimes referred to as "intellectual assets," is neither easily recorded within the organization nor easily shared among employees.

PART 1: ADMINISTRATOR

Purpose: The Knowledge Management Assessment Tool is primarily intended to generate dialogue, inquiry, and action planning organization-wide. It also can be used to examine the effectiveness of knowledge management practices within or between departments and/or external clients—customers, partners, vendors, and suppliers—and identify "information flow" and knowledge-sharing bottlenecks.

Audience: The tool is intended to be completed by all of the employees within an organization. Although administration within a work unit would certainly yield valuable data, sustainability is more an organization-wide concept.

Content: The Knowledge Management Assessment Tool consists of thirty statements, six for each of the five dimensions of the knowledge management process. Individuals completing the assessment read each statement and reflect on how it pertains to their work. These reflections are quantified from 6 (strongly agree) to 1 (strongly disagree).

Timing: The instrument takes approximately thirty minutes to complete.

Administration: It is recommended that administration of the assessment be done online and scoring accomplished electronically if at all possible.

Reliability and Validity: The Knowledge Management Assessment Tool was piloted with corporate managers responsible for organization development, information management, and process improvement and revised based on their feedback. The population that piloted the survey concurred on both content and face validity. Content validity is

(Continued)

the degree to which items on the survey represent the content that the survey is designed to measure. Face validity is the subjective appraisal of what the content of the survey measures. Reliability data for the Knowledge Management Assessment Tool is not available. The authors suggest being mindful of stability over time and increasing the number of survey items to test reliability.

Scoring Process: The Knowledge Management Assessment Tool Scoring Sheet is in three sections. Section 1 is to be completed by the employee. Sections 2 and 3, containing aggregated data, are to be completed by an organizational administrator. If large quantities of data are anticipated for aggregation, an online instrument with electronic scoring is recommended, thus providing an easy way to collect and score the data. For smaller data sets, administration can be conducted with paper and pencil, with scoring done manually, by following the instructions provided in Sections, 1, 2, and 3 of the Scoring Sheet. All responses are best kept confidential and scores revealed as organizational or departmental averages only.

Section 1

1. Participants transfer their responses from the survey pages to the appropriate spaces in Section 1 of the KMAT Scoring Sheet.
2. Participants add their responses for each dimension and record these sums.

Section 2

1. An administrator (unless scoring is done electronically) places the aggregate totals for each dimension in the appropriate total box in Section 2 of the KMAT Scoring Sheet.
2. The number of respondents in each category is written in each N box.
3. The adjusted total (the average score) is calculated by dividing the total of each dimension by N.

Section 3

1. An administrator (unless scoring is done electronically) adds the total scores of all participants for each question and places this value in the appropriate subtotal box.
2. Then he or she adds the subtotals for both explicit and tacit knowledge and places this value in the proper total box and places the total number of participants in the N box.
3. Then the administrator divides the total for each dimension by N to find the adjusted totals (averages).

Interpretation of Scores: Two different Scoring Sheets (Sections 2 and 3) are provided to make it easier to interpret the aggregated results. Section 2 presents scores according to the five knowledge management dimensions and should be evaluated using the following scale for each of the five dimensions:

Score	Interpretation
31 to 36	The organization (or department) exhibits highly effective knowledge management practices in this area.
26 to 30	The organization (or department) exhibits very effective knowledge management practices on this dimension.
21 to 25	The organization (or department) exhibits moderately effective knowledge management practices on this dimension.

(Continued)

16 to 20	The organization (or department) exhibits moderately ineffective knowledge management practices in this area.
11 to 15	The organization (or department) exhibits very ineffective knowledge management practices on this dimension.
6 to 10	The organization (or department) exhibits extremely ineffective knowledge management practices on this dimension.

Section 3 of the Scoring Sheet arrays responses by the type of knowledge—explicit or tacit—and should be evaluated using the following scale for each of the two types of knowledge.

Score	Type of Knowledge
79 to 90	The organization (or department) exhibits highly effective knowledge management practices in this area.
66 to 78	The organization (or department) exhibits very effective knowledge management practices on this dimension.
53 to 65	The organization (or department) exhibits moderately effective knowledge management practices on this dimension.
40 to 52	The organization (or department) exhibits moderately ineffective knowledge management practices in this area.
27 to 39	The organization (or department) exhibits very ineffective knowledge management practices on this dimension.
15 to 26	The organization (or department) exhibits extremely ineffective knowledge management practices on this dimension.

Posting the Data: The results can be posted and compared with previous assessments to show progress for the entire organization. The scores can be presented in a number of ways, including:

- Scores for the entire organization;
- Breakdowns of scores by business unit (human resources, engineering, marketing, accounting, and so forth);
- Breakdowns of scores by knowledge management dimension (identification and creation, collection and capture, storage and organization, sharing and dissemination, and application and use); or
- Breakdowns of scores by type of knowledge: explicit or tacit.

Care should be taken to ensure that there are at least five respondents from each business unit to assure anonymity.

(*Continued*)

Instructions: This survey is designed to allow you to register your opinions regarding your organization and its external relationships. Please review each of the following statements and circle the response that best represents your opinion about your organization, using the following scale:

Item	Strongly Disagree	Disagree	Mildly Disagree	Mildly Agree	Agree	Strongly Agree
	1	2	3	4	5	6
1. The generation of new ideas and knowledge is highly valued.	1	2	3	4	5	6
2. Job analyses are frequently performed to determine job duties and requirements.	1	2	3	4	5	6
3 An electronic knowledge base exists to store new ideas, knowledge, solutions, and best practices.	1	2	3	4	5	6
4. Documents are proactively shared with employees.	1	2	3	4	5	6
5. The collective experience of employees is an integral part of decision making.	1	2	3	4	5	6
6. Suggestions and multiple viewpoints are often sought for decision making and organization development.	1	2	3	4	5	6
7. The development of job documentation is encouraged.	1	2	3	4	5	6
8. Information from many sources is stored in an integrated manner and cross-referenced, facilitating better communication and decision making.	1	2	3	4	5	6
9. No policies or technical security issues prevent the sharing of information and knowledge.	1	2	3	4	5	6
10. Job responsibilities are carried out and decisions are made based on all the necessary information and knowledge.	1	2	3	4	5	6
11. Experience is highly valued.	1	2	3	4	5	6
12. Documents can be posted on an organizational intranet portal or saved on a network server.	1	2	3	4	5	6
13. The information and knowledge you receive is accurate and up-to-date.	1	2	3	4	5	6
14. An organizational intranet portal exists where information and knowledge relevant to job requirements may be retrieved.	1	2	3	4	5	6

(Continued)

15.	New ideas and knowledge are frequently applied.	1	2	3	4	5	6
16.	Brainstorming and other similar techniques are often used to generate and record new ideas and knowledge.	1	2	3	4	5	6
17.	New ideas and knowledge are recorded for future use.	1	2	3	4	5	6
18.	It is common practice to store work documents on an organizational server, rather than on personal computers.	1	2	3	4	5	6
19.	Electronic and/or non-electronic collaboration, teamwork, and cooperation are a part of doing business.	1	2	3	4	5	6
20.	Recorded knowledge and best practices are used for training, staff development, and organizational development.	1	2	3	4	5	6
21.	Tips and tools, job aids, and case studies of best practices are available for performance objectives.	1	2	3	4	5	6
22.	On-the-job time is available to gather information and knowledge from others.	1	2	3	4	5	6
23.	Information is stored and organized in a way that makes it intuitively easy and quick to locate.	1	2	3	4	5	6
24.	Collaborative meetings to gather information and share knowledge are productive.	1	2	3	4	5	6
25.	Advanced technologies, such as data warehousing, mining, and modeling, are used to leverage data and information for strategic and operational decision making.	1	2	3	4	5	6
26.	There is a directory of experts for each major knowledge domain.	1	2	3	4	5	6
27.	Concept mapping, sometimes called "mind mapping," is a common technique used to gather new information and knowledge.	1	2	3	4	5	6
28.	Documents stored on an organizational server or intranet contains timely and useful knowledge for our job responsibilities.	1	2	3	4	5	6
29.	Incentives are in place that motivates staff to share knowledge.	1	2	3	4	5	6
30.	Expert systems and knowledge bases are used to aid in decision making.	1	2	3	4	5	6

(Continued)

EMPLOYEE SCORING SHEET

Instructions:

1. Enter the department or business unit for which you work in the space provided.
2. Transfer your score on each item from the Knowledge Management Assessment Tool to the corresponding numbered blank.
3. Add your responses for each dimension vertically and place the total in the appropriate blank at the bottom of the column.

Section 1

Your department or business unit: _____

Knowledge Identification and Creation	Knowledge Collection and Capture	Knowledge Storage and Organization	Knowledge Sharing and Dissemination	Knowledge Application and Use
1.	2.	3.	4.	5.
6.	7.	8.	9.	10.
11.	12.	13.	14.	15.
16.	17.	18.	19.	20.
21.	22.	23.	24.	25.
26.	27.	28.	29.	30.
Total:	Total:	Total:	Total:	Total:

(Continued)

KNOWLEDGE MANAGEMENT ASSESSMENT TOOL ADMINISTRATOR SCORING SHEET 1: FIVE-DIMENSIONAL ANALYSIS

Instructions:

1. Add the total scores of all participants within whatever subunit or organizational division you have chosen for each dimension and place this value in the total box.
2. Place the total number of respondents in the N box.
3. Divide the total number for each dimension by N to find the adjusted total (average score for that dimension).

Section 2

Dimension	Total	N	Adjusted Total (Total/N)
Knowledge Identification and Creation			
Knowledge Collection and Capture			
Knowledge Storage and Organization			
Knowledge Sharing and Dissemination			
Knowledge Application and Use			

(Continued)

KMAT Administrator Scoring Sheet 2: Explicit/Tacit Analysis

Instructions:

1. Add the total scores of all respondents for *each question* and place this value in the respective subtotal box.
2. Add the subtotals in each column to obtain total scores for explicit knowledge and for tacit knowledge.
3. Place the total number of participants in the N box for each column.
4. Divide the total for each dimension by N to find the adjusted total (average for that dimension).

(Continued)

Section 3

Explicit Knowledge and Management Practices

Question	Subtotal
2	
4	
7	
9	
12	
14	
16	
18	
20	
21	
23	
24	
25	
28	
30	
Total	
N	
Adjusted Total (Total/N)	

Tacit Knowledge and Management Practices

Question	Subtotal
1	
3	
5	
6	
8	
10	
11	
13	
15	
17	
19	
22	
26	
27	
29	
Total	
N	
Adjusted Total (Total/N)	

Source: D.J. Maier and J.L. Moseley (2003). The knowledge management assessment tool (KMAT). In E. Biech (Ed.), *The 2003 annual, volume 1: Training.* San Francisco: Pfeiffer. Used with permission.

- *Shared Vision:* This commitment is experienced by employees when they all share in knowing what to do and in making the organization a better place for themselves and for the outside world. The alignment of one's personal goals with the organization's goals is primary.
- *Mental Models:* These are our assumptions about the world and how it works, testing those assumptions with new input and data, and fashioning the decisions we make accordingly.
- *Personal Mastery:* This is our legacy, what we strive for in life, what we want the world to remember about us and how we go about fulfilling that purpose and following that dream.[14]

Argyris and Schön identify types of organizational learning that have significantly impacted the field: The first occurs when an organization realizes a problem and takes corrective action to fix it; the second occurs when the organization makes a concerted effort to determine why the problem exists in the first place so that it will never occur again; the third occurs when the first and second types of learning are in place and the organization wants to find out how to continuously improve the situation and what lessons may be learned from the encounters.[15]

Workplace Implementation. The following suggestions help the performance practitioner to focus thinking about organizational learning. The practitioner begins by considering the organization's personality and looks at its culture, its mission, values, goals, critical business issues, strategies, and shared vision. The practitioner focuses on the organization's corporate social responsibility, that is, what the organization does to instill value in the external neighborhood or community and how the organization is contributing to its social world. The practitioner considers the type of dialogue that occurs within the organization: Do employees have a sense of their responsibility to contribute to corporate intelligence? Are leaders and managers redefining their roles by getting their hands and feet wet—management by walking around? Are sustainable management practices employed to survive our tenure in the organization? What are we doing to provide appropriate balance between work and life and how can we learn from these experiences?[16]

Learning Management System (LMS)

Definition. A learning management system is a software system used to manage and deliver learning content and resources to students and other learners. Since most learning management systems are web-based, they facilitate on-the-spot, any time, anywhere access.[17]

Scope. Global and regional training groups and teams through intranet and/or Internet "often use a network-based aggregation system that manages learning content, member activity reports, and member information . . . content flows to its members based on assignments, job functions, roles, and requirements . . . content may or may not have assessments to track the performance of the users."[18] The learning management system can be highly developed or something much simpler depending on the functions, needs, or priorities of the organization. It can also provide performance management functions such as performance appraisals and reviews, competency management, skill gap assessments, succession planning, and retention efforts and specifications.[19]

Ellis, in an American Society for Training and Development (ASTD) report, says that a viable and robust learning management system should be capable of personalizing content, enabling knowledge reuse, assembling and delivering training content rapidly, consolidating training initiatives on a scalable web-based platform, and so forth.[20]

Typical LMSs include, but are not limited to, Blackboard, Moodle, Desire2Learn, and Sakai. These are also course management and collaborative learning systems.[21]

Workplace Implementation. A performance practitioner selects and implements a learning management system by determining the learning strategy and its administration, tracking, and reporting options, researching learning management companies and issuing requests for proposals (RFP), scheduling demonstrations, and demanding pilots and prototypes.[22]

Content Management System (CMS)

Definition. A content management system "allows its members to authenticate their personal identification and gain access to digital files, such as customer records, documents, spreadsheets, presentations, and audio and video files from practically anywhere."[23]

Scope. A collaborative space within a secure Internet connection allows employees to work together "when accessing, uploading, editing, storing, and managing documents [with] a single point of search and distribution of these files."[24] The procedures used are computer-based or manual. In a content management system many individuals can contribute and share information; can control access to data based on their roles and responsibilities within the organization; provide for easy storage and retrieval of data; reduce repetition; enhance and enrich the communication among users at all levels of the organization.[25] There are also learning content management systems (LCMS), which support "the creation, storage, reuse, and management of courses in a central depository."[26]

Workplace Implementation. The organization from top down must support a CMS. This goes far beyond providing lip service to the enterprise. In order to access digital files, there must be a secure Internet in place. Employees at various levels in the organization must have access to the central depository, and the machinery must be available and in working order for effective and efficient retrieval of data as needed. Designated individuals or a team must be responsible for updating the data, checking for errors and redundancies, and controlling and dating the versions.

Education

Definition. Education is the process that improves work performance in a focused direction beyond the person's current job or station in life. The emphasis is on broad knowledge, understanding, comprehension, analysis, synthesis, and evaluation and on transferring knowledge to future objectives, as well as to immediate life experiences and to job-related applications.

Scope. Individual and organizational change are the outcomes of educational programs.[27] In order for these changes to occur, "education should be seen as a fundamental and ongoing process. . . . The education process should emphasize immediate application of learnings."[28] Traditionally, the term *education* refers to learning in a K–12 environment or K–20 environment with curricula designed for early childhood, primary, elementary, mid-level, high school, as well as undergraduate, graduate school, and beyond. With today's emphasis on lifelong learning, the focus shifts to educating people of all ages in multiple settings using various low- or high-tech modalities and media. The employer or the employee can act on the need for education on an immediate and on an as-needed basis.

Workplace Implementation. The Greek philosopher Maimonides offered advice to people seeking a broader, more global educational perspective when he said: "May there never develop in me the notion that my education is complete but give me the strength and leisure and zeal continually to enlarge my knowledge." Learning is a lifelong privilege. Education is not a task to be completed, but a process to be continued.

Training

Definition. There are a variety of training designs that provide instruction to employees by employers to establish, improve, maintain, or extinguish performance as it relates to business needs. Training develops employee knowledge, abilities, skills, and attitudes to "maximize the human resource contribution to an enterprise."[29]

Scope. Training is a four-part performance intervention wherein:

- Objectives describe the outcomes (what the trainees are expected to know or do when the training ends)
- Content provides information to help the trainees learn
- Interaction gives the trainees a chance to demonstrate what they have learned
- Feedback provides the trainees (and the instructor) with information and data to compare the interaction to an *exemplary model*[30]

Moskowitz cites essential training elements as change and goal-focused with alignment of all organizational systems. These elements also include extreme training such as scavenger hunts, ropes courses, whitewater rafting, and other kinds of adventures.[31]

Workplace Implementation. Training is big business, and it is appropriate only when knowledge, skills, and mandated experiences are necessary; otherwise, other interventions are required to close gaps or to realize opportunities or challenges. The performance practitioner is positioned to work with clients to determine whether or not training is both an appropriate and effective intervention. These points of guidance help the practitioner implement training:

1. Analyze the situation
2. Write learning objectives
3. Choose the delivery method
4. Identify content

5. Plan the learning activities
6. Structure a training program
7. Develop materials and validate the program
8. Evaluate the results[32]

Self-Directed Learning

Definition. Self-directed learning is training designed to allow the employee to master material independently, at the employee's own pace.

Scope. Self-directed learning is the tendency of adult learners to prefer to take charge of their own learning; however, we can all name some people who are chronologically adult but do not behave in a self-directed manner.[33] Self-directed learning is critical for success in higher education, in organizational learning, and in selecting, training, and retaining adults who are savvy in the new interactive technologies. As self-motivated and self-directed employees are given opportunities and trust to work from home or any place at any time with laptop in hand, business opportunities and challenges will be realized and addressed. In their award-winning book about older workers and learners, Moseley and Dessinger cite research that says late-life self-directed learners "prefer self-study modules or hands-on experiences in which they can control what they learn, when they learn it, where they learn, how they learn, and why they learn."[34] Table 10.1 lists major advantages and disadvantages of self-directed learning.

Workplace Implementation. A self-directed individual is one who is motivated to fulfill the demands of the work that is required, responsible to follow through when the going gets tough, trustworthy to work in a collaborative posture with peers, clients, and various stake-holders, and accountable for his or her actions. All of these characteristics demand a person who exhibits the wisdom of Solomon and the patience of Job and who can perform with

TABLE 10.1.   Self-Directed Learning Guidelines

Trainee	Trainer Developer	Corporation
Advantages	*Advantages*	*Advantages*
Based on trainee readiness	Fewer repeated classes	Allows multiple site training
Material individually selected	Increase in development time	Allows continuous learning process to begin
Learner sets pace	Time to serve as coach or mentor of resources	Foundational to learning organization and teaching organization
Disadvantages	*Disadvantages*	*Disadvantages*
Learner unable to function in a self-directed capacity	Difficult to develop	Cost factor is high (production, reproduction, distribution, revision)
Uncomfortable relying on objectives	Context in which self-directed learning is used must be carefully analyzed	Allows continuous learning process to begin
Uncomfortable with self-evaluation	Study habits of target population must be fully known	

humility and perseverance. In an organizational setting, a supervisor creates a suitable climate for self-directed learning to occur by providing time for the trainee to do the learning; allowing flexibility for the employee to choose those components of training that will enhance current and future status; empowering the trainee to practice the skills gained in the self-directed format; coaching the trainee to remain focused; guiding the trainee on a journey that is personally fulfilling and one that meets the organization's strategic vision and mission.[35]

On-the-Job Learning

Definition. On-the-job learning is a "strategy used to train new employees . . . it has been melded with just-in-time training and has become part of a seamless, on-the-job learning continuum for workers."[36] It is a "real-time change strategy"[37] that is defined by time, place, and resources. It is individual or small group training conducted at or on the worksite by one or more expert performers (peers or supervisors) during work hours.

Scope. It is formal (structured) when it is planned and it may involve a combination of classroom learning, role playing and simulations, job-related practice scenarios, and various assessment exercises. It is informal (unstructured) when it is the practice of asking a skilled employee to teach a new employee the tricks of the trade.[38] It enjoys both strengths and limitations. The fact that is does not require special training facilities, for example, takes less time to train on the job than in a classroom, and does not require the expert to leave the worksite are considered strengths. On the other hand, the fact that it may disrupt the workplace, that experts may lack training skills, and hands-on or practice time may vary are considered limitations.[39]

Workplace Implementation. On-the-job learning is "smart" when it "is directly related to the work of the unit . . . the trainer is completely familiar with the topics . . . when it can be given in short modules . . . when the trainee can see what he or she is supposed to learn . . . when it is given by genuine experts."[40] In addition, myriad opportunities should be provided for the novice to practice, practice, and do more practice under the guidance and direction of a designated expert coach who will communicate regularly and furnish frequent and timely constructive feedback.

Just-in-Time Learning

Definition. Just-in-time learning is a training design that takes place just before or concurrent with the trainee's need to use a specific knowledge or skill. It is real-time learning and marks the convergence of workplace learning, performance, and accomplishment.

Scope. Just-in-time learning has its origins in the manufacturing world, where it "is a company-wide philosophy oriented toward eliminating waste throughout all operations and improving materials throughout."[41] Gradually, it moved to other arenas of productivity. It is a learn-and-do intervention that focuses on need-to-know rather than nice-to-know content. Moseley and Dessinger believe "It is best suited to situations in which workers need immediate practice to master new knowledge or skills and when it is possible to roll out a new procedure throughout an organization or in pockets of the organization."[42]

Workplace Implementation. Just-in-time learning places substantial reliance on the employee to secure the most relevant, recent, and useful information with appropriate resources for achieving a particular purpose. It suggests that the learner is self-directed and self-motivated and that an expert guide or coach who can influence with integrity is present to answer questions, to help establish patterns and priorities, and to serve as a "sounding board" for the employee's need-to-know.

Action Learning

Definition. Action learning is both a process and a program that builds opportunities for learning around real problems and work-related issues brought to the workplace by people. Through training and education, an individual's skill advancement is enhanced which, in turn, strengthens the operational effectiveness of the organization.[43]

Scope. The concept of action learning was developed more than seventy years ago as a way to improve performance. Action learning groups focus on problems that are complex, systemic issues, important to the organization, and not easily solved by experts or ready-made right answers.[44] There are two basic types of action learning programs: programs presented by the organization and everyone in the group works on its solution under the guidance of a champion; programs wherein each group member brings a problem forward and group members take turns at being the client by focusing on results, taking a systems view, adding value, and establishing partnerships.[45]

Workplace Implementation. Table 10.2 provides guidelines and process elements for action learning.[46]

TABLE 10.2. Action Learning Guidelines

Components	How the Process Works
Groups of 6 to 30 employees	Representatives from different businesses or from different functional areas
Reflection on lessons learned from previous experiences	Apply knowledge to create more effective future performance
Take action on issues or problems brought to the group	Group wrestles with problem; finds alternative with help of group process expert
Selection of appropriate problems	Lasts weeks, months, or years, depending on projects selected and needs of members
Action learning vehicle: common problems and tasks	Action learning focus: learning and development of group members
Highly charged environment	Collaborative efforts with keen listening skills

Source: Froiland, 1994, pp. 27–34. Used with permission.

Blended Learning

Definition. Blended learning is a "system which combines face-to-face instruction and learning with computer-mediated instruction."[47]

Scope. Historically, it is "the ongoing convergence of two archetypal learning environments . . . traditional-face-to-face learning environments . . . [and] distributed learning environments (learning resources distributed in space and time to support learners anywhere and everywhere) that have begun to grow and expand."[48] Why would one want to choose a blended

EXHIBIT 10.1. THE PRACTITIONER'S VOICE: ACTION LEARNING

"Action learning takes a slightly different approach to workplace problem solving. While the primary goal is still to advance the organization's progress toward goal attainment, the secondary goal is to enhance individual and organizational knowledge in preparation for future tasks and challenges. What is unique to action learning is that there is a conscientious effort to recognize and encourage the element of learning surrounding a decision or an event. Such organizations allocate time so the staff can reflect upon or *process* the learning tied to a recent task or challenge. They do this to build the skill and knowledge capacity of the organization to be better prepared for future tasks. An overlooked, yet often equally important secondary purpose of action learning is its role in helping the organization weather workforce or industry shifts that often affect an organization's ability to recruit and retain strong performers. By purposefully enhancing knowledge and capacity of their staff, organizations become less reliant on outside talent to help move them forward. Action learning represents a mindset that is reflected in the overall organizational health."

Robert W. Lion, Ph.D.

Assistant Dean, College of Business

Northern Michigan University

Marquette, Michigan, USA

learning modality over other types of learning? Osguthorpe and Graham's research suggest reasons for designing, developing, and implementing a blended learning system:[49]

> "A blended learning system provides pedagogical richness, access to knowledge, and social interaction; since it is cost effective and easy to revise, blending occurs at the activity level, the course level, the program level or the institutional level."[50]

Workplace Implementation. There are many challenges to designing blended learning systems. Practitioners need to be good instructional designers who can deliver content with an effective blend of technologies. They also need to pilot blended systems, teach teams the elements of a blended learning experience through action, and prepare organizations, always remembering that learning is a life-long process of mastering change.[51]

Technical and Non-Technical Learning

Definition. Technical training is "instruction intended to help people perform the unique aspects of a special kind of work and apply the special tools, equipment, and processes of that work, usually in one organizational setting."[52] Clark defines it as "a structured learning environment engineered to improve workplace performance in ways that are aligned with bottom-line business goals."[53]

Non-technical training is another name for soft skills training, which is "training to help people learn how to interact with other people."[54] It involves changing attitudes rather than knowledge or skills.

Scope. Rothwell and Benkowski see it as purely hard skills training that differs from soft skills training and basic skills training; whereas Clark believes that it includes both hard and soft skills. In a technical training environment, the trainee must process and learn the content by remembering essential information and data, by applying the information and data to a particular job-related problem, opportunity, or challenge, and by evaluating the process and reflecting upon it.[55] The audience for technical training includes workers who are responsible for the following tasks;

- Producing, packing, or distributing tangible products (automobiles, electronic components, soap, batteries) or services (customer billing, sales, selection, hiring, retention)
- Using equipment or technologies (forklifts, computer applications, magnetic resonance imaging, total quality management, techniques, tools, digital technologies)
- Servicing or maintaining equipment, technologies, or processes
- Troubleshooting equipment, technologies, or processes

One way to determine whether the skill or task is technical or non-technical is to ask: Is there one right or wrong way to perform? If *yes*, then the skill or task is technical; if *no*, then the skill or task is soft; if *sometimes*, then the skill or task may be a hybrid with hard and soft components, for example, troubleshooting, which requires thought and skill for resolution.

Workplace Implementation. Whether technical or non-technical, the performance practitioner makes certain that the training supports the organization's needs and critical issues and is aligned

---

EXHIBIT 10.2. THE PRACTITIONER'S VOICE: TECHNICAL AND NON-TECHNICAL LEARNING

"Changes in student preferences and increased globalization have had strong impacts on delivering technical and non-technical learning. In the past, global learner analysis showed distinct differences in preferred technical learning delivery methods from country to country. Current analyses show that these differences have diminished and that most common delivery methods have become acceptable, if not preferred. Short, targeted learning/training backed by adequate job aids and local expertise have become essential methods since global workers want more control over their learning and more support while performing their jobs. Globalization and learner preferences for non-technical learning/training show the same trends, but issues with non-technical or soft skills training may be more difficult to resolve. There may be a need for communization of internal processes and performance standards before training can take place. In addition, the learning/training organization may have to decide whether or not to adapt learning/training to local cultures and practices or to make content acultural. Global audiences for non-technical learning/training may prefer conversation around the content, or may have cultural norms that reduce sharing in a classroom setting. However, as with technical learning/training, non-training audiences also show a preference for shorter targeted learning/training and adequate support supplemented by asynchronous opportunities to share information."

Carol K. Diroff, Ph.D.

Instructional Design Manager

Ford Learning & Development

Ford Motor Company

Dearborn, Michigan, USA

to the organization's strategies, vision, mission, and goals. Participants for the training have to be properly identified and have the appropriate resources to perform the job. The practitioner checks the expertise and credibility of vendors and external consultants who can offer specialized services and makes certain that appropriate delivery methods, including blended ones, are selected based on learning effectiveness, cost effectiveness, and time allocation and, finally, evaluate and reflect and reflect and evaluate.[56]

Social Learning

Definition. Social learning is learning from each other; it is "collaborative, immediate, relevant, and presented in the context of an individual's unique work environment."[57]

Scope. By harnessing social media to facilitate social learning, workplaces can build a collaborative culture within the organization and leverage new technologies and strategies to support and sustain social learning at work. Social media help people in organizations learn faster, innovate frequently, exchange new knowledge and data, collaborate with peers, form partnerships with customers, and add value to services or products. Researchers from the United Kingdom say that to be considered social learning, a process must:

- Demonstrate that change in understanding has taken place in the individuals involved,
- Demonstrate that this change goes beyond the individual and becomes situated within wider social units or communities of practice, and
- Occur through social interactions and processes between actors (people) within a social network.[58]

Bingham and Conner have this to say: "The new social learning provides people at every level, in every nook of the organization, and every corner of the globe, a way to reclaim their natural capacity to learn non-stop. Social learning can help the pilot fly more safely, the saleswoman be more persuasive, and the doctor keep up-to-date."[59]

Workplace Implementation. Today's and tomorrow's workplaces will continue to change, thanks to social media and the powerful social learning that takes place in organizations as employees gather to solve problems and realize opportunities in real time. Social learning and the social competence that results represent a fundamental shift in how people work and learn and how they see themselves functioning within corporate social responsibility in the greater society.

Employers have an obligation to make corporate learning fun, engaging, participatory, and well-integrated within the fabric and threads of work. Ralph Lauren says, "I don't design clothes; I design dreams." Working within a framework of Web 2.0, social learning, through various social media, will help organizations design and fulfill dreams by sustaining competitive advantage, maintaining market position, and building brand loyalty. A social media strategy leads to powerful social learning by identifying business drivers, forming a coalition of stakeholders, hosting a social media boot camp, creating a launch plan, developing a pilot offering, designing a communication plan, and agreeing on metrics.[60] It is particularly wise from an evidence-based perspective to choose metrics that are appropriate to the organization's strategic plan, identify key performance indicators, and track performance on a regular basis.

Interactive Learning Technologies

Definition. Interactive learning technologies are more than software and hardware. They are any learning technology (method or media) that encourages and supports the active involvement of the learner with the content, the instructor, the technology, other learners, and the learning resources.

Scope. Interactive learning technologies help learners "learn to learn" by encouraging engagement and dialogue among learners, clarifying performance expectations, and helping learners with information needed to manage scope, depth, and breadth of new content. Recognizing and accepting individual differences along with cross-fertilization of ideas that comes from sharing, empowers learners to be self-directed.[61]

Workplace Implementation. In order for the many learning technologies to be effective with multiple generations of learners, each selected technology requires a thorough understanding of the target population; a curriculum or course of study that is needs-driven and meticulously designed; special instructional techniques to accommodate effective and efficient usage; practice sessions that are monitored and feedback that is constructive and timely; an evaluation plan that answers what worked and didn't work, why, and how it can be improved; and special administrative and organizational arrangements that are linked to critical business issues and strategic planning. Remaining cognizant of organizational goals and objectives, project management tools and

---

EXHIBIT 10.3. THE PRACTITIONER'S VOICE: INTERACTIVE TECHNOLOGIES

"Interactive technologies continue to evolve and converge at escalating speeds resulting in single devices that meet a dizzying number of needs, including training and performance support. At Chrysler Academy, we strive to stay ahead of the curve by integrating the latest technology into our learning solutions that will engage and serve the needs of our learners. But we always keep the 'person' in mind. We think the most effective marriage of technology and human performance starts with the fundamental principles and guidelines for effective learning design. In other words, human performance solutions start with the human.

"The mobile revolution is creating a host of challenges and opportunities for us. Given the prediction that in the near future the mobile device will replace the pc as the primary tool for getting work done, we are asking a whole host of new questions before designing any learning solution. Learners' preferences and way of working change as the technology changes. Staying connected with the wants and needs of learners is a critical success factor in our world."

Laura Rutkowski, M.B.A., M.Ed.

Senior Instructional Designer, Chrysler Academy

Past President, Michigan Chapter, ISPI

Chrysler Group LLC

Auburn Hills, Michigan, USA

techniques, and the realization that interactive learning technologies are best approached as a team effort will also guide the implementation journey.

Enterprise Learning

Definition. Enterprise learning is a training design system that delivers instruction that is critical to the entire organization and must be disseminated to a large number of people dispersed over a wide geographic area.

Scope. Enterprise training is both a driver and client of interactive learning technologies. It is largely defined by scope and that scope is BIG. The logistics and time elements for enterprise training are daunting, and the budget can be staggering.[62] Enterprise resource planning (ERP) drives the need for enterprise training. For example, many companies are faced with backing up process change with massive software implementation that *touches a lot of jobs* and requires enterprise-wide training and e-commerce.[63] The major concept behind enterprise training is that "training delivered via the web has no boundaries, that it can reach anyone in any far-flung corner of a global business organization, twenty-four hours a day."[64]

Workplace Implementation. The performance improvement practitioner is well-positioned as both a generalist and a synthesizer to assist organizations to initiate and implement major steps for integrating enterprise learning technologies into the overall education and training strategy by:

- Selecting an infrastructure (learning management system and/or content management system) to support enterprise-wide learning
- Deciding how to populate the system with courses, for example, analyze learner and organizational needs, existing courses, available technology, instructional standards, and the like
- Identifying vendors to provide off-the-shelf or customer-designed courses
- Identifying consultants who can help organizations with data allocation and maintenance[65]
- Integrating learning with the organization's business needs and requirements

Classroom Learning

Definition. Classroom learning is education or training delivered by a live instructor to a group of learners at a location separated from the actual worksite.

Scope. Live classroom learning is used for all types of learning: facts, concepts, rules, principles, verbal information, attitudes, and so forth.[66] When the learning is interactive, it becomes more interesting, more challenging, more engaging, and fun. Live classroom learning is a "legitimate, creative, and rewarding" workplace learning and performance intervention if it is well-designed and suitable for solving a specific performance problem.[67] "Despite the continued growth of e-learning and newer technology-driven methods . . . and tightened purse strings, . . . classroom learning remains resilient and dominant . . . in today's learning organizations."[68]

Chief Learning Officer magazine reports learning delivery survey data conducted by their Business Intelligence Board (BIB) from 1,500 professionals in the learning and development industry. "According to the survey, 41 percent of learning executives indicated they continue to use classroom training as the primary learning delivery method. Formal on-the-job training tied asynchronous e-learning for the second highest ranked instructional delivery method (18 percent), followed by synchronous e-learning (11 percent), text-based training (4 percent), satellite video (4 percent), and portable technology (1 percent)."[69] BIB adds that "For delivering soft skills training, the classroom-based method is even more prevalent and has proven to be remarkably resilient . . . use of instructor led training for soft skills is only slightly down this year (2011, 65 percent) after its peak in 2009, when 69 percent of executives employed it as their delivery method of choice."[70]

Workplace Implementation. The key to determining whether or not classroom instruction is the appropriate and most efficient and effective vehicle for learning and problem solving is to conduct a thorough performance analysis. The PT practitioner is well-positioned to do this based on human performance knowledge, the systems perspective, and the value-added viewpoint. Practitioners "need to analyze the learning or performance problem, the organization, the type of knowledge and skills required to solve the problem, and the available delivery strategies before deciding to select live classroom learning as the best performance improvement intervention."[71] Based on a thorough analysis, the practitioner determines whether live classroom learning is possible, appropriate, and the best solution and whether live classroom learning should stand alone.

Distance/Distributed Learning

Definitions. Distance learning is a system for delivering instruction to learners who are separated by time and/or space. Synchronous distance learning is instructional delivery that occurs at the same time but not necessarily in the same place. Asynchronous distance learning is instructional delivery where time and place are different.

Distributed learning is a form of distance learning that adapts to and supports the expressed needs of the learner. While the terms distance learning and distributed learning are often used synonymously, there are operational differences between the two. For example, distributed learning has a just-in-time, just-for-me orientation.

Scope. The idea behind these systems is moving information rather than moving people; it is delivering instruction in nontraditional ways via myriad technologies that are currently available. They enjoy a rich history, which evolved from correspondence courses to live interactive instruction.[72] Broad categories of distance/distributed learning are

- Audio-based—audio cassettes, CDs, radio, audio teleconferencing, podcasts, mobile devices, and other media;
- Video-based—DVDs, broadcast television, satellite and microwave transmission, closed-circuit and cable systems, Internet;

- Computer-based—interactive computer-based media with audio and video capabilities and linkages to inter or intranets; and
- Internet-based—e-mail, chat, instant messaging, online discussion forums, webinars, blogs and wikis, audio and video conferencing, web-based instruction.[73]

Workplace Implementation. Careful planning is necessary for success of any distance learning modalities. The performance practitioner begins with an understanding of the distance learner and the reasons for choosing the distance format and whether or not that learner has had previous experience with these systems of instructional delivery. The practitioner provides a distance learning module with the "need to know" essentials prior to the beginning of delivery and follows with explicit directions, timelines, guidelines, back-up plans, browser settings, software, and frequently asked questions (FAQs) for learner access, properly configured browser settings, and necessary software.

The practitioner is always mindful of cost, technical difficulty, and the need for training and support. Finally, the practitioner realizes that not all content is compatible with distance learning. You would not want to have your heart surgery performed by the surgeon who has learned the skill via the Internet and medical school lectures. Here hands-on experience working with small animals, cadavers, and actual operating room practice and guided coaching with an expert heart surgeon and team are necessary.[74]

Online/e-Learning

Definition. Online/e-learning is a system for delivering instruction to learners using intranet or Internet technology. It is also called web-based learning, web-based training, distance learning, distributed learning, e-learning. e-Learning is "the use of electronic technology to deliver education and training applications, monitor learner performance, and report learner progress."[75]

Scope. e-Learning is networked to allow instant updating, storage, and retrieval. It is delivered via computer, and it focuses on the broadest views of learning from traditional training to tools that improve performance.[76]

It is most effective for the acquisition of knowledge and as part of a systematic approach to learning with appropriate support. It provides strength for communities of professional practice. It is least effective when interpersonal interaction is necessary.[77]

According to an ASTD *State of the Industry Report*, a survey that includes responses from many practitioners including various corporations, government, military, and selected professional groups, nearly one-third of all the training content delivered through myriad modalities is now delivered electronically.[78] Among the most frequently occurring e-learning practices are programs that support tests and knowledge, those which present content and opportunities to practice and receive feedback, and job-specific programs that allow tracking.[79]

Rosenberg lists many benefits to e-learning such as lowering costs, enhancing business responsiveness, messaging that is consistent or customized, timely and dependable content, learning 24/7, building community, leveraging the corporate investment in the web, and others.[80] There are, however, constraints to e-learning involving cost, change in employee attitudes, unprepared infrastructure, and others.

Workplace Implementation. Piskurich says: "Accommodation of e-learning solutions will require a thorough review of your learning program. From the instructional systems design model to the delivery mechanisms, from learning professional skills to the expectations of learners, there are few systems and processes that will emerge from the transition to e-learning in their present form."[81] Now is the time, as Rosenberg says, "to move from e-learning *talk* to e-learning *action* . . . and you do this by having a strategy."[82] The performance improvement practitioner is well-positioned to work with the organization to develop a robust performance strategy using the Performance Improvement/HPT Model introduced in the earlier chapters.

By determining the target population, analyzing the current and desired state and determining the gap or performance challenge, by considering vision and mission, conducting force-field and SWOT analyses, the practitioner is positioned to suggest recommendations that lead to a robust action plan.

EXHIBIT 10.4. THE PRACTITIONER'S VOICE: ONLINE OR E-LEARNING

"Online learning represents the highest level of proper utilization of existing technology. It has destroyed all traditional barriers to sharing knowledge, skills, and thoughts. The impact of online education is tremendous at all levels and in all disciplines. In healthcare, in particular, online education helps minimize the gap in quality between wealthy and poor countries. In addition, it has contributed greatly in elevating the standards of practice of healthcare providers who lack access to traditional means of continuing education. When properly designed and utilized, online education is expected to efficiently improve local, regional, and international healthcare quality."

Adnan D. Alwadie, Ph.D., RRT, RPFT

Respiratory Care Department

King Fahad Medical City (KFMC)

Riyadh, Saudi Arabia

Wikis

Definition. A wiki is "a collection of web pages which can be easily created and edited by individuals who visit them."[83] The best-known example is *Wikipedia*, the free online encyclopedia.

Scope. A wiki resembles a blog. Individuals can collaborate with others to create and edit web page text using a web browser like Internet Explorer or Mozilla Firefox. A collaboratively focused environment permits content to be changed by anyone who visits the site. Changes are tracked and, if desired, users can roll back older versions of a page. There are also many communication avenues.[84]

Workplace Implementation. Wikis can be found in business, healthcare, management, education, the arts, physical and natural sciences, social sciences, and other areas and disciplines as well. However, their content needs to be frequently evaluated for accuracy, comprehensiveness, integration, value, completeness, and effectiveness. An excellent evaluation checklist for a wiki user is available in the Toker, Moseley, and Chow article cited at the end of this section and in the references.[85]

Avatars

Definition. Avatars are "digital representations of computer users . . . characters or images that represent one person in an interactive exchange . . . avatars function from either a first person or third person perspective."[86]

Scope. Avatars are gaining popularity as an emerging technology, especially in learning environments in higher education chat rooms They function in two ways: "In e-learning environments, avatars almost always operate as agents of the e-learning application and help guide users through the environment. By contrast, in virtual worlds, which are computer-based simulated environments, users represent themselves with avatars and interact with other users' avatars."[87] There are potential benefits of avatars in educational and performance environments as well as constraints and obstacles. Blake and Moseley[88] provide criteria for the design and use of avatars in educational settings and suggest questions to ask when considering avatar use.

Workplace Implementation. Avatars provide a balance between interactive modalities and traditional modalities. They fit nicely within a constructivist learning environment because they give learners the opportunity to learn on their own or to use coaches or facilitators as "peripheral advisors." Learners need to be prepared in advance. Instructors need a contingency plan if technical difficulties arise. Since they are time-consuming to design and develop, avatars should be considered only if they enhance learning and instruction.

And More . . .

It is impossible to list all potential interactive technologies. The reader should also consider email, chat, instant messaging, online discussion forums, podcasting, webinars, blogs, video conferencing, virtual learning systems like Second Life, and others. A good resource on educational technology or on teaching and learning with technology should provide solid background information for the anywhere and any time novice worker in interactive technologies. For example, consider books by Bonk,[89] Carliner and Shank,[90] Tarlow and Tarlow,[91] Silberman,[92] and Boone.[93]

Games

Definition. Games are experiential learning activities that contain elements of fun, surprise, and challenge. They are designed for two or more participants who follow rules for problem solving and decision making.

Scope. We are all familiar with popular board games or TV game shows; however, the emphasis here is on games for instructional purposes in different workplaces. Organizations are using games to motivate trainees, encourage their learning, and sharpen their work-related repertory of knowledge and skills. Games are particularly useful for team development activities where game characteristics and instructional context are cohesively joined. Perhaps the most pertinent finding from Sitzmann's research is that "Trainees who participate in game play retained 9 percent more information than trainees who did not."[94]

A successful game meets these criteria:

- Provides a simple, single-purpose activity that focuses the participants on a job-related concern
- Incorporates on-the-job application of the learning
- Provides just-in-time training
- Is carefully integrated into the total training session
- Uses a short and clear procedure of two to four steps
- Access is available as often as needed[95]

Workplace Implementation. Experience and research indicate that solid learning must be "goal-oriented, contextual, interesting, challenging, and interactive and . . . most effective learning experiences are also engaging . . . and hard fun."[96] So too with games. Designing a game requires considerable up-front planning. Knowing the learning goals and integrating them to the game, developing all component parts and piloting them before implementation, and following up with a debriefing session to determine the lessons learned are further guidelines.[97]

Here is a tremendous opportunity for the performance improvement practitioner who knows the organizational content, the business needs, the learning needs, and the performance needs to work very closely with an instructional designer who knows learning theory, goals and objectives formulation, instructional design principles and strategies, interactive technologies, and evaluation procedures and best practices.

Simulations

Definition. Simulations are highly interactive experiential learning activities that mirror reality and allow participants to manipulate equipment or situations to practice a task; for example, land a plane, troubleshoot car mechanics or electrical circuits, trace pulmonary functions, learn anatomical procedures without harming the patient, or decide on how to handle a workplace conflict between a manager and an employee.

Scope. Simulations are useful when training requires a show-and-do approach and it is impossible to "do" it in the real world because of exorbitant cost and/or safety factors. Simulations "vary greatly in the extent to which they fully reflect the realities of the situation they are intended to model . . . simulations are by design active . . . provide realistic practice with feedback in a realistic context."[98] They range in complexity from paper-based to computer-assisted; from simple linear video to interactive video; from role play to digital.

Simulations are used in instruction when role plays or open-ended interaction among people is required, and they are well-suited for teaching motor skills, complex skills, social interaction, human relations skills, and decision-making skills in varieties of disciplines.[99] They are an excellent way to engage participants in the learning situation since participants are challenged with solving a problem that has direct bearing on an aspect of the job.

There are also simulation games, experiential learning activities that combine the characteristics of a game and a simulation. A game has rules and regulations; a simulation has a modicum of reality with role play.

Workplace Implementation. The performance improvement practitioner becomes familiar with the types of simulations that are available and feasible in the current organizational environment. Preparation for a simulation is essential as well as knowing the target population, the learning objectives, and the linkages between simulations and the real world of work. The practitioner prepares the facility, the timeline, and the coach.

In delivering the simulation, the practitioner establishes ground rules, observes, communicates, and knows when to intervene. Debriefing is critical for success; the practitioner should ask:

- How did you feel?
- What happened?
- What did you learn?
- How does this relate to your work life?
- What if . . . ?
- What next?
- Why? Why? Why?[100]

"Students are changing. They are increasingly pragmatic. They crave interaction and personalization . . . are highly visual . . . problem solvers . . . averse to reading . . . want more in less time . . . are computer savvy."[101] Simulations can keep learners motivated, engaged, challenged, and committed.

Citations

1. Dalkir, 2005, p. 21
2. Knight & Howes, 2003, p. 12
3. Fitter, 1999, p. 55
4. Whiting, 1999, p. 2
5. Charney, 1999, p. 96
6. Barclay & Murray, 1997, p. 13
7. Barclay & Murray, 1997, pp. 5–6
8. Rossett, 2000, pp. 62–69
9. Fitter, 1990, p. 60
10. Maier & Moseley, 2003, pp. 168–184

11. What Is Organizational Learning?, 2005
12. Silber & Kearny, 2010, p. 240
13. Senge, 1990, pp. 139–269
14. Silber & Kearny, 2010, p. 241
15. Silber & Kearny, 2010, pp. 241–243
16. What Is Organizational Learning?, 2005
17. Learning Management System (LMS), (n.d.) (n.p.)
18. Clemons & Kroth, 2011, p. 19
19. Clemons & Kroth, 2011, pp. 19–20
20. Ellis, 2009, p. 1
21. DeLoose, Unger, Zhang, & Moseley, 2009, pp. 28–32
22. Ellis, 2009, pp. 5–6
23. Clemons & Kroth, 2011, p. 19
24. Clemons & Kroth, 2011, p. 19
25. Personal interview with Ann Chow, February 7, 2011
26. Rosen, 2009, p. 224
27. Caffarella, 1994, p. 2
28. Jewell & Jewell, 1992, p. 226
29. Pepitone, 1995, p. 13
30. Langdon, 1999, pp. 382–383
31. Moskowitz, 2008, pp. 2–32
32. Chan, 2010, pp. v-vii
33. Brookfield, 1994, p. 25
34. Moseley & Dessinger, 2007, pp. 132–133
35. Piskurich, 1993, p. 167
36. Moseley & Dessinger, 2007, p. 249
37. Jacobs, 1999, p. 608
38. Moseley & Dessinger, 2007, p. 249
39. Rothwell, 2005, pp. 237–242
40. Carr, 1992, pp. 189–191
41. Bateman & Snell, 1999, p. 319
42. Moseley & Dessinger, 2007, p. 249
43. Marquardt, 1999, pp. 23–25
44. Marquardt, 1999a, p. 2
45. Marquardt, 1999b, pp. 43–45
46. Froiland, 1994
47. Bonk & Graham, 2006, p. 5
48. Graham, Allen, & Ure, 2003, p. 4
49. Bonk & Graham, 2006, p. 5
50. Graham, 2006, p. 5
51. Osguthorpe & Graham, 2003, p. 8
52. Bonk & Graham, 2006, pp. 10–16
53. Hoffman in Bonk & Graham, 2006, pp. 27–40

54. Rothwell & Benkowski, 2002, p. 7
55. Clark, 2008, pp. 10–11
56. Clark, 1994, pp. 124–125
57. Rothwell & Benkowski, 2002, pp. 52–58
58. Meister & Willyerd, 2010, p. 265
59. Peterson, 2010
60. Peterson, 2010
61. Bingham & Conner, 2010, p. 6
62. Meister & Willyerd, 2010, p. 6
63. Vazquez-Abad & Winer, 1992, p. 676
64. Stamps, 1999b, p. 40–46
65. Stamps, 1999a, pp. 40–48
66. Moseley & Dessinger, 2007, p. 270
67. Yelon, 1999, p. 486
68. Yelon, 1999, pp. 485–517
69. Prokopeak, 2011, n.p.
70. Prokopeak, 2011, n.p.
71. Prokopeak, 2011, n.p.
72. Lever-Duffy, McDonald, & Mizell, 2005, pp. 346–349
73. Newby, Stepich, Lehman, Russell, & Ottenbreit-Leftwich, 2011, pp. 211–217
74. Newby, Stepich, Lehamn, Russell, & Ottenbreit-Leftwich, 2011, pp. 211–217
75. Sales, 2002, p. 3
76. Rosenberg, 2001, pp. 28–28
77. Sloman, 2002, p. xvii
78. *ASTD State of the Industry Report*, 2008, p. 35
79. Rossett & Marshall, 2010, pp. 34–38
80. Rosenberg, 2001, pp. 30–31
81. Piskurich, 2003, p. 77
82. Rosenberg, 2001, p. 291
83. Toker, Moseley, & Chow, 2008, p. 22
84. Toker, Moseley & Chow, 2008, pp. 24–26
85. Toker, Moseley & Chow, 2008, p. 27
86. Blake & Moseley, 2010, p. 14
87. Blake & Moseley, 2010, p. 14
88. Blake & Moseley, 2010, pp. 16–19
89. Bonk, 2009
90. Carliner & Shank, 2008
91. Tarlow & Tarlow, 2002
92. Silberman, 2007
93. Boone, 2001
94. Sitzmann, 2010, p. 20
95. Salopek & Kesting, 1999, p. 28
96. Quinn, 2005, pp. 9–17

97. Giunta, 2010, pp. 76–77

98. Smaldino, Russell, Heinrich, & Molenda, 2005, p. 33

99. Smaldino, Russell, Heinrich, & Molenda, 2005, pp. 33–34

100. Browner & Preziosi, 1995, pp. 179–181

101. Aldrich, 2005, p. xxix

References

Aldrich, C. (2005). *Learning by doing: A comprehensive guide to simulations, computer games, and pedagogy in e-learning and other educational experiences.* San Francisco: Pfeiffer.

ASTD (2008). *State of the industry report.* Alexandria, VA: American Society for Training & Development.

Barclay, R.O., & Murray, P.C. (1997). What is knowledge management? Retrieved online: www.media.access.com/whatishtml.

Bateman, T.S., & Snell, S.A. (1999). *Management: Building competitive advantage* (4th ed.) New York: Irwin/McGraw-Hill.

Bingham, T., & Conner, M. (2010). *The new social learning; A guide to transforming organizations through social media.* Alexandria, VA: American Society for Training & Development.

Blake, A.M., & Moseley, J.L. (2010, March/April). The emerging technology of avatars: Some educational considerations. *Educational Technology, 50*(2), 13–20.

Bonk, C.J. (2009). *The world is open.* San Francisco: Jossey-Bass.

Bonk, C.J., & Graham, C.R. (2006). *The handbook of blended learning: Global perspectives, local designs.* San Francisco: Jossey-Bass.

Boone, M.E. (2001). *Managing inter@ctively: Executing business strategy, improving communication, and creating a knowledge-sharing culture.* New York: McGraw-Hill.

Brookfield, S.D. (1994). *Understanding and facilitating adult learning.* San Francisco: Jossey-Bass.

Browner, E.S., & Preziosi, R.C. (1995). Using experiential learning to improve quality. In J.W. Pfeiffer (Ed.), *The 1995 annual: Volume 1, training* (pp. 168–174). San Francisco: Pfeiffer.

Caffarella, R.S. (1994). *Planning programs for adult learners: A practical guide for educators, trainers, and staff developers.* San Francisco: Jossey-Bass.

Carliner, S. & Shank, P. (Ed.). (2008). *The e-learning handbook: Past promises, present challenges.* San Francisco: Pfeiffer.

Carr, C. (1992). *Smart training: The manager's guide to training for improved performance.* New York: McGraw-Hill.

Chan, J.F. (2010). *Designing and developing training programs.* San Francisco: Pfeiffer.

Charney, M. (1999, June). KM from the ground up. *Knowledge Management, 296*(6).

Chow, A. (2011, February 7). Personal interview.

Clark, R.C. (1994). *Developing technical training: A structured approach for developing classroom and computer-based instructional materials.* Phoenix, AZ: Performance Technology Press.

Clark, R.C. (2008). *Developing technical training: A structured approach for developing classroom and computer-based instructional materials* (3rd ed.). San Francisco: Pfeiffer.

Clemons, D., & Kroth, M. (2011). *Managing the mobile workforce: Leading, building, and sustaining virtual teams.* New York: McGraw-Hill.

Dalkir, K. (2005). *Knowledge management in theory and practice.* Oxford, England: Elsevier Butterworth-Heinemann.

DeLoose, S., Unger, K.L., Zhang, L., & Moseley, J.L. (2009, September/October). Moodling around: A tool for interactive technologies. *Educational Technology, 49*(1), 28–32.

Ellis, R.K. (Ed.) (2009). *Learning Circuits' field guide to learning management systems.* Alexandria, VA: American Society for Training & Development.

Fitter, F. (1999, June). The human factor. *Knowledge Management, 2*(6).

Froiland, P. (1994, January). Action learning: Taming real problems in real time. *Training, 31*, 27–34.

Giunta, J.P. (2010, June). Designing games that really teach. *T + D, 64*(6), 76–77.

Graham, C.R. (2006). Blended learning systems: Definition, current trends, and future directions. In C.J. Bonk & C.R. Graham (Eds.), *The handbook of blended learning: Global perspectives, local designs* (pp. 5–21). San Francisco: Pfeiffer.

Graham, C.R., Allen, S., & Ure, D. (2003). Blended learning environments: A review of the research literature. Unpublished manuscript, Provo, UT.

Hoffman, J. (2006). Why blended learning hasn't (yet) fulfilled its promises: Answers to those questions that keep you up at night. In C.J. Bonk & C.R. Graham (Eds.), *The handbook of blended learning: Global perspectives, local designs* (pp. 27–40). San Francisco: Pfeiffer.

Jacobs, R.L. (1999). Structured on-the-job training. In H.D. Stolovitch & E.J. Keeps (Eds.), *Handbook of human performance technology: Improving individual and organizational performance worldwide* (2nd ed.) (pp. 606–625). San Francisco: Pfeiffer/ISPI.

Jewell, S.F., & Jewell, D.O. (1992). Organization design. In H.D. Stolovitch & E.J. Keeps (Eds.), *Handbook of human performance technology: A comprehensive guide for analyzing and solving performance problems in organizations* (pp. 211–232). San Francisco: Jossey-Bass/ISPI.

Knight, T., & Howes, T. (2003). *Knowledge management: A blueprint for delivery*. Oxford, England: Butterworth/Heinemann.

Langdon, D.G., Whiteside, K.S.. & McKenna, M.M. (Eds.) (1999). *Intervention resource guide: 50 performance improvement tools*. San Francisco: Pfeiffer.

Learning management system. (n.d.). Retrieved .from www.networkdictionary.com/software/1.php.

Lever-Duffy, J., McDonald, J.B., & Mizell, A.P. (2005). *Teaching and learning with technology* (2nd ed.). Boston: Pearson/Allyn Bacon.

Maier, D.J., & Moseley, J.L. (2003). The knowledge management assessment tool (KMAT). In E. Biech (Ed.), *The 2003 annual: Volume 1, training*. San Francisco: Pfeiffer.

Marquardt, M.J. (1996a, May 26). Action learning in action: The key to building learning organizations. Presentation at the American Society for Training and Development International Conference and Exposition, Atlanta, GA. Session Handout W406.

Marquardt, M.J. (1996b). *Action learning in action: Transforming problems and people for world-class organizational learning*. Palo Alto, CA: Davies-Black.

Moseley, J.L., & Dessinger, J.C. (2007). *Training older workers and learners: Maximizing the performance of an aging workforce*. San Francisco: Pfeiffer.

Moskowitz, M. (2008). *A practical guide to training and development: Assess, design, deliver, and evaluate*. San Francisco: Pfeiffer.

Newby, T.J., Stepich, D.A., Lehman, J.D., Russell, J.D., & Ottenbreit-Leftwich, A. (2011). *Educational technology for teaching and learning* (4th ed.). Boston: Pearson.

Osguthorpe, R.T., & Graham, C.R. (2003). Blended learning systems: Definitions and directions. *Quarterly Review of Distance Education, 4*(3), 227–234.

Pepitone, J.S. (1995). *Future training: A roadmap for restructuring the training function*. Dallas, TX: AddVantage Learning Press.

Peterson, G. (2010, November). What is social learning? Retrieved from www.rs.resalliance.org/2010/11/03/what-os-social-learning/

Piskurich, G.M. (1993). *Self-directed learning: A practical guide to design, development, and implementation*. San Francisco: Jossey-Bass.

Piskurich, G.M. (Ed.). (2003). *Preparing learners for e-learning*. San Francisco: Pfeiffer.

Prokopeak, M. (2011, February). Learning delivery: Classroom is still king. *Chief Learning Officer Online*. http://clomedia.com/articles/view.learning-delivery-2011-classroom-is-still-king/1.

Quinn, C.N. (2005). *Designing e-learning simulation games*. San Francisco: Pfeiffer.

Rosen, A. (2009). *e-Learning 2.0: Proven practices and emerging technologies to achieve real results*. New York: AMACOM.

Rosenberg, M.J. (2001). *e-Learning: Strategies for developing knowledge in the digital age.* New York: McGraw-Hill.

Rossett, A. (2000, May). Knowledge management meets analysis. *T + D, 53*(5), 62–69.

Rossett, A., & Marshall, J. (2010, January). e-Learning: What's old is new again. *T + D, 64*(1), 34–38.

Rothwell, W.J. (2005). *Beyond training and development* (2nd ed.) New York: AMACOM.

Rothwell, W.J., & Benkowski, J.A. (2002). *Building effective technical training: How to develop hard skills within organizations.* San Francisco: Pfeiffer.

Sales, G.C. (2002). *A quick guide to e-learning: A "how to" guide for organizations implementing e-learning.* Andover, MN: Expert Publishers, Inc.

Salopek, J.J., & Kesting, B. (1999, February). Stop playing games. *T + D, 53*(2), 28.

Senge, P.M. (1990). *The fifth discipline: The art & practice of the learning organization.* New York: Doubleday/Currency.

Silber, K.H., & Kearny, L. (2010). *Organizational intelligence: A guide to understanding the business of your organization for HR, training, and performance consulting.* San Francisco: Pfeiffer.

Silberman, M. (Ed.). (2007). *The handbook of experiential learning.* San Francisco: Pfeiffer.

Sitzmann, T. (2010, October). Game on? The effectiveness of game use in the workplace depends on context and design. *T + D, 64*(10), 20.

Sloman, M. (2002). *The e-learning revolution: How technology is driving a new training paradigm.* New York: AMACOM.

Smaldino, S.E., Russell, J.D., Heinrich, R., & Molenda, M. (2005). *Instructional technology and media for learning* (8th ed.). Upper Saddle River, NJ: Pearson/Merrill/Prentice-Hall.

Stamps, D. (1999a). Enterprise training: This changes everything. *Training, 36*(1), 40–48.

Stamps, D. (1999b). Wired, wired world. *Training, 36*(8), 40–46.

Tarlow, M., & Tarlow, P. (2002). *Digital aboriginal: The direction of business now: Instinctive, nomadic, and ever-changing.* New York: Warner Books.

Toker, S., Moseley, J.L., & Chow, A. (2008, September/October). Is there a wiki in your future? Applications for education, instructional design, and general use. *Educational Technology, 48*(5), 22–26.

Vazquez-Abad, J., & Winer, L.R. (1992). Emerging trends in instructional interventions. In H.D. Stolovitch & E.J. Keeps (Eds.), *Handbook of human performance technology: A comprehensive guide for analyzing and solving performance problems in organizations* (pp. 672–687). San Francisco: Jossey-Bass/ISPI.

What is organizational learning? (2005). Pegasus Communications, Inc. Retrieved from www.pegasus.com/aboutol.html.

Whiting, R. (1999, November 22). Myths and realities: What's behind one of the most misunderstood IT strategies. *Internet Week ONLINE News.* www.informationweek.com/762/know2.htm.

Yelon, S.L. (1999). Live classroom instruction. In H.D. Stolovitch & E.J. Keeps (Eds.), *Handbook of human performance technology: Improving individual and organizational performance worldwide* (pp. 485–517). San Francisco: Pfeiffer/ISPI.

Performance Support Interventions

Performance support interventions are available to the performer on the job and just in time, and they may enhance or replace learning interventions such as training. Performance support interventions share these characteristics:

- *Intuitiveness*—provides guidance even if the user has minimal or no prior learning or experience
- *Integration*—presents a seamless union of people, process, and devices
- *Immediacy*—offers on-demand access to tools, information, advice, training, communication, and so forth
- *Individualization*—supports needs of novices, competent performers, and experts at the individual, group, or organizational level
- *Interactivity*—opens a "dynamic dialogue" between user and performance support tool[1]

Performance support interventions stress the integration of "doing" and "technology"; improve individual, group, or team performance; improve processes, products, services; and guide business plans, deliverables, results, and success measures. Typical performance support interventions are listed in Figure 11.1 and will be covered in this chapter. Listen carefully—the voice of the practitioner may be heard commenting on a specific intervention.

In order to determine whether or not a performance support intervention is appropriate and targeted requires careful performance analysis since change beats at the heart of this type of intervention. The performance improvement practitioner begins with a planned change mindset;

FIGURE 11.1.   Scope of Performance Support Interventions

Performance Support
• Performance Support Tool (PST) or Job Aid
• Electronic Performance Support Systems (EPSS)
• Documentation and Standards
• Expert Systems

remains solution neutral; *listens, listens, listens*; and then confirms with the client—What I heard you say was. . . .

Performance Support Tools (PSTs)/Job Aids

Definition. Performance support tools (job aids) provide just-in-time, on-the-job learning and just-enough information to enable a worker to perform a task efficiently and successfully without special training or reliance on memory. They may inform, support procedures, or support decisions.

Scope. Performance support tools are used during a task to facilitate job performance and efficiency. They provide guidance and, usually, they do not instruct. They are useful when employees need immediate assistance to help them get the job done. Tasks that are performed infrequently and are not part of a person's regular job are ideal situations for performance support tools.

On the other hand, PSTs that are quickly outdated, that convey complex information, or that compromise performance are inappropriate.[2] Performance support tools can be checklists or worksheets, matrix/decision tables, flowcharts, mixed varieties, and virtual reality. Those that guide job performance, reduce the length of time recall is necessary, signal when to take some action, and give directions or actions are successful performance support tools. Table 11.1 illustrates a traditional versus expanded view of performance support tools/job aids.[3]

Workplace Implementation. Performance improvement practitioners, as members of the design team, do not usually become involved in implementing job aids until after the fact . . . when the design of a system has already been agreed to, a task has been identified, and it has become apparent that the skills required to perform the task may exceed the skills currently available in those who must perform (it).[4] The skilled practitioner should conduct an environmental analysis (see Chapter 5) and help to design both the job and the performance support tool. In addition to strong analysis skills, designing performance support tools calls for creativity, problem-solving skills, and knowledge of how new technologies can enhance their design and development. Performance Support Tool 11.1 can be used to select or evaluate the use of a format.

TABLE 11.1.   Performance Support Tools/Job Aids: Traditional and Expanded Views

	Traditional View	*Expanded View*
What PST/Job Aids Do	Provide information	Provide information
	Support procedures	Support procedures
		Influence perspective and decision making
When PST/Job Aids Are Useful	During performance	Prior to performance
		During performance
		After performance

PERFORMANCE SUPPORT TOOL 11.1. WHEN TO USE STANDARD PST OR JOB AID FORMATS

Directions: Use the following checklist to select the most appropriate format for a PST or job aid. The formats are adaptable to print-based or electronic-based support tools.

Numbered List

❑ Performance requires a simple, linear action sequence

❑ Performance may become so repetitious that steps may be left out

❑ Task is performed infrequently

Checklist

❑ Performance involves inspecting, observing, or planning

❑ Performance requires documentation

❑ Performance requires user to calculate or record data

Matrix or Decision Table

❑ Performance is simple but involves making a maximum of two decisions

❑ Performance requires identification of particular conditions to continue action

Flow Chart

❑ Performance is complex; requires branching to explore alternatives

❑ Performance is enhanced by visualizing relationships between components

Hybrid (mixture of two or more formats)

❑ Performance requires a complex set of instructions involving both sequence and decision making

❑ Users range from novice to advanced

Source: J.C. Dessinger and J.L. Moseley (1992). *Designing and evaluating job performance aids,* pp. 23–24. St. Clair Shores, MI.: The Lake Group, Inc. Used with permission.

Electronic Performance Support Systems (EPSS)

Definition. Electronic performance support system (EPSS) is an electronic, computer-mediated infrastructure that empowers the user as performer and learner, enhances organizational learning, and enables knowledge management. It uses software to integrate performance-based content, knowledge, learning, and structure into a user-friendly performance and learning support system.

Scope. Electronic performance support systems are neither an intelligent performance support tool nor a type of computer-based training (CBT). However, both PSTs and CBT are considered subsets of EPSS. EPSS has these advantages:

- Access to large databases of information,
- Designed to coach the user through questioning, assessing answers, evaluating responses and offering recommendations, and
- User-friendly[5]

The benefits of using an EPSS are for both the user and the organization. For the user, EPSS can "match the learning context to the operational context . . . integrate with the work process so learners get up to speed faster and work more efficiently . . . manages complexity and work flow . . . structures the activities necessary to complete tasks, represents knowledge with graphics, sound, or animation, provides data related to the task, and provides built-in tools such as calculating fields for carrying out tasks."[6] For the organization, EPSS can provide return on investment by:

- Enhancing productivity and work flow
- Reducing training costs
- Increasing worker autonomy
- Increasing quality due to uniform work practices
- Enabling knowledge capitalization[7]

Workplace Implementation. The performance improvement practitioner is well-positioned to work with employees in this arena by becoming familiar with EPSS from the user perspective and from the organization framework. A review of recent research in this area is a good beginning. Then get involved with an EPSS project team that is working to develop a new system or improve an existing system. Here is an opportunity to exercise all "tool chest" skills, from assessment and analysis through evaluation. Performance Support Tool 11.2 is a decision tool you can use to help decide whether to select EPSS as the intervention or choice—or not.

The practitioner can assist with system maintenance by handling process and task issues and helping all employees, from novice to expert, make appropriate decisions about selecting an EPSS intervention based on sound evidence, sound practical and informed judgment, and cultural dynamics influencing individual and organizational critical thinking. This is where project management, communication, and change management knowledge and skills come in handy.

Knowledge of basic electronic performance support system design standards and design/ development activities is essential; the ability to find the right experts and convince them to

PERFORMANCE SUPPORT TOOL 11.2. TO EPSS OR NOT?

When Not to Use EPSS

1. A computer is not practical for the task.
2. Task is simple and repetitive
3. Task is constantly changing, which would increase maintenance costs and cancel out performance gains.
4. Adequate development funds are not available.
5. Experts are not available to design, program and maintain the EPSS.

When to Use EPSS

1. A computer is fundamental to the task.
2. Task complexity is wide and deep with many paths and many variables.
3. After design and programming is complete, systems maintenance can handle process and task changes.
4. System must support all levels of performers—novice to expert.
5. Inadequate performance has significant business consequences, even if number of performers is limited.
6. Turnover is high so there is a regular need to train new performers.
7. There is a need to redesign an old system or develop a new system.
8. There is a large performer population.
9. Performers must gather or create and share knowledge.

Adapted from G.L. Gery (1999). Electronic performance support systems (EPSS). In D.G. Langdon, K.S. Whiteside, and M.M. McKenna (Eds.), *Intervention resource guide: 50 performance improvement tools* (pp. 144–145). San Francisco: Pfeiffer. Used with permission.

> **EXHIBIT 11.1. THE PRACTITIONER'S VOICE: EPSS**
>
> "As an HPT practitioner, I love the concept of electronic performance support systems (EPSS). I believe the 'holy grail' in our business is to make learning an indistinguishable part of doing the work. I've worked for software companies where the EPSS approach works very well—make it intuitive enough that no training is needed or at least provide training at the exact point of use. My challenge now is to figure out how to apply the same concept in the development of leadership and interpersonal skills. Since technology continues to evolve rapidly, we need to be creative and look for ways to get there."
>
> Shonn Colbrunn, M.A., SPHR
>
> Vice President, Learning Solutions
>
> Grand Rapids, Michigan, USA

design and/or produce the EPSS is priceless. And finally, EPSS is an expensive intervention, and the practitioner will need to be able to make a business case for implementing EPSS. Feasibility and sustainability issues are also a factor when selecting this intervention. (See Chapter 19, Making the Business Case.)

Documentation and Standards

Definitions. Documentation codifies information to preserve it and to make it accessible in the workplace through written descriptions, policies, procedures, guidelines, reference manuals, quality assurance plans, bylaws, articles of incorporation, partnership agreements, contracts, letters of intent, and so forth.[8] Performance standards are concise statements or principles of ethical conduct that serve as a gauge for measuring accomplishment. The organization sets the standards around which performance is judged and the criteria that guide the performer. (See Standards of Performance Technology in Appendix A.)

Scope. Documentation may be in manuals and printed form or developed and distributed as electronic files. "Interventions in this family make information continuously accessible . . . it is important that people be able to retrieve and reference information on an as-needed basis."[9]

Documentation has many uses:

- Codifies and records progress, accomplishments, failures, lessons learned, policies, procedures, job specifications, standards, problems, and decisions;
- Provides feedback and data to analyze, validate, clarify, track, report, and record information for current and future (history) reference; and
- Helps institutionalize best practices and lessons learned.

Today's highly complex and global organizations require documentation that is more than anecdotal, so they often use documents such as process maps and procedures, customer-driven measures, process control charts, accident reports, and other documentary information about current and past performance; process management team meeting minutes and annual business plans; process improvement suggestions, procedures, and vehicles for solving process problems and capitalizing on process improvements; and similar items.[10]

Organizations that have well-documented rules, regulations, policies, procedures, practices, and the other important information and data often avoid legal and ethical problems. Standards support total quality management (TQM), performance improvement, job design or redesign, as well as other organization-wide initiatives. They improve interfaces, allow for an appropriate type of flexibility, and result in lower costs because they permit economies of scale.[11]

Workplace Implementation. Performance improvement specialists must understand when to select documentation and standards as performance interventions and how to design, develop, and disseminate the documentation or standards. This may include initiating change management initiatives to "win over" employees and other stakeholders who are affected by new procedures or standards. Performance Support Tool 11.3, based on Hale's research, provides excellent guidance.[12]

Expert Systems

Definition. Expert systems fall under the computer applications category of artificial intelligence. They are computer systems that demonstrate expert reasoning and engage in tasks that normally would be performed by a human expert to assist in decision making and problem solving.[13]

Scope. An expert system has three components: (1) a knowledge base or data base of facts, information, heuristics, and experiential knowledge used for problem solving; (2) an inference system, that is, the logic that allows a system to think through problems based on complementary psychological and mathematical theories; and (3) a human-machine interface that includes speech recognition and speech production by the computer.[14]

Workplace Implementation. Expert systems are used to diagnose human illnesses after the physician conducts a thorough physical examination. They are often used in the business world to make financial forecasts and in industry and sales to determine the shortest routes for delivery vehicles. They can be used to solve problems that are too costly, too complex, too time-consuming, and too labor-intensive. One of the hallmarks of expert systems is their use in memory capacity for organizations, that is, when an employee is forced out of the job or retires, the knowledge and expertise of that individual remains within the organizational structure.[15]

The performance improvement practitioner needs a basic knowledge of expert systems. The practitioner also needs the ability to data-mine and find out more about expert systems, or identify experts that may be able to help design, develop, and/or implement an expert system to solve a diagnosed performance problem. Feasibility and sustainability issues are also a factor when selecting this intervention. (See Chapter 19, Making the Business Case.)

PERFORMANCE SUPPORT TOOL 11.3. DOCUMENTATION OR STANDARDS?

If these conditions currently exist . . .	and you are certain that . . .	then implement documentation
• Variance in behavior is undesirable • Variance exists • Variance is caused by operating inefficiency, waste, or unnecessary costs • Information can reduce variance • Information is not currently accessible over time • Information is very complex • Job aids, manuals, help screens are not available, inadequate, inaccurate, or not easy to access	• It is possible to document required information in a form that is accurate, user friendly, and easily accessible • Documentation will facilitate consistent interpretation or compliance • Documentation will contribute to efficiency • The cost of not doing anything or doing something else is greater than the cost of gathering, communicating, and maintaining documentation	• Form a project team of stakeholders (including experts and technical support staff as appropriate) • Identify what information is required to improve performance • Determine how to codify information for easy accessibility and user friendliness • Prepare standards for measuring effectiveness of documentation • Develop documentation • Pilot documentation • Manage (distribution) and maintain (update) documentation

If these conditions currently exist . . .	and you are certain that . . .	then implement standards
• Deviation in equipment, materials, specifications, procedures, common practices, and so on • Adds extra cost • Results in lower yields • Causes variance in the quality of the work • Industry, government, and/or customers mandate standardization	• Stakeholders agree that lack of standardization is the cause of the problem • Stakeholders agree to standardize • Stakeholders agree that standardization will meet business needs • Stakeholders agree standardization will fit the organizational culture or the culture will adapt to it • Stakeholders agree standardization is essential for gaining or maintaining competitive advantage	• Conduct a feasibility and/or cost-benefit analysis • Identify industry standards • Identify existing internal standards • Prepare measurement criteria • Develop appropriate standards for organization • Implement change management interventions • Pilot standards • Implement standards Control and maintain standards

Adapted from J.A. Hale (2006). *The performance consultant's fieldbook: Tools and techniques for improving organizations and people* (2nd ed.) (pp. 136, 155–157, 161). San Francisco: Pfeiffer. Used with permission.

EXHIBIT 11.2. THE PRACTITIONER'S VOICE: EXPERT SYSTEMS

"Computer systems that usually are built on artificial intelligence utilize a collection of experts' knowledge in a domain. There are two main components of expert systems: knowledge base and reasoning or inference. While knowledge bases store and organize all detailed information, reasoning components recognize conditions and foster decision making to utilize timely and important information at the most appropriate place and time. Expert systems have great potential in the workplace since experts' performance is always critical. They can collect all experts' knowledge under one common system, and they can execute decision-making processes, even though experts are not physically present. They can automate tasks or processes regularly relied on by experts. However, developing an expert system as an in-house application takes significant time and is resource-consuming. Available software products exist but they cannot fulfill an organization's specific needs since these are usually packaged products. They also offer customization, but this increases the cost of the product."

Sacip Toker, Ph.D.

Independent Performance Consultant

Mersin, Turkey

Citations

1. Villachica & Stone, 1999, p. 444
2. Rossett & Gautier-Downes, 1991
3. Rossett & Gautier-Downes, 1991
4. Rossett, 1996
5. Gery, 1999, p. 143
6. Winer, Rushby, & Vazquez-Abad, 1999, p. 879
7. Dean, 1998, p. 11
8. Hale, 2006
9. Rummler & Brache, 1995, p. 168
10. Hale, 1998, p. 136
11. Hale, 1998, p. 136; 155–157; 161
12. Hale, 1998, p. 136; 155–157; 161
13. Expert Systems (n.d.)
14. Simonson & Thompson, 1997, pp. 29–31
15. Simonson & Thompson, 1997, pp. 29–31

References

Dean, P.J. (1998). Performance improvement interventions: Methods for organizational learning. In P.J. Dean & D.E. Ripley (Eds.), *Performance improvement interventions: Culture & systems change* (pp. 2–19). Silver Spring, MD: International Society for Performance Improvement.

Expert Systems. (n.d.). Retrieved from www.dayarayan.info/english-Glossary%20.php;services.eliteral .com/glossary/decision-support-systems-glossary.php

Gery, G.J. (1999). Electronic performance support system (EPSS). In D.J. Langdon, K.S. Whiteside, & M.M. McKenna (Eds.), *Intervention resource guide: 50 performance improvement tools* (pp. 142–148). San Francisco: Pfeiffer.

Hale, J. (2006). *The performance consultant's fieldbook: Tools and techniques for improving organizations and people* (2nd ed.). San Francisco: Pfeiffer.

Rossett, A. (1996). Job aids and electronic performance support systems. In R.L. Craig (Ed.), *The ASTD training & development handbook: A guide to human resource development* (4th ed.) (pp. 557–578). New York: McGraw-Hill.

Rossett, A., & Gautier-Downes, J. (1991). *A handbook of job aids.* San Francisco: Pfeiffer.

Rummler, G.A., & Brache, A.P. (1995). *Improving performance: How to manage the white space on the organization chart* (2nd ed.) San Francisco: Jossey-Bass.

Simonson M.R., & Thompson, A. (1997). *Educational computing foundations.* Upper Saddle River, NJ: Prentice-Hall.

Villachica, S.W., & Stone, D.L. (1999). Performance support systems. In H.D. Stolovitch & E.J. Keeps (Eds.), *Handbook of human performance technology: Improving organizational performance worldwide* (2nd ed.) (pp. 441–463). San Francisco: Pfeiffer/ISPI.

Winer, L.R., Rushby, N., & Vazquez-Abad, J. (1999). Emerging trends in instructional interventions, In H.D. Stolovitch & E.J. Keeps (Eds.), *Handbook of human performance technology: Improving individual and organizational performance worldwide* (2nd ed.) (pp. 867–894). San Francisco: Pfeiffer/ISPI.

Job Analysis/Work Design Interventions

12

Sociologists define work as "the creation of material goods or services, which may be directly consumed by the worker or sold to someone else . . . includes not only paid labor but also self-employed labor and unpaid labor. . . . provides material and personal benefits."[1] A performance improvement practitioner says that work is "one version of performance" or what the worker must do on the job.[2] No matter the type, function, or industry represented, all organizations perform three different types of work:

- *Direct work* fulfills the mission and goals of the organization.
- *Management work* guides personnel, material, and organizational resources and aligns the organization with the direct work that needs to be accomplished and with the organization's external environment and world commitment.
- *Support work* provides the necessary products or services that need to be accomplished.[3]

Job analysis and work design are complimentary intervention categories that maximize organizational efficiency and employee satisfaction and well-being. This chapter will provide information on definition, scope, and work implementation for job analysis and work design performance improvement interventions. (See Figure 12.1.) Listen carefully—the voice of the practitioner may also be heard commenting on a specific intervention.

Job Analysis Interventions

Definition. Job analysis looks at the job itself and the kind of person necessary to fulfill the job. It is a systematic and technical process of collecting job information by identifying appropriate skills, duties, knowledge, and accountability issues.

Scope. Although it may be considered a performance intervention on its own merit, in the performance improvement arena it is part of the up-front performance analysis occurring prior to gap analysis, cause analysis, and selection or design of appropriate interventions.[4] In the human resource development arena, "job analysis is necessary for legally validating the methods used in making employment decisions, such as selection, promotion, and performance appraisal."[5] Job analysis interventions include job descriptions and job specifications.

Workplace Implementation. Job analysis answers questions regarding inputs, processes, outputs, or outcomes of specific jobs. Consideration is given to purpose, location, frequency, importance, qualifications, and tools for input. Procedures and job difficulties are the domain of processes.

FIGURE 12.1.   Job Analysis/Work Design Interventions

Job Analysis/Work Design Interventions			
Job Analysis	**Work Design**	**Human Factors**	**Quality Improvement**
• Job Descriptions • Job Specifications	• Job Design • Job Enlargement • Job Rotation • Job Enrichment • Reengineering, Realignment, Restructuring	• Ergonomics • Safety Engineering • Security Management • Green Workplace	• Total Quality Management (TQM) • Continuous Improvement • Preventive Maintenance (PM) • Six Sigma • Lean Organizations

Outputs or outcomes focus on standards, consequences, and feedback.[6,7] Performance Support Tool 12.1 is an example of a job analysis survey to gather data about a specific job in an organization.

Job Descriptions

Definition. A job description is a written account highlighting the tasks and functions of a job, including what is done on the job, how it is done, and under what circumstances. A job analysis makes it possible to write efficient, concise, and effective job descriptions.

Scope. The following data may be generated through job analysis and applied to job descriptions: work activities, worker activities, job resources, job tangibles and intangibles, work performance, job content, and special job requirements.[8]

Workplace Implementation. Although individual organizations may have specific requirements; there is no standard form used for writing a job description. In general, sufficient consistency and attention to detail are necessary so that performers understand:

- Major tasks performed
- Percentage of time devoted to each task
- Performance standards
- Working conditions
- Reporting chain
- Non-human resources used on the job[9]

Job descriptions are also useful components of other interventions such as job classification, compensation, design and redesign; employee recruitment, selection, staffing, training and development; performance appraisal; and retention.

PERFORMANCE SUPPORT TOOL 12.1. JOB ANALYSIS SURVEY

Directions: Use the following job analysis survey or adapt the survey to gather data about a specific job in your organization. It is helpful to use the same survey with *all* the internal and external stakeholders including performer, manager, supervisor, customer, supplier, or others.

1. **Demographic Data**

   Name of organization: _____

   Name of performer: _____

   Title/position of performer: _____

   Division/Department/Unit: _____

2. **Describe the job:**

   Work processes (action over time, such as completing a form, assembling a door)

   Work activities (tasks performed to complete a process)

   Work procedures (how processes/tasks are performed)

   Work expectations:

   • Performer

(Continued)

- Supervisor

- Customer

3. What are the results of the job?

4. Describe specific task attributes related to the job:
What does the performer need to know to perform the job successfully?

What skills does the performer need to perform the job successfully?

What abilities does the performer need to perform the job successfully?

What attitudes support successful completion of the job?

5. Identify the non-human resources required for the job (technology, machines, equipment, tools, or others):

6. List any actions faced on the job that may endanger health and safety:

7. List the direct report chain from the performer to the person holding ultimate responsibility for the job (internal or external):

8. List the people who report to the job performer (internal or external):

Job Specifications

Definition. Job specifications list the minimum qualifications that a person needs to perform the job successfully. These are performer-focused, while job descriptions are job-focused.

Scope. Job specification categories include knowledge, skills, abilities, aptitudes, attitudes, experience, and capacity limits, given appropriate training, tools, equipment, and environment.

Workplace Implementation. The performance improvement practitioner focuses on the basic knowledge, skills, abilities, attitude, and experience that are necessary to perform the job successfully; determines which requirements are absolutely necessary and those which are nice to have; and addresses the legal implications of the job specifications.

Work Design Interventions

Definition. Work design is an umbrella term that includes job design and other job-related components. It is tied directly to the strategy and goals of the organization. It is a blueprint of job tasks structured to improve organizational efficiency and employee satisfaction.

Scope. The way work is organized and how people are grouped together to accomplish the organization's mission and goals provide the far-reaching scope of the work design process. Work design interventions include job design, enlargement, rotation, enrichment, reengineering, realignment, and restructuring.

Workplace Implementation. Work design concepts are applied at several levels of the organization. The content of individual jobs, the organization of work units, and the coordination of work both within and between divisions and departments are designed effectively only when the work requirements are understood.

Job Design

Definition. Job design is the process of putting isolated tasks together to form complete jobs.[10]

Scope. Rothwell sees job design as a four-fold function involving work duties, activities, responsibilities, and desired outcomes.[11] It determines "how the job is performed, who is to perform it, and where it is to be performed."[12]

Workplace Implementation. Job design is all about change: recognizing the need for change; approaching the change effort; determining how, when, where and why to change the job; and, if it is appropriate to do so, diagnosing workflow and processes and providing training and support, making job changes, and evaluating the job changes.[13]

Job Enlargement

Definition. Job enlargement is a work design option that increases the job scope by expanding a performer's job duties. For example, job enlargement may require a worker to perform traditionally unrelated tasks or may increase the knowledge requirements for a specific job.

Scope. Task enlargement and knowledge enlargement help workers experience more job satisfaction, fewer job errors, and enhanced customer satisfaction.[14] See the Job Enlargement Scenario in Exhibit 12.1.

EXHIBIT 12.1. JOB ENLARGEMENT SCENARIO

Darlene, Joan, and Jim are employed by XYZ Friendly, Inc. Their responsibilities are as follows: Darlene makes the product, Joan packages the product, and Jim distributes the product. All three workers are valued employees; however, their enthusiasm for their jobs is decreasing.

In an attempt to retain their interest and enthusiasm and challenge their potential, their immediate supervisor enlarged their jobs. Under the new arrangement the following occurs:

- Darlene continues to make the product but also takes over the packaging duty of preparing and attaching the bill of lading, describing the merchandise being transported, and the conditions that apply to the transportation.
- Joan is still the lead packager but also schedules inspection and completes the bill of lading.
- Jim is still responsible for distribution, but also takes over two warehousing tasks that were formerly assigned to another worker.

Workplace Implementation. There are major up-front activities related to implementing job enlargement:

1. Determine the tasks required and the frequency of repetition required for each task;
2. Focus on the type of work—direct work, management work, and/or support work; and
3. Consult with a supervisor to clarify specific job or political dimensions. Once these three tasks are completed, select one or two jobs for enlargement, monitor the scope and selection, and seek frequent and pointed feedback from the employees about the process.

Job Rotation

Definition. Job rotation is a form of job enlargement that occurs when employees do numerous and entirely different jobs on a flexible, revolving schedule without disrupting the workflow. Job rotation usually involves cross-training.

Scope. Employers rotate people into jobs in order to facilitate their learning and development and help employees see the bigger organizational picture.[15] On an assembly line, for example, a worker whose job is to install tires that come off a conveyor belt may be rotated to another station to install fenders. Later, she may rotate to a third workstation to inspect certain components of the cars once they leave the assembly line. This is a proactive way of dealing with absenteeism and general worker dissatisfaction, and it supports career advancement because workers are trained to perform a variety of jobs.

Workplace Implementation. The performance improvement practitioner selects jobs that could be rotated based on a predetermined set of criteria and employees who are in the early phases of their careers or are the top performers in their job classifications. The practitioner assigns employees to a variety of jobs within the organization, monitors their job skills, and records their progress. The practitioner provides feedback to employees regarding career opportunities, promotion, and salary adjustments.[16]

Job Enrichment

Definition. Job enrichment is a job design option that makes a job more rewarding and satisfying by adding tasks (horizontal job enrichment) or responsibilities (vertical job enrichment).

Scope. Job enrichment is a job-enhancing process with effects that can be traced to intrinsic and extrinsic performance motivation factors. Intrinsic motivation comes from within the individual performer; the performer feels that "doing a good job is its own reward." Extrinsic motivation comes from outside the individual and may include rewards for increasing production or consequences for producing poor quality products or services. Job enrichment may provide opportunities for autonomy, feedback, and decision making; for example, the worker may have input in work scheduling, methodology, and so forth.[17]

Workplace Implementation. A performance practitioner uses a number of strategies to enrich jobs: form natural work groups; alter the job so that each employee owns a unique body of work; combine the tasks and empower the employee to perform the complete job; establish client relationships by allowing employee and client to confer about the product; vertically load the job and permit the employee to plan and control it; open feedback channels; and provide opportunities for efficient and timely sharing of information.[18] Again, this is a perfect opportunity to be creative and think outside the box.

Job Reengineering, Realignment, Restructuring

Definitions. Reengineering is the radical redesign of processes for the purpose of extensive rather than gradual performance improvement. Realignment is all about getting the organization refocused on its core competencies. Restructuring reorganizes the units, divisions, or departments of an organization, which usually results in a new organizational chart and new responsibilities and may also involve new reporting relationships.

Scope. The three R's are management processes that focus on increasing efficiency, implementing lessons learned, streamlining process flow, and creating an organizational foundation on which to grow and prosper. They should be integrated into strategic planning as performance improvement initiatives.

Workplace Implementation. The three R's can correct imbalances and make the workplace more efficient and the work assignments more challenging.[19] However, the three R's also affect employees on a daily basis by changing work configuration and, indeed, the culture of work groups. It is important to prepare employees thoroughly for any type of management change and involve them in the decision-making process.

Human Factors Interventions

Definition. Human factors is an interdisciplinary approach in which work, work environments, machines, equipment, and processes are married to human physical and cognitive characteristics—in which machine and person are consciously and purposefully linked to produce results.[20]

Scope. Four areas of human factors that interface in a performance environment are ergonomics, safety engineering, security management, and the green workplace. Each area may be a focus for human-factors-based performance improvement interventions.

Work Implementation. Each area has a variety of strategies for implementation. Basically, the performance improvement practitioner needs a foundational knowledge of human factor principles and the ability to data-mine and network to obtain the needed information and resources to implement human factors interventions.

Ergonomics

Definition. Ergonomics is the scientific study and design of workstations, work practices, workflow, equipment, and tools to accommodate the physical and psychological capabilities and limitations of employees. It "seeks to fit the machine to the person rather than the person to the machine . . . [and] to minimize the harmful effects of carelessness, negligence, and other human fallibilities that otherwise may cause product defects, damage to equipment, or even injury or death of employees."[21]

Scope. The two major areas of ergonomics are physical ergonomics and cognitive ergonomics. Physical ergonomics deals with the visible physical work. Decisions are made about appropriate chair heights, proximity of equipment to perform the job successfully, how to reach, bend, flex, lift, squat—or not. "Cognitive ergonomics refers to the impact of the physical/sensory ergonomic environment on our mental or cognitive process."[22] It deals with mental work, the worker's ability to process information, and the effect or ergonomic factors on the efficiency and effectiveness of information processing. Trying to think on the floor of a steel manufacturing plant is a good, if extreme, example of cognitive function under ergonomic stress.

Workplace Implementation. Three key pillars of ergonomics are (1) fitting the task and workplace to the individual; (2) designing the workplace for individuals with a range of body sizes;

and (3) designing the workplace for individuals at the extremes of the body-size range.[23] Ergonomists and performance improvement practitioners may be called upon to perform tasks such as select ergonomically designed chairs for good posture and comfort; select properly sized tools to accommodate the hand sizes of both men and women; adjust lifting capacities; design task components to require minimum force; eliminate distractions such as outside noise, glare, and intense lighting.[24]

Safety Engineering

Definition. Safety engineering is a planned process to reduce the symptoms and costs of poor safety and health and make the work environment safer and healthier for employees.

Scope. The benefits of safe and healthy work environments are greater productivity, lower absenteeism, increased efficiency for involved workers, lower medical and insurance costs, lower workers' compensation rates because fewer claims are filed, and so on.[25] Today's organizations need to be vigilant regarding a variety of workplace issues and concerns. Among these are workplace bullying and violence, blood-borne pathogens, exposure to hazardous chemicals, chemical dependency issues, particularly smoking and drinking on the job, occupational respiratory diseases, and job stress and burnout.

Workplace Implementation. The Occupational Safety and Health Administration (OSHA) sets safety and health standards for workers. OSHA requires organizations to maintain adequate records of the incidences of injuries and illness. Once a performance analysis is conducted, the performance improvement practitioner should verify that a "real" problem exists, determine the nature of the problem, justify the need for a safety engineering intervention, and select or design an intervention targeted at the high-risk area(s) based on OSHA or other industry standards. Table 12.1 offers suggestions for selecting safety engineering interventions.

Security Management

Definition. Security management is a broad field of management "for programs designed to protect the physical and intellectual property of the firm and the employees, clients, and suppliers of an organization."[26]

Scope. The focus of security management is on protecting company property, personnel, and information. Other responsibilities include information technology infrastructure and security management, including network architecture design, bandwidth management, virus scans, and organizational troubleshooting.[27]

Workplace Implementation. Risk assessment and risk analysis are used to recognize threats, rate system vulnerabilities, and determine the probability of any predictions or if . . . then scenarios. (See Chapter 19, Making the Business Case.) The performance improvement practitioner working with the security management team identifies the potential risks, determines the costs of a particular problem and ways to eliminate or minimize it, and suggests how to allocate resources that will protect the organization.[28]

TABLE 12.1. Suggestions for Selecting Safety Engineering Interventions

If the problem is . . .	You may want to suggest . . .
Accidents	• Redesigning the work environment
	• Setting goals and objectives for accident prevention
	• Establishing safety committees
	• Training in health and safety
	• Encouraging financial incentives for good health and safety practices
Diseases	• Discussing the work environment
	• Setting goals and objectives for preventing occupational diseases
	• Analyzing incidence, severity, and frequency of illness and accidents
Stress	• Establishing organizational stress programs
	• Establishing individual stress strategies
	• Monitoring employees' progress toward stress reduction

Green Workplace

Definition. A green workplace is devoted to environmentally sensitive green business initiatives and practices with a strategy that shows solid relationships with people, long-term profitability, and a commitment to improving the planet. A green workplace creates a culture of environmental awareness.

Scope. Going green enjoys many meanings. For some it means reducing pollution, conserving resources and ecosystems, being energy-efficient, and reducing climate changes. Some see it as being aware of social issues like abject human poverty or disparities in health care. Green initiatives save organizations money and help enhance profitability.

Workplace Implementation. Performance improvement practitioners support a green work environment by becoming catalysts for change and for sustainable thinking. "The changes must occur throughout, from the actions of individual employees and how they are rewarded, to how the organization measures its success, to how green roles and responsibilities are distributed across the organization."[29]

Greening a workplace involves mobilizing a green strategy team that is empowered to make the necessary green changes in the work environment. The green team develops strategies according to their potential organizational impact, makes recommendations for implementing green initiatives, and tracks and monitors successes and failures. The key here is to align all green initiatives within the organizational culture.[30] These areas are major roles for involvement of the performance practitioner.

Performance Support Tool 12.2 is a guide to help assess the importance of selected green practices. The form and survey process may be used with a variety of stakeholders within and outside of a specific workplace.

Quality Improvement Interventions

Definition. Quality improvement is a formal and systematic approach to the analysis of performance that focuses on how to improve the quality of the process, performance, performer, or product.

Scope. Quality improvement is about conducting business right the first time, every time. Quality and efficiency—the economical production of goods and/or services using minimal resources—are the chief goals of quality improvement. There are numerous performance improvement interventions for improving quality: total quality management (TQM), continuous improvement, preventive maintenance (PI), six sigma, and lean organizations.

Work Implementation. Three activities support world-class competence in a global marketplace, and each one implies commitment to continuous quality improvement:

- Encourage continuous improvement
- Empower continuous change
- Enable continuous learning

Total Quality Management (TQM)

Definition. Total quality management is "both a philosophy and a set of guiding principles that represent the foundation of a continuously improving organization."[31] Smith defines it as a "holistic approach to workplace management . . . [and] the engagement of all workplace stakeholders to define, build, measure, and assess quality by controlling products, services, and people through planning, assurance, control, and continuous improvement feedback activities."[32]

Scope. TQM focuses on doing things right the first time, striving for continuous improvement, and addressing customer needs and satisfaction.[33] The goal of TQM is the highest quality that can be produced from the perspectives of product quality—achieving or exceeding production standards; service quality—responding to customers' needs before, during, and after product or service are delivered; and customer quality—meeting or exceeding customer expectations.[34] An historical display in the history room at Chicago's Marshall Field's store, now the May Company, quotes Marshall Field, the icon of retail merchandising, as saying: "Quality is remembered long after the price is forgotten."

Workplace Implementation. Total quality management supports a committed and involved management who can form partnerships with internal and external customers, suppliers, and vendors, determine performance measures to track processes, and balance and align the organization's continuous improvement efforts.[35]

Table 12.2 describes some of the tools that TQM practitioners use.[36,37,38]

PERFORMANCE SUPPORT TOOL 12.2. GREEN PRACTICES IN HUMAN PERFORMANCE ARENAS

Directions: The following items represent green practices in human performance arenas. Check each item in the column that indicates your perception of its importance. Discuss the items with your co-workers to see whether there is consistency in your thinking about green practices. Then develop a green roadmap to guide the greening of your workplace.

	Extremely Important	Definitely Important	Some Importance	Slight, If Any, Importance
1. Become a change agent for working green every day.	☐	☐	☐	☐
2. Go digital—keep files on computers instead of in a filing cabinet.	☐	☐	☐	☐
3. Review documents on screen rather than printing them out.	☐	☐	☐	☐
4. Send emails instead of paper letters.	☐	☐	☐	☐
5. Print on both sides of the paper.	☐	☐	☐	☐
6. Turn off lights when leaving a room for fifteen minutes or longer.	☐	☐	☐	☐
7. Set computers to energy saving settings and shut them down when you leave for the day.	☐	☐	☐	☐
8. Write letters to your representatives to support green initiatives.	☐	☐	☐	☐
9. Mark unwanted newsletters, catalogs, and magazines "Return to sender" and ask to be removed from the list.	☐	☐	☐	☐
10. Recycle old papers.	☐	☐	☐	☐
11. Spearhead green discussion at monthly meetings. Typical discussions might include reducing pollution in the organization; developing an energy-efficient mindset for the organization; buying electricity from green power companies; emphasizing recycling and promoting the use of bio-degradable materials; allowing employees to work remotely either occasionally or full-time.	☐	☐	☐	☐
12. Encourage green bag lunches: employees take turns briefly summarizing an appropriate journal article from the scholarly or popular press and then informally discuss it.	☐	☐	☐	☐
13. Connect the organization's green efforts with the community in which the organization is located.	☐	☐	☐	☐
14. Network with other individuals in similar organizations to encourage green efforts.	☐	☐	☐	☐
15. Partner with a librarian to provide the necessary resources to maintain interest in going green.	☐	☐	☐	☐

(Continued)

	Extremely Important	Definitely Important	Some Importance	Any Importance
16. Help your organization develop key performance indicators (KPIs), a series of metrics that your green team will use to help define and measure your organization's progress toward goals. These indicators may be ecological (transportation of people and products, for example), social (health, safety, and welfare in the workplace, for example), economic (community economic development, for example).	☐	☐	☐	☐
17. Encourage the organization to develop a "green toolkit" to show employees how they can save money and energy.	☐	☐	☐	☐
18. Encourage the company to change to new compact fluorescent light bulbs, which use 70 percent less electricity than incandescent light bulbs.	☐	☐	☐	☐
19. Set the thermostat a few degrees lower in the winter and a few degrees higher in the summer.	☐	☐	☐	☐
20. Ask about adding a filtration device to the drinking water and stop drinking bottled water.	☐	☐	☐	☐
21. Set up a workplace recycling system.	☐	☐	☐	☐
22. Save laser toner and ink jet empties and return them to manufacturers.	☐	☐	☐	☐
23. Buy recycled printer paper.	☐	☐	☐	☐
24. Encourage videoconferencing and telecommuting whenever possible.	☐	☐	☐	☐
25. Recycle old electronics. Outdated but usable computers can be donated to groups that will refurbish them to help schools who can't otherwise afford them.	☐	☐	☐	☐
26. Donate old cell phones to charitable organizations that will give them to the elderly or homebound.	☐	☐	☐	☐
27. Learn about sustainability as a key driver of innovation.	☐	☐	☐	☐
28. Prepare a press release on what the organization is doing regarding green technology.	☐	☐	☐	☐
29. Use recycled, refurbished, or reconditioned products and materials whenever possible.	☐	☐	☐	☐
30. Encourage the organization to develop a green research and development policy.	☐	☐	☐	☐
31. Encourage the organization to develop a green purchasing policy.	☐	☐	☐	☐
32. Encourage the marketing department to conduct green marketing research.	☐	☐	☐	☐
33. Encourage the organization's leadership to develop a green vision statement.	☐	☐	☐	☐
34. Draft an environmental statement that embraces your organization's green philosophy.	☐	☐	☐	☐
35. Provide training about green technology to employees.	☐	☐	☐	☐

Adapted from J.L. Moseley and A.M. Blake (2012). Green practices in human performance arenas. (unpublished manuscript). Used with permission.

TABLE 12.2. TQM Toolkit

This tool . . .	Provides . . .	For the purpose of . . .
Affinity Diagram*	Simple characterization process linking factors with one another, for example, people, strategies, resources, etc.	Illustrating the relationships between causes and effects
Check Sheet or Checklist*	List of items to verify, validate, or monitor; each item is preceded by a box that may be checked off upon completion of the monitoring task	Verifying, monitoring, or validating factors related to process, performance, or product; for example, verifying that all criteria for completing a task successfully have been met
Control or Process Control Chart	Horizontal axis display of the variation in an ongoing process, for example, plotting the variable 'time' against upper, average, and lower control limits	Discovering how much variability is due to random variation and how much is due to unique events or individual performance Determining whether a process is within statistical control Determining whether to change the process or the specifications
Cross Impact Matrix*	A format for organizing consequences and related factors; consequences are recorded in vertical columns and related factors in horizontal columns	Discovering relationship between factors and consequences Analyzing impact or effect of a specific factor on a specific consequence
Decision Wheel*	Thinking tool for probable effects of actions taken: A decision is recorded in the center "bubble." A circle with four bubbles is drawn around the center bubble; each of the four bubbles is used to record the effects of the decision. A second circle with four bubbles is drawn around the first circle and each bubble is labeled with the effects of the first set of effects	Showing probable effects of actions taken or decisions made Showing both intended and unintended effects Showing how one effect may cause another effect (often unanticipated)
Fishbone Diagram (aka Cause and Effect Diagram or Ishikawa Diagram	Graphic presentation of root causes that also sorts causes and show relationships	Identifying causes responsible for an existing effect (problem)
Five Whys	Process for surfacing real cause of a problem: 1. Ask question; 2. Listen to and record response; 3. Ask "Why?" 4. Repeat Steps 2 and 3 five times—no more, no less!	Determining true or real cause of a problem
Flowchart	Diagram of steps in a process in sequential order	Thinking through processes before implementation or redesign
Force Field Analysis*	Process for identifying, analyzing, and graphically displaying the forces (what and who) that may drive or restrain a specific organizational change	Analyzing and graphically representing forces pushing for and against a specific change Determining which forces will have the most impact on successful change implementation Developing an action plan
Histogram	Bar chart representing the spread of variable data over time	Showing the natural distribution of data Showing how results of a repeated event vary over time Showing variability or deviations from standard or normal range and how much of a deviation exists
Pareto Chart	Vertical bar chart that highlights process factors in descending order of importance or frequency of occurrence	Identifying basic cause of a problem Prioritizing which problem to solve first, second, and so on Monitoring progress

This tool . . .	Provides . . .	For the purpose of . . .
Plan, Do, Check, Act (PDCA) Cycle	Systematic process used to get jobs or projects completed	Analyzing, designing, developing, implementing, and evaluating continuous improvement processes
Scatter Diagram	Plotted points that show correlations between two variables by plotting points for the variables on an X (vertical) axis and a Y (horizontal) axis, for example, X = time and Y = cost	Proving that a relationship exists between two variables
		Indicating the strength of the relationship
		Determining whether the relationship is positive or negative
		Not used for proving that one variable causes another

Note: Tools marked with an asterisk are not "traditional" TQM tools; however, they are frequently included in a TQM practitioner's toolkit.
Sources: Bonstingl, 1992, pp. 51–68, and Rothwell, 2005, pp. 166–168. Used with permission.

Continuous Improvement

Definition. Continuous improvement is an ongoing, systematic process to assure, maintain, and improve processes, products, and services based on predetermined standards and customer satisfaction. The entire organization, including internal and external stakeholders, is committed to and involved in the process.

Scope. Continuous improvement has a long-range focus that addresses organizational well-being and is built upon solid foundational pillars that give customers a voice in the issues that affect them.[39] "Continuous improvement means undertaking improvement projects that range from fixing things that fail to creating new processes, services, and products. It means forming and empowering teams of people to deal with existing problems and opportunities at work."[40]

Workplace Implementation. Continuous improvement is integral to an organization's vision, mission, values, goals, strategies, and critical business issues. Practical organizing guidelines for continuous improvement exist throughout the literature on quality:

- Select a champion from top management to plan and communicate continuous improvement goals.
- Encourage total workforce involvement; plan individual and team efforts.
- Emphasize skill and knowledge training in continuous improvement approaches that are applicable to the job.
- Hold employees accountable for performance; link quality indicators to customer requirements.
- Reward and recognize personnel who both talk and model continuous improvement at the various organizational levels.
- Evaluate continuous improvement goals regularly and frequently.
- Publish and celebrate continuous improvement successes, both within the organization and its external geographical area and range.

EXHIBIT 12.2. THE PRACTITIONER'S VOICE: CONTINUOUS IMPROVEMENT

"It [continuous improvement] is all about establishing many lines of communication, interactions, and feedback lines with our customers . . . we want to hear about their preferences, their stay with us, their thoughts, feelings, opinions. We encourage among all our employees a culture of feedback. Consistency of experience is most important. . . . We have twelve service standards we believe we deliver on a consistent basis. Among them are getting it right the first time, greet the guest by name, smile and always make eye contact, first impressions count, no request is too small—these are some of the standards. We also learn from our mistakes."

Malcolm Hendry

General Manager

The Rubens at the Palace

Buckingham Palace Road

London, England, UK

Preventive Maintenance

Definition. Preventive maintenance (PM) is a manufacturing term for a proactive approach to equipment maintenance that focuses on repair and adjustment issues within a production system. However, the concept of preventive maintenance can be applied to any operating system, including management systems, human resource systems, information systems, technical systems, and so on.

Scope. Changing the organization's climate through analysis and diagnosis of the context in all areas of production are foundational elements in prevention-based thinking. Preventive maintenance is everybody's business; it is performer-centered and is integrated within all job functions in all industries.

Workplace Implementation. The performance improvement practitioner who selects and implements preventive maintenance aims for zero failure, zero trouble, and zero waste by taking a proactive approach with a focus on:

- Maintaining normal machine conditions through frequent inspections, regular cleaning, tightening of screws, nuts, bolts; observing correct operating procedures;
- Determining abnormal production conditions in a timely manner by using the five senses and sophisticated diagnostic equipment; and
- Developing and implementing countermeasures to reinstitute normal machine efficiency.

Six Sigma

Definition. Six sigma is a systematic quality improvement process that is used on both the production and transactional sides of the business to design, manufacture, and market goods and services that customers may desire to purchase. Six sigma principles require that "acceptable [product or service] variations fall within six standard deviations from the average [so] six sigma measures changing statistical properties in a very precise and detailed manner."[41]

Scope. As a philosophy, six sigma's focus is on continuous quality improvement as viewed through a customer's lens. As a practice, its focus is on reducing the variation in product or service quality.[42] It uses different application methods for implementation:

- DMAIC—define, measure, analyze, improve, control—is used to find and fix defects on existing projects;
- DMADV—define, measure, analyze, design, validate—prevents defects; and
- DMEDI—define, measure, explore, develop, implement—focuses on exploring other options, alternatives, risk factors, and so on before development and implementation.[43]

Workplace Implementation. Six sigma "delivers measurable, tangible economic benefits."[44] Table 12.3 shows the parallel constructions between the Performance Improvement/HPT Model and the Six Sigma Process.

TABLE 12.3.   Human Performance and Six Sigma: Parallel Constructions

Performance Improvement/HPT Model	Six Sigma Process Steps
Analysis: Performance, Gap, Cause	Analyze, Define, Measure, Explore
Intervention Selection, Design, Development	Design, Improve, Explore
Intervention Implementation and Change	Implement, Improve
Evaluation	Measure, Control

Source: Dessinger, 2006. Used with permission.

The performance improvement practitioner may want to become involved on the people side of six sigma as a champion, a senior-level manager who promotes six sigma methodology, "owns" the process, monitors projects, and measures the savings realized; master black belt, an expert in six sigma tools and tactics and serves as a trainer, mentor and guide; black belt, a full-time leader of a defined project working strictly on processes to reach desired outcomes; or green belt, a part-time leader who assists black belts in a functional area and who drives bottom-line results.[45]

Six sigma and performance improvement are comprehensive and complementary approaches to establishing a culture of quality. Van Tiem, Dessinger, and Moseley show how performance improvement practitioners benefit from adopting and adapting the principles of six sigma to human performance improvement. They also provide a very useful six sigma toolbox for the human performance practitioner.[46]

Lean Organizations

Definition. A lean organization "maximizes customer value while minimizing waste . . . creating more value for customers with fewer resources."[47] Lean organizations are customer-focused, organizationally aligned and have empowered trusting employees who can solve problems.

Scope. The term "lean" can be applied to any process within an organization; however, its greatest benefit is its application to *all* organizational systems. Lean organizations focus on value generation and growth, relationships between organizations, their functions and their place in the external value chain, and people who respond to the demands and requirements of getting work done.[48] Lean organizations are efficient and effective and employ management principles within a framework of least cost and zero waste.

Workplace Implementation. Performance improvement practitioners who select and/or implement this intervention in their organizations need to be able to "think lean," understand the internal and external cultures of the organization, and be adroit at facilitating change. Lean organizations begin with lean thinking from top management down to all employee levels. Sources of waste such as defective products, overproduction, unnecessary transportation, delays in production or time spent waiting, inventory waste, and so on need to be identified with an appropriate action plan for minimizing their effect or eliminating them altogether. Interventions are identified and implementation is monitored and recorded. Research shows that lean organizations experienced "higher rates of change; were likely to be more responsive to business strategy, costs, and volume flexibility; were significantly different; were more aware of customer requirements because of direct contact; and established as priority direct involvement with customers, vendors, and within their own organizations."[49]

Citations

1. Hodson & Sullivan, 2002, pp. 3–4
2. Langdon, 1995, p. 12
3. Shortell & Kaluzny, 1997, pp. 205–207
4. Van Tiem, Moseley, & Dessinger, 2000
5. Schuler & Huber, 1993, p. 153
6. Langdon, 1995, pp. 71–93
7. Spitzer, 1989, p. 37
8. Mondy, Noe, & Premeaux, 1999, p. 110
9. Mondy, Noe, & Premeaux, 1999, p. 115
10. Robbins & Coulter, 2010, p. 439
11. Rothwell, 2005, p. 226
12. Rue & Byars, 1989, p. 225
13. Schuler & Huber, 1993, pp. 568–569
14. Campion & McClelland, 1993, pp. 339–352
15. Jackson & Schuler, 2006, p. 337
16. Ewald & Burnett, 1997, pp. 440–456
17. Owings & Kaplan, 2012, pp. 215–219
18. Hackman, Oldham, Janson, & Purdy, 1975, pp. 57–71
19. DuBain, 1996
20. Sherman, Bohlander, & Snell, 1996, p. 140
21. Sherman, Bohlander, & Snell, 1996, p. 140
22. Kearny & Smith, 1999, p. 11

23. Ostrom, 1993, p. 8
24. Ostrom, 1993, pp. 8–11
25. Schuler & Huber, 1993, p. 660
26. Phillips, 2008, p. 521
27. IBM Service Management Resource Center, 2011
28. Phillips, 2008, pp. 521–522
29. Stringer, 2009, p. 37
30. Stringer, 2009, pp. 60–76
31. Besterfield, Besterfield-Michna, Besterfield, & Besterfield–Sacre, 1999, p. 1
32. Smith, 2010, pp. 326–327
33. Mescon, Bovee, & Thill, 1999, p. 169
34. Foster, 2001, pp. 3–26
35. Besterfield, Besterfield-Michna, Besterfield, & Besterfield-Sacre, 1999, p. 2
36. Bonstingl, 1992, pp. 51–68
37. Rothwell, 2005 p. 177
38. *Memory Jogger*, 1998
39. DeCenzo & Robbins, 2010
40. McLaughlin & Kaluzny, 2006, pp. 3–18
41. Cappelli, 1998, p. 1
42. Van Tiem, Dessinger, & Moseley, 2006, pp. 693–694
43. Smith, 2010, p. 333
44. Brisgaard & Freisleben, 2004, p. 57
45. Pande, Neuman, & Cavanagh, 2000, pp. 117–129
46. Van Tiem, Dessinger, & Moseley, 2006, pp. 692–716
47. *What Is Lean?*, 2009
48. Knuf & Lauer, 2006, pp. 721–723
49. Uday-Riley & Guerra-Lopez, 2010, p. 422

References

Besterfield, D.H., Besterfield-Michna, C., Besterfield, G.H., & Besterfield-Sacre, M. (1999). *Total quality management* (2nd ed.). Upper Saddle River, NJ: Prentice Hall.

Bonstingl, J.J. (1992). *Schools of quality: An introduction to total quality management in education*. Alexandria, VA: Association for Supervision and Curriculum Development.

Brisgaard, S., & Freisleben, J. (2004, September). Six sigma and the bottom line. *Quality Progress, 37*(9), 547–62.

Campion, M., & McClelland, C. (1993). Follow-up and extension of the interdisciplinary costs and benefits of enlarged jobs. *Journal of Applied Psychology, 78*(3), 339–352.

Cappelli, W. (1998, July 17). Six sigma: The new wave in quality management. Retrieved from www.rlis.ford.com/giga/jul98/o79981-WC98.html.

DeCenzo, D.A., & Robbins, S.P. (2010). *Human resource management* (10th ed.). Hoboken, NJ: John Wiley & Sons.

DuBain, A.J. (1996). *Reengineering survival guide: Managing and succeeding in the changing workplace*. Cincinnati, OH: Thomson Executive Press.

Ewald, H.R., & Burnett, R.E. (1997). *Business communication*. Upper Saddle River, NJ: Prentice Hall.

Foster, F.T. (2001). *Managing quality: An integrative approach*. Upper Saddle River, NJ: Prentice Hall.

Hackman, J.R., Oldham, G., Janson, R., & Purdy, K. (1975, Summer). A new strategy for job enrichment. *California Management Review, 17*(4), 57–71.

Hodson, R., & Sullivan, T.A. (2002). *The social organization of work* (3rd ed.). Belmont, CA: Wadsworth/Thomson Learning.

IBM Service Management Resource Center. Resources for security management professionals. www.servicemanagementcenter.com/Main/Pages/IBMRBMS.

Jackson, S.E., & Schuler, R.S. (2006). *Managing human resources: Through strategic partnerships*. Mason, OH: Thomson South-Western.

Kearny, L., & Smith, P. (1999, January). Creating workplaces where people can think: Cognitive ergonomics. *Performance Improvement, 38*(1), 10–15.

Knuf, J., & Lauer, M. (2006). Normal excellence: Lean human performance technology and the Toyota production system. In J.A. Pershing (Ed.), *Handbook of human performance technology: Principles, practices, potential* (3rd ed.) (pp. 717–742). San Francisco: Pfeiffer/ISPI.

Langdon, D.G. (1995). *The language of work*. Amherst, MA: HRD Press.

McLaughlin, C.P., & Kaluzny, A.D. (2006). *Continuous quality improvement in health care: Theory, implementation, and applications* (3rd ed.). Sudbury, MA: Jones and Bartlett Publishers.

Memory Jogger: A pocket guide of tools for continuous improvement. (1998). Methuen, MA: Goal/QPC.

Mescon, M.H., Bovee, C.L., & Thill, J.V. (1999). *Business today* (9th ed.). Upper Saddle River, NJ: Prentice Hall.

Mondy, R.W., Noe, R.M., & Premeaux, S.R. (1999). *Human resource management* (7th ed.). Upper Saddle River, NJ: Prentice Hall.

Moseley, J.L., & Blake, A.M. (2012). Green practices in human performance arenas (unpublished manuscript). Grosse Pointe Farms, MI.

Ostrom, L.T. (1993). *Creating the ergonomically sound workplace*. San Francisco: Jossey-Bass.

Owings, W.A., & Kaplan, L.S. (2012). *Leadership and organizational behavior in education: Theory into practice*. Upper Saddle River, NJ: Pearson Education, Inc.

Pande, P.S., Neuman, R.P., & Cavanagh, R.R. (2000). *The six sigma way: How GE, Motorola, and other top companies are honing their performance*. New York: McGraw-Hill.

Phillips, L. (2008). *SPHR exam prep* (2nd ed.). Upper Saddle River, NJ: Pearson Education.

Robbins, S.P., & Coulter, M. (2010). *Management* (11th ed.). Upper Saddle River, NJ: Prentice Hall.

Rothwell, W.J. (2005). *Beyond training and development* (2nd ed.) New York: AMACOM.

Rue, L.W., & Byars, L.L. (1989). *Management: Theory and application* (5th ed.). Homewood, IL: Irwin.

Schuler, R.S., & Huber, V.L. (1993). *Personnel and human resource management* (5th ed.). St. Paul, MN: West Publishing Company.

Sherman, A., Bohlander, G., & Snell, S. (1996). *Managing human resources* (10th ed.). Cincinnati, OH: South-Western.

Shortell, S.M., & Kaluzny, A.D. (1997). *Essentials of health care management*. Albany, NY: Delmar Publishers.

Smith, D.M. (2010). New kids on the block: Evaluation in practice. In J.L. Moseley & J.C. Dessinger (Eds.), *Handbook of improving performance in the workplace, volume 3: Measurement and evaluation* (pp. 314–338). San Francisco: Pfeiffer/ISPI.

Spitzer, D.R. (May/June, 1989). Best performer analysis. *Performance and Instruction, 28*(5).

Stringer, L. (2009). *The green workplace: Sustainable strategies that benefit employees, the environment, and the bottom line*. New York: Palgrave Macmillan.

Uday-Riley, M., & Guerra-Lopez, I. (2010). Process improvement. In R. Watkins & D. Leigh (Eds.), *Handbook of improving performance in the workplace, volume 2: Selecting and implementing performance interventions* (pp. 418–437). San Francisco: Pfeiffer/ISPI.

Van Tiem, D.M., Moseley, J.L., & Dessinger, J.C. (2000). *Fundamentals of performance technology: A guide to improving people, process, and performance.* Silver Spring, MD: International Society for Performance Improvement.

Van Tiem, D.M., Moseley, J.L., & Dessinger, J.C. (2006). Six sigma: Increasing human performance technology value and results. In J.A. Pershing (Ed.), *Handbook of human performance technology: Principles, practices, potential* (3rd ed.) (pp. 692–716). San Francisco: Pfeiffer/ISPI.

What is lean? (2009). Retrieved from www/lean.org/what'slean/

Personal Development Interventions

Ownership and accountability for personal professional development in the workplace are the responsibilities of the individual. The demand for new knowledge, new skills, tolerant attitudes, and new ways of doing things is constant. Moving beyond short-term fixes and solutions to long-term goals helps position people for future success.

One way to approach any personal development intervention is to help the employee develop an action plan as part of the intervention. Reasonable long- and short-term goals are set, guideposts for achieving them are determined, and measures of success are noted. An action plan should focus on long-term career plans, current position, effective strategies and tactics to achieve the goal, and personal assessment and satisfaction.

Personal development interventions outlined in Figure 13.1 are considered personal development or growth interventions because individuals assume ownership. Each intervention is determined by how it fits into the employee's personal action plan. Listen carefully—the voice of the practitioner may also be heard commenting on a specific intervention.

Feedback

Definition. Feedback means informing people about how others perceive their actions and communications. It is one way of helping employees determine whether they are on track in meeting their personal goals and expectations.

FIGURE 13.1. Personal Development Interventions

PERSONAL DEVELOPMENT INTERVENTIONS
• Feedback
• Coaching
• Mentoring
• Emotional intelligence
• Social intelligence
• Cultural intelligence
• Communities of professional practice

Scope. Everyone appreciates constructive feedback, whether it is positive or negative. The chef at the restaurant wants to hear about the special dish that was created for your wedding party. The priest wants to know how you liked the Sunday homily and how it applies to you. The teenager wants to know whether the purple shirt looks good with the recently purchased red pants. The belly dancer, well, she wants feedback, too. Feedback about on-the-job performance strengthens learning and transfer. It also increases self-efficacy, and people with high self-efficacy tend to be more motivated and, in the long run, achieve more.[1] Feedback tells employees whether or not their responses are correct, allowing for adjustments in behavior; it makes an activity more interesting, encouraging people to continue; it can lead to specific goals for maintaining or improving performance.[2]

In receiving feedback, employees must convert the feedback into an action or proposal for self-improvement. This is an important step in personal growth. Feedback helps in monitoring everyday work events. To receive feedback, employees must often ask for the information. Feedback boosts self-confidence and helps in developing career goals and new job skills. In giving feedback, the individual focuses on the behavior or issue and not on the personality.

Feedback should be timely, concise, and pertinent to the behavior or issue.[3] Some organizations are using the 360-degree feedback approach rather than the traditional performance appraisal approach. Organizations using this approach indicate that multi-rater measures seem more reliable, valid, and credible to employees receiving feedback than the traditional single-source feedback provided solely by one's supervisor. The 360-degree feedback approach is based on the premise that the collective intelligence of many raters is more likely to provide a clearer picture of specific behaviors and skills from which an individual can structure a meaningful personal plan for growth.

Workplace Implementation. Excellent feedback preserves an individual's dignity and integrity while allowing for improvement in behavior. Here are some suggestions for giving feedback:

- Offering feedback on observed behavior, not on perceived attitudes
- Offering a description of what was seen or felt, rather than on a judgment
- Focusing on behavior that can be changed
- Commenting on the things that an employee did well, as well as areas for improvement
- Observing personal limits by avoiding giving too much feedback at once

Performance Support Tool 13.1 is a checklist that describes how consistently workers and others use certain feedback behaviors in the workplace. But first, listen to the voice of a practitioner.

Coaching

Definition. Coaching is the help that managers give to employees by examining and guiding on-the-job performance. A coach teaches, supports, and motivates the performer and facilitates

EXHIBIT 13.1. THE PRACTITIONER'S VOICE: FEEDBACK

"Understanding positive and negative connections is a critical dynamic in creating, maintaining, and improving human performance processes and systems."

"Positive feedback in our work, worker, and workplace processes is the motivator that helps us to continue to engage and meet our goals. Positive data streams allow our processes to grow in the same direction they were designed. Unfortunately, too much positive can have cumulative, often debilitating, effects; like one dish of ice cream—delicious; the whole carton—diabetic coma. A positive feedback loop left to itself can lead to decline and ultimate destruction of the system.

"On the other hand, as painful as it sometimes is, negative feedback challenges us to reverse our current behaviors to maintain stability and equilibrium in the system. Previous experience with over indulging the negative feedback loop helps me learn from my mistakes and enjoy sugary desserts wisely and perhaps even redirect my eating habits (the system) in a new direction."

Eileen Banchoff, Ph.D., CPT

Independent Consultant

Banchoff Associates, Inc.

Southgate, Michigan, USA

good performance by providing relevant positive and negative feedback to improve both performance and potential.

Scope. Coaching builds on the assumption that most employees want to fulfill their jobs in an efficient and effective manner and contribute to their organization's successes, well-being, and market share. It can be formal and planned or immediate and just-in-time. The coach is usually a manager or supervisor of a unit, department, division, or team who possesses solid communication and listening skills along with abilities to praise jobs that are well done and provide corrective feedback as needed. Expert performers may also serve as coaches.

Coaching allows for rehearsing and practicing. In job performance, coaches help employees realize goals and opportunities, provide necessary support, analyze barriers, and help employees develop action plans for future success. They are people who set good example, inspire loyalty, celebrate successes, and empower by saying "we" instead of "I."

Many organizations today invest in developing and nurturing their leaders by providing opportunities for executive leadership coaching, which facilitates behavioral change and, ultimately, makes the leader more skilled, more sensitive to employee issues and concerns, and more reflective in personal action. This is a win-win situation; both the leader and the organization have potential for great success.[5] For the coaching experience to be successful, the process has to be highly valued, carefully planned, and thoughtfully and thoroughly implemented in order for both the organization and the individual to realize positive outcomes.[6]

PERFORMANCE SUPPORT TOOL 13.1. FEEDBACK CHECKLIST

Directions: For each statement, check the appropriate response to describe how consistently you use the described behavior in the workplace.

	Rarely	Sometimes	Often
1. I provide frequent opportunities for feedback.	☐	☐	☐
2. I promote feedback when I work with teams.	☐	☐	☐
3. I provide constructive feedback that is both positive and negative.	☐	☐	☐
4. I time my feedback appropriately.	☐	☐	☐
5. I encourage feedback that indicates an employee can master a task.	☐	☐	☐
6. I listen before I provide feedback.	☐	☐	☐
7. I like to provide reinforcing feedback.	☐	☐	☐
8. I encourage formative feedback (modifying or changing performance from unacceptable to acceptable).	☐	☐	☐
9. I use language that is appropriate and understandable in providing constructive feedback.	☐	☐	☐
10. I tailor my feedback to fit the needs of the performer and the performance.	☐	☐	☐
11. I refrain from using punitive feedback.	☐	☐	☐
12. I help people understand that some kinds of performance depend on a continuous flow of feedback.	☐	☐	☐
13. I use a nonjudgmental attitude in providing feedback.	☐	☐	☐
14. I often provide feedback that deals with correctable items over which the employee has some control.	☐	☐	☐
15. In giving feedback, I provide clear and concrete data.	☐	☐	☐
16. I refrain from delivering feedback that is delivered inconsiderately or that is vague.	☐	☐	☐
17. When new employees come aboard, I orient them to the feedback improvement effort.	☐	☐	☐
18. I use nonverbal cues (smiles, nods, and so forth) to give feedback.	☐	☐	☐
19. I consistently try to improve my feedback efforts.	☐	☐	☐
20. Before giving feedback, I consider its value to the employee.			

Workplace Implementation. The coaching process has a preparation phase whereby the coach observes the client's workplace and leadership skills. The coach then discusses and shares findings with the client and listens for openness to the coaching process. The ongoing dialogue phase serves as a reality check for the action plan, where goals, objectives, and progress are recorded. A follow-up phase determines successes and failures of the coaching experience and looks for opportunities for improvement.[7]

Performance Support Tool 13.2 is a self-assessment tool to help the potential coach identify coaching strengths and areas for improvement.

Mentoring

Definition. In mythology, when Odysseus, King of Ithaca, went to fight in the Trojan War, he entrusted the care of his kingdom to Mentor. Mentor served as the teacher and overseer of Odysseus' son, Telemachus. From then on, mentoring has become the offering of experience, emotional support, and guidance by an experienced person to a less experienced one. It is a relationship of mutual trust and respect between two people with a common goal of professional development and learning. The relationship may continue over an extended period of time.

Scope. Mentoring is a powerful, dynamic process. A mentor knows the organization, has exemplary managerial and leadership skills, can give and share credit, has good common sense, and, above all, is generally a patient individual. A mentor shares personal experiences, wisdom, and political knowledge to enable the mentee to develop skills and capabilities necessary for future success. A mentor helps a mentee make connections. The mentor plays four key roles during the mentoring process:

- *Role model*—practices the values that the organization endorses,
- *Coach*—clarifies the organization's culture and political structure so mentees can correctly direct their efforts,
- *Broker*—helps the mentee establish the contacts needed to succeed, and
- *Advocate*—recommends and supports the mentee for projects and task groups.

Not every employee is suitable to be mentored. A likely candidate for mentoring needs to be open to learning and appreciate the wisdom that is offered. The mentee should have a track record of success, a desire to achieve, willingness to take on challenges and responsibilities, self-motivation, and loyalty to the organization.[8]

Workplace Implementation. Mentoring is a valuable retention tool and a critical element in employee development.[9] Mentoring programs also play an important role in career development and information resource by helping the mentee define purpose and direction, seek advancement opportunities, and realize future dreams.[10] Here are some suggestions for developing a mentoring program:

1. Create a business case for why the program is necessary (see Chapter 19).
2. Develop a roadmap for guidance including goals, success factors and desired outcomes, duration of the program, and budget parameters.

PERFORMANCE SUPPORT TOOL 13.2. COACHING SKILLS SELF-ASSESSMENT

Directions: Use this performance support tool to assess your coaching strengths and areas for improvement. Rate yourself on each statement. Reflect on situations when you exhibited that behavior. Jot down ideas for your own personal performance improvement based on your reflection. Be your own coach!

	Yes	No
1. I provide frequent, timely, and specific feedback.		
2. I ask open-ended questions and listen to the responses.		
3. I never assume what motivates an employee. I ask.		
4. I applaud employee successes.		
5. I work with employees to develop measurable and attainable goals.		
6. I provide the resources employees need to succeed.		
7. I take time to discuss new ideas and initiatives with employees.		
8. I solicit and follow up on employee suggestions.		
9. I encourage creative problem solving.		
10. I encourage open and honest communication.		

3. Gain commitment and support from top management and begin to match mentors with mentees.

4. Establish a mentoring agreement and an action plan that will measure and record successes and then celebrate the milestones.

5. Evaluate, evaluate, evaluate. Use formative evaluation throughout the program, summative evaluation when the program has completed its cycle, and confirmative evaluation for continuing competence, job transfer, continuing effectiveness, and organizational impact. Also measure the return on investment.[11]

Emotional Intelligence

Definition. Emotional intelligence (EI) is "the ability to accurately identify and understand one's own emotional reactions and those of others. It also includes the ability to regulate one's emotions and to use them to make good decisions and to act effectively."[12]

Scope. Emotional intelligence is critical to the well-being and success of organizations and is the heartstring of effective leadership. The ability to influence others is contingent on connecting with them on an emotional level and making sense of what they are feeling, why they are feeling that way, and how their feelings influence their decisions.

There is substantial evidence that emotional intelligence is more important than job-specific technical skills and knowledge or IQ (intelligence quotient). Emotional intelligence involves social awareness—empathy and organizational awareness; relationship management—positive impact on others; self-management—adaptability, positive outlook, achievement orientation, emotional self-control; and self-awareness—emotional understanding of oneself.[13] EI can be developed at any age; however, it takes time, effort, and robust commitment.

Workplace Implementation. Emotional intelligence can improve relationships with peers; help individuals control themselves and remain motivated and relatively stress free; and assist them in communicating well without conflict. Individuals should periodically reflect on their emotional reactions to other people and be self-aware and self-regulating; they should think before they act.

Emotional intelligence is very personal; however, performance improvement practitioners can encourage employees to measure their individual emotional intelligence level to determine strengths and limitations. The practitioner also increases employee awareness and improves the workplace environment by researching and suggesting self-assessment tools and providing information and a chance to dialogue about emotional intelligence too. Dialogue starter questions could include: How well do you react to the viewpoints of others? Do you communicate and listen to others when they do not share your thoughts?[14]

Social Intelligence

Definition. Social intelligence (SI) is "the ability to get along well with others while winning their cooperation. It is a combination of sensitivity to the needs and interests of others, sometimes called your 'social radar,' an attitude of generosity and consideration, and a set of practical skills for interacting with people in any setting."[15] It is competence in surveying one's personal landscape and environment and responding with socially successful conduct.

Scope. Social intelligence is the new science of success in our highly competitive and global world. It goes beyond IQ and emotional intelligence by applying multiple intelligence theory to human interaction. Social intelligence is the ability to read situations and interpret how people behave. It is about the behavior that others use to judge a person as fair, honest, and trustworthy. It is about connecting with people and empathizing with them. It is a daily journey of observing, learning, developing, and reflecting that begins with the individual and extends to others.[16]

Workplace Implementation. The performance practitioner observes the behavior of people and listens to their issues and concerns. A typical activity would consist of observing persons in multiple situations, either virtually or in real time, and analyzing and reflecting upon their actions, paying particular attention to personal behaviors and how others react to what has been said and done. Discussion questions include the following:

- Is the person well-intentioned, open, ethical, and deserving of trust?
- Are the person's verbal and nonverbal messages communicated clearly and concisely?
- Do people listen to what the person has to say?
- Does the person empathize with others by understanding their feelings and actions and connecting with their thoughts?
- Does the person ask for feedback from others regarding socially successful conduct?

Cultural Intelligence

Definition. Cultural intelligence is the "capability to function effectively across national, ethnic, and organizational cultures."[17] This is accomplished by seriously studying and observing the culture and gradually learning more about it, by developing new ways of thinking, and by interacting with members of the culture.[18]

Scope. Cultural intelligence begins with the motivational cycle, which provides energy and self-confidence to pursue cross-cultural deliberations; the cognitive dimension, which provides an understanding of cultural issues and values; the meta-cognitive dimension, which plans and interprets a situation; and the behavioral dimension for engaging in effective leadership patterns. Cultural intelligence picks up where emotional intelligence leaves off. Emotional intelligence is a person's ability to led socially and emotionally; cultural intelligence helps individuals to work with people from different cultural orientations.[19]

Workplace Implementation. Cultural intelligence can be both developed and learned and starts with developing strengths and overcoming weaknesses. The performance improvement practitioner begins by developing a personal self-assessment and follows this by selecting appropriate training to remedy weaknesses and by applying training to everyday occurrences. These can lead to broader, more specific actions in time by helping employees organize personal resources, workload demands, and time constraints for enhancing cultural intelligence. Follow this by encouraging employees to enter into the cultural setting that needs to be perfected. Secure feedback from peers and others in the group or organization. Finally, assess and evaluate the skills and competencies that have developed, learned, and applied.[20]

Communities of Practice

Definition. Communities of professional practice are individuals who join together with a specific and genuine shared interest in a discipline, a field of study, or some other organizing format. The community members reflect on and share ideas, collaborate with one another, and learn from each other's contributions, successes, and failures.[21]

Scope. Communities of professional practice find solid ground in "bigness"—big business, big industry, big government, big education—as well as in other avenues where professional men and women gather to discuss the impact that their environment has on engaging learning. Peer-to-peer interaction "will increasingly be accepted as an effective means of maintaining and updating professional level skills."[22]

Workplace Implementation. The performance improvement practitioner helps initiate and organize face-to-face or online or mobile communities of professional practice by discussing the importance of learning from others. The practitioner can help create a community among potential participants. Initially, the practitioner can help the group determine what it is they want or need to learn to maintain and advance their professional skill levels. Then the practitioner can help the members clarify priorities, sharpen their focus, and decide on a realistic plan, with targets and timelines, to achieve their goals. The practitioner may also help identify individual and group behaviors that promote or inhibit community collaboration actions and the sharing of responsibility for learning. The practitioner can also facilitate discussions and feedback, record the groups' deliberations and findings, and identify individuals who will keep the learning elements on track and relate them to the nuts and bolts of the professional skills that are identified. Finally, the performance improvement practitioner can evaluate the process by looking at individual gains and group gains and discuss how the experience has improved performance at the job level, the process level, and/or the organization level.

Citations

1. Bandura, 1991
2. Locke & Latham, 1990
3. Whetten & Cameron, 2011, pp. 348–351
4. Wood & Scott, 1989, pp. 48–51
5. White, 2010, pp. 646–650
6. De Filippo, 2010, pp. 24–26
7. Harvard ManageMentor, 2011
8. Stone, 1999, pp. 98–99
9. Segal, 2000, p. 157

10. Kuo, 2000
11. Best Practices: Mentoring, 2008
12. Cherniss & Goleman, 2006, p. 400
13. Mckee, Johnston, Mwelwa, & Rotondo, 2009, p. 54
14. Emotional Intelligence Checklist, 2006, pp. 446–447
15. Albrecht, 2006, pp. 3–10
16. Albrecht, 2006, pp. 28–31
17. Ang & VanDyne, 2008, p. 3
18. Thomas & Inkson, 2005, p. 7
19. Livermore, 2010, pp. 23–32
20. Earley & Mosakowski, 2004, pp. 139–146
21. Chyung & Berg, 2010, p. 41
22. Ziob & Moser, 2006, pp. 94–98.

References

Albrecht, K. (2006). *Social intelligence: The new science of success: Beyond IQ, beyond EI, applying multiple intelligence theory to human interaction.* San Francisco: Pfeiffer.

Ang, S., & Van Dyne, L. (2008). Conceptualization of cultural intelligence. In S. Ang & L. Van Dyne (Eds.), *Handbook of cultural intelligence: Theory, measurement, and applications.* Armonk, NY: M.E. Sharpe.

Bandura, A. (1991). Social cognitive theory of self-regulation. *Organizational Behavior and Human Decision Processes, 50,* 248–287.

Best practices: Mentoring. (2008, September). Washington, DC: United States Office of Personnel Management.

Cherniss, C., & Goleman, D. (2006). *Emotional intelligence. Business: The ultimate resource.* Cambridge, MA: Basic Books.

Chyung, S.Y., & Berg, S.A. (2010). Linking practice and theory. In R. Watkins & D. Leigh (Eds.), *Handbook of human performance in the workplace, volume 2: Selecting and implementing performance interventions* (pp. 27–50). San Francisco: Pfeiffer/ISPI.

DeFilippo, D. (2010, June). Coaching in context. *Talent Management, 6*(6), 25.

Earley, C., & Mosakowski, E. (2004, October). Cultural intelligence. *Harvard Business Review, 82*(10), 139–146.

Emotional Intelligence (EI) Checklist, (2006). *Business: The ultimate resource.* Cambridge, MA: Basic Books.

Harvard ManageMentor. (2011). Coaching: Four steps. http://learndirecthmmdemo.Immattersonline.com/course/html10/coaching.

Kuo, K. (2000, March/April). The power of mentoring. *Educause Review, 35*(2), pp. 9–11.

Livermore, D. (2010). *Leading with cultural intelligence: The secret of success.* New York: AMACOM.

Locke, E., & Latham, G. (1990). *A theory of goal setting and task performance.* Englewood Cliffs, NJ: Prentice Hall.

Mckee, A., Johnston, F., Mwelwa, E., & Rotondo, S. (2009). Resonant leadership for results: An emotional and social intelligence program for change in South Africa and Cambodia. In M. Hughes, H.L. Thompson, & J. Bradford Terrell (Eds.), *Handbook of developing emotional and social intelligences: Best practices, case studies, and strategies* (pp. 49–71). San Francisco: Pfeiffer.

Segal, J. (2000, March/April). Mirror-image mentoring. *HR Magazine, 45*(3), 157.

Stone, F.M. (1999). *Coaching, counseling & mentoring.* New York: AMACOM.

Thomas, D.C., & Inkson, K. (2005, March). Cultural intelligence: People skills for a global workplace. *Consulting to Management, 16*(1), 5–9.

Whetten, D.A., & Cameron, K.S. (2011). *Developing management skills* (8th ed.). Upper Saddle River, NJ: Prentice Hall.

White, D. (2010). Executive leadership coaching. In R. Watkins & D. Leigh (Eds.), *Handbook of improving performance in the workplace, volume 2: Selecting and implementing performance interventions* (pp. 646–671). San Francisco: Pfeiffer/ISPI.

Wood, B., & Scott, A. (1989, April). The gentle art of feedback. *Personnel Management, 26*(4), 48–51.

Ziob, L., & Mosher, B. (2006). Putting customers first at Microsoft: Blending learning capabilities with customer needs. In C.J. Bonk & C.R. Graham (Eds.), *The handbook of blended learning: Global perspectives, local designs* (pp. 92–104). San Francisco: Pfeiffer.

HRD
Interventions

14

Human resource development (HRD) is the systematic and planned practice designed by an organization to enhance employee knowledge, skills, abilities, and attitudes. It begins when an employee is hired and continues throughout the employee's tenure with the organization. The activities, designed for employees at all levels of the career ladder, help direct current and future job demands so that efficient and effective use of valuable resources are maintained. It is centralized or decentralized depending upon the structure and functions of the organization.[1]

Human resource management (HRM) is the business area that strategically plans and executes human resource functions. It is the utilization of employees joined together to achieve the mission, vision, goals, and strategic initiatives of the organization.[2] Human resource management activities include equal employment opportunity (EEO) compliance, job analysis, human resource planning, training and development, safety, health, and wellness, labor relations, employee recruitment and selection, and other activities concerned about people in the workplace.

While the human resource management designation is widely used, talent management, one of the current buzzwords in corporate human resources, is becoming more and more popular as organizations face a shortage of available talent. In the 1970s and 1980s ,the organization's personnel department hired employees and paid their salaries and benefits. The department fulfilled a business function role. In the late 1980s and 1990s, human resources assumed the role of a strategic business partner. Human resources took on greater roles with employees by hiring the right person for the right job at the right time, by training them, and by providing them with total compensation packages and by serving as a "one stop" communication channel for employee well-being.

Organizations are now facing new human resource demands that call for integrating human resources and learning management with business management processes. As organizations meet their business goals, all human resource functions must come together and interact synergistically if the organization is to remain viable and the value of its products and/or services becomes sustainable.[3]

The agricultural age was a land-driven economy; the industrial age, a manufacturing-driven economy; the knowledge age, an information assets economy. In the vortex of the knowledge age, the competitive environment focuses on talent quality and the search for the best people since they are the determinants of value and sustainability. Today's many challenging workforce issues require new thinking and a new talent mindset if the organization is positioned to achieve business success.[4]

In this chapter, human resource management interventions are divided into subcategories:

- Talent management (Figure 14.1) focuses on core employee-oriented business functions: staffing, employee development, retention of employees, compensation and benefits, health and wellness, retirement planning, and labor relations.
- Individual growth (Figure 14.2) focuses on the organization's need to encourage high-performance employees: motivation systems, performance management and key performance indicators, performance appraisals and 360-degree feedback, and competency testing.
- Organizational growth (Figure 14.3) focuses on the organization's need for long-term success: succession planning, career pathing, leadership development, executive development, management development, and supervisory development.

Listen carefully—the voice of the practitioner may be heard commenting on a specific intervention.

Talent Management

Definition. Talent management "refers to the concept of bringing together—in a unified technology platform—the functions of recruitment, selection, and assessment, learning and development, performance management, workforce planning, compensation, and other human resource functions."[5] It is a systematic process to meet the organization's human capital needs by placing the right people in the right jobs at the right time.[6]

Scope. Talent management is a new way of looking at human resource management (HRM). While many of the essential human resource principles are similar, talent management requires a new mindset and a new way of thinking to achieve business success. Human resource management is more tactical; talent management, more strategic.

In the talent management lifecycle, employees are empowered to think and act while they create a unique brand of value for the organization. Engagement is important as individuals work with

FIGURE 14.1. Talent Management Interventions

Talent Management
• Staffing
• Employee Development
• Retention
• Compensation/Benefits
• Health and Wellness
• Retirement Planning
• Labor Relations

teams to advocate for the organization and go that extra mile to complete a task. This process is continuous and ongoing, and it impacts not just human resources but the entire fabric and culture of the organization. Yves Saint Laurent, one of the world's most influential fashion designers, says: "Dressing is a way of life." As corporate America focuses more on strategic thinking, strategic processes, and talent management strategies and conducts business reviews to align organizational and talent needs, the talent age is the new "way of life."

Workplace Implementation. When an organization embraces talent management processes, it achieves its overall goal of making money and responding to changes in the competitive environment.[7] Focusing on talent and a complementary corporate culture guides sustained organizational performance. "Talent management is action-oriented, people-oriented, globally oriented, and future-oriented."[8] This is a prime example of why a performance improvement practitioner must remain current and up-to-date on new concepts and strategies in the field of performance improvement and is able to integrate the best of what was with what is required now. When selecting interventions, the practitioner needs to re-focus on whether or not the interventions will help the organization concentrate on talent management and create a "complementary corporate culture" that supports talent management.

EXHIBIT 14.1. THE PRACTITIONER'S VOICE: TALENT MANAGEMENT

"Talent management refers to integrated strategies to increase workforce productivity and growth through having the right people with the right skills, behaviors, and aptitudes to meet current and future business needs . . . talent alignment drives your strategy around talent acquisition, talent assessment, talent identification, and talent development. You can't have an engaged workforce without talent management."

Bill Tarnacki II, M.Ed., M.B.A., MHCS

Director, Talent Management and Corporate Human Resources

Pulte Group, Inc.

Bloomfield Hills, Michigan, USA

Staffing

Definition. Staffing is the talent management function that anticipates and fills open positions within organizations.

Scope. Staffing is a critical talent management function, and both the organization and the employee benefit from careful planning. Unfortunately, this does not consistently occur. As Drucker, the management guru, said: "No other decisions are so long lasting in their consequences or so difficult to unmake. And yet, by and large, executives make poor promotion and staffing decisions."[9] Staffing includes strategic personnel planning (the right number and kinds of capable people, strategies for hiring, training, and retaining, and so forth);[10,11] recruitment (the process of attracting qualified applicants who drive new thinking and possess talent acumen to achieve robust business results); selection (screening and selecting the best candidates from applications, résumés, and interviews and from such external resources as executive recruiters, college recruiting, referrals and walk-ins, gray power, Internet, and other advertising mechanisms).[12] A peak performance staffing function includes:

1. Analyzing jobs
2. Conducting strategic human resource planning
3. Recruiting applicants
4. Interviewing candidates
5. Administering employment tests
6. Checking references and backgrounds
7. Selecting candidate(s)
8. Arranging for physical, medical exam(s)
9. Making final offer to the candidate
10. Retaining talent (added by authors)[13]

Workplace Implementation. Performance improvement practitioners play unique roles in the talent management process by utilizing their competencies to develop strategic partnerships. They begin by analyzing jobs and the people and resources necessary to complete them effectively and efficiently. Then they write concise job descriptions and state realistic job specifications. Use Performance Support Tool 12.1. Job Analysis Survey as a model.

Performance practitioners contribute to talent management strategy by following industry trends and remaining current in local, national, and global marketplace developments and by designing performance support tools, various human resource forms, checklists and other support tools, by training talent managers to implement activities, and by facilitating strategic planning sessions. Finally, the performance improvement practitioner can play a vital role with the talent manager in evaluating the recruits and in verifying resources and vendors. (See the exhibit at the end of Section 3 to read about a real-world talent management intervention.)

Employee Development

Definition. Employee development is the process that begins after the candidate accepts the final offer of employment and continues throughout the employee's life with the organization.

Scope. Table 14.1 provides an overview of employee development components, focus, purpose, and potential interventions. It is based on the work of Van Tiem, Moseley, Dessinger, and others.[14] Further discussion of employee development with an implementation and maintenance focus appears in Chapter 22.

TABLE 14.1.   Employee Development Overview

Components	Focus and Purpose	Interventions
Employee Training	• Focus on skills and knowledge • Introduce new employees to the organization • Help employees acquire, maintain, or improve current job skills	• Employee orientation • Just-in-time training • On-the-job training • Coaching and mentoring • Job aids
Employee Development	• Focus on education • Plan for future business needs • Enhance employee's ability to understand and interpret knowledge	• Orientation handbook • Traditional or technology-based instruction • Corporate university • Job rotation • Team/committee assignments • Seminars • Simulations • Experiential learning (survival training, and so forth)
Career Development	• Focus on long-term career effectiveness and success • Assist employees in advancing their work lives • Provide information and assessment to realize career goals	• Challenging job assignments (job rotation/ enrichment) • Career counseling • Career workshops • Career pathing • Continuing education and training • Professional associations
Organization Development	• Focus on system-wide organizational change • Change attitudes and values of employees • Help employees adapt to change (unfreeze status quo, change, refreeze)	• Feedback activities (surveys and other means) • Team-building activities • Third-party interventions (change management, conflict resolution, and so forth)

Source: DeCenzo and Robbins, 1999, pp. 13–14, 218–270. Used with permission.

Workplace Implementation. Employers and employees have shared responsibility for employee development. If an organization chooses to remain competitive with cutting-edge business acumen and with a talent management mindset, it must integrate learning with working. Continuous learning is the key, and this is manifested in learning organizations and in professional communities of practice. Organizations often support employees in advanced schooling through tuition reimbursement programs. Brown-bag lunches, where topics range from current affairs to leadership books, anywhere workers to next-gen mobility and everything in between can help employees learn about cutting-edge topics. Joining professional organizations and attending conferences add further perspective. The performance improvement practitioner supports the work of the talent manager in these areas and can also plan and design appropriate programs that strengthen employee commitment and organization growth.

EXHIBIT 14.2. THE PRACTITIONER'S VOICE: EMPLOYEE DEVELOPMENT

"We have a fundamentally very strong marketplace training plan written by professional career personnel. It begins with needs analysis, goals, ambitions, and direct organizational targets involving our HR person and the heads of our departments; it's a business within a business. We have a menu of development and training opportunities; 105 training courses per week in blocks of eight weeks focusing on core skills and individual potential skills. I also participate in training with courses like health and safety management, employment management (new laws and regulations), and appraisal skills. . . . Our infrastructure lets people take advantage of the many opportunities available. There is management support and department support. We are developing a culture within our organization. We have a company-led management mentoring program where twelve to fourteen employees are paired off with another manager. We provide training for our mentors. . . . We need to be good listeners."

Malcolm Hendry

General Manager

The Rubens at the Palace

Buckingham Palace Road

London, England, UK

Performance Support Tool 14.1 asks people to determine who is responsible for current employee development activities—the organization or the individual employee. Discuss the results with peers over a brown-bag lunch.

Retention

Definition. Retention is the final step in the selection process and refers to the organization's ability to retain qualified employees.

Scope. Retention implies what is controllable and desirable. It is a proactive concept. Organizations need to retain top talent in good times and in bad and "in managing retention, especially for the pivotal roles and A-list players."[15] Value to the organization is enhanced when it engages in improving retention. Value for the organization is gained by reduced recruiting costs, reduced training costs, less supervisory time required, and, in general, improved quality, innovation, productivity, and service.[16] Employees leave an organization voluntarily because of poor behavior and lack of trust in their supervisors, the perceived lack of advancement opportunities, and the stress involved in work/life balance. Effective retention programs that are planned collaboratively with the performance practitioner and the talent manager focus on supervisory training, career management, and stress reduction.[17]

Workplace Implementation. Since retention shares direct relationships with customer satisfaction, customer loyalty, quality outcomes, operating effectiveness, and financial performance,

PERFORMANCE SUPPORT TOOL 14.1. EMPLOYEE DEVELOPMENT: WHO IS RESPONSIBLE FOR SUCCESS?

This instrument has multiple uses:

1. Identify current employee development activities; identify who is responsible for the success of each activity—the organization or the individual employee—and explain your perception of the current situation.
2. Identify current activities and who is responsible, and explain why you *agree* or *disagree* with the current situation.
3. Identify potential employee development activities, suggest who *should* be responsible for success, and justify the suggestions.

Directions: List the current employee development activities and assign responsibility by checking ORG for organization or IND for individual employee. Use the Why? Column to explain your perceptions of the current situation, agree or disagree with the current situation, or justify suggestions for future employee development interventions.

Employee Development Activity	Responsible?		Why?
	ORG	IND	

retention is a pivotal player and indicator of strategic business outcomes. There are several predictors of retention:

- Overall job and work satisfaction
- Organization commitment
- Quality of the leader and member relationship
- Clarity of role
- Person-to-job fit—how well employees' skills and interests are matched to job requirements
- Level of conflict (this could be conflict within or across groups)
- The extent to which one is embedded in the community, such as social, religious, hobby, or political activities
- Job search intentions[18]

The retention chief at MGM Mirage used many retention drivers to "help keep them in the house."[19]

- Job security
- A safe working environment
- Competitive compensation and benefits
- Culture and work unit that meets their affiliation needs
- Work flexibility
- Interesting work
- Decision-making opportunities
- Growth and ability to get ahead

The performance improvement practitioner utilizes skills from the performance consulting tool chest to support the retention drivers that are mentioned here because they have direct bearing on business outcomes and capabilities. Furthermore, the practitioner should continuously study the talent market and benchmark the organization's retention efforts and how they influence strategic thinking and planning.

In Performance Support Tool 14.2, Rothwell[20] provides an instrument that has been developed and successfully used to focus leadership attention on what to do to improve organizational retention efforts. This tool provides an organized framework by which organizational leaders can compare their retention practices to best practices as identified by theory, research, and practice on retention.

Compensation/Benefits

Definitions. Compensation programs are monetary and in-kind payments used by organizations as tangible rewards for employee service. Benefits are the non-cash portion of compensation programs intended to improve the quality of work life for an organization's employees. They are a central rather than a peripheral part of the organization's pay structure.

Text continues on page 339

PERFORMANCE SUPPORT TOOL 14.2. ORGANIZATIONAL RETENTION ASSESSMENT (ORA)

DESCRIPTION OF THE INSTRUMENT

The Organizational Retention Assessment (ORA) consists of a set of one hundred criteria by which to assess how well an organization's retention practices match up to what theory, research, and practice on employee retention indicate are desirable. These criteria must, of course, be tailored to the unique organizational and industry characteristics affecting an employer. But the instrument is intended to permit employers to focus their retention efforts, examining how much and how well they are doing to address retention issues.

THEORY BEHIND ORA

Much has been written about employee retention. This instrument is intended to pull together a large amount of research and practice information on employee retention, essentially "boiling it down" so that it may be effectively used as a focus for taking action.

ADMINISTRATION OF ORA

To maximize the effectiveness of the Organizational Retention Assessment, facilitators should provide the instrument to managers and to selected employees. The scores should be computed by group and then compared in a management setting as a starting point to identify action strategies to improve employee retention.

SCORING THE ASSESSMENT

The scoring is simple. The higher the score, the more an organization's retention practices are aligned to best practice; the lower the score, the less an organization's retention practices are aligned to best practice. A score of 80 or higher is generally indicative of an organization that is taking concerted action on retention. Lower scores indicate a need to improve retention efforts.

RELIABILITY AND VALIDITY OF THE ASSESSMENT

The instrument is intended for management use only, to focus attention on how to improve employee retention efforts. It is not designed to measure more enduring or general organizational characteristics.

Instructions: Read each criterion below. Then place a check mark in the box in the column that indicates whether your organization is presently using this practice to retain employees. When you finish, add up your scores. A "yes" counts as 1 and a "no" counts as 0.

Yes	No	Does Your Organization . . .
____	____	1. Build in a message about the importance of long service to the organization in all recruitment literature?
____	____	2. Examine the work records of all job applicants, looking for individuals who have shown long service with other organizations?
____	____	3. Ask new hires to sign lawyer-prepared non-compete agreements?

(Continued)

Yes	No	Does Your Organization . . .
____	____	4. Describe to job applicants how the organization recognizes long service (that is, employee recognition programs)?
____	____	5. Include a question on all job applications to ask all job applicants what they would regard as long service (that is, surface expectations about employee loyalty during the selection process)?
____	____	6. Track turnover by department?
____	____	7. Track turnover by location?
____	____	8. Track turnover by employee performance and potential so as to monitor the percentage of high-potentials leaving the organization?
____	____	9. Communicate turnover figures widely in the organization, focusing attention on ways to reduce it?
____	____	10. Track absenteeism by department, since absenteeism is a "leading indicator" (advance warning indicator) of future turnover?
____	____	11. Track absenteeism by location?
____	____	12. Track absenteeism by employee performance and potential so as to monitor the percentage of high-potentials who may be about to leave the organization?
____	____	13. Communicate absenteeism figures widely in the organization, focusing attention on ways to reduce it?
____	____	14. Recognize employees with long service with the organization?
____	____	15. Recognize managers whose employees have long service with the organization?
____	____	16. Encourage employees with long service records in the organization to refer prospective job applicants who are also likely to become long-service employees?
____	____	17. Conduct regular attitude or climate surveys in the organization, focusing attention on identifying problems that can lead to turnover and addressing them?
____	____	18. Hold employee focus groups periodically to identify reasons for employee turnover and address them?
____	____	19. Hold manager focus groups periodically to identify management-supported ideas to encourage longevity/discourage turnover?
____	____	20. Conduct regular exit interviews with departing employees to discover *why they are leaving?*
____	____	21. Conduct performance appraisals of departing employees so that the quality of workers leaving the organization can be specifically monitored?
____	____	22. Conduct interviews with long-service employees to discover *why they stay* with the organization?
____	____	23. Examine the organization's pay practices to ensure that outstanding performance is recognized as quickly as possible?
____	____	24. Examine the organization's bonus plans and reward programs to ensure that managers are rewarded or recognized for encouraging employee retention?
____	____	25. Take action to dispel the misconception that investments in employee training lead to higher turnover when, in fact, research reveals that training is an employee retention strategy because it builds employee loyalty?

(Continued)

Yes	No	Does Your Organization . . .
____	____	26. Experiment with innovative reward systems, including both pay and alternative rewards, to encourage employee retention and discourage employee turnover (for example, annual retention bonuses)?
____	____	27. Use employee sign-on/sign-up bonuses?
____	____	28. Provide employee benefits that encourage retention but discourage turnover (such as tuition reimbursement that is forgiven as more length of service is accumulated)?
____	____	29. Provide a planned employee orientation program that mentions the importance of long-service employment to the organization?
____	____	30. Provide a planned employee orientation program that mentions the importance of long-service employment to individuals (what's in it for them)?
____	____	31. Provide planned employee socialization programs (such as peer mentors) that make workers feel welcome in the organization?
____	____	32. Train managers on how to make new hires feel welcome?
____	____	33. Train managers on how to show appreciation on a periodic basis to long-service workers for their longevity with the organization?
____	____	34. Train workers on how to show appreciation on a periodic basis to long-service workers for their longevity with the organization?
____	____	35. Provide employee training periodically, in a way that compares favorably to other organizations in the industry, to keep workers current in their jobs and fields/occupations?
____	____	36. Use spot bonuses to show appreciation for instances in which individual employee performance goes "above and beyond the call of duty"?
____	____	37. Make clear to whom employees should go for help and counseling when they experience conflicts with supervisors, managers, or co-workers (for example, a widely publicized employee relations program)?
____	____	38. Make clear to whom employees should go for help and counseling when they experience personal problems such as legal, marital, drug-related, alcohol-related, or other personal problems (for example, a widely publicized employee assistance program)?
____	____	39. Make clear to whom employees should go for help and counseling before they decide to resign from the organization (that is, an early warning system to try to avoid turnover before it occurs)?
____	____	40. Reduce or eliminate waiting periods for benefits' eligibility, since that may encourage turnover?
____	____	41. Make career planning programs available to workers, showing qualifications required to qualify for advancement?
____	____	42. Base employee benefits, in part, on longevity with the organization?
____	____	43. Base employee promotion decisions, in part, on longevity with the organization?
____	____	44. Provide financial support for child care?
____	____	45. Provide time off, with or without pay, for child care?

(Continued)

Yes	No	Does Your Organization . . .
____	____	46. Provide essential personal services, such as dry cleaning services, on site with or without company financial support?
____	____	47. Provide personal services, such as retirement or financial planning, on site with or without company financial support?
____	____	48. Provide alternative rewards, such as stock options or purchase plans (with or without company financial support)?
____	____	49. Provide opportunities for paid or unpaid sabbaticals?
____	____	50. Provide opportunities for paid or unpaid shadowing experiences?
____	____	51. Provide opportunities for employee tuition reimbursement?
____	____	52. Provide opportunities for employee rotation experiences?
____	____	53. Encourage employee task forces to identify programs to reduce employee turnover?
____	____	54. Provide opportunities for flex-time work?
____	____	55. Provide opportunities for flex-place work?
____	____	56. Relax formal dress codes in favor of relaxed dress for employees?
____	____	57. Allow redeployment (applications for alternative employment in the organization) in the event of downsizings or other reductions in force?
____	____	58. Allow employees the opportunity to increase their income if they wish through voluntary overtime?
____	____	59. Work to reduce or eliminate mandatory overtime?
____	____	60. Train supervisors, managers, and executives on how to demonstrate effective competencies in working with employees (such as how to coach, counsel, etc.)?
____	____	61. Provide regular performance appraisals that balance discussions of "what to fix" with "what employees are doing well and right"?
____	____	62. Encourage supervisors or managers to provide daily positive feedback to workers about their work?
____	____	63. Encourage workers to provide daily positive feedback to co-workers about their work?
____	____	64. Encourage celebration of employees' personal events (birthdays, anniversaries, and others)?
____	____	65. Use formal, written contracts with employees to specify employment periods?
____	____	66. Hold meetings between management and non-management workers to discuss issues facing the organization so that workers understand key issues influencing their future employment prospects?
____	____	67. Encourage senior managers to "manage by walking around" and take action on employment practices that they notice that may influence employee retention?
____	____	68. Encourage senior managers to work side-by-side with workers at least one day per year so that they experience working conditions first-hand?
____	____	69. Open the books to show the organization's financial condition to workers?
____	____	70. Focus suggestion systems around ways to improve retention, providing (for instance) higher rewards for new ideas that slash turnover?

(Continued)

Yes	No	Does Your Organization . . .
____	____	71. Encourage "town hall" meetings between senior managers and workers to surface concerns and send the message that management listens—and acts on—worker concerns?
____	____	72. Identify and use a pool of contingent workers, such as retirees, so that regular workers can meet work/life balance priorities as they need to?
____	____	73. Find compelling ways to show how the work that each employee performs contributes to the organization's mission, such as annual reports for each worker that facilitate that discussion and provide a structure for management to provide that feedback?
____	____	74. Give employees the opportunity to work on community projects during work time if they so desire?
____	____	75. Permit employees to purchase the organization's products or services at special discounts?
____	____	76. Give employees financial or non-financial support for relocations, even when not organizationally related?
____	____	77. Give employees access to spiritual/religious help/counseling during work time?
____	____	78. Celebrate diversity of all kinds, including differences in outlook?
____	____	79. Encourage social relationships, such as organizational picnics, without forcing employees to participate if they do not wish to do so?
____	____	80. Encourage the use of appropriate humor to reduce stress and improve the quality of work life?
____	____	81. Allow workers freedom in how they do their work so long as they accomplish results in legal, moral, and ethical ways in line with the organization's policies?
____	____	82. Take steps to compare the organization's pay, benefits, and other employment features to competitors' and take steps to equal or surpass them?
____	____	83. Take special steps to encourage retention of employees within the first three years of employment, since most-recent hires are at greatest potential for loss? (The rule is usually "last in, first out" because new hires still have their résumés floating and they have the least emotional investment with their current employer).
____	____	84. Take steps to ensure that individuals are treated consistently and managers are not accused of undue favoritism for reasons other than productivity?
____	____	85. Monitor individuals' personal situations, taking steps to address issues that may lead to turnover (such as a spouse who is forced to move or care giving concerns)?
____	____	86. Take special steps to identify high-potential workers early in their job tenure with the organization and improve their retention?
____	____	87. Take steps to *encourage* the turnover of workers whose productivity is not adequate?
____	____	88. Provide real rewards for worker success and not give truth to the old saying that "the reward for outstanding performance is not more pay or a promotion but more and harder work"?
____	____	89. Encourage managers to monitor the workload of all workers to ensure that some people are not overworked while others escape work?

(*Continued*)

Yes	No	Does Your Organization . . .
____	____	90. Make a decided effort to monitor research and best practices on employee retention and apply the results of that research and best practice?
____	____	91. Consider the track record of managers in employee development *explicitly* when considering their own promotability?
____	____	92. Consider the track record of managers in employee retention *explicitly* when considering their own promotability?
____	____	93. Conduct an annual review of each department and location, reporting on their turnover rates and reporting those to all senior managers on a regular basis?
____	____	94. Include information about the cost of turnover and organizational efforts to reduce turnover in the organization's communication efforts with employees?
____	____	95. Include information about the cost of turnover and organizational efforts to reduce turnover in the organization's training efforts with employees?
____	____	96. Display charts of turnover by department or location prominently in those departments or locations?
____	____	97. Survey managers periodically on how the organization's policies and practices could be changed to encourage retention more effectively?
____	____	98. Target areas of the organization with the highest turnover for special programs/management attention and action?
____	____	99. Monitor how the turnover of special groups (such as women, minorities, and other protected class workers) compares to general organizational turnover and take steps to address higher turnover with special groups?
____	____	100. Communicate with customers, investors, suppliers, and distributors about the organization's efforts to reduce turnover and the results secured from those efforts?

Additional comments:

While this questionnaire is intended to be anonymous, some information about you is important. Check one for each of the following:

❑ Male   ❑ Female

❑ Non-management   ❑ Management

Source: W.J. Rothwell (2007). The organizational retention assessment (ORA). In E. Biech (Ed.), *The 2007 Pfeiffer annual, volume 2: Consulting* (pp. 177–188). San Francisco: Pfeiffer. Used with permission.

Scope. Goals of compensation policies include rewarding employees' past performance, remaining competitive in the labor market, maintaining salary equity among employees, motivating employees' future performances, maintaining the budget, attracting and retaining new talent, and reducing unnecessary turnover.[21] *Compensation* typically includes pay for work and performance, disability income, deferred income, health, accident, and liability protection, loss-of-job income, and continuation of spousal income when there is a loss. *Benefits* include the employer's share of legally required payments, for example, FICA, unemployment compensation, retirement and savings plan payments, 401(k), profit sharing, stock bonuses, medical benefit payments, and so forth.[22] In realizing that talent drives performance, employers often dangle job benefits to attract new personnel. These may include gym memberships or on-site recreation rooms, meals when working late, tickets to movies and sporting events, on-site dry cleaning service, cosmetology services, paid week off between major holidays, and various and sundry kinds of discounts for computer hardware and software, auto purchases, day care, elder care, and more.[23]

Workplace Implementation. In order to plan and design an equitable compensation system, the performance improvement practitioner works with the organization's talent management division to conduct a job analysis, identify job specifications, and write concise job descriptions. "The most important factor influencing the rate of pay of an employee is the kind of job the person performs. In classifying or differentiating jobs for pay purposes, no one single factor carries greater significance than the knowledge and skills required of the job holder."[24]

The performance practitioner must also remain proactive in helping talent managers keep abreast of new talent management processes that affect performance. "Organizations have to be sure their compensation management strategies are shaped to reward excellence, not pay for subpar performance."[25] By thinking better, thinking more effectively, and thinking more powerfully, the performance improvement practitioner is able to help organizations generate fresh solutions to global and business challenges that have direct bearing on compensation and benefits.[26]

Health and Wellness

Definition. Health and wellness programs are organization-sponsored initiatives that focus on health promotion (life style changes), health protection (prolonging life), and prevention (preventing disease). Wellness programs focus on the employee's total physical and mental condition.[27]

Scope. Employee health and wellness programs are significantly changing corporate America, as more organizations are investing in wellness programs for their key leaders to ensure they are up to the job. Good health among employees translates into productive work environments and influences the culture of the organization. Employee assistance programs (EAPs) are available "to deal with a wide range of stress-related problems, both work and non-work related, including behavioral and emotional difficulties, substance abuse, family, and marital discord, and other personal problems."[28] Employee assistance programs include diagnosis, treatment, screening, and prevention.[29] Wellness programs "identify and assist in preventing or correcting specific health problems, health hazards, or negative health habits . . . such programs are those emphasizing hypertension identification and control, smoking cessation, physical fitness and exercise, nutrition and diet control, and job and personal stress management."[30] For example, wellness programs at Johnson & Johnson "cumulatively saved the company $250 million on health care costs over the past decade."[31]

Workplace Implementation. Health and wellness programs are inextricably linked to corporate culture because they are extensions of benefit packages, robust recruitment efforts to capture the talent mindset, and retention efforts. The performance improvement practitioner works with the talent management division to plan, design, develop, and implement health and wellness programs that educate and instruct employees on health-related issues (workplace health and safety classes, health screening, and so forth) that modify or alter behavior (smoking cessation programs, including second and third-hand smoke, physical fitness classes, and so forth); that create an organizational environment that helps employees maintain healthy lifestyles (specific programs that combine educational, personal, and organizational value).[32] The performance practitioner who is skilled in evaluation offers strength in developing and evaluating instruments from health status and risk factors data. The practitioner can also monitor key performance indicators or impact measurements like absenteeism, turnover, retention, costs, productivity, accident frequency and severity rates, medical expenses, defects, rework, stress reduction, and so forth.

EXHIBIT 14.3. THE PRACTITIONER'S VOICE: HEALTH AND WELLNESS

"High-performing organizations recognize the link between maintaining employee health and wellness and performance in the workplace. With increased pressures on the workforce and longer work hours, organizations play pivotal roles in promoting healthy lifestyle choices that lead to healthier employees and organizational productivity including reduced sick time and injuries. Data indicate up to 80 percent of all illnesses, disabilities, and preventable death from chronic diseases are attributable to modifiable factors—factors that individuals can change, such as tobacco use, physical inactivity, unhealthy eating, and obesity. Many organizations are now developing and adopting formal, comprehensive workplace health and wellness policies that promote healthier workplace environments. Workplaces have integrated programs and activities directly into the workday, such as providing on-site fitness facilities, mini fitness classes during lunch, rest breaks with massage therapy, and "lunch and learn" workshops focused on stress reduction and burnout prevention, challenges of shift work, and maintaining work/life balance."

Linda A. Morrow, Ph.D.

Manager, Learning and Workplace Development

Windsor Regional Hospital

Windsor, Ontario, Canada

Retirement Planning

Definition. Retirement is a life event, a time of transition and change. The noted social gerontologist Atchley offers three views:

1. The institutional arrangements that provide retirement pensions and rules of eligibility for retirement,
2. The transition between a position of employment and the position of retired person, and
3. The life stage following retirement from the labor force.[33]

Scope. Retirement is changing, but so are the words we use to describe it. The new words for retirement are embedded in a lexicon of Rs: reorientation, recommitment, reinvention, reinvolvement, regeneration, renewal, renovation, redirection, rethinking, revitalizing, reinvestigation, replenishment, reexploration, redeciding, and more. "*Retirees* and *seniors* are now *rebounders, primetimers,* or *recareerers.* In short, the term *retirement* is being retired, or at least redefined."[34] Another gerontologist says: "Retirement challenges your identity, changes your relationships, and may leave you feeling rootless if you have no purpose."[35] However, having an adequate income, role models to follow, a healthy self-concept with a proactive approach to life, and mattering to the community can help individuals adjust.

Workplace Implementation. Retirement is part of other performance interventions such as career pathing, rewards and incentives, compensation and benefits, succession planning, and so on. The performance practitioner has the necessary leadership and organizational skills to help employees transition into retirement. Helping talent managers train employees in areas of housing, financial affairs, elder care, elder law, elder boomer issues, long-term care opportunities, anti-aging, and more will help employees frame retirement decisions and position the organization to be proactive in its negotiations with older workers.

It is time to rethink talent management practices regarding retirement: "The recession has caused older workers to reconsider their exit strategy from the workforce. As those plans change, talent managers should rethink their practices and policies to support the new workplace reality."[36] The performance practitioner can aid in developing this area. Performance Support Tool 14.3 is a planning tool to help individuals think or act and come to grips with issues related to retirement.

Labor Relations

Definition. Labor relations is the system of continuous relationships that exists between workers and management in regard to employee fair treatment, working conditions, wages, and other issues.[37]

Scope. The relationship includes "the negotiation of a written contract concerning pay, hours, and other terms and conditions of employment as well as the interpretation and administration of the contract over its period of coverage."[38] Employee rights are protected by federal

PERFORMANCE SUPPORT TOOL 14.3. ISSUES TO CONSIDER WHEN PLANNING FOR RETIREMENT

Directions: Planning for retirement includes thinking about and/or acting on many of the issues listed below. Ask potential retirees to code each issue according to the scale provided in the second column and to explain their responses. This will provide information on individual needs as well as workforce trends. For example, John needs to examine his financial situation before he retires, or 50 percent of the plant's workers have not thought about retirement goals.

Issues to Consider When Planning Retirement	Where I Stand on This Issue
1. Retirement Goals Comments:	❑ I have acted on this issue ❑ I have thought a lot about this issue ❑ I have given this issue some thought ❑ I have not thought about this issue ❑ This issue does not concern me
2. Legal Affairs Comments:	❑ I have acted on this issue ❑ I have thought a lot about this issue ❑ I have given this issue some thought ❑ I have not thought about this issue ❑ This issue does not concern me
3. Health and Wellness Comments:	❑ I have acted on this issue ❑ I have thought a lot about this issue ❑ I have given this issue some thought ❑ I have not thought about this issue ❑ This issue does not concern me
4. Financial Issues Comments:	❑ I have acted on this issue ❑ I have thought a lot about this issue ❑ I have given this issue some thought ❑ I have not thought about this issue ❑ This issue does not concern me

(Continued)

Issues to Consider When Planning Retirement	Where I Stand on This Issue
5. Retirement Housing Comments:	❑ I have acted on this issue ❑ I have thought a lot about this issue ❑ I have given this issue some thought ❑ I have not thought about this issue ❑ This issue does not concern me
6. Leisure Activities Comments:	❑ I have acted on this issue ❑ I have thought a lot about this issue ❑ I have given this issue some thought ❑ I have not thought about this issue ❑ This issue does not concern me
7. Working After Retirement Comments:	❑ I have acted on this issue ❑ I have thought a lot about this issue ❑ I have given this issue some thought ❑ I have not thought about this issue ❑ This issue does not concern me
8. Volunteering After Retirement Comments:	❑ I have acted on this issue ❑ I have thought a lot about this issue ❑ I have given this issue some thought ❑ I have not thought about this issue ❑ This issue does not concern me

legislation, specifically by the National Labor Relations Act (also called the Wagner Act), the Labor-Management Relations Act (also called the Taft-Hartley Act), and the Labor-Management Reporting and Disclosure Act (also called the Landrum-Griffin Act). Other influential pieces of legislation protecting employees include the Fair Labor Standards Act, the Equal Pay Act, Age Discrimination in Employment Act (ADEA) and the Occupational Safety and Health Act (OSHA). The two areas that are integral to labor relations are unionization and collective bargaining. Employees join unions for economic needs, job satisfaction, beliefs in union power, and union image.[39] Collective bargaining involves management and unions negotiating an equitable and fair agreement over economic needs (wages and hours) and working conditions.

Workplace Implementation. The performance improvement practitioner works with the labor relations division to prepare information on job attitudes among employees, benchmark salaries for particular industries, traces historical milestones regarding labor laws, and, in general, works with talent managers to improve interactions between workers and management regarding incentives and rewards, job security, health issues, and other areas. The practitioner partners with a business librarian and becomes familiar with the major statutes and regulations administered by the U.S. Department of Labor (DOL) that affect business and workers.

The practitioner also provides information and protocol on engaging the multigenerational workforce and serves as a resource for recent state legislation pertaining to employment law. Performance improvement practitioners in the United Kingdom, the European Union, and in other countries of the global world of business should similarly be mindful of and respect the spirit of the labor laws in their countries and places of employment to guarantee fair and equitable treatment of employees.

Individual Growth Interventions

Individual growth is that part of human resources that focuses on the organizational need to encourage and retain high-performance personnel. It is crucial for organizations to have policies and practices aimed at meeting short- and long-range needs and opportunities. To do so requires that employees remain energized, engaged, enthusiastic, and committed to job excellence and career enhancement.

Individuals are responsible for their own competitiveness, productivity, continuous learning, and professional development. Individuals are encouraged to develop a unique talent management mindset that impacts the overall mission and objectives of the organization. Performance improvement specialists should be mindful of *Training* magazine's advertisement charging and challenging employees to reexamine their learning, reframe their perceptions, redefine the impact of their learning experiences, rethink their roles as change agents, and reignite their passion for knowing and doing well.[40] Individual growth is fostered by a number of interventions. The individual growth interventions covered in this chapter are listed in Figure 14.2.

FIGURE 14.2.   Individual Growth Interventions

Individual Growth Interventions
• Motivation
• Performance Management
• Key Performance Indicators (KPIs)
• Performance Appraisals
• 360-Degree Appraisals
• Competencies
• Compentency Testing

Motivation

Definition. Motivation is an inner drive, a state of feeling or thinking that energizes, directs, and sustains human behavior.[41]

Scope. Many theories of motivation contribute to work and job experiences. They are categorized as *content* and *process* theories.

Content theories are about *what* energizes behavior. Familiar content theories include Maslow's hierarchy of needs, Alderfer's ERG (existence, relatedness, growth) theory of needs, McClelland's learned need theory (achievement, power, affiliation), and Herzberg's two-factor (motivation and hygiene) theory. Process theories are about *how* behavior is energized. Typical process theories are equity theory (individuals value and seek fairness), expectancy theory (expending effort on work that leads to desired rewards), and goal-setting theory (a goal provides the foundation for how much work effort to expend).[42] A solid resource on organizational behavior or on managing human resources can provide detail about these theories.

A discussion on motivation is incomplete unless the topics of rewards and incentives are noted. *Reward systems* are designed to change and reinforce behavior through techniques, such as public recognition, gift certificates, or vacations and travel based on meeting sales quotas. Reward programs attract qualified talent, sustain the desire to continue work, and motivate employees for producing their best results.[43] *Incentive systems*, both short-term and long-term, link pay with a standard for performance, such as salary, differential pay, allowances, time off with pay, deferred income, loss-of-job coverage, desirable working conditions, training, adequate equipment and materials, and so forth.

Workplace Implementation. Motivation is a shared responsibility between employer and employee. Performance improvement practitioners work with management to recognize valuable employees, promote constructive relationships; develop job analyses, job specifications, and job descriptions for creative and challenging jobs; identify and secure appropriate resources to perform a job; monitor employees' needs, abilities, goals, and preferences; and other activities that promote employees to remain energized, engaged, enthusiastic, and committed to job excellence and talent growth. Performance Support Tool 14.4 identifies ways an organization motivates employees. Discuss the results with your peers and your organization's talent management team.

PERFORMANCE SUPPORT TOOL 14.4. HOW MOTIVATING IS YOUR ORGANIZATION?

Directions: Use this performance support tool to identify ways your organization motivates employees. Put a check in the (+) column if motivation occurs and a check in the (–) column if improvement is needed.

+	–	Rules and Regulations
		The organization has clearly defined vision, mission, goals, and objectives.
		Performance criteria are clearly defined and communicated to all employees.
		Resources are provided to help employees attain their goals and objectives.
		Rewards and recognition are a part of the culture.
		A support network is in place so employees know where to go for assistance when needed.
		Whenever possible, the organization takes advantage of employees' expertise by including them in meetings, discussions, and other fact-finding initiatives.
		Timely information sharing, including lessons learned, occurs at all levels of the organization.
		Communication is open and encouraged.
		The organization has a conflict resolution model available to all employees.
		The organization celebrates the successes of its team and employees.
		The organization supports personal growth with training opportunities and tuition reimbursement.

Performance Management

Definition. Performance management is the process by which upper management links and aligns organizational goals to employee performance.[44]

Scope. Performance management is an ongoing management process and system that helps the organization become more efficient by motivating, training, rewarding, and promoting employees.[45] Its scope includes "strategic goal setting, development of performance standards, performance appraisal, development and coaching, and discipline and reward; all integrated to achieve organizational goals."[46] In short, a performance management system, when carefully conceived, planned, and orchestrated, defines, measures, monitors, and gives feedback to employees. It serves a strategic purpose in linking employee functions with the organization's vision, mission, goals, critical issues, and overall strategic plan. It also serves a communication purpose in helping employees recognize the effects of their activities and what the organizational expectations are. It serves as a basis for employment decisions regarding promotion, termination, transfer, train, and other options.[47]

Workplace Implementation. The performance practitioner is influential in the design, development, and implementation of a performance management system. The practitioner identifies all key stakeholders; creates and orchestrates cross-functional teams to design, advocate, and communicate the benefits of a performance management system; creates a needs assessment, complete with needs analysis and gap analysis; helps to develop a performance culture by raising the bar on expectations; develops training materials to improve managers' coaching skills; plans and monitors the organization's performance measurement system; and preps for classes, webinars, and other vehicles that will describe and enhance the benefits of a performance management system. Above all, the performance improvement practitioner uses business language in communicating the process to management and employees, rather than the language of human relations.[48]

Key Performance Indicators (KPIs)

Definition. Key performance indicators are quantitative performance measures that define the critical success factors of an organization, help the organization measure progress toward its organizational goals and objectives, and identify areas for organizational performance and improvement.[49]

Scope. Key performance indicators differ depending on the organization, so businesses, schools, healthcare facilities, social service agencies, the oil industry, and the like all have different key performance indicators, which may change as the organization's goals change. A school, for example, may focus its key performance indicators on students passing a standardized test at grade level or a graduation rate. An assisted living facility may focus its key performance indicators on the number of clients it services quarterly.[50] Key performance indicators are nonfinancial; yet, frequently measured; they are team responsibility with high impact yield.[51] If key performance indicators are valuable and sustainable in an organization, there have to be ways to accurately define and measure them. Targets also need to be in place for each key performance indicator.[52]

Workplace Implementation. A performance improvement practitioner plays an important training role in introducing key performance indicators in the organization, how they will be developed, and how they will be used. By providing workshops on defining and measuring them and determining targets for each of them, the practitioner sets him- or herself apart from other practitioners (instructional designers, analysts, organization development personnel, and others) in the organization. There are evaluation roles to play in implementing, monitoring, and evaluating key performance indicators over time and as the organization moves closer to achieving its goal. Timelines need to be established, and the performance culture needs to be carefully and effectively monitored and progress reported to the appropriate management levels.

EXHIBIT 14.4. THE PRACTITIONER'S VOICE: KEY PERFORMANCE INDICATORS

"As critical real-time quantifiable success markers, key performance indicators (KPIs) provide strategic and operational value to drive individual and organizational goals and benchmarks. KPIs are characterized by definable elements, prioritization, measurement, and quantification regardless of type and size of the organization. Detailing KPIs reduces uncertainty and ensures better performance management when values are effectively communicated among all stakeholders. Depending on the type of organization, KPIs range from efficient use of resources to industrial plan efficiency. Performance improvement practitioners are particularly interested in KPIs for internal and external accountability, such as value-based processing systems, efficient data and information flow among employees and departments, cost-effectiveness, employee turnover, customer satisfaction, and annual sales performance."

Josephine A. Larbi-Apau, Ph.D.

Instructional and Performance Improvement Technologies Consultant

Ghana, West Africa

Performance Appraisal

Definition. Performance appraisal is a structured and systematic process used by managers to provide feedback on an individual's performance to encourage improvement. Sometimes appraisals provide information for salary decisions, promotions, and improving job performance.

Scope. Informal performance appraisal occurs when management expresses an opinion about how well an employee is doing. This approach is often influenced by political, cultural, social, and interpersonal processes so that employees who are liked better stand a good chance of obtaining a positive appraisal. Formal performance appraisal is conducted to evaluate employee performance regularly and systematically.[53] These two approaches often exist simultaneously in organizations.

Performance must be based on established criteria for quality and quantity of work. Criteria need to be reliable, relevant, sensitive, and practical. In most organizations, the immediate supervisor conducts the performance appraisal; however, other approaches are gaining in popularity. Among these are rating by a committee of several supervisors, rating by the employee's co-workers, rating by the employee's subordinates, rating by someone outside the immediate work situation, self-evaluation, and rating by a combination of approaches.[54] Examples of performance appraisal methods used by organizations include checklists; weighted checklists, graphic rating scales, mixed scales, forced-choice scales, behaviorally anchored rating scales (BARS), and critical incidents, which are written descriptions of a highly effective or highly ineffective performance.[55] The human resource development literature is filled with positive techniques for conducting effective performance reviews. It also reports stories of anxiety, frustration, uncertainty, and ambiguity when performance appraisals are handled improperly.

Workplace Implementation. The performance improvement practitioner works with the human resource division and immediate supervisors of employees to inform and train them in the use of performance appraisal methods. The practitioner keeps abreast of performance appraisal best practices and shares them with the many individuals who appraise employees' performance. Practitioners play vital roles in creating the performance appraisal process, tracking annual feedback meetings, and coaching managers regarding follow-up to improvement plans. Their expertise extends from designing appraisal systems to evaluating performance appraisal processes.

360-Degree Appraisals

Definition. A 360-degree appraisal is a comprehensive approach to performance appraisal that uses self-ratings, customer ratings, and ratings by others to evaluate the performance of an employee.

Scope. The approach has gained popularity over the years. It is reported that as many as one-quarter of U.S. organizations are now using 360-degree appraisals in order to obtain as much information as possible to make informed and ethical decisions about employee activities.[56] It is similarly being used in human resource departments in the United Kingdom and in some European Union settings too.

This approach to appraisals provides performance feedback from bosses, peers, and subordinates but also from others with whom the performer has had direct contact. The result is excellent information that can be used for such developmental purposes as identifying strengths, identifying career goals, creating career plans, coaching, mentoring, training, and identifying areas for general improvement. On the other hand, there are limitations imposed by administrative paperwork and the fact that outside raters have different expectations regarding what constitutes effective job performance and job accomplishment.[57] This approach to appraisal is "made to order for the new, flatter, team-oriented organizations that emphasize total quality or high performance management, whereby input from many sources is crucial."[58]

Workplace Implementation. The performance improvement practitioner works with human resource and information technology personnel in facilitating the collection and analysis of 360-degree appraisals. The practitioner is also well-positioned to assist employees in identifying career goals and career plans and assist them in formulating individual development plans to include training and other work- and job-related educational needs. The practitioner sets up coaching and mentoring experiences for the employee that will ultimately affect the entire organization's growth and development plans and positioning priorities. Since there is great variability in the ratings provided by outside raters, the practitioner provides workshops and other training opportunities—especially those online activities like podcasts and webinars—to discuss expectations regarding performance and uses role plays and simulations to concretize the practices.

EXHIBIT 14.5. THE PRACTITIONER'S VOICE: 360-DEGREE FEEDBACK

"Feedback is crucial to professional development, and 360-degree surveys provide a good source of this valued input. Often, employees receiving 360-degree feedback say that the insights are crucial to their growth as leaders. Delivery of the results needs to be well-designed to enable employees to safely process how others perceive them. An amazing best practice calls for senior leaders to share their own feedback, with all its warts, and discuss what they learned and what actions they will take to improve. When leaders show their vulnerability and their own need for development and growth, they send a powerful message regarding the organization's commitment to continuous improvement. While it's not always practical to secure a high response rate, if the 360 feedback is an important evaluation, research suggests that six or seven responses are needed to generate reliable feedback. Too few responses may bias the results, making the feedback less valuable."

Bonnie Beresford, M.B.A.

Vice President, Client Services

Capital Analytics, Inc.

Durham, North Carolina, USA

Competencies and Competency Testing

Definition. Competencies are those characteristics or capabilities of an individual that result in successful job performance. They enable performance and include knowledge, skills, abilities, behavior, accomplishment, performance outcomes, motivation, determination, and proper attitude for the tasks involved. Competencies are also organizational capabilities that align employee behavior and action with the organization's vision, mission, goals, and business issues for strategic balance and optimal success.[59] Competency testing examines the current job knowledge and skills that are necessary for present and future job performance through a variety of testing modalities that give direct evidence of an individual's ability and skill to perform a job to the best of his or her capabilities.

Scope. Competencies are "a cluster of related knowledge, skills, and attitudes that affects a major part of one's job (a role or responsibility), that correlates with performance in the job, that can be measured against well-accepted standards, and that can be improved via training and development."[60] Specifically, they involve customer satisfaction, communication and listening skills, resolving disputes, thinking, and using technology as appropriate. Rothwell identifies specific competencies associated with the roles performance improvement specialists play in human performance work, namely, the roles of analyst, intervention specialist, change manager, and evaluator.[61] As organizations become more specialized, the need to develop the competencies of their employees will be a primary component to determining success and market share.

Workplace Implementation—Competency Development. Performance improvement practitioners play an important role in helping management develop competencies for jobs. They have strengths in job analysis, writing goals and objectives, and describing behaviors, and their academic background and experiences position them to provide the leadership and development that is needed in handling the core and role-related competencies associated with human performance. They design and develop training protocols; help their organizations develop a systems thinking approach to talent management; plan scenarios and role-play adventures on problem solving, coping, and consulting skills; identify knowledge and skill requirements of individuals and teams; select appropriate interventions; improve communication channels; evaluate individual and program results; provide feedback; and more.

Workplace Implementation—Competency Testing. It is important for organizations to determine the breadth of knowledge, skills, and abilities of their employees in this global and specialized world of work. It is particularly significant, and even crucial, in regulated industries such as healthcare, pharmaceuticals, energy, and others. Organizations test employees to determine and verify their competencies and capabilities to do the job for which they were hired.

Tests may be verbal; for example, customer service representatives or managers are often asked how they would handle a particular situation that impacts their unit. Tests may focus on motor or other skills; for example, a finish carpenter gives evidence of ability to build bookshelves and a mantle, a nurse, the ability to take a blood pressure, an architect, the ability to read a blueprint, and so on. Whatever testing mechanism is used, testing should be carefully constructed and planned for so that employees are treated fairly and appropriately.

To ascertain the validity of the testing, the appropriate job tasks and specific requirements must be in place. Directions must be provided, time allotted must be reasonable, and cost factors must be considered. It is important for an organization to study its jobs to identify and assign weights to the knowledge and skills each one requires. Testing people for current job skills or for attributes or skills needed for future performance helps the organization fulfill its strategic goals for talent management. Interviews, psychological profiles, intelligence testing, aptitude and preference tests, and the like are also used in competency testing.

A word of caution here. For those performance improvement practitioners without a background in psychometrics, an industrial psychologist should be hired to work with measurement and to determine the validity and reliability of the testing mechanisms that are ultimately used.

Organizational Growth Interventions

An organization is a group of people working together to pursue a goal, a desire or other areas of value that cannot be achieved by individuals acting alone. It is formally and consciously established and it allows people to "increase specialization and division of labor, use large-scale technology, manage the external environment, economize on transaction costs, and exert power and control which increases the value that an organization can create."[62]

A company's organizational growth is only as strong as its investment in talent. Organizations need talent who understand vision, mission, strategy, goals, and culture. They need people who possess problem-solving skills, interpersonal relationship skills, and performance understanding. They need personnel who possess the "big picture" mindset within the framework of systems thinking and understanding. Just as these characteristics and functions make a major impact on the organization, the organization similarly makes an impact on its workforce by requiring an educated, highly motivated, technologically sophisticated talent mindset where self-determination, self-discipline, and ethical principles are recognized. (See Figure 14.3.)

FIGURE 14.3. Organizational Growth Interventions

Organizational Growth Interventions
• Succession Planning
• Career Pathing
• Leadership Development
• Executive Development
• Management Development
• Supervisory Development

Succession Planning

Definition. Succession planning ensures that qualified talent will be available to fill job vacancies for future positions. It is a long-term plan and an integral part of a comprehensive career planning program primarily designed for managerial and executive positions.

Scope. Succession planning is a process of identifying key individuals by their productivity and work ethics, developing these individuals through formal training, coaching, and mentoring, and tracking this group through job successes and creative dynamics and their value-added leverage. In both large and small firms, succession planning is receiving considerable attention since turnover rates for upper-level executives are on the rise. Retirement is a distinct possibility for many executives who are aging and no longer wish to assume the stresses their jobs require. Then, too, there are losses to competitors or to death, which makes succession planning a way of coping with anticipated departures. The landscape of succession planning is changing rapidly, shown by the following:

- A move from meeting promotion needs to meeting knowledge transfer needs
- An increased reliance on rethinking retirement and on retirees
- A transition from focusing on strategic succession to tactical, daily succession
- A greater integration of succession planning with career development[63]

Workplace Implementation. After appropriate talent is identified, the performance practitioner engages individuals in training and development programs, in mentoring programs, participating in task forces, serving as gatekeeper while the organization's succession plan is generated, and acting as a change catalyst when the plan is implemented. The practitioner helps revise the plan as the organization undergoes transformation. The practitioner also plays an administrative role in helping the members of the organization remain focused on their vision, mission, goals, and objectives and keeps them on track as they pursue their business and economic needs.

EXHIBIT 14.6. THE PRACTITIONER'S VOICE: SUCCESSION PLANNING

"Succession planning is important if you truly believe in the mission of your organization and department, and want the mission to continue, even if the faces change. One aspect is knowledge management systems. Faculty or administrators who write a grant, for example, must ensure that electronic and paper documents are stored reliably and accessibly, in the event that someone else writes a grant the following year. A second important aspect is personnel recruitment and development. When we consider new hires, we evaluate their ability to fill all the roles in our department, including leadership roles. We make certain that our faculty development program grooms people to take over in emergencies, and also for normal succession such as retirement."

Mike Dosch, M.S., Ph.D., CRNA

Chair, Nurse Anesthesia Program

University of Detroit Mercy

Detroit, Michigan, USA

Career Pathing

Definition. Career pathing communicates potential job advancement as employees move up the career ladder; it is a plotting of positions through which an organization moves an employee in preparation for future job opportunities.

Scope. Career pathing is viewed from two equally important and equally significant perspectives. From the organization's perspective, career paths help determine an adequate supply of talent for a variety of jobs and from the individual's perspective, a career path represents the myriad jobs the employee undertakes along the journey to successfully achieve career goals, advancements, and the fulfilling of personal goals and objectives for a better life style.[64] While it is impossible to thoroughly integrate both perspectives in the design of career paths, a systematic career plan helps to close the gap between the two.[65]

Workplace Implementation. The performance improvement practitioner is well-positioned to work with multiple approaches to implementing career paths within an organization. The practitioner can analyze paths previously followed and note business trends to establish job markers and job transitions; chart entry and exit points into the career path; identify required education, specialized training and skills, certifications, licenses, and so on; remain focused on the organization's business needs since these determine workforce talent—number, kind, background, experiences, new mindsets; encourage feedback from coaching, mentoring, and counseling; offer seminars and guide career discussions on the types of career paths available and supported by the organization; and help employees adjust to the many changes that will result from the integration of career pathing.[66]

Leadership Development

Definition. Leadership development is "the expansion of a person's capacity to be effective in leadership roles and processes . . . to work together in productive and meaningful ways."[67] It prepares employees to cope with changes through prioritizing, overcoming obstacles and assumptions, and initiating action; it is necessary at all levels of an organization.

Scope. Leadership is the vehicle through which leadership development is accomplished. Leadership is a multi-dimensional experience and process; it is influencing and intentional, with goal accomplishment as the objective. Successful leaders use different styles of leadership influenced by traits and skills and follower and situation characteristics. Successful leaders incorporate multiple intelligences—emotional, cultural, and social—as they "walk the talk" of leadership. Their goals are to help employees become more effective and efficient in their jobs, more performance and accomplishment oriented, and more satisfied and self-directed as they contribute to organizational health and well-being. Books by Kouzes and Posner,[68] Hesselbein and Goldsmith,[69] Blanchard,[70] Drucker,[71] and Schein[72] provide information on the leadership challenge.

Workplace Implementation. New approaches to leadership and leadership development demand new skills for the performance improvement practitioner. The practitioner begins by thoroughly studying or reviewing the leadership process and the characteristics that determine the business needs of the organization. The practitioner centers the leadership development activities within an organizational context, alters learning methodologies as needed, changes leadership development from an event to a career process lasting a lifetime, creates opportunities to help everyone in the organization learn from their mistakes, and realizes that leadership and talent are everyone's responsibility.[73] Performance Support Tool 14.5 can be used as an individual or group activity to determine the alignment of an organization's leaders in terms of their individual approaches to leadership.

Executive Development

Definition. Executive development is the systematic development of an organization's executives through specific skill programs, managerial skill programs, or personal improvement programs that enhance senior management's ability to create vision, values, and business strategies.

Scope. Executive leaders are the top managers, the chief executive officers, chief financial officers, chief information officers, chief knowledge managers, chief learning officers, chief marketing officers, chief sustainability officers, presidents and vice presidents, and other top officials of organizations whose mission is to lay the foundation for the strategic planning, implementation, and monitoring of the organization. The road to the top is shifting in boundary-less organizations.

PERFORMANCE SUPPORT TOOL 14.5. HOW DO INDIVIDUAL MANAGERS APPROACH LEADERSHIP?

Use this instrument as an individual and/or group activity to determine the alignment of an organization's leaders in terms of their individual approaches to leadership.

Directions: The respondents will read each statement, check their level of agreement from 5 = Strongly Agree to 1 = Strongly Disagree, and explain why they selected the response. After everyone has completed the instrument, the facilitator may ask the group to share and discuss the responses. The facilitator may also tally the responses for each statement to determine how closely aligned the leaders are in their approach to leadership.

	5 Strongly Agree	4 Agree	3 Not Sure	2 Disagree	1 Strongly Disagree
NATURE APPROACH People are born with leadership traits or develop them very early in life. *I selected this response because:*					
NURTURE APPROACH Traits provide the foundation upon which abilities and behavior develop. *I selected this response because:*					
CHARISMATIC APPROACH Traits, abilities, behaviors, situation are important, but visionary, inspirational, and empowering qualities are primary. *I selected this response because:*					
SITUATIONAL APPROACH Traits, abilities, behaviors, are important, but situational characteristics are primary. *I selected this response because:*					

"Once people reach the C-suite, technical and functional expertise matter less than leadership skills and a strong grasp of business fundamentals."[74] The chief executive is an actor who plays many roles on the organization's competitive stage: a visionary who presents clear direction, a sponsor who champions new initiatives, a governor who controls functions and directions for evaluating effectiveness, a subject-matter expert and thought leader for the company's business, a teacher who teaches by example, a learner who models continuous learning, and a chief marketing agent who promotes the organization.[75]

The next generation of leaders is poised to bring a new mindset to the corporate board room. At an earlier time the top manager's biggest concern was handing the consequences of change; now, more worrisome and unsettling is uncertainty.[76] Ralph Lauren, who heads a major fashion empire today, says, "I don't design clothes; I design dreams." Executive development is not about "designing clothes"; it is about designing dreams, about making innovation work and how to manage it, measure it, and profit from it. It is about leveraging foresight by capitalizing on emerging ideas and growth potentials and strategizing how to make them work before competitors do.[77] It is about the wisdom to spot opportunity and recognize risk. It is about breaking the chains of organizational structure and developing a corporate mindset and corporate empathy where talent excellence is empowered, appreciated, and valued. The C-suite champion must "manage the present, selectively forget the past, and create the future."[78]

Workplace Implementation. The performance improvement practitioner helps an organization generate an executive development plan or a formal program in several areas by linking development to vision, mission, goals, and strategies; integrating all organizational systems and aligning them with the products or services provided by the organization; matching educational activities for executives with the development needs of the organization; providing and monitoring coaching and feedback mechanisms; committing to continuous learning and knowledge creation for organizations; helping top managers develop and implement large-scale interventions focusing on the organization's priorities, and other areas that help center executive leadership in an age of transparency.[79]

Management Development

Definition. Management development, a level of leadership development, prepares managers to support the organization's mission, strategy, goals, objectives, and critical business issues. It fosters learning experiences that upgrade skills, knowledge, attitudes, and ways of thinking required in current and future managerial positions.

Scope. Leadership and management are complementary terms: leaders create change, while managers control complexity and produce short-term results. Kotter's research shows leadership as establishing direction, aligning, motivating, and inspiring people, whereas management involves planning, budgeting, organizing, staffing controlling, and problem solving.[80] In addition to the critical knowledge and skills provided by an organization's development programs, management development "requires personal commitment of the individual manager. In fact, taking responsibility for one's own development may be the most important aspect."[81]

Learning experiences that promote management development either in-house or outside the organization may include inter- and intrapersonal skills; technical, administrative, and conceptual skills; decision making, delegating, and self-management and networking skills; change management, coping, and trusting skills; clear thinking, logic, and listening skills; and ethical choice skills, among others.

Workplace Implementation. There is a major role for the performance improvement practitioner to play in designing management development programs by reaching into the design principles section of one's performance tool chest. The practitioner conducts a thorough needs assessment focusing on current and future skill categories; establishes program objectives and performance objectives for all talent management programs; oversees internal and external programs supported by the organization; mentors employees in self-development programs; evaluates the programs formatively, summatively, confirmatively; fosters organizational culture and teamwork; embraces change and change management; and sets up role plays and other support mechanisms for those who are resistant. Above all, the performance improvement practitioner should be certain that the management development programs and practices put forth are inextricably linked to the organization's strategic planning, thinking, and market position.

Supervisory Development

Definition. Supervisory development offers improvement opportunities to supervisors who are part of the organization's management team while they oversee the work of operative employees.

Scope. Supervisors are involved in myriad and multiple tasks involving motivation, feedback, dispute resolution, alignment, communication, career assessment, and gate-keeping. They "set objectives, plan work, assign people to do the work, and follow up on the results of the work."[82]

Their competencies extend from analyzing and diagnosing complex situations to capitalizing on specialized knowledge and expertise to establishing a power base and networking connections.[83]

Workplace Implementation. Supervisory personnel learn best from reality-oriented practice and concrete examples. The performance improvement practitioner works cooperatively with the talent management division to plan and design supervisory development activities. These collaborative efforts are based on:

- Ability to recognize qualifications and aspirations of supervisors participating in improvement activities
- Knowledge of core and key competencies of supervisors in various work assignments
- Sensitivity and empathy to roles and relationships imposed upon supervisors by the organization
- Realization that supervision is a continuously evolving role
- Flexibility, open-mindedness, and thinking outside the box[84]

Citations

1. DeSimone & Harris, 1998
2. Van Tiem, Moseley, & Dessinger, 2001
3. Bersin, 2006
4. Taleo Research, 2011
5. Oakes, 2006, p. 21
6. Cappelli, 2008, p. 1
7. Cappelli. 2008, p. 5
8. Ivancevich, 2007, p. 5
9. Drucker, 1985, p. 22
10. DeCenzo & Robbins, 1999, p. 130
11. Dessler, 2000, pp. 21–26
12. Dessler, 2000, pp. 134–154
13. DeCenzo & Robbins, 1999, pp. 12–13; 169–174
14. Van Tiem, Moseley, & Dessinger, 2000, pp. 138–144; 208
15. Schiemann, 2009, p. 223
16. Fitz-enz, 2009, pp. 115–116
17. Fitz-enz, 2009, pp. 116; 140–141
18. Hom, 2009, pp. 226–227
19. Vosburgh, 2009, pp. 226–227
20. Rothwell, 2007, pp. 177–188
21. Sherman, Bohlander, & Snell, 1996, pp. 344–345
22. Sherman, Bohlander, & Snell, 1996
23. Kozlowski, 2000, p. 4A
24. Henderson, 2000, p. 31
25. Ovsyannikov, 2010, p. 16
26. Hurson, 2008, pp. 5–8
27. Robbins, 2001, p. 572
28. Gibson, Ivancevich, Donnelly, & Konopaske, 2006, p. 217
29. Dolezalek, 2010, pp. 26–28
30. Gibson, Ivancevich, Donnelly, & Konopaske, 2006, p. 218
31. Berry, Mirabito, & Baun, 2010, p. 105
32. Berry, Mirabito, & Baun, 2010, p. 105
33. Atchley, 1996, p. 437
34. Robinson & Lakin, 2007, p. 4
35. Schlossberg, 2009, p. 15
36. Prokopeak, 2010. p. 24
37. Bateman & Snell, 1999, pp. 354–355
38. Ivancevich, 2007, p. 483
39. Bateman & Snell, 1999, pp. 355–359
40. Lakewood Media Group, p. 4
41. Gomez-Mejia, Balkin, & Cardy, 2001, p. 60

42. Burns, Bradley, & Weiner, 2012, pp. 91–104

43. Gibson, Ivancevich, Donnelly, & Konopaske, 2006, p. 177

44. Phillips, 2008, p. 311

45. Gliddon, 2010, p. 299

46. Phillips, 2008, p. 311

47. Cascio & Aguinis, 2005, pp. 82–844

48. Gliddon, 2010, pp. 311–312

49. Editors' Discussion, 2010, p. 848

50. Reh, 2011

51. Parmenter, 2010, p. 6

52. Reh, 2011

53. Ivancevich, 2007, p. 253

54. Ivancevich, 2007, pp. 257–258

55. Anthony, Perrewe, & Kacmar, 1996

56. Schermerhorn, Hunt, & Osborn, 2008, p. 162

57. Phillips, 2008, pp. 312–315

58. Schermerhorn, Hunt, & Osborn, 2008, p. 162

59. Phillips, 2008, p. 193

60. Parry, 1996, p. 50

61. Rothwell, 1996, pp. 18–19

62. Jones, 2007, p. 5

63. Rothwell, 2010, pp. 51–54

64. Ivancevich, 2007, p. 463

65. Gainshaw, Beynon, Rubery, & Ward, 2002, pp. 89–110

66. Cascio, 1998, pp. 170–171

67. McCauley, Moxley, & Van Velsor, 1998, p. 4

68. Kouzes & Posner, 1995

69. Hesselbein & Goldsmith, 2006

70. Blanchard, 2007

71. Drucker, 2002

72. Schein, 2010

73. Zenger, Ulrich, & Smallwood, 2000, pp. 22–27

74. Groysberg, Kelly, & MacDonald, 2011, p. 61

75. Meister & Willyerd, 2000, pp. 52–58

76. Galagan, 2011, pp. 27–28

77. Emelo, 2011, pp. 20–23

78. Govindarajan & Trimble, 2011, p. 109

79. Wertz, 1996, p. 634

80. Kotter, 1990, pp. 103–111

81. Mondy, Noe, & Premeaux, 2002, p. 229

82. Gibson, Ivancevich, Donnelly, & Konopaske, 2006, p. 315

83. Katz, 1974, pp. 90–102

84. Bittel & Newstrom, 1996, pp. 656–657

References

Anthony, W.P., Perrewe. P.L., & Kacmar, K.M. (1996). *Strategic human resource management* (2nd ed.) Fort Worth, TX: The Dryden Press/Harcourt Brace College Publishers.

Atchley, R.C. (1996). Retirement. In J.E. Birren (Ed.), *Encyclopedia of gerontology: Age, aging, and the aged, volume 2* (pp. 437–449). San Diego: Academic Press.

Bateman, T.S., & Snell, S.A. (1999). *Management: Building competitive advantage* (4th ed.) Boston: Irwin/McGraw-Hill.

Berry, L.L., Mirabito, A.M., & Baun, W.B. (2010, December). *Harvard Business Review, 88*(12), 104–112.

Bersin, J. (2006, May). Talent management: What is it? Why not? Retrieved from www.bf.umich.edu/docs?KeyReferenceArticles.pdf.

Bittel, L.R., & Newstrom, J.W. (1996). Supervisor development. In R.L. Craig (Ed.), *The ASTD training and development handbook: A guide to human resource development* (pp. 656–657). New York: McGraw-Hill.

Blanchard, K. (2007). *Leading at a higher level: Blanchard on leadership and creating high performing organizations.* Upper Saddle River, NJ: Pearson/Prentice Hall.

Burns, L.R., Bradley, E.H., & Weiner, B.J. (2012). *Shortell and Kaluzny's health care management: Organization design & behavior* (6th ed.). Clifton Park, NY: Delmar/Cengage Learning.

Cappelli, P. (2008). *Talent on demand: Managing talent in an age of uncertainty.* Boston: Harvard Business School Press.

Cascio, W.F. (1998). *Applied psychology in human resource management* (5th ed.). Upper Saddle River, NJ: Prentice Hall.

Cascio, W.F., & Aguinis, H. (2005). *Applied psychology in human resource management* (6th ed.). Upper Saddle River, NJ: Pearson/Prentice Hall.

DeCenzo, D.A., & Robbins, S.P. (1999). *Human resource management* (6th ed.). Hoboken, NJ: John Wiley & Sons.

DeSimone, R.L., & Harris, D.M. (1998). *Human resource development* (2nd ed.). Fort Worth, TX: The Dryden Press.

Dessler, G. (2000). *Human resource management* (8th ed.) Upper Saddle River, NJ: Prentice Hall.

Dolezalek, H. (2010, January). Executive training. *Training, 47*(1), 26–28.

Drucker, P.F. (1985). Getting things done: How to make people decisions. *Harvard Business Review, 63*(4), 22.

Drucker, P.F. (2002). *Managing in the next society.* New York: St. Martin's Press.

Editors' discussion. (2010). Key performance indicators (KPIs). In R. Watkins & D. Leigh (Eds.), *Handbook of improving performance in the workplace, volume 2: Selecting and implementing performance interventions* (p. 848). San Francisco: Pfeiffer/ISPI.

Emelo, R. (2011, January). Foresight as a leadership attribute. *Talent Management, 7*(1). 20–23.

Fitz-enz, J. (2009). *The ROI of human capital: Measuring the economic value of employee performance* (2nd ed.). New York: AMACOM.

Gainshaw, D., Beynon, H., Rubery, J., & Ward, K. (2002, February). The restructuring of career paths in large service sector organizations: Delayering, upskilling and polarization. *Sociological Review,* pp. 89–110.

Galagan, P. (2011, January). What worries CEOs now? *T + D, 65*(1), 27–28.

Gliddon, D.G. (2010). Performance management systems. In R. Watkins & D. Leigh (Eds.), *Handbook of improving performance in the workplace, volume 2: Selecting and implementing performance interventions* (pp. 299–318). San Francisco: Pfeiffer/ISPI.

Gomez-Mejia, L.R., Balkin, D.B., & Cardy, R.L. (2001). *Managing human resources* (3rd ed.). Upper Saddle River, NJ: Prentice Hall.

Govindarajan, V., & Trimble, C. (2011, January/February). The CEO's role in business model reinvention. *Harvard Business Review, 89*(1/2), 108–114.

Groysberg, B., Kelly, L.K., & MacDonald, B. (2011, March). The new path to the C-suite. *Harvard Business Review, 89*(3), 60–68.

Henderson, R.I. (2000). *Compensation management in a knowledge-based world* (8th ed.) Upper Saddle River, NJ: Prentice Hall.

Hesselbein, F., & Goldsmith, M. (Eds.). (2006). *The leader of the future 2: Visions, strategies, and practices for the new era*. San Francisco: Jossey-Bass.

Hom, P., as cited in W.A. Schiemann. (2009). *Reinventing talent management: How to maximize performance in the new marketplace*. Hoboken, NJ: John Wiley & Sons.

Hurson, T. (2008). *Think better: Your company's future depends on it . . . and so does yours*. New York: McGraw-Hill.

Ivancevich, J.M. (2007). *Human resource management* (10th ed.). Boston: McGraw-Hill/Irwin.

Jones, G.R. (2007). *Organizational theory, design, and change* (5th ed.). Upper Saddle River, NJ: Pearson/ Prentice Hall.

Katz, R.L. (1974). Skills of an effective administrator. *Harvard Business Review, 52*(5) 90–102.

Kotter, J.P. (1990, May/June). What leaders really do. *Harvard Business Review, 68*(3), 103–111.

Kouzes, J.M., & Posner, B.Z. (1995). *The leadership challenge: How to keep getting extraordinary things done in organizations*. San Francisco: Jossey-Bass.

Kozlowski, K. (2000, January 19). Teachers' union chief calls for big raises. *The Detroit News*.

Lakewood Media Group. Training 2011 Conference & Expo advertisement, p. 4.

McCauley, C.D., Moxley. R.S., & Van Velsor, E. (Eds.). (1998). *Handbook of leadership development*. San Francisco: Jossey-Bass.

Meister, J.C., & Willyerd, K. (2000). The CEO-driven learning culture. *Training and Development, 54*(6), pp. 52–58.

Mondy, R.W., Noe, R.M., & Premeaux, S.R. (2002). *Human resource management* (8th ed.). Upper Saddle River, NJ: Prentice Hall.

Oakes, K. (2006, April). The emergence of talent management. *T + D, 60*(4), 21–24.

Ovsyannikov, M. (2010, May). Pay to perform vs. pay to fail. *Talent Management, 6*(5), 16–19.

Parmenter, D. (2010). *Key performance indicators: Developing, implementing, and using winning KPIs* (2nd ed.). Hoboken, NJ: John Wiley & Sons.

Parry, S.P. (1996, July). The quest for competencies. *Training, 33*, 48–56.

Phillips, L. (2008). *SPHR exam prep* (2nd ed.). Upper Saddle River, NJ: Pearson Education.

Prokopeak, M. (2010, May). Rethinking retirement. *Talent Management, 6*(5), 24–27.

Reh, F.J. (2011). Key performance indicators (KPI): How an organization defines and measures progress toward its goals. Retrieved from http://about.com/cs/. . ./keyperfindic.htm?p=1

Robbins, S.P. (2001). *Organizational behavior* (9th ed.). Upper Saddle River, NJ: Prentice Hall.

Robinson, S.P., & Lakin, M.B. (2007). *Framing new terrain: Older adults & higher education* (p. 4). Washington, DC: American Council on Education.

Rothwell, W.J. (1996). *ASTD models for human performance improvement: Roles, competencies, and outputs*. Alexandria, VA: American Society for Training & Development.

Rothwell, W.J. (2007). The organizational retention assessment (ORA). In E. Biech (Ed.), *The 2007 Pfeiffer annual, volume 2: Consulting* (pp. 177–188). San Francisco: Pfeiffer.

Rothwell, W.J. (2010, September). The future of succession planning. *T + D, 64*(9), 50–54.

Schein, E.H. (2010). *Organizational culture and leadership* (4th ed.). San Francisco: Jossey-Bass.

Schermerhorn, J.R., Jr., Hunt, J.G., & Osborn R.N. (2008). *Organizational behavior* (10th ed.). Hoboken, NJ: John Wiley & Sons.

Schiemann, W.A. (2009). *Reinventing talent management: How to maximize performance in the new marketplace*. Hoboken, NJ: John Wiley & Sons.

Schlossberg, N.K. (2009). *Revitalizing retirement: Reshaping your identity, relationships, and purpose*. Washington, DC: American Psychological Association.

Sherman, A., Bohlander, G., & Snell, S. (1996). *Managing human resources* (10th ed.). Cincinnati, OH: South-Western Publishing.

Taleo Research. What is talent management? Retrieved from www.taleo.com/researcharticle1/what-talent-management/

Van Tiem, D.M., Moseley, J.L., & Dessinger, J.C. (2001). *Performance improvement interventions: Enhancing people, process, and organizations through performance technology.* Silver Spring, MD: International Society for Performance Improvement.

Van Tiem, D.M., Moseley, J.L. ,& Dessinger, J.C. (2000, 2004). *Fundamentals of performance technology: A guide to improving people, process, and performance.* Silver Spring, MD: International Society for Performance Improvement.

Vosburgh, as cited in W.A. Schiemann (2009). *Reinventing talent management: How to maximize performance in the new marketplace.* Hoboken, NJ: John Wiley & Sons.

Wertz, L.H. (1996). Executive development. In R. Craig (Ed.), *The ASTD training and development handbook: A guide to human resource development* (4th ed.) (pp. 622–635). New York: McGraw-Hill.

Zenger, J., Ulrich, D., & Smallwood, N. (2000, March). The new leadership development. *T + D, 54*(3), 22–27.

Organizational Communication Interventions

Although the word *communication* has multiple meanings, it is basically defined as the transfer of meaning between sender and receiver. The sender has an idea that is put into an email, memo, or conversation so that it can be sent to the receiver, thereby encoding and distributing the message. The transmitted idea is then received, whereupon the receiver interprets or decodes the message and provides feedback. The message is sent through channels selected by the sender, receiver, or an external source such as technology, geographic distance, and so forth.

A message may be oral, using face-to-face, telephone, teleconference, webinars, and similar techniques, or written in faxes, emails, electronic bulletin boards, and so forth. Noise may filter, block, or distort the message. Feedback confirms the success or failure of the communication. In order for understanding to occur, the sender must provide a clear message, the channel must be free from noise, and the receiver must interpret the message and respond with appropriate feedback.

More broadly, communication is a process through which people, acting together, create, sustain, and manage meanings through the use of verbal and nonverbal signs and symbols within a particular context. An organization's success depends on the effectiveness of its people working together, supporting common goals, and understanding critical issues, all of which is dependent on effective communication. Organizational communication is the process by which messages are sent, the monitoring of what types of messages are sent, the values associated with those messages, the amount of information conveyed, the rules and norms under which messages are sent, and organizational variables like structure and outcome measures that affect the processes.

Organizational communication is a wide-ranging field of study encompassing behavioral science disciplines such as anthropology, sociology, and psychology and business specializations such as marketing, public relations, talent management, and leadership. Communication in various organizational settings "requires an open mind . . . willingness to take on ideas and explore new perspectives . . . is particularly challenging due to factors such as formal structures, cultural diversity, political, financial and time pressures, though efforts to improve communication practices can make a real difference to performance."[1]

This chapter will provide information on the definition, scope, and work implementation for the organizational communication interventions outlined in Figure 15.1. Listen carefully—the voice of the practitioner may also be heard commenting on a specific intervention.

FIGURE 15.1. Organizational Communication Interventions

Organizational Communication
• Communication Networks
• Information Systems
• Suggestion Systems
• Grievance Systems
• Dispute Resolution
• Social Media

Communication Networks

Definition. Communication networks are the patterns that form when messages move from sender to receiver; they illustrate the relationships and interactions between and among individuals and organizations and provide the infrastructure for both communication and collaboration.

Networks are patterns of communication interactions. They are defined channels within an organization that expedite the timely transmission of messages to their intended receivers. Defined network channels add predictability to an organization by directing the access of information.

Scope. Communication networks facilitate the dissemination and collection of information, the coordination of work effort, and the achievement of goals. The networks are either formal or informal and flow top down, bottom up, or horizontally. They influence job performance and job satisfaction. Many smaller networks exist within the larger organizational networking system. For example, there are personnel and individual networks, and there are departmental networks.[2] Individuals have studied network structures, formal and informal networks, communication roles of networks, descriptive properties, and network analysis.

Workplace Implementation. Performance improvement practitioners are well-positioned to solve problems that involve an organization's communication network. They begin by conducting a communication audit or analysis, which includes elements of communication, attributes of communication networks, and the organization's management style and climate. Then they select the appropriate intervention based on the findings and outcomes:

- *System interventions*—change the direction or flow, amount, frequency, availability, and/or usability of exchanged information.
- *Interactive interventions*—influence direct or indirect communication patterns
- *Message campaign interventions*—create unifying themes that direct performance[3]

Information Systems

Definition. Information systems are any combination of information technology and people's activities using that technology to support operations, management, and decision making.[4]

Information systems store, process, disseminate, and sometimes even analyze information for those who need it.

Scope. Information systems are made up of technology, documentation, data, and people. Technology, including computer hardware, networks, and software, is most commonly associated with information systems; however, even more important is the interaction among people; algorithmic processes for collecting, storing, organizing, and retrieving information; instructions; and data. Use of information systems, if handled correctly, has increased over the past decade because information systems offer many advantages over other organizational communication devices. There are information systems dedicated to supporting management, decision making, and the processing of various business transactions, as well as keeping the C-suite informed. Among the many advantages are these:

- Immediate dissemination of information to employees, suppliers, customers, and any other constituents;
- Synchronous or asynchronous text, audio and visual communication unobstructed by geographic separation;
- Dissemination of the most up-to-date information;
- Training on demand;
- Integration of departmental data and information for executive decision making;
- Facilitation of collaborative teamwork unobstructed by geographic separation; and
- Multimedia communication.

Depending on the decisions they are required to make, people at different levels of an organization require different information. An executive who engages in long-range strategic planning, for example, needs new product information and innovation mechanisms. Middle managers need forecasting trends and budget analysis. First-line managers need information for short-term operational decisions. Individual workers need information that affects daily work decisions.[5]

Workplace Implementation. The introduction of information systems as an organizational communication mechanism carries with it many implementation considerations:

- *Security.* Sensitive information made available by and transmitted through information systems must be protected with passwords, encryption, firewalls, and virus protection.
- *Integration.* Information systems should ideally be integrated. However, when this is not possible, consideration should be given to making the various systems, as much as possible, compatible with other departments as well as with suppliers and customers.
- *Consistency.* An important consideration, especially in nonintegrated systems, is maintaining consistency to avoid the use of inaccurate or out-of-date information.
- *Policies.* Consideration must be given to ensure that information systems are used in a manner compliant with organization policies, codes of ethics, and governmental regulations.
- *Ease-of-use and training.* Information systems bring with them new and sometimes more complicated methods of use and thus require development of user-friendly interfaces and, when necessary, the appropriate training on their use.

- *Dehumanization.* Information systems should only be used as an organizational communication instrument when face-to-face communication is not possible or necessary. Examples where information systems, in isolation, are not advisable include employee terminations, diversity or safety training, and labor relations.

Performance improvement practitioners need to know how to enhance their own performance by developing a personal information system that makes it easy to store and share information and resources, communicate with clients and resources at a distance, make presentations, and facilitate information or training sessions. At the organizational level, the practitioner must remain up-to-date on new and improved information technologies and actively maintain a network of experts who can provide support during new system implementation or existing system upgrades or maintenance.

Suggestion Systems

Definition. Suggestion systems are planned procedures used by organizations to gather ideas from employees about improvements in organization effectiveness. Rewards are often provided for suggestions that bring positive results to the organization.

Scope. Suggestion systems allow employees to increase workplace responsibility and accountability by offering ideas for improving products, policies, procedures, practices, and services. Ideas generally focus on increasing productivity, fostering genuine employee relations, cutting costs, and improving working conditions, especially in areas of safety, health, and wellness.[6] "The objective of a suggestion program is to promote employee involvement, creative thinking, and continuous improvement."[7] Successful suggestion systems include leadership commitment, clearly defined goals and objectives, carefully articulated reward systems, regular publicity, and immediate response to each suggestion.[8]

Workplace Implementation. A suggestion system is supplemental to regular channels of communication within an organization. The performance improvement practitioner opens lines of communication between the organization and employees by suggesting the implementation of a new suggestion system or by improving an existing one. The practitioner can also ensure that the system is uniquely structured to match the mission, vision, goals, and strategic thinking and planning within the organization.

A suggestion system committee representing all levels of the organization should be formed. The committee, under the guidance and capable direction of the performance improvement practitioner, establishes a procedural format for submitting, evaluating, providing feedback, and implementing suggestions. Once the suggestions are implemented, they need to be targeted to the business needs, the performance needs, and the individual workplace needs of the organization. Performance Support Tool 15.1 offers guidance in implementing a suggestion system in the workplace.

Grievance Systems

Definition. Grievance systems are formal or informal processes for communicating, reviewing, and resolving employee complaints. An employment-related issue is brought to the attention of

PERFORMANCE SUPPORT TOOL 15.1. PLANNING A SUGGESTION SYSTEM

Purpose: Use this performance support tool to gather information, document the planning process, make decisions regarding systems structure, format, incentives, feedback, communication, and so on, and to evaluate the outcomes.

Directions: Fill in the information for all the sections. Revise the questions or add new ones as needed to adapt this performance support tool to a specific situation.

1. **Structure the Suggestion System**
   - Why is the suggestion system needed?

   - How will a suggestion system contribute to upward communication within the organization?

   - What will the suggestion system look like (submission, evaluation, feedback, implementation, maintenance)?

   - Who is responsible for implementing and maintaining the suggestion system?

   - When will the suggestion system be inaugurated within the organization?

   - Where are the strategic locations for the system?

2. **Gather Input from Stakeholders**
   - Which population is being targeted?

   - Which stakeholders have input?

   - Who else might be beneficial contributors?

3. **Procedural Format**
   - How will the suggestion system be used?

   - Are written suggestions required?   ❏ Yes   ❏ No
   - How is feedback given for rejection or acceptance of ideas?

(Continued)

4. Nature of Incentives

- Will the rewards be   ❑ monetary   ❑ non-monetary   ❑ both?

- If the rewards are non-monetary, what type of incentives will be included?

- Will the incentives be commensurate with the benefits of the suggestion to the company?   ❑ Yes   ❑ No

- If yes, how will the benefit be established?

5. Driving Forces

- Who champions the establishment of a suggestion system?

- What communication barriers are the forces behind the suggestion system?

6. Communicate the Message

- How is the suggestion system marketed throughout the organization?

- How is the suggestion system advertised throughout the organization?

- How is the suggestion system integrated within the organization?

the appropriate person or persons, who consider the issue impartially and resolve it as quickly as possible.

Scope. Grievances have several causes and are often symptoms of underlying problems. Employees often cite wages, hours, or conditions of employment as the basis for a grievance. Some grievances are more serious and far more time-consuming than others; for example, discipline cases and seniority problems, including promotions, transfers, and layoffs, are problematic.[9] Grievance systems are most frequently found in unionized settings; however, they can operate in a non-union environment, too; for example, an ombudsperson may facilitate a grievance resolution and represent the worker to management. When the organizational climate is positive and when employees feel they are heard, grievances are more likely to be settled favorably.

Workplace Implementation. The performance improvement practitioner plays a key role in helping the organization design and implement or improve a grievance system. The practitioner can make certain that procedures are in place to handle grievances promptly and that those procedures and forms for airing grievances are user-friendly. Generating process flowcharts for handling grievances; analyzing, designing, repurposing, and piloting grievance forms; and designing and developing training programs, information packets, and/or performance support tools ensure that employees and supervisors are thoroughly familiar with grievance procedures and policies. Finally, the performance improvement practitioner works with management to keep channels of communication open to support a healthy organizational climate that fosters productivity, quality, and continuous improvement.

Dispute Resolution

Definition. Dispute or conflict resolution involves alleviating a disagreement between two or more people who share differing views.

Scope. The literature reports three types of conflict:

1. *Task content conflict*—disagreements about the actual tasks being performed;
2. *Emotional conflict*—awareness of interpersonal incompatibilities among people working together on a task, including negative emotions and dislike of people involved;
3. *Administrative conflict*—awareness by people involved that there are controversies about how task accomplishment will proceed.[10]

A moderate amount of task content conflict is critical to effective group functioning, whereas administrative conflict and emotional conflict can result in group dysfunction. Conflict is categorized at the individual level and at the group level. Individual or intrapersonal conflict occurs when the locus of the dispute is the individual. Interpersonal conflict occurs between two or more individuals.

Workplace Implementation. The performance improvement practitioner should keep eyes and ears open to spot potential signs of conflict within the organization, monitor the work climate to detect early warning signs, take time to find out whether the real cause of the conflict is individual or group generated, see who is involved, and speculate on the potential effects the conflict may have on individuals, groups, and the organization. The practitioner offers dispute resolution training that focuses on developing the communication skills needed to resolve gridlock in relationships. Because the goal of dispute resolution should be to resolve, rather than win, communicating the process should never be hostile or negative; it should be clear, direct, and as open as possible. Table 15.1 lists some useful tips for successful dispute resolution.

TABLE 15.1.   Dispute Resolution Do's and Don'ts

Do	Don't
Ask for feedback and reflect on what you think the other person is saying	Use "You should/shouldn't" statements
Give nonverbal supportive messages	Use overly long statements
Make sure the problem is clear, concise, and specific	Use putdowns and sarcasm
Express problems as soon as you are aware of them	Interrupt others in mid-sentence
Admit when you are wrong	React defensively
Argue only one point at a time and resist temptation to get off the subject	Fight about an issue as a way to avoid a more serious issue
Keep discussions private when appropriate	Ignore the statements of others
Create neutral atmospheres when mutual agreements are more likely to be reached	Act in a commanding or threatening manner
Express facts and feelings regarding the problem, ensuring everyone has an equal chance to speak	Respond to an unfair comment with an equally unfair remark
Back up from solutions to needs	Use double messages
Depersonalize the argument	Hold resentments
List possible solutions, being as creative as possible and considering all solutions	Express more anger than you really feel just to intimidate the person
Develop specific actions that have a good chance of being successful and that are developed from shared input	Give up before the issue is resolved just to keep peace
Try to keep a sense of humor	Make unfair comparisons

Social Media

Definition. Social media is a "range of Web 2.0 tools such as blogs, wikis, and RSS feeds by means of which people create and disseminate content to individuals and groups."[11]

Scope. Social media "typically refers to the many relatively inexpensive and widely accessible electronic tools that enable anyone to publish and access information, collaborate on a common effort, or build relationships. . . . It is about participation and . . . interactions between people."[12] Social media as an organizational communication mechanism is represented by discussion forums, blogs, wikis, podcasts, videos, and pictures. Each of these tools uses a communication platform called Web 2.0 that enables anyone to create information on line. Typical social media tools include:

- *Facebook:* A social utility that connects people with friends and others who work, study, and live around them
- *Twitter:* A free social networking and micro-blogging service that enables its users to send and read messages known as tweet
- *LinkedIn:* A business-oriented social networking site
- *Blog:* A type of website, usually maintained by an individual with regular entries of commentary, descriptions of events, or other material such as graphics or video
- *Wiki:* Wiki, short for "quick," is a website that allows the easy creation and editing of any number of interlinked web pages via a web browser using a simple markup language
- *Digg:* A social news website
- *Flickr:* An online photo management system
- *Wikipedia:* Website for collaborating and sharing knowledge
- *Discussion Forums:* A place to pose questions with answers and comments able to be viewed by all

Workplace Implementation. The performance improvement practitioner utilizes information about social technology and interfaces to help the organization and its employees gain knowledge about, and skill sophistication in, the use of social media tools. The practitioner assists the organization in incorporating social media into the everyday life of the organization. The practitioner must remain current with advancements in software technology that enable social connection. The use of social media gives an organization more ways to work collaboratively with other organizations, accelerates productivity, and helps an organization develop a culture clothed in social technology.[13]

EXHIBIT 15.1. THE PRACTITIONER'S VOICE: SOCIAL MEDIA

"Social media has an amazing potential to increase knowledge sharing among employees. Informal learning can be expanded from the proverbial 'water cooler' talk to rapid global response through the use of social media tools. As any hobbyist can attest, a simple post to a content-specific Internet forum can yield tremendous information gains. Social media can increase the scope and speed of such information transfer. Organizations must cautiously approach the use of such tools. While the potential productivity gains cannot be ignored, social media is inherently 'social' and may actually contribute to lower productivity. In addition, security concerns, such as leaked information, must be carefully considered before incorporating social media tools in the workplace."

Jason Paul Siko, M.Ed., M.S.

Science Educator

Clarkston High School

Clarkston, MI, USA

Citations

1. Blundel & Ippolito, 2008, p. 18
2. Gibson & Hodgetts, 1986, p. 228
3. Swenson, 1999, p. 92
4. *Software Engineering*, 1998
5. Dessler, 1998, p. 617
6. Levine, Belman, Charness, Groshen, & O'Shaughnessy, 2001
7. Suggestion Program, 2006, p. 1633
8. Rynes & Gerhart, 2000
9. Dessler, 2011, pp. 566–569
10 Shortell & Kaluzny, 2006, pp. 152–153
11 Meister & Willyerd, 2010, p. 124
12 Jue, Alcaldemarr, & Kassotakis, 2010, pp. 4–5
13 Jue, Alcaldemarr & Kassotakis, 2010, p. 18

References

Blundel, R., & Ippolito, K. (2008). *Effective organisational communication* (3rd ed.). Harlow, UK: Prentice Hall/*Financial Times*.

Dessler, G. (1998). *Leading people and organizations in the 21st century*. Upper Saddle River, NJ: Prentice Hall.

Dessler, G. (2011). *Human resource management* (12th ed.) Boston, MA: Pearson.

Gibson, J.W., & Hodgetts, R.M. (1986). *Organizational communication: A managerial perspective*. Orlando, FL: Academic Press.

Jue, A.L., Alcaldemarr, J., & Kassotakis, M.E. (2010). *Social media at work: How networking tools propel organizational performance*. San Francisco: Jossey-Bass.

Levine, D., Belman, D., Charness, G., Groshen, E., & O'Shaughnessy, K.C. (2001). *The new employment contract: Evidence from how little wage structures have changed*. Kalamazoo, MI: Upjohn Institute.

Meister, J.C., & Willyerd, K. (2010). *The 2020 workplace: How innovative companies attract, develop, and keep tomorrow's employees today*. New York: Harper Business.

Rynes, S.L., & Gerhart, B. (Eds.). (2000). *Compensation in organizations: Current research and practice*. San Francisco: Jossey-Bass.

Shortell, S.M., & Kaluzny, A.D. (2006). *Health care management: Organization design and behavior* (5th ed.) Clifton Park, NY: Thomson Delmar Learning.

Software engineering institute report: Glossary. (1998). Pittsburg, PA: Carnegie Mellon University. www.seicmu/publications/documents 03 reports/03tr002/03tr002glossary.html.

Suggestion program. (2006). In *Business: The ultimate resource*. Cambridge, MA: Basic Books.

Swenson, J. (1999). Communication. In D.L. Langdon, K.S. Whiteside, & M.M. McKenna (Eds.), *Intervention resource guide: 50 performance improvement tools*, (pp. 91–97). San Francisco: Pfeiffer.

Organization Design and Development

16

The onset of the Information Age has forced industry to continuously seek new and innovative business practices to remain competitive. This has compelled organizations to examine the way they do business and to restructure their organizations through organization design and development interventions.

This chapter provides information on definition, scope, and work implementation for the organization design and development interventions outlined in Figure 16.1. Listen carefully—the voice of the practitioner may also be heard commenting on a specific intervention.

FIGURE 16.1. Organization Design and Development Intervention Components

Empowerment	Organizational Pro-Action	Organizational Values
• Team Strategies	• Strategic Planning	• Culture
• Virtual Teams	• Environmental Scanning	• Diversity
• Problem Solving	• Appreciative Inquiry	• Inclusion Strategies
	• Outsourcing	• Globalization
	• Benchmarking	• Localization
	• Balance Scorecard	• Social Responsibility
	• Dashboards	• Ethics
		• Decision Making

Definition and Scope

Organization design and development is a process that examines the operation and management of an organization in an effort to reshape the organization if necessary to ensure efficiency and competitiveness. Organization design and development focuses on aligning all the aspects of the organization, from structures to roles, with the organization's business strategy.

One process for organization design and development is Galbraith's STAR model,[1] which is both organization- and people-focused. STAR begins by examining the organization's strategy or direction and then moves on to examine the organization's structure to locate the decision-making power, processes to determine information flow, rewards to examine motivation and align the goals of employees and organization, and finally, human resource policies to determine the impact on employee attitudes and skills.

Organizational operations are affected by both internal and external factors. Political environments, the economy, technology, and social norms all have an impact on how an organization does business. Successful organization leaders incorporate a variety of interventions to address these factors and to maintain an edge in their respective markets. The intervention categories frequently used to affect organization design and development fall into three areas: empowerment, organizational pro-action, and organizational values.

Empowerment Interventions

Empowerment means enabling people to work to their highest levels by believing in them and establishing processes and systems that support their efforts. Workers should be empowered to think, overcome obstacles, and resolve problems. Empowerment interventions encourage all employees to do their best to continuously improve the workplace by identifying situations that create challenges and looking for better ways of doing things. Empowerment interventions discussed here are based on team strategies, virtual teams, and problem solving.

Team Strategies

Definition. A team is a group of people working together as a cohesive unit to accomplish a common goal. Team strategies are the methods team members work out in advance for accomplishing the objectives at hand.

Scope. Teaming is based on the philosophy that people work better and more creatively in groups than they do alone. Team participation leads to greater commitment to common goals and action plans. It focuses on trust, collaboration, openness, and other interpersonal factors. Teamwork is the ability to work together toward a common vision and to direct individual accomplishment toward organizational objectives. It is the fuel that allows common people to attain uncommon results.

Committing to a team approach is affected by team characteristics such as composition, size, norms, cohesiveness; the nature of the task, team goals and task interdependence; the environmental context within the organizational culture, and the external environment. Teams work together through decisions, problem solving, and work accomplishment either independently or in interaction with peers. Diversity of team members, such as age, gender, job assignment, job level, and so forth, are often an advantage because team thinking is more divergent, ideas are more innovative, and outcomes more robust. The result is satisfied workers who produce quality products and who take pride in their work.

Implementation. The performance improvement practitioner assists the team through the forming stage, where the team becomes acquainted and members learn to trust one another. In the storming stage the team manages its disputes. In norming, the team aligns responsibilities and commits to goals. Performing leads to actualizing the work plans, while adjourning leads to closure.[2]

The practitioner is positioned to work with teams in setting clear performance objectives, documenting procedures and methods, providing effective coaching and reinforcement, training on interpersonal relationships, and infusing change management techniques to keep the team working through times of constant change.

EXHIBIT 16.1. THE PRACTITIONER'S VOICE: TEAMS

"A choice to implement teams, especially in a multinational corporation, is not entered into haphazardly. As an intervention sponsor one must understand the time, effort, financial support, and commitment that will be required to effectively implement teams and achieve a sustainable competitive advantage through the process and into the future, too. Team-based performance improvement initiatives require a comprehensive design of sub-interventions that range from broad goals to invasive performance management systems. Effective designs must include instructional and non-instructional performance support interventions and take a systems approach to tackle performance issues at four organizational levels: individuals, processes, work groups, and business units. Self-directed work teams must have a purpose and specific objectives that complement the organization's mission overall. A compelling purpose allows people to commit effort in service of issues larger than themselves and increases the probability of team and organizational goal achievement."

David Shall, Ph.D., CSP, CRSP

Executive Vice President

Choctaw-Kaul Distribution Company

Detroit, MI, USA

Use Performance Support Tool 16.1 on the next page to determine how team members feel about their teams and the jobs they are doing.

Virtual Teams

Definition. A virtual team is "a group of individuals who work across time, space, and organizational boundaries with links strengthened by webs of communication technology."[3]

Scope. Virtual teams interact electronically from geographically different sites to achieve common organizational goals. Virtual team members "have complementary skills and are committed to a common purpose, have interdependent performance goals, and share an approach to work for which they hold themselves mutually accountable."[4] There are many reasons for fostering virtual teams: demands of globalization, the 24/7 workday-into-week, competitive and responsive flexible organizations, environments that necessitate inter-organizational cooperation, and increasing technological sophistication, among others.

PERFORMANCE SUPPORT TOOL 16.1. EVALUATING TEAM ATTITUDES

Directions: Use this instrument to acquire information about how team members feel about their team and the job they are doing. Areas with lower scores indicate potential areas for team-building intervention. Use the following scale to respond to each statement: 3 = Agree 2 = Don't Know 1 = Disagree

	Agree	Don't Know	Disagree
1. Self-Perceptions	3	2	1
a. I communicate with members of my team regularly.			
b. I contribute to team discussions.			
c. I participate in team activities.			
d. I work well with the other members of my team.			
e. I respect the members of my team.			
f. The members of my team respect me.			
g. I value the contributions of other team members.			
h. The other team members value my ideas.			
2. Perception of Team Members	3	2	1
a. Everyone on my team contributes to its success.			
b. Everyone on my team contributes to problem solving.			
c. My team works well together.			
d. Everyone on my team is shown respect.			
e. Everyone on my team participates in team discussions.			
3. Ideas	3	2	1
a. My team has good ideas.			
b. All ideas have potential.			
c. All ideas presented are considered and discussed.			
d. There are no bad ideas.			
e. All ideas presented to my team are shown respect.			
4. Team Work	3	2	1
a. Everyone on my team listens with an open mind.			
b. All ideas have potential.			
c. Everyone on my team is encouraged to participate.			
d. No one monopolizes the team discussions.			
e. Team members work together to solve problems.			

(Continued)

	Agree	Don't Know	Disagree
5. Group Dynamics	3	2	1
a. My team is diverse in age.			
b. My team is diverse in gender.			
c. My team is diverse in ethnicity.			
d. My team is diverse in knowledge.			
e. My team is diverse in experience.			
f. The diversity of my team makes it easier to solve problems.			
g. The diversity of my team is a valuable asset.			
6. Progress	3	2	1
a. My team works efficiently most of the time.			
b. Work in my team is completed on time.			
c. Recommendations from my team have been implemented in the organization.			
d. My team consistently achieves success.			
e. My team does not always succeed in reaching our goals.			
f. My team solves problems well.			
g. We have achieved more as a group than we would have working individually.			
h. Management has denied some of our recommendations.			
7. Satisfaction	3	2	1
a. Working with my team has been a positive experience.			
b. It is easier to solve problems when working as a group.			
c. I have learned from group solutions that did not work out.			
d. I enjoy working as part of a group.			
e. Group work promotes creativity.			
f. Working as part of a group has helped me personally.			
g. I look forward to working with my team.			

Virtual teams are supported by hardware such as telephones, PCs, modems or equivalent, communication links, and local area networks and by software including electronic mail, meeting facilitation software, time management systems, and collaborative software suites, among others.[5]

Workplace Implementation. The performance improvement practitioner seizes an opportunity to tap efficiency and team synergy uncommon in traditional teaming. The performance improvement practitioner works with others in the organization to explain the purpose of virtual teaming and engages teams with the varieties of virtual communication tools available on the marketplace. Finally, the practitioner assists virtual teams to work in collaboration, coach others to be productive talented partners, and provide professional assistance when it is asked for and necessary.[6]

Problem Solving

Definition. Problem solving is the structured process of defining a problem, gathering data about the situation and causes, considering alternatives, making choices, evaluating the new situation, and making adjustments based on evaluation.

Scope. A successful problem-solving intervention is an outcome of empowered teams and empowered individuals working in a healthy and high-performing organization. As an intervention, problem solving focuses on understanding the problem and its causes. Jonassen's research classifies problems using this typology: "puzzles, algorithms, story problems, rule-using problems, decision making, troubleshooting, diagnosis-solution problems, strategic performance, systems analysis, design problems, and dilemmas."[7] Since problems differ in structure, complexity, and context, they generate multiple kinds of problem solving processes.

EXHIBIT 16.2. THE PRACTITIONER'S VOICE: PROBLEM SOLVING

"Problem solving is a high-order cognitive skill. It entails examining a problem from multiple perspectives and discovering alternative solutions. A problem can be viewed as either a challenge or an opportunity. When a problem is viewed from a different perspective or through a different lens, the outcome may be different. Since individuals use multiple frames of reference to tackle problems, a solution generated by an individual may differ from a team-generated solution. The process of problem solving does not always follow a linear pattern. It is helpful to stand back, reflect on action, and make appropriate adjustments in order to move forward with the problem-solving process."

Misa Mi, Ph.D., MLIS, AHIP

Associate Professor

Oakland University

William Beaumont School of Medicine Library

Rochester, Michigan, USA

Workplace Implementation. Problem solving is usually structured to proceed in stages; however, the actual step-by-step approach can be varied to meet the needs of the situation. Common steps in the problem-solving process are these:

1. Explore the problem issues and define the problem.
2. Gather information and intelligence on the situation and causes.
3. Choose criteria for judging the information and determine their relative importance.
4. Explore an ideal solution and generate possible realistic options.
5. Evaluate the realistic options and choose the most appropriate.
6. Implement the choice and evaluate the decision.
7. Adjust implementation based on evaluation.

The performance improvement practitioner works with individuals and teams before and during the problem solving process by using methods like brainstorming, brainwriting (a creative problem-solving technique with ideas recorded by their originator and then passed on to the next person, who uses them as triggers for generating his or her own ideas), and affinity diagrams (group process tool that organizes ideas into their natural relationships), among others. Performance Support Tool 16.2 can be used to guide the seven step process indicated above.

Pro-Action Interventions

Pro-active organization design and development interventions provide direction that may create radical change, which can be stressful even if the change is warranted. Before implementation, senior management should thoroughly consider interventions. Change efforts need strong commitment by senior-level champions who are prepared to see the change process through successfully. Change planning needs to involve participative cross-functional and cross level approaches. Organizational pro-action interventions include strategic planning, environmental scanning, appreciative inquiry, outsourcing, benchmarking, balanced scorecards, and dashboards.

Strategic Planning

Definition. Strategic planning is the process by which an organization envisions its future and develops the necessary goals and procedures to achieve that vision.

Scope. Strategic planning is the core intervention of organizational design and development. Successful strategic planning is at the heart of an organization and reflects the essence of what the organization does. When organizations change, strategic planning provides direction to employees and serves as a guide to organizational purpose. This is expressed in terms of the mission or purpose of the organization and the vision or how the organization will appear when it achieves success. To garner support and achieve success, a strategic plan must be easily communicated and must apply to the entire organization.

PERFORMANCE SUPPORT TOOL 16.2. PROBLEM-SOLVING WORKSHEET

Directions: Use this performance support tool to follow seven steps to problem solving.

1. Describe the problem. The problem is. . .

   _____

   _____

2. Define desired state and current state, and delineate the gap.

   Desired state: _____

   Current state: _____

   Gap: _____

3. Analyze information and equipment, individual capacities, and motivation to determine causes.

   Information and equipment: _____

   _____

   Individual Capacities: _____

   _____

   Motivation: _____

   _____

4. Brainstorm and prioritize possible solutions.

   _____

   _____

   Rank Results: _____

5. Select and plan solution to alleviate problem and minimize cause.

   Action plan: _____

6. Implement plan (timeline, steps, responsibilities, measurable outcomes).

   Timeline: _____

   Steps: _____

   _____

   Responsibilities: _____

   _____

   Measurable outcomes: _____

7. Evaluate solution (measure outcomes and determine return on investment).

   Measure outcomes: _____

   Determine return on investment: _____

Strategic planning creates the blueprint for an organization. It documents directional goals and performance objectives based on internal capabilities and competencies and external environmental conditions. Strategic planning, as an intervention, provides direction, focus, and the organizational target. Strategic plans are usually developed for a five-year time period; however, given the swiftly changing external environment in which organizations function, the plans should be reviewed and updated yearly.

Workplace Implementation. Performance improvement practitioners support strategic planning by using their expertise in systematic and systemic thinking and helping the organization identify its vision, mission, values, and critical issues. They can help gather data that are crucial to the strategic planning process by conducting a SWOT analysis of strengths, weaknesses, opportunities, and threats; an internal scan of the organization, including the organization's culture, talent management, resources, and capabilities; and an external scan based on trend analysis to identify future directions.

Environmental Scanning

Definition. Environmental scanning is a strategic planning technique for monitoring trends in the external environment of an organization. These trends could include any political, economic, technical, social, national, or international factors that affect the operation of an organization.

Scope. The strategic planning process provides opportunities for organizations to tune in to their internal activities and functions as well as carefully scrutinizing the external environment. Environmental scanning should be an ongoing activity, since analyzing the environment contributes to understanding which factors threaten the organization and what opportunities can be observed and maximized.

Environmental scanning provides management with much of the information needed to develop and implement its strategic plan. The process focuses on trends and issues that may have an effect on the organization's future. It can also help determine the education and training needs of current or future employees and assist in developing plans to meet those needs. Internal and external scanning help both employees and management to understand the inner and outer aspects of the organization's policies, procedures, and practices. The approach to scanning should be thorough and balanced, including the organizational level, the people level, and the work level.

Workplace Implementation. Performance improvement practitioners explore the internal categories of environmental scanning by considering such areas as state-of-the-art alternatives; relationships between and among individuals, including communication patterns; effective utilization of resources; opportunities for dialogue and idea exchange regarding political roles and the effectiveness and efficiency of organizational structure. External categories such as political, economic, social, technological, and demographic trends should be evaluated as well. Environmental scanning empowers every employee to be observant and suggests changes that could have a positive effect on the organization.

Appreciative Inquiry

Definition. Appreciative inquiry (AI) is both a philosophy and a process to determine what is working successfully within an organization. It is systematic in approach and it brings out the best in people, in the processes that are crucial to their work, and in the dynamic environment in which accomplishment is primary.

Scope. Choosing a glass that is half full versus half empty is at the heart of the practice of appreciative inquiry. "By analyzing positive factors instead of focusing on problems, causes, and gaps, appreciative inquiry focuses on the achievement of the best possible outcomes and practices . . . of what is successful and working well."[8]

By asking positively-framed questions, the four-D framework of *discovering* what is working well in an organization; of *dreaming* about optimal performance and outcomes; of *designing* new and user-friendly systems for the organization; of *destinying* or shaping, implementing, and sustaining potential growth, your mindset is positioned for a synergistic culture-based approach to success.[9,10] The four phases of the AI framework are inextricably related so that the output of one phase becomes the input for the next.

Workplace Implementation. Within the AI framework, the performance improvement practitioner views the organization as high performing and capable, with all policies, procedures, and practices aligned with mission, goals, and strategies, and optimal performance as achievable. By working with executive and managerial personnel, the practitioner becomes the organization's appreciative inquiry spokesperson; provides examples of practical applications from a variety of situations, industries, and nonprofits; implements and monitors the four D process; and can orchestrate the positive approach to change that will result. A useful and practical framework can be drawn between appreciative inquiry and evaluation practices; this should be fertile territory for the performance improvement practitioner.

Outsourcing

Definition. Outsourcing is the process of contracting out to another organization or transferring responsibility for an area of work that had been performed inside the organization to a source outside of the organization.

Scope. Most operational, nonstrategic human resource functions are outsourced. In organizations of three thousand or more employees, nonstrategic functions such as wellness programs, reference checking, benefits and pension administration, and payroll processes are frequently outsourced. Employee-related outsourcing functions may include pre-employment testing, applicant screening, interviewing, equal employment opportunity (EEO) tracking, libraries, tracking continuing education units (CEUs), among others.

The drivers of outsourcing include downsizing or rightsizing, rapid growth or decline of business, globalization, increased competition, restructuring, and the inability of training arenas to exhibit value.[11] The key to outsourcing success "is to determine which functions to outsource, the extent to which they should be outsourced, and which ones to keep in-house."[12] The implications involved are quite significant both to the organization's bottom line and to internal and external worker-organization relationships.

Workplace Implementation. The performance practitioner assists the executive and managerial levels of the organization to be clear in their expectations and what they want to achieve from an outsourcing relationship. Helping key leadership determine what to outsource and the corresponding extent of outsourcing are crucial to maintaining those parts of the business of the organization that are most important to the organization as a whole. The practitioner is also positioned to evaluate the potential benefits of outsourcing and to select and use appropriate external resources.

Benchmarking

Definition. Benchmarking is the systematic process of comparing an organization to other organizations for purposes of identifying better work methods and determining best practices.

Scope. Through benchmarking, organizations compare themselves to the best industry practices in their fields and sometimes outside of their fields. Understanding best practices helps the organization's leadership identify what must be changed to achieve the vision. Benchmarking helps define customer requirements, establish effective goals and objectives, develop true measures of productivity, and identify education and training needs for current and future employees. While business processes and business practices are most often benchmarked, other areas, such as physical products produced, services provided, or levels of customer satisfaction, can be benchmarked.[13]

Workplace Implementation. The performance improvement practitioner works with executive and managerial leadership in developing the benchmarking process steps for the organization through deliberate planning, careful analysis, well-conceived integration of findings, and successfully implementing action plans.[14]

The performance improvement practitioner also evaluates and monitors the benchmarking process. Performance Support Tool 16.3 is a useful reality check while planning the benchmarking challenge.

Balanced Scorecard

Definition. The balanced scorecard (BSC) is a management tool that measures and manages an organization's progress toward strategic goals and objectives. The balanced scorecard is also called a performance measurement and management system and a strategic framework for action. It incorporates financial indicators with perspectives from the customer, internal business processes, and learning and growth.

PERFORMANCE SUPPORT TOOL 16.3. BENCHMARKING PLANNER

Directions: Complete the following questionnaire as a "reality check" while planning the benchmarking project. Check the appropriate box. Add any notes in the space provided.

Have the parameters of the benchmark study been determined?	☐ Yes	☐ No
Has a champion be3en identified?	☐ Yes	☐ No
Has a self-assessment been completed to understand the current situation within the organization	☐ Yes	☐ No
Have high-performing organizations been identified?	☐ Yes	☐ No
Have partnership sharing opportunities (such as benchmarking networks) been investigated?	☐ Yes	☐ No
Has the benchmarking questionnaire been developed?	☐ Yes	☐ No
Have standardized guidelines for the interview been developed?	☐ Yes	☐ No
Are existing benchmarking strategies available for adaptation, or will it be necessary to create a unique strategy for the organization?	☐ Yes	☐ No
Is it understood what is confidential and what should be discussed only in the context of the benchmark study and not with external sources?	☐ Yes	☐ No

Scope. Objectives and performance indicators are developed for each perspective and data are collected and analyzed. Kaplan and Norton, the architects of the balanced scorecard, have this to say: "The BSC provides managers with the instrumentation they need to navigate to future competitive success. . . . translates an organization's mission and strategy into a comprehensive set of performance measures that provides the framework for a strategic measurement and management system."[15]

Workplace Implementation. The performance improvement practitioner may not be well-versed in the "hard" financial measures of the balanced scorecard; however, the "soft" quantifiable operational measures provide opportunities for involvement in the process. The practitioner monitors how the organization is perceived by its customers and their likes and dislikes, the areas in which an organization must excel and grow in order to maintain competitive strength, and areas in which an organization must improve and add value to maintain brand recognition and sustainable growth. The practitioner is positioned to assist the organization in developing goals and appropriate measures for each of the four perspectives.

Dashboards

Definition. Dashboards are business intelligence tools that display performance indicators, present data and information at both summary and detailed levels, and assist decision-makers to act on the information presented in the dashboard.

Scope. Many different businesses benefit from dashboards. The information is carefully selected to meet the information needs of the organization, useful in decision making and thoughtful reflection, and actionable to permit the organization to move forward using appropriate trend analyses and forecasting tools.[16] "Modern dashboards meet business needs in a practical and actionable ways when they can give quick snapshots of the big picture on one hand while offering detail on the other . . . dashboards must have as much business brain as technological muscle."[17]

Dashboards use a variety of data visualization tools like charts, grids, gauges, and maps to display data in a visually effective, user-friendly, efficient, and sophisticated manner with clarity and immediacy. An effective business dashboard is simple, instructive, and aesthetically appealing. It communicates with clarity and keeps distracters to a minimum. It organizes business information to support meaning and use. It incorporates the latest research in visual presentation of information.[18]

Performance dashboards are becoming the preferred way for busy executives to monitor key business metrics at a glance. They "translate the organization's strategy into objectives, metrics, initiatives, and tasks customized to each group and individual in the organization . . . they let business people monitor critical business processes and activities, analyze the root cause of problems, and manage people and processes to improve decisions, optimize performance, and steer the organization in the right direction."[19]

Workplace Implementation. The performance improvement practitioner works with the information technologist in designing dashboards that have direct relevance to critical business activities. The practitioner customizes the dashboard, assures easy administration, ensures plenty of support so that the dashboard can be efficient and trouble-free, keeps the design focused on business critical information, and limits the information to what is essential and necessary.[20] The practitioner with graphic skills designs dashboards that show effective color use and have a visually appealing interface.

Values

Organizational values interventions help people succeed by supporting the "right" decisions; maximizing the significance of employee, supplier, customer, and client; encouraging workers to think globally; and treating people with respect and trust. Organizational values interventions include culture, diversity and inclusion strategies, globalization, localization, social responsibility, ethics, and decision making.

Culture/Organizational Culture

Definition. Culture is a shared system of values, beliefs, and behaviors that characterizes a group or organization.

Scope. In business, culture is demonstrated in the way that things are done. Culture often originates from an organization's mission and vision. It consists of the key values of the organization and the practices that support those values. Culture is pervasive; it virtually shapes and controls employee behavior. Most of culture is unwritten and often is not discussed, except informally among close friends and colleagues. Culture change is the alteration or modification of an organization's values, beliefs, or behavior system. Culture interventions redefine, clarify, emphasize, or create desired practices within a group. The goal is to influence both employee behavior and performance output.

Organizational culture is made up of the collective human behavior of employees, as witnessed through decision making, speech, writing, and actions that are based on mutual acceptance of values, myths, heroes, symbols, and artifacts.[21] Organizational and individual values are the basic concepts and beliefs, the heart of culture. They are evidenced in standards, such as "if you do this, this will happen." *Heroes* are the role models, the visionaries, the memorable people who "made it." Representative organizational heroes include Thomas Edison as an inventor, Jack Welsh as an Information Era chief executive officer, Alfred Sloan as a crafter of corporation structure, and Gabrielle "Coco" Chanel who revolutionized fashion with her many rows of pearls, little black dress, timeless, classic suits and accessories, and, of course, her fragrance, Chanel No. 5.

Rites and rituals refer to the methods of celebrating successes, holidays, and customs relative to daily organization life, such as whether employees drink coffee in groups gathered around lunch tables or individually at their own desks. The wearing of academic regalia for commencement exercises celebrates rites and rituals. *Symbols* are the posters, awards and plaques, lobby pictures and decorations, and organizational logo. And, finally, *artifacts* include the annual report, newsletters, brochures, and "giveaways," such as coffee mugs and ballpoint pens.[22]

Workplace Implementation. The performance improvement practitioner should be quite familiar with cultural issues since culture is an important component of The Performance Improvement/ HPT Model. The practitioner is capable of assessing the culture and identifying strengths and limitations. The practitioner's background in change management provides the experiences necessary to lead or support any cultural improvement initiatives. Furthermore, the practitioner leads efforts to conduct a culture audit of the organization. This is an analysis procedure that focuses on workers, work processes, and the workplace and answers the question: "How do we think about things or do things in our organization?"

Diversity/Inclusion Strategies

Definition. Diversity refers to the physical and cultural human differences of age, ethnicity, gender, physical attributes, race, and sexual/affectional orientation. It also includes secondary dimensions like educational background, marital status, religious beliefs, health disabilities, and work experience. Inclusion refers to the degree to which the culture respects and values diversity and is open to anyone who can perform a job, regardless of his or her diversity attributes.[23]

Scope. Diversity is an element of organizational culture. Diversity means differences in employees' ethnic, cultural, and religious backgrounds; education; values; attitudes; and gender. A diverse workforce enhances creative output because people are able to contribute from their varied experiences. Diversity can be viewed as an organizational asset that should be used to the fullest.

Maximizing the unique perspectives of individual employees from diverse backgrounds is a tremendous, potentially untapped resource. Diversity and inclusion strategies build productivity, innovation, and creativity and ensure business success. They are effective and sustainable when they:

- Directly align with and help achieve key business strategies and plans,
- Measure progress in ways that the chief executive officer agrees are important to the business,
- Have the full support and engagement of the CEO and senior executive team, and
- Take account of the company's organizational culture and readiness and capacity for change.[24]

Workplace Implementation. Performance improvement practitioners lead diversity initiatives. They create teams and determine interventions that are meaningful and specific to affect change in the organization. They track accomplishments against goals and expected outcomes; help the organization determine its diversity quotient; plan and deliver diversity training; and monitor implementation and follow up. Diversity requires sensitivity to people issues and the capacity to understand data and the impact of information on planning and reporting. Performance Support Tool 16.4 can assist practitioners in determining their organizations' diversity quotient.

PERFORMANCE SUPPORT TOOL 16.4. DIVERSITY QUOTIENT ASSESSMENT

Directions: Use the questions to determine your organization's "diversity quotient." Discuss your answers with your peers.

1. Are the *leaders of the organization* informed and supportive of cultural and diversity issues?
   ☐ Always ☐ Sometimes ☐ Never ☐ Not Sure

2. Has *input from all employees* been integrated into diversity planning?
   ☐ Always ☐ Sometimes ☐ Never ☐ Not Sure

3. Does the diversity planning integrate the *core strategic objectives* of the overall organization?
   ☐ Always ☐ Sometimes ☐ Never ☐ Not Sure

4. Is diversity viewed as an *advantage* and *essential* to good organizational operations?
   ☐ Always ☐ Sometimes ☐ Never ☐ Not Sure

5. Is a *self-assessment* used to help employees identify stereotypes and possible areas of personal challenge?
   ☐ Always ☐ Sometimes ☐ Never ☐ Not Sure

6. Does the diversity training build on the success of current diversity situations and cover major issues of all "protected" categories?
   ☐ Always ☐ Sometimes ☐ Never ☐ Not Sure

7. Is there a steering committee set up to facilitate open dialogue and discussion groups within the department?
   ☐ Always ☐ Sometimes ☐ Never ☐ Not Sure

8. Are members of management role models for diversity and culturally sensitive issues?
   ☐ Always ☐ Sometimes ☐ Never ☐ Not Sure

9. Are employees given scenarios or examples of sensitive situations to discuss and resolve so that they recognize diversity issues?
   ☐ Always ☐ Sometimes ☐ Never ☐ Not Sure

List the names of people who will serve as diversity resources, such as coaches or mentors for problem situation:

_____

_____

_____

_____

_____

_____

_____

Globalization/Localization

Definitions. *Globalization* is the process of achieving higher productivity and efficiency by identifying and focusing on an organization's efforts and resources in major world markets. It focuses on the "'interdependency of transportation, distribution, communication, and economic networks across international borders."[25] *Localization* is the process of customizing and adapting a global application for a particular culture and locale.

Scope. The fundamental ideals behind globalization are free flow of commerce, capital, and labor and the belief that individuals can significantly influence large social and economic systems. Globalization is accomplished in several ways. Outsourcing noncore activities, combining purchasing volumes, and centralizing key support activities are examples of globalization techniques. Production and distribution activities are often consolidated to create more efficient operations. Success is based on the ability to quickly adjust to the needs of the customer. For this reason, globalization is often more successful in smaller organizations.

Globalization affects employees, customers, and suppliers. It encourages people to attain a new awareness of both their organization and the world in which they live. Through this realization come new opportunities for personal and professional advancement and satisfaction.[26] Localization, on the other hand, of documents primarily includes:

- Translating text content, software source code, websites, or database content;
- Adjusting graphic and visual elements and examples to make them culturally appropriate;
- Post-production quality control of content, systems, and the integrated product; and
- A market focused on software, documentation (packaging information, technical booklets, user manuals, training equipment, and so forth), websites, and applications.[27]

Workplace Implementation. As performance improvement interventions, globalization and localization require learning about and respecting customs, etiquette, workplace expectations, and the heritage of people with whom an employee directly or indirectly interacts. Performance improvement practitioners orchestrate these functions. They participate in the globalization efforts of their organization by using The Performance Improvement/HPT Model and this book to help analyze issues or activities in various locations, determine internal best practices, and help document common practices. They help with the implementation by using their skills in change management and process consulting.

In the localization arena, performance improvement practitioners determine cultural appropriateness. They also oversee the design and development of technical books and training manuals, monitor selection and use of training equipment, and work with information technology personnel to develop efficient and effective web sites.

Social Responsibility

Definition. Social responsibility is a genuine interest and concern for the well-being of individuals that leads an individual to plan, think, do, and act in a socially responsible way and to be a sensitive team member in personal and professional relationships. When it is applied to the corporate world, social responsibility "is a commitment to improve community well-being through discretionary business practices and contributions of corporate resources."[28]

Scope. Gantt, from Gantt Chart fame, believed that management had distinct obligations and responsibilities to the community at large and that an organization that enjoys a high profile, high productivity, and high profits had a duty toward the welfare of society.[29] There are social activities and initiatives that fulfill commitments to corporate social responsibility. However an organization responds to these social responsibility initiatives, the organization as an aligned system must remain ethical and be sensitive to its internal and external environment.

Workplace Implementation. Corporations are moving away from "doing good to look good," "do good as easily as possible," "doing well and doing good" to "doing all we can to do the most good, not just some good." Corporate conscience tells us that we have a responsibility for our organization's actions by encouraging and providing positive, ethical, and sensitive impact through the goods it produces, the services it provides, and the customers with whom it forms partnerships. Sharing similar goods and services, working on projects that employees and customers really care about, volunteering employee expertise and time, and forming strategic alliances with external partners are ways to implement and weave social responsibility into the fabric of the organization.[30] The bottom-line benefits are many.

Ethics

Definition. Ethics defines good and bad standards of conduct. Standards of conduct are cultural and vary among countries, organizations, incidents, and situations. Ethics is realizing what is right and wrong and then doing what is right.

Scope. Ethics support and help define the culture of an organization. *Societal* ethics, professional ethics, and individual ethics influence organizational ethics. Societal ethics are codified in a society's legal system, its customs and practices, and in unwritten norms and values. *Professional* ethics are the moral rules and values that people use to control the way they perform. *Individual* ethics are the personal and moral standards used for interacting with others.[31] When discussing the ethics of an organization, it is important to establish guidelines for the organization that everyone is aware of, willing to follow, and committed to enforcing.

Successful implementation of ethical standards requires that they be applied to every person within a group or organization, as well as to outside individuals or groups that do business with the organization.[32] Benefits to ethics management are that they cultivate strong teamwork and productivity, support employee growth and give personal and professional meaning to work, and serve as a marketing and human relations beacon for the organization.[33]

Workplace Implementation. Performance improvement practitioners assist organizations in developing an ethics policy by focusing on societal, professional, and individual ethics. They can create scenarios that help employees face sundry ethical dilemmas in the workplace. (See examples of scenarios in Performance Support Tool 16.5.) Practitioners encourage ethical thinking and practices and help employees realize that practicing ethics is not a one-time experience; rather, it is continuous and permeates every aspect of the organization's fabric.

PERFORMANCE SUPPORT TOOL 16.5. ETHICAL DILEMMAS IN THE WORKPLACE

Directions: Read each scenario and decide what is the correct approach for your organization or for an appropriate organization with which you are familiar. Share and discuss the results with your work group.

Department	Scenario	What would you do?	Whom would you contact?
Purchasing	Purchasing decides not to conduct a fair bidding process but rather to predetermine awards and use the actual bidding as a "showcase" (a sham) to justify a decision.		
Purchasing	Buyers accept substantial gifts of money, dinners, entertainment, or vacations to overlook errors or quality flaws.		
Staffing–HR	Recruiters ask inappropriate questions during pre-employment interviews about family status or family planning interventions, forcing interviewees to believe that if they resist answering the questions they will not be seriously considered for the position.		
Restructuring –HR	Downsizing plans favor certain age groups and discriminate against protected employees.		
Compensation	Hourly workers falsify timesheets, often to cover "legitimate" needs, such as dental appointments.		
Finance	Finance department keeps two sets of books to disguise certain practices.		
Finance	Accounts receivable insists on payment terms from customers that the organization would not be willing to pay out to its own suppliers.		
Legal	Employees are encouraged to photocopy materials that are protected by copyright because the organization lacks sufficient funds to pay the copyright holder for use of the materials.		
Any Department	People watch and do nothing while one employee is singled out and treated unfairly or subjected to a form of harassment.		

Decision Making

Definition. Decision making is the act of making judgments and drawing conclusions.

Scope. Decision making as an intervention involves placing values on ideas or options and determining resulting actions. This can lead to ethical dilemmas. Ethical decisions are not determined by a single moral standard, but they are influenced by gender, age, moral philosophy, education, work experience, organizational culture, stated and unstated codes of ethics, awareness and knowledge of the situation, rewards and sanctions, and opinions of significant others such as co-workers or peers.[34]

For example, one study found that younger males make more utilitarian decisions and older males make more legalistic choices. Women, on the other hand, tend to be more interested in fairness and justice.[35] Executives are accustomed to creating directives, defining strategies, and expecting implementation from others and often believe that making decisions is their privilege. Teams also make decisions and use a number of methods, including consensus decision making, to guide their thought processes. The concept of empowerment also extends to individual workers who should also be involved in the decision-making process.

Workplace Implementation. Performance improvement practitioners play key roles in changing the decision making dynamics of an organization. Due to its systematic and thorough approach, The Performance Improvement /HPT Model relies on careful and honest decision making throughout. Decision making improvements often mean changes in organizational culture, such as viewing employees as partners with valuable information and insight and empowering them to make sound decisions based on solid evidence. Performance improvement practitioners can help establish a culture that encourages risk taking, innovation, and creativity and where new thinking is not about the dollars you invest. It is about the people you invest in.

Citations

1. Galbraith, n.d.
2. Shortell & Kaluzny, 2006, p. 182
3. Virtual Teams: Definition, n.d.
4. Virtual Teams, 2011
5. Ubell, 2010, pp. 55, 57
6. Ubell, 2010, p. 55
7. Jonassen, 2004, p. 7
8. Lewis & Van Tiem, 2004, p. 19
9. Lewis & Van Tiem, 2004, pp. 19–21
10. Smith, 2010, pp. 322–326
11. Hale, 2010, pp. 681–696
12. Mondy, Noe, & Premeaux, 2002, p. 9
13. Camp, 1989, p. 42

14. Camp, 1989, p. 17

15. Kaplan & Norton, 1996, p. 2

16. Hetherington, 2009

17. Fuchs, 2011

18. Hetherington, 2009

19. Eckerson, 2011, pp. 4–5

20. Fuchs, 2011

21. Deal & Kennedy, 1982

22. Kilmann, Saxton, Serpa, & Associates, 1985

23. Thomas & Woodruff, 1999

24. MDB Group, Inc., n.d.

25. Gibson, Ivancevich, Donnelly, & Konopaske, 2006, p. 56

26. Shepperd, 1998

27. Localization, p. 2.

28. Kotler & Lee, 2005, p. 33

29. Gantt, 2006, pp. 1206–1207

30. Kotler & Lee, 2005, pp. 2–18

31. Jones, 2007, pp. 45–47

32. Westgaard, 1992

33. McNamara, 1998

34. Hatcher & Aragon, 2000, pp. 179–185

35. Shea, 1988, p. 27

References

Camp, R.C. (1989). *Benchmarking: The search for industry best practices that lead to superior performance.* Milwaukee, WI: ASQC Quality Press.

Deal, T.E., & Kennedy, A.A. (1982). *Corporate cultures: The rites and rituals of corporate life.* Reading, MA: Addison-Wesley.

Eckerson, E. (2011). *Performance dashboards: Measuring, monitoring, and managing your business.* Hoboken, NJ: John Wiley & Sons.

Fuchs, G. (2011). Dashboard best practices: White paper from LogiXML, Inc. Retrieved from http://pages. logixml.com?WP-DashboardBestPracticesC.html?Activit.

Gailbraith, J. (n.d.). The STAR model. Retrieved from www.jaygailbraith.com/pdf.

Gantt, H.L. (2006). The Gantt chart. *Business: The ultimate resource.* Cambridge, MA: Basic Books.

Gibson, J.L., Ivancevich, J.M., Donnelly, Jr., J.H., & Konopaske, R. (2006). *Organizations: Behavior, structure, processes* (12th ed.). Boston: McGraw-Hill/Irwin.

Hale, J.A. (2010). Outsourcing. In R. Watkins & D. Leigh (Eds.), *Handbook of improving performance in the workplace, volume 2: Selecting and implementing performance interventions* (pp. 681–696). San Francisco: Pfeiffer/ISPI.

Hatcher, T., & Aragon, S.R. (2000, Summer). A code of ethics and integrity for HRD research and practice. *Human Resource Development Quarterly, 11*(2).

Hetherington, V. (2009). The dashboard demystified. Retrieved from www.dashboardinsight.com/articles/digital-dashboards/fundam.

Jonassen, D.H. (2004). *Learning to solve problems: An instructional design guide.* San Francisco: Pfeiffer.

Jones, G.R. (2007). *Organizational theory, design, and change* (5th ed.). Upper Saddle River, NJ: Pearson/Prentice Hall.

Kaplan, R.S., & Norton, D.P. (1996). *The balanced scorecard: Translating strategy into action*. Boston: Harvard Business School Press.

Kilmann, R.H., Saxton, M.J., Serpa, R., & Associates. (1985). *Gaining control of the corporate culture*. San Francisco: Jossey-Bass.

Kotler, P., & Lee, N. (2005). *Corporate social responsibility: Doing the most good for your company and your cause*. Hoboken, NJ: John Wiley & Sons.

Lawler, E.E., III, Ulrich, D., Fitz-enz, J., Madden, J., & Maruca, R. (2004). *Human resources business process outsourcing*. San Francisco: Jossey-Bass.

Lewis, J., & Van Tiem, D. (2004, September). Appreciative inquiry: A view of a glass half full. *Performance Improvement, 43*(8), 19–24.

Localization, Internationalization and Globalization. Retrieved from http://philip.pristine.net/glit/en/

McNamara, C. (1998). Complete guide to ethics management: An ethics toolkit for managers. Retrieved from www.mapnp.org/library/ethics/ethxgde.htm.

MDB Group, Inc. (n.d.). Diversity and inclusion strategy to grow your organization. Retrieved from www.mdbgroup.com/strategies 1.htm.

Mondy, R.W., Noe, R.M., & Premeaux, S.R. (2002). *Human resource management* (8th ed.). Upper Saddle River, NJ: Prentice Hall.

Shea, G.F. (1988). *Practical ethics*. New York: American Management Association.

Shepperd, F.M. (1998). What is globalization? Retrieved from www.quadalgroup.com/globis.htm.

Shortell, S.M., & Kaluzny, A.D. (1997). *Health care management: Organization design and behavior* (5th ed.). Clifton Park, NY: Thomson Delmar Learning.

Smith, D.M. (2010). New kinds on the block: Evaluation in practice. In J.L. Moseley & J.C. Dessinger (Eds.), *Handbook of improving performance in the workplace, volume 3: Measurement and evaluation* (pp. 314–338). San Francisco: Pfeiffer/ISPI.

Thomas, R.R., Jr., & Woodruff, M.I. (1999). *Building a house for diversity*. New York: AMACOM.

Ubell, R. (2010, August). Virtual team learning. *T + D, 64*(8), 53–57.

Virtual Teams: Definition and why virtual teams. (2011). Retrieved from http://managementhelp.org/grp_skll/virtual.htm#anchor5002

Westgaard, O. (1992). Standards and ethics for practitioners. In H.S. Stolovitch & E.J. Keeps (Eds.), *Handbook of human performance technology* (pp. 576–584). San Francisco: Jossey-Bass/NSPI.

Financial Systems Interventions

17

Economic activity affects small and large businesses, interest and mortgage rates, the stock market, and the global marketplace. In a sense, it affects the entire world's purchasing power. The financial system's primary role is to move savings from one business or individual into investments for another business or individual. It is extremely important to have general familiarity with basic financial concepts to communicate with the finance division or the accountant or the marketing specialist or with anyone in the organization concerned about money and its true cost.

All employees benefit by understanding the role their job assignments play in value creation for their organization. To be a key decision-maker, the performance improvement practitioner assumes a proactive role in the organization's financial planning. While it is true that the practitioner may not be directly responsible for orchestrating the organization's financial systems, the practitioner must be ready and willing to use wise financial intelligence and judgment when implementing interventions and be involved in communicating the organization's financial picture to employees, clients, stakeholders, and other audiences. The financial picture is pivotal to determining business, organizational, performance, and learning needs.

As performance improvement interventions, financial systems deal with economics and decisions tied to the financial aspects of business. The financial systems interventions considered here are summarized in Figure 17.1. The last three are multi-organizational arrangements, included here because of their bottom-line results. This chapter will provide information on definition, scope, and work implementation for these financial systems interventions. Listen carefully—the voice of the practitioner may also be heard.

FIGURE 17.1. Financial Systems Interventions

Financial Systems Interventions
• Open Book Management
• Profit Versus Cost Center
• Financial Forecasting
• Capital Investment and Spending
• Cash Flow Analysis
• Mergers, Acquisitions, Joint Ventures

EXHIBIT 17.1. THE PRACTITIONER'S VOICE: FINANCIAL INTELLIGENCE

"Performance practitioners need to know finance (not financials) in order to demonstrate their worth to business in the language that business understands. Financial intelligence helps employees and other personnel prove their value to the organization's bottom line. . . . Practitioners who possess finance competencies have a better chance to gain the attention of and rub elbows with top management and ultimately make a difference in the culture of the organization's business functions."

Ann Chow, Ph.D.

Independent Consultant

Andersen, Indiana, USA

Open Book Management

Definition. Organizations that adopt open book policies present key financial documents, income and cash flow statements, balance sheets, inventory flow methods, ratio analysis, and so forth to their employees for thoughtful review, discussion, advice, and corrective action.[1] Open book management occurs when everyone in the organization helps the business make money. Financial status is fully shared and employees become active participants in financial performance.

Scope. As an intervention, open book management improves team functioning and provides information to help employees understand issues and make better judgments. For open book management to be successful, the organization must be open and aligned, which means sharing financial information with employees to help them track financial data, learning the art and science of financial information, and showing them how knowledge of financial data helps them make a difference in the organization. Although open book management takes many forms and is often practiced differently, elements common to most of these interventions are open books, empowerment, planning and decision making, profit sharing, highly participative management, and weekly alignment meetings.[2]

Workplace Implementation. The performance improvement practitioner plays a crucial role in orchestrating open book management by reinforcing its purpose among employees, providing resources, spearheading discussions, leading and monitoring financial literacy training, and evaluating the entire process so that employees see the financial picture in the context of what is happening in the global world of finance.[3]

Profit Centers Versus Cost Centers

Definition. A profit or revenue center is charged with controlling costs and generating revenues; it has an expense and a revenue budget. A cost center is charged with managing costs; it has neither a revenue budget nor an obligation to earn revenues.

Scope. Most companies are expected to make money or profit. By definition, non-profit organizations do not make profits. However, internal departments of both profit and non-profit organizations can be cost or revenue centers.

An internal department as a cost center provides services without charging back the services to the department that received the services. An internal department that is a revenue or profit center charges back the services to the department receiving the services. Examples of profit or revenue centers are in-hospital laboratories, in-hospital pharmacies, hospital cafeterias, and cafeterias on military bases that service enlisted men, officers, and civilians. Some training departments are obliged to generate revenue by selling some form of product or services to external or internal customers. "Training organizations usually have three products they can sell externally: training programs, training facilities, and training expertise."[4]

A cost center is "overhead." It is an organizational unit that contributes costs without offsetting them with revenue. Typical cost centers in organizations are administrative units, talent management departments, housekeeping services, maintenance and repair, and clerical and office pools. "Being a cost center does not make a unit any less important than any other unit in the organization."[5] Cost centers need to be lean, efficient, effective, and flexible.

To remain successful and maintain market share, organizations need to reduce costs and increase their revenue holdings. Profit versus cost centers as an intervention determines the best mode of service delivery relative to financial factors.

Workplace Implementation. In many instances, a cost center can become more responsive if it becomes a revenue center. As a cost center, there is no competition since the organization relies on the services provided. When a cost center converts to a profit center, there is usually the opportunity to choose another provider outside the organization.

With training, for example, it is possible for a departmental manager to send employees outside of the organization to an external training organization or send the employees to the internal training department. This choice often leads training departments to increase their responsiveness. In other words, will a training or performance department be a cost or a profit center? When it is a cost center, the training department is an "overhead" expense. The performance improvement practitioner helps a training or performance department position itself to generate revenue by also selling the products or services developed for internal use to external customers, such as suppliers or customers. A department can "sell or license programs . . . sublease training classroom space . . . contract out experienced training staff to external clients."[6] The performance improvement practitioner conducts a SWOT analysis prior to offsetting training costs with revenue.

The performance improvement practitioner also assists financial personnel in developing a business plan that answers questions like these:

- What products or services are involved?
- Where is the business and why?
- Who is the competition and where is it located?

PERFORMANCE SUPPORT TOOL 17.1. RESPONSIBILITY CENTER ANALYSIS

Directions: Conduct an in-depth analysis of your organization to find its responsibility centers. List them on the form. Then answer the question.

Cost Centers	Organizational Units
	• _____
	• _____
	• _____
	• _____
	• _____
	• _____

Profit (Revenue) Centers	Organizational Units
	• _____
	• _____
	• _____
	• _____
	• _____
	• _____

How would a training or performance department repurpose itself from a cost center to a profit (revenue) center? Consider:

What:

Who:

When:

Where:

Why:

How:

- How will the products and services be marketed and advertised?
- What resources will be required?

Performance Support Tool 17.1 may be used to help the practitioner identify those organizational units that are and should be profit (revenue) or cost centers and decide how to repurpose a training or other performance department from a cost center to a profit center.

Financial Forecasting

Definition. Financial forecasting is predicting future trends, events, and outcomes with business perspectives in mind, that is, profit, interest, supply, demand, and similar issues.

Scope. Financial forecasting is anticipating the future cash needs for a particular business. Financial managers use financial forecasts to help senior management determine whether their financial plans are aligned and consistent with their business goals and objectives. Financial forecasts play a major role in planning business strategies, monitoring the organization's financial affairs, and controlling and investing cash. Forecasts help management anticipate the financial positions of their businesses and make realistic and prudent business decisions. These activities help to increase profits and reduce risk and are, therefore, vital components in the continuing effort to make businesses successful.

Financial forecasting methods are scientific in nature; yet, financial forecasts do not guarantee desired results nor can they predict unexpected circumstances. Rather, financial forecasts provide roadmaps that measure the progress of businesses. Financial forecasts are living documents that are reviewed and adjusted to reflect current business opportunities, practices, and congruence with external markets.

Successful forecasting relies on solid judgment combined with objective analysis of available data. All variables, domestic, and global, must be reviewed to come up with a financial forecast that is accurate and reliable. Information for financial forecasts may come from various locations, such as the balance sheet, the income statement or cash-flow forecasts, or trend forecasts. Forecasting techniques can be classified into *qualitative*, which use expert judgments and opinions to predict the future, and *quantitative*, which use mathematical and statistical rules and analyses of data banks to predict the future.

Workplace Implementation. Forecasting is one of the most important and complex tools a performance improvement practitioner can master because every organization needs to conduct financial forecasts. The wise practitioner should become proficient in at least two qualitative forecasting techniques, such as Delphi (elicits expert opinions) and the nominal group technique (group-based judgment forecasting method), and two quantitative techniques, such as time series analysis (uses evenly spaced data points—weekly, monthly, quarterly, and so forth, to predict with historical data), and regression models (predict on the basis of dependent and independent variables). The performance improvement practitioner plays a crucial role in planning, gathering data, and monitoring financial forecasting processes.

Capital Investment and Spending

Definition. Capital investment refers to commitment or use of money and other assets made in anticipation of greater financial returns in the future, usually involving large sums of money. Capital spending involves risk-return tradeoff analyses in order to secure long-term financial advantage.

Scope. Capital investments yield returns during future periods and may include property, buildings, equipment, and securities of other companies. Property may include the land on which the organization's facilities are located. Equipment may include furniture, tools, computers, and machinery that the company uses to produce the goods that it sells to customers. Resources and cash often are committed for long periods, so it may be difficult to reverse the effects of a bad decision. Uncertainty about return on investments is a risk factor.

Investment Decisions. To decide whether an investment or strategy should be pursued, the analyst must decide whether it has the potential of value for the firm's stakeholders. To create value, the investment or strategy's returns must exceed its costs. Determining which costs and benefits are relevant to the particular investment or strategy must also be determined. Capital invested in new products has a cost. To use capital, the organization has to pay for its use. Money invested in new products, equipment, or facilities could be diverted to other uses, such as paying off debt, making a pay-out to stockholders, or investing in stocks or bonds. These all result in economic benefits to the organization. Organizations normally take into consideration that the value of money will not be the same in the future; this is known as discounting the value of money, primarily due to inflation.

Funding Decisions. Once management has decided to make an investment in property, plant, equipment, or working capital, a decision must then be made to fund the project. Funds that are invested in these types of endeavors may come from stockholders and/or bondholders. The capital budgeting problem is essentially balancing the benefits from these new capital expenditures with the costs needed to finance them. The cost of this capital, adjusted to a minimum acceptable rate of return, plays an essential role in ranking the relative effectiveness of different types of capital projects and in establishing acceptable guidelines for project acceptance. A sound capital expenditure program recognizes the need to search for investment opportunities, conduct long-term planning, estimate future benefits from projects, appraise the state of the economy, establish guidelines for return on investment, and review all completed projects.

Many organizations experience uneven cash flow during the year. An example is department stores, which generate a large portion of their revenue during the months of November and December, resulting in a large cash inflow during the holiday season. In many instances, these large amounts of cash are not immediately needed to fund the operations of the organization. Many of the organizations may elect to put some of their excess cash into short-term investments until the cash is needed for operations. These investments usually produce higher earnings than those available from bank accounts, enabling organizations to increase their earnings.

The "time value of money" is a key concept in investment analysis. The term refers to the fact that a dollar received today is more valuable than a dollar received one year from now. The dollar received today can be invested at some interest rate so that it will be worth more than the dollar received one year from now, which cannot be invested until that time.[7]

Most workers do not understand the strategies involved in deciding whether money should be invested in capital equipment, land, facility expansion, or securities. The company hires people and purchases new machinery to build products, products are sold to make money, and money pays the bills and gives people their paychecks. However, these investments must create value, which means that they must be able to produce a product that, when sold, will produce revenues that exceed the cost of the production of that product. These decisions are important, especially when one bad decision can bankrupt an organization or stress it enough financially that it can never fully recover. In other words, the decision to invest in new computers for training means that the organization believes that the value of worker training exceeds the cost of the computers and installation and maintenance of the computers.

Workplace Implementation. Overseeing the entire capital investment and spending practices of an organization resides with the accountants and the financial team. The performance improvement practitioner assists in the focusing phases of capital investment and spending and in monitoring, implementing, and evaluating the procedures. Beyond this, the following guidance is helpful:

- Know how the organization internally defines capital and how this is reflected on balance sheets and profit and loss sheets;
- Understand and be able to articulate the larger concepts under which capital investment and spending decisions are made;
- Read *The Wall Street Journal, Baron's,* and other financial dailies and/or quarterlies to increase business acumen and innovative capital investment and spending practices and solutions.[8]

Cash Flow Analysis/Cash Flow Forecast

Definition. Cash flow analysis is a financial tool or process used by businesses and banks to determine the various sources and uses of an organization's cash and to make accurate projections of cash inflow and outflow for forecasting purposes.

Scope. Cash flow analysis provides information about the inflow and outflow of cash during a specific period. The ability of a business to generate cash is important because it affects its ability to pay debt obligations and make a profit. Cash also enables the organization to replace old equipment, to expand product lines, and to provide dividends to shareholders. Cash flow is the difference between revenues—the amount of money taken in from the sale of a product or service and the cost of the product or service that was sold. These costs could include materials, labor, equipment, and overhead, among others. However, not all healthy businesses have a large, positive cash flow. Businesses that are experiencing extensive growth often use their excess cash to expand their production facilities, acquiring new equipment and labor and thus reducing the amount of cash on hand.

Cash flow forecasting is an essential tool because an organization must know its financial cycles and ensure that adequate cash is available at all times to support its activities. During periods when cash outflow exceed cash inflow, short-term financing must be available. When the production-to-receivables-to-cash cycle is completed, short-term financing can be paid down.[9] The cash flow forecast uses basic economic assumptions and forecasts of sales and production (in a manufacturing environment) to arrive at a schedule of the organization's cash cycle. Cash outflow often exceeds cash inflow, especially early in the business cycle, and it is at these times that organizations require short-term external financing. A cash flow forecast provides the organization with a schedule of when the short-term financing will be required throughout the year, and in what dollar amounts.[10]

Workplace Implementation. The extent of many employees' knowledge of cash flow analysis and cash flow forecasting is that they want the organization to have enough money in its bank account so that their weekly paychecks are covered on payday. However, cash flow plays a very important role in the everyday running of any organization. Being able to pay obligations in a timely manner is just one part of doing business. Cash flow also makes it possible to produce profitable products, to replace old or defective equipment, expand productive and profitable product lines, and provide dividends to shareholders.

Employees need to understand how cash flow operates. If workers know how cash flow operates, they may be able to suggest ways that money could be saved when cash is at a minimum. Because these areas are in the domain of managerial accounting and financial management, the performance improvement practitioner may not be directly involved. However, the practitioner must understand the process.

The business needs of the organization drive performance needs, which drive the learning needs, which drive the workplace needs. Performance improvement practitioners analyze and use accounting reports provided by the finance department, monitor spending, and plan budgets based on data. They then use their understanding of cash flow and forecasting to help set tuition, determine compensation for vendors and consultants, and help make analysis-based decisions relative to cost versus profit centers. The practitioner benchmarks successful organizations to observe their cash flow analysis and forecasting activities and asks myriad questions of accountants and financial managers to gain a better understanding of these vital areas.

Mergers, Acquisitions, Joint Ventures

Definitions. *Mergers* occur when two separate organizations combine operations to become one organization. *Acquisitions* occur when one organization acquires more than 50 percent of the voting stock of another organization and controls that organization. *Joint ventures* are cooperative efforts by competitors for a specific purpose, such as developing a new technology, entering new markets, generating new products, or meeting customer demands quickly.

Scope. A substantial body of literature describes mergers and acquisitions and, to a lesser degree, joint ventures. Each strategy or alliance involves changes in the organization's assets and activities.

For purposes of this discussion, the three terms are treated collectively. Organizations engage in mergers, acquisitions, and joint ventures for these reasons:

- Provide improved capacity utilization;
- Make better use of existing sales force;
- Reduce managerial staff;
- Gain economies of scale;
- Smooth out seasonal trends in sales;
- Gain access to new suppliers, distributors, customers, products, and creditors;
- Gain new technology;
- Reduce tax obligations; and
- Experience synergism in being privately and publicly held.[11]

The Harvard Business School suggests that "most mergers and acquisitions fail. That's because most acquirers don't know how to think systematically about what they're buying and what it might do for them."[12] In addition, there are often cultural conflicts when combining organizations, leading to reduced productivity and strained workplace environments.

Workplace Implementation. Performance improvement practitioners are trained to think systematically and to predict conflicts that may arise from a major change initiative. Often morale drops during mergers and acquisitions because of concerns about an uncertain future, the stress of change, and job losses. However, if employees know the ramifications of a merger, acquisition, or joint venture beforehand, they may be able to position themselves better by acquiring additional training to reduce the risk of job loss.

The performance improvement practitioner minimizes the problems by conducting a cultural audit of both organizations and making plans to align the organizations. Only in rare situations is the performance improvement practitioner directly involved in mergers, acquisitions, and joint ventures. However, the practitioner plays a pivotal role in working with the organization's personnel who are displaced by these alliances, however friendly or hostile. Specifically, the performance improvement practitioner can:

- Anticipate the changing organizational environment by conducting a thorough performance analysis;
- Recognize channels of organization change efforts by focusing on the organizational mindset about change, change process, structures for managing change, personal responses to change, communication networks, environmental factors, financial boundaries, and client demands;
- Suggest interventions to enhance change outcomes;
- Monitor those people who are resistant to change efforts and provide appropriate support for them as they go through the process, with a focus on minimizing resistance, control, and politics; and
- Engage employees in completing Performance Support Tool 17.2.

PERFORMANCE SUPPORT TOOL 17.2. ASSESSING STRATEGIC ALLIANCES

Directions: Indicate the strengths and limitations associated with mergers, acquisitions, and joint ventures. Share your ideas with colleagues to see whether your views and theirs are similar. Discuss reasons for differences. Then, individually or collectively, answer the question that follows.

Alliances	Strengths	Limitations
Mergers		
Acquisitions		
Joint Ventures		

Speculate on how other employees feel about being involved in these alliances, covering issues like:

• Loss of knowledge of the organization

• Loss of control

• Loss of friends

• Loss of physical location

• Loss of organizational synergy

• Loss of cultural compatibility

• Other concerns

Citations

1. Proudfit, 1999
2. Burlingham, 1999, p. 3
3. Berman & Knight, 2006, p. xiii
4. Waagen, 2000, p. 9
5. McLean, 1997, p. 136
6. Waagen, 2000, p. 9
7. Cox, Stout, & Vetter, 1995
8. Deku, 1996, pp. 1–2
9. Witucki, 2000, p. 1
10. Witucki, 2000, p. 3
11. Mescon, Bovie, & Thill, 1999, p. 118
12. Christensen, Alton, Rising, & Waldeck, 2011, p. 51

References

Berman, K., & Knight, J. (2006). *Financial intelligence: A manager's guide to knowing what the numbers really mean.* Boston: Harvard Business School Press.

Burlingham, B. (1999, September). Open book management. Retrieved from www.fed.org/leadingcompmics/nov96/motiv.html.

Christensen, C.M., Alton, R., Rising, C., & Waldeck, A. (2011, March). The new M&A playbook. *Harvard Business Review, 89*(3), 48–57.

Cox, R.A.K., Stout, R.G., & Vetter, D.E. (1995). *Financial administration and control.* Cambridge, MA: Blackwell.

Deku, B. (1999). Capital investment and spending (Report #4: IT 7320). Detroit, MI: Wayne State University College of Education.

McLean, R.A. (1997). *Financial management in health care organizations.* Albany, NY: Delmar Publishers.

Mescon, M.H., Bovie, C.L., & Thill, J.V. (1999). *Business today* (9th ed.). Upper Saddle River, NJ: Prentice Hall.

Proudfit, C. (1999, September). The open book management opportunity. Retrieved from www.tsbj.com/editorial/02050914.htm.

Waagen, A.K. (2000). How to budget training. *Infoline, 0007.* Alexandria, VA: American Society for Training & Development.

Witucki, A.P. (2000). Cash flow analysis (Report #4: IT 7320). Detroit, MI: Wayne State University College of Education.

Intervention Design

18

The first two editions of *Fundamentals* did not discuss design of the performance intervention(s) as a discrete step in the selection, design, and development phase of the Performance Improvement/HPT Model. This third edition of *Fundamentals* will discuss design and development separately; however, sometimes the discussion will blend both activities the way they are blended in the real world. (See Figure 18.1.)

Definition and Scope

Design is the "systems planning" activity of the intervention selection, design, and development phase. The performance improvement practitioner, functioning as intervention designer, developer, or both, "finds or creates plans, materials, and media by which to transform that intervention selection decision into reality."[1] The purpose of the intervention design activity is to plan who, what, where, and when to create "learning and other interventions that help to address the specific root causes of human performance gaps."[2]

Inputs and Outputs

The inputs to the design process are the outcomes of the Performance Analysis and the Intervention Selection decisions. The output of the design activity is a detailed plan or design document in which the designer describes how the intervention will look and feel and how it will happen in an effective and efficient manner. The design document includes performance objectives, process plans, detailed outlines for materials and media, and criteria for evaluating the results.

Blended Process—Or Not?

Rothwell suggests an intervention system design model that blends design and development. Design activities would include verifying the analysis of performer characteristics and competencies and work environment, and formulating performance objectives and methods for measuring performance objectives; development activities would include creating detailed project, communication, and marketing plans and making, buying, or buying and modifying materials and media to support implementation.[3]

FIGURE 18.1. Performance Improvement/HPT Model: Design Component

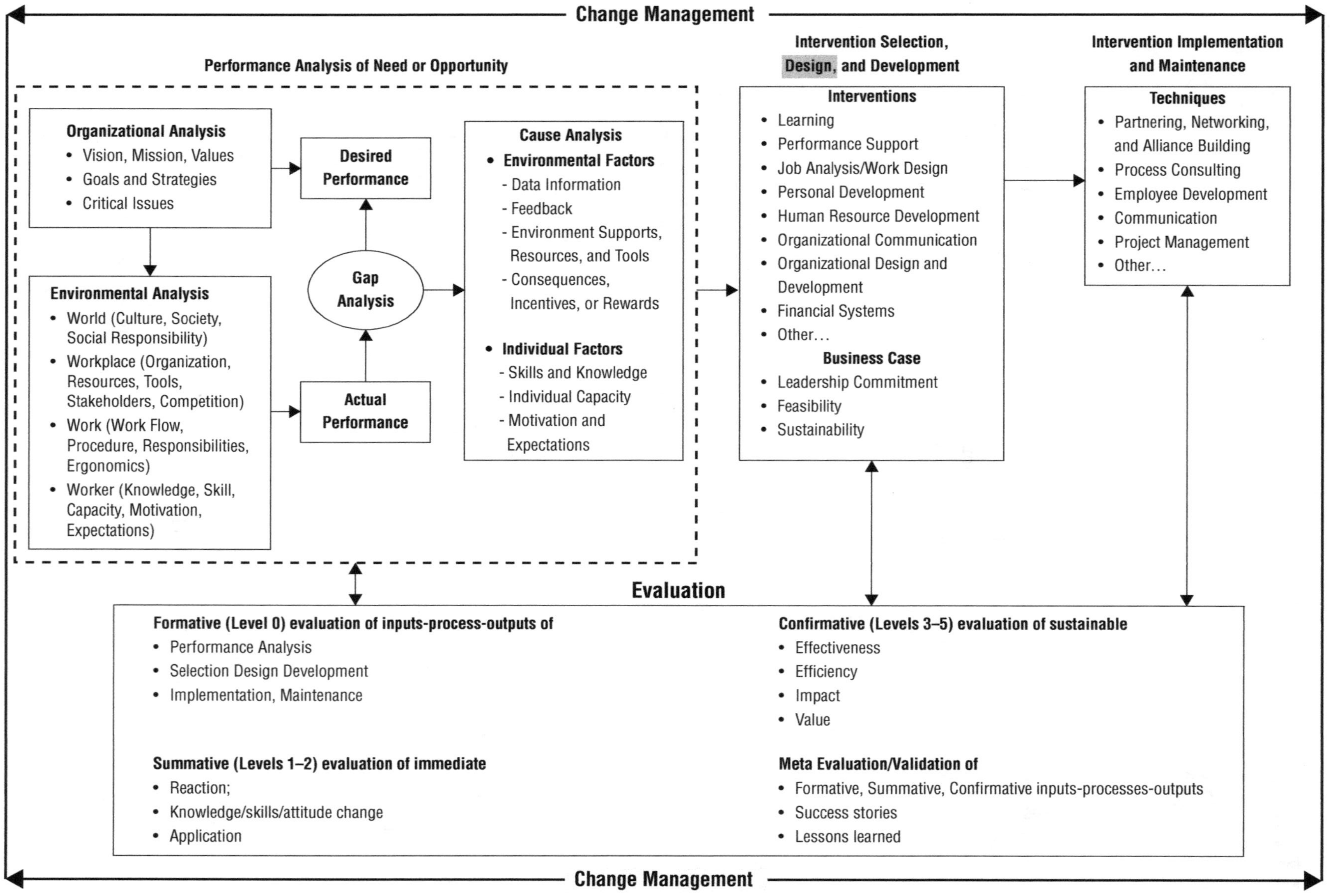

Change Management

Performance Analysis of Need or Opportunity

Organizational Analysis
- Vision, Mission, Values
- Goals and Strategies
- Critical Issues

Environmental Analysis
- World (Culture, Society, Social Responsibility)
- Workplace (Organization, Resources, Tools, Stakeholders, Competition)
- Work (Work Flow, Procedure, Responsibilities, Ergonomics)
- Worker (Knowledge, Skill, Capacity, Motivation, Expectations)

Desired Performance

Gap Analysis

Actual Performance

Cause Analysis

Environmental Factors
- Data Information
- Feedback
- Environment Supports, Resources, and Tools
- Consequences, Incentives, or Rewards

Individual Factors
- Skills and Knowledge
- Individual Capacity
- Motivation and Expectations

Intervention Selection, Design, and Development

Interventions
- Learning
- Performance Support
- Job Analysis/Work Design
- Personal Development
- Human Resource Development
- Organizational Communication
- Organizational Design and Development
- Financial Systems
- Other…

Business Case
- Leadership Commitment
- Feasibility
- Sustainability

Intervention Implementation and Maintenance

Techniques
- Partnering, Networking, and Alliance Building
- Process Consulting
- Employee Development
- Communication
- Project Management
- Other…

Evaluation

Formative (Level 0) evaluation of inputs-process-outputs of
- Performance Analysis
- Selection Design Development
- Implementation, Maintenance

Summative (Levels 1–2) evaluation of immediate
- Reaction;
- Knowledge/skills/attitude change
- Application

Confirmative (Levels 3–5) evaluation of sustainable
- Effectiveness
- Efficiency
- Impact
- Value

Meta Evaluation/Validation of
- Formative, Summative, Confirmative inputs-processes-outputs
- Success stories
- Lessons learned

Change Management

On the other hand, Watkins' "designing for performance" process blends design, development, and selection activities. The first step in this blended process is to align performance expectations with performance objectives. Then Watkins suggests "before choosing any interventions you must define the performance assessments linked to each performance objective."[4]

The Performance Improvement/HPT Model presents each component of the intervention selection, design, and development phase as discrete activities within the phase. Whether design (and development?) should earn its own "phase" remains open for future consideration.

Foundation for Successful Design

The first four Performance Technology Standards (RSVP) (see Appendix A) provide a strong foundation for the performance improvement intervention designer. These guidelines have been expanded and reinforced over the years by practitioners in the field:[5]

- Focus on the expected *results* generated during the Performance Analysis Phase of the Performance Improvement/HPT Model. The design should be based on a comprehensive understanding of the situation and the expected results. Is additional analysis necessary? Are expectations clear? Are specific requirements or specifications clear?
- Use *systemic and systematic* design processes. The Instructional Systems Design (ISD) process is a good place to start. Formative evaluation should be an integral part of the design phase. The design should also include processes and products to conduct summative, confirmative, and meta evaluation of the implemented intervention as needed.
- Add *value* to the performance improvement effort by aligning the intervention design with the expected results. The design should be feasible; it should be mindful of the human and other resources required to plan and map the intervention as well as implement, maintain, and evaluate the intervention. The design of a long-term intervention should be sustainable; it should be adaptable and have built-in mechanisms to allow for change over time.
- *Partner or collaborate* with champions and other stakeholders during the design process. The process should be collaborative. The intervention should have a sponsor who will champion the activities and be active in the design process along with other stakeholders. There will be challenges and unanticipated situations along the way. Project team members, developers, implementers, or others associated with the effort may not continue to participate. The sponsor or champion will assist in securing the needed personnel, protect budgets and timelines and generally stand behind the effort. A major issue is sustainability of the intervention effort. The champion will be able to represent the long-term view so that the project will be sufficiently developed and implemented and will not disappear when the original funding and effort go away.

Steps to Successful Design

The intervention designer follows in the footsteps of the instructional systems design (ISD) professional. However, "the instructional systems design model must be broadened to become the intervention system design model" because workplace performance improvement practitioners design both learning and non-learning interventions.[6] A successful design phase is a collaborative effort that is characterized by reflection, discussion, iteration, planning, revision, and finally approval.

The steps to successful design are based on ISPI Performance Standard 7: Be Systematic—Design,[7] and on years of experience in the field as an instructional and/or performance system designer. Like the Performance Improvement/HPT Model, design steps may be adapted to the situation and the designer. The steps include:

1. Verify and/or clarify the situation based on input from Performance Analysis Phase—performance gaps and causes, desired results, assumptions, environmental parameters, and so forth;
2. Identify and/or clarify all the elements or components of the intervention—strategies, processes, activities, materials, and so forth;
3. Create a performance goal and performance objectives for each element;
4. Identify criteria and/or metrics to evaluate the results;
5. Decide whether it is best to purchase, develop, and/or customize the elements of the intervention;
6. Create an action plan or design document that describes *how* to develop, implement, and evaluate the intervention;
7. Communicate action plan to leadership and other stakeholders to seek approval; and
8. Initiate a request for proposal process *or* begin internal development phase.

Performance Support Tool 18.3 at the end of the chapter is a guide and checklist that focuses the designer on the results for each step in the intervention design process. The rest of this chapter discusses intervention elements, performance objectives, evaluation criteria and metrics, options for developing the intervention in-house or by partnering with outside vendors or consultants, and the action plan or design document.

Intervention Elements

Intervention elements are the components of the intervention that must be in place to implement the intervention. Elements may be processes or materials. For example, if the intervention is to conduct an informational meeting (organizational communication), then the elements may include (1) the process for selecting the attendees, (2) the content or agenda for the meeting, (3) the processes for scheduling, communicating with attendees, preparing the meeting room and/or electronic media, and so forth, and (4) the materials—agenda, visuals, script, documents, and so forth—needed to conduct the meeting and record the results. If the intervention involves a change in the reward structure for submitting a successful idea to the suggestion system, the design may include outlines of both the informational and communication or marketing materials to be developed and the deployment plan for the materials, including audience, media, timing, resource requirement, and so forth.

Performance Objectives

"Performance objectives describe the results to be accomplished, the criteria that will define success, and the ways those criteria will be assessed" and are "derived from the strategic goals of the organization and its partners."[8] They clearly describe what the performer must do to accomplish the goals that were defined during the Performance Analysis Phase of the Performance Improvement/HPT Model.

Purpose

Performance objectives serve a double purpose: they guide the design and development of the performance improvement intervention(s) and establish the criteria for evaluating the effectiveness, efficiency, impact, and value of the intervention during and after implementation. When performance objectives are established prior to selecting the intervention, they also guide the selection process.[9]

Describing Performance

Langdon developed a "six-word lexicon . . . a set of work performance words arranged in a meaningful relationship to one another" to describe performance.[10] The six words, which Langdon also called the "work syntax" or "performance paradigm" are inputs, conditions, process, outputs, consequences, and feedback. Each of these words should be clearly described to make a complete performance objective:

- *Inputs*—What does the performer need to know or be able to do to accomplish the performance?
- *Conditions*—What factors influence how the performance is accomplished?
- *Process*—What does the performer need to do to initiate, conduct, and complete the performance?
- *Outputs*—What will the performer produce as a result of the performance?
- *Consequences*—What will happen if the performer fails to initiate, conduct, or complete the performance? What will happen if the performer succeeds?
- *Feedback*—How will the performer know whether the performance is a success or a failure?

Evaluation Criteria, Metrics, Methods

At this stage in the performance improvement process, evaluation should include formative evaluation of the design process and plans for:

- Formative evaluation of the development and implementation processes;
- Summative evaluation of immediate reaction, learning, and application when the intervention is developed and implemented; and

- Confirmative evaluation of the long-term efficiency, effectiveness, impact, and value of the intervention and each element for interventions that extend beyond three months.

Chapters 23 and 24 contain information on each type of evaluation, including various methods.

The methods, criteria, and metrics for evaluating interventions or their elements will vary depending on the type of intervention or element and the requirements of the organization. Criteria and metrics should measure the accomplishment of the desired results. Evaluation methods should be feasible in terms of the resources required and the value the outputs bring to the organization. For example, establishing metrics that require statistical analysis may involve hiring a statistician or acquiring statistical process software, which will add time and cost to the evaluation process. If the organization is not committed to evaluation and/or making decisions based on the results of evaluation, a less costly method or different metrics should be selected.

Options for Development

Once the intervention project is defined and clarified and the objectives and evaluation criteria are formulated, a variety of development options are available to the designer:

- Develop all the intervention processes and materials in-house,
- Purchase an intervention package from an outside vendor or consultant that contains all the elements of the intervention,
- Purchase an intervention package and customize it in partnership with the vendor/consultant or in-house, or
- Develop elements in-house and purchase elements from a vendor or consultant.

Exhibit 18.1 provides three examples of situations when the purchased intervention package needed to be customized. In the case of customizing, the pricing of the materials and documentation reflects the degree of effort as well as the value of the vendor supplied input.

EXHIBIT 18.1. THREE EXAMPLES OF CUSTOMIZATION

Example 1

An intervention involves new work processes, which in turn require the purchase of new equipment, tools, and software to implement the intervention. However, the manufacturer's documentation may not meet specific user needs so some support documents or systems may be produced internally. In addition, some of the software may need to be customized to align with specific organizational standards or process requirements.

EXAMPLE 2

A course on hydraulics might need a picture of the actual equipment in the documentation and the supplier of the materials or vendor might only have a generic picture. In that case, the vendor could come to the site of the hydraulics equipment and take a picture of the actual piece of equipment or the organization could send the vendor a digital picture. Then, once the specific picture is placed into the documents, they would be completely accurate. This may be particularly important in regulated industries.

EXAMPLE 3

Customizing may mean adapting the materials to include a company logo, cultural customs, or particular forms and policies. In that case, to protect the copyright and trademarks of each party, a dual copyright is agreed on, which often means that the generic materials written and owned by the vendor retain the vendor copyright. The vendor is free to use the same generic materials with other customers. However, copyright for the logo, policies, and cultural customs or forms is retained by the organization contracting for the material. In that way, the vendor cannot use those customized materials to demonstrate his or her capability with other clients or potential clients.

Feasibility

A decision to search for an outside vendor or consultant will involve internal approvals and budgets sufficient to fund the effort. Using external resources involves considerable management of and interaction with the vendor. It is important to plan time and commit to communicating and seeing interim examples. Using a turnkey approach or asking a vendor to provide an end product without sufficient interaction is unrealistic in most cases and often results in disappointment. A feasibility assessment must be part of the initial planning process.

Requests for Proposals

Requests for proposals (RFP) are issued to vendors or suppliers of equipment, tools, software, performance support tools, materials and documents, workshops, and so forth. The organization writes specifications for exactly what is needed for the intervention effort.

RFP Contents. The request for proposal includes organizational goals and overall expectations, anticipated measures of success or results, a description of the requirements and specifications, the target audience, and a description of the scope of the project. There also should be a statement about how and when the competing vendors will be notified as to whether or not they won the bid.

Major project design factors, including a Gantt chart and report expectations, should be documented. There should be clear descriptions of role expectations. Will subject-matter experts provide insight, guidance, and content as needed? What is the process for securing organizational "know how," such as subject-matter experts or participants to test simulations or other materials?

Cost targets are helpful so that the vendor has an idea as to whether a first-class intervention is desired or a more modest version, whether a racing or mountain bicycle is expected, whether the organization wants fixed price or single price for the entire project or whether the organization will accept time on the project plus materials and expenses. Time, materials, and expenses means charging all costs to the client, including the time of each person assigned to the project. Fixed cost can be a benefit if the entire project goes smoothly. Time, materials, and expenses can lead to a more relaxed pace of work, and, therefore, a more expensive product. Often, when the extent of the development effort is difficult to predict, it is necessary to do time, materials, and expenses.

Quality expectations should be set; for example, as a result of the training everyone will be able to use the software package correctly or the vendor must re-train the concepts and materials. On training materials, the standard could be 90 percent of the people get 90 percent correct during a workplace simulation activity. On the other hand, that might not be a sufficiently stringent standard. Getting 90 percent of the information correct on a loan application would not be sufficient; in that case, it would probably be a 100 percent standard.

Invoicing needs to be described. It is best for the organization to pay based on deliverables, such as vendor designs, prototypes, and materials that meet approval. Perhaps the first draft would be 25 percent of the price, second draft and pilot would be 25 percent, and final revisions, meeting quality standards, and implementation would be 50 percent.

Cover Letter. The RFP usually contains a cover letter inviting vendors to submit a proposal for the project. The cover letter usually includes a contact person for vendor questions the exact date and time when the proposal is due and the name, building, desk, or office location of the person who will receive the proposals.

Pre-Bid Meeting. If the project is sufficiently large, there is usually a pre-bid meeting. Invitations are prepared and distributed to all potential bidders. The meeting allows all the bidders to hear the same introduction to the project and hear the responses to their own and other vendors' questions.

Review-Revise-Approve Cycle. The approval process or review-revise-approve cycle must be planned and documented. For example, will the proposal be first screened for content and later screened for price? or Will price be the key factor? If there is an approval committee, knowing who is on the decision team or their job titles will help the vendors be sure to include information of particular importance to the approval team.

Many vendors want to know why they did not obtain the bid, and their requests for explanation should be honored. It takes a great deal of time and effort to create a proposal, so the purchasing organization should respect the efforts of the competing vendors by providing an explanation.

Bidders' List. It is best to qualify the bidders on a project. Each vendor has different specialties, employee strengths, and rates of success and customer satisfaction. The organization needing the vendor services should set up a selection process similar to the one used when hiring an employee. The organization must decide what is important and then request information in order to qualify for the bidders' list. Common bidder criteria might include relevant experience of the overall organization and its staff, financial stability, size of the organization's core staff and network of associates, reputation, and trust factors. Typically, information from the vendor might also include resumes of associates who are likely to be on a project, examples of previous projects, and a list of references. Then the organization should narrow the bidders to a manageable number. This is primarily because creating proposals is costly and time-consuming. It is easy to ask so many vendors to prepare a proposal that the cumulative cost of the proposals exceeds the value of the work. Once the organization has determined a bidders' list, then the organization selects vendors with the particular strengths that are needed for an intervention effort. Selection of the vendors for the bidders' list should be by an internal team because it is difficult for one person to judge everything. The purchasing department in the organization is likely to be part of the team. (See Performance Support Tool 18.1.)

Proposal Selection Criteria and Weighting. Vendors are going to want to know how their proposals will be judged. Providing them with the information helps them target their proposal appropriately. They need to know the criteria and the weighting. The organization may weigh one aspect of the proposal more heavily than another. Content and innovativeness of the ideas may be more important than cost, or vice versa. Vendors need to know the priorities and how each criterion is weighted.

Vendor Guidelines. The RFP should help vendors to prepare well-defined proposals that match what was requested. All aspects must be spelled out in the RFP in order to receive proposals that can be compared with one another. Nothing should be assumed. However, there are times when the vendor believes that he or she has a better idea or an innovative alternative. The vendor should include that idea only after responding exactly to the RFP. It is essential that the vendor also claim copyright of the proposal and that its content be the sole property of the vendor. It is imperative that the purchasing organization honor the ideas of each vendor and not use ideas without providing fair compensation and recognition to vendors.

ISPI Toolkit. The Development and Implementation Section of the online *ISPI Performance Technology Toolkit* provides a Customer Recommendations Report for providing feedback to customers "in an organized and consistent format," a Training Supplier Assessment to evaluate the capability and compare the value of outside vendors, and a Vendor Proposal Evaluation Instrument to evaluate vendor proposals.

Intervention Design Document

The major output of the intervention design activity is a detailed, comprehensive design document. The purpose of the document is to ensure that (1) the developer or development team has enough information to transform the design plan into a complete intervention package of "tangible products and services"[11] and (2) the approvers will have enough detail to accept, ask for revision, or reject the development and implementation of the intervention. The design document must create confidence and gain support and approval from stakeholders, including senior leadership and the developer(s) who must develop the plan.

PERFORMANCE SUPPORT TOOL 18.1. BIDDER SELECTION MATRIX

Directions: Use this performance support tool to rate vendors during the selection process. Apply the following rating scale:

1 = Poor; 2 = Fair; 3 = Good; 4 = Very Good; 5 = Excellent

Selection Criteria	Candidate 1	Candidate 2	Candidate 3
Overall appropriate experience			
Experience related to this project			
Quality of samples			
Organization's financial stability (if large project and high risk)			
Organization's ability to meet deadlines			
Ability of the organization to fit into culture			
Reputation of the organization			
Other:			
Total Scores			

Source: D.M. Van Tiem (2000). *Coursepack for EDT514: Application of instructional design.* Dearborn, MI: University of Michigan–Dearborn. Used with permission.

The design document requires collaboration. As a result, preparing this document will probably be iterative as feedback from stakeholders is sought and received.

Purpose-Based Content

An intervention design document includes an executive summary and a detailed discussion of each of the elements of the intervention. There may also be associated documents or figures, such as a Gantt chart or other project management tools, storyboards, prototypes, and sample resources. Based on the two major goals of the design document, the content should

1. Acquire the support of stakeholders, who must approve the intervention plan prior to development and implementation, and the performance improvement practitioner, who must clearly identify why the intervention was selected, what is to be accomplished, how it will be accomplished, and how the results will be evaluated.
2. Provide a map for developing and implementing the intervention, with enough detail for internal or external developers to design and produce all the materials required to implement the intervention and align them with desired results and expectations.

The design document may be part of the business case (see Chapter 19) or a stand-alone document. The difference between a design document and a business case is that the design document provides a level of detail that may or may not be required to justify the intervention selection, but is necessary for developing the various components of the intervention.

A design document should be developed, even if the processes and products required to implement the intervention are already available from external vendors or consultants. In this case, the design document will be used as part of a request for proposal from outside suppliers. The design document may also be used to describe how the "off-the-shelf" product may have to be customized to meet the specific situation.

PERFORMANCE SUPPORT TOOL 18.2. DESIGN DOCUMENT TEMPLATE

Purpose: The purpose of this performance support tool is to outline the contents of a typical intervention design document.

Degree of Detail: The degree of detail required varies with each organization and the needs of the intervention effort. For some large efforts, it may be necessary to have exact details, which may include "storyboards" or illustrations and ideas for text, media, and so forth. For other design situations, the expectations may be more general. For example, for an online training program that includes visuals, complex responses, and opportunities for further learning, there would be a need for storyboards and prototypes. In the case of a mentoring intervention, there would be a need for definition of the mentor-mentee relationship and other details of mentoring selection and tracking, but probably not storyboards and prototypes. It may be that the development of full specifications, storyboards, and prototypes will be part of the development process.

Use of Terminology: Although each design document may vary in order of the headings, most if not all, of the headings listed in the content outline should be included. In addition, the following perspectives should be addressed as applicable:

- World is important to document cultural or language issues. Many times the intervention will be planned for several locations, and some may span the globe. However, if the improvement effort is internal, there may or may not need to be a discussion of world characteristics that apply.
- Workplace should be used to describe the current situation so leadership and developers can understand the context of the effort.
- Work and Worker need to be explained in terms of job titles and roles, current skills, knowledge, and abilities, plus motivation and attitudinal issues.

DOCUMENT OUTLINE

1. Executive Summary

Give a brief summary of the entire document in one page or less. The C-suite executives may read only this part of the document! Stress the benefits of approving the intervention.

2. Problem or Opportunity

Define the opportunity and include the current situation, desired situation, gap, and cause based on the performance analysis.

3. Results, Objectives, Evaluation Criteria/Metrics

State the performance goals and objectives for each intervention and element. Use definite, observable, measureable terms. Align them with the desired results and match them to the evaluation criteria, metrics, and methods that will be used to measure accomplishment. A table format may be useful.

(Continued)

4. Intervention(s) and Elements

Why is the element important? What are the benefits? Who will be involved? What needs to be developed to implement the element? Where and when will it be implemented? What change management actions are required for each element? How will each element be evaluated—method, criteria, metrics? A flowchart may help illustrate how the interventions and/or intervention elements integrate with each other. For example, a flowchart could show how the elements of a new skill development intervention will move the participant from the awareness level to the application level.

5. Development Plan

Include recommendations for developing in-house, purchasing, or customizing. Describe tasks, responsibilities, finances and other resources, timelines, and so forth required for developing the intervention package. Use project management tools such as Gantt charts or spreadsheets to illustrate timelines, milestones, and so forth. Illustrations help stakeholders see the process at a glance and can be used later to report progress to the stakeholders.

6. Implementation Plan

Describe tasks, responsibilities, finances and other resources, timelines, and so forth required for implementing the intervention package. Use project management tools and illustrations (see number 5).

7. Evaluation Plan

Describe tasks, responsibilities, finances and other resources, timelines, and so forth for evaluating the intervention package at the formative, summative, confirmative, and/or meta level. Use project management tools and illustrations (see number 5).

8. Conclusion

Summarize the design document and ask for action. This section may include the directions for how to provide feedback and approve the design document or ask for revisions.

Source: J.C. Dessinger (2011). Successful intervention design. White paper #108. Used with permission.

PERFORMANCE SUPPORT TOOL 18.3. STAY FOCUSED: A GUIDE TO SUCCESSFUL INTERVENTION DESIGN

Purpose: The purpose of this performance support tool is to keep the performance intervention designer focused on results during the design process.

Directions: Use this tool as a guide during the design process and a checklist to verify that the results for each step in the design process are accomplished. You may not need or be able to accomplish all the results, or you may need to add results based on your specific situation. This tool is just a guide to get you started!

Note: The word "intervention" is used here to include both a *single* type of intervention such as performance incentives and *blended* interventions such as job redesign plus performance support tools plus incentives.

Intervention Design Step	Results
1. Verify/clarify situation	❑ Desired results clearly defined ❑ Selected intervention clearly defined ❑ Performance analysis results clear, complete, and unambiguous ❑ Situation changes since analysis phase identified ❑ Organization, leadership, and worker assumptions clear ❑ Other:
2. Identify/clarify all the elements or parts of the intervention—strategies, processes, activities, materials, and so forth	❑ Each element of the intervention clearly identified ❑ Sequence or priorities identified if applicable ❑ Feasibility assessment for each element conducted ❑ Other:
3. Write a performance goal and performance objectives for each element	❑ Goals aligned with desired results ❑ Objectives include input, process, output, conditions, consequences, feedback as appropriate ❑ Other:
4. Identify criteria/metrics to evaluate the results	❑ Criteria/metrics established for each goal and objective ❑ Criteria/metrics feasible in terms of available resources ❑ Criteria/metrics feasible in terms of organizational environment ❑ Criteria/metrics aligned with desired performance results ❑ Other:

(Continued)

5. Prepare an action plan that outlines *how* to develop, implement, and evaluate the intervention.	❑ Who will participate in development, implementation, and evaluation
	❑ When development, implementation, and evaluation will take place
	❑ What processes and materials need to be developed or purchased to accomplish the objectives of each intervention and each element
	❑ What resources will be required to accomplish successful development, implementation, and evaluation
	❑ What the development, implementation, and evaluation plans will include—who, when, where, what, why, how
	❑ The plan will accomplish the desired results
	❑ Other:
6. Recommend whether to purchase, develop, customize the elements of the intervention	❑ Vendor products identified that may be appropriate
	❑ Vendor products identified that may need to be customized
	❑ In-house development is feasible
	❑ Issue a request for proposals from outside vendors
	❑ Other:
7. Communicate design plan to leadership and workers	❑ Communication includes rationale, design specifications, action plan, and recommendations
	❑ Most appropriate method(s) of communication selected
	❑ Review-revise-approve cycle initiated if appropriate
	❑ Communication asks for commitment
	❑ Other:
8. Initiate request for proposal process or internal development phase	❑ Development phase begins
	❑ or
	❑ Request for proposal developed
	❑ Review-revise-approve cycle completed for proposals
	❑ Development or implementation partnership with outside vendor begins
	❑ Other:

Source: J.C. Dessinger (2011). Successful intervention design. White paper #108. Used with permission.

Citations

1. Rothwell, 2000, p. 71
2. Rothwell, 2000, p. 89
3. Rothwell, 2000, p. 72
4. Watkins, 2007a, p. 12
5. Spitzer, 1992, 1999; Rothwell, 2000
6. Rothwell, 2000, p. 71
7. Standards, 2011
8. Watkins, 2007a, p. 11
9. Watkins, 2007b, p. 12
10. Langdon, 1995, pp. 12–17
11. Rothwell, 2000, p. 71

References

Langdon, D. (1995). *The new language of work* (pp. 12–17). Amherst, MA: HRD Press.

Rothwell, W.J. (2000). *The intervention selector designer & developer implementor: A self-guided job aid with assessments based on ASTD Models for Workplace Learning and Performance*. Alexandria, VA: American Society for Training and Development.

Spitzer, D.R. (1992). The design and development of effective interventions. In H.D. Stolovitch & E.J. Keeps (Eds.), *Handbook of human performance technology: A comprehensive guide for analyzing and solving performance problems in organizations* (pp. 114–129). San Francisco: Jossey-Bass.

Spitzer, D.R. (1999). The design and development of high impact interventions. In H.D. Stolovitch & E.J. Keeps (Eds.), *Handbook of human performance technology: Improving individual and organizational performance worldwide* (2nd ed.) (pp. 163–184). San Francisco: Pfeiffer/ISPI.

Watkins, R. (2007a). Designing for performance, part 1: Aligning your HPT decisions from top to bottom. *Performance Improvement Journal, 46*(1), 7–13.

Watkins, R. (2007b). Designing for performance, part 2: Selecting your performance technologies. *Performance Improvement Journal, 46*(2), 9–15.

Making the Business Case

19

Business case methodology resides in management science; however, it is rarely found in the best practices, including performance improvement efforts. The business case process *is* "integrated with the organization's procurement process" because purchasing expenditures for resources, human or non-human, are usually required to develop and implement the intervention.[1] Business cases *should* be integrated into performance improvement initiatives because:

> "It is not enough to have a good idea; it is not sufficient to have totally appropriate and helpful intervention plans and designs. In many instances, the organization and decision-makers want to know more. They want to know exactly what the performance improvement effort will cost, what be the value of the benefit will be, how the project will affect other departments and individuals, and how it will impact the culture. Developing and documenting a business case will foster senior leadership support, accomplish the confidence of finance, and provide the justification needed by purchasing agents."[2]

Definition and Scope

A number of definitions are applicable to the performance improvement field. "A business case is a management argument supporting an investment or a procurement judgment. . . . An investment or procurement judgment assesses the value of a design."[3] It is also "a recommendation to decision-makers to take a particular course of action for the organization, supported by an analysis of its benefits, costs, and risks compared to the realistic alternatives, with an explanation of how it can best be implemented."[4]

The second definition adapts particularly well to the performance improvement mindset; the business case for a performance improvement intervention should present a specific, analysis-based recommendation for an intervention(s) addressed to people with the authority to make a decision at the organizational or major business unit level. The business case should include a cost-benefit comparison for realistic alternative interventions.

For some performance improvement practitioners, such as those working in the primary, secondary (K–12), or higher education arena, a business case may sound similar to a *proposal*. Educators often write proposals when they recommend adopting new curriculums, courses, programs, textbooks, or school equipment. Performance improvement practitioners may write proposals when they are seeking consultants or vendors to help design and develop intervention components. (See Chapter 18.) In the latter case, the proposal may or may not be part of the business case.

Business cases are usually written on behalf of champions and senior stakeholders. Sometimes, performance improvement practitioners write business cases for a single intervention or a combination of interventions, as many needs or opportunities are complex.[5] Highly structured business cases include background of the effort, expected business outcomes, options for alleviating the need or optimizing the opportunity, the gap between the current and anticipated end state, expenses, costs of the effort and estimated value, risks to implement or doing nothing, project timeframe, roles, and more.

Purpose

Business cases present the reason for the intervention "and are used to prevent *blue sky ideas* from taking root without justifiable or provable value to the organization."[6] Whether the business case is a long, comprehensive document, or a short business brief, the point is to justify the expenditure of money and capital resources to support a specific business need. For example, the business case for an enterprise-wide software upgrade will provide the costs of implementation and maintenance plus the benefit or value to the organization using *discounted* money calculations. It may also include plans for design, development, implementation, and evaluation of the upgrade.

The term *capital* is used when referring to investments, such as land, equipment, and buildings that are used to provide goods and services. They are not consumed while providing goods and services; they gradually depreciate or lose value due to usage, such as desks, chairs, or machinery. *Discounting of money* refers to money losing value each year, due to inflation and other economic factors. In other words, one dollar spent in one year may need a return of one dollar plus five cents the next year in order to break even.

A business case also "supports the adoption by a specific organization of a specific solution, and is centered around what people might actually do."[7] The purpose of the case is to convince decision makers that the tangible and intangible benefits of implementing the intervention outweigh the costs and risks, in other words, that the change is worth doing![8].

Rationale

"A business case is not an end in itself but a means to an end; rationally justified (and justifiable) investment decisions."[9] From a project management perspective, in addition to helping the decision-makers make the right decision, the purpose of the business case is to provide documentation that will help mobilize and sustain the project [intervention], meet any compliance requirements, provide a "platform for managing the project" intervention development, implementation, and maintenance, and provide a "baseline for measuring the project [sustainable intervention effectiveness, efficiency, impact, and results]."[10]

Looking at performance improvement intervention development, implementation, and maintenance from a project management perspective, the reason for expending the resources and effort to develop a business case is clear:

As the project [intervention] moves forward, particularly in its early stages when it still may be politically vulnerable and may well run into teething trouble, it is bound to be challenged to justify itself afresh and demonstrate that it is really going to deliver.[11] By setting out a schedule of deliverables, benefits, and costs in the business case, the document becomes an authoritative reference point, both for the project [intervention] team and for the wider organization, and reduces the chances of the goal posts being moved.[12]

Performance Improvement Practitioner Role

The business case process is gradual and iterative; it builds gradually as consensus develops when more details are decided and outcomes are more fully explained. The role of the performance improvement practitioner is to collect, analyze, and synthesize information for the case during the performance analysis; select or design an appropriate intervention(s); develop a convincing business case that weighs the costs, benefits, and risks associated with implementing the intervention; and facilitate the development and acceptance of the case; develop, implement, and maintain the intervention within the parameters set by the business case; and evaluate the intervention in terms of alignment with the business case objectives. (See Figure 19.1.)

Performance improvement practitioners collaborate with the intervention team, which may be the same team that guided the performance analysis phase as well. Practitioners may initiate, help collect, and record discussion and other feedback from informal and formal leadership, including the intervention sponsor, financial experts, purchasing agents, and/or representatives from each department or organizational segment involved in the effort.

Performance Improvement Practitioner Competencies

One of the major competencies for developing a business case is the ability to analyze and synthesize information that surfaces during the Performance Analysis Phase in order to design and develop a business case that is concise, complete, and compelling. The process also involves cooperation and give and take among the stakeholders so it also requires negotiation skills. In addition:

> "People are more likely to be persuaded by someone who knows what they are talking about and in whose intentions and abilities they have confidence . . . . Do the work thoroughly, systematically and professionally and decision-makers will be persuaded by your competence and expertise. Demonstrate integrity and show the positive energy and commitment to get behind your team and your task, and your decision makers will want to be persuaded."[13]

Building a business case may falter without project management skills and subject matter expertise, or access to subject-matter experts (SMEs). Due to the complexity of some intervention projects, the business case document may involve discussions of whether to produce the interventions or buy the interventions through consultants or suppliers. Complex intervention projects may require the use of project management tables, Gantt charts, and other graphics that may also need to be included in a business case.

Competencies may include collecting and analyzing costs, revenue, benefits, and risks; understanding business strategy; managing and communicating with stakeholders throughout the business case process; writing and editing drafts and reports, managing a review/revise cycle; and facilitating a presentation.[14] Presentations are important to establish context; verify compliance to expectations, standards, and regulations; and document future changes, so the performance improvement practitioner may need oral presentation design and communication skills.

The Business Case Process

According to Veryard,[15] the business case is not a "static product"; it is a "process" of building the case and then adapting as more input is acquired: "The formulation of the business case is part of the solution process." When the business case has been accepted it should be embedded into the development and implementation of the intervention and, as far as possible, should "remain true . . . and valid." The basic process for making a business case is illustrated in Figure 19.1.

FIGURE 19.1.   Business Case: An Iterative Process

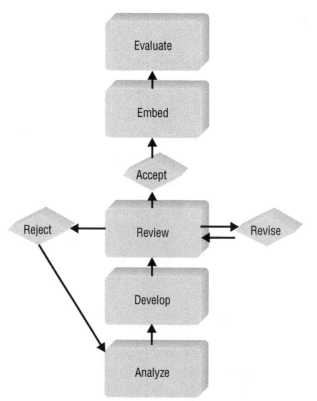

Source: Dessinger, 2011. Used with permission.

Content and Focus

Unfortunately, "Instead of a due diligence on an investment opportunity, business cases often deteriorate into pitch-and-forget sales tools."[16] Business cases are more effective if they are not just a set of claims but also include analysis to back up those claims and provide the decision-makers with all the information they need, plus compelling reasons why they should accept the recommended intervention. Statements regarding feasibility and sustainability are included to justify the proposed change.

Format

Usually, a document is an important part of the business case. However:

> "A business case should never be seen primarily as a document. . . . a business case is an analytically supported recommendation. In fact it could be a series of structured presentations to key decision-makers supported by some key numbers and lots of dialogue and debate."[17]

In more formal organizations there may be a template or a set of specific requirements for developing the business case document and/or presentation.

Issue of Integrity

Credibility plays a big role in moving decision-makers to accept a performance intervention, and integrity is a factor in establishing the credibility of the person or team that produces the business case and the *goodness* of the case itself. A good business case should be demonstrably legal; decent, that is, politically correct; honest; regarding issues of self-interest or bias; truthful regarding costs and benefits; convincing, that is, making a strong case for the change; and bold enough to present an "innovative argument" despite "potential risks." Gambles discusses "degrees" of integrity, which he labels strong, misleading, weak, and token. When the business case demonstrates strong integrity it is usually accepted, when it is misleading or weak the decision makers may make the wrong decision, and token business cases may lead to revisions or outright rejection.[18]

Designing and Developing the Business Case

The process of developing the business case should be "a learning experience with a minimum of thrashing about to gain agreement among the participants and a reasonable expenditure of time and resources."[19] The process should be gradual and requires agreement among the stakeholders. The practitioner who is leading the design and development effort should:

- Identify and ask the right questions to establish clear objectives and understand the nature of the intervention for which you are doing the business case;
- Clarify open-ended questions (no right or wrong answer) before asking close-ended questions (select right answer from options); and
- Identify and clarify prior decisions that may affect implementation.[20]

Clarifying the budget is one time when the practitioner needs to ask the right questions. Issues that may need clarifying are the process or acceptability of cost estimation, confidentiality, and access to and use of proprietary information. Determining whether the budget will be derived bottom-up or top-down is also critical. Bottom-up budgets are based on the cost of the intervention activities and deliverables; top-down budgets are based on the high-level allocation of funds and reflect how management prioritizes the intervention in the context of available resources and competing demands. Finally, questions must be asked to clarify the status of the budget. Is the budget fixed or variable through the life of the intervention?

Steps to Take

Some activities related to preparing the business case are iterative, some are parallel, and some are completed simultaneously.[21] The steps to a successful business case include:

1. Define the task clearly up-front by asking the right questions of the right people and analyzing the responses;
2. Build a coalition of leaders and subject-matter experts;
3. Select a shortlist of realistic alternative options: "If you understand the strategic space you are working in and what you are really trying to achieve, structured, creative thinking will produce winning options"[22];
4. Identify and quantify the costs and benefits of each option;
5. Assess how well each option will deliver costs and benefits; and
6. Develop a strong case for change that is accurate. Demonstrate that the recommended option is the best option because it is closest fit to the business strategy and delivers greatest benefits in most cost-effective way.[23]

Leadership Commitment

Leadership commitment is vital. A well-placed and credible supporter, sponsor, or champion should participate throughout the business case process, and the business case should be compelling enough to mobilize and maintain the commitment of the major decision-makers and senior leadership. It is important for the performance improvement practitioner to fully understand the concerns and priorities of each senior leader and key decision-maker and include aspects of the intervention effort that support their priorities.

Throughout the effort, unanticipated occurrences arise, leading to adjustments and possibly recommitment by senior leadership. Including the priorities of senior leadership in the beginning helps maintain leadership confidence though maintenance and sustaining the effort long term. For example, the project sponsor may receive a promotion and the new person in the position would not be aware of the need for the intervention. By building the confidence of several senior leaders, the other leaders can convey the importance of the project and encourage the new person to retain the role of intervention sponsor.

The sponsor or champion will assist in securing the needed personnel, protect budgets, and timelines and generally stand behind the effort. A major issue is sustainability of the intervention effort. The champion will be able to represent the long-term view so that the project will be sufficiently developed and implemented and not be vulnerable when the original funding and effort go away. Sustainability is discussed later in this chapter.

Feasibility

"Advocating a tough, risky option may be the right thing to do. Advocating it without understanding and explaining the risks and practicalities of implementation never is."[24] It is always essential to balance attractiveness with achievability and practicality.

The greatest ideas in the world need to be implementable or achievable; stakeholders need to believe that an idea makes sense. After brainstorming and thinking an idea through from an initial point of view, momentum increases as those involved visualize the idea and describe the value and outcomes of the idea. In fact, the first steps in assessing feasibility involve RSVP: defining desired *results*, thinking in a *systematic* and *systemic* fashion, determining that there will be *value*, and beginning to establish the collaboration and *partnering* that will be part of the initiative. Whether the effort is a quality, instructional design, industrial engineering, leadership, or strategic planning effort, it is critical to anticipate the entire effort to determine if the effort makes sense and is feasible.

Feasibility Studies

A business feasibility study is "a controlled process for identifying problems and opportunities, determining objectives, describing situations, defining successful outcomes and assessing the range of costs and benefits associated with several alternatives for solving a problem." The Business Feasibility Study is used to support the decision-making process based on a cost-benefit analysis of the actual business or project viability.[25]

Feasibility studies use deliberate processes to determine viability of the initiative: analyze the situation, enable the creation of recommendations, and document limitations. The studies are detailed and document all aspects to determine whether the desired improvement effort is realistic. Feasibility studies help decision-makers determine which projects will be effective and which are not likely to be successful.

Planning Feasibility

It is critical to plan carefully to secure champion and leadership support and sufficient resources so that the outcomes will be lasting. In addition, if sustainability and future support for the project are not considered during feasibility studies, it is very likely that the performance improvement effort will not be ongoing. (See the discussion of sustainability later in this chapter.) Lack of long-term leadership commitment can lead to skepticism and the belief that the performance improvement effort is merely a "flavor of the year" or annual priority. By resisting change, employees believe that the intervention effort will fizzle out and revert back to the "way we do things here."

Feasibility planning includes four methods of advanced planning, structured, deductive, inductive, and narrated.[26]

Structured. Feasibility is considered when planning projects and covers the various aspects of projects, such as work-breakdown structure (WBS), project phases, critical pathing or optimal progress, linkages and ordering of the steps, and cost-benefit analysis, in other words documenting each step, sub-step, sub-sub-step, and so forth in the project. The project is described in phases, activities, tasks, and deliverables or milestones so that objectives can be accomplished and unanticipated situations can be corrected as they occur.

Critical pathing, linkages between aspects and activities, and ordering of the steps make it possible to determine which steps need to be completed prior to other steps, which can be done simultaneously, which may be postponed for a while, and so forth. Cost-benefit analysis determines at what point the costs of the project and the anticipated benefits will be equal, known as the break-even point. It is a process to evaluate whether the anticipated effort would be worthwhile organizationally and financially.

Deductive. Backward or deductive planning occurs when the final outcomes are defined, such as desired results and the gap between the current situation and the desired situation. Then the team needs to consider how to accomplish the final expectations in the most feasible way.

Inductive. Forward or inductive thinking occurs in pre-thinking while the exact end of the project has not been defined. It is also important for intermediary planning, such as to figure out the costs of aspects that are less defined. It is a process of visualizing interim situations. Most projects have many aspects that need to be integrated, and future-looking descriptions of the intermediary stages help realize success as the project progresses.

Narrated. Descriptive writing is needed to define project scope, purpose, desired outcomes and goals, and value-added and to communicate with collaborators and partners. Narratives enable all stakeholders to agree on the intentions, expectations, stages, costs, and benefits prior to beginning the effort.

Performance Improvement Feasibility Planning

Performance improvement efforts are often viewed as projects, but are considerably varied in purpose, methods, and intended outcomes. Many projects have commonalities within industries, such as health care, manufacturing, non-profit social agencies, governmental or military, education, or retail to name a few examples. However, each project may use the Performance Improvement/HPT Model for planning the feasibility study. Feasibility is a consideration throughout the model. There is no one time that represents the culmination of feasibility; for example, formative evaluation is iterative and continues throughout improvement effort, setting the stage for further work.

Performance Support Tool 19.1 provides a structure for feasibility studies. It is not entirely complete because it is generic. Each project will have unique considerations that will add aspects to the study.

PERFORMANCE SUPPORT TOOL 19.1. PERFORMANCE IMPROVEMENT FEASIBILITY STUDY OUTLINE

Discussion of this topic . . .	Should contain this content . . .
Performance Improvement	Describe intended improvement, what will be the initial focus, and the improvement to be sustained.
	Describe benefits to each stakeholder.
	Describe RSVP (results orientation, systemic approach, value added, and partnership) and collaboration.
Intended Beneficiaries	Identify and describe all stakeholders.
	Describe champion (person who will shepherd the project, ensure resources, and minimize resistance within the organization.
	Define all beneficiaries, including demographic factors and other relevant factors.
Communications and Marketing Strategies	Discuss types of communication, such as newsletters, emails, videos, and marketing efforts.
	Describe initial and ongoing efforts needed to keep all stakeholders informed.
	Determine feedback to and from stakeholders.
Intervention Strategies	Since feasibility is iterative, it may be necessary to provide initial feasibility prior to determining interventions.
	Determine strategic partnerships needed to implement intervention.
Steps to Implementation	List of proposed key managers, responsibilities, experience, skills, and costs.
	Resources: champion, financial, facilities, technology, equipment, and other.
Financial Analysis	Break-even analysis: short-term point where the benefits equal the initial costs. If the project has a multi-year break-even calculation, then financial experts can adjust calculations for time-based factors of money.
	Cost/benefit analysis: long-term benefit based on fixed and variable costs and benefits, taking into consideration employee retention, quality improvements, ergonomics factors, environmental sustainability issues, government regulations compliance, and others.

Source: Van Tiem, 2012. Used with permission.

Sustainability

Sustainability refers to enduring over time supported by adequate emphasis, resources, and structure. It is an aspect of performance improvement intervention planning that organizations utilize when the interventions need to be maintained for the long term.[27] They are intervention efforts that are viewed as helpful to stakeholders and worth keeping in place.

"Sustainability isn't a one-size-fits-all strategy that a company can implement by following a set of rules. Rather, it springs from challenges each company faces in its own markets."[28] While there are some common elements in how companies accomplish sustainability, decisions are based on specific critical issues (see Chapter 5). Fromartz explained:

> "Sustainability is less a target than an approach, which is why it is continually being refined. As companies ramp up understanding, they also push the envelope of what can be accomplished. In short, learning more about what they do has led companies to change how they do it. Though it takes investment and commitment, the rewards are measured in energy cost savings, new product design, customer engagement and employee commitment. Together, all these attributes amount to the one thing any business understands: competitive advantage."[29]

Sustainability in the Performance Improvement/HPT Context

Sustainability is one of the most challenging issues in performance improvement. After following the Performance Improvement/HPT Model and creating a timely and effective solution using a carefully crafted combination of interventions that are determined to be successful in resolving the problem, the effort could be discontinued or neglected, thus becoming ineffective. How could something that is meeting a recognized need and providing a positive resolution be ignored or discontinued?

There are, unfortunately, many factors or circumstances that lead to discontinuing a seemingly very successful effort. Change in leadership is probably the most common cause, as change in leadership may lead to a change in direction. Just when the project is implemented and progressing well, there can be an organizational change of emphasis, leading to a situation referred to as "flavor of the year" or annual change of emphasis. When an organization has a history of beginning initiatives and then changing interests, there is a tendency of employees to wait and not take change seriously because they believe that the change is likely to be temporary. In other words, the employees become conditioned to resist change.

Several strategies can enable or encourage sustainability of performance improvement efforts. Applying the Performance Improvement/HPT Model is important to the long-term success of performance improvement efforts. Three other strategies are RSVP, capacity building, and implement for sustainability.

RSVP

It is critical to apply the first four Performance Technology Standards (Figure 19.2) to sustainability planning. The four standards, known as RSVP, are **F**ocus on results, be **S**ystemic, add **V**alue, and **P**artner with others.[30]

Results. Focusing on results and helping the clients focus on results is vital in sustainability planning. When there are identified problems and failures within the organization, it is easy to agree on where to begin. However, it is not wise to begin without agreement regarding the results or desired outcomes. If the leadership and those who are affected by the effort have not defined and agreed to the meaning of success, then there will be differing ideas about what the end result should look like.

Systemic Approach. Look at situations systemically, taking into consideration the larger context, including competing pressures, resource constraints, and anticipated change. Gaining consensus on measures of tangible or intangible outcomes, such as production quotas, phones calls answered, project management timelines, sales productivity, or performance appraisals objectives met, is the critical first step. To not have agreement means the effort has no clear destination, similar to taking a vacation without knowing exactly where you are going. While this may make sense for an informal family trip, it leads to disorientation in organizations.

Within organizations, almost everything is interdependent. The success of a disaster recovery effort relies on communication, portable medical facilities, food, water, shelter, search and rescue teams, and heavy equipment to dig through rubble. A successful computer software upgrade project relies on careful programming based on sound processes, strong help desk support, consistent and clear technical manuals, and concise and well-designed training. The entire initiative needs to be aligned with the organization in order to be sustainable.

Value. Determining value is challenging because value includes tangible and intangible elements. On the *tangible* side, the highest level of evaluation includes determining the value of an intervention relative to cost-benefit or the total costs of the intervention minus the total benefits. Determining the costs and the benefits of a long-term intervention may require many years of complex analysis. At a minimum, the analysis must take into account the discounted or changing value of money over time due to inflation or the anticipated increases in supplies, wages, rent,

FIGURE 19.2.   RSVP

and so forth. In addition, profit-making organizations may set internal rates of return or anticipated profit margins or establish an internal minimum acceptable rate of return or "hurdle" rate that a manager or company is willing to accept before implementing an intervention.

Interventions also have *intangible* value. Just as brand image has value to marketing and sales, changes in organizational culture can increase employee retention or the ability to attract desired employees. Enhanced employee engagement and empowerment can make a great deal of difference for customer service.[31] Opportunities for advancement can be motivational. Human capital literature can be very helpful in determining intangible value.

Partnerships. Utilizing partnerships or collaborations with clients and other experts is essential for sustainability. All too often, changes in leadership or changes in priorities are the most important reasons for discontinuing or dismantling change. When one single champion retains the vision and the energy and the champion moves on, then the effort can falter. Establishing a broad base of involvement enables the changes to be retained. An RSVP example is shown in Exhibit 19.1.

EXHIBIT 19.1. RSVP: AN EXAMPLE

A high-tech U.S. manufacturing plant had all areas and all shifts meeting quota and quality goals, except for one team. This manufacturing team seemed just like the other teams in education, training, and ability. The differences seemed to be culture of origin and first language.

The performance improvement manager established a leadership team composed of the plant manager, human resources manager, lean manufacturing manager, operations manager, line supervisor, and a member of the manufacturing team who was accomplished in the language of the manufacturing team and English. The performance improvement manager used the Performance Improvement/HPT Model as the basis to accomplish consistent quality and quota goals for this manufacturing team.

The effort was widely embraced by key leadership. In the end, there seemed to be a need for this group and the entire plant to better understand their role in meeting the company goals, vision, and mission. Key leadership conducted meetings with the various shifts and groups, including the target manufacturing team. Within a few weeks, their goals and quotas were met and retained, as they could see the importance of their efforts and how their work was aligned with the entire process.

Not only was this first performance improvement effort successful, but the company is planning to use the Performance Improvement/HPT Model with other improvement projects in the same and other locations. Broad collaboration, with clear success measures, and applying a systematic process generated confidence to use the approach elsewhere.

Adapted from Beish, 2011. Used with permission.

Building Capacity

Due to the essential need to sustain and expand on school improvements, the Certification Standards for School Improvement explicitly covers capacity building as necessary for sustainability. For example, a great deal of research and observation has lead to the development of standards for kindergarten through grade twelve. However, the capacity concept can be generalized to all performance improvement projects, and it is already common to many improvement efforts involved at the international development level.

Capacity building is an approach to organization development that begins with understanding the inhibitors or obstacles to successful performance and then focuses on how to build on the existing capabilities of the organization to accomplish measurable and sustainable results. Not only do those directly involved need to have considerable capacity and understanding, but key leadership also must have capacity in order to make good decisions. An example is shown in Exhibit 19.2.

EXHIBIT 19.2. BUILDING CAPACITY: AN EXAMPLE

Sometimes elements of improvement are retained over thirty years, although the actual project is long forgotten. In the mid-1980s, a small city in Nevada was challenged with workforce legal battles. A performance improvement specialist applied a systemic HPT approach to create some new initiatives: the first city-wide management and training program, an employee recognition scheme, a suggestion and innovation program, an employee assistance (EAP) service, an arbitration procedure, and others. As a result, hundreds of thousands of legal savings occurred. (See Section 1 of Case Study 1.3. Reducing Municipal Strife Through Engagement.)

After two years, the city manager departed and the arbitration piece was discontinued. But the rest of the elements remained in one form or another. "This is a rare example of what can happen when a broad group of stakeholders is able to truly define needs, a capable leader presses forth to implement and support changes for a few years, and the interventions instituted actually begin to produce performance results (and reduced cost)."

Based on a personal communication with Steve Kelly, March 6, 2011. Used with permission.

Interventions. The strategies or interventions for improvement have to align with desired outcomes and measures of success. Improvement professionals need to coach and provide feedback. In order to maximize potential and see new possibilities in complex situations, it is important to reflect on progress. It is essential to not only track progress of the improvement project directly, but also to confirm that key leaders are developing capacity. Sharing improvements and success measures are essential to build confidence in all constituencies associated with the effort.[32]

Implement for Sustainability

Performance improvement professionals need to assure that a wide variety of stakeholders remain committed to improving and sustaining the improvements throughout the life of the intervention. This means establishing and preparing for the transfer of ownership from the initial project team. It is essential to retain and also adapt measures of success while celebrating early accomplishments. This builds confidence and energy. Report leading indicators of change in order to sustain new processes, recognize achievements, and gradually gain more support for long-term transformation. An example is shown in Exhibit 19.3.

EXHIBIT 19.3. IMPLEMENT FOR SUSTAINABILITY: AN EXAMPLE

This example comes from Eastern Europe beginning in 1992. A major automobile manufacturer desired to enhance their sales and distribution from five dealership/service centers to a national headquarters and eighty dealerships throughout Eastern Europe. In the communist days, sales were based on customers (ordering cars from binders with photos) who paid full cash up-front, and waited eight to twelve months for delivery. There were no test drives, and sellers often took bribes to advance delivery dates. This effort involved training new dealers/owners in Western management techniques and building an effective sales and service force to sell and maintain vehicles in a competitive environment. Due to a comprehensive approach, by the mid-1990s, the import auto company had taken over first place by establishing a complete dealer network and had a cadre of several hundred successful sales representatives and capable service personnel.

This effort relied on clear objectives, trusted internal leaders, highly motivated staff, and excellent product, with strong marketing support and fair compensation. "The key for any successful and sustained PI initiative . . . is the involvement of the leadership. This really needs to be more than 'buy-in,' rather they need to be the initiators and drivers of the change . . . and seen as such by the workforce. The most usual situations when initiatives dissolve or do not add value is when this leadership role is missing from the start, such as for HR or global HQ driven efforts, and key leaders are changed, or overridden by broader cultural or political factors. Such changes as this make it very hard to sustain change, except when the middle level of leadership has begun to gain benefits from improved performance and will press forward."

Based on a personal communication with Steve Kelly, February 28, 2011. Used with permission.

Challenges to Sustainability

Clearly, in a workplace world that changes rapidly, with unexpected competitive pressures and priorities, sustaining progress is challenging. Performance improvement efforts are often project driven with recognized beginning and end dates. Yet, the gains and the accomplishments need to continue.

Establish Sponsorship

Establishing a broad base of sponsorship is essential. All too often, the champion has received accolades regarding the positive impact of the improvement effort and is then assigned to new opportunities. Having a broad leadership foundation that includes representation from all aspects of the initiative enables the improvement effort to continue and adapt.

Set Expectations

Although sponsors and champions are pleased with the outcomes, the gains are often smaller in the beginning than later when momentum has added greater value. It is important to establish the expectation to measure and evaluate efforts on an ongoing basis. It is essential to publicize success stories in newsletters and other forms of communication, establishing the expectation that the success is the new norm.

See the example of sustained success in Exhibit 19.4.

EXHIBIT 19.4. MEETING THE CHALLENGES: AN EXAMPLE

A sustained success on a global sales project happened because:

- "The leader of the corporate learning organization, which owns the initiative, had a clear vision of the importance of this work and of what the solution needed to include.
- This leader effectively communicated this vision and our progress to executive leadership at corporate and globally, and obtained their support for the effort.
- This leader identified and assigned roles to internal and external team members that effectively leveraged their expertise.
- The sales regions were actively included in the development and implementation of the curriculum architecture. They provided expert performers, subject-matter experts, trainers, and even funding.
- With strong executive support for the initiative globally, sufficient budget was provided to enable achievement of initiative's evolving goals. This enabled the team to adhere to best practice in its efforts; no one had to "make do."
- The various regions were not compelled to all adopt the curriculum at the same time; the situations in their various markets guided the adoption timeline. Similarly, the regions were encouraged to map the curriculum architecture against their existing curricula and leverage where possible. Further, all training was localized to each region.
- Finally, a significant contributor to sustainability is positive business results. The positive sales results achieved as the curriculum architecture began to be implemented played a strong role in reinforcing commitment to the initiative."

Based on a personal communication with Lisa Toenniges, March 12, 2011. Used with permission.

PERFORMANCE SUPPORT TOOL 19.2. TEMPLATE FOR A BUSINESS CASE

Purpose: Business cases provide evidence of the value of interventions and document the important aspects of the intervention scenarios or options. They include financial considerations that involve working with financial experts and purchasing issues that involve purchasing agents within the organization. Performance improvement interventions require leadership support for sustained success, and the business case represents current leader-supporters, reaches out to other leaders for support, and helps to sustain continuing leadership support. As they collaborate while the business case is prepared, many stakeholders develop consensus and partnerships that are maintained throughout the intervention life cycle and beyond.

Business Case Table of Contents

Executive Summary

Introduction

    Statement of the Gap and Measures of Success

    Justification

Assumptions and Methods

    Financial Metrics

    Assumptions and Risks

Project Planning

    Scenarios

Business Impacts

Conclusions and Recommendations

EXECUTIVE SUMMARY

The executive summary is often the only part of the business case that is read by senior leadership and those not directly involved in the case. It is written after the entire document has been crafted to present information succinctly.

INTRODUCTION

Statement of the Gap and Measures of Success. The opportunity or problem should be defined based on the performance analysis, including the gap and cause analysis. Goals and objectives are described in definite, observable, measureable terms. Baseline status, which defines the current situation, should to be documented. Definite results, goals, and objectives need to align with the desired state. Accomplishment of alignment will indicate success, known as measures of success.

Justification. Benefits of the intervention effort should include statements aligned with strategic direction and emphasis of the organization. The benefits are the value of accomplishing the project's measures of success. Intervention efforts should demonstrate impact, including return on investment. The project could increase brand

(Continued)

reputation, customer focus, culture, or innovative and excellent products or services. For example, an effort to empower customer call center representatives would provide an innovative new service option and could please customers, which would lead to improved brand reputation and making customers feel valued. This, in turn, could create a more positive culture for the entire call center. It is likely that there would also be a positive return on investment.

ASSUMPTIONS AND METHODS

Financial Metrics. Describe the types of measures that the business case is based on. It is likely that the performance improvement practitioner will work with someone from the finance department to determine which of these measures apply. The list below represents customary, generic measures for any organization.

- Net cash flow
- Net present value
- Payback period
- Return on investment
- Discounted cash flow
- Internal rate of return
- Return on assets
- Price/performance ratio

Also, intangible measures should be documented, such as increased brand loyalty, improved collaboration, faster decisions, or higher ratings on annual employee cultural surveys.

Assumptions and Risks. List all assumptions taken for granted. Also identify and define the consequences and risks of not implementing the interventions.

PROJECT PLANNING

Projects need to be visualized in terms of tasks, responsibilities, financial and other resources, timelines, and so forth.[33] It is important to anticipate and document the tasks that would be involved in the effort.[34] Project management software can be quite easy to learn because the software is an electronic performance support tool based on spreadsheet software. The software has artificial intelligence built in so that it is easy to create reports that track tasks on time, tasks delayed, contingency planning using critical pathing, plus resources over-utilized, and so forth. Attaching Gantt charts, with milestones and timelines (see Figure 19.3) helps stakeholders see at a glance what is expected. Gantt charts are also helpful for documenting the importance of timing of resources to prevent delaying the effort.

(Continued)

FIGURE 19.3.　Example of Project Management Gantt Chart

D	Task Name	Duration	Start	Finish	January / Jan	February / Feb	March / Mar	April / Apr	May / May	June / Jun	July / Jul
1	**Company Profile**	**6d**	**1/13/99**	**1/20/99**	▰						
2	Group Resumes	6d	1/13/99	1/20/99	▮						
3	Individual Matrices	6d	1/13/99	1/20/99	▮						
4	**Situational Analysis**	**6d**	**1/20/99**	**1/27/99**	▮						
5	**Justification**	**11d**	**1/27/99**	**2/10/99**	▮						
6	**Proposal**	**6d**	**2/10/99**	**2/17/99**		▮					
7	**Design Documents**	**6d**	**2/17/99**	**2/24/99**		▮					
8	**Prerequisite/Testing**	**16d**	**2/24/99**	**3/17/99**			▰				
9	Prerequisite Skills Assessment	16d	2/24/99	3/17/99			▮				
10	Pretest and Post-Test	16d	2/24/99	3/17/99			▮				
11	**Prototypes**	**6d**	**3/17/99**	**3/24/99**			▰				
12	Manual	6d	3/17/99	3/24/99			▮				
13	Job Aid	6d	3/17/99	3/24/99			▮				
14	**Handouts**	**6d**	**3/24/99**	**3/31/99**			▰				
15	Self-Study Materials	6d	3/24/99	3/31/99			▮				
16	Walk-Through Materials	6d	3/24/99	3/31/99			▮				
17	**Evaluation Forms**	**11d**	**3/31/99**	**4/14/99**				▮			
18	**Final Presentations**	**11d**	**3/31/99**	**4/14/99**				▮			

Project: Date: 4/14/99	Task ▬▬▬ Progress ▬▬▬ Milestone ◆	Summary ◤▬▬◥ Rolled Up Task ◤▬▬◥ Rolled Up Milestone ◇	Rolled Up Progress ▬▬▬

Scenarios. Scenarios provide narrative visualizations of the potential of the intervention project and the risks and consequences of not doing the intervention effort. Typically, more than one scenario is presented if more than one plan is appropriate. Benefits and limitations of each scenario are presented.

BUSINESS IMPACTS

For each scenario, highlight the main outcomes and the benefits. It is also important to point out the downsides and risks of each approach. Charts and other graphics may be helpful to illustrate the features of each option.

CONCLUSIONS AND RECOMMENDATIONS

Summarize the main points of the scenarios and options, along with the benefits and consequences of each choice. Recommendations should be concise and describe the optimal intervention scenario, as well as briefly describe the other scenario options.

Citations

1. Veryard, 1999, p. 4
2. Ali, Boulden, Brake, Bruce, Eaton, Holden, Johnson, Langdon, Osborne, Renshaw, Seymour, Shervington, & Tee, 2002, p. 614
3. Veryard, 1999, pp. 3–4
4. Gamble, 2009, p. 1
5. McElyea & Van Tiem, 2008
6. *Business: The Ultimate Resource*, 2002, p. 1195
7. Veryard, 1999, p. 3
8. Leatherman, Berwick, Iles, Lewin, Davidoff, Nolan, & Bisognano, 2003
9. Veryard, 1999, p. 21
10. Gambles, 2007
11. Van Tiem, 2002, p. 2
12. Gambles, 2009, p. 9
13. Gambles, 2009, p. 155
14. Gambles, 2009, p. 31
15. Veryard, 1999, p. 22
16. Finneran, 2007, n.p.
17. Gambles, 2009, p. 27
18. Gambles, 2009, pp. 10–19
19. Veryard, 1999, p. 4
20. Gambles, 2009
21. Gambles, 2009, pp. 20–25
22. Gambles, 2009, p. 4
23. Gambles, 2009, p. 117
24. Gambles, 2009, p. 117
25. Thompson, 2005, p. 185
26. Dekom, 1991, pp. 23–24
27. USAID, 2006
28. Fromartz, 2009, p. 4
29. Fromartz, 2009, p. 41
30. International Society for Performance Improvement, 2011b
31. Gargiulo, Pangarkar, Kirkwood, & Bunzel, 2006
32. International Society for Performance Improvement, 2011a; Watkins, Meiers, & Visser, 2012
33. Doyle, Mansfield, & Van Tiem, 1995; Greer, 1996; Kerzner, 1995; Lewis, 2002
34. Frame, 1987; Knutson & Bitz, 1991

References

Ali, J., Boulden, G., Brake, T., Bruce, A., Eaton, J., Holden, R., Johnson, R., Langdon, K., Osborne, C., Renshaw, B., Seymour, J., Shervington, M., & Tee, R. (2002). *Successful manager's handbook*. London: Dorling Kindersley.

Beish, K. (2011). Using the HPT model to identify and resolve issues for foreign workers in a lean U.S. assembly plant: A case study. Unpublished dissertation. Minneapolis, MN: Capella University.

Business: The ultimate resource. (2002). Cambridge, MA: Perseus Books.

Dekom, A.K. (1991). Systems feasibility: Studying the possibilities. *Journal of Systems Management, 42*(6), 23.

Dessinger, J.C. (2012). Designing performance interventions. White paper #108. St. Clair Shores, MI: The Lake Group.

Doyle, T., Mansfield, A., & Van Tiem, D. (1995). Technical and skills training suppliers. In L. Kelly (Ed.), *The ASTD technical and skills training handbook.* New York: McGraw-Hill.

Finneran, J.F. (2007). Shaky spreadsheets: Making the business case believable. Retrieved from www.gant-thead.com/content/articles/237413.cfm.

Frame, J.D. (1987). *Managing projects in organizations: How to make the best use of time, techniques, and people.* San Francisco: Jossey-Bass.

Fromartz, S. (2009, Fall). The mini cases: 5 companies, 5 strategies, 5 transformations. *MIT Sloan Management Review, 51*(1), 41–45.

Gambles, I. (2009). *Making the business case.* London: Gower.

Gargiulo, T.J., Pangarkar, A., Kirkwood, T., & Bunzel, T. (2006). *Business acumen for trainers: Skills to empower the learning function.* San Francisco: Pfeiffer.

Greer, M. (1996). *The project manager's partner: A step-by-step guide to project management.* Amherst, MA: HRD Press.

International Society for Performance Improvement. (2011a). *Performance improvement standards.* Silver Spring, MD: Author.

International Society for Performance Improvement. (2011b). *10 standards of school improvement.* Silver Spring, MD: Author.

Kelly, S. (2011, February 28). Personal communication.

Kelly, S. (2011, March 6). Personal communication.

Kerzner, H. (1995). *Project management: A systems approach to planning, scheduling, and controlling* (5th ed.). New York: Van Nostrand Reinhold.

Knutson, J., & Bitz, I. (1991). *Project management: How to plan and manage successful projects.* New York: AMACOM.

Leatherman, S., Berwick, D., Iles, D., Lewis, L.S., Davidoff, F., Nolan, T., & Bisognano, M. (2003, March). The business case for quality: Case studies and an analysis. *Health Affairs, 22*(2), 17–30.

Lewis, J.P. (2002). *Fundamentals of project management: Developing core competencies to help outperform the competition* (2nd ed.) New York: AMACOM.

McElyea, J.E., & Van Tiem, D.M. (2008, April). HPT and small business: Gold mine or land mine. *Performance Improvement, 47*(4), 33–38.

Thompson, A. (2005). Business feasibility study outline. In *Entrepreneurship and business innovation: The art or successful business start-ups and business planning.* Retrieved from bestentrepreneur.murdock.au/business_feasibility_study_outline.pdf.

Toenniges, L. (2011, March 12). Personal communication.

USAID. (2006). Strategic plan (2006–2011). Zels: Association of the Units of Local Self-Government of the Republic of Macedonia.

Van Tiem, D.M. (2002). EDT 514 course pack–Application of instructional design. Dearborn, MI: University of Michigan–Dearborn.

Veryard, R. (1999, February 10). Making the business case. Retrieved from www.scipio.org.

Watkins, R., Meiers, M.W., & Visser, Y.L. (2012). *A guide to assessing needs: Essential tools for collecting information, making decisions, and achieving development results.* Washington, DC: The World Bank.

Wyckham, R.G., & Wedley, W.C. (1990). Factors related to venture feasibility analysis and business plan preparation. *Journal of Small Business Management, 28*(4), 48.

Intervention Development

20

The first two editions of *Fundamentals* did not discuss development of the performance intervention as a discrete step in the selection and design phase of the HPT Model. In fact, "there is not always a well-defined distinction between design and development."[1] In addition, very little has been written about development in the PI/HPT literature. This chapter will synthesize the available literature and provide guidelines for developing various types of performance improvement interventions.

Definition and Scope

Definition. *Development* is sometimes used as an umbrella term that includes design and sometimes even implementation. According to Spitzer[2] development is "an extension of design. It prepares the design for implementation." ISPI Performance Standard 8 states that "Development is about the creation of some or all of the elements of the solution. It can be done by an individual or by a team. The output is a product, process, system, or technology."[3]

Whether interventions are selected or designed, in whole or in part, there is a phase when the intervention needs to be developed prior to implementation. Development takes an "off-the-shelf" "performance intervention package or an intervention design document or a combination and does whatever is required to "make it happen." Development translates the intervention selection decisions into a program or product that supports action and change. It literally produces the intervention.

Scope. Rummler and Brache[4] suggest that, taken together, design and development "may include a broad range of actions" and the processes and materials required to support those actions, including "the process that will be used to evaluate the effectiveness of the treatment [interventions]." Whether customizing a purchased or "off-the shelf" team-building program or working from a design document, the performance improvement practitioner as the developer will be faced with a variety of development scenarios.

"Some interventions require extensive development . . . others require very little."[5] Spitzer provides the following examples: a new sales incentive program may only require an announcement containing details for earning the incentive and email follow-ups to encourage participation in the program, while setting up a new manufacturing system may include writing and producing procedures and job aids, setting up a performance measurement system, developing instructor and learner materials for multiple training program, writing and producing communication materials, and so forth.

FIGURE 20.1. Performance Improvement/HPT Model: Intervention Development Component

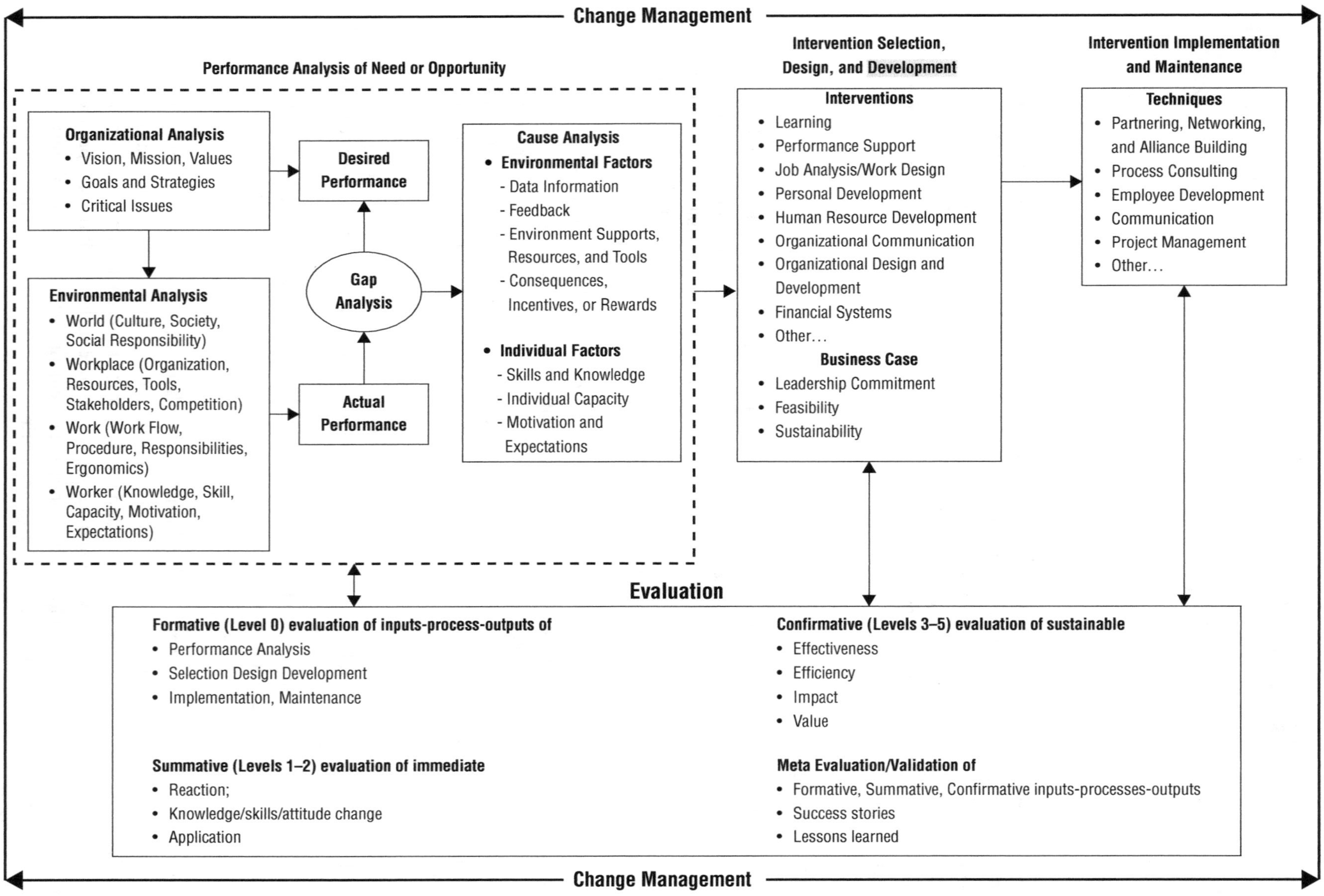

444

The scope of development activities needs to be taken into account when selecting the most appropriate intervention. Developing new interventions "from scratch" is the most resource-consuming process. The resources needed for working with off-the shelf packages vary depending on the degree of change required to make the package fit the solution.

New Intervention Packages. Performance intervention packages that are new to the industry or the organization and cannot rely on off-the-shelf products or programs require the most extensive development. If the intervention is global and targets a wide variety of audiences with different languages and cultures, development can be especially challenging.

Off-the-Shelf Packages. When a large pharmaceutical company decided to reorganize their nationwide sales units into teams, the company selected an off-the-shelf team building program with an accompanying train-the-trainer program so their internal training department staff could facilitate team-building workshops. The company also decided to provide travel incentives to the sales teams who completed the training and met their target sales goals within the twelve months after the training. The company outsourced the administration and distribution of the incentives to an outside company. The internal performance improvement practitioner had minimal involvement; she acted as a liaison between the vendors and the company and worked with the internal training department and sales department to collect data on attendance, training evaluations, and sales performance.

On the other hand, when off-the-shelf interventions require customization of materials or even content to adapt them to the culture of an organization, customization may be done in-house. A management consulting company purchased the same off-the-shelf team training program as the pharmaceutical company; however, their in-house trainer developed the customized material and delivered the training.

Environmental Impact. The extent of development required may also be impacted by environmental issues. Developing a new intervention for a company with a strong corporate culture may require producing all new components or elaborating, building on, customizing, or otherwise changing existing components to meet the needs of the organization or audience. Updating an existing intervention may require the acquisition of new technology or the adaptation of existing technology to implement the intervention. At a minimum, development involves using technology to produce materials that support changes in performance as well as support change management, evaluation, communication, reporting, scheduling, and other activities required for successful implementation and maintenance.

Purpose

Silber[6] states that the purpose of development is to "turn existing specifications for the performance solution into a product." Rummler and Brache[7] look at design and development as an important step in the HPT process and suggest "the objective of this step is to design and develop the recommended changes—treatments—that were specified as part of the analysis step." The development step makes sure that everything is in place—scheduled, organized, supported, and validated—prior to implementation. After the selection and/or design of an intervention, the purpose of development is to produce all the pieces and put them together before implementation.

Timing

From a linear perspective, development activities occur *after* performance analysis, intervention selection and/or design, and acceptance of the business case. Development should also occur just *before* intervention implementation and maintenance. However, in the real world, Spitzer suggests that development **and** implementation activities should be "proactively" considered during the design phase because during design it is "important to consider the feasibility and cost of subsequent phases."[8] Concurrent design and development is also part of the rapid prototyping movement for just-in-time or right-now implementation of performance improvement interventions.

Practitioner Role and Competencies

Development skills are different and broader than design skills. Successful development may require collaboration with graphic designers, computer or video producers, evaluators, statisticians, marketing experts, writers and editors, instructors, work redesign experts, salary or benefits experts, and others with specific skills to produce the various components of an intervention. Project management skills are essential for keeping the development activities on time and within budget. Communication skills are vital for working with a team of development professionals. ISPI Standard 8 (Appendix A) shows the iterative nature of development and the broad skills required of the performance improvement practitioner in the role of intervention developer.

Guidelines for Successful Intervention Development

Development is both an art and a science. It has a creative side and a systematic side. On the one hand, the developer turns a task description into a performance support tool or job aid that separates nice to know from need to know, captures and holds the performer's attention, contains all the need-to-know information required to perform the task, and facilitates rapid on-the-job comprehension. On the other hand, the developer develops the components of an online learning simulation within the strict parameters set by the simulation system.

Developers must be able to stay focused on the objectives and the desired results of the intervention elements as well as the criteria or metrics that will be used to evaluate the elements. They also need to be consistent in the use of terminology and voice, especially when they are developing materials such as posters, training manuals, or business forms. All the materials for the intervention must have the same look and feel so the performance improvement practitioner or lead developer must monitor the development outputs.

Involving subject-matter experts and other stakeholders in the development process is vital and helps to maintain commitment for the upcoming implementation phase. Content experts and expert

FIGURE 20.2.   Intervention Development Process Model

performers can review training materials or supporting documentation for accuracy and/or appeal and provide feedback to the developer before it becomes difficult to incorporate changes. This also gives the experts a sense of ownership and makes them more committed to the intervention's success. The process is shown in Figure 20.2.

Development Process

Development may be conducted by one person or by a team that includes, at the very minimum, the performance improvement practitioner and a production person. Development teams may also include a person for scheduling activities and tracking delivery of the various components of the intervention. Spitzer[9] suggests a five-step development process: (1) select the development team, (2) prepare the development plan, (3) develop and test the prototype, (4) revise the development plan as needed, and (5) produce the final intervention materials. The list of steps that follows builds on Spitzer's five steps and adds steps based on ISPI Standard 8 and experience in the field. The steps also assume that a design document was completed during the design phase which includes a detailed development plan:

1. Prepare:
   a. Gather the development plan in the design document, off-the-shelf product documentation, and standards or other requirements that will guide the development process;
   b. Select the development team—unless this was done earlier during design;
   c. Review the development plan with the team;
   d. Review the purchased intervention program or products or the intervention design blueprint;
   e. Review the goals and objectives of the intervention;
   f. Review what needs to be developed to implement, maintain, and evaluate the intervention;
   g. Review or plan the resource requirements for development; and
   h. Sequence and organize the intervention delivery activities and materials for maximum effectiveness.

2. Freeze the design document; no changes until the first draft is completed and reviewed.

3. Develop:

    a. Draft the processes and materials required to support the implementation of the intervention and

    b. Revise the materials as needed.

4. Test:

    a. Validate drafts with content or performance experts;

    b. Test the intervention components with a "typical" audience, stakeholders, and/or other designers or developers;

    c. Make revisions as needed; and

    d. Initiate review-revise-approve cycle as needed.

5. Produce the complete performance improvement intervention package.

Throughout the development process, the developer should conduct formative evaluations of the process and the products and make adjustments based on the results. During the pilot, the developer can also conduct an initial summative evaluation of the participants' immediate reactions and observed or perceived changes in knowledge, skills, or attitude (see Chapters 23 and 24 on Evaluation).

Feasibility, Sustainability, Change Management

During the development phase, the developer should ensure that the development activities maintain the feasibility and sustainability standards established in the business case (see Chapter 19). For example, changes in resource requirements to develop computer-based materials may increase the original cost estimate or expand the timelines and require verification from a decision-maker.

The developer should also pay special attention to creating the processes and materials related to the sustainability and change management strategies that are designed into a long-term intervention. This will ensure that the intervention can be maintained and remain successful over its intended life cycle.

Conclusion

Intervention development is all about transformation—about turning a performance improvement intervention *design* into a real-life *intervention*. The development team, and it usually does take a team, creates whatever elements and components are needed to implement the performance improvement intervention and accomplish the desire results. The first step in the development process—Prepare—lays the foundation for a successful development phase. Performance Support Tool 20.1 helps the performance improvement practitioner and the development team document the results they achieve during Step 1.

PERFORMANCE SUPPORT TOOL 20.1. OUTPUTS MATRIX FOR STEP 1: PREPARE FOR DEVELOPMENT

Directions: Use this matrix to record the outputs of the Prepare step. Use a separate outputs matrix for *each* design element of the intervention.

Design Element: _____

_____

What component(s) need to be developed to implement this element?

_____

Are there any special requirements, standards, or constraints to development of this element?

_____

What design document sections support development of this element?

_____

If this is a purchased element, what user support is available? (Documentation? Technician? Training? Other?)

_____

Who has the knowledge and/or skill to help develop the components of this element?

_____

Who can provide leadership support for this element of the intervention?

_____

What production tools or other resources are required to develop the intervention process and materials?

_____

What are the timelines? Milestones? (Prepare a separate Gantt chart or spreadsheet.)

_____

What is the budget for developing this element?

_____

What is the communication plan for the development phase of this element? (Scheduled status reports? "Yellow flag" notices for potential time or cost overages? Other?)

_____

Other:

Source: J.C. Dessinger (2011). Preparing for development. White paper #109. Used with permission.

Citations

1. Spitzer, 1999, p. 180
2. Spitzer, 1999, p. 164
3. *ISPI Standards*, 2011, p. 25
4. Rummler & Brache, 1992, p. 44
5. Spitzer, 1999, p. 181
6. Silber, 1992, p. 62
7. Rummler & Brache, 1992, p. 44
8. Spitzer, 1999, p. 180
9. Spitzer, 1999, pp. 181–182.

References

ISPI standards. (2011). www.ispi.org.

Rummler, G.A., & Brache, A.P. (1992). Transforming organizations through human performance technology. In H.D. Stolovitch & E.J. Keeps (Eds.), *Handbook of human performance technology: A comprehensive guide for analyzing and solving performance problems in organizations* (1st ed.) (pp. 32–49). San Francisco: Jossey-Bass/ISPI.

Silber, K.H. (1992). Intervening at different levels in organizations. In H.D. Stolovitch & E.J. Keeps (Eds.), *Handbook of human performance technology: A comprehensive guide for analyzing and solving performance problems in organizations* (1st ed.) (pp. 50–65). San Francisco: Jossey-Bass/ISPI.

Spitzer, D. (1999). The design and development of high impact interventions. In H.D. Stolovitch & E.J. Keeps (Eds.), *Handbook of human performance technology: Improving individual and organizational performance worldwide* (2nd ed.) (pp. 163–184). San Francisco: Pfeiffer/ISPI.

No Room for Error: Saving a Multi-Office Dental Practice in Michigan

Topic: *Business Case*

Jeffrey E. McElyea, M.S., M.A., *President and Lead Consultant, Lucid Business Strategies, Shelby Township, Michigan, USA*

Background

A Michigan dentist built a very successful practice over a period of twenty-five years. As the practice became larger, the owner decided that he no longer wanted to practice dentistry full-time, but would rather hire associate doctors to fill his current role. The dentist would change his focus to purchasing under-performing practices and turning them into high-profit offices.

The client dentist located a practice that had been in operation fifteen years. Despite a very desirable location, solid patient base, and capable staff, the practice had been declining in production (sales) over the previous five years. After a brief negotiation, the dentist successfully purchased the practice.

Critical Business Issue

After the purchase, the dentists asked the office manager and two key personnel from the first practice to work temporarily at the new office to implement their systems and to reverse the trend of declining production. Six months later production and operations at the new practice stabilized, but did not grow. The original practice began loaning cash to the new practice to help pay vendors and to make the loan payments to the bank for the purchase of the practice.

During the time the personnel worked at the new office, problems developed at the original practice. Patients began leaving the practice, causing a significant decline in cash flow. This, combined with the money that was loaned to the new practice, began to cause the original practice to struggle to meet payroll and pay their vendors.

In an effort to keep both practices financially viable, the dentist used all of his personal cash reserves and began taking out lines of credit until lenders would not extend any further credit. This doctor, who had worked his entire career to build a successful practice and position himself for a comfortable retirement, was now in a position of impending insolvency.

Building the Initial Business Case

The client's original request was to "conduct a marketing campaign to attract new patients for both practices." We needed to convince the dentist that conducting a performance analysis would be a better starting point than a marketing campaign; putting the solution first would not address the larger issues of why patients were leaving, why the financial condition of both practices was deteriorating, and why the original practice began declining so rapidly after the acquisition of the second practice.

The consulting team began building a business case to demonstrate our point. We decided that we should build a business case for only the performance analysis, instead of a full performance improvement project, since it would be easier to gain buy-in for this instead of trying to convince the clients to completely abandon their preferred intervention, the marketing campaign.

We began building the case by identifying the points that were important to the dentist and increase our chances of obtaining his buy-in. The points we agreed to make were:

1. To shift the dentist's focus off marketing by pointing out that his real objective was to improve the business situation.
2. To clearly explain what a performance analysis is and what would be involved.
3. To emphasize that it was very important to be certain that the solutions would improve the business situation, and the only way to determine what was truly causing the challenges was a performance analysis.
4. That conducting a performance analysis would save money.
5. The performance analysis would be done quickly so that we could begin correcting the business problems as soon as possible.
6. The performance analysis would actually support his marketing campaign if marketing was the solution.

The consulting team assembled data from the practice's financial statements, practice management software, and from similar projects the team had worked on in the past. We analyzed the data, prepared the business case presentation, and set an appointment to present the case to the dentist and the office manager.

The Presentation

The team decided that a case that was based on data had the best chance of convincing the dentist and office manager that performance analysis was the best approach. We decided that we would:

1. Present the data and lead the client through interpreting it, instead of presenting our opinions. In this way we would be collaborators rather than salespeople.
2. Be certain to not say that a marketing campaign was wrong, as we had no data to support that statement, and we might alienate the client.
3. Relate everything to the client's ultimate goal of improving the business situation.

We began our presentation by asking the dentist and office manager to identify their biggest concerns. They quickly identified cash flow, loss of patients, decline in production, and lack of new patients. Then we asked what turned out to be the most important question in our entire engagement: "What happens if these challenges are not corrected quickly?" The response was: "We're out of business!"

From this point forward, our presentation focused entirely on making sure we correctly identified causes and implemented solutions in the most expedient and cost-effective way possible. We demonstrated what the cost of a marketing campaign would likely be and asked, "How confident are you that a marketing campaign will correct all of your issues?" They answered, "We hope that it will be successful in bringing in new patients, and that will correct our cash flow issues." We pointed out that, even if that were true, it would not correct the long-term situation, as it would not address the problem of losing patients.

Next, we demonstrated how much the current problems had cost them. The challenges were costing the practice a *minimum* of $800,000 each year; the actual cost was more in opportunity costs because each practice should be growing each year. The dentist and office manager were unaware of this fact. This opened the door for us to present the concept of conducting a performance analysis.

We explained what a performance analysis was, and why we recommended it. We emphasized that we would analyze every facet of both practices and provide conclusive evidence to them about what was causing their performance challenges. From there, we would work with them to decide the best courses of action. We explained that we could complete this analysis in less than thirty days. The dentist and office manager quickly agreed.

Focus on Results

Since small business owners are typically very results-oriented, we decided to not only identify the problems but also to create the performance goals. We agreed on and wrote specific goals for each of the following:

1. Identify the causes of the cash flow challenges.
2. Reduce the loss of patients.

3. Identify and eliminate the internal or non-marketing barriers to growth at both practices.
4. Increase the number of new patients.

Given the gravity of the situation, it was imperative that the consulting team be as comprehensive as possible in analyzing the situation. They began with an extensive review of daily schedules, scheduling trends, billing records and processes, patient attrition, accounts receivable, profit and loss statements, and other such data. This was followed by structured interviews of every staff member of both practices. Patient satisfaction surveys were conducted, and interviews were conducted with new patients, current patients, and former patients.

Focus on Systems View

As important as it was to evaluate each individual practice, it was equally important to evaluate the impact of adding the second practice and the impact of the combining the challenges from both practices. The consulting team conducted a second round of interviews with staff members to understand the impact of the office manager covering both offices. They also evaluated data to understand the differences in how each practice performed when the office manager was at that location instead of the other. The key performance challenges were that:

1. The division of the office manager's time between practices made it nearly impossible to devote sufficient time to managing the key performance drivers of either practice. Each practice performed better on days that the office manager was at that location.
2. The office manager used to oversee the billing at the original office. When her time was divided between offices, these duties were delegated to other persons. These individuals did not have the knowledge to perform these duties and did not want to do them. Consequently, billing fell behind, collection calls were not made, the amount of accounts receivable more than doubled within sixty days. This almost stopped the flow of cash coming into both practices.
3. The way in which patient records were entered into the practice management software made it extremely difficult to identify which patients were past due for treatment so staff could not contact those patients to fill the dentists' schedules.
4. Front desk personnel perceived that the economy made patients postpone treatment so they allowed the patients to leave the office without making their next appointments. This information was not entered into the practice management software, so there was no effective way to contact these patients to schedule their next appointments.
5. Front desk personnel began creating payment plans for treatment to help patients afford treatment. Approximately 25 percent of these patients did not make the agreed-on payments.
6. As production began dropping, management stepped up pressure on the staff to turn the situation around and fill the schedule. This caused the staff to over-schedule their day, which caused the staff to run behind so appointments took two to three times longer than patients had anticipated. This caused patients to refuse to schedule their next appointments. Records indicated that both practices had more than doubled the attrition rate.
7. As cash flow became tighter, both practices stopped all external marketing efforts in an effort to conserve cash. This almost completely stopped the flow of new patients.

8. When patients needed major treatment, they needed help having the procedures explained to them and navigating insurance, financial arrangements, and scheduling. The staff was unable to do this, as they were extremely busy answering phones and checking patients in and out. This meant that many patients left the practice without this treatment being scheduled.

Interventions

The consulting team presented the findings from the analysis. The clients agreed with the findings, especially since they were involved in conducting the analysis. The consulting team then brainstormed interventions that we collectively agreed could solve the business issues and achieve our performance goals. These interventions were to:

1. Assemble a triage team to address billing and collections, record treatment plans in the practice management software, and recall patients who were due for treatment.
2. Hire an office manager for the second practice.
3. Hire a dedicated billing and collections person and centralize billing for both offices.
4. Identify and train a specific person in each office to present treatment to patients, and gain their commitment to proceed with the doctor's recommendations.
5. Implement a daily scheduling template to maximize production and ensure that all patient appointments would start and end on time.
6. Locate external sources of financing for patients so that we could eliminate internal payment plans.
7. Develop and post a daily performance dashboard in an employee area to show the number of patients who left without appointments, amount of refused treatment, and so forth. Use these metrics in daily pre-shift meetings to understand the causes and to train the staff in methods of handling these situations.
8. Develop incentive programs for both staff and patients to reward referrals to new patients.
9. Design a "new patient experience" program to ensure each practice far exceeds the expectations of the patients.
10. Implement an extensive training program to script and standardize every facet of patient care and administrative procedures.
11. Implement an Internet marketing strategy for new patients only after all other interventions are successfully implemented.

The dentist and office manager were in agreement that each of these interventions was needed; however, they were hesitant to proceed with any of them until they knew more information about cost and impact. As is often the case, we needed to build a second business case to prove the value of the interventions.

The Second Business Case—Feasibility

The consulting team began building the business case by identifying the costs associated with implementing each intervention. The cost of implementing all of the interventions was estimated to be $150,000. Our challenge now became to build a case that would convince the client that he could afford $150,000, and that it was a wise investment. It was time to collaborate with him once again.

We met with the dentist and office manager to reveal the costs associated with each intervention and work with them to structure a way to afford this expense. We did this by:

1. Showing that the interventions would be implemented over time, so the cost could be spread out over a period of several months.
2. Prioritizing which interventions would have the greatest financial impact at the lowest cost. We would use the financial gains from these interventions to invest in the future ones.
3. Promising to track the results of every intervention versus cost to determine an ROI for each, and to refine interventions that were not producing as expected.

The clients were still apprehensive, but were comforted by spreading out the implementation time-frame. They also felt comfortable knowing that we were evaluating every intervention and would not be spending money that did not show a positive ROI. They approved the interventions pending the results of the first implementation—assembling a triage team.

Designing the Interventions

The success of interventions was dependent upon the acceptance and buy-in of the staff members at each practice. Sustained success was dependent on the staff members seeing the interventions as being led by the dentist and office manager instead of the consultant team. The consultant team coached the clients on identifying a team of exemplary performers from both practices to work side-by-side with the dentist, the office manager, and consultants and to lead the team through the process of implementing the interventions in their respective practice and creating solutions to any obstacles. A project plan was created to identify the steps, resources, and support material that would be required to develop each intervention.

Developing the Interventions—Sustainability

The same team that was involved in the design of the interventions worked to develop them. The team met once a week with the dentist and office manager to review the progress each had made, resolve issues, and provide input to each intervention. To ensure buy-in, the development team members were encouraged to discuss their intervention with other members of the team and to obtain their input. By the time the interventions were fully developed, every person in each practice was fully aware of the changes that were coming and had been involved in helping bring the interventions to life.

Implementing the Interventions

The interventions were implemented in phases. The first intervention implemented was the triage team. This team was comprised of exemplary performers from each practice and focused entirely on cash-generating activities. This intervention cost little to implement, as it was performed by the existing staff. This intervention was extremely successful—more than $20,000 in receivables that were previously thought uncollectable were collected, and more than one hundred appointments were made with patients who had unscheduled treatment. The practices now had the cash to move ahead with other interventions.

The remaining interventions were implemented by the staff themselves. The managers, dentist, and consultants conducted a staff meeting to introduce each intervention. This was followed by daily fifteen-minute meetings to evaluate the prior day's success and brainstorm solutions to any challenges that occurred. These meetings continued until the intervention was fully in place and became normal operating procedure.

Evaluating Results

Given the urgency of this engagement, it was critical to evaluate results literally on a daily basis to determine whether the cost of the intervention exceeded the results. Every intervention had its own evaluation metric and method for measuring that metric. Each metric was analyzed daily. If the daily performance was less than our goal, the teams evaluated what caused the under-performance and decided whether an adjustment was needed or not. If an adjustment was required, it was done that day and introduced in the following day's morning meeting. The teams also studied any unusually positive performance to decide whether something had occurred that we should take advantage of and implement as part of our systems.

The final results of this engagement were overwhelmingly positive:

1. Both practices were cash flow neutral in sixty days or less and had positive cash flow in less than six months.
2. During the first twelve months, production in the new practice doubled and production in the second practice increased by 20 percent.
3. The new practice averaged thirty-five new patients per month within six months; the existing practice averaged thirty new patients per month within twelve months.
4. Patient attrition for the twelve months following implementation was less than 10 percent at both practices.

It is important to evaluate not only results versus goals, but also the cost of the interventions versus the benefit gained. This project brought a return on investment of 6:1 in the first year of implementation.

■　■　■

Lessons Learned from the Case
- A business case is an essential component of any performance improvement project—creating buy-in and demonstrating the feasibility of the proposed interventions.
- More than one business case may be required. It is an iterative process—the first business case achieves sufficient buy-in to start a project, but another may be required to continue the project.

- Having the stakeholders implement interventions with consultant guidance greatly enhances the sustainability of the results achieved.
- The business case demonstrates both projected and actual results and builds the credibility of the consulting team for future projects!

Jeff McElyea, M.S., M.A., is the president and lead consultant of Lucid Business Strategies, a management consulting firm that applies the principles of performance improvement to help small business owners build successful enterprises. McElyea received his master's degree with high distinction in performance improvement and instructional design from the University of Michigan, Dearborn. He also received his master's degree in integrated marketing communications from Eastern Michigan University. He earned the Human Performance Improvement (HPI) certificate from ASTD. McElyea is the past-president of the Michigan Chapter of ISPI and a past board member of the Greater Detroit ASTD. He has published articles in *Performance Improvement Journal* and *ASTD Links* and frequently contributes to business publications in southeastern Michigan. He may be reached at jmcelyea@lucidbusiness.com.

Acquisition of Westford Bank by Spring Harbor Bank

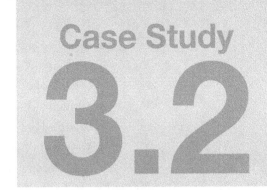

Topic: *Design-Development*

Alicia Stephens, M.Ed., *Training and Communications Manager of a Michigan Commercial Bank, USA*

Background

Spring Harbor Bank is a domestic financial institution with a focus in commercial banking services. The company, headquartered in Detroit, Michigan, has a strong footprint in Michigan, Ohio, and northern Indiana. It employs approximately seven thousand associates and holds over $40 billion in assets. The company's competitive advantage lies within its ability to offer custom financial solutions, enabling it to compete with significantly larger institutions. The leadership manages its expenses by balancing the maintenance of these custom solutions with the economies of scale needed to achieve operational efficiency benchmarks.

Situation

In an effort to diversify the company's loan portfolio, Spring Harbor purchased Westford Bank, a small commercial institution headquartered in Atlanta, Georgia. This purchase (1) increased the geographic distribution of their customer base and (2) provided access to banking technology that would be a benefit to Spring Harbor's existing employees.

In the last three years, Westford had experienced severe employee turnover due to a significant percentage of their workforce entering retirement. As a result, the company had a relatively inexperienced sales force that struggled with their performance.

As a part of the due diligence process prior to the acquisition, Spring Harbor's and Westford's senior management teams made the following observations:

- Westford had a strong sales prospecting system. When interviewed, both seasoned and new employees attributed the system for identifying strong cross-sale leads. Despite lagging overall sales, their cross-sale ratios were best in class for a bank of their asset size.
- Spring Harbor's sales prospecting tool was antiquated compared to the Westford technology.
- Westford did not have a strong sales training program.
- Spring Harbor's sales training program was more developed than Westford's, but was in need of refreshing to make it more applicable to the current sales environment.

Critical Business Issue

What Was

After the acquisition was complete, Spring Harbor had two sets of employees with different sales philosophies. The Westford sales process was ineffective for its inexperienced sales force and conflicted with Spring Harbor's lending strategy.

Spring Harbor's original employee base had strong sales, but lacked the data to execute strong cross-sales. In addition to these challenges, the company was carrying the cost of maintaining two different sales prospecting systems.

What Should Have Been

Spring Harbor should have had a sales process that met the strategic goals of the company and created a support network for sales staff. Additionally, the company should have been on a single sales prospecting system, enabling them to operate within industry standard benchmarks for technology costs.

Focus on Outcomes or Results

Spring Harbor's consolidated senior management team set out to project the financial impact of their desired end state:

- Increased sales of the Westford associates by 5 percent over the next six quarters.
- Increased cross-sale ratios of the original Spring Harbor associates by 7 percent over the same time period.
- Decreased technology costs of $1.7 million per year by eliminating one of the sales prospecting systems and implementing the surviving system company-wide.

The senior management team believed that this could be accomplished by creating a new sales training program that fit the needs of Spring Harbor's joint team. They also planned to train all applicable employees on the legacy Westford sales prospecting system. This would provide Spring Harbor the data needed to improve its cross-sale ratios.

In order to ensure that these action items were appropriate, the senior management team set out to *validate them using a systematic approach*. They wanted to ensure that training and the expansion of the Westford system would actually bridge the performance gap. An incorrect assumption at this stage in the process could prove detrimental to the success of the initiative.

Focus on Systems View

Inputs. The management team actively solicited feedback from the impacted employees and managers from both organizations. It was important to involve not only the sales force, but also the associates who would be key to a successful *technical* system implementation.

The feedback was collected by an electronic survey and by small group sessions conducted via webcast. Both collection methods focused on gathering data points regarding how the employees felt about the approach selected to achieve the desired outcomes and what they believed would ensure the initiative's success.

Process. After the data were collected, the results were analyzed by the senior management team. A small number of Spring Harbor and Westford employees representing all markets and lines of businesses were included in the exercise to maintain objectivity.

Outputs. The output of this exercise was a document that summarized the findings and included the highlights below:

- Spring Harbor associates had mixed feelings regarding the adoption of a new sales prospecting system. Forty percent had moderate to very positive feelings regarding the proposed implementation. The balance of the associates had varying levels of concern regarding their ability to learn the new system.
- Westford associates had a strong interest in adopting a new sales training program and process, but were concerned that Spring Harbor management would not adequately support it.
- Employees from both organizations believed that having onsite support during this transition period would help to alleviate anxiety.

Constraints. The senior management team recognized that a major constraint of this initiative would be the diffusion and adoption of the changes to come. Additionally, implementing an onsite support strategy for every impacted location would be cost-prohibitive based on the footprint of the combined company.

Focus on Value

The senior management team determined that this initiative required strong marketing to help generate employee and managerial support for the plan. The team produced a brief recorded presentation that focused on (1) increasing awareness of the desired end-state and (2) highlighting the value that it would add at an organizational level and employee level. Spring Harbor associates would have access to a state-of-the-art sales prospecting system that would help them to increase their cross-sell ratios; Westford associates would have a new sales model that provided strong support to boost their overall sales.

The presentation also explained that a project team would be assembled to manage this process. This marketing piece was distributed to all impacted employees and was well received.

Focus on Establishing Partnerships

In order to make sure the appropriate stakeholders were brought to the table, the senior management team nominated two associates, one from Spring Harbor and one from Westford, to act as executive project sponsors. Next, a project team was assembled. This team would include members of HR, training, communications, technical support, and sales employees and managers from both banks. This group was carefully selected to ensure that the interests of all lines of businesses were represented.

Be Systematic in the Assessment of the Need, Opportunity, or Challenge

The project team understood that simply completing research to vet out the *organizational* impact of the action items was not enough; the *workplace environment* needed to be analyzed as well. This analysis would consider the impact of the changes to the individual workers, department policies and procedures, as well as how the sales trends would be reported to internal stakeholders and external stockholders.

Armed with this information, the project team believed that they could design a plan that would successfully close the performance gap. They scheduled a series of brainstorming sessions to look at this process from various points of view.

Be Systematic in the Analysis of Work, Worker, Workplace, and World View

The output of the brainstorming sessions provided the project team a more holistic view of the initiative:

- *Worker Level*—It would be key that each affected associate (1) understood how the new sales process and system implementation would change his or her everyday work and (2) directly benefit from changes.
- *Work Level*—Managers and supervisors involvement would be needed to make required adjustments in departmental policies and procedures.
- *Workplace Level*—HR and training managers should be engaged to support the learning and change management process; technical expertise should be leveraged to ensure the company's infrastructure would be appropriately supported.
- *Worldview Level*—Spring Harbor's leadership encouraged innovative solutions that reflected the integrity of the company, as well as their commitment to "greener" business operations. The design of the program would have to take this into consideration as well.

Be Systematic in the Design of the Solution

After analyzing the data, the project team set out to design a program that would meet the educational needs identified, provide the associates the appropriate tools to perform their jobs, and leverage technology. These performance interventions would also attempt to minimize the amount of travel and paper consumed in support of the company's "green" strategic vision.

The new sales process would combine the best practices from the Spring Harbor program with an added coaching component to support new sales associates. The initial training would be delivered via webcast to accommodate the geographic distribution of the attendees. Each manager would be required to join his or her new associates on a series of sales calls.

After these calls, the pair would use a provided checklist to help rate the success of the client interactions and to focus on areas of improvement. The program also would include quarterly educational webcasts on sales-related topics, such as product training.

The sales prospecting system training would be delivered online. This self-paced program would include interactive simulations and feedback to boost knowledge transfer. Once the Spring Harbor associates became competent on this platform, they would have access to the information needed to improve their cross-sell ratios.

An email help line would be available to field system questions. Also, system SMEs from Westford would host quarterly calls to share best practices regarding the system. Frequently asked questions (FAQs) from the email help line would also be included as agenda topics during these events.

The project team included critical information in the design plan, such as the development timeline, required resources, technical considerations, and who would approve each item. The team also obtained signoff from the project sponsors before development began.

Be Systematic in the Development of the Solution

Once the design of the program was approved, the project team was able to manage the development of the deliverables. By scheduling frequent review sessions of the products, the internal developers, project team, and sponsors felt well-informed and were able to quickly resolve differences of opinion. By using pre-established corporate templates for the online training and program checklists, the development timeline was shortened without detracting from the quality of the product.

Be Systematic in the Implementation of the Solution

Due to the high impact of this initiative, the project team believed that it was critical to pilot this program. The project team wanted to assess the practicality and effectiveness of the program deliverables. It was very important that the pilot group be reflective of the diversity of the organization. Without this diversity, the team might miss critical data points in the feedback.

The pilot lasted for one quarter. This exercise revealed key action items that better positioned Spring Harbor to achieve its goals. Adjustments were made to the usability of the online course and to the contents of the coaching checklists.

Be Systematic in the Evaluation of the Process and the Results

Early in the process, the project team understood that this initiative contained action items that had both short-term and long-term impact. Checkpoints conducted via small group session were established to analyze the following points of interest:

- The effectiveness of the sales training and the system training from a qualitative and quantitative perspective
- The quality of the coaching program, email help line, and quarterly webcast sessions

Data points from managers and end-users were collected monthly during the three-month pilot. The results were reported to the senior management team and project sponsors. Using this information, the project team created a list of revisions to make to the program prior to the company-wide rollout.

Once the program was implemented company-wide, data points were collected and reported quarterly to the appropriate stakeholders. This information was tracked carefully to ensure that the goals of the program were being achieved. In addition, the project team also documented important lessons learned and laid out a strategy to periodically evaluate the programs value in the future.

Spring Harbor was pleased with the outcome of this initiative, as it positively influenced performance.

■   ■   ■

Lessons Learned from the Case
- Invest the time to understand the diverse needs of your stakeholders. If you can clearly document their goals, concerns, and motivations, then you will be better equipped to meet and/or exceed their performance improvement expectations.
- If performance interventions are selected before an appropriate analysis of the situation has been completed, validate that those methods will actually close the performance gap before moving forward.
- Diffusion and adoption of major changes can be a challenge. Level set the expectations of your stakeholders early in the process. Investing time in the up-front planning process will yield positive returns later.

Alicia R. Stephens, M.Ed., is a training and communications manager for a domestic commercial bank. She has an interest in corporate education programs that support process and system training. You may contact Alicia at Alicia_R_Stephens@yahoo.com.

Exhibit

3.1

Information Technology Company Aligns Workforce to Business Strategy and Direction

Bill Tarnacki II, M.Ed., M.B.A., MHCS *Director, Talent Management and Corporate Human Resources, Pulte Group, Inc., Bloomfield Hills, Michigan, USA*

Talent management refers to integrated strategies to increase workforce productivity and growth through having the right people with the right skills, behaviors and aptitudes meet current and future business needs . . . talent alignment drives your strategy around talent acquisition, talent assessment, talent identification, and talent development. You can't have an engaged workforce without talent management.

Situation

ProQuest, an information technology company located in Ann Arbor, Michigan, focuses on aggregated information publishing and research support. ProQuest's beginnings date back to its founding in 1938 as a pioneer in microfilm. Today, ProQuest creates specialized information resources and technologies that support researchers around the world.

Early in 2007, ProQuest Company sold its largest business unit, ProQuest Information and Learning, to Cambridge Information Group (CIG). CIG's focus for the remainder of 2007 was the integration of ProQuest Information and Learning and Cambridge Scientific Abstracts (CSA), which was previously a competitor, under the Cambridge Information Group umbrella. 2008 kicked off with much of the tactical integration work complete, and the organization turned its attention to aligning the workforce to the overall business strategy and direction.

Cambridge Information Group was intent on growing ProQuest and, more generally, that part of the business that focused on facilitating and supporting research activities around the world, both organically and through further acquisitions. In order to do so, CIG leadership recognized the importance of having a talent strategy for the organization and the need to invest in the execution of that talent strategy.

Talent Management Intervention

As the new, consolidated ProQuest embarked on its talent management effort, it quickly became apparent that the organization would have to assess the similarities and differences between the standard talent management processes (performance management, compensation planning, recruiting, and so on) that had been employed by CSA compared to those employed by ProQuest Information and Learning.

The HR team gathered feedback from various members of leadership as well as from the different field locations and then collaborated on addressing the primary issues to ensure standardization of practices and accountability at all levels for the talent imperative. Three issues in particular were identified as core to successfully moving forward with the talent management agenda:

- The organization lacked alignment on what talent management meant and who was ultimately accountable.
- There was confusion and inconsistency around how employee performance was measured and evaluated.
- There were data integrity and reporting issues hindering leaders' abilities to determine and execute basic talent management processes.

Dialogue. The leadership team recognized that problems existed and engaged the HR team. Each senior leader provided input for addressing the issues in the context of ensuring a competent, informed, and agile workforce for the future. The HR team then formulated a plan for addressing the issues, focusing on three specific goals: (1) align the talent strategy with the business strategy; (2) ensure accountability for performance and development; and (3) improve data integrity and availability to enhance consistency, speed, and quality of people decisions.

Alignment. Accomplishment of these goals required ongoing dialogue between the HR team and the senior leadership of the organization, as well as confirmation and calibration activities with the broader organizational population to avoid introducing something that was too high level and overly complicated. Through their analysis, HR determined that alignment, or lack thereof, was at the root of the problem because the organization had just been formed and minimal work had been done to establish a unified talent culture among the various business units.

The first order of business was to create a model and elicit buy-in, particularly among the senior leadership, for definition and a philosophy supporting talent management. After several iterations, the exercise yielded a workable definition, philosophy and principles of talent management in the organization. From there a model was developed (Figure 1), which was intended to show the key elements of talent management and the continuous and interrelated nature of

EXHIBIT 3.1. INFORMATION TECHNOLOGY COMPANY ALIGNS WORKFORCE   467

EXHIBIT 3.1. FIGURE 1.   ProQuest Talent Management Model

Copyright William Tarnacki II. Used with permission.

those elements. It provided a simple picture of what talent management encompasses and was supplemented with materials that explained each element in detail, from a process and activity perspective, so that every employee could understand his or her role in executing the model in day-to-day operations.

ProQuest defined talent management as "integrated strategies to increase workforce productivity and growth through having the right people with the right skills, behaviors and aptitudes meet current and future business needs." They established the accountability parameters shown in the following table.

EXHIBIT 3.1. TABLE 1.   ProQuest Accountability Parameters: Philosophy and Principles

Philosophy	Principles
• Strong talent management is at the core of executing the growth and innovation strategy of the business • The organizational culture promotes creativity and risk awareness • Development of key talent starts with challenging stretch assignments • Metrics and measurement define success • Reward systems are structured to differentiate based on level of performance and the behaviors demonstrated to achieve results	• People are responsible for their own development • Senior leadership is responsible for recognizing talent and providing opportunities for development • HR helps to facilitate the talent management process • Organizational leaders must always be searching for new talent • Hiring managers should seek to fill roles with individuals who have potential beyond that role

Copyright William Tarnacki II. Used with permission.

Finally, ProQuest defined the elements of the talent management model in terms of the core activities associated with each one, as shown in the next table.

EXHIBIT 3.1. TABLE 2. Elements of Talent Management: Details

Alignment	Acquisition	Assessment	Identification	Development
• Communications Plan and Strategy Cascading	• Talent Gap Assessment	• Metrics and Reporting	• Competency Planning	• Critical Jobs and Performance Feedback
• Operations Planning	• Market Trend Analysis	• Individual Objectives and Competency Ratings	• Career Ladders and Position Profiles	• Gap Assessment— Strengths and Weaknesses Identification
• Organization Design and Workforce Planning	• Branding and Sourcing	• Calibration	• Pipeline Review	• Coaching and Mentoring
• Change Management Strategy	• Internal Rotations	• Profile and Leadership Assessment	• Succession Planning	• Skills and Competency Training
• Goal Creation and Cascading	• College Graduate Programs	• 360 Evaluation	• Potential Assessment	• Leadership Development
• Reward and Retention Strategy	• Internships and Co-ops	• Compensation Planning	• Talent Ranking and Matrix	• Special Projects and Assignments
• On-Boarding and Orientation	• Interviewing and Selection	• Monthly, Quarterly, and Annual Progress Checks	• Calibration	

Copyright William Tarnacki II. Used with permission.

Talent Assessment. With the "launch" of the common talent management platform accomplished and clear alignment of the talent management program linked to the business model and strategy, the HR team focused its attention on the talent assessment element and, specifically, what personal success looked like in the context of organizational success. The business leadership was responsible for identifying the business priorities for any given year during the strategic planning process, but there was not a consistent translation of those business priorities to individual accountabilities across the business. Additionally, development planning and management were hindered by the organization's multiple competency models and differing definitions of competencies for various groups of employees.

As a result of the merger of various business units into a single structure, there were multiple processes being employed to evaluate and differentiate performance. Within the ProQuest Information and Learning business unit itself, there was misalignment between the performance management process and the pay for performance philosophy, creating confusion and inconsistencies in how performance was planned and assessed. To address this issue, the HR team revamped the process to standardize how performance objectives were aligned, cascaded, and finalized and introduced a common set of behavioral competencies for individual contributors and leaders (the two "categories" of employees based solely on whether they formally had people reporting to them or not) that aligned to the organizational values and competencies.

A standard performance management calendar was established to ensure consistent and timely planning and feedback, and expectations were made clear through a balanced weighting between the performance objectives (what people accomplished) and the behavioral competencies (how

EXHIBIT 3.1. INFORMATION TECHNOLOGY COMPANY ALIGNS WORKFORCE   **469**

people accomplished their goals). In defining the "how" with respect to the behavioral competencies, a tiered definition structure was put in place to help individuals understand how each competency related to the newly defined career path for individual contributors and leaders and how expectations grew along the hierarchical continuum.

Ultimately, the new framework and process were designed to achieve three primary outcomes from the performance management process: (1) all employees were provided goals that aligned their focus and efforts to the overall success of ProQuest; (2) development planning that was robust and two-dimensionally focused on excellence in role and preparation for future roles; (3) consistency in how employees were evaluated and rated to promote a pay for performance culture, where pay was differentiated based on assessed level of performance and behavioral competence. Figures 2, 3, and 4 show the organizational competency model and the alternative career paths for individual contributors and leaders along with the associated definition for each level.

EXHIBIT 3.1. FIGURE 2.   ProQuest Organizational Competency Model

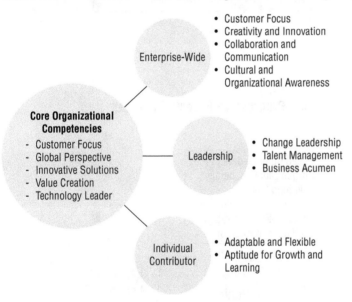

Education and Communication Intervention

In order to effectively introduce the new organizational talent management model and restructure the process and framework for the performance management process, a great deal of time and energy were invested in education and communication to the global workforce. Materials were developed internally to allow for in-person and web-based delivery, presented to senior leadership for buy-in, and then "tested" with small focus groups from across the business to ensure both the materials and the concepts themselves were clear and comprehensible. Once all the input was incorporated and leadership signed off, everything was launched over the course of a few weeks so that all employees were on the same page within a reasonable period of time. A communications plan also was established with follow-up refresher messages delivered from HR and business leadership to demonstrate ownership and accountability.

EXHIBIT 3.1. FIGURE 3. ProQuest Individual Contributor Progressive Expectations Map

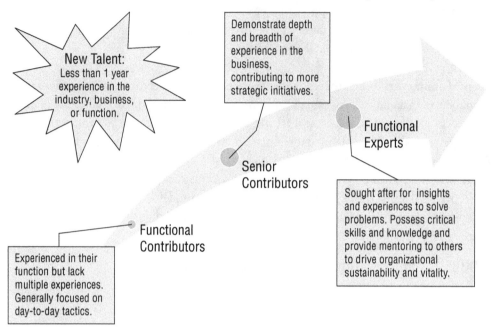

Copyright by William Tarnacki II. Used with permission.

EXHIBIT 3.1. FIGURE 4. ProQuest Leadership Progressive Expectations Map

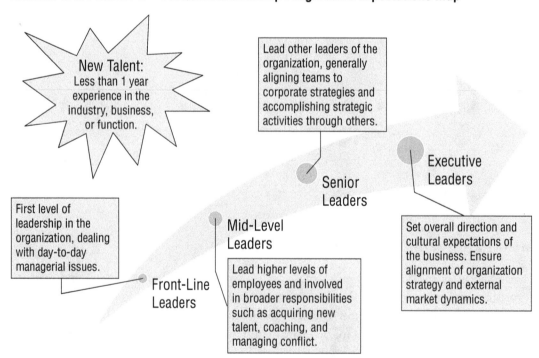

Copyright by William Tarnacki II. Used with permission.

HRD System Intervention

The final issue that remained was the lack of data integrity and analysis with respect to talent, resulting from the fast-paced growth and integration of various global business units into a single entity. This issue was that multiple systems were not scalable to match the needs of the business

EXHIBIT 3.1. INFORMATION TECHNOLOGY COMPANY ALIGNS WORKFORCE   471

as the organization grew globally. In addition, there was misalignment between the systems in place and their ultimate purpose, that is, what defined "system of record" for the various aspects of the talent life cycle. The focus of this particular intervention was the systems associated with managing talent, not the systems associated with managing the day-to-day operations.

The difference between the other two interventions and this one was the involvement of all CIG HR resources in the process of evaluating and selecting the appropriate system(s) based on everyone's needs. In other words, the baseline expectation was to identify the appropriate systems that were scalable not only to match ProQuest's growth expectations, but also Cambridge Information Group's other businesses, too. ProQuest elected to expand the scope to include a system that could facilitate implementation of and reporting on the core talent management processes of performance management, development planning, and succession.

The resulting intervention was the selection and deployment of a new human resources information system (HRIS) for all of CIG and a new integrated talent management system for ProQuest. The keys to the selection process were consensus on "system of record" requirements in terms of the types of employee data that would have to be stored and could be extracted for reporting purposes, and alignment of the systems to the core talent management processes that had just been launched across the enterprise.

As was the case with the talent management model and strategy deployment, a comprehensive training plan was compiled to ensure complete and pertinent training to all areas of the organization. Various tools were employed, including web meeting forums, ProQuest's intranet site, and SharePoint sites, to facilitate timely delivery in line with actual process timing to ensure real-time access to tools and job aids designed for each type of system user. These tools and training materials are reviewed and revised annually based on changes and enhancements to the systems themselves. The end result is an integrated talent management program aligned with the business strategy and owned by organizational leadership that is fully supported by relevant processes, systems, training, documentation and job aids.

■   ■   ■

Lessons Learned

- *Systems View:* Taking and maintaining a systems view of things when identifying performance gaps and devising solutions is absolutely critical to ensuring ongoing applicability of those solutions. Too often, organizations experience diminishing returns on their performance interventions because the scope was not scalable to adapt to growth and changes in organizational dynamics. In the case of ProQuest, if a systems approach had not been taken, then there would have been issues with different "translations" of the competencies in different geographic regions and the systems would not have been able to accommodate interactivity and communication with other talent management systems amassed through acquisitions.

- *Electronic Systems Are Tools, Not Solutions:* Many organizations are convinced that a system, especially a talent management system, can solve their problems with respect to aligning talent to common objectives and consistently assessing, identifying, developing, and rewarding their talent. It is imperative to solidify the model for managing talent across the organization and perfecting the processes associated with each element of that model *before* introducing a system that can help tie it all together. Systems can absolutely be beneficial in speeding up execution of processes and facilitating reporting, but if the overall strategy and processes are not accepted and owned by the business, then the system itself will only accentuate problems that already exist. Although ProQuest established the strategy, direction, and processes ahead of time, it might have been more effective to only take on one system of record launch at a time and allow for a full year of implementing the revised talent processes.

- *Alignment Is Key:* This is true in every sense of the word. Leaders must be aligned and accept responsibility for "owning" the talent strategy, just as they own the business strategy; expectations and rewards for employees must be aligned with the high-level organizational goals and the values and culture of the organization; and systems must be aligned with the processes and functions they are designed to support. Without alignment, any solution is doomed to be labeled a "flavor of the month" (transitory) or outright ignored, and the business will continue to suffer. The approach the ProQuest HR team took of involving senior leadership in problem identification and solution formulation and utilizing focus groups to confirm the legitimacy and explicitness of the solutions reduced confusion and expedited deployment.

- *Plan for the Future, But Act in the Moment:* Like any gap assessment, the analysis performed to identify root causes is steeped in historical data and reflection versus projection. To a large extent, this is unavoidable. The key for ensuring longevity of solutions is to make sure they are tested against macro and micro business trends with an eye on what future success looks like. Additionally, it is important to always think in terms of outcomes versus activities, which can be difficult since business professionals are typically motivated to solve problems quickly, rather than slow down and plan with a long-term end goal in mind. The problem is that, without considering this at the outset, it becomes very difficult to measure success or failure over time. By involving senior leadership in the process, there was an immediate perspective on the validity of the talent strategy as it relates to the longer term business strategy and further iterations of that strategy have called out a confirmative review as part of the business strategic planning process.

William Tarnacki II is director of talent management and corporate human resources for PulteGroup, Inc., Bloomfield Hills, Michigan. Bill is a graduate of Wayne State University's Instructional Technology Program and The University of Michigan's Ross School of Business MBA Program. He is currently pursuing a doctorate in education in the University of Pennsylvania's Wharton School Executive Program in Work-Based Learning Leadership. Bill can be reached at 505.681.1190 or btarnacki2@gmail.com.

SECTION 4
INTERVENTION IMPLEMENTATION AND MAINTENANCE

"I TOLD YOU TO GET THE OXYGEN!"

Intervention Implementation and Maintenance

21

The performance analysis is complete, and it has painted a credible portrait of the organizational and environmental parameters from the actual state of performance to the ideal state of performance; from what *is* to what *should be*. The gaps and their causes have been identified and prioritized. Appropriate, cost-effective, and sustainable interventions have been selected or designed. The interventions are ethically sound. So far, the performance improvement effort has been results-driven, systemic in scope, systematic in process, value-added in quality, and partnership-based. But the process is not complete until the performance practitioner considers the implementation and maintenance of interventions, shown in Figure 21.1.

Change permeates the intervention implementation and maintenance phases. Implementation needs to include plans for (1) introducing the initiative, (2) consolidating and supporting the change effort, and (3) minimizing resistance. Measurement throughout implementation activities will help monitor progress and clarify decisions for corrective actions to sustain the intervention over time. Establishing tracking systems that are designed to compare actual with ideal progress helps people realize that interventions lead to results. Financial and nonfinancial metrics allow determination of the value of the change activities and enable performance improvement practitioners to calculate return on investment and return on expectations.

Intervention Implementation

This chapter addresses implementation and maintenance. Since these two activities are often intertwined, the authors may use both terms while discussing what happens during this phase of the Performance Improvement/HPT Model.

Definition and Scope

"Implementation is the process of communicating, piloting, launching, monitoring, and modifying interventions. Its intended outcome is the institutionalization of the planned intervention, resulting in long-term change within the organization."[1] Although analysis and intervention selection and design are critical to the success of any performance improvement effort, actual changes in performance are incomplete until the intervention is implemented. As car-loving Detroiters say, "That's when the rubber hits the road." As interventions are implemented,

475

FIGURE 21.1. Performance Improvement/HPT Model: Implementation and Maintenance Phase

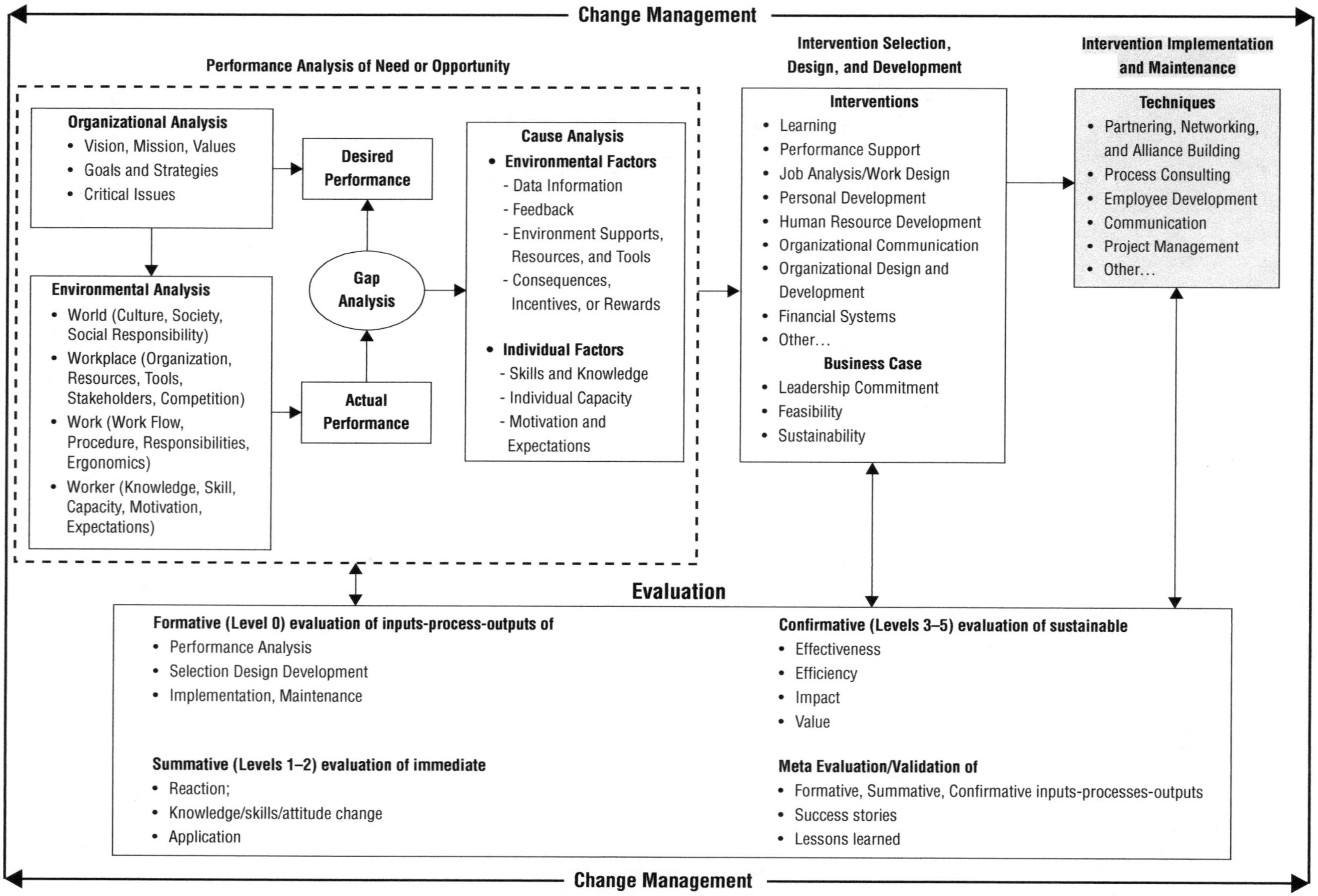

changes begin to affect the worker, the work, the workplace, and the world. Some changes are desired and anticipated, but much of the change occurs as people adapt to the interventions.

Importance of Successful Implementation

Intervention implementation is critical to performance improvement. It protects organizational investments, encourages and empowers employees, improves accountability, enhances the likelihood that interventions will target specific needs, helps supervisors maintain focus on the performance environment, and enables success.[2] It helps the practitioners identify *why* successful implementation is important to the organization and *which* implementation model best suits the organization's needs.

Models Lead the Way

Models help performance improvement practitioners visualize implementation. Because each model has a different focus, taken together they provide optional approaches to successful implementation.

Dormant—Cross-Functional Model

An early and influential implementation model is a cross-functional model suggested by Dormant. It focuses on information exchanges between developers and implementers. The team model "places implementation activities parallel in time with development activities, [which] results in benefits to the organization and the users, as well as to the developers and implementers."[3]

Hale—Sustainability Model

Hale's implementation model focuses on sustaining interventions by institutionalizing new behaviors. The model employs a multi-faceted implementation approach:

- *Governance*, which includes establishing leadership structure, communication patterns, and platforms to revolve issues and clarify roles and responsibilities
- *Attention*, which includes focusing on goals and status of interventions that are on management's agenda for extended time periods;
- *Measurement*, which includes tracking and reporting changes in indicators of success; and
- *Self-regulation*, which includes generating tools and standards to monitor behaviors and rate of adoption.[4]

Moseley and Hastings—Four-Stage Process Model

Moseley and Hastings developed the intervention implementation process model, which leverages intervention selection and design by focusing on resources, strategic goals, competencies, and collective learning. The model consists of four stages of implementation with a variety of activities common to each step. Practitioners are reminded that each stage must be completed sequentially to facilitate change.[5] (See Table 21.1 for a closer look at this model.)

TABLE 21.1. Stages of Moseley and Hastings' Model

Stage	Suggested Activities for Communication, Action, Auditing, and Feedback
Planning	Publicize upper management support
	Confirm stakeholder commitment
	Secure resources
	Conduct pilots
	Assess intervention fit
	Identify barriers to success
	Provide directions for subsequent stages
	Modify processes for future interventions
Doing	Market the intervention
	Disseminate and launch the intervention
	Identify transfer issues
	Review ethical considerations
	Provide direction for subsequent stages
	Modify processes
Stabilizing	Align with the organization's values and goals
	Keep stakeholders informed
	Fine-tune the intervention
	Assess the impact on work, worker, workplace, world
	Provide direction for subsequent stages
	Modify processes
Institutionalizing	Publicize success
	Prevent backsliding
	Measure organizational impact
	Identify and eliminate political barriers to success
	Signal completion
	Modify processes for future interventions.

Source: Moseley and Hastings, 2005, pp. 8–14. Used with permission.

Dublin—I³ Change-Focused Implementation Model

Dublin's I³ Change Implementation Model, an approach to sustainable implementation, ensures that the implementation of an organizational change becomes integral to the organization so that the change is sustainable.[6] The model consists of three stages:

- *Inform or Awareness*—Generates an awareness about change using a consumer marketing approach consisting of branding, positioning, tagline creation, and so forth;

- *Involve or Engagement*—Focuses on knowing the change and engaging and internalizing it; and
- *Integrate or Commitment*—Ensures that change becomes embedded within the organization's culture.[7] Each of the stages is customized to fit the norms and expectations of the organization. It involves employees at all levels in planning the change, monitoring progress, making adjustments, and evaluating results.[8] Since all performance improvement interventions imply change, this implementation model is easily adapted to use during the intervention implementation and maintenance phase of the Performance Improvement/ HPT Model.

Implementation Design

In order for the implementation process to be successful, it must be carefully designed, creatively framed, and adroitly monitored. Addison, Haig, and Kearney suggest that these elements should be part of any intervention implementation design:

- Expected results clearly linked to the business,
- Extensive communication exchanges with stakeholder representatives,
- Active inclusion of affected employees,
- Visible support of senior management,
- Identification of all affected processes, and
- Careful consideration of the organization's cultural norms.[9]

Process Design Steps

Swinney suggests general steps for designing an intervention implementation process (see Table 21.2).

When prodded for additional thoughts regarding implementation, Swinney offered these thoughts:

- Implementation design starts at the end of the analysis phase, and some might even argue it begins during analysis.
- A good implementation process can salvage an "ok" performance intervention or training project, but the best project in the world will not survive poor implementation.
- Implementation is a shared process. Performance improvement must be looked at within the entire organizational structure.
- You don't need management support. You need management involvement. If managers don't have an active role, you don't have a good implementation plan.
- Implementation must be considered in the language of the work, not in the language of human performance.
- Pilot test the implementation process the same way you would pilot test a performance intervention. Will the implementation plan be successful the way it is designed?[10]

TABLE 21.2.   Steps for Designing an Intervention Implementation Process

Steps	*Components*
1. Identify Target Results	Who is the target population?
	Under what conditions will they be expected to perform?
	What results are expected?
	How should success be measured?
2. Identify Potential Obstacles	What conditions in the environment could interfere with desired performance?
	Who are the stakeholders and who will benefit if the performance improves?
	Who are the key influencers of the target population?
	Do the influencers agree that this performance is desired?
	Who influences the influencers?
3. Identify Expectations	What are the expectations for members of the target population?
	For supervisors or influencers of the target population?
	For key members of the organizational hierarchy?
4. Identify Feedback and Reinforcement (sources of and recipients of)	For members of the target population
	For supervisors or influencers of the target population
	For key members of the organizational hierarchy
	Systemic (more powerful and effective if it is a built-in part of the work environment instead of a separate function
5. Identify Skill and Knowledge Issues	For the target population
	For key influencers.
6. Map the Implementation Process	Cross-functional; include all influencers and support functions
7. Get Buy-In and Commitment to the Process from Key Players	Modify as needed
	Use the language of the business, not the language of performance improvement
	Not necessarily a discrete step—"selling" the concept should start as early as Step 2 to obtain ideas from key players and influencers about what they could do or recommend to make things work
8. Test the Process	Alpha—internal; using other team members
	Beta—using various members of the target population or extended target population
	Pilot—stand-alone—as it would be expected to work in the real world
9. Revise as Needed	
10. Monitor the System	

Source: Swinney, 2000. Used with permission.

Feasibility Issues

Kirkey and Benjamin's thoughts on feasibility analysis provided guidelines to consider prior to engaging in detailed design and development activities, and again before and during implementation.[11] The guidelines are also applicable to implementing interventions by taking into account practical, political, and cultural considerations:

- Practical considerations focus on administering, preparing, communicating, accessing, supporting, timing, and continuing organizational context as well as environmental constraints and technology-mediated solutions.
- Political considerations focus on appropriate leadership support, involvement of key stakeholders, the formal and informal power structure, and the benefits and adverse consequences that may affect any or all participants.
- Cultural considerations ask how the implementation plan fits within the organization's norms and values, stories, heroes and heroines, myths, and rituals. They consider audience deployment, the need for monitoring and intervening, and the impact that the implementation process will have on the organization's members. And they address readiness for change.[12]

Design for Sustainability

Hale, in a document entitled "Sustaining Results: Adding Value to the Future," lists ten steps for successful implementation that will last as long as the intervention is aligned with the need or opportunity:

1. Agree on the goals, scope, target audience, measures, critical mass
2. Set the baseline
3. Assess feasibility
4. Develop a strategy, game plan to actualize the goal
5. Identify and track leading indicators
6. Put an oversight structure in place
7. Sustain attention
8. Measure the rate of adoption and report
9. Shift ownership
10. Reward adoption[13]

Additional steps to take during intervention implementation include monitoring change, providing meaningful and sufficient feedback, framing reinforcement options, and recording and celebrating successes and failures.

Success or Failure?

While it is important to capitalize on the successes along the way, it is far more important to reflect on and learn from failures. Some reasons for implementation failure and derailment include a lack of a compelling vision or sense of urgency, leaders not accountable, failure to learn, insufficient communication, lack of a critical mass, insufficient change in the culture of the organization, insufficient infrastructure, disconnect between vision and action, and no outside perspective.[14]

Variables Affecting Successful Implementation

Of the many variables that potentially affect intervention implementation, three are discussed here—characteristics of the intervention, the organization, and interpersonal relations.

Characteristics of the intervention itself. Is the intervention routine or radical, technical or administrative, central or peripheral? These variables may require changes in employee behavior, organization structure, degrees of formalization, power issues, impact on work design, and individual, group, and team involvement.

Characteristics of the organization. What are the organization's structure, history, and size? What strategies are employed? How does culture influence organizational learning? These variables direct the performance improvement practitioner to view the organization as a participative entity with open communication channels rather than one governed by rules, regulations, and ambiguity. The size of the organization and its place in history impact the strategies that are used. The values and beliefs of employees, influenced by culture and organizational learning, directly or indirectly impact how interventions are implemented and maintained.

Characteristics associated with interpersonal processes. How are employees involved in the intervention? How do politics, communication patterns, and leadership styles influence intervention implementation? Involving employees from the get-go adds growth points to implementation success as do the frequency and direction of communication patterns. Organizational politics and its influence in decision making, as well as the leadership styles of key personnel, add to successful intervention implementation.[15] A performance improvement practitioner "ensures that interventions are implemented in ways consistent with desired results and that they help individuals and groups achieve results."[16]

Implementation Strategies

Rothwell believes that performance improvement practitioners play a pivotal role in helping the organization prepare to install an intervention. He goes on to say that the results of intervention implementation "usually are a clear sense of the desired outcomes . . . an action plan that enjoys the ownership of key stakeholders, and the assembly of talent necessary to implement the intervention."[17]

Intervention Maintenance

An automobile is an appropriate tool for traveling great distances, and re-fueling helps ensure an arrival at the destination. For purposes of this chapter, we view the automobile as the *intervention*, then re-fueling is the *maintenance*. Intervention maintenance requires conscious and deliberate commitment by all those involved in the maintenance process. Careful monitoring of change dynamics will substantially influence sustainability and institutionalization.

Definition and Scope

Maintenance is "the process of continuing to use new skills over time, even when opportunities to practice are limited, and work constraints (such as time, pressures, stress, or lack of manager support) exist."[18]

The maintenance of interventions over time is not an easy process because it is filled with risk and reward, success and failure, and readiness and resistance to change. However, if the performance improvement practitioner assumes leadership for planning, orchestrating, nurturing, guiding, maintaining and evaluating the interventions within the organization culture as well as its internal and external clients, sustainability will be realized.

Sustainability

Sustainability means endurance. Sustainability here refers to the extent to which a program's legacy is continued over time.[19] It is an engaging and synergistic journey, not a final destination. Organizations are beginning to engage and employ sustainability champions to guide their legacy. These change agent individuals are organized and possess an action-oriented mindset.

The Sustainability Thinker. The sustainability thinker, also known as the *change agent*, thinks systemically by looking at the larger picture or context, including competing pressures, resource constraints, and anticipated change pressure points. The sustainable thinker's work is guided by the value-added dimensions of the interventions and their maintenance. And the wise sustainable thinker utilizes partnerships and collaborates with all stakeholders in the sustainable effort. The change agent, as sustainable thinker, is likely to scope out answers to questions such as these:

1. Does the business of the organization continue to deliver value for all its constituents?
2. Is the organization well-run with appropriate talent management to assure success for the long term?
3. Do all stakeholders involved in the implementation process favor program continuation?
4. Is there an evidence-based need or a compelling case to continue the interventions?
5. How are authority and responsibility for program continuation assigned to achieve maximum accountability?
6. How do sustainability issues address budget continuation processes, procedures, and practices?
7. How are communication patterns and other issues regarding the change process resolved in a timely and effective manner?[20]
8. How do collaboration and transparency transition to sustainable excellence?[21]

There are also personality traits and leadership and business-related skills that will guide the sustainability thinker through both the implementation and maintenance of interventions. The personality traits include a thirst for knowledge, a strong sense of principles and work ethic, and a willingness to share and celebrate success and praise. Leadership and business skills include understanding of the relationship between risks and rewards, talent for building team spirit and managing projects, and the ability to create new paradigms.[22]

In addition to the traits and skills already emphasized, the change agent must create a sustainability plan that begins with the performance improvement efforts which have been emphasized throughout this book.

Institutionalization

Embedding an intervention into an organization is institutionalizing it. "Institutionalization involves making a particular change a permanent part of the organization's normal functioning. It ensures that the results of successful change programs persist over time."[23] The process of institutionalization is a four-task process involving communication, action, auditing, and feedback. The communication task publicizes successes through success stories, celebrations, and rewards. It also reaffirms the organization's commitment to change and resolves lingering issues involving stakeholder commitment and sustainability of the intervention over time. The action task requires support from the intervention sponsor, usually upper management, through both verbal and non-verbal communication. Enthusiasm and commitment for change must also be ongoing if the intervention is to be assimilated into the culture of the organization. Sufficient resources must similarly be appropriated and allocated to prevent backsliding.

The auditing task involves collecting and interpreting data to determine the success of the intervention at closing gaps, its alignment with the mission, values, and beliefs, and identifying barriers to success.

The feedback task brings closure to the implementation process. Here the emphasis is on successes, failures, and lessons learned. Processes are modified for future interventions. Feedback "lays the foundation for the confirmative evaluation process, which goes beyond formative and summative evaluation to judge the continued merit, worth, or value of a long-term intervention."[24]

Performance Support Tool 21.1 raises general questions about the change management process. It is designed as a guide to focus thinking prior to intervention implementation or evaluate the process during and after implementation.

Citations

1. Moseley & Hastings 2005, p. 8
2. Steiner, 2009
3. Dormant, 1992
4. Hale, 2005, pp. 10–11
5. Moseley & Hastings, 2005, p. 10
6. Haig & Addison, 2007, p. 4

7. Dublin, 2007, cited in Haig & Addison, 2007, pp. 4–6

8. Dublin, 2007, cited in Haig & Addison, 2007, p. 5

9. Addison, Haig, & Kearney, 2009, p. 85

10. Swinney, 2000

11. Kirkey & Benjamin, 2010

12. Kirkey & Benjamin, 2010

13. Hale, 2010

14. Gelinas & James, 1998

15. Hedge & Pulakos, 2002, pp. 7–8

16. Rothwell, 1996, p. 15

17. Rothwell, 1996, p. 15

18. Kraiger, 2002, p. 57

19. Stufflebeam, 2002

20. Stufflebeam, 2002

21. Cramer & Karabell, 2010, p. 9

22. Swallow, 2009, pp. 36–38

23. Evaluating and Institutionalizing Organization Development Interventions, 2011

24. Moseley & Hastings, 2005, p. 13

References

Addison, R, Haig, C., & Kearny, L. (2009). *Performance architecture: The art and science of improving organizations*. San Francisco: Pfeiffer/ISPI.

Cramer, A., & Karabell, Z. (2010). *Sustainable excellence: The future of business in a fast-changing world*. New York: Rodale.

Dormant, D. (1992). Implementing human performance technology in organizations. In H.D. Stolovitch & E.J. Keeps (Eds.), *Handbook of human performance technology: A comprehensive guide for analyzing and solving performance problems in organizations* (pp. 167–187). San Francisco: Jossey-Bass.

Evaluating and institutionalizing organization development interventions. Retrieved from www.zainbooks .com/books/management/organization-develop.

Gelinas, M., & James, R. (1998). *Collaborative change*. San Francisco: Pfeiffer.

Haig, C., & Addison, R. (2007, August). TrendSpotters: I3 Change implementation model. *PerformanceXpress*, pp. 4–5.

Hale, J.A. (2005, October). Implementation: Assuring adoption. *PerformanceXpress*, pp. 10–11.

Hale, J.A. (2010). Sustaining results: Adding value to the future. Workshop handout, available from Haleassoci@aol.com.

Hedge, J.W., & Pulakos, E.D. (Eds.) (2002). *Implementing organizational interventions: Steps, processes, and best practices*. San Francisco: Jossey-Bass.

Kirkey, D., & Benjamin, C.M. (2010, April). Feasibility analysis: Practical, political, and cultural considerations in implementation. San Francisco: ISPI Conference Handout.

Kraiger, K. (Ed.). (2002). *Creating, implementing, and maintaining effective training and development: State-of-the-art lessons for practice*. San Francisco: Jossey-Bass.

Moseley, J.L., & Hastings, N.B. (2005, April). Implementation: The forgotten link on the intervention chain. *Performance Improvement*, 44(4), 8–14.

Rothwell, W.J. (1996). *ASTD models for human performance improvement: Roles, competencies, and outputs*. Alexandria, VA: American Society for Training and Development.

Steiner, A. (2009). Implementation planning that works! Orlando, FL: ISPI Conference Handout.

Stufflebeam, D.L. (2002, June). CIPP evaluation model checklist: Evaluation checklists project. Retrieved from www.wmich.edu/evalctr/checklists.

Swallow, L. (2009). *Green business practices for dummies*. Hoboken, NJ: John Wiley & Sons.

Swinney, J.M. (2000). Implementing training and performance improvement interventions. Cincinnati, OH: ISPI Conference Handout.

PERFORMANCE SUPPORT TOOL 21.1. EVALUATING SUSTAINABILITY FROM A CHANGE MANAGEMENT PERSPECTIVE

Directions: Answer the following questions and use your answers to analyze the effects of change on sustainability.

Has the change expectation been thoroughly defined?

How will this change disrupt the current organization?

Does the organization have a history of implementation problems? Is so, describe them.

Are the sponsors sufficiently committed to the project? If not, would education or replacing sponsors help?

Does synergy exist among sponsors, employees, and change targets? If not, what can be done to improve relationships?

What resistance is anticipated?

Is planned change consistent with organizational culture?

Are employees sufficiently ready for a change effort? Would training help?

Are the right people, right communication plan, and right measurements in place?

Techniques for Implementation and Maintenance

22

Intervention implementation and maintenance are as important as the previous stages of the Human Performance/HPT Model. Rothwell points out that "A good solution that's poorly implemented becomes a poor solution."[1] In addition to the change management techniques that are used throughout the performance improvement process there are eight typical methods or techniques for interventions implementation and maintenance:

1. Partnering, networking, and alliance building,
2. Process consulting,
3. Employee development,
4. Communication to develop support,
5. Change management,
6. Project management,
7. Feasibility, and
8. Sustainability.

This chapter explores each technique as it applies to successful intervention implementation and maintenance, with the exception of feasibility analysis techniques, which are covered in Chapter 19, Making the Business Case. As it does throughout all the performance improvement/HPT model phases, RSVP—Results, Systems view, Value, and Partnerships, guide implementation and maintenance processes and techniques. (See Appendix A, CPT Standards.) Since partnership, networking, and alliance building work in tandem and should begin even before initiating any performance improvement effort, they will be the first technique discussed in this chapter. Listen carefully and you may also hear the Practitioner's Voice discussing a technique.

Partnering, Networking, and Alliance Building

Partnering, networking, and alliance building allow individuals and organizations to team up with others who already perform the desired behaviors. These activities are ingrained in continuous improvement and professional development.

Partnering

ISPI Performance Standard 4 suggests working in partnership with our internal and external clients as necessary and required. A partnership is a relationship built on trust, and cultivating strong relationships is critical to ensuring organizational results. Partnership building is also a collaborative effort that involves fact finding, planning, and decision processes. "Partnerships provide not only a wealth of strategies to help us achieve shared objectives, but they also produce the criteria by which we and our partners will jointly measure the success of our ventures. In this way we are in motion with our partners."[2] Solid listening and communication skills are paramount.

Gargiulo suggests key qualitative indicators for judging a successful partnership:

- Strength of the relationship, including trust, dialogue, values, degree of reciprocity, and level of respect;
- Flexibility in requirements, design, delivery, and measurement;
- Facilitation skills, including process, communication, listening, managerial, instrument development, and other skills and abilities as well as personal qualities;
- Results orientation with focus and validation of the vision, mission, strategies, and critical business goals of the organization; and
- Business focus, which shows benefits to organizational and individual success.[3]

Among their many contributions to performance consulting, the Robinsons suggest the ACT approach to partnering with clients. ACT stands for gaining **A**ccess by establishing and gaining "face" time with clients; building **C**redibility or the client's confidence in the consultant's capability to know the "business of the business"; and building **T**rust or the client's confidence in the consultant's integrity and reliability.[4]

Human performance practitioners do other things to build successful partnerships, such as being an integral part of the organization's functional areas, sitting at the executive table, supporting partner activities to celebrate successes, and reinventing the partnership.[5] The practices work for establishing internal as well as external partnerships.

Networking

Networking, or forming informal relationships with people who have common interests or experiences, is an essential part of getting work done. Networks have no formal structure and no obvious authority. They can consist of vast numbers of people, including outsiders, peers, bosses' bosses, and subordinates' subordinates.[6] Successful career models have vast contact networks, are involved in professional and community activities outside their businesses, and encourage opportunities to be visible.[7]

Individuals form their own personal networks based on integrity, trust, mutual benefit, and knowledge that can be shared. Networks are cooperative relationships with people who respond to questions or requests for information or assistance. Performance improvement practitioners need real-time or online networks to affirm direction and ideas. External networks provide examples or ways to discuss similar experiences, helping the practitioner anticipate change. Internal networks explain actions and rally support.

Networks depend on mutual advantage and must be nurtured and appreciated through reciprocation. Effective networking assumes political sensitivity and trust that shared information will be used discreetly. Coleman says: "Networking is the single most valuable source of continued professional development . . . [and] should always be a reciprocal arrangement . . . works best when human performance practitioners are willing to give as well as receive help and support."[8]

Networks can be built and nurtured by joining professional associations, such as the International Society for Performance Improvement (ISPI), the American Society for Training and Development (ASTD), the Association for Educational Communications and Technology (AECT), the Society for Human Resource Management (SHRM), and others. A professional would not necessarily join all these organizations; it is best to select the organization(s) that fits personal career goals and leverages individual talent.

In addition, graduate schools, study groups, and alumni organizations provide opportunities for frequent contact with people with similar interests. LinkedIn and other online networks are an opportunity for people to connect and form business as well as social networks.[9] Networking should be ingrained in the way professionals do things and, as such, it should be done all the time. Suggestions include creating contact lists, self-marketing, networking, being diplomatic, polite, and respectful of others, and so forth.[10]

Alliance Building

Performance improvement practitioners should create and sustain alliances. These agreements increase service delivery capabilities and encourage the sharing of resources. For example, non-competitive organizations in close proximity enroll each other's employees into unfilled training seats on an equity basis. Each organization will have more training sessions filled to capacity, and each organization can offer greater educational variety to meet individual needs.

Networks are handy because they are readily accessed, informal, and personal. Alliances, on the other hand, are based on the mutual benefit of all parties. They are more formal or more organized, and often have protocol, rules, and restrictions. Typically, alliances are limited in scope.[11] Alliances are based on agreements relative to partnership participation, operations, and influence, but are non-conflicting organizations or entities. Each partner keeps autonomy, but needs flexibility to cooperate, as required.

A word of caution is in order, however. "Too often, companies enter into business with the wrong partner or for the wrong reasons, and they end up regretting this decision. Even when an alliance looks great on paper, cultural differences between the parties or mismatched expectations can undermine the arrangement."[12]

Process Consulting

In this competitive, rapidly changing, global marketplace, the need for flexibility and the willingness to adapt are necessary for survival. In many cases, it is possible for departments or work groups to observe a need, analyze the situation to understand it better, brainstorm alternative solutions, and implement the most favorable idea with minimal discomfort. In those situations, change is welcomed because it alleviates outmoded practices.

Sometimes business practices and processes become entrenched because they involve many departments or include processes that have served well in the past. Often, the need to change is not obvious to all employees and, as a result, change may be resisted. Ambiguous situations, multi-departmental concerns, or problems with little agreement are often best suited for process consulting. As a result, process consulting can lead, at times, to significant reengineering.

Definition and Scope

Process consulting involves designing processes and jobs, leading to significant organizational reengineering. It results in revising processes and often involves restructuring an entire organization. The process consultant is either an internal or an external person who responds to a problem, opportunity, or challenge.

Organizations change continually in subtle ways, and solutions to correct minor issues are implemented daily. However, there are times when process consulting is needed to ensure that change is coordinated and sustained. Process consulting is usually spearheaded by one leader or team, such as a performance improvement practitioner, who works closely with a sponsor and a project team.

For smaller problems, work groups can accomplish change using traditional continuous improvement techniques. Process consultants, on the other hand, work in a mutual, collegial relationship on the larger organizational issues. It is important that consulting recommendations be beneficial to employees.[13]

Process consultants use specialized skills to observe and interpret group dynamics, bring insight to work process concerns, and manage the stress and ambiguity of change relationships. Performance improvement practitioners, as process consultants, observe interactions among and between various constituent groups such as executives, managers, and workers and, perhaps, customers or suppliers, create process flowcharts, and analyze policies, procedures, and work standards to identify or confirm work problems. In addition, they prepare for resistance and the frustration of people who do not welcome the change effort.

Determining Performance Relative to Business Needs

Frequently, people fear process consulting efforts because they believe that chaos and anxiety, as well as the loss of power and jobs, usually come with major change initiatives. Employees become defensive because change efforts seem to imply that everything in the past was wrong.

Actually, process consulting is usually triggered by changes in stakeholder expectations, increased competition, or a need to increase productivity and maximize the possibilities available through technology. Typically, the results of process consulting are increased productivity, consolidated functions, or the elimination of unnecessary work.

Consulting Phases

Many consulting approaches are reported in the literature. The reader is encouraged to review the writings of Lippitt and Lippitt,[14] Robinson and Robinson,[15] Block,[16] Weiss,[17] Carucci and Tetenbaum,[18] Biech,[19] and Scott.[20] This discussion highlights the work of Hale and Rummler, who have substantially changed the consulting landscape in the performance improvement field.

Hale's work is a foundational resource that has influenced consultants worldwide. She models how to maintain integrity with facts, accept the perceptions of others, obtain useful information creatively, involve the clients throughout the process, and apply what is learned to help organizations and people become successful.[21] Hale offers seven process consulting phases that document and communicate her approach. Figure 22.1 is a detailed exploration into these phases.

Rummler's work about serious performance consulting encourages us to become proactive and find opportunities for improving results. Serious performance consulting is different from "lite" performance consulting because serious consulting consists of closing the measurable gap between what is and what should be, applying a systematic results improvement process, and a rigorous performance analysis.[22]

Although no intervention implementation and maintenance project adheres rigidly to each of the approaches and phases listed here, using a similar overall process consulting plan promotes successful interventions. Performance improvement practitioners, as process consultants, listen and watch diligently, empathize with the entire workforce, and partner with the organization to achieve excellence and to institute exemplary processes and practices.[23] Performance Support Tool 22.1 can help a performance improvement practitioner focus on the objectives of a process consulting initiative.

Employee Development

Techniques for implementing and maintaining a focus on interventions may include techniques from the learning side of employee development. Most performance improvement initiatives require learning new skills and knowledge to implement and maintain them. Employee development is the organizational structure that supports such learning. Employee development involves acquiring knowledge, skills, and attitudes through a number of learning techniques, including (1) traditional instruction; (2) newer technology-oriented formats; (3) informally by means of mentoring, coaching, and on-the-job training; or (4) team participation.

FIGURE 22.1.   The Consulting Process

Phase I: Defining the request

- Qualify the job.
- Qualify the client.
- Determine expectations.
- Define work protocols.
- Define roles, relationships, and responsibilities.
- Scope out a plan.

Phase II: Fact-finding

- Start with hypotheses.
- Include all voices.
- Use more than one method.
- Look for corroborating evidence.
- Apply rigor to control bias.
- Consider the environment.

Phase III: Analyzing your findings

- Compile the results.
- Apply analytical techniques.
- Look for significant findings and differences.
- Identify the costs.
- Find out the consequences on costs, satisfaction, image, and so on.
- Report the results.

Phase IV: Designing the solution

- Describe the audiences (direct and indirect).
- Specify the requirements.
- Specify the long-term support.
- Specify communication and implementation requirements.
- Specify the costs and benefits.
- Specify other relevant success measures.
- Specify the pilot test and rollout plans.
- Specify how and who will measure results.

Phase V: Developing the solution

- Prepare or secure materials, systems, and other required elements.
- Prepare collateral and management support materials.
- Prepare public relations materials.

Phase VI: Implementing the Solution

- Set up an implementation team.
- Conduct the pilot test.
- Analyze the findings.
- Launch the rollout.

Phase VII: Measuring the Results

- Gather the data.
- Compare to pre-established measures.
- Report the results.

Source: Hale, 1998, p. 18. Used with permission.

PERFORMANCE SUPPORT TOOL 22.1. PROCESS CONSULTING PLANNER

Consulting Objective	Initial Observations and Issues
Describe situation and improvement opportunities.	
Why is the proposed process consulting project necessary?	
List project team members and document executive-level support.	
Sketch out consulting activities and sponsor's expectations.	

Definition and Scope

Employee development enhances workforce capabilities in an organized manner to maintain competitive advantage and prepare the organization for anticipated knowledge and skills requirements. The knowledge era requires workers to continuously develop new skills due to advances in technology, improved processes to increase productivity, and the need to be competitive.[24] Employee development is critical for succession planning and aligning leadership practices with business objectives.

Learning Organizations

Organizations are becoming *learning* organizations that encourage, support, and celebrate personal mastery of knowledge. Motivation to learn has come along with tuition reimbursement; structured on-the-job training; performance support tools or job aids; handy online, mobile, or pocket guides; podcasts; webinars; or special assignments. In addition, formal instruction can be offered in traditional classroom settings or via newer online, mobile, or social media platforms that merge personal involvement with the convenience of learning at the worksite. A learning organization is committed to and practices the belief that individuals and teams can learn continuously and cooperatively to foster an organization's competitive advantage. Senge describes the hallmarks of learning organizations, which include sharing the organization's vision, striving for individual excellence, team learning, creating common mental models, and applying systemic and systematic thinking to enhance the use of knowledge as a competitive strategy.[25]

Learning organizations constantly strive to transform themselves by encouraging all employees to participate in decision making and view management decisions as "experiments" rather than edicts. They link customers, suppliers, and the neighborhood community with employees to increase communication and cooperation and produce a climate of self-development and inquiry. Organizational information, formerly viewed as confidential, is used to inform and empower people, as accounting and control systems are opened up and designed to support employee inquiry. Employees are rewarded for ideas and actions that contribute to innovation and progress.

Four Basic Techniques

Four basic techniques are used to implement employee development learning initiatives: formal instruction, learning support, job experiences, and interpersonal relationships.[26] Formal instruction can be traditional, classroom-based training, college courses attended through tuition assistance, distance learning events such as podcasts and webinars, videoconferences, self-study, and more. Topics may range from problem solving to new product launch, and audiences may range from executives to clerical or line workers.

Learning support may include conference participation; assessment such as performance appraisals, 360-degree feedback, and career inventories; and performance support such as embedded computer software help, telephone help desks, or corporate libraries. Job experiences may include on-the-job training, performance support tools or job aids, reference manuals, job rotation and special assignments, or team involvement. Interpersonal relationships may involve mentoring and coaching, online social or professional networking, informal suggestions, or advice received at lunch and breaks.

Responsibility

Both the employee and the organization are responsible for employee development. In most cases, employees are responsible for learning and implementing changes in the workplace as a result of the learning opportunity. Employees are also responsible for enrolling themselves in the learning activity. Organizations have the responsibility to provide learning opportunities, to provide sufficient information about future jobs, and to honestly appraise current performance, allowing people to make useful education and learning selections.

Issues

Questions can be raised about who should attend training, about establishing good relations between departments and the training and development providers, about working with requesting departments to see whether an intervention will alleviate a problem or enhance competence, and managing vendors and consultants. All of the issues will advance and enhance the linkage between employee development and organizational success.

Performance Support Tool 22.2 is useful to identify and assess various issues related to employee development interventions that impact either the results or the feasibility of the intervention.

Communication

Developing support through effective communication is the quickest, most basic technique for ensuring the success of the intervention implementation—and that the success can be maintained. Communication is critical for creating and sustaining a clear understanding of the organization's direction and change efforts.

Communication focuses the organization on the positive value of intervention implementation, maintenance, and the inevitable changes that occur as a result of the intervention. It is like an old-fashioned elixir. It is good for this and good for that and it usually leaves a pleasant taste on the palate. In fact, nothing works well without it.

Communication is the glue that holds all of the pieces of a well-designed intervention together. Communication helps people understand what is happening and why it is happening. It gives them a chance to talk. It is the process of sharing thoughts and ideas to develop a common understanding. It is not necessary for people to agree with the idea. It is okay to disagree. However, communicators need to agree about what was actually said. Each communicator needs to be able to paraphrase, or repeat, the essence of what was said.

PERFORMANCE SUPPORT TOOL 22.2. ASSESSING EMPLOYEE DEVELOPMENT SUCCESS STANDARDS

Purpose: Use this tool to identify and assess various issues related to employee development interventions that impact either the results or the feasibility of the intervention.

Questions	Yes	No
Objectives and Target Population		
Does the employee development intervention meet objectives through clear links to job performance?	☐	☐
Will the employee development intervention benefit people and the organization?	☐	☐
Will management and workers endorse the employee development intervention and apply the learning?	☐	☐
Does the employee development intervention match learner characteristics?	☐	☐
Does the employee development intervention include balanced learning in cognitive (knowledge), affective (feelings), and psychomotor (manual skill) domains or procedures?	☐	☐
Design Integrity		
Does the employee development intervention match findings of gap analysis and cause analysis?	☐	☐
Is the employee development intervention based on action learning? (Action learning means working on projects related to actual job issues.)	☐	☐
Is the employee intervention interactive?	☐	☐
Is the employee development intervention modular? (Modular learning allows flexibility for scheduling employee development.)	☐	☐
Does the employee development intervention contain a variety of learning strategies? (Variety should enable employees with diverse learning styles and sensory needs to have opportunities to learn effectively.)	☐	☐
Does the employee development intervention focus on "need to know" and minimize "nice to know"?	☐	☐
Does the employee development intervention include accelerated learning features designed to simplify and enhance learning? (Accelerated learning features tap various parts of the brain to encourage learning.)	☐	☐
Culture and Context		
Does the employee development intervention support current organizational initiatives?	☐	☐
Does the employee development intervention accommodate quality, health, and safety standards?	☐	☐
Does the employee development intervention include language and illustrations compatible with the organization's culture and ideals?	☐	☐

(Continued)

Questions	Yes	No
Cost and Usability		
Is the employee development intervention available in-house? (In-house training is usually targeted to the organization and work environment and supports the organization because it is designed to meet the organization's needs, be cost-effective, and minimize impact to cash flow.)	☐	☐
Is the employee development intervention cost-effective? (Calculate costs: development, material purchase, instructor/facilitator delivery, facility [location, equipment, and food], and compare estimated total costs against estimated value to organization and employees. Some organizations also calculate participating employee wages and benefits as an expense. Other organizations consider employee development as a routine part of the job and not an additional expense.)	☐	☐
Quality Assurance		
Was the employee development event designed by a team containing a performance improvement practitioner or an instructional technologist?	☐	☐
Was the employee development event designed by a team containing a subject-matter expert?	☐	☐
Does the employee development event contain a variety of pre-assessments and post-assessments that are job-related? (Evaluation tools should measure cognitive [knowledge], affective [feeling], and psychomotor [manual skills] outcomes.)	☐	☐
Does the employee development event contain a reasonable quality standard? (A quality target of 90/90 percent is recommended. That means 90 percent of the participants will score 90 percent or better on the post-assessment.)	☐	☐
Other Standards Based on Organizational Requirements		

Conclusions and Comments

> ### EXHIBIT 22.1. THE PRACTITIONER'S VOICE: EMPLOYEE DEVELOPMENT
>
> "Employee development is defined by the needs of both the organization and the employee. The best employee development plan provides a review process at least once each year to ensure that the organization and employee have the same expectations and to provide guidance to the employee for the future.
>
> "From an organization's viewpoint, development can be seen as a method of linking employees to the company's mission and ideals, assisting employees to maintain or update skills to provide efficient, effective products or services, and maintaining certification or licensure from external regulating bodies. From an employee's standpoint, development can be a benefit that helps with advancement (tuition assistance for an advanced degree or enhancement of management skills) or learning that can make the current position more efficient and effective.
>
> "Some organizations also include mentoring and coaching with frequent feedback as methods for increasing employee skills and providing employee development and talent management. This can be especially useful for daily job functioning, promotion, leadership skills, and succession planning.
>
> "When an organization invests time and money to enhance their skills, employees feel that they are valued and contributing members of the team. Each employer must determine how employees can be encouraged to grow and learn to meet both personal goals and the organization's goals. The organization's culture, types of employees and their work ethic, and management styles will determine a successful employment development system that works for all."
>
> Ireta Ekstrom, Ph.D., CPT
>
> Instructional Developer
>
> Central Michigan University
>
> College of Medicine
>
> Mount Pleasant, Michigan, USA

Frame of Reference

"The typical components of the communication process are the information source, the message, auditory and visual channels, noise, environment, and information receiver including the receiver's cultural background and previous experiences, interpretation of meaning, and feedback."[27] Communication involves understanding another's frame of reference. People encode messages by putting feelings and ideas into the message and decode when they receive the message and internally translate the words or visual elements into personal meaning. Each participant in the communication translates the message differently based on his or her own frame of reference.

People understand verbal messages based on their unique experiences, educational background, race, gender, attitudes, personality, and values. Frame of reference influences everything. Effective communicators need to predict how the listener will receive a verbal or visual statement. It is not sufficient to use perfectly accurate and clear descriptions. If the receiver has no way of grasping the ideas or visualizing the experience, miscommunication will result. *"The message that counts is the one received. . . . Therefore, the burden of communication lies with you, the sender."*[28]

Communication Patterns

Communication is more than words; it includes the entire body and its surrounding contextual environment. Communication patterns are not actual messages but the way the messages are carried. Three basic patterns are used to communicate messages: verbal (spoken or written language); paralanguage (tone, pitch, rate, volume, and emphasis); nonverbal (muscle movements, gestures, facial expressions, eye contact, appearance, posture).[29]

Birdwhistell's research shows that "probably no more than 30 to 35 percent of the social meaning of a conversation or an interaction is carried in the words."[30] As a result, communicators should realize that 65 to 70 percent of the message comes from paralanguage and nonverbal means.

Interpersonal Relationships

Performance improvement practitioners establish trust and work closely with others. Without effective intrapersonal and interpersonal communication, resistance ensues and confidence is not established. Effective communication depends on the ability to make personal expectations clear and to understand and respect the beliefs, values, and attitudes of others. This requires empathy and understanding differences among people.

Active Listening

Active listening requires the ability to accurately absorb what the speaker is saying with an understanding of the speaker's point of view. Effective listeners are able to paraphrase, or accurately restate, the speaker's ideas and feelings using similar words. Good paraphrasing requires listeners to minimize the influence of personal values, past experiences, background, and educational level. Listening is an active process that focuses on the speaker's message. It requires the listener to test the accuracy of understanding by questioning the speaker. Active listening involves a positive outlook towards the speaker's message.

Change Management

Change management is "any action or process taken to smoothly transition an individual or group from the current state to a future desired state of being."[31] Using change management techniques during intervention implementation and maintenance provides opportunities for the performance improvement practitioner to help organizations plan, adapt, communicate, evaluate, and manage change. Change represents a transition state and a critical mass of employees have to be on board the change train or they will be left on the tracks in the station.

Chapter 3 contains a complete discussion of change management—definition and scope, purpose, and techniques. Chapter 4 explains some analysis techniques and tools that are useful for change management activities. Here are some highlights:

- *Visioning*—Varkey and Antonio suggest creating an implementation plan that challenges members of the organization to engage in visioning how the intended change will affect the people, culture, performance, technology, structure, workday, and processes of the organization.[32] (Read the discussion in Chapter 3.)

- *Binder's Six Boxes Model*—This is an update of Gilbert's Behavior Engineering Model that is effective for anticipating and pinpointing change-related behavior and developing an implementation plan that aligns performance improvement, supports management practices, and communicates organization change efforts. (Read about the Six Boxes in Chapter 4.)

- *Sponsors and Change Managers*—Change management efforts involve individuals who fulfill the roles of sponsors and change managers. The sponsor is a true advocate of the intervention and has both the time and authority to make things happen. The change manager facilitates the change process and develops, leads, and supports the change effort throughout the organization. (Read more about sponsors and change managers in Chapter 3.)

- *Minimizing Resistance*—Dormant proposes five strategies to optimize intervention implementation and minimize resistance to change and new ideas. (See the full explanation in Chapter 3.)

- *Five Stages of Change*—Remember that change is a process, not an event, and it is accomplished in five stages; each stage has its corresponding strategy for gaining acceptance.[33] (Read about the stages in Chapter 3.)

- *Monitoring Strategies*—When the intervention is implemented in the workplace, the human performance practitioner, along with the change manager, diligently monitors the process. Rothwell suggests asking questions that will help to focus the change management process.[34] (Questions are listed in Chapter 3.)

Project Management

Project management is the structure that supports successful intervention implementation and maintenance. Project management is also a technique for enabling successful change.

Definition and Scope

Project management is a "specialized management technique to plan and control projects . . . an appropriate way to bring about sudden, revolutionary, or purposeful change."[35] Its origins are found in the U.S. government space program, and other arenas have since adopted the discipline. The European Commission, for example, uses project management for budget support and formulation. Other countries use project management to align multi-national projects and plan alliances and joint ventures. The Association for Project Management in the United Kingdom promotes widespread use of project management for business, industry, healthcare, tourism, and so forth.

PERFORMANCE SUPPORT TOOL 22.3. THE MAINTENANCE EVALUATOR

Purpose: The Maintenance Evaluator raises general questions about the intervention maintenance process. It is designed as a guide to focus thinking during maintenance activities and to evaluate the success of the maintenance efforts.

Directions: Answer the following questions and then discuss them with your team members.

Is implementation maintenance being accomplished in a timely and efficient manner? If not, why not?

Is the implementation maintenance disrupting the organization? If so, how so?

Does the organization have a history of maintenance problems? If so, describe them.

Are the sponsors sufficiently committed to maintaining the interventions? If not, would education and/or training help?

Does synergy exist among stakeholders, team members, and change targets? If not, why not?

How will resistance be handled if/when it is encountered?

Is maintaining the interventions consistent with the organization's culture? Describe the plan.

Are organization members ready for maintaining the change effort? If not, why not?

Are the right people, right communication plan, and right measurements in place? Describe the positioning of each.

What evidence supports the sustainability of interventions?

Is there committed involvement for sustainability? If not, why not?

How will success over failure be measured over time?

EXHIBIT 22.2. THE PRACTITIONER'S VOICE: PROJECT MANAGEMENT

"Project management can be approached through the answers to three questions. The answers enable both a novice and an experienced project manager to meet client expectations effectively.

"The first question is 'What are we going to do?' Answering this question provides you with the project details; it defines the project and identifies what will be part of the project work and what will be excluded.

"The second question is 'How long will it take?' To answer this question, match the project requirements with the activities needed to produce them. Estimate the amount of time needed to complete each activity. Put the activities in order and assign a resource who will be responsible for completing each activity.

"The third question is 'How much will it cost?' Armed with the answers to the first two questions, assemble your material and resource costs, add your overhead. Be sure to include the time you will spend planning, organizing, and directing your resources during the project. Your project cost is the sum of these numbers.

"Use this foundation to develop your quality plans, assess project risks, determine whether suppliers are needed, and establish a communication plan to help you guide your resources to meet the client's requirements.

"Three simple questions, three answers, and you are managing a project!"

Debra M. Smith, M.B.A., PMP

Instructional Consultant

Wayne State University

Office of Teaching and Learning

Detroit, Michigan, USA

A project consists of multiple activities, involving myriad resources, and timely accomplishment. Quality, cost, and schedule drive the project. Projects have life cycles: they begin slowly, gain momentum, reach a climax, begin to decline, and, finally, are terminated. Project management techniques can be applied to any area of activity within an organization since "everyone wants *high performance* within a very *short time*, at *minimum cost*."[36]

Success Factors

Successful management focuses and supports emphases on business, people, and control. Projects that engage critical business issues involve defining and focusing the targets and determining the benefits to business.

People are the primary doers for successful project completion, and project managers, sponsors and champions are held accountable for their actions. These individuals follow a course of action, assess risks, determine sufficient resources, and guarantee target completion.[37]

While there are other areas that compete for the project manager's time and resources, the manager must realize that some aspects will require more attention than others, but time, communication, and risks are the ones that require the most.[38]

Feasibility

Feasibility studies are essential techniques to use during the performance improvement process. The studies are triggered by the need to provide detailed and broad documentation of all aspects of a performance improvement project to determine whether the effort is realistic in terms of resources, cost-benefit, value, risk, and so forth. Feasibility is covered in Chapter 19, Making the Business Case. During intervention implementation and maintenance, the performance improvement practitioner monitors whether the results of the original feasibility study are still valid or whether the implementation process requires some adjustment and/or additional study.

Sustainability

Sustainability of performance improvement speaks to legacy issues and the institutionalization of efforts over time. Sustainability efforts built into an intervention during design and development become part of the maintenance process. Refer to Chapter 21 for a more detailed description of sustainability, including sustainability champions and change agents, sustainability thinkers, sustainability plans, and institutionalization.

Citations

1. Rothwell, 1996, p. 9
2. Gargiulo, Pangarkar, Kirkwood, & Bunzel, 2006, p. 179
3. Gargiulo, Pangarkar, Kirkwood, & Bunzel, 2006, pp. 179–191
4. Robinson & Robinson, 2007
5. Gargiulo, Pangarkar, Kirkwood, & Bunzel, 2006, pp. 191–199
6. Kotter, 1982, p. 67
7. Networking and Marketing Yourself in Business, 2006, p. 857
8. Coleman, 1992, p. 638
9. Bozarth, 2010
10. Networking and Marketing Yourself in Business, 2006, pp. 857–858
11. Simon and Sexton, 1994, pp. 14–17
12. How to Build Business Alliances, 2010
13. Bellman, 1990, p. 66
14. Lippitt & Lippitt, 1978
15. Robinson & Robinson, 1995
16. Block, 2011
17. Weiss, 2002a; 2002b; 2003
18. Carucci & Tetenbaum, 2000
19. Biech, 2007

20. Scott, 2000
21. Hale, 1998
22. Rummler, 2007, p. 8
23. Robinson & Robinson, 1995
24. Carnegie Commission on Higher Education, 1993
25. Senge, 1990
26. Noe, 1998
27. Richey, Klein, & Tracey, 2011, p. 49
28. Hamilton, 1997, p. 11
29. Hamilton, 1997, p. 13
30. Birdwhistell, 1970, p. 158
31. Varkey & Antonio, 2010, p. 268
32. Varkey & Antonio, 2010, p. 271
33. Dormant, 1999, pp. 246–247
34. Rothwell, 1996, p. 15
35. Burke, 2000, p. 568
36. Understanding the Basics of Project Management, 2006, p. 973
37. Understanding the Basics of Project Management, 2006, p. 974
38. Haney & Driggers, 2010, p. 381

References

Bellman, G.M. (1990). *The consultant's calling: Bringing who you are to what you do.* San Francisco: Jossey-Bass.

Biech, E. (2007). *The business of consulting: The basics and beyond* (2nd ed.). San Francisco: Pfeiffer.

Birdwhistell, R.J. (1970). Kinesics and context: Essays on body motion communication. Quoted in C. Hamilton with C. Parker (1997), *Communicating for results: A guide for business and the professions* (p. 158). Belmont, CA: International Thomson Publishing.

Block, P. (2011). *Flawless consulting: A guide to getting your expertise used* (3rd ed.). San Francisco: Pfeiffer.

Bozarth, J. (2010). *Social media for trainers: Techniques for enhancing and extending learning.* San Francisco: Pfeiffer.

Burke, R. (2000). *Project management: Planning and control techniques* (3rd ed.). Hoboken, NJ: John Wiley & Sons.

Carnegie Commission on Higher Education. (1993). *Towards a learning society: Alternative channels to life, work, and service* (p. 43). New York: McGraw-Hill.

Carucci, R.A., & Tetenbaum, T.J. (2000). *The value-creating consultant: How to build and sustain lasting client relationships.* New York: AMACOM.

Coleman, M.E. (1992). Developing skills and enhancing professional competence. In H.D. Stolovitch & E.J. Keeps (Eds.), *Handbook of human performance technology: A comprehensive guide for analyzing and solving performance problems in organizations* (pp. 634–647). San Francisco: Jossey-Bass/ISPI.

Dormant, D. (1999). Implementing human performance technology in organizations. In H.D. Stolovitch & E.J. Keeps (Eds.), *Handbook of human performance technology: Improving individual and organizational performance worldwide* (2nd ed.) (pp. 237–259). San Francisco: Pfeiffer.

Gargiulo, T.L., with A.M. Pangarkar, T. Kirkwood, & T. Bunzel. (2006). *Building business acumen for trainers: Skills to empower the learning function.* San Francisco: Pfeiffer.

Hale, J.A. (1998). *The performance consultant's fieldbook: Tools and techniques for improving organizations and people.* San Francisco: Pfeiffer.

Hamilton, C., with C. Parker. (1997). *Communicating for results: A guide for business and the professions.* Belmont, CA: International Thomson Publishing.

Haney, D., & Driggers, J.T. (2010). Knowledge management. In R. Watkins & D. Leigh (Eds.), *Handbook of improving performance in the workplace, volume 2: Selecting and implementing performance interventions* (pp. 366–391). San Francisco: Pfeiffer.

How to build business alliances. (2010, June). Retrieved from www.com.magazine.20100601/how-to-build-business-alli

Kotter, J.P. (1982). *The general managers.* New York: The Free Press.

Lippitt, G., & Lippitt, R. (1978). *The consulting process in action.* San Francisco: Pfeiffer.

Networking and marketing yourself in business. (2006). In *Business: The ultimate resource.* Cambridge, MA: Basic Books.

Noe, R.A. (1998). *Employee training and development.* Boston: Irwin/McGraw-Hill.

Richey, R.C., Klein, J.D., & Tracey, M.W. (2011). *The instructional design knowledge base: Theory, research, and practice.* New York: Routledge.

Robinson, J.C., & Robinson, D.G. (2007). The ACT approach to partnering with clients. In Strategic business partner: Taking performance consulting to the next level. San Francisco: ISPI Conference Handout.

Robinson, D.G., & Robinson, J.C. (1995). *Performance consulting: Moving beyond training.* San Francisco: Berrett-Koehler.

Rothwell, W.J. (1996). *ASTD models for human performance improvement: Roles, competencies, and outputs.* Alexandria, VA: American Society for Training & Development.

Rummler, G.A. (2007). *Serious performance consulting: According to Rummler.* San Francisco: Pfeiffer.

Scott, B. (2000). *Consulting on the inside: An internal consultant's guide to living and working inside organizations.* Alexandria, VA: American Society for Training & Development and San Francisco: Pfeiffer.

Senge, P.M. (1990). *The fifth discipline: The art and practice of the learning organization.* New York: Doubleday/Currency.

Simon, F.L., & Sexton, D.E. (1994). International business: Formulating and implementing a business strategy. In J.J. Hampton (Ed.), *AMA management handbook* (3rd ed.). New York: AMACOM.

Understanding the basics of project management. (2006). *Business: The ultimate resource.* Cambridge, MA: Basic Books.

Varkey, P., & Antonio, K. (2010). Change management for effective quality improvement: A primer. *American Journal of Medical Quality, 25*(4), 268–273.

Weiss, A. (2002a). *How to acquire clients: Powerful techniques for the successful practitioner.* San Francisco: Pfeiffer.

Weiss, A. (2002b). *Value-based fees: How to charge—and get—what you're worth.* San Francisco: Pfeiffer.

Weiss, A. (2003). *Great consulting challenges and how to surmount them.* San Francisco: Pfeiffer.

Church Pension Fund: The GREAT Model

Topic: *Intervention Maintenance*

Pat Rasile, M.A., CPT, *Operations Training Manager for Client Engagement, Church Pension Group Services Corporation, New York, New York, USA*

Background

The Church Pension Fund (CPF) is a not-for-profit organization that provides pensions and other benefits and services to employees of the Episcopal Church. It contributes to their lifetime economic, physical, emotional, and spiritual well-being.

CPF came into existence in 1914 and, until recent years, the business units of pension, medical services, and life insurance had team members answering client calls. In 2005, a centralized call center was chartered under the direction of a new vice president of "client engagement" whose goal was to deliver excellent, compassionate, and consistent client service. One of CPF's corporate goals is client focus, measured through client satisfaction studies.

Situation

In 2006, Client Engagement (CE) implemented a reputable industry call strategy, which proved to be too cumbersome to use for the client engagement representatives (CERs) as well as being unresponsive to clients' needs. In addition to its awkwardness, the CERs were frustrated with the strategy because it lacked easy-to-use performance support tools.

Managers of CERs were inconsistent with their evaluations and coaching, leading to sporadic feedback and, in some cases, undesirable performance. The culture at CPF was also problematic. There was little documentation provided on how policies, procedures, and practices were accomplished. Employees were not used to being held accountable for their performance, and there was resistance to change.

Intervention

In 2007, after receiving the latest, and lower than desired, client satisfaction survey scores, the VP of client engagement called for a reassessment and redesign of the current call strategy, including its performance and management.

If successful, the right call strategy would increase client satisfaction and meet one of CPF's key corporate goals, thereby showing the value of the new call center. It would also prevent current "call backs" from clients due to incomplete or inconsistent information. If prevented, the call center would experience increased productivity, resulting in better service at lower cost.

If unsuccessful, CE could incur decreased client satisfaction, increased operational costs, and reputation risks for CPF. This possibility could potentially lead to lost business for CPF.

Critical Business Issue

What Is. Client satisfaction was lower than desired and the current strategy neither met client expectations nor needs. In addition, performance of the client engagement representatives (CERs) was not where we wanted it to be and management of the strategy was ineffective.

What Should Be. Client satisfaction should meet desired results and the call center strategy should be focused on meeting our clients' expectations and be easy for CERs to perform. Managers should be effective supporters and champion mechanisms for the CERs to obtain and maintain desired and optimal performance levels. Clients should perceive and receive world class service by the call center.

Focus on Outcomes or Results

The outcomes focused on both the external clients and the performance needs of the client engagement representatives. The desired result was to:

- Achieve increased client satisfaction scores in service skills to support the corporate goal on client focus and show the effectiveness of the new call center
- Support a call strategy that was customized to the needs of CPF clients
- Engage all CERs in using the call strategy consistently and accurately
- Train the client engagement managers to evaluate CER performance consistently

The effectiveness was determined by client satisfaction in service skills as measured by client surveys. We partnered with an external vendor, the Center for Client Retention, to conduct the surveys. The effective and consistent performance of CERs was measured by the quality assurance manager, call center managers, and trainers through our quality program (call monitoring and evaluation).

Focus on Systems View

There were three main areas of foci: our clients, CPF as an organization, and the call center. Our current strategy was not providing our desired results. Client satisfaction top box was only in the 70 percent range (top box equals the percent of clients who rated us a 5 on a 5-point scale, with 5 being the highest). It was important to gather as much information as possible on what our clients valued and design a customized call strategy.

Because CPF had recently implemented an organizational change effort that formed Client Engagement, there was a time-sensitive issue to show the value and effectiveness of the new centralized call center. We needed results as soon as possible.

The frustration and lack of commitment to the call strategy from the CERs was a huge concern. Because the current call strategy was cumbersome and frustrating, it was important to address their concerns and learn what currently worked and did not work. In addition, we needed to figure out how to effectively implement the change to such a resistant culture, especially when it addressed accountability and measurement. Being more inclusive early in the analysis, design, and development could help overcome this obstacle. Proper measurement, coaching, and performance management were the other key factors. We knew overall client satisfaction was also dependent on the work of other business units, but the immediate focus was on the call center and service skills.

Focus on Value

By focusing on both the client and the CERs, we were able to design a strategy directly correlated with the CERs desired performance to the client needs and expectations. Clients received what they wanted, and the CERs were able to easily and effectively meet performance standards.

The training and support materials were performance-based and attainable on every level of experience. This allowed existing and new CERs to quickly obtain desired performance and deliver better service. Managers were able to successfully evaluate, coach, and manage performance.

Focus on Establishing Partnerships

There were two main areas of foci: our clients and the CERs. We listened to our clients and made changes to deliver on their expectations and needs. We then listened to our CERs to determine the necessary support to help them better service our clients consistently. And we empowered both.

The VP of CE was instrumental with her vision of facilitating the resources and influencing the project. We created a quality team consisting of the training manager, the Client Engagement managers, and the quality assurance manager. The team provided input, conducted research, reviewed materials, provided consensus on the recommended solution, and designed the implementation strategy and evaluation.

The CERs provided in-depth feedback and presented new ideas, allowing us to customize the training and performance materials. Feedback during the implementation helped us increase the alignment of expectations between the CERs and their managers.

The assistant vice president of human resources was kept in the loop, since this was a large training initiative and a change for the call center, not to mention the new approach in client service. HR also asked Client Engagement to develop a version for all CPF employees as an integral part of new hire orientation.

Be Systematic in Assessment of Need, Opportunity, or Challenge

The fundamental need/opportunity was established by comparing CE's goal of providing world class service to the client survey results. It was imperative to find out two things: first, how our clients' perception and definition of great service compared to what we defined as great and, therefore, measurable, and second, how the current performance of the CERs compared to the desired performance.

The quality team gathered current data on client satisfaction, including overall satisfaction, and on individual service skills. Client verbatim and in-depth analysis helped us learn exactly what our client expectations and needs were. We compared what our clients valued to the conclusions from industry standards on how organizations and individuals judge service and quality. It was important that we not only meet the spoken needs of our clients, but also that we consider other service areas that could represent their unspoken needs.

Call center managers and CERs were interviewed to learn their perspectives on the current strategy, performance levels, and what they felt or heard was important to our clients. We reviewed existing evaluations and listened to client calls to assess the current CER performance levels and ensure that the quality scores were consistent with their performance. We also used existing calls (using the current strategy) to find opportunities to meet the newly learned client expectations in order to build them into the design of the new call strategy.

We assessed the current measurements we had in place to see whether we were placing enough "weight" on the specific areas voiced as being valued most by our clients. We evaluated the current process for assessing, coaching, and managing performance, including consequences for not utilizing the strategy to standard. Comparisons of evaluations were conducted by the quality team to see how well we were aligned.

Be Systematic in the Analysis of Work, Worker, Workplace, and World View to Identify the Causes or Factors That Limit Performance

The biggest discovery was realizing that the current strategy did not have the right focus for our clients. There were service elements either missing or without proper emphasis. In addition, our client service was not "good enough" to reach our desired levels of excellent service. One key differentiator was "compassionate" service. Although the current call strategy was producing some results, we wanted to raise the bar.

The CERs were not fully executing the current call strategy. It was difficult to follow because it did not match the flow of our calls and had too many areas to remember. Definitions were lacking and there was genuine ambiguity, which led to inconsistency in both performance among the CERs and measurement among the managers. Coaching was neither executed regularly nor consistently. Support materials were ineffective. In addition, it appeared the CERs lacked some soft skills necessary to make a personal connection with our clients. Consequences for inadequately performing the strategy were not great enough to help overcome the obstacles of accountability and change.

Be Systematic in the Design of the Solution

The recommendation was to create a new call strategy addressing the needs, desires, and values of CPF clients. The strategy would be implemented with performance-based training and support materials, measurement, coaching, and proper management.

Our VP suggested we build the components of the call flow around the word GREAT (Greet, Research, Educate, Agree, and Thank). This was consistent with the principles of information mapping and would make it easy for CERs to remember and follow. And so the GREAT Model was born. Each component had two to five parts within it, which correlated directly to a service or need of our clients. Emphasis was placed on the *educate* component, since our clients valued this the most.

The training would include an online training introduction (which could be reused as refresher training), classroom training (including skill building), and support materials with examples to be used on the job. Both the CERs and managers would use the materials as a reference for performance and measurement so that both parties would be in alignment.

Evaluations would be conducted by the quality assurance manager, CE managers, and trainers and would constitute 50 percent of the CERs' annual performance reviews. Formal coaching would occur on a weekly basis by the managers, and the quality team would meet weekly for calibration on a client call. In addition, managers would conduct informal "just in time" coaching, where they would listen to a CER's call live and provide immediate feedback. CERs would have the ability to appeal an evaluation to resolve a discrepancy on a particular call.

Be Systematic in the Development of the Solution

The feasibility and workability of the solution were considerations throughout the project and were addressed regularly by the quality team. During development, we established review points for the GREAT Model communication, training and support materials, evaluations, and an appeal process. We applied a draft of the GREAT Model to real client calls to ensure that it covered all the service areas desired and that the flow seemed natural.

The training manager worked with external consultants in the instructional design and development of the online tutorial and was responsible for ensuring that the implementation was done on time and within budget. At the same time, the training manager developed a version of the GREAT Model for the company-wide new hire orientation with the assistant vice president of HR. He shared the full implementation strategy, including measurement, coaching, and management, but HR did not secure buy-in from managers on anything beyond initial training.

Be Systematic in the Implementation of the Solution

Implementation for the GREAT Model would have been a huge challenge, but by including the CERs from the very beginning, the transition was much smoother. We already had their buy-in to change to a more client-focused, easily followed strategy. Now it was a matter of proving its value and providing the proper support.

The CERs were notified of the new strategy several weeks before the training and implementation and were given the support materials ahead of time. Advance review of the materials was at their own discretion. During the training session, a full explanation and rationale of the GREAT Model (tied to our clients' wants, needs, and expectations) were delivered along with the performance support tools. The first step was gaining agreement on the term "world class service." This was done with an exercise in which the CERs told us what it meant to them, and we were able to turn it around to show them that everything they wanted was exactly what our clients wanted. It all made sense.

Next was learning the strategy and deepening their service skills. The training was performance-based, using exercises and scenarios and using the support materials as they would on the job. The training focused on the "why, what, and how." We also responded to feedback from the CERs, including suggestions for improvement, areas that needed clarity, or additional help in skill building. Because we trained managers ahead of time, they were a support mechanism during the training and continued to work with and coach the CERs during the early stages of implementation. So as not to distract from the training, managers discussed evaluations with the CERs at a different time.

The measurement process was used to track and analyze individual and team performance and improvement. Based on scores, individual coaching plans were created. The monthly averages were used to determine each CER's level of performance and related directly to his or her performance appraisal. CERs with consistently high scores were recognized among their peers and rewarded with either a salary increase and/or bonus, and CERs whose average scores consistently fell below the threshold were put on development or corrective action paths, which could lead to termination.

During the initial implementation we used competition to motivate the CERs. We awarded CERs who had the best calls or were the most improved. After each evaluation, the call and score were published individually for each CER to see, review, and learn from. The appeals process gave each CER the opportunity to have his or her call reviewed or reevaluated by the quality team.

To ensure that the quality team was consistent and fair in its evaluations, weekly calibration sessions were held during which every team member evaluated the same call and compared evaluations. This resulted in one collective score for a CER by the entire team to count toward his or her performance appraisal.

CE managers met with CERs weekly to review performance on their calls and, more informally, provided immediate feedback. Monthly reports were sent to the quality team and the CERs to track and monitor individual and team performance, showing both overall service and individual service areas within the GREAT Model. This information was used for both individual coaching plans and additional team skill building.

Be Systematic in the Evaluation of the Process and the Results

We continued to use the Center for Client Retention to conduct our client satisfaction surveys and benchmark our data. The results showed a steep improvement over the first twelve to sixteen months of the GREAT Model implementation, with client satisfaction top box scores increasing from 78 percent to 88 percent. Client Engagement took the results and incorporated some additional process improvements. Six months later, top box scores had improved to 93 percent. More importantly, we had our client satisfaction numbers in the 90s—reaching our desired client service levels. We continue to conduct surveys on a regular basis and use the data to measure and improve the service we deliver.

The internal measurement showed that the GREAT Model strategy immediately enabled the CERs to gain better control and take ownership of their calls, be more personable, educate our clients with accurate and complete information, and resolve problems more efficiently. CE internal call evaluations improved by 20 percent after the first month and 33 percent after six months. The current standard is 85 percent for proficiency. CERs who excelled were rewarded with year-end merit increases and bonuses. CERs who fell below received coaching plans, extended corrective action, and, when warranted, were terminated.

Managers are measured by their commitment to evaluating calls and providing feedback and coaching to the CERs, as well as their responsibility for CERs overall performance. The quality team continues to meet for weekly calibration and to address any concerns about performance of the GREAT Model.

The solution had a tremendously positive impact on both client satisfaction and the CERs' performance. Human resources stopped introducing the GREAT Model during the new hire orientation. It was discovered that, without setting proper expectations and management, new hires (not in Client Engagement) were confused and didn't use it. However, HR has remained supportive of the strategy.

■ ■ ■

Lessons Learned from the Case
- Knowing about your clients and asking about what they value most will allow you to customize your services to their needs.
- Involving the people who actually do the performance and their managers gives you a better understanding of their needs and gives them a sense of ownership. This not only

deepens the relationship they have with their managers but increases the implementation rate and employee job satisfaction.

- Management needs to be aligned, follow through on commitments, and be a strong support system. Otherwise, no one will take them seriously.
- If you are going to measure performance, have appropriate rewards and consequences.
- Implementation goes beyond training. It is the end-to-end process from the introduction of the initiative to proficiency or desired result. Having check points during implementation, as well as during development, allows you to revise areas that are deficient so that you can improve and reach your desired outcome.
- It is important to have proper metrics in place so that you can measure the extent to which you have reached the desired outcome. Proven success is always looked upon well by senior management.
- Be patient and be professional in your working relationships and be passionate in your desire to orchestrate a change strategy.

Pat Rasile, CPT, is the operations training manager for Client Engagement of the Church Pension Group Services Corporation, where he leads performance improvement initiatives for the call center and the pension services department. He is a Certified Performance Technologist (CPT) through the International Society for Performance Improvement and holds instructional designer certification from Darryl L. Sink and Associates, Inc. He is the recipient of a bachelor of science degree in applied mathematics from Rochester Institute of Technology and a master's degree in music composition from NYU. He can be reached at patrasile@aol.com or by phone at 646.872.1865.

St. Luke Lutheran Church and School

Topic: Intervention Implementation

Keith Vieregge, M.C.M., M.Ed., *Independent Consultant, Eastpointe, Michigan, USA*

Background

St. Luke Lutheran Church is a congregation located in a suburb of Detroit, Michigan. The congregation is led by two pastors, assisted by the church office staff consisting of two secretaries. The congregation also owns and operates a Lutheran school with a preschool through eighth grade enrollment of about 140. The school employs eight teachers, one of whom serves as a teacher and the principal of the school. Assisting in the administration of the school is the school secretary.

In general, the organization is well-established, with many of its people having held membership in the church for many years. The school serves as an excellent means to serve younger families within the congregation and to attract new families to the congregation. Additionally, the church offers many opportunities for members to involve themselves in a variety of activities oriented toward fellowship, instruction in the faith, and service to the church and the community.

Situation

In recent years, the organization has encountered stagnation, which the leadership fears could lead to a general decline in the church's membership. The school has already seen several years of declining enrollment. Although some of the decline could be attributed to a recent economic recession, feedback from membership and staff indicates systemic issues within the organization are also contributing to the situation.

Congregation members report they have little timely awareness of events and activities in the church. Frequent miscommunication or non-communication between various individuals or entities in the school and congregation has caused confusion and sometimes conflict within the organization. The staff spends much of its time "putting out fires" instead of focusing on their given jobs. In general, the staff is experiencing low morale and little satisfaction, while congregation members and school parents feel increasingly detached from the organization. Realizing these are serious problems in need of effective solutions, the leadership enlisted a consultant to identify the issues and their causes and to recommend a course of action that would resolve the issues.

Intervention

During the initial meeting, the pastors and the principal (the team) described a number of issues spanning every aspect of the organization. It was apparent that the team was overwhelmed by the prospect of having to deal with so many issues at once. After some discussion, the consultant persuaded the team to narrow the scope of the project, concentrating on one area that they felt would make the most impact on the organization's performance. The team decided to concentrate on matters pertaining to the organization's communication systems and processes. With the scope of the project narrowed, the consultant developed a proposal for an assessment and analysis of the organization's communication systems.

During the next two months, the consultant gathered data pertaining to organizational communication. He reviewed organization documents, including policy manuals, procedural documents, intra-staff memos, newsletters, worship bulletins, signage around and in the facility, and the organization's website. He sent out questionnaires to school parents, congregation members, and faculty. He conducted interviews with individual workers in the organization, including members of the governing boards of the congregation, pastors, principal, faculty, and secretaries.

At the conclusion of the survey activities, the consultant compiled the data and offered his preliminary findings to the team. After discussing the findings, the team accepted the preliminary findings. The consultant then performed a cause analysis for each of the identified performance gaps (Table C.4.1) and presented his analysis to the team. After the team had reviewed the analysis, the consultant asked the team to consider each gap relative to the impact that closing the gap would have on the organization's overall performance and the level of time and other resources required to close each gap. Then, using a criticality matrix (Exhibit C.4.1), the team members rated each gap according to the priority they would assign to closing that gap.

Based on discussions with the team and their rankings of the criticality of the gaps, the consultant developed a set of recommendations comprised of five "action areas," summarized in Exhibit C.4.2. For each action area, the consultant described the action to be taken, a rationale for taking the action, the steps required to achieve the action, and the performance gaps that each step would address. This approach was taken, in large part, as a way of quieting feelings of being overwhelmed that the team expressed. From the point of view of the team, presenting a plan of five action areas was much more manageable than dealing with eighteen separate performance gaps. The approach also had the benefit of demonstrating to the team that many of the performance gaps were interrelated or shared common causes.

The team enthusiastically embraced the recommendations and, as of this writing, is working with the consultant to design, develop, and implement a program of interventions aimed at effectively addressing each of the action areas.

TABLE C.4.1.   Cause Analysis for Communication Performance Gaps

	Performance Gap	Causes	Recommendations
1	The organization lacks strategic communications plan that aligns with the organization's strategic plan.	No deliberate, clearly articulated strategic plan May lack some expertise required to develop a robust communication plan	Develop an organizational strategic plan Consult with marketing and graphic design talent to develop a robust strategic organizational communication
2	The pastors are often distracted by attending to concerns that are rightly the responsibility of others.	Members are often unaware of where their concerns should be voiced Member knowledge of who serves in which capacity is limited The work and responsibilities of boards and other elected officials have little visibility among congregation members	After elections, publish a directory of church officials and board membership Develop a strategy for making the work and responsibilities of the boards known to the congregation Pastors develop a strategy for kindly redirecting members to the appropriate group or person
4	Boards and individuals often do not report important information to the church or school offices.	Guidelines in the form of printed directions and job aids are not available to board members Feedback system for bringing accountability for board communication practices is not available	Provide boards with guidelines that make clear communication expectations Provide job aids in the form of examples of well-written minutes, announcements Develop a feedback system for alerting board members when communications are lacking
5	The church and school website is underutilized.	Website has not been consistently updated Website design lacks functionality desired by those who would use it Website is not well publicized Website is not integral to a robust organizational communications plan	Integrate the website into communications plan Web redesign that serves the organization's strategic goals and objectives Develop a plan for ensuring the website can be updated easily and often Include the web address on all publications
6	The church marquee and the bulletin boards appear to lack attention to content and appearance.	No clearly articulated goal or objective for the marquis to serve No known person in charge of the appearance and/or content	Set standards that will align the content of marquee and bulletin boards with strategic goals and objectives Assign care, appearance, updating, to an individual, board, or committee
7	Signage inside and outside the building does not adequately direct those unfamiliar with the facilities.	Some signs are weathered and difficult to read Signs that exist are not noticeable to newcomers	Repair, repaint, or replace weathered signs Consider interior signs that mount perpendicular to the wall so people can read them as they look down the halls Post an easily recognizable directory by key entrances to the building

(continued)

TABLE C.4.1. (Continued)

	Performance Gap	*Causes*	*Recommendations*
8	The church's methods of communicating are not likely to reach inactive or less active members of the congregation.	Current communications are only available to those who attend church	Develop a communication plan that includes objectives for reaching all the membership
		Information on website does not consistently relay the most current information, as one would find in "News and Notes," for example	Web design that is updated easily and often
			Provide periodic mailings of congregation news and events (newsletter)
9	The organization's publications do not convey an identifiable organization brand.	Organization's logo has changed several times over the past years	Develop a communication plan that includes standards for logo, colors, and formatting of church and school documents
		Depending on when documents have been updated, different logos may be shown	Create templates for documents, which will standardize document look and feel throughout the organization
		Lack of organization-wide document formatting standards	
10	Many existing organization policy and procedure documents are in need of review and updating.	In many cases, probably a result of the fact that the documents are not often referenced	Review organization's policies and procedures
		No scheduled plan of review for these documents	Update documents, as necessary
			Discard documents no longer needed
		Docs may not be relevant to what actually happens	Create new documents to answer new needs
11	The organization's Internet connection is unreliable, particularly in the school.	The cause of this is unknown at this time	Acquire the services of someone competent to diagnose problems and resolve issue(s)
12	Intra-staff communication methods are often unreliable.	There is not a single prescribed method by which staff know they should expect to send and receive intra-staff communications	Review options for intra-staff communications
		Although the preferred method is email, unreliability of the system effectively discourages consistent use of this method	Select one method that all staff know will be an acceptable means of communicating, and stick to it
			Diagnosis and resolution of reliability issues with email service
13	School communication is often untimely, unclear, or inaccurate.	Writer is often rushed; last-minute completion	Schedule enough lead time so communications are not completed in a rush
		Frequent distractions and interruptions prevent concentration necessary for accuracy	Work on communications at a time when interruptions are minimal
		Principal sometimes finds himself making schedules that others on staff are in a better position to decide	Compose communications at a time that will minimize distractions or interruptions
			Ask a reliable person to proofread docs
			Enlist faculty to create schedules or documents when they pertain to their own work

	Performance Gap	Causes	Recommendations
14	Current methods of school-parent communications do not reflect communication preferences of many parents.	Many parents would prefer the posting of school news on the school website Several parents indicate a preference for personal communication via email and Power School	Ensure website redesign accommodates frequent posting and updating of school news Acquire the services of someone competent to diagnose Internet connection problem and fix it Get parent email addresses at the start of the school year
15	Staff follow-up communication with parents and each other is often insufficient.	Unreliable Internet connection makes access to email and Power School records unreliable Unreliability of system is a disincentive to communication efforts	Acquire the services of someone competent to diagnose Internet connection problem and fix it In the absence of a reliable connection, develop an alternative strategy as a work-around
16	Workers receive little formal timely and helpful feedback on their job performance.	No formal feedback system Informal feedback is not consistently timely or helpful	Develop a feedback system that includes periodic worker reviews
17	Member information updates received by one office is not readily available to the other office.	School and church operate from separate databases	Consider combining data into a commonly shared database In the absence of a common database, develop a system for communicating updated member information between offices
18	Matters pertaining to personnel compensation are not always readily accessible to the business manager.	Sometimes compensation information has been stored in personnel files in school office and is not relayed to the business manager When special compensation arrangements are made, it is not always communicated to the business manager No policy governing how these matters should be handled	Set a policy governing where compensation information should be stored and how compensation matters should be communicated to the business manager This should be addressed immediately, as there may be legal compliance issues involved

EXHIBIT C.4.1. CRITICALITY RANKING OF COMMUNICATION PERFORMANCE GAPS

In the chart below, shaded areas indicate the range of responses. The (X) indicates the average of all the responses.

	Low 1	2	3	4	5	6	7	8	9	High 10
1. The organization lacks strategic communications plan that aligns with the organization's strategic plan.						X				
2. The pastors are often distracted by attending to concerns that are rightly the responsibility of others.								X		
3. The work and responsibilities of boards and other elected officials have little visibility among congregation members.								X		
4. Boards and individuals often do not report important information to the church or school offices.						X				
5. The church and school website is underutilized.							X			
6. The church marquee and the bulletin boards appear to lack attention to content and appearance.							X			
7. Signage inside and outside the building does not adequately direct those unfamiliar with the facilities.									X	
8. The church's methods of communicating are not likely to reach inactive or less active members of the congregation.									X	
9. The organization's publications do not convey an identifiable organization brand.						X				
10. Many of the organization's policy and procedure documents have not undergone content review or revision for many years.							X			
11. The organization's Internet connection is unreliable, particularly in the school.					X					
12. Intra-staff communication methods are often unreliable.					X					
13. School communication is often untimely, unclear, or inaccurate.						X				
14. Current methods of school-parent communications do not reflect communication preferences of many parents.						X				
15. Staff follow-up communication with parents and each other is often insufficient.							X			
16. Workers receive little formal timely and helpful feedback on their job performance from their supervisors.							X			
17. Member information updates received by one office is not readily available to the other office.						X				
18. Matters pertaining to personnel compensation are not always readily accessible to the business manager.			X							

Based on the work of D.M. Van Tiem, J.L. Moseley, and J.C. Dessinger, 2004. Used with permission.

EXHIBIT C.4.2. SUMMARY OF RECOMMENDATIONS

Action Area 1	As soon as possible, the organization should develop a strategic plan that includes statements of the organization's vision, mission, and values, strategic goals, and objectives. Included in the plan should be goals and objectives for the organization's communication systems.
Action Area 2	Take steps immediately to ensure reliable access to the Internet and email.
Action Area 3	Review organizational policies and procedures, particularly as they relate to organizational communication systems. Update existing documents and create new documents, as necessary.
Action Area 4	As soon as possible, develop and initiate a feedback system for employees and those holding office in the church.
Action Area 5	Reinstitute the mailing of a monthly (or some other regular interval) newsletter to the membership of the congregation.

Critical Business Issue

What Is. Existing policies and procedures do not adequately address the communication needs of the congregation. Consequently, frequent miscommunication, non-communication, and misdirected communication are resulting in frustration and confusion; and the absence of a strategic plan is resulting in a general lack of direction among the membership, staff, and governing boards of the congregation.

What Should Be. The organization has a strategic plan that is clearly communicated to all boards, workers, and members. Supporting the strategic plan is a communication plan that defines communication expectations and procedures that facilitate communication across organizational entities.

Focus on Outcomes or Results

The desired outcome of the project was to identify the causes of misdirected communication, as well as inadequate intra-staff, school-parent, and church-membership communications, and to develop recommendations for addressing these communication issues.

Focus on Systems View

At its core, a communication system has four basic components that need to be considered:

- *Message encoded*—Policies and procedures should state communication expectations and processes for what, when, how, and to whom information should be communicated. Messages should align with and support the organization's strategic plan.
- *Medium*—The print media, including the organization's website, should have a clearly recognizable brand that is attractive and inviting to the reader. Internet access should be

reliable so that email can be sent and received with confidence that the message will reach its destination.

- *Message decoded*—Well-formed and purposeful messages attractively presented will help ensure that the message is "heard" by the intended audience. Up-to-date mailing and emailing lists ensure that the intended recipient receives the message.
- Noise—Publications should be free of visual clutter and convey an organizational brand that sets the publication apart from other bulk mailings the membership may receive. The website should also have a clean appearance that draws the eye to the main message of the page. Navigation should be simple and clear to encourage reading and further exploration of the website.

Focus on Value

The process of assessing and analyzing the organization's communication systems focused on bringing value to the organization and its constituents in several ways. First, by collecting objective data the team was able to develop a clear, objective understanding of what was happening in the organization. This, in turn, allowed the team to understand the causes of the performance gaps. Finally, the recommendations provided an understandable blueprint for actions aimed at closing the communication gaps.

According to the clients, for them, the immediate value of the project was that the sense of being overwhelmed and paralyzed had been lifted. Despair had been replaced by hope, and there was an eagerness to implement the recommendations. Should they effectively implement the recommendations, the long-term value to the organization will include a sense of direction and purpose that is supported and driven by the organization's communication systems, a better informed and more active membership, and greater worker productivity and job satisfaction.

Focus on Establishing Partnerships

Establishing partnerships took place on several levels. The consultant established a trusting partnership with the team by inviting their input and review of all aspects of the project. The principal, who had been the target of much criticism from faculty and parents, was initially resistant to participating in the project. As the project proceeded, however, his attitude shifted from resistance to eager participant and valued problem-solver.

Likewise, the faculty were invited to provide their insights into the identification and causes of communication issues and to consider possible solutions to those issues. The discussions highlighted how the faculty, accustomed to working in isolation from one another, could benefit from frequent conversation and collaboration. In the future, partnerships between the governing boards, staff, and individual congregation members will be necessary to establish strategic plans that will drive the congregation toward accomplishing strategic goals.

Be Systematic in the Analysis of the Need, Opportunity, or Challenge

By surveying each stakeholder group and interviewing individuals and groups within the organization, the consultant was able to establish multiple data points. The data collected were carefully examined in order to objectively establish the communication needs, opportunities, and challenges facing the organization. The data also provided valuable insight to the causes of identified performance gaps, as well as clues about possible solutions.

Be Systematic in the Analysis of Work, Worker, Workplace, and Worldview to Identify Factors That Limit Performance

The consultant asked each worker interviewed to describe his or her work and to reflect on perceived barriers to that work. Many of the barriers identified were related to inadequate communication between the workers and their supervisor or between the workers and the people they serve.

Unreliable Internet access for email was cited as a key barrier to prompt, effective communication. Workers reported that timely and relevant feedback on their job performance was virtually nonexistent. As a result, they often felt isolated, left to decide for themselves how to perform their jobs. Each person interviewed stated he or she would like some kind of regular performance review with his or her supervisor.

Be Systematic in the Design of Solutions

Although the scope of the project did not include the development, implementation, or evaluation of solutions, the recommendations provide a blueprint for the design of solutions for closing communication performance gaps. The recommendations are the logical conclusion of a careful and systematic assessment of the current situation, including the identification of performance gaps and their causes.

Prior to settling on the recommendations, the consultant tested the ideas with several stakeholders in order to gauge how well stakeholders perceived they would work and how willingly stakeholders would embrace their implementation. As a result, the project team is confident that the recommendations provide a solid plan that will enjoy stakeholder support and will effectively close the organization's communication gaps.

Be Systematic in the Evaluation of the Process and Results

The project plan included an iterative evaluation plan for the processes and outcomes for each step of the project. During each of the data sweeps, the team evaluated each of the assessment instruments on the basis of its accuracy and likely ability to achieve the data collection objectives for which it was developed. After each of the data sweeps, the team evaluated the data to determine whether the information collected was valid and satisfied the assessment objectives. The team evaluated the findings to ensure they were supported by the data. Finally, the team evaluated and prioritized the final recommendations.

■ ■ ■

Lessons Learned from the Case
- Establishing a trusting partnership with clients and stakeholders early in the process was critical to uncovering critical information and issues that might otherwise remain

undetected. At the beginning of the project, it seemed as if the principal would present obstacles to the assessment and analysis process. As his trust in the consultant and the process grew, he became an indispensable asset to the process, particularly in the identification of performance gap causes and the formulation of solutions. This will pay dividends well into the future, as his input and support will be a key to the successful implementation of many of the solutions.

- Limiting the scope of the project and keeping the clients focused on defined objectives was more difficult than expected. The team had been anxious and overwhelmed for quite a while by myriad issues in the organization, and those feelings persisted at the beginning of the project. The consultant patiently and repeatedly directed their attention to the objectives of the project and demonstrated to them how applying the correct solutions to their communication issues would have a positive effect on the entire performance of the organization. Over the course of the project, the team gradually became more relaxed and better focused on the project objectives.

- Involving the stakeholders in the process of developing and testing solution recommendations was an important component of gaining stakeholder buy-in and support for the recommendations. This was most noticeable among the faculty. One teacher remarked after a meeting with the consultant that at the beginning of the meeting she was dreading the process. Now she was very enthusiastic about the prospect of improvements to her work situation.

Keith Vieregge, M.C.M., M.Ed., is an independent consultant in Eastpointe, Michigan. He is a graduate of Wayne State University's Instructional Technology program with an emphasis in human performance improvement. He holds a master's in church music and a master's in education. Keith can be reached at 586.218.7348 or kvieregge@gmail.com.

SECTION 5
INTERVENTION EVALUATION

"WHAT TYPE OF STRING DID YOU USE?"

Overview of
Evaluation

23

The International Society for Performance Improvement (ISPI) has long supported "the integral role of evaluation in performance technology and in the ongoing functioning of any organization."[1]. In this chapter we will discuss the definition, scope, and purpose of evaluation and present several models of evaluation.

Definition of Evaluation

The *definition* of evaluation has not changed substantially since 2000 when the first edition of *Fundamentals* was published. What has changed is the *scope* of evaluation. In 2000, evaluation was defined primarily from a training and development or program evaluation perspective, with definitions adapted for performance improvement (PI) and human performance technology (HPT) applications. Today, evaluation concepts apply to all performance improvement activities and efforts.

Authors and practitioners in all fields still agree that "to evaluate is to place a value on or judge the worth of a person, place, thing, or event"[2]—with some variations:

- "In the context of *performance*, evaluation is still considered as a way to compare results with intentions and delve into the usefulness of methods and resources so that we may move toward the required results."[3]
- "In the world of learning and performance, evaluation is the act of passing judgment on the value of a problem and its proposed solution."[4]

Scope of Evaluation

The term *scope* refers to range or possibilities and is open to a variety of interpretations. Russ-Eft[5] looks at the scope of evaluation from the perspective of *approaches* to evaluation: "As evaluation expands into different contexts, the approaches to evaluation also expand." She categorizes the approach as "outcome-based or process- and systems-based." The evaluation models discussed later in this chapter provide examples of both approaches. For example, Kirkpatrick's model is an outcome-based model and Brinkerhoff's model is a process-based model.

Dessinger and Moseley[6] discuss scope in terms of *types* of evaluation—formative, summative, confirmative, and meta evaluation—that may be applied to both outcome-based and process- and system-based approaches to evaluation. *Formative* evaluation is diagnostic and is "used to

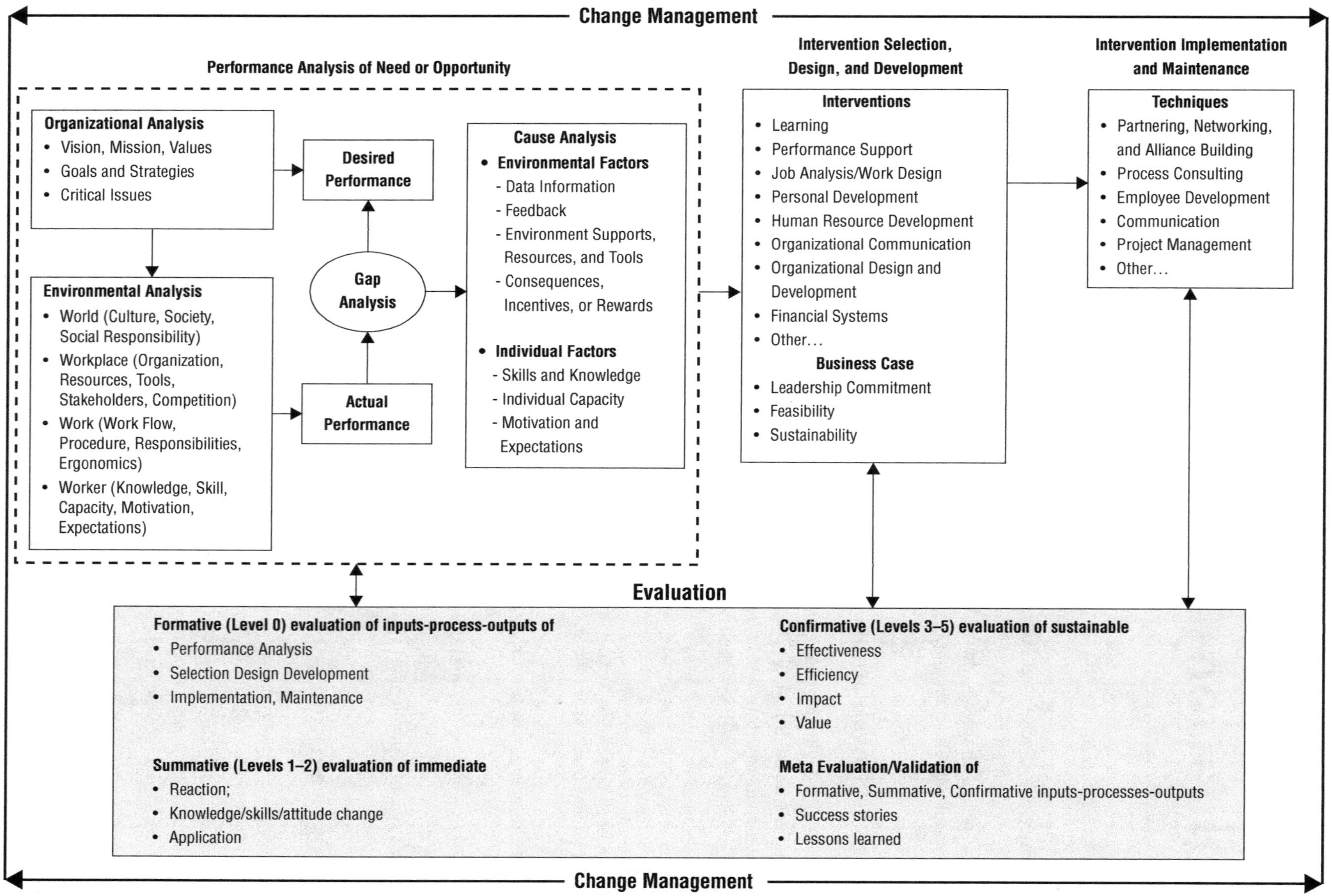

FIGURE 23.1. Performance Improvement/HPT Model: The Evaluation Step

shape or mold an ongoing process . . . to provide information for improvement."[7] *Summative* evaluation focuses on the immediate effectiveness of a performance intervention after it is implemented. *Confirmative* evaluation identifies and explains the long-term effectiveness, efficiency, impact, and value of the intervention. *Meta* evaluation is a process for "assuring and checking the quality of evaluation."[8] All four types of evaluation will be discussed in this chapter and in Chapter 24.

Purpose of Evaluation

Establishing the purpose of an evaluation is an up-front and vital part of the evaluation process. The purpose or "why" of any evaluation drives decisions regarding what to evaluate, when to evaluate, and how to evaluate. If the purpose is (1) explicit, that is, clear, specific, and detailed; (2) true or real and undistorted; (3) aligned with the organization's mission and values, and (4) determined in advance by all the stakeholders, then the resulting what, when, and how will flow more smoothly and truly. (See Figure 23.2.)

The purpose of evaluation varies depending on stakeholder needs and expectations and the specific context or issues involved. In broad terms, "the purpose of evaluation is to illuminate and improve the organization . . . [and] also to affect decision making."[9] For example, feedback from the evaluation of a performance improvement intervention can help decision-makers determine whether to maintain, change, or end the intervention based on its impact on the world, work, workplace, and/or worker.

Geis and Smith[10] suggest that, to provide effective and targeted feedback, the performance improvement practitioner or evaluator may focus the evaluation on one or more of the following purposes:

- Confirm that a particular intervention is being carried out as designed;
- Indicate the effectiveness of a treatment or intervention in order to describe whether to continue, expand, or eliminate the intervention,
- Audit the current state of affairs; and/or
- Determine whether the cost of an intervention is justified by its effects.

FIGURE 23.2.   Flow of Evaluation Decisions: Why to How

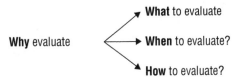

Why evaluate
What to evaluate
When to evaluate?
How to evaluate?

Earlier in this chapter it was stated that the purpose of evaluation determines which type of evaluation—formative, summative, confirmative, or meta—will be used to evaluate a performance improvement intervention.

Evaluation Models

Evaluation models from instructional systems design (ISD) and program evaluation perspectives still form the basis for evaluating performance interventions, although new evaluation models specifically related to performance improvement/HPT are surfacing. The age of the model has little impact on its applicability today, perhaps proving that evaluation is an "ageless" activity because it is based on theory and practice that only gets better with age. Here are some ageless models that are useful for the current practice of performance improvement.

Kirkpatrick Evaluation Model (1959–Present)

The most well-known model of evaluation is the Kirkpatrick four levels model. Kirkpatrick originally developed the four levels in 1959 to help users establish criteria for evaluating training. Kirkpatrick later explained that, for simplicity's sake, he uses the word "training" to include development.[11] Today, Kirkpatrick's model (see Table 23.1) is widely used by both ISD and performance improvement practitioners because it provides a common language, a common tool, and an emphasis on targeted results that practitioners and their clients can both understand and adapt to evaluate a variety of performance improvement interventions.

A visit to the Kirkpatrick Partners website[12] shows the subtle evolution of the basic Kirkpatrick model since 1959. At Level 1 there is an emphasis on measuring *positive* reaction. Level 2 now measures *learning* of *targeted* knowledge, skills, and attitudes rather than *changes* in attitude, knowledge, and/or skills. Level 3 has shifted from measuring *change in behavior* to measuring on-the-job *transfer*. Level 4 *now* measures *targeted* results after training *and reinforcement*. The website also lists five foundational principles: (1) begin with the desired results, (2) identify and focus on return on expectations (ROE), (3) partner with clients to maximize results, (4) create value before demonstrating value, and (5) develop a chain of evidence using all four levels to demonstrate value.

TABLE 23.1.   Kirkpatrick's Four Levels of Evaluation

Level 1—Reaction
Level 2—Learning
Level 3—Behavior
Level 4—Results

Source: Kirkpatrick, 1959. Used with permission.

Brinkerhoff's Six-Stage Model (1987–present)

Brinkerhoff's process model focuses on evaluating learning interventions, specifically training program evaluation. The original six-stage model is iterative in nature, viewing evaluation as a cycle. Brinkerhoff states that his model "responds to the decisions necessary for programs to proceed productively and defensibly . . . enabling and facilitating quality efforts."[13] In performance improvement terms, the six-stage model evaluates the following:

1. *Needs and goals*—the value and importance of the problems of opportunities that trigger the intervention
2. *Design*—the practicality, soundness, and responsiveness to the needs and goals
3. *Operation*—the "goodness" of the installation and implementation of the performance intervention in relation to the needs, goals, and design
4. *Learning*—the level of the user's knowledge, skills, and attitude when he or she first uses the intervention on the job
5. *Usage and endurance*—how well the intervention achieves the intended results over time
6. *Payoff*—the return on investment from the implementation of the intervention

In later work, Brinkerhoff and Mooney[14] focus on how to evaluate HRD training programs in order to demonstrate their worth and value to the organization, determine results, implement and debug new programs, and refine existing programs. Brinkerhoff also aligns his approach to evaluation with Kirkpatrick's levels of evaluation, discussed later in this chapter, and stresses that "level three is the most important and productive of all the levels of evaluation."[15]

Geis and Smith Model (1992)

Geis and Smith's model uses the basic ISD ADDIE model—Analyze, Design, Develop, Implement, Evaluate.[16] The importance of the Geis and Smith model (see Figure 23.3) is that it reconfigures the traditional ADDIE model into ADDI/E to suggest a proactive, integrated approach to the evaluation of learning interventions. This model is helpful when deploying rapid intervention design techniques that compress the analysis, design, development, and implementation phases for right-now or just-in-time deployment of learning or other performance improvement interventions.

FIGURE 23.3.   Geis and Smith Evaluation Model

Analyze→ *Evaluate*→Revise→ **Design**→*Evaluate*→Revise→ **Develop**→

Evaluate→Revise→ **Implement**→**Evaluate**→Revise→

Source: Geis and Smith, 1992. Used with permission.

Kaufman-Keller-Watkins Model (1996–Present)

Recognizing the limits of the Kirkpatrick model, Kaufman, Keller, and Watkins offered an expanded version designed to fit the broader dimensions of the performance improvement environment:

"We suggest that these levels (Kirkpatrick Level 1–4) are incomplete, however, in terms of assessing performance and consequences, and as such they have encouraged many to focus narrowly on evaluating training. . . . Including interventions other than training into the general evaluation design will require some modification to the four levels, while incorporating existing aspects of program evaluation. . . . We propose that the principles and processes of training evaluation be expanded to consider all interventions associated with strategic and tactical planning, performance improvement, organizational development, customer satisfaction/total quality, and societal *contributions*."[17]

Kaufman and his colleagues offered an expanded version of Kirkpatrick's model designed to fit the broader dimensions of the performance improvement environment (see Table 23.2).

Dessinger-Moseley Full-Scope Evaluation Model (1997–Present)

Originally, Dessinger and Moseley expanded on the Geis and Smith model, using spiraling concentric circles to represent "the proactive and iterative nature of evaluation" within the ADDI/E process.[18] The original model evolved into the Dessinger-Moseley full-scope evaluation model (Figure 23.4). The concept of full-scope evaluation was used as the basis for integrating the evaluation phase into the performance analysis, intervention selection, design, and development, and intervention implementation phases for the 2000 and 2004 versions of the HPT Model.

The concept of full-scope evaluation is based on three types of evaluation—formative, summative, and confirmative plus a process called meta evaluation, which literally evaluates

TABLE 23.2. Kaufman-Keller-Watkins Adaptation of Kirkpatrick Model

Level 1	Input and Reaction—The availability and quality of human, financial, and physical resources (input) and the perceived acceptability and efficiency of method and processes (reaction)
Level 2	Aquisition—Individual and small-group mastery and competence
Level 3	Successful Application—Individual and small-group utilization within the organization
Level 4	Organizational Results—Organizational contributions and payoff
Level 5	Societal Consequences—Societal and client responsiveness, contributions, and payoffs

Source: Kaufman, Keller, and Watkins, 1997. Used with permission.

FIGURE 23.4. **Dessinger-Moseley Full-Scope Evaluation Model**

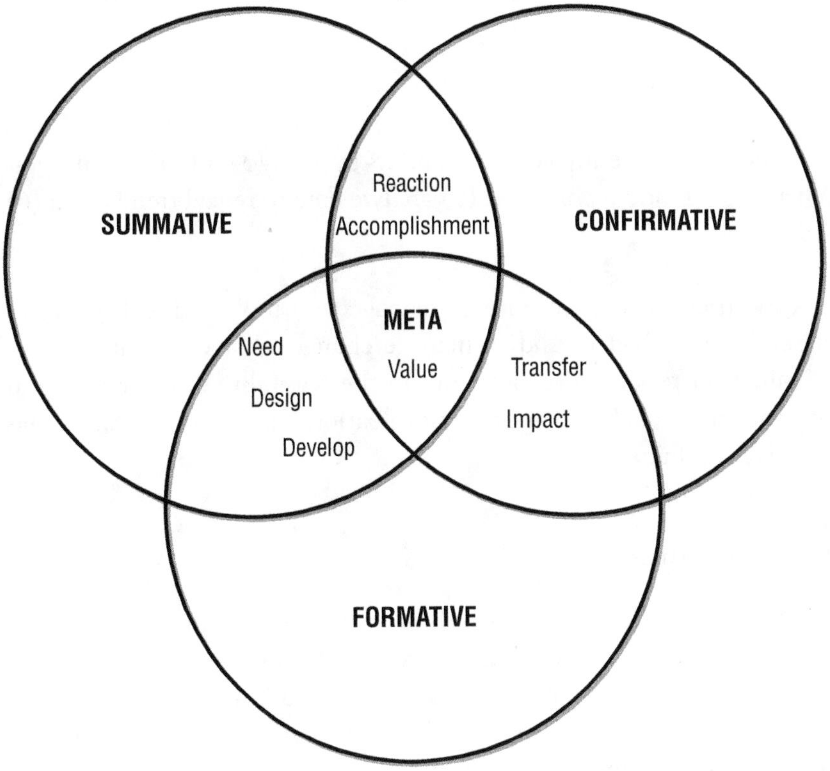

Source: Dessinger and Moseley, 2006, p. 318. Used with permission.

TABLE 23.3. Full-Scope Evaluation: Type, Purpose, and Timing

Type (What)	Purpose (Why)	Timing (When)
Formative	Diagnose and improve analysis, selection or design, and development inputs, processes and outputs	During Analysis, Selection, Design, Development and sometimes Implementation phases
Summative	Assess immediate effectiveness, efficiency, impact, and value of intervention	During Implementation phase
Confirmative	Assess effectiveness, efficiency, impact, and value of intervention over time	Begins 3 to 12 months *after* Implementation to evaluate sustainability
Meta Evaluation	Validate evaluation inputs, processes and outputs	Contiguous with or after completion of other evaluation phases

Source: Kaufman, Keller, and Watkins, 1997. Used with permission.

the evaluation.[19] Full-scope evaluation is an integral part of the life cycle of a performance intervention, guiding the decision-making processes that occur during and after the analysis, selection or design, development, implementation, and, yes, evaluation phases of the PI/HPT Model. Table 23.3 describes each type of evaluation in terms of its purpose and timing within the Performance Improvement/HPT Model.

Combs and Falletta Targeted Evaluation Model (2000–Present)

Combs and Falletta's targeted evaluation model provides a flexible, six-step approach to evaluating performance interventions. The model focuses on determining whether the intervention achieved the goals of the stakeholders. The six steps include (1) identify and partner with the appropriate stakeholders, (2) understand the intervention and its impact, (3) ask the right questions, (4) use the right evaluation tools and techniques, (5) analyze data to reveal trends, and (6) report results to the organization.[20]

The targeted evaluation process stresses the use of project-management tools and techniques to keep the activities on time and within budget and to manage changes that occur during the evaluation. The targeted evaluation process also help ensure the feasibility of the evaluation project by verifying up-front that the stakeholders support evaluation and the organization has the necessary resources to conduct evaluation.

Predictive Approach to Evaluation

Earlier in this chapter we discussed the expanding scope of evaluation in the workplace. Using evaluation to predict outcomes is becoming more and more popular as the need to resolve accountability requirements goes beyond government and education and into business, industry, and other sectors. Predictive evaluation, also known as predictive analytics, may not be perfect, but it is possible and it helps to reduce risk and uncertainty.

Predictive Evaluation

Predictive evaluation is an approach to evaluation driven by business data. It seeks to isolate business impact using predictive analytics to determine where and for whom the investments are having the greatest impact. The data may include predictions of successful intention, adoption, and impact; leading indicators of adoption or transfer; impact or business results; and recommendations for continuous improvement.[21]

Foundations. According to Basarab,[22] Predictive evaluation is built on the work of Kirkpatrick and Brinkerhoff. Beresford feels that predictive evaluation is actually Kirkparick's Level 4 "as he would have wanted it to be," the level that allows evaluation of isolated impacts. Predictive evaluation actually goes beyond the Phillips' survey-based methodology, or Level 5, to become the new business data-driven Level 6, which allows the practitioner to evaluate isolated impacts; for example, which populations—new hires or veterans—will succeed given this intervention?

Beresford also feels that, outside of the learning department, senior executives do not care about learning's four levels of evaluation—they just want authentic business impact. For example:

> "When an organization's budget comes under scrutiny, learning and HR professionals often find themselves vulnerable to cuts. They discover that their traditional and well-loved survey-based business impact and ROI results don't pass muster with the CFO. Thus, many organizations are turning to their own company's operational business data to show their value.

Following a standard research protocol of test and control groups and prior and post-performance, they evaluate the change business metrics over time. Using statistical methods, they can quantify and isolate the impact of their human capital investments . . . in a way that is credible in the C-suite."[23]

Planning and Conducting Predictive Evaluation. Basarab[24] provides tips, tools, and techniques for planning and conducting predictive evaluation. Predictive evaluation uses a combination of interview, survey, and statistical analyses. Data from the performance analysis as well as documentation of the design phase are collected and analyzed to help the evaluator understand the program being evaluated. Real-time and virtual meetings are used to collect data from company stakeholders. For example, a steering committee of eight to twelve stakeholders is formed to meet and create an impact matrix. Company records also provide impact data. Methods for collecting participant data for predictive evaluation are self-reports, including dashboard reports, surveys, questionnaires, interviews, and success stories from high performers. Predictive evaluation also requires statistical analysis of the collected data.

Predictive Analytics

Predictive analytics is making an impact in the field of evaluation because it brings a different methodology to learning evaluation, namely a research methodology familiar to the field of psychology. The idea of using current and historical data and statistical modeling to make predictions about future outcomes is commonplace in some fields; for example, insurance premiums and credit scoring. This science of predictive analytics is finally making its way into the HR and learning space—and is greatly enhancing decision making.

Organizations are using their own HR, training, and business performance data to determine whether an initiative is working, that is, driving business results, and with whom and where is it working best. They can use the data to compare populations and situations, for example, to determine which segments of employees—millennials or boomers, those working in small offices or large offices, and so forth—are benefiting most and least from an initiative and by how much.

Benefits. Predictive analytics provides a degree of certainty that HR and training departments have never had before, enabling them to make data-driven decisions to improve future investments. They make it possible to be systemic, focus on outcomes, and access data beyond the training department. They increase the credibility of HR and training departments.

Implementation. Predictive evaluation is not for the faint of heart and not for a short-term or infrequent program. This sort of evaluation is typically reserved for highly visible, expensive initiatives for which the organization will really want to know the results and will act on the information.

The basic steps for using predictive analytics are

- Engage stakeholders—ideally up-front during analysis or later if necessary; engagement leads to commitment; commitment leads to data access;

- Link everything through a needs assessment, performance map, or impact map;
- Ask stakeholders to establish outcome metrics. What metrics do they expect this initiative to impact?;
- Access and review related business data. Access to data is key;
- Use statistical methods to find out whether training is really responsible for a change in behavior; for example, if you have a group of people in the same environment and you know the demographics, you can do a regression analysis and isolate control factors before and after on both trained and untrained populations and over time;
- Analyze and compare the outcome metrics of the populations; and
- Recommend action.

Roles and Competencies

The performance improvement practitioner should be aware of the possibilities that predictive analytics brings to the evaluation table and be able to articulate the benefits of it to the client. The practitioner also needs a basic knowledge of statistics and/or access to a statistician. In addition, the practitioner must have the credibility and political clout to approach a person with the power to access business data and support action once the results of the evaluation are communicated.

Integrating Evaluation into the PI/HPT Model

When the Performance Improvement/HPT Model was first introduced in 1992 by Deterline and Rosenberg, the last step in the model was "evaluation of results." Marc Rosenberg, one of the authors of the original Performance Improvement/HPT Model, summarized the evaluation component of the model and its purpose as follows: "After applying or implementing the PT solution, it's important to monitor it to determine its effect on performance improvement and on the organization."[25]

The current positioning of evaluation in the Performance Improvement/HPT Model illustrates the integration of evaluation into every phase of the performance improvement process—performance analysis, intervention selection and design, and development, intervention implementation, and evaluation itself. The revised Performance Improvement/HPT Model (Figure 23.1) also suggests which type of evaluation to use during each performance improvement phase and what to evaluate. However, as Hastings[26] cautions: "We must allow process (formative), product (summative), and impact (confirmative) evaluation efforts to permeate the entire performance improvement process."

Performance improvement practitioners should not think of evaluation as an afterthought or a one-time event: "Evaluation may occur at any time and with any frequency. The timing depends on the purpose of the evaluation"; for example:

> "During analysis one often carries out the activities earlier defined as evaluative: clarifying decisions to be made, collecting information, and feeding it into the decision process. A good part of the needs assessment—of front-end analysis in general—is evaluation."[27]

Rothwell also suggests: "Establish a framework for accountability during the selection and implementation phases and ensure the personal involvement of key decision makers in choosing bottom-line measures to demonstrate the value of their efforts."[28]

Role of the PI/HPT Practitioner as Integrator

"The increasing responsibilities of professionals for the results, consequences and payoffs of their activities has led us into a new era of professionalism. For the performance professional this era requires a renewed focus on the scientific basis for decision making."[29] Full-scope evaluation is an ideal which, while it may not be appropriate for all interventions, helps to ensure the validity and reliability of the data upon which business decisions are based. Organizations subject to audits or governed by standards and regulations can benefit greatly from the integration of full-scope evaluation into their performance improvement efforts. Performance Support Tool 23.1, located on page 542, is a guide for the performance improvement practitioner or evaluator who is responsible for integrating full-scope evaluation into the process.

Citations

1. Geis & Smith, 1992, p. 130
2. Van Tiem, Moseley, & Dessinger, 2000, p. 156
3. Kaufman, Keller, & Watkins, 1997, p. 9
4. Hale, 2010, p. 180
5. Russ Eft, 2010, p. 341
6. Dessinger & Moseley, 2004
7. Geis & Smith, 1992, p. 134
8. Madaus, Scriven, & Stufflebeam, 1987, p. 16
9. Geis & Smith, 1992, p. 132–133
10. Geis & Smith, 1992, p. 134
11. Kirkpatrick, 1994, p. xiv
12. Our Philosophy, 2011
13. Brinkerhoff, 1987, p. 26
14. Brinkerhoff & Mooney, 2008
15. Brinkerhoff, 2009, n.p.
16. Geis & Smith, 1992
17. Kaufman, Keller, & Watkins, 1996, p. 9
18. Moseley & Dessinger, 1998, p. 247
19. Moseley & Dessinger, 1998; Dessinger & Moseley, 2004
20. Combs & Falletta, 2000
21. Basarab, 2011
22. Basarab, 2011
23. Beresford, personal communication, August 2011
24. Basarab, 2011
25. Rosenberg, 1996, p. 9

26. Hastings, 2010, p. 254
27. Geis & Smith, 1992, pp. 138–139
28. Rothwell, 1996, p. 283
29. Kaufman & Watkins, 2002, p. 1

References

Basarab, D. (2011). *Predictive evaluation: Ensuring training delivers business and organizational results*. San Francisco: Berrett-Koehler.

Brinkerhoff, R.O. (1987). *Achieving results from training: How to evaluate human resource development to strengthen programs and increase impact*. San Francisco: Jossey-Bass.

Brinkerhoff, R.O. (2009). *Achieving results from training: How to evaluate human resource development to strengthen programs and increase impact*. San Francisco: Pfeiffer.

Brinkerhoff, R.O., & Mooney, T. (2008). *Courageous training*. San Francisco: Berrett-Koehler

Combs, W.L., & Falletta, S.V. (2000). *The targeted evaluation process: A performance consultant's guide to asking the right questions and getting the results you trust*. Alexandria, VA: American Society for Training & Development.

Dessinger, J.C., & Moseley, J.L. (2004). *Confirmative evaluation: Practical strategies for valuing continuous improvement*. San Francisco: Pfeiffer.

Dessinger, J.C., & Moseley, J.L. (2006). The full scoop on full-scope evaluation. In J.A. Pershing (Ed.), *Handbook of human performance technology: Principles, practices, potential* (3rd ed.). (pp. 312–333). San Francisco: Pfeiffer/ISPI.

Geis, G.L., & Smith, M.E. (1992). The function of evaluation. In H.D. Stolovitch & E.J. Keeps (Eds.), *Handbook of human performance technology* (pp. 130–150). San Francisco: Jossey-Bass/ISPI.

Hale, J.A. (2009). Performance-based evaluation: Tools, techniques, and tips. In J.L. Moseley & J.C. Dessinger (Eds.), *Handbook of improving performance in the workplace: Volume 3: Measurement and evaluation* (pp. 179–199). San Francisco: Pfeiffer/ISPI.

Hastings, N.B. (2010). Integrated evaluation: Improving performance improvement. In J.L Moseley & J.C. Dessinger (Eds.), *Handbook of improving performance in the workplace: Volume 3: Measurement and evaluation* (pp. 240–255). San Francisco: Pfeiffer/ISPI.

Kaufman, R., Keller, J., & Watkins, R. (1997).What works and what doesn't: Evaluation beyond Kirkpatrick. *Performance and Instruction, 35*(2), 8–12.

Kaufman, R., & Watkins, R. (2002). Getting serious about results and payoffs: We are what we say, do, and deliver. Modification of an article in a special issue of *Performance Improvement*, April 2000. Retrieved from www.ispi.org/archives/Glossary/Kaufman_Watkin.pdf.

Kirkpatrick, D.L. (1994). *Evaluating training programs: The four levels*. San Francisco: Berrett-Koehler.

Madaus, R.F., Scriven, M.S., & Stufflebeam, D.L. (1987). *Evaluation models: Viewpoints on educational and human services evaluation*. Boston: Kluwer-Nijhoff Publishing.

Moseley, J.L., & Dessinger, J.C. (1998). Dessinger-Moseley evaluation model: A comprehensive approach to training evaluation. In P.J. Dean & D.R. Ripley (Eds.), *Performance improvement interventions: Instructional design and training: Methods for organizational learning* (pp. 233–260). Washington, DC: International Society for Performance Improvement.

Our philosophy: The Kirkpatrick model. (2011). Retrieved from www.kirkpatrickpartners.com/OurPhilosophy/tabid/66/Default.aspx.

Rosenberg, M.J. (1996). Human performance technology: Foundations for human improvement. In W.J. Rothwell (Ed.), *ASTD models for human performance: Roles, competencies, and outputs* (pp. 5–10). Alexandria, VA: American Society for Training and Development.

Rothwell, W.J. (1996). *Beyond training and development: State-of-the-art strategies for enhancing human performance*. New York: AMACOM.

Russ-Eft, D. (2010). Expanding scope of evaluation in today's organizations. In J.L. Moseley and J.C. Dessinger (Eds.), *Handbook of improving performance in the workplace: Volume 3: Measurement and evaluation*. San Francisco: Pfeiffer/ISPI.

Van Tiem, D.M., Moseley, J.L., & Dessinger, J.C. (2000). *Fundamentals of performance technology: A guide to improving people, process, and performance* (1st ed.). Washington, DC: ISPI.

PERFORMANCE SUPPORT TOOL 23.1. WHAT THE PERFORMANCE IMPROVEMENT/HPT PRACTITIONER OR EVALUATOR CAN DO TO INTEGRATE FULL-SCOPE EVALUATION INTO THE PERFORMANCE IMPROVEMENT PROCESS

Formative Evaluation

1. Decide feasibility of conducting a formative evaluation:

   a. Do the organization and stakeholders need to validate the "goodness" of the intervention analysis, selection/design, and development processes and outputs?

   b. Does the organization have the resources (time, money, expertise) and desire to support formative evaluation?

   c. If the answer is *yes to both* a and b, go to Step 2; if the answer is *no to either* a or b, go to Step 4.

2. Establish purpose, goals, objectives, and scope of the evaluation.

3. Design, develop, and implement a formative evaluation plan that aligns with the purpose of the intervention and establishes criteria for revising, maintaining, rejecting, or replacing components of the intervention prior to full implementation.

4. Report findings to organization and stakeholders.

5. Change intervention as needed.

Summative Evaluation

1. Review the analysis outputs and outcomes to decide feasibility of conducting a summative evaluation:

   a. Do the organization and stakeholders need data on the immediate effectiveness, efficiency, impact, and/or value of the intervention?

   b. Does the organization have the resources (time, money, expertise) and desire to support summative evaluation?

   d. If the answer is *yes to both* a and b, go to Step 2; if the answer is *no to either* a or b, go to Step 4.

2. Establish purpose, goals, objectives, and scope.

3. Design, develop, and implement a summative evaluation plan that aligns with the purpose of the intervention and the immediate data needs of the organization/stakeholders.

4. Report findings to organization and stakeholders.

5. Change intervention as needed.

(Continued)

Confirmative Evaluation

1. Review the analysis outputs and outcomes to decide feasibility of conducting confirmative evaluation:

    a. Is it a long-term intervention?

    b. Do the organization and/or stakeholders need to confirm long-term effectiveness, efficiency, impact, and/or value of the intervention?

    c. Does the organization have the resources (time, money, expertise) and desire to support confirmative evaluation?

    e. If the answer is *yes to a, b, and c,* go to Step 2; if the answer is *no to a, b, and/or c,* go to Step 4.

2. Establish purpose, goals, objectives, and scope.

3. Design, develop, and implement a confirmative evaluation plan that aligns with the purpose of the intervention and the long-term data needs of the organization/stakeholders.

4. Report findings to organization and stakeholders.

5. Make life-cycle decisions: maintain, revise, reject, or replace intervention or components.

Meta Evaluation

1. Decide feasibility of conducting meta evaluation:

    a. Do certification, standards, licensing, quality, or other external or internal accountability factors require meta evaluation?

    b. Does organization have resources (time, money, expertise) and desire to support meta evaluation?

    c. If the answer is *yes to both* a and b, go to Step 2; if the answer is *no to either* a or b, go to Step 6.

2. Establish purpose, goals, objective, and scope.

3. Select a professional evaluator or performance improvement practitioner.

4. Select type of meta evaluation:

    a. Type One: monitor and evaluate the evaluation processes, outputs, and outcomes during each evaluation—formative, summative, confirmative.

    b. Type Two: Collect and evaluate the data from each evaluation—formative, summative, confirmative.

5. Design, develop, and implement meta evaluation.

6. Report findings to organization and stakeholders.

7. Make life-cycle decisions: maintain, revise, reject, replace intervention or components.

Source: J.C. Dessinger and J.L. Moseley (2006). The full scoop on full scope evaluation. In J.A. Pershing (Ed.), *Handbook of human performance technology: Principles, practices, potential* (3rd ed.), pp. 324–325. San Francisco: Pfeiffer. Copyright 2006 by Dessinger/The Lake Group. Used with permission.

Planning and Conducting Evaluation

24

Evaluation is more than a phase of the Performance Improvement/HPT Model; it is the integrating force that proves the merit, worth, and value of the entire performance improvement effort. This chapter is a guide to planning and conducting the four types of evaluation introduced in Chapter 23—formative, summative, confirmative, and meta evaluation.

The performance improvement practitioner and/or evaluator takes a leadership role in planning and conducting evaluation. During the evaluation phase, shown in Figure 24.1, the performance improvement practitioner or evaluator is traditionally responsible for performing or monitoring seven major tasks,[1] whether the evaluation is formative, summative, confirmative, or meta:

- Establishing the purpose, goals, objectives, criteria, and scope of the evaluation;
- Establishing the feasibility of conducting the evaluation;
- Selecting the appropriate method(s) based on the purpose and context of the evaluation—social and political environment—and available resources such as time, money, and expertise;
- Collecting all the data that are feasible, available, and relevant;
- Analyzing the data using appropriate sound qualitative and/or quantitative methods;
- Reporting the findings after first determining who needs to know, what they need to know, how best to inform them, and how often to keep them informed. This may also include setting up a review-revise-approve cycle for stakeholders; and
- Making recommendations based on the evaluation results.

This chapter offers resources and guidance to the performance improvement practitioner or evaluator who is planning and/or conducting the four types of evaluation: formative, summative, confirmative, and/or meta. The author concludes that the practitioner or evaluator should really begin setting the stage for evaluation even before the planning begins.

Formative Evaluation

Some performance improvement practitioners think of formative evaluation as a type of *up-front analysis*. Others consider it a *continuous improvement* or *quality control* tool. Planning formative evaluation depends on purpose, timing, and feasibility. Conducting an effective and efficient formative evaluation depends in large part on the *goodness* of the planning process.

FIGURE 24.1. Performance Improvement/HPT Model: Evaluation Phase

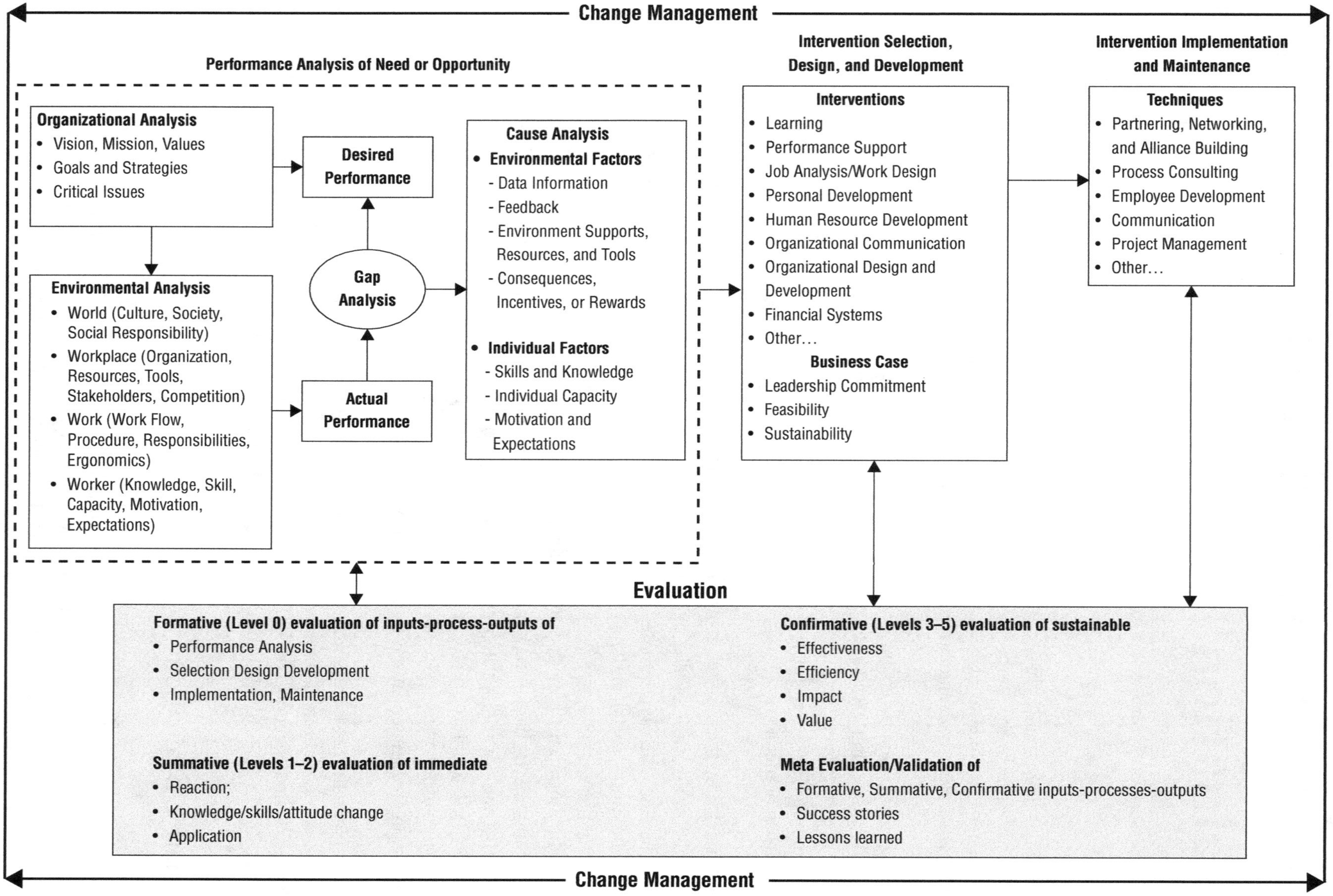

Definition and Scope

By any other name, formative evaluation would be called *continuous improvement* or *quality control*. Originally coined to describe a "systematic process of revision and tryout,"[2] to improve curriculum and instruction, formative evaluation has become a major technique for ensuring quality and consistency of performance improvement processes. Formative evaluation is diagnostic and is "used to shape or mold an ongoing process . . . to provide information for improvement."[3]

Formative evaluation is set apart from summative or confirmative evaluation because it is "a quality control method to improve, not prove . . . effectiveness."[4] The word *improve* is key to understanding why formative evaluation is such an important tool in the performance improvement practitioner's toolkit. "The immediate output of formative evaluation is an improved (performance intervention) package that provides consistent results."[5] The term *performance intervention package* is defined as "any combination of products and procedures designed to improve the performance of individuals and/or organizations."[6]

Purpose

Formative evaluation is largely defined by its purpose. The general purpose of formative evaluation is to validate that the performance intervention package is

- Designed to do what the designers/developers promise it will do,
- Grounded in the mission and values of the organization, and
- Aligned with the objectives of the performance improvement effort.

Timing

Traditionally, formative evaluation begins during the analysis, design, and development of the Performance Improvement/HPT Model.[7] However, performance improvement practitioners are beginning to take a less traditional look at when to conduct formative evaluation. Here are some of their views:

- Integrate formative evaluation with all four levels of Kirkpatrick's Evaluation Model (see Table 23.1 in Chapter 23). Formative evaluation is usually associated with Level 1 (immediate reaction) and Level 2 (immediate knowledge and skill change) of Kirkpatrick's model. Integrating formative evaluation with Level 3 (on-the-job transfer) and Level 4 (organizational results) "is consistent with current approaches to performance technology, and provides an opportunity for the designer to become knowledgeable about the workplace, and to use that knowledge to facilitate the transfer of learning from the classroom to the performance context."[8]
- Consider formative evaluation as "an ongoing process for updating and upgrading the performance improvement package even after it has been implemented in the workplace."[9]

This is similar to the process of maintaining and upgrading a computer system throughout its life cycle.

- Beer and Bloomer[10] also discussed *concurrent* use of summative and formative evaluation during design, development, and implementation as long as the intervention is *revisable* and concurrent use of confirmative and formative evaluation to evaluate relevancy and usefulness after implementation.

The concept of ongoing formative evaluation is consistent with the practice of *rapid design*, which omits or shortcuts some of the up-front analysis and design activities and begins with a basic intervention package that is improved as it is implemented. The concepts of concurrent formative evaluation is consistent with the practice of *rapid design* which eliminates or shortcuts some of the up-front analysis activities and often begins with a basic performance improvement package that is revised as it is implemented.

Planning a Formative Evaluation

Planning formative evaluation begins by working with the stakeholders to define and clarify the intended purpose of the formative evaluation. The stakeholders should agree on the purpose first, since it drives how the evaluation is planned and conducted; then they can discuss the ongoing issue of feasibility. Feasibility analysis balances the resource requirements for conducting the formative evaluation against the purpose or reason why the evaluation is being conducted. Is the goal of the evaluation and/or the use of the selected evaluation methodology worth the cost? (See Chapter 19, Making the Business Case.) As the evaluation expert, the performance improvement practitioner or evaluator is positioned to offer alternative methods for making the formative evaluation as effective and efficient as possible while accomplishing the intended results. The practitioner or evaluator can use Performance Support Tool 24.3 on page 569 to initiate dialogue with the stakeholders, make decisions, and develop the basis for a situation-specific formative evaluation plan that is effective and efficient and will accomplish the desired results.

Conducting a Formative Evaluation

There are four traditional methods for conducting formative evaluation and eight alternative methods.[11] Table 24.1 outlines Tessmer's traditional and alternative methods and has been updated to include new and emerging technologies.

Traditional Methods

The four traditional methods are expert review, on-to-one, small group, and field test. The methods described below may be used to review the entire performance intervention package products and procedures throughout the entire performance improvement process. Thanks to new and emerging technologies for implementing these methodologies, formative evaluation can now be implemented using real-time or virtual activities.

TABLE 24.1. Traditional and Alternative Formative Evaluation Methods

Traditional Method	Alternative Methods
1. Real-time or online expert review	• Self-Evaluation • Panel Review
2. Real time or online one-to-one evaluation	• Two-on-One Evaluation • Think-Aloud Protocols • Interviews
3. Real-time or online small-group evaluation	• Evaluation Meetings • Journals • Blogs or Tweets
4. Real-time or online field-test evaluations	• Online Journals • Blogs and Tweets • Rapid Prototyping

Expert Review. A content or performance expert(s) provides information that aids in the selection or design of the intervention and/or reviews draft components of the intervention before implementation. The performance improvement practitioner or evaluator then "reviews the review," clarifies any remaining issues, and revises the intervention.

One-to-One. A potential performer or user reviews draft components of the selected or designed intervention before implementation. The performance improvement practitioner or evaluator takes part in the review and revises the intervention as needed.

Small Group. Potential performers or users review draft components of the selected or designed intervention before implementation. The performance improvement practitioner or evaluator may or may not participate directly in the review, but is responsible for establishing what the group will focus on during the review, clarifying issues that arise during the review and making the necessary revisions.

Field Test. The selected or designed intervention is tried out with target performers/users before full-scale implementation. This method is frequently followed by a debriefing session involving the practitioner or evaluator, who makes any necessary revisions.

Alternative Methods

Despite the usefulness and proven validity of traditional methods for conducting formative evaluation, Tessmer[12] lists two major factors that call for alternatives:

1. Special circumstances such as time or resource pressure, geographic distances, complexity of performance, or political goals may require altering the basic methods; and

2. New technologies such as computer and electronic communication technologies have created new tools for gathering and evaluating information that expand real-time methods for conducting formative evaluation.

The alternative methods help the performance improvement practitioner to customize traditional formative evaluation processes to fit the context in which the package was designed and will be implemented. No matter which alternative is selected and implemented, the outcome is that the practitioner, in the role of evaluator, designer, and/or developer, guides the focus and criteria for the evaluation process and revises the performance improvement package based on the feedback. The following discussion is updated based on original suggestions from Tessmer,[13] Thiagarajan,[14] and other practitioners. They can be implemented using available real-time or online technologies.

Self-Evaluation (Initial Debugging)

The designer, developer, or several members of the design team try out and evaluate the intervention before presenting it to experts or performers for evaluation. This process is frequently called an *internal review* and is conducted before presenting material to the client for an external review-revise-approve cycle. For self-evaluation to work effectively, the designer or developer should complete the following tasks:

- Develop a set of evaluation criteria. The criteria may be the same as or different from the criteria set for the expert, performer, or client review, but it should include all the items the client or external reviewers will focus on, plus any design or development issues that the design team needs to resolve.
- Set the intervention material aside for several days to gain distance from the intervention's content and intent.
- Literally become the performer and try out the intervention.
- Record both positive and negative feedback.

Panel Reviews

The performance improvement practitioner directs and structures the evaluation process, preparing a set of questions to guide two or more groups of experts through their review of the performance improvement package. Ideally, the experts review the package before meeting the practitioner so that they can focus on areas of concern during the meeting. The practitioner facilitates the meeting and records the outcomes. The panel review may take place in person or using videoconferencing technology.

Two-on-One Evaluation

Two performers review the performance intervention package with the performance improvement practitioner. The performers discuss their reactions as they move through the processes and products that compose the package. The discussion may be conducted online using chat room or videoconferencing technologies or in-person.

Think-Aloud Protocols

This method involves only one performer at a time. The performer walks through the package and verbalizes all of his or her thoughts and reactions. The PT practitioner or evaluator prompts the performer to continue thinking aloud whenever the performer becomes silent. The "walk through" may be conducted in real time or online using video conferencing technologies.

Interviews

Interviews may be conducted in person, by telephone or mobile technology, or online; using email, bulletin board, videoconferencing, or chat room technology. The PT practitioner or evaluator can send, retrieve, analyze, and respond to the email, or use a software program that automatically send questions, collects and analyzes responses to open- or closed-ended questions, and even generates and distributes a customized report.

Using online technology, the practitioner or evaluator can post performance improvement package products, procedures, or issues that arise during design or development. Experts or performers then go into a bulletin board area, read the postings, and react to the postings by leaving messages. Bulletin boards allow for ongoing dialogue among and between the PT practitioner or evaluator, the experts, and the performers. This technology is especially helpful during rapid prototyping when analysis, design, and development of the performance intervention package are conducted simultaneously.

Videoconferencing technology and chat rooms allow the practitioner or evaluator to conduct real-time interviews with one of more experts or performers and to share the discussion for further analysis. Facilitation of real-time, online interviews requires practice. For example, when chat rooms contain more than two people the facilitator must set up protocols to keep the interview focused and allow respondents to complete their responses before another respondent cuts in. The difficulty level rises exponentially with the number of people in the room.

Evaluation Meetings

Evaluation meetings bring together users and/or participants, designer, and evaluator to review and discuss the performance improvement package. Evaluation meetings may be repeated several times to validate revisions to the original package.

Journals, Blogs, and Tweets

Networking technology gives the PT practitioner or evaluator the option of gathering information from online journals, blogs, or tweets. The expert or novice performer records reactions to the intervention and makes suggestions for improvement. The PT practitioner or evaluator may then follow up by using some of the computer interviewing methods discussed above.

Rapid Prototyping

Rapid prototyping is an alternative to full systematic design of performance intervention packages. The designer or practitioner simultaneously analyzes, selects or designs, develops, and implements the package components instead of working in a linear fashion. In the PT environment, the sequence of activities may look as follows:

1. Analyze, select or design, and develop one component or more components of the performance improvement package.
2. Develop the support products required to implement the component(s).
3. Field tests the component(s) immediately with experts or performers.
4. Revise as needed.
5. Repeat the process until the entire performance improvement package is completed.

During rapid prototyping, formative evaluation is similar to a pilot except the users or experts provide feedback during the initial implementation of the performance improvement package. Reviewer input is used to revise the prototype and, in time, to develop the final version.

Advantages and Disadvantages of Alternative Methods

Table 24.2. was updated from Tessmer[15] to provide an overview of the advantages and disadvantages of the alternative methods of formative evaluation. Use of the various methods should be based on feasibility issues such as the need to collect data, determine time and resources available, and check level of support from stakeholders.

TABLE 24.2.   Advantages and Disadvantages of Alternative Formative Evaluation Methods

Method	Advantages	Disadvantages
Self-Evaluation	• easy to conduct • insider's viewpoint	• not rigorously conducted • sometimes don't "see the forest for the trees"
Panel Reviews	• expert dialogue • negotiated agreement	• may move off task • less independence
Two-on-One	• performer dialogue • performer agreement • possible time savings	• no pace/time data • no individual opinions • dialogue distraction
Think-Aloud Protocol	• data on mental errors • process data	• intrusive • awkward to use
Computer Interviewing	• access to remote subjects • continuous evaluation	• time-consuming • training required • equipment required
Evaluation Meetings	• amount of group info • quick tryout and revision	• only easy changes made
Computer Journals, Blogs, Tweets	• continuous evaluation • environmental variations • cost- and time-effective	• hardware and software requirements • computer experience levels of users • no evaluator present
Rapid Prototyping	• assess new strategies • assess new technologies	• time and cost to develop • undisciplined design

Summative Evaluation

Formative evaluation helps the organization to determine whether or not to put the *soup* on its performance improvement *menu*; summative evaluation helps the organization determine whether or not to *keep* the soup on the menu. "When the cook tastes the soup, that's formative; when the guest taste the soup, that's summative."[16] During formative evaluation, the "cooks" who prepare the performance intervention package—analysts, designers, developers—both conduct and benefit from the evaluation. On the other hand, an external evaluator frequently stirs the pot during summative evaluation and the "guests" who are tasting the soup may be major organizational decision-makers and stakeholders "who provide the political and economic support for the program or intervention."[17]

Definition and Scope

Summative evaluation focuses on the immediate effectiveness, efficiency, impact, and value of the intervention when it is implemented. Basically, summative evaluation looks at the immediate results of a performance intervention package during implementation and gathers information that will be useful to the decision-makers in the organization. The results being evaluated may include the following:

- What is the immediate or short-term reaction of the performers or other stakeholders to the intervention?
- What immediate or short-term changes in knowledge, skills, and/or attitude occur? To what degree do the changes occur?
- Are the intervention and/or resulting changes applied on the job by the performers and/or accepted by other stakeholders?

Purpose

Summative evaluation seeks to answer two major questions:

1. Did the performance intervention package solve, eliminate, or reduce the original performance improvement opportunity, problem, or gap?
2. Does the performance improvement package meet the needs of the organization?[17]

Changes to the intervention may or may not take place based on this immediate feedback.

Planning a Summative Evaluation

Summative evaluation takes place during the implementation and maintenance phase of the Performance Improvement/HPT Model. In fact, Smith and Brandenburg refer to summative evaluation as "rear end analysis," as opposed to front-end or performance analysis.[18] Traditional steps to follow when planning a summative evaluation based on Smith and Brandenburg are

1. Indentify the decision-maker and the stakeholders and conduct interviews to specify what decision(s) needs to be made and what data are needed to make the decision(s).

2. Translate decision(s) into targeted evaluation questions and ask the decision-maker to validate the questions.

3. Analyze constraints, resources, and opportunities to determine what is feasible given the existing situation.

4. Make a plan:

— Select the evaluation strategies, standards, and participants or population.

— Specify instruments, procedures, and sampling strategies that will collect the required data.

— Specify administration plan requirements for staffing, scheduling, budgeting, and reporting.

5. Conduct a reality check to validate that the evaluation plan components are feasible and will accomplish the intended results.

6. Distribute the evaluation plan to the stakeholders as needed.

Use Performance Support Tool 24.3 on page 569 as a guideline for planning a summative evaluation plan.

Conducting a Summative Evaluation

The process of collecting and analyzing data is more formalized during summative evaluation than it is during formative evaluation. Summative evaluation may use some of the same tools as formative evaluation—interviews, observation, group processes, and surveys—to collect data on immediate participant reaction, on-the-job transfer, and/or organizational results and impact. However, summative evaluation uses assessment techniques to test and measure immediate changes in knowledge, skill, and/or attitude, and statistical analysis to establish significance and develop an objective basis for decision making. Frequently, an expert evaluator develops test questions and a statistician analyzes the test results.

New technology and software have improved the PT practitioner's ability to collect, analyze, store, and distribute summative evaluation data.[19] Software such as SPSSX® simplifies the use of statistical analysis techniques. Statistical analysis software can collect, analyze, and store data and prepare graphics and reports. There is also increasing use of computer and/or mobile technologies to deliver and evaluate the education, training, and/or information required for performance improvement. Computer technology is also capable of facilitating interactivity between the participants and the materials and collecting data on whether the participants have understood and used the education, training, or information to change their knowledge, skills, or attitudes and their immediate reaction to the delivery content and strategy. Mobile technology has some interactivity and collection capability and is continually increasing its potential.

Confirmative Evaluation

Thirty-three years ago Misanchuk[20] introduced confirmative evaluation as a logical next step to formative and summative evaluation of instructional materials or learners. Twenty-six years later, Seels and Richey[21] suggested that "Quality control requires continuous evaluation including extending the cycle beyond summative evaluation," and a decade after that Dessinger and

Moseley[22] moved confirmative evaluation into the realm of performance improvement with their book: *Confirmative Evaluation: Practical Strategies for Valuing Continuous Improvement.* Confirmative evaluation builds on the findings and recommendations generated during formative and summative evaluation. It enables evaluators to confirm the *continuing* worth of performance improvement packages and performers and helps organizations decide how to manage continuous performance improvement efforts. The Dessinger-Moseley model is shown in Figure 24.2.

Definition and Scope

The following definition of confirmative evaluation, although written for ISD practitioners, is easily adapted to the broader context of PT: "Confirmative evaluation is the process of collecting, examining, and interpreting data and information in order to determine the continuing competence of the learners (performers) or the continuing effectiveness of the instructional materials (performance improvement intervention)."[23] Confirmative evaluation "challenges us to jettison linear models and integrate evaluative process throughout every phase of [performance improvement]."[24] For further insight into what confirmative evaluation is all about, it is necessary to examine its purpose and timing.

Purpose

The major purpose of confirmative evaluation is to provide continuous quality control over the life cycle of the performance improvement package. Confirmative evaluation does this by placing a value on the endurance of the performance improvement package and by helping the decision-makers establish what to do next.[25]

Confirmative evaluation identifies, explains, and confirms the long-term or enduring efficiency, effectiveness, impact, and value of the intervention.[26] It judges the actual and perceived value to the user in terms of competence and "usefulness" and the impact on the organization in terms of performance improvement, return on investment (ROI), and other measurable factors.

"Enduring or long-term effects" refer to those changes that can be identified after the passage of time and are directly linked to the performance improvement package."[27] Figure 24.3 illustrates how the value of a performance intervention is equal to the continuing competence of the performers who participate in the intervention and the continuing effectiveness of the entire performance improvement package, including products and processes.

In addition to confirming the competency of the performers and the effectiveness of the performance improvement package, there are two other reasons why performance improvement practitioners or evaluators should conduct confirmative evaluation. First, confirmative evaluation may be used to link the intervention to broader accomplishments that directly affect the organization and to establish actual costs and benefits.[28] Second, long-term formative evaluation or confirmative evaluation not only supports and strengthens continuous improvement efforts within an organization, but can also "feed back valuable hypotheses to research in pursuit of a better understanding of human behavior, performance, and accomplishment," helping to build a scientific base for PT.[29]

FIGURE 24.2. Dessinger-Moseley Confirmative Evaluation Model

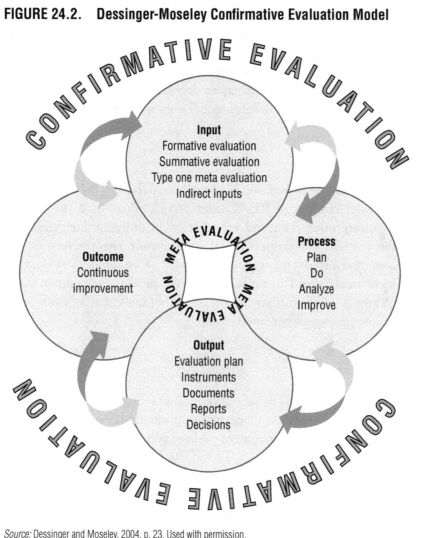

Source: Dessinger and Moseley, 2004, p. 23. Used with permission.

Planning and Conducting Confirmative Evaluation

In 1997 Moseley and Solomon[30] published a model of confirmative evaluation. The model divides confirmative evaluation into four processes: planning, doing, assessing, and improving. The focus of the model is on continuous improvement driven by customer expectations. The model and its companion checklist are shown in Figures 24.4 and 24.5.

Moseley and Solomon[31] suggest that the following tasks should be conducted during each phase of their confirmative evaluation model. The tasks are listed in Table 24.3.

Planning Confirmative Evaluation

Moseley and Solomon[32] suggest that during the planning phase of confirmative evaluation the performance improvement practitioner or evaluator should partner with the stakeholders to focus and design the evaluation (see the first row in Table 24.3). Questions to ask during the planning phase that help the PI practitioner focus and design the confirmative evaluation are outlined in Performance Support Tool 24.3 on page 569.

FIGURE 24.3.   Equation for Confirming the Value of a Performance Intervention

Value of the Intervention	=	Continuing competence of the performers	+	Continuing effectiveness of the performance package

FIGURE 24.4.   Moseley-Solomon Confirmative Evaluation Model

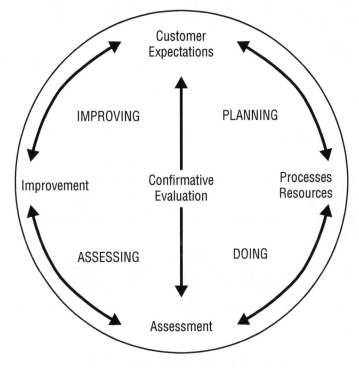

Source: Moseley and Solomon, 1997, p. 13. Used with permission.

During the planning stage the performance improvement practitioner or evaluator will also determine when to conduct the confirmative evaluation, what resources will be required to conduct and support the confirmative evaluation, for example, people, materials, and cost. The decision will also be made whether to develop or purpose or customize the evaluation materials.

Deciding when to conduct confirmative evaluation is a major planning task. There are two viewpoints on when to use confirmative evaluation. The first views confirmative evaluation as an extension of formative evaluation, and the second views confirmative evaluation as a separate and distinct form of evaluation that goes beyond formative and summative evaluation.

FIGURE 24.5. **Preliminary Checklist for Confirmative Evaluation**

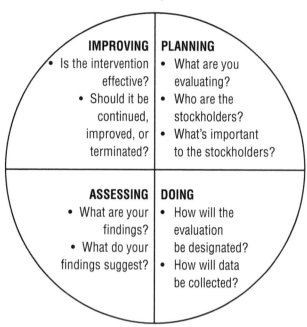

IMPROVING
- Is the intervention effective?
- Should it be continued, improved, or terminated?

PLANNING
- What are you evaluating?
- Who are the stockholders?
- What's important to the stockholders?

ASSESSING
- What are your findings?
- What do your findings suggest?

DOING
- How will the evaluation be designated?
- How will data be collected?

Source: Moseley and Solomon, 1997, p. 13. Used with permission.

TABLE 24.3. Tasks to Perform During Confirmative Evaluation Phases

During this phase . . .	*The evaluator will . . .*
Planning	• focus the evaluation • design the evaluation
Doing	• collect information • use multiple information gathering techniques such as questionnaires, interviews, observations, focus groups, work sample analysis, performance analysis, context studies, peer-supervisor self-reports, cost-benefit analysis, analysis of formative and summative evaluation data
Assessing	• organize data • interpret data
Improving	• consider the impact, value added, and effectiveness • recommend whether to continue, improve, or terminate the intervention

Source: Moseley and Solomon, 1997, p. 13. Used with permission.

Ongoing Process

The first viewpoint stresses that confirmative evaluation should be "an ongoing process designed to 'take a pulse' before, during, and after an intervention is implemented. Confirmative evaluation must be woven into the fabric of an intervention."[33] This viewpoint is in line with the concept of "long-term formative evaluation," which extends formative evaluation beyond implementation and summative evaluation. "Long-term formative evaluation is conducted after the newly installed intervention has been in effect for some time and after its novelty has worn off. Ideally, this evaluation should be repeated every six months or so."[34]

After Implementation

The second and more traditional viewpoint is that "the major element which distinguishes confirmative evaluation from formative and summative evaluation is the time factor. Confirmative evaluation . . . takes place after implementation."[35] The heuristic, or rule of thumb, is that confirmative evaluation should take place three months to a year after implementation of the performance improvement package. The following guidelines suggest that confirmative evaluation should not begin until and unless:

- The criteria for the formative and summative evaluation phases have been met;
- Detailed assessment information on the participants is available; and
- Instrumentation is available to assess the areas of possible effect and other intervening factors.[36]

Resolving the Time Issue

One way to determine when to conduct confirmative evaluation is to use these three criteria: criticality, complexity, and frequency.[37] Performance Support Tool 24.1 offers some heuristics or rules of thumb for determining when to conduct confirmative evaluation based on Hellebrandt and Russell's criteria and best practices in the field.

Conducting Confirmative Evaluation

Because long-term formative evaluation and confirmative evaluation are so similar in intent, Thiagarajan's[38] guidelines for conducting long-term formative evaluation also apply to the process of confirmative evaluation, with some modifications based on best practices:

1. Collect data every six months or more or less, depending on the criticality of the intervention results.
2. Be as unobtrusive as possible; for example, incorporate data collection into ongoing activities such as performance appraisals or audits.
3. Focus on the typical effects of the package such as long-term productivity, return on investment (ROI), accountability or standards requirements.
4. Methods for conducting confirmative evaluation may include, but are not limited to, the following:
   — Checklists for desired or optimal performance;
   — Interviews with stakeholders;
   — Observation and/or performance tests;
   — Rating scales to quantify level of actual performance;
   — Assessment tests of knowledge and skill, pre- and post-intervention; and
   — Review of existing information such as before-and-after data, safety reports, production reports, suggestions.

PERFORMANCE SUPPORT TOOL 24.1. WHEN TO CONDUCT A CONFIRMATIVE EVALUATION

Directions: Gather responses from as many stakeholders as possible: performers, their supervisors, managers, customers, vendors, suppliers, and organization decision-makers. Then use this performance support tool to determine when to conduct the confirmative evaluation.

Learning/Performance Factor	Rating	Confirm Every . . .
Criticality: How critical is the performance to the success of the organization?	High	3 to 6 months
	Medium	6 to 12 months
	Low	12 months
Complexity: How complex is the performance?	High	3 to 6 months
	Medium	6 to 12 months
	Low	12 months
Frequency: How often is the performance required?	Regularly	3 to 6 months
	Monthly	6 to 12 months
	Annually	12 months
	One time only	Do not confirm
Frequency: How often is the performance intervention implemented?	Regularly	3 to 12 months
	Monthly	6 to 12 months
	Annually	12 months
	One time only	do not confirm

Role of the Performance Improvement Practitioner/Evaluator

Confirmative evaluation requires a special perspective and strong analysis skills. One option is to use an "unbiased" external evaluator or external evaluation team, to determine whether or not the performers have maintained the level of competence they achieved after the performance intervention was implemented and whether or not the intervention itself still meets the original objectives. The external evaluator or team could partner with an internal expert who is familiar with the performance and/or the environment in which the performers function.

The performance improvement practitioner should be an active member of the evaluation team. The automotive example in Exhibit 24.1 shows how an internal performance improvement practitioner and outside observers and evaluators confirmed the effectiveness of a critical, long-term performance improvement intervention.

EXHIBIT 24.1. TEAM ROLES IN A CONFIRMATIVE EVALUATION

One task assigned to the field service managers at automotive dealerships is to appraise leased vehicles that have been turned in at the end of a lease. In this situation, the managers were not consistent in their appraisals so, to minimize the variance between the appraisers, a performance improvement intervention was implemented. The intervention included classroom and hands-on training, performance support tools (PST), and incentives. The standards for performance were known. The evaluation plan called for formative, summative, and confirmative evaluation.

The performance improvement practitioner led all the evaluation elements of the intervention plan. For the confirmative evaluation element, the practitioner designed and developed checklists, which included a list of conditions, rating standards or criteria for desired performance, and a rating scale for each desired performance. The practitioner trained external observers to use the checklists and rating scale to conduct the confirmative evaluation.

Immediately after the initial implementation of the new inspection program, and again six months later, the trained observers watched the managers as they appraised a series of vehicles with preset conditions and recorded their observations on the checklists. An external evaluator used statistical analysis techniques to analyze the data and determine the continuing competence of the performers and the continuing effectiveness of the intervention. The evaluator submitted the report to the evaluation team and the team communicated the results with their recommendations to the intervention champion, who was also the project lead at the organizational level.

Meta Evaluation

Meta evaluation is a process for "assuring and checking the quality of evaluations."[39] Through meta evaluation, a professional evaluator or a trained performance improvement practitioner validates the formative, summative, and confirmative evaluation processes and products. Meta evaluation is especially important for long-term, strategic, performance improvement interventions. Changes to the intervention may or may not occur depending on the results of the meta evaluation.

Michael Scriven coined the term "meta evaluation" in 1969. His website contains information and tools such as a meta evaluation checklist.[40] Meta evaluation has been around since then; however, organizational buy-in to implementing meta evaluation is spotty at best because of time, cost, and skill requirement constraints.

Definition

Meta evaluation stands apart from the three types of evaluation discussed in the previous sections. Meta evaluation is the process of evaluating formative, summative, and confirmative evaluation by literally zooming in on the evaluation processes, products, results, and recommendations to take a closer look at what happened and why. It is a quality control process that is applied to the inputs, processes, and outputs of formative, summative, and confirmative evaluation and to success stories and lessons learned. Those who do implement meta evaluation find that it enables them to:

- Improve the quality of formative, summative, and confirmative evaluation,
- Test whether or not the formative, summative, and confirmative evaluations delivered what they promised, and
- Increase the probability that evaluation results will be used effectively.[41]

Scope

There are two types of meta evaluation: Type One and Type Two. What sets the two types apart is timing and purpose, as shown in Table 24.4.

Type One Meta Evaluation. Type One is very much like formative evaluation because it is concurrent and proactive. Many times an outside evaluator observes and analyzes the formative, summative, and confirmative stages of evaluation as they occur and makes recommendation for improving the evaluation process before the process is finalized.

Type Two Meta Evaluation. Type Two resembles summative evaluation because it places a value on the evaluation processes after they occur. Type Two is the more frequently used form of meta evaluation. It requires fewer resources like time, money, personnel, or materials and can be tied directly to the bottom line of the performance intervention. Therefore, we focus here on Type Two.

TABLE 24.4. Timing and Purpose for Type One and Type Two Meta Evaluation

Type of Meta Evaluation	Timing and Purpose
Type One	Conducted *during* formative, summative, and confirmative evaluation
	Guides the evaluator through the planning, design, and implementation of all three stages of evaluation
Type Two	Conducted *after* the formative, summative, and confirmative evaluations are completed
	Provides *feedback* on the reliability and validity of the evaluation process, products, and results

Purpose of Type Two

The concept of Type Two meta evaluation fits in quite well with the concepts of quality control and accountability. "Evaluators will be more likely to see their studies effectively utilized when they demonstrate that their work can stand the test of careful analysis and that they themselves are open to growth through criticism."[42]

The specific purpose for conducting Type Two meta evaluation may vary, but usually involves placing a value on basic issues such as:

- Technical adequacy of the formative, summative, and/or confirmative evaluation processes and products;
- Usefulness of the formative, summative, and/or confirmative evaluation results in guiding decision making;
- Ethical significance of policies for dealing with people during formative, summative, and/or confirmative evaluation;
- Practical use of resources during formative, summative, and/or confirmative evaluation;
- Whether the formative, summative, and/or confirmative evaluations served the information needs of the client;
- Whether or not the formative, summative, and/or confirmative evaluations adequately addressed the goals and values of the performance improvement intervention and the organization;
- How well the formative, summative, and/or confirmative evaluation met the requirements of honesty and integrity; and
- Other . . . as determined by the organization for which the intervention was implemented.[43]

Planning Type Two Meta Evaluation

The performance improvement practitioner or evaluator could rephrase the purposes stated above as questions and use the questions to focus the meta evaluations. Performance Support Tool 24.2 suggests questions to ask to help focus the meta evaluation.

Conducting Type Two Meta Evaluation

There are three basic methods for conducting a Type Two meta evaluation: review the documentation, do it again, or compare it to similar evaluations.[44]

Review the Documentation

The performance improvement practitioner or evaluator reviews the evaluation proposal, evaluation plan, status or other interim reports, and/or final report. The purpose of the review is to determine whether the reviewer agrees with the data collection, data analysis, conclusions, and

PERFORMANCE SUPPORT TOOL 24.2. FOCUSING THE META EVALUATION: WHAT'S THE GOAL?

Directions: Ask these questions of the stakeholder to help decide the goal(s) or purpose(s) of the meta evaluation. Then stay focused on the goal(s) as you plan what to evaluate, how to evaluate, what resources will be required, when to evaluate, and how to communicate the results and recommendations. Circle either "yes" or "no" for each item.

Technical adequacy of the evaluation process and products?	Yes	No
Usefulness of the results in guiding decision making?	Yes	No
Ethical significance of policies for dealing with people?	Yes	No
Practical use of resources?	Yes	No
Whether it served the information needs of the client?	Yes	No
Whether it adequately addressed the goals/visions of the performance improvement package?	Yes	No
Whether it adequately addressed the goals/values of the organization?	Yes	No
How well it dealt with situational realities?	Yes	No
Whether it met the requirements of honesty and integrity?	Yes	No
How well it satisfied the need to truthfulness?	Yes	No
Other?	Yes	No

recommendations of the original evaluator(s). Documentation review is particularly helpful when the outcomes of an evaluation are qualitative rather than quantitative. Qualitative outcomes are based on feelings and experience, and the information is often gathered through interviews that are self-reporting. Quantitative outcomes are based on more objective measurement, and the information is often gathered using statistical methods.

Do It All Over Again

The performance improvement practitioner or evaluators reanalyze the quantitative data from the original evaluation to determine the reliability and validity of the data and the analysis techniques. The practitioner or evaluator may replicate all or part of the original evaluation or examine the effects of using different statistical procedures or asking different questions. Reanalysis is costly in terms of time and resources and is usually reserved for evaluation projects that involve major policy changes.

Find Others Who Did the Same Thing and Combine the Results

If an evaluation has been repeated in different settings, it is possible to gather together and integrate the results from all the evaluations. This is a statistical process that makes it feasible to draw general conclusions about the processes, products, and results of all the evaluations. The current popularity of internal or external benchmarking could be a selling point for implementing this method of meta evaluation; benchmarking compares internal performance to industry standards or practices.

Role of the PI/HPT Practitioner or Evaluator

The performance improvement practitioner or evaluator conducts the meta evaluation with input and support from the performance intervention stakeholders. The stakeholders should be involved in the meta evaluation, particularly if an outside evaluator conducts the evaluation. Stakeholders can help make decisions regarding the purpose for conducting the meta evaluation and can also help select the methods to use when conducting the evaluation. The services of an external evaluator, or an internal evaluator who has not participated in planning, designing, or implementing the performance improvement package, is generally preferred to gain a fresh perspective.

Conclusion: But Are They Ready?

This chapter has been all about planning and conducting the four types of evaluation. However, before the planning or conducting begins, the practitioner or evaluator should really determine whether the organization is willing and able to *do* an evaluation. The Full-Scope Evaluation

Pre-Planning Inventory developed by Dessinger and Moseley is a performance support tool that is designed to be used with all the stakeholders to assess or audit the following:

- Does the organization have "the will and the resources" to conduct an evaluation?
- Is the failure or success of the performance improvement intervention *really* important to the organization? The stakeholders?
- What is the most effective and efficient way to evaluate the performance improvement intervention?[45]

The inventory "sets the stage for successful evaluation by exploring the environment in which the evaluation will take place and ensuring that the stakeholders . . . *oughta* and *wanna* evaluate."[46]

Citations

1. Herman, Scriven, & Stufflebeam, 1987
2. Tessmer, 1994, p. 16
3. Geis & Smith, 1992, p. 134
4. Thiagarajan, 1991, p. 22
5. Thiagarajan, 1991, p. 24
6. Thiagarajan, 1991, p. 22
7. Moseley & Dessinger, 1998, p. 245
8. Dick & King, 1994, p. 8
9. Thiagarajan, 1991, p. 31
10. Beer & Bloomer, 1986
11. Tessmer, 1994
12. Tessmer, 1994, p. 5
13. Tessmer, 1994
14. Thiagarajan, 1991
15. Tessmer, 1994
16. Seels & Richey, 1994, p. 58
17. Dessinger & Moseley, 2010, p. 139
18. Smith & Brandenburg, 1991, p. 35
19. Rothwell & Whiteford, 2010
20. Misanchuk, 1978
21. Seels & Richey, 1994, p. 59
22. Dessinger & Moseley, 2004
23. Hellebrandt & Russell, 1993, p. 22
24. Moseley & Solomon, 1997, p. 12
25. Brinkerhoff, 1987
26. Hanson & Siegel, 1995, p. 27
27. Hanson & Siegel, 1995, pp. 27–28
28. Hanson & Siegel, 1995

29. Thiagarajan, 1991, p. 13

30. Moseley & Solomon, 1997, p. 13

31. Moseley & Solomon, 1997, p. 12–13

32. Moseley & Solomon, 1997

33. Hellebrandt & Russell, 1993, p. 24

34. Hanson & Siegel, 1995, p. 28

35. Hellebrandt & Russell, 1993

36. Thiagarajan, 1991, p. 31

37. Madaus, Scriven, & Stufflebeam, 1987, p. 16

38. Thiagarajan, 1991

39. Posavac & Carey, 1989, p. 284

40. Scriven, 2011

41. Posavac & Carey, 1989, p. 282

42. Posavac & Carey, 1989, p. 284

43. Posavac & Carey, 1989, p. 282

44. Posavac & Carey, 1989, pp. 282–284

45. Dessinger & Moseley, 2010, p. 132

46. Dessinger & Moseley, 2010, p. 140

References

Beer, V., & Bloomer, A.C. (1986). Levels of evaluation. *Educational Evaluation and Policy Analysis, 8*(4), 335–345.

Brinkerhoff, R.O. (2009). *Achieving results from training: How to evaluate human resource development to strengthen programs and increase impact.* San Francisco: Pfeiffer.

Dessinger, J.C., & Moseley, J.L. (2004). *Confirmative evaluation: Practical strategies for valuing continuous improvement.* San Francisco: Pfeiffer.

Dessinger, J.C., & Moseley, J.L. (2006). The full scoop on full-scope evaluation. In J.A. Pershing (Ed.), *Handbook of human performance technology: Principles, practices, potential* (3rd ed.). (pp. 312–333). San Francisco: Pfeiffer/ISPI.

Dessinger, J.C., & Moseley, J.L. (2010). Full scope evaluation. In J.S. Moseley & J.C. Dessinger. (Eds.), *Handbook of improving performance in the workplace: Volume 3: Measurement and evaluation* (pp. 128–141). San Francisco: Pfeiffer/ISPI.

Dick, W., & King, G. (1994). Formative evaluation in the performance context. *Performance and Instruction, 33*(9), 8.

Geis, G.L., & Smith, M.E. (1992). The function of evaluation. In H.S. Stolovitch & E.J. Keeps (Eds.), *Handbook of human performance technology* (pp. 130–150). San Francisco: Jossey-Bass/ISPI.

Hanson, R.A., & Siegel, D.F. (1995, April 3–7). The three phases of evaluation: Formative, summative, and confirmative. Updated draft of paper originally presented at the 1991 meeting of the American Educational Research Association (AERA), Chicago, Illinois.

Hastings, N.B. (2010). Integrated evaluation: Improving performance improvement. In J.L Moseley & J.C. Dessinger (Eds.), *Handbook of human performance technology: Volume 3: Measurement and evaluation* (pp. 240–255). San Francisco: Pfeiffer/ISPI.

Hellebrandt, J., & Russell, J.D. (1993, July). Confirmative evaluation of instructional materials and learners. *Performance and Instruction, 32*(6), 22–27.

Madaus, R.F., Scriven, M.S., & Stufflebeam, D.L. (1987). *Evaluation models: Viewpoints on educational and human services evaluation*. Boston: Kluwer-Nijhoff Publishing.

Misanchuk, E.R. (1978). Descriptors of evaluation in instructional development: Beyond the formative-summative distinction. *Journal of Instructional Development, 2*(1), 15–19.

Moseley, J.L., & Dessinger, J.C. (1998). Dessinger-Moseley evaluation model: A comprehensive approach to training evaluation. In P.J. Dean & D.R. Ripley (Eds.), *Performance improvement interventions: Instructional design and training: Methods for organizational learning* (pp. 233–260). Washington, DC: International Society for Performance Improvement.

Moseley, J.L., & Solomon, D.L. (1997). Confirmative evaluation: A new paradigm for continuous improvement. *Performance Improvement, 36*(5), 12–16.

Posavac, E.J., & Carey, R.G. (1989). *Program evaluation: Methods and case studies* (3rd ed.). Englewood Cliffs, NJ: Prentice Hall.

Rothwell, W.J., & Whiteford, A.P. (2010). Using new technology to create a use-friendly evaluation process. In J.L. Moseley & J.C. Dessinger (Eds.), *Handbook of improving performance in the workplace: Volume 3: Measurement and evaluation*.

Scriven, M. (2011, February). Evaluating evaluations: A meta evaluation checklist. Retrieved from michaelscriven.info/images/EvaluatingEvals-Checklist.pdf.

Smith, M.E., & Brandenburg, D.C. (1991). Summative evaluation. *Performance Improvement Quarterly, 4*(2), 35–58.

Tessmer, M. (1994). Formative evaluation alternatives. *Performance Improvement Quarterly, 7*(1), 3–18.

Thiagarajan, S. (1991). Formative evaluation in performance technology. *Performance Improvement Quarterly, 4*(2), 22–34.

Van Tiem, D.M., Moseley, J.L., & Dessinger, J.C. (2004). *Fundamentals of performance technology: A guide to improving people, process, and performance*. Silver Spring, MD: ISPI.

PERFORMANCE SUPPORT TOOL 24.3. PLANNING THE FORMATIVE, SUMMATIVE, AND CONFIRMATIVE EVALUATION OF A PERFORMANCE IMPROVEMENT INTERVENTION

Directions:

1. Check the type of evaluation you are planning.
   ☐ Formative   ☐ Summative   ☐ Confirmative   ☐ Meta

2. Meet with the stakeholders and fill in the matrix below. The columns are labeled with the first three phases of ISPI's Performance Improvement/HPT Model. The rows are labeled with the issues that you need to address when planning a successful evaluation. Start with the first phase—Analysis and fill in each cell.

3. The rows and columns also form the basic outline for an evaluation plan. The information may be supplemented with project management–type timelines and milestone charts and an executive summary.

	Performance Analysis	Intervention Selection, Design, and Development	Intervention Implementation, Maintenance
What do we want to accomplish in this phase?			
When do we evaluate this phase?			
What resources do we need to evaluate this phase (people, time, materials, other)?			
What basic and alternative methods will we use to evaluate this phase?			
What data will we collect to evaluate this phase? How? Who will analyze it?			
What type of report do we need at the end of the evaluation? Who is our audience? What do they need to know?			
What will it cost to evaluate during this phase?			

Source: J.C. Dessinger and J.L. Moseley (2010). Full-scope evaluation. In J.L. Moseley and J.C. Dessinger (Eds.), *Handbook of improving performance in the workplace: Volume 3: Evaluation and measurement.* San Francisco: Pfeiffer. Used with permission.

ABC Automotive Company—Dealership Sales and Marketing Academy

Getting to the Business Impact of Training
Topic: Predicting Outcomes

Bonnie Beresford, M.B.A., *VP of Client Services, Capital Analytics, USA*

Background

ABC Automotive is a major automobile manufacturer with a global network of dealerships selling its cars and trucks. The Dealership Sales and Marketing Academy is responsible for the training and development of the U.S.-based dealership sales force of some fifteen thousand employees. The Academy's sales curriculum is structured as a certification program, which is voluntary for dealership sales consultants. Certification is granted to sales consultants upon completion of the core curriculum; consultants maintain certification by keeping current on new products as the associated training rolls out. The Academy's training offerings have historically focused on product information because corporate managers believed dealers would train their own staffs to their own sales processes. Courseware was delivered through a combination of web-based and instructor-led courses.

Training is partially funded by the company. However, dealers must also pay for courses, making the need to offer high-quality training that will drive results an imperative for the Academy. If dealers do not see a return on their investment in the Academy's offerings, they simply will not enroll their employees.

Situation

A disappointing new vehicle launch led company executives to blame the Academy's sales training for the lackluster sales. Tired of being the "fall guy" for sales shortfalls (and never the "hero" for sales successes), the director of the Academy set out to understand the business impact of his curriculum. While data showed that trained salespeople outsold untrained ones by thirty-five vehicles per year, it was unknown how many of these sales were actually attributable to training versus other variables, for example, attractive financing, exciting products, new advertising campaign, and so forth. He established a measurement task force, with a charter to (1) determine the relationships between training and business results and (2) improve the quality and relevance of the Academy's services. The task force consisted of Academy representatives from sales, service, parts, and technical training teams and the Academy's long-term third-party training partner. The first order of business was to get the curriculum aligned with the needs of the retail audience—the personnel at the dealerships. Then it would be time to measure—and prove—the impact of the Academy's training on business results.

Intervention

Over the next year, the measurement task force (MTF) led the Academy on a performance improvement journey. They sought to improve their internal processes, especially in front-end analysis, and then sought to improve the quality of courseware. Through improved courseware, the Academy believed they would drive dealership performance. Wrapped around this was the awareness that any performance improvement must be measurable. With the help of outside performance improvement experts, the MTF framed their charter, strategies, and a game plan for turning the Academy into a performance-based organization with a culture of measurement. The plan included six key elements:

1. Standardized Measurement
2. Performance Mapping
3. Gap Analysis
4. Redesigned Curriculum
5. Measurement
6. Communication of Results

The MTF gained some early wins by introducing Kirkpatrick's four levels and implementing measurement standards for Levels 1 and 2. Results encouraged department managers to become engaged in understanding how consistent, systematic measurement could improve the quality of their courses. Soon managers were asking for and talking about their "Level 1's."

Knowing that those initial measurement stages would not align the curriculum with business impact, the task force again engaged an outside performance improvement expert to assist in defining the required skills and associated performance gaps among the sales force. Eight sets of high-performing sales consultants participated in an iterative process to create a performance map. This enhanced task analysis adds valuable insights about the tasks, such as importance, difficulty to learn, frequency, and risk of not doing it. A key finding of the mapping was the distinction between "applied selling time" (when a customer is present) and "unapplied selling time" (what a consultant does when no customers are in the dealership).

Based on the map, the task force conducted a gap analysis to determine areas of highest need and to help prioritize new course development. The analysis revealed that only top performers made effective use of "unapplied selling time," such as prospecting and having a daily game plan. Gaps were also found in some of the "applied selling time" skills, especially around presenting the offer.

A new curriculum was structured to align with the performance map. Course development was prioritized based on needs identified in the gap analysis. Some courses in the new curriculum leveraged existing content, while others required completely new content. Many of the skills-based courses called for live training to enable consultants to practice and receive feedback on new skills. Knowledge-based courses were created for the web and served as foundational prerequisites for the live training.

As soon as a sufficient numbers of consultants had completed the new curriculum, the task force was ready to measure the impact. The performance metrics included sales volume, sales consultant retention, and customer satisfaction scores. In order to isolate how many of the thirty-five additional vehicles sold by trained sales consultants per year were actually attributable to training, the MTF utilized the services of Capital Analytics, a consultancy that specializes in isolating the impact of human capital investments. The approach considered sales consultant performance both before and after training to determine how performance improved. Untrained personnel were evaluated over the same time period to provide comparative data. Multivariate analysis, including general linear modeling, was used to isolate the effect of training on performance.

The measurement results were powerful. They isolated fifteen of the thirty-five additional vehicles, showing that this gain could be attributed to the new curriculum versus other factors such as advertising, financing, or new products. Training also contributed to a dramatic increase in retention, especially among new hires—38 percent retention of untrained versus 98 percent retention of trained new hires.

With results like these, the Academy was eager to promote the benefits of training to the dealers and throughout the company. The combination of the performance map and the business results guided future investment decisions. The impact of training on retention led the Academy to offer special incentives for dealers to train their new hires.

Today, the Academy has a repeatable process for determining needs, defining gaps, and measuring impact. In addition to better serving their stakeholders, their work has won Excellence in Practice and Business Impact industry awards.

Critical Business Issue

What Is. Sales training needs had been largely driven by corporate mandate rather than a formal needs analysis. Training's contribution to the business in terms of sales performance was speculated but not known for sure.

What Should Be. The sales training curriculum should be driven by a task and needs analysis and aligned with the dealer and company goals. The relationship between training and those goals should be understood, measured, and communicated to stakeholders.

Focus on Outcomes or Results

The Academy's objective was to align training with business goals so that a revamped curriculum would intentionally impact business results, specifically sales volume, customer satisfaction, and sales consultant retention.

Focus on Systems View

Inputs. The inputs for the needs analysis had to come from the field, for example, from sales consultants. Insights from top performers would shape the new curriculum. Once launched, impact would be measured using data from the personnel, learning management, and sales reporting systems.

Process. An iterative interview process was used to create the performance map. The online gap analysis sent to all sales consultants and managers determined areas of greatest need. This repeatable process helped prioritize curriculum development. The subsequent measurement process used existing company data to isolate the impact of training on performance.

Outputs. There were several key outputs, including the performance map and gap analysis, the new curriculum, and the quantifiable evidence of training's impact.

Constraints. The marketplace does not stand still, and with the infusion of technology, in time the performance map will likely need updating and the gap analysis will have to be re-done. If the Academy wants to continue providing value-added training, the map and associated curriculum must be kept current.

Focus on Value

This entire initiative was all about the value of training. The task force's charter was to show relationships between training and business results and to improve the quality and relevance of the Academy's services. The mapping enabled the Academy to design the right training to fill the skill gaps. The business results illustrated the value to the organization and to dealers.

Focus on Establishing Partnerships

The Academy realized that creating a culture of measurement and implementing a performance improvement/HPT approach would require a team effort. The formation of the measurement task force built internal partnerships. Their training partner and other third-party human performance improvement experts brought needed expertise to the team. Through these partnerships, the team gained a working knowledge of the tools of HPT.

Be Systematic in Assessment of Need, Opportunity, or Challenge

ABC Automotive has a dealer council that includes a subcommittee on training. The Academy met with this engaged group of dealers to understand dealer perspectives on current training practices. Knowing that the company expected training to contribute to sales, the Academy was anxious to quantify training's business impact. The establishment of the measurement task force put a formal entity in place to get the curriculum aligned with dealer and company goals.

Be Systematic in the Analysis of Work, Worker, Workplace, and Worldview to Identify the Causes or Factors That Limit Performance

The measurement task force designed a game plan and followed it. The performance mapping/gap analysis process provided a structured approach to define the key skills needed among the sales force. The performance mapping process included tasks and tools as well as importance, risk, and difficulty of each task. Sales managers and trainers critiqued and refined the final map.

Be Systematic in the Design of the Solution

The new curriculum's design was based on the map. Priorities were determined by the biggest skill gaps (as defined by the gap analysis). The associated impact analysis was designed to use existing data and a standard research methodology (test and control groups). The task force actively participated with Capital Analytics in the design of the impact study.

Be Systematic in the Development of the Solution

The Academy built the new curriculum according to priorities laid out by the gap analysis (unapplied selling time, followed by applied selling time skills). The analysis, design, development, implementation, and evaluation (ADDIE) model is the standard approach employed using the performance map and the Academy's new Level 1 and 2 measurement standards. All courses were piloted (web and live) to refine the content as needed. Online tools were implemented to deliver the Level 1 and 2 instruments.

Be Systematic in the Implementation of the Solution

New courses were announced to the sales force with the new year's certification program. Trainers were engaged in extensive "train-the-trainer" sessions to learn the new content. The Academy monitored enrollment rates and Academy managers and instructional design teams keenly reviewed Level 1 results. Despite these new courses adding more requirements to the certification program, the sales consultants' response to the new and targeted content was overwhelmingly positive.

Be Systematic in the Evaluation of the Process and the Results

The measurement standards applied to all courses, enabling the Academy to compare courses to each other over time. Reporting timetables were established for new courses to provide rapid feedback on Level 1 and 2 results. Results of sales and retention of trained versus untrained sales consultants were tabulated each quarter in anticipation of the planned impact study.

As a result of the statistical analysis, the Academy *proved* the value of their new curriculum, as well as *improved* its deployment and impact. They could now confidently communicate to the company and to dealers that training did indeed contribute to sales success and sales consultant retention. They introduced a "ninety-day protection plan," leveraging the new hire-training-retention linkage. The plan encourages dealers to train their new consultants sooner by lowering the risk of investing in the training.

■ ■ ■

Lessons Learned from the Case

- Engaging outside experts can bring needed perspective and capabilities. Be sure the chemistry is a good fit; leverage their expertise and learn from them.
- Building a culture of measurement takes time, but it's worth it: start small and share results. Making decisions based on data increases your credibility.
- Measuring for business impact isn't just to prove; it's also to improve.

Bonnie Beresford, M.B.A., has extensive experience in measurement and evaluation, process improvement, training, and performance support. As VP of client services at Capital Analytics, she leads consulting teams in evaluating and isolating the business impact of human capital investments. Bonnie holds a business degree from Central Michigan University and an MBA from Wayne State University. She is currently pursuing a Ph.D. in human capital management at Bellevue University in Omaha, Nebraska. She can be reached at 248.366.4507 or bberesford@capanalytics.com.

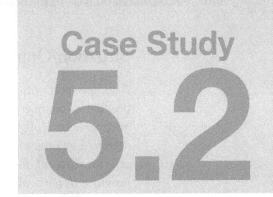

Community Healthcare Association of the Dakotas: A Five-Level Evaluation Model

Topic: *Five-Level Evaluation Model*

Holly Burkett, Ph.D., SPHR, CPT, *and Principal, Evaluation Works, Davis, California, USA*

Background

The Community Healthcare Association of the Dakotas (CHAD) faced accelerating demands for more diversified, compliance-oriented training and technical assistance services. The consultant used collaborative processes to build a sustainable, outcome-based service model for addressing volatile changes associated with increased pressures for efficiency and effectiveness and for measuring the value of federally funded community partnership and collaboration services.

The Community Health Care Association of the Dakotas is the bi-state primary care association for federally supported health clinics in North and South Dakota. CHAD's membership includes eleven health clinics, four in North Dakota and seven in South Dakota. As the primary care association for two rural, frontier states with widely disbursed populations, CHAD serves a community health clinic network through consultation, technical assistance, training, resource development, financial management, and human resource advocacy for the purpose of increasing capacity and sustainability of community health clinics. CHAD's mission is to lead the Dakotas in quality primary health care through public policy and community-driven health services. Its vision is to be recognized and valued for its network of services and expertise that facilitates the missions of "safety net provider" CHC members.

Situation/Opportunity

An expansion of health clinics in the Dakotas has created an accelerated demand for CHAD to provide its members with more diversified and compliance-oriented training and technical assistance services. In light of increased pressures for utility and efficiency and a political climate characterized by ongoing resource and budget constraints, the board of directors established strategic priorities around determining the value and payback of "partnership and collaboration activities" provided to network members.

Intervention

The key objective of this two-year consulting engagement was to create, implement, and standardize a sustainable, results-based evaluation model to ensure that CHAD's "suite" of educational and technical assistance services were designed, delivered, and monitored to achieve desired results and make optimal use of resources.

In order to address those needs, the ROI process methodology was selected as the evaluation framework and results-based service model for this project. The ROI process expands Kirkpatrick's four-level framework for evaluation—reaction, learning, behavior, and results—to incorporate a fifth level of evaluation, which captures return-on-investment (ROI). The ROI process model also includes techniques for isolating the effects of a program and for capturing a sixth data measure, intangible benefits.

Solution implementation began with an organizational analysis consisting of extant data review and focused interviews with key stakeholders and select CHC network members. Work products, processes, policies, and procedures were also examined to identify enablers and barriers to technical service design and delivery.

A logic model approach was used to help program staff and key stakeholders define and document key interim outcomes for tracking the progress of technical assistance (TA) initiatives and to create shared understanding about how TA activities contributed to desired long-term outcomes, such as capacity building and improved patient care. Once service needs, objectives, outcomes, and influencing enablers and barriers were identified, project sponsors and stakeholders agreed to introduce the ROI process on a pilot basis. A comprehensive TA project, known as OC3, was chosen as the pilot program. OC3 curriculum helped members manage compliance issues related to federal regulations.

Critical Business Issue

What Is. By 2015, it is estimated that health centers will double their current capacity to forty million patients while facing estimated federal budget cuts of $1.3 billion nationwide. Given increased demands to double capacity while also bringing down costs, more and more funding sources are requiring evidence of demonstrable results to justify continued investments.

What Should Be. Utilization of an outcome-based evaluation framework ensures that decision-makers have a durable, credible process for helping to focus on programs or services that provide the most value. The framework can also be used internally to measure the efficiency and effectiveness of community partnership and collaboration services and define continuous improvement opportunities.

Focus on Outcomes or Results

Stakeholders identified key desired outcomes, including: (1) enhancing methods for collecting, organizing, and presenting data about outcomes; (2) increasing member utilization of the association's support services, resources, and products; (3) increasing member satisfaction with technical assistance services; and (4) improving resource allocation by defining the services or products that add the most member value.

Focus on Systems View

Inputs. Critical inputs for this project included analysis findings from (1) review of extant data (mission, vision, strategic plans, site visit reports by funding sources, member satisfaction surveys, policies, and procedures); (2) individual and focus group interviews with key stakeholders; (3) work process observation and flow mapping; and (4) job/task analysis.

Process. Stakeholders participated in a logic model process to link immediate, intermediate, and ultimate outcomes with program activities and processes. Then a data collection plan was collaboratively developed to document expected outcomes and define the type of evidence needed to determine success. The plan also described what outcome and activity data would be collected; how it would be collected; when it would be collected; and who was responsible for collecting it.

Output. Several outputs were developed during analysis, design, development, implementation, and evaluation. These included a logic model; data collection, transition, communication, and implementation plans; training and education materials, job aids; data collection instruments; and reporting templates.

Constraints. Predominant barriers to internalizing a new service model included staffing, time, and budget issues. Evaluation planning and pilot project implementation plans incorporated experts' input about expected and potential unexpected constraints to project success, along with suggested approaches to counter obstacles.

Focus on Value

By emphasizing a collaborative process, the consultant brought value to the client in several ways. Collaboration activities provided stakeholders with a clear and realistic direction about the schedule, scope, and resource requirements involved with implementing and internalizing a results-based evaluation process; helped stakeholders make informed decisions; encouraged shared ownership among stakeholders and CHC members; and helped participants focus on value-added aspects of the effort.

Focus on Establishing Partnerships

Multiple partnerships were formed during the course of this two-year consulting engagement. Collaboration was a critical component throughout each phase of analysis, solution design, development, implementation, and evaluation. Strategies that promoted partnerships and emphasized shared ownership for project success included logic model development, data collection planning, transition planning (including communication planning and briefings), evaluation capacity building, implementation project planning, and the ROI process pilot project.

Be Systematic in Assessment of Need, Opportunity, or Challenge

The performance needs, opportunities, and challenges in this project were explored from multiple systemic perspectives. For example, the perspectives of project sponsors, stakeholders, members, staff were collected and integrated during all phases of the project.

Be Systematic in the Analysis of Work, Worker, Workplace, and Worldview to Identify the Causes or Factors That Limit Performance

Evaluation planning including working with stakeholders, community network members, and CHAD specialists from four functional areas to (1) define roles and (2) identify real or potential work, worker, workplace, or world challenges that might limit achievement of objectives; and identify possible countermeasures for addressing these barriers.

Be Systematic in the Design of the Solution

Long-term outcomes are difficult to measure using traditional evaluation methods.-CHAD staff and the consultant worked together to design a logic model to link immediate, intermediate, and ultimate outcomes with program activities/processes. This approach helped staff to stay focused on outcomes; visualize *relationships* between inputs, outputs, and interim and long-term outcomes; graphically link association activities, services, and processes to desired outcomes; keep underlying assumptions and influencing factors at the forefront; and identify intangible benefits and long-term outcomes.

The process of developing the logic model provided a focal point for discussion and shared understanding about how ROI process implementation could support, monitor, and measure assumptions. In addition, the solution design incorporated project management and change leadership strategies to address issues related to increased accountability, new work process demands, and new performance expectations.

Be Systematic in the Development of the Solution

Implementing a results-oriented evaluation focus into the public service sector represents a fundamental and dramatic shift in business thinking, acting, and managing that requires moving away from a focus on activities and outputs to a focus on outcomes and results. Therefore, solution development included such planned transition elements as policy and purpose statements;

infrastructures to support results-based efforts; communication plans and briefings with association members around their role in creating and field testing a results-based focus; creating and field testing data collection protocol and instruments; establishing implementation project plans with specific, measurable, and achievable target dates and milestones; updating roles and responsibilities to include performance expectations; and enhancing performance support and feedback mechanisms.

Be Systematic in the Implementation of the Solution

Leaders and staff worked with the consultant to purposely select pilot participants. Staff called each selected participant and explained the purpose and importance of the project. All who were invited agreed to participate voluntarily. A letter and email follow-up was then generated.

Post-training meetings were held to orient individuals to the impact questionnaire and the summative evaluation process. Participants were assured that they would receive evaluation results and that individual responses would be part of an aggregate.

Following the pilot, action planning sessions were conducted with stakeholders to identify lessons learned and continuous improvement opportunities. This input was used in subsequent strategy development for sustaining and internalizing the ROI process.

Be Systematic in the Evaluation of the Process and the Results

Implementation results were systematically collected, analyzed, and reported across multiple levels:

Level 1: Reaction; Planned Action. 100 percent of participants indicated that OC3 participation was a worthwhile investment, identified planned actions they would take as a result of participation, and stated that they would recommend OC3 training to others.

Level 2: Learning. Participants reported the highest success with the following learning objectives:

- Enhance methods for collecting and organizing data about agency outcomes.
- Enhance methods for analyzing data relevant to client outcomes.
- Increase awareness of partner networks.

Level 3: Application. Participants assigned a high value to the use of (1) financial management, document control, and medical record management tools; and (2) human resource materials for performance appraisals and risk management analysis. Time and staffing constraints were reported as the most common barrier, and training and education was being reported as the most valuable enabler.

Level 4: Impact. Specific work measures significantly influenced by application of OC3 tools and resources included:

- Compliance with funding (grant) requirements
- Cost control, cost conversions

- Operational performance
- Risk management
- Compliance with program requirements
- Customer (patient) satisfaction

The category of "improved compliance with funding requirements" was the most frequently reported business measure that was significantly influenced by the training intervention.

Isolation and Data Conversion. The evaluation strategy also included methods for isolating the program's effect and then converting improvement data to monetary value. Data gathered in this step pinpointed the amount of improvement directly related to the project under review. Assumptions included that (1)participants were credible sources of improvement data to senior management, (2) unresponsive participants had realized no improvement, and (3) cost-benefit ratios were factored on an annualized basis only.

Once the isolation factors were determined, the Level 4 impact data were converted to monetary value. In accordance with the ROI process methodology, these values were then adjusted to account for potential error and the impact of other influences. The business improvement value *most relevant* to stakeholders was an estimated cost benefit for prevention of grant incidents of $3,087.96 per incident. This and other values are typically used as cost-benefit data and compared to program costs in the final ROI analysis and calculation. However, for various reasons, it was ultimately determined by the staff that ROI calculations were not going to be captured for this pilot effort.

Intangible Benefits. Intangible benefits are those benefits linked directly to the program, but not converted to monetary value. Intangible benefits from the pilot of most interest to stakeholders included increased knowledge of operational and business issues and improved ability to complete a health care plan with achievable, measurable goal statements. Improved personal effectiveness in (1) organizing and prioritizing work; (2) utilizing association resources; (3) analyzing continuous improvement opportunities; and (4) and implementing continuous improvement processes were also noteworthy.

Reporting Results. Upon completion of the pilot study, a one-hour briefing was presented to executive sponsors, participants, and board members. Results were also communicated to the association's member network on the agency's website.

Finally, at a subsequent regional conference, CHAD's deputy director and the consultant presented concurrent conference sessions in which the ROI methodology was introduced as CHAD's newly adopted, outcome-based approach for meeting strategic health care imperatives on a national level and member needs on a regional level.

Next Steps

After completing the pilot evaluation project, CHAD's board incorporated the ROI process as an outcome-based service model by integrating it into subsequent strategic plans and executive board reports. However, despite dedicated efforts to maintain progress, many predictable and unpredictable challenges have compromised ongoing attempts to fully internalize ROI as a standardized service strategy and business process for CHAD' technical assistance function. The challenges include volatile changes in the healthcare and economic environment as well as dynamic changes in the organization related to staff resource constraints, attrition of key sponsors, and conflicting priorities around allocation of resources, particularly those dedicated to evaluation of service outcomes.

Summary

Findings from the pilot implementation suggest that an outcome-based service model can be used as a continuous improvement tool for enhancing the sustainability of community health clinics and ensuring that federally funded partnership and collaboration services meet member needs.

■ ■ ■

Lessons Learned from the Case

- Effective adaptability and utilization of an outcome-based evaluation framework ensures that decision-makers will have a durable, credible process for helping to focus on programs or services that provide the most value returned for resources invested.

- Establishing a collaborative approach to defining and evaluating service outcomes adds value to partners and improves the potential for implementation success.

- Context matters. Simply focusing on the technical aspects of an intervention or its methodology without fully assessing the environmental, political, and cultural contexts in which the methodology is meant to function will deter efforts to implement and sustain the process.

- Sustainability of the return on investment process is directly related to the quality of the planning, design, delivery, and follow-up approaches used to implement it. Implementation plans must be manageable in scope, adequately staffed and funded, routinely monitored for progress or risk factors, and appropriately aligned with organizational needs.

- Utility and sustainability go hand in hand. A results-based measurement system that has no utility will not be sustained. The use of results data for continuous improvement and institutional knowledge-sharing is a characteristic of sustainable ROI process implementation.

- Building evaluation capacity and capability is an evolutionary, developmental process that takes time, commitment, constant reinforcement, and dedicated resources. For instance, underestimating the "lead time" needed to create compatible infrastructures has proven to be a common barrier.

- While there is no best way to sustain an outcome-based service model in the face of omnipresent change, recognition of the change issues associated with sustainable implementation can help organizations target interventions and allocate resources to those leverage points that will have the greatest influence on its change adaptability and utility.

Holly Burkett, Ph.D., SPHR, CPT, is principal of Evaluation Works in Davis, California. A certified ROI professional, she has more than twenty years of experience assisting public- and private-sector clients design and implement outcome-based systems and measures of program effectiveness. Recognized as an evaluation expert with the U.S. Department of Health and Human Services, Health Resources and Services Administration (HRSA) Office of Performance Review (OPR), she is a frequent conference presenter, workshop leader, and author on performance measurement issues. Sample clients include The International Union Against Tuberculosis and Lung Disease; Apple Computer; Federation of State Medical Boards; and Kansas Association of the Medically Underserved (KAMU). Former editor of the *Performance Improvement Journal*, her publications include the "Action Planning" chapter in the *ASTD Handbook of Measuring & Evaluating Training* (2010) and co-authoring *The ROI Fieldbook* (2006) with Jack and Patti Phillips and Ron Stone. She holds a Ph.D. in human capital development and a master's degree in human resources and organization development from the University of San Francisco. Holly can be reached at burketth@earthlink.net.

APPENDICES

"DON'T YOU THINK IT'S TIME HE
LEARNED TO FLY ON HIS OWN?"

ISPI's Performance Technology Standards

Copyright 2012 by the International Society for Performance Improvement (ISPI). These materials or any part thereof may not be reused or reproduced in any form, known now or hereafter created, without written permission of the International Society for Performance Improvement. Questions and comments should be directed to:

International Society for Performance Improvement

1400 Spring Street, Suite 400

Silver Spring, Maryland 20910

301.587.8570

www.ispi.org   info@ispi.org

International Society for Performance Improvement

WHERE KNOWLEDGE BECOMES KNOW-HOW

Table of Contents

Performance Standard 1

Focus on Outcomes

Focusing on outcomes—that is, results—puts you in a position to question, confirm and reconfirm that people share the same vision and goals, the job procedures support efficiency, and that people have the skills and knowledge they require. You determine what it is you are trying to solve. You measure the outcomes or results of an intervention and assess whether performance has improved as a result of it. Sometimes it is necessary to challenge the assumed answer to a problem or the expected event or activity of an intervention, and to focus instead on the accomplishment or business need that is the client's true priority.

Focus on Outcomes		
Performances	**Criteria**	**Development Resources/ Opportunities**
You—	*So that you and the client can—*	*(Note your personal development plans here.)*
1. Determine the outcome or expected result of the assignment. You may: — Help clients specify what they expect to change, or what benefit they expect to gain as a result of the effort or assignment. — Help clients come to agreement on what they expect to accomplish. — Guide or facilitate clients in focusing on accomplishments in deference to activities or events. 2. Determine what will be measured or accepted as evidence that the business need was met. 3. Explain the importance of focusing on accomplishments.	• Better evaluate if the effort was successful and produced outcomes of worth. • Determine in the beginning what information will be collected and how it will be collected to measure accomplishment of the desired outcome. • Communicate what the expected outcome is to team members and other stakeholders. • Establish goals and performance measures with staff and key clients. • Design your fact-finding (analysis) efforts and recommend solutions that are more likely to accomplish the desired outcome. • Celebrate and recognize those efforts that accomplished desired outcomes. *So that—* • The results of your work and how you went about producing those results supported the client, the organization, or society's goals	

Examples (Note: The following list is illustrative rather than exhaustive.)

For example, you—

- Ask what it is the client wants to be different as a result of your doing the work.
- Confirm what the desired outcome is so you can better design your analysis, present a set of viable options, and judge how to best honor and fulfill the request.

— Desired outcomes may include job or task proficiency, information dissemination, compliance with regulations, retention of employees, professional development, higher productivity, fewer errors, reduced costs, increased customer retention, etc.

- Determine what your client is trying to accomplish and what prevents them from accomplishing it, so together you can identify what your function has to provide in terms of training and performance improvement.
- Identify what staff require(s) to be outcome focused.
- Direct and train staff to be outcome focused.
- Act as a liaison between staff and clients to ensure both are working toward the same outcome.

Performance Standard 2

Take a Systemic View

Taking a systemic view is vital, because organizations are very complex open systems that affect the performance of the individuals that work within them.

It is important to distinguish a systemic approach from a process model. A process contains inputs and outputs and has feedback loops. An open system implies an interconnected complex of functionally related components. The effectiveness of each unit depends on how it fits into the whole, and the effectiveness of the whole depends on the way each unit functions. A systemic approach considers the larger environment that affects processes and other work. The environment includes inputs, but, more importantly, it includes pressures, expectations, constraints, and consequences.

Take a Systems View

Performances	Criteria	Development Resources/ Opportunities
You—	*So that you and the client can—*	*(Note your personal development plans here.)*
1. Identify the current work, workplace, or market environment in terms of how it affects organizational and group performance.	• Determine if and how the work, workplace, or industry environment supports or impedes the desired organizational and group performance.	
2. Identify the environment and culture of the work and workplace and how it affects organizational and group performance.	• Determine if and how the current culture supports or impedes the professed performance.	
3. Identify if there is a lack of alignment between or among—	• Identify if and where there is a lack of alignment between or among key factors affecting the success of the solution.	
— Goals and objectives	• Determine if and how the barriers and leverage points support or impede the proposed solutions and the desired organizational and group performance.	
— Performance measures		
— Rewards and incentives		
— Job/work/or process designs		
— Available systems, tools, and equipment	• Analyze how the proposed solutions will affect the greater environment of the organization as a whole.	
— Expectations and capacity		
4. Identify barriers and leverage points, both in the workplace and surrounding your project, in terms of how these factors could affect processes; organizational and group performance; and the development, implementation, and outcome of your proposed solutions. You may identify—	• Determine whether and how the results of your work and how you plan on going about producing those results might jeopardize the client, the organization, or society's well-being.	
— Key political players and stakeholders		
— Issues affecting the larger environment		

Take a Systems View (Continued)

Performances	Criteria	Development Resources/ Opportunities
— Pressures on key players, the business, the audience, managers, etc. — Expectations around the project — Workplace constraints and surrounding the project — Consequences of various solutions or in not pursuing a solution 5. Drive conversations around the barriers and leverage points that have been identified. Discussions could include the following issues: — Constraints or pressures related to: — Deadlines — Budget — Politics — Time — Regulatory issues — Product launch — Safety — Leverage points, including— — Political players — Stakeholder support — Related initiatives within the workplace that support the goals of the proposed solution 6. Explain the benefits of taking a systems approach in a conversation, design document, or project plan. You may— — Point out the knowledge gained by looking at the larger picture surrounding a project or performance issue. — Show how identified leverage points could be used to positively affect the project. — Discuss how identified barriers needed to be considered in order to increase the probability of a project's success.	• Help ensure that the methods of deploying and the results of the project will have a positive impact on the client, the larger environment, and society. • Increase awareness throughout the workplace of the benefits of a systems approach.	

Examples (Note: The following list is illustrative rather than exhaustive.)

For example, you—

- Orient and train staff to have a systemic view.
- Develop processes that enable staff to have a systems view.
- Model a systems view in your exchanges with other functional managers and key influencers in the organization.

Performance Standard 3

Add Value

Did you **add value** in the way you worked with the client and your suggested intervention? This is an assessment your client will be asked to make. You can set the stage for this by offering your clients a process that will help them fully understand the implications of their choices, set appropriate measures, identify barriers and tradeoffs, and take control.

Add Value

Performances	Criteria	Development Resources/ Opportunities
You—	*So that you and the client can—*	*(Note your personal development plans here.)*
1. Identify two or more possible solutions or courses of action.	• Establish at the start what will be used as evidence of success, accomplishment, or worth and communicate that to all vested parties (stakeholders).	
2. Identify the worth of the requested solution or those under consideration, by comparing factors such as—	• Determine that a mechanism exists to determine whether the gain was realized and to track early indicators of success so corrections are made.	
— Cost to design, develop, implement, and maintain each.	• Determine if the assumptive base and the argument for or against a course of action is documented and communicated.	
— Likelihood of adoption or use by the target audience.	• State what tradeoffs were made and what value was gained, and conclude that the value outweighed the cost.	
— Probability of each solution achieving the desired goals.	• State that what you do adds value and how you go about your work adds value.	
— Implication or possible impact on the target audience, other employees, consumers, the community, etc.	*So that—*	
— Ability of the organization to support each solution (reward the appropriate behaviors and results, provide the appropriate communication/information systems and tools and equipment, maintain sponsorship, etc.).	• The product of the assignment or the goal of the task is sound and beneficial to the organization	
— Risks associated with the success or failure of each solution in terms of threats to safety, health, financial return, customer satisfaction, etc.		
3. Recommend solutions that add value, are feasible, and are more likely to accomplish the goals or aims of the project with minimal risk.		
4. Describe the potential value added and how that value will be measured, such as—		
— Increased safety, utility, or customer or community satisfaction.		
— Increased revenues.		

Performances	Criteria	Development Resources/ Opportunities
— Avoided costs. — Decreased errors, lost time accidents, time to market, cycle time, processing time, wait time, etc. — Increased on-time delivery. — Increased customer and employee retention. 5. Point out the risks, tradeoffs, and assumptions on which decisions or choices are based. 6. Document—using a contract, memo of understanding, or description in project description—the expected value added, the costs (materials, resources, time, etc.), and a schedule of deliverables. 7. Explain the importance of doing work that adds value and the importance of demonstrating the value gained. 8. Contribute insights and call out implications throughout the work. 9. Display honesty; push back, challenge assumptions. 10. Represent yourself honestly, not as having expertise beyond your capabilities.		

Add Value (Continued)

Examples (Note: The following list is illustrative rather than exhaustive.)

For example, you—

- Identify the driver, the reason for the request, the assumptions on which it is based, and what need or opportunity your solution is expected to satisfy.
- Distinguish between requests for solutions that—
  - Are required to bring new hires to proficiency
  - Are required to satisfy regulations
  - Are desired to satisfy an organization need or opportunity
- Present facts related to the request and point out the costs, risks, and odds of success, such as the following:
  - Lack of field support
  - Lack of technological infrastructure
  - Significant change in culture
  - Lack of incentive or consequence for using the solution

- Point out what other interventions may be required to fully realize the opportunity or satisfy the need, such as a change in rewards, a change in the way to give feedback, the need to adopt new or different tools, and the consequences of not providing these.
- Help the client identify success factors, risks, and associated direct and indirect costs.
- Guide the client or team in choosing the solution with the best value added.

For example, as a manager, you—

- Find out where the pain is or where the opportunities lie for the organization or key clients.
- You facilitate or participate in meetings on how to best relieve the pain or seize the opportunity.
- You challenge ideas that are based on faulty assumptions.
- You focus your function on providing those solutions that are aligned with the organization's goals and capability to actualize.
- You set up systems to track how your function adds value.

Performance Standard 4

Work in Partnership with Clients and Other Specialists

Work in partnership with clients and other specialists—that is, collaboratively. This means that you involve all stakeholders in the decision making around every phase of the process and that you involve specialists in their areas of expertise. Working collaboratively means that decisions about goals, next steps to take in the process, and implementation are all shared responsibilities. Partnerships are created from listening closely to your client and trusting and respecting each other's knowledge and expertise, so you both can make the best choices about accomplishments, priorities, and solutions.

Work in Partnership with Clients and Other Specialists, That Is Collaboratively		
Performances	**Criteria**	**Development Resources/ Opportunities**
You—	*So you and the client can—*	*(Note your personal development plans here.)*
1. Collaborate with stakeholders, experts, and specialists, making use of their knowledge, capabilities, and influence. You may— — Identify stakeholders. — Determine if other content expertise is required. — Solicit other content expertise as needed. — Incorporate stakeholders, experts, and specialists as part of the team, involving them as required. — Establish collaborative relationships. — Leverage the expertise and influence of others for the benefit of the client. 2. Take the initiative to define your expectations, working relationships, roles, responsibilities, etc. You may do the following: — Point out the benefits of collaboration and partnering. — Increasingly expect to work in collaboration or in a partnership with each other. — Anticipate resistance and respond accordingly. — Anticipate issues and barriers. — Bring misunderstandings to the surface to reconcile them. — Give credit and acknowledge the support, endorsement, and contributions of your partners.	• Trust and respect each other's roles, knowledge, and expertise. • Leverage expertise and influence of others to the client's benefit. • Assure the voices of all vested parties are sought and integrated into the design of the instructional program. • Share responsibility for all decisions concerning goals, next steps to take in the process and implementation. • Make the best choices about accomplishments, priorities and solutions because you understand your client's needs, challenges, and culture. • Support the product of the assignment or the goal of the task. *So that—* • All stakeholders are involved in the decision making around every phase of the process and specialists are involved in their areas of expertise.	

Examples (Note: The following list is illustrative rather than exhaustive.)

For example, you—

- Ensure there is a program sponsor.
- Negotiate the sponsor's level of involvement and desired outcomes.
- Establish relationships with management from those functions that are your key clients and benefactors of your function.
- Establish relationships with all departments that are key to providing essential information, data, or assistance to ensure the following:
  — Their knowledge is brought to bear.
  — Their needs are satisfied.
  — You have a solid business case for change or the recommended solution.
  — You have the required support when it comes time for implementation.
- Engage those from other functions in ways that are mutually beneficial.
- Recommend specialists to assist in the design of solutions or interventions outside of your expertise (for example, compensation specialists, interior designers to help redesign work space and tools, information system specialists, etc.).
- Draw on the knowledge and expertise of specialists who can contribute to the development of the instructional strategy, materials, or delivery mechanisms.
- Convene clients and, either personally or through staff, facilitate meetings related to fact finding, uncovering resistance, setting priorities, weighing alternatives, etc.
- Convene partners and facilitate meetings related to fact finding, uncovering resistance, setting priorities, weighing alternatives, etc.
- Identify your clients' issues and needs and help support them in their efforts.
- Seek the voices of the learner, the learner's boss, and customers and integrated them into the design of the instructional program.
- Recognize the contributions of the subject matter experts and specialists.

Performance Standard 5

Be Systematic—Needs or Opportunity Analysis

Being systematic is extremely complex since it touches the remaining six standards that describe the human performance technology process. Each part relies on your having processes in place. All performances may or may not be performed, and all parts may or may not be completed in a specific order, based on the specific circumstances.

Analysis occurs in the beginning of the project. **Needs or opportunity analysis** is about examining the current situation at any level (society, organizational, process, or work group) to identify the external and internal pressures affecting it. Based on the examination, you determine if the situation is worthy of action or further study. The output is a statement describing the current state, the projected future state, and the rationale or business case for action or non-action.

As a specialist, you need to determine the scope of the analysis and identify the external and internal pressures affecting it to determine, in collaboration with your client, whether there are any needs worthy of further examination or action. The goal is to align the client's activities and priorities with that of the group being studied.

Functional analysis is about identifying what causes a gap between actual and desired performance. Given that you have results from a needs or opportunity analysis or a request from a client to solve a problem, you may identify what is required for performance at any level (societal, organizational, or work group). This type of analysis may be referred to as a functional, performance, or job/task analysis. The output is a description of activities; resources used or consumed; desired or required outputs and accomplishments; and other attributes of a well-performing society, organization, work effort, or process.

For the specialist, this standard is about identifying what currently makes up performance and what is required.

The types of analyses include the following:

- Job or Task Analysis—Identifies the required activities, information, processes used, and outputs produced and then compares that to actual practice.
- Process Analysis—Identifies the cycle time compared to process time; time at task compared to time on rework, waiting, or checking; resources consumed and the cost of those resources; and what drives activity (customer or product requirements).
- Work Environment Analysis—Identifies and evaluates the effectiveness and efficiency of feedback, the reward and incentive system, information and communication systems, work and process designs, and work tools and equipment.
- User or Audience Analysis—Identifies current expectations, perceptions, physical capability and capacity, and knowledge and skills.

- Communication Systems Analysis—Identifies and evaluates the availability, capability, capacity, upgrade ability, and cost to use and maintain.
- Market Analysis—Identifies the size, competition, growth, current and potential constraints or limitations, organizational expectations, initiatives, capabilities, and capacity.
- Data System Analysis—Identifies and evaluates the capability, capacity, availability, upgrade ability, and cost to use and maintain.

Be Systematic—Needs or Opportunity Analysis

Performances	Criteria	Development Resources/ Opportunities
You—	*So that you and the client can—*	*(Note your personal development plans here.)*
1. Determine the type of analysis required. 2. Develop a plan or process for conducting the analysis, including any of the following: — Hypotheses — Data-collection methods — Audiences to be polled — Sampling method — Statistical treatment — Sequence of activities — Timeline — Resources required 3. Develop any tools or documents, such as interviews, surveys, or observation forms, required to capture the data. 4. Conduct the analysis. 5. Analyze the data. 6. Interpret the results. You may— — Determine the magnitude of the gap in terms of criticality, frequency, cost or exposure, or lost benefit. 7. Build a business case for action or non-action. 8. Make recommendations based on the results.	• Use analysis methods appropriate to the situation. • Determine the question (hypothesis) you want to answer. • Carry out the analysis at the appropriate level: individual, group, process, organizational, or societal. • Develop recommendations on whether to act on the findings and how. • Use data-gathering methods appropriate to the situation. • Use sampling methods that follow recommended practices. — If a representative sample was used, it lists the criteria for being selected. — If a random sample was used, it (1) was of sufficient size to generalize from the results and support the statistical analysis used, (2) lists the criteria for being part of the population, and (3) describes how the sample was chosen. — If a stratified sample was used, the strata are listed, the size of the strata is shown, and the size of the sample by strata is shown. • Use a survey format that complies with recommended practice, if a survey is used: — Consistent use of scales — Sufficient number of questions for statistical analysis — Clear directions on how to complete the survey — Piloted to confirm the questions and directions work as intended — Standard method of analysis — Documented method of analysis	

| | Be Systematic—Needs or Opportunity Analysis (Continued) | |
Performances	Criteria	Development Resources/ Opportunities
	• Use an interview format that complies with recommended practice, if interviews or observation used: — Documented format — Piloted questions — Documented analysis method — Accepted analysis method • Correctly use documents or work products as a source of data: — Documented sampling method — Accepted sampling method — Documented evaluation or comparison criteria for documentation or work products • Identify the physical and technological opportunities and constraints in the work environment. • Identify the actual work processes used to accomplish work. • Identify the actual and expected outputs of the work. • Identify the consequences and who the receivers of those consequences are. • Identify what feedback systems are or are not in use and how effective they are. • Identify the inputs that the workgroup has available. (Inputs include information, directions, requirements, expectations, etc.) • Identify gaps between what is required and what actually occurs. • Discriminate causes due to lack of information, knowledge, or skill from those due to inadequacies in the work environment, poor job design, inadequate feedback systems, lack of consequences, or poorly designed processes. • Determine the feasibility or probability of eliminating the gap. *So that—* • The plan is feasible given organizational time and resource constraints. • The results are useful and valid. • The process for conducting the analysis is cost and time efficient. • Findings serve as guides for future work and provide information for later evaluation. • The process for conducting the analysis is administered consistently and includes the voices of all stakeholders. • The analysis method is applied to the level of completeness and accuracy required by the problem and its risks, and no more.	

Examples (Note: The following list is illustrative rather than exhaustive.)

For example, you, in collaboration with your client—

- Identify the objectives of the analysis, who to involve, what data you require, how best to get the data, how the data will be used and by whom, and when you want to begin and end.
- Interview, observe, and check documents.
- Determine which needs or opportunities lend themselves to further analysis or a solution and what type of solution.
- Develop hypotheses regarding why the current situation exists. Some examples of this include (but are not limited to)—
  — Turnover due to ineffective supervisory practices
  — Current employees' abilities underutilized by the company
  — Purchasing practices having a negative impact on the local economy
  — One work group lacks troubleshooting skills

Performance Standard 6

Be Systematic—Cause Analysis

Cause analysis is about determining why a gap in performance or expectations exists. Some causes are obvious, such as new hires lack the required skills to do the expected task and, therefore, the solution must eliminate that gap. The output is a statement of why performance is not happening or will not happen without some intervention.

Be Systematic—Cause Analysis		
Performances	**Criteria**	**Development Resources/ Opportunities**
You—	*So that you and the client can—*	*(Note your personal development plans here.)*
1. Use the gap to help determine the worth of determining the cause and establish criteria for measuring the effectiveness of a chosen solution. 2. Develop a hypothesis for why the gap exists. 3. Develop a plan or approach to test your hypothesis and identify the cause of the gap. 4. Implement the plan and identify the cause of the gap, such as— — Lack of skills or knowledge — Insufficient environmental support — Inappropriate rewards or incentives or measures — Poorly designed jobs or processes 5. Report your findings.	• Differentiate performance problems that are caused by lack of knowledge and skill from those that are due to environmental, job, or process design; inadequate feedback or performance support systems; insufficient or inappropriate tools and equipment; conflicting objectives; or inappropriate performance measures. • Determine how much certainty is required to support a solution. • Determine which hypotheses (the cause of turnover, high cost of recruitment, poor morale, customer dissatisfaction, etc.) are supported by the data. • Note those instances where a solution is predetermined, such as training done in order to comply with regulations or for new hires who are known to lack the required skills and knowledge. *So that—* • Future design and development will cost effectively address the real need(s).	

Examples (Note: The following list is illustrative rather than exhaustive.)

For example, you, in collaboration with your client, point out—

- Those performance deficiencies due to a lack of knowledge and skill that lend themselves to instructional solutions, such as training for new hires or for new systems, technology, or products.
- Where training is done to satisfy regulatory requirements, such as safety, hazmat, sexual harassment.

- Why a performance deficiency exists, such as—
  - Excessive turnover
  - Product defects
  - Poor performance
  - Inability to attract more qualified candidates
  - Poor morale and employee satisfaction
- Those performance deficiencies that are due to inadequate or insufficient environmental, job design, feedback, or performance support systems and that lend themselves to a non-instructional solution.

Performance Standard 7

Be Systematic—Design

Design is about identifying the key attributes of a solution. The output is a communication that describes the features, attributes, and elements of a solution and the resources required to actualize it.

For the specialist, you identify and describe one or more solutions in detail, what will be required to develop and implement them, which is preferred, and why.

Be Systematic—Design		
Performances	**Criteria**	**Development Resources/ Opportunities**
You—	*So that—*	*(Note your personal development plans here.)*
1. Decide on one or more solution set(s), such as— — Process redesign — Training — Change/benefit 2. Define the desired performance. 3. Identify the objectives of the solution and all elements of the solution. 4. Develop a plan for accomplishing the objectives and elements that includes strategy and tactics. 5. Agree on roles and responsibilities for stakeholders, high performers, and subject matter experts to be involved in the development and implementation of the solution. 6. Identify key attributes of the proposed solution—such as learning strategy and tactics, transfer systems, feedback, etc.—for— — Data and communication systems — Job or process elements — Management practices (feedback, rewards, scheduling, promoting, performance measures, etc.) 7. Identify how the solution will be produced or actualized. 8. Identify the resources required. 9. Identify methods for delivering or deploying the solution.	• The objectives, conditions, performances, performance elements, and criteria for judging learning, transfer, or adoption are sufficiently detailed. • The assumptions, the aims or intent of the solution, the strategy for development and deployment, and the criteria for judging adoption and success are sufficiently detailed and sound. • The required terms, concepts, rules, heuristics, principles, and procedures key to performance are present. • The sequence of the content and tactics is sufficiently detailed. • The materials used to actualize the solution are designed following instructional methods designed to enhance the likelihood of attaining the intended outcomes. • The strategy and tactics for accomplishing the objectives (transferring knowledge, building skills, supporting performance, redesigning work processes and feedback systems, and aligning rewards and consequences) are sufficiently detailed. • The method for evaluating the accomplishment of the objective and the effectiveness of the solution is feasible and sufficiently detailed.	

Be Systematic—Design (Continued)		
Performances	**Criteria**	**Development Resources/ Opportunities**

10. Identify how the solution will be maintained or reinforced.
11. Identify methods for evaluating the effectiveness of the solution.
12. Explain the rationale for the proposed methods, such as—
   — Evaluation
   — Strategy and tactics
	So that—
	• The methods for deploying the solution are described.
	• The methods for maintaining or reinforcing the solution over time are described.
	• The client understands the investment in time and resources necessary to develop and implement the solution and can provide the resources to actualize the design.
	• The target audience can participate in testing the solution.
	• The information serves as a guide for future work and provides information for later evaluation.	

Examples (Note: The following list is illustrative rather than exhaustive.)

For example, you develop a plan for how you intend to do the following:

- Accomplish the objectives. The plan includes a strategy, tactics, and key content elements (terms, concepts, principles, rules, heuristics, steps, procedures).
- Develop, produce, deploy, and maintain instructional materials.
- Confirm the accuracy of the content and the content elements, the usability of the materials and media—*or* to do a formative evaluation.
- Redesign a process, job, or system.
- Change management practices.
- Evaluate the effectiveness of the solution (summative evaluation).
- Change what behaviors and results get rewarded.

Performance Standard 8

Be Systematic—Development

Development is about the creation of some or all of the elements of the solution. It can be done by an individual or by a team. The output is a product, process, system, or technology. Examples include training, performance support tools, a new or re-engineered process, the redesign of a workspace, or a change in compensation or benefits.

For specialists, this standard is about creating or acquiring all or parts of the solution. You may choose to do it personally or, as part of a team, or you might outsource the effort.

Be Systematic—Development		
Performances	**Criteria**	**Development Resources/ Opportunities**
You—	*So that you and the client can—*	*(Note your personal development plans here.)*
1. Ensure that the chosen solution is developed according to design specifications. You may— — Assist in the development of electronic support systems, such as help screens or help desks. — Participate in the development of a job, task, or process redesign. — Participate in the development of a feedback system, reward and recognition system, communication system, or information system. — Participate in the development of a change strategy. — Develop materials or methods to improve team processes, job procedures, work practices, or individual or group decision-making.	• Determine if the physical elements of the solution support the objective(s), are usable to the target audience, can be administered in the way intended, and can be maintained over time. • Get timely, relevant data for the pilot or user tests. • Ensure that learnings are fed back into the development. *So that—* • The solution is effective or performs as expected and accomplishes the desired goal.	

Be Systematic—Development (Continued)		
Performances	**Criteria**	**Development Resources/ Opportunities**
2. Conduct formative, pilot, and user evaluations of all elements of the chosen solution/product to determine if it performs as expected and accomplishes the desired goal(s). You may— — Engage high performers or experts in reviewing all materials or in creating a new process or system. — Design and/or conduct a formative evaluation of all elements of the solution. — Design and/or conduct pilot and/or user tests to determine readability, functionality, usability, etc. — Compare formative, pilot, and user test results against design standards. — Determine if the physical elements of the solution support the objective(s), are usable to the target audience, can be administered in the way intended, and can be maintained over time. — Ensure that learnings are fed back into development.		

Examples (Note: The following list is illustrative rather than exhaustive.)

For example, you—

- Write or develop instructional materials or performance support materials, such as job aids, in a print or electronic.
- Coordinate the efforts of others who are developing materials.
- Participate on teams engaged in the design of work processes, feedback systems, performance support tools, work tools, and reward and incentive systems.

Performance Standard 9

Be Systematic—Implementation

Implementation is about deploying the solution and managing the change required to sustain it. The outputs are changes in or adoption of the behaviors that are believed to produce the anticipated results or benefits.

This standard is about helping clients adopt new behaviors or use new or different tools. You develop an implementation plan that includes how you or the client will track change, identify and respond to problems, and communicate the results.

Be Systematic—Implementation		
Performances	**Criteria**	**Development Resources/ Opportunities**
You—	*So that you and the client can—*	*(Note your personal development plans here.)*
1. Design a change strategy that includes the following: — How the effort (the message) will be communicated and to whom. — What implementation materials and messages will be required and how they will be produced. — A schedule of the rollout, including milestones, timelines, etc. — How the new behaviors and other evidence of adoption will be recognized and rewarded. — What to do in case of resistance. — Who will provide support and reinforcement during deployment. — Roles and responsibilities of management, the target audience, and other vested parties. 2. Develop tools and procedures to help those involved in the implementation. For example: — Train the trainer sessions — Job aids — FAQs	• Send a uniform message about the why, what, and how of the solution. • Determine what tools and procedures the team responsible for implementation or deployment requires to effectively support implementation. • Determine how best to track the speed of the deployment and any resistance. • Determine how to identify and best handle resistance. *So that—* • The information serves as a guide for future work and provides information for ongoing evaluation. • The solution is delivered to the target audience. • Change is sustained over time.	

	Be Systematic—Implementation (Continued)	
Performances	**Criteria**	**Development Resources/ Opportunities**
3. Participate in the implementation or deployment of the solution. 4. During implementation, solicit feedback related to the utility and relevance of the solution and use the information obtained in the following ways: — As a guide for future work and evaluation. — To look at what worked and feed it back into the solution. — By sharing it among key players to improve the solution and ongoing rollout.		

Examples (Note: The following list is illustrative rather than exhaustive.)

For example, you—

- Participate on a team to design a change or implementation strategy.
- Help develop implementation materials and messages.
- Help train people who will deliver the training, or assist the target audience in adopting the new behaviors, executing the new process, or using the new tools.

Performance Standard 10

Be Systematic—Evaluation

Evaluation is about measuring the efficiency and effectiveness of what you did, how you did it, and the degree to which the solution produced the desired results so you can compare the cost incurred to the benefits gained.

This standard is about identifying and acting on opportunities throughout the systematic process to identify measures and capture data that will help identify needs, adoption, and results.

Be Systematic—Evaluation		
Performances	**Criteria**	**Development Resources/ Opportunities**
You—	*So that you and the client can—*	*(Note your personal development plans here.)*
1. State outcomes of the evaluation effort in measurable terms. 2. Design a measurement strategy or plan based on the program's or project's goals and outcomes. The plan includes the following: — The program or project's key success indicators or goals in measurable terms — How data will be collected and results validated — The standard or goal against which results will be compared — How data from others will be incorporated or leveraged — If and how evaluation expertise may be required 3. Develop the tools, instruments, and guidelines for collecting and interpreting data and selecting samples. 4. Measure the results of the solution or help the client evaluate the impact of the solution. 5. Identify what can be done in the future to improve the way in which needs and opportunities are identified and solutions selected, valued, developed, and deployed. 6. Report your findings and recommendations. 7. Explain the value of evaluating (ethics).	• Determine whether the solution fulfilled the goal or satisfied the need. • Determine whether data are valid and useful. • Determine if the measurement methods and metrics are valid and useful. • Make timely decisions about the need to change, alter, or intervene to better ensure the effectiveness of the solution. *So that—* • Reports are useful and relevant to the reader(s). • Your methods and processes for analysis, selection and comparison of alternative solutions, and the design, development, deployment, and maintenance of solutions, are improved. • The efficacy of the solution is ensured.	

Examples (Note: The following list is illustrative rather than exhaustive.)

For example, you—

- Partner with clients and the target audience to identify ways to capture and track performance data.
- Evaluate the results of a program or project by gathering data and comparing what you find to some standard, goal, or client expectation.
- Model the importance of evaluation by evaluating your own methods and processes.
- Coach clients in issues related to sampling, the design of data-gathering instruments, how best to capture data, and how to interpret data.

Certified School Improvement Specialist Standards

B

1. **Analyze and Apply Critical Judgment**
   1.1 Facilitate the collection, analysis, validation, corroboration, and interpretation of quantitative and qualitative data regarding the multiple factors impacting student, teacher, leader, and school performance.
   1.2 Demonstrate deep knowledge of the work of school improvement and transformation and the underlying research and best practices, particularly in improving curriculum, instruction, assessment, and facilitating solutions and breakthroughs.
   1.3 Present evidence so that conclusions and solutions are supported, and so that others have a clear model to follow.

2. **Facilitate Meaning and Engagement**
   2.1 Help others create meaning from findings, research, and inquiry.
   2.2 Help others comprehend the implications of their actions, recognize patterns, and accept new responsibilities.
   2.3 Build supportive relationships among stakeholders by initiating and sustaining dialogue between individuals and groups.
   2.4 Develop commitment so that people act in new ways, feel engaged, and believe change is possible.

3. **Focus on Systemic Factors**
   3.1 Focus on the systemic and interdependent factors in the school context that impact students' learning, school improvement, and transformation efforts.
   3.2 Demonstrate use and alignment of a portfolio of improvement options and approaches.
   3.3 Ensure improvement and transformation efforts result in school teams and students demonstrating higher order thinking skills, collaboration, effective use of technology, and other skills that create value.

4. **Plan and Record**
   4.1 Recommend methods, resources, high leverage, and high impact practices and information about what works to address the factors impacting performance.
   4.2 Facilitate development and recording of sound improvement and transformation plans with related action or project plans and progress measures.

4.3 Facilitate the planning, recording, and communicating of the work ahead and the individual and team performance expectations, so that people's efforts are aligned and focused on meaningful activities that are more likely to lead to the desired outcomes in support of student learning and school improvement and transformation.

4.4 Document the practices and progress so that best practices can be replicated with fidelity, and taught and disseminated to others.

5. Organize and Manage Efforts and Resources

5.1 Organize work tasks by breaking them down into feasible steps.

5.2 Effectively distribute work, responsibility and accountability, authority, and leadership so that people are empowered and feel that their time is respected.

5.3 Coordinate efforts, schedules, and human and financial resources in ways that lead to important, agreed-to outcomes with effective stewardship of resources, including time.

6. Guide and Focus Collaborative Improvement

6.1 Influence the behaviors and decisions of stakeholders within a personal circle of influence.

6.2 Leverage the cooperation and support of others to influence a wider circle of stakeholders.

6.3 Facilitate the collaborative development of clear mission, vision, purpose, values, goals, and performance targets.

6.4 Provide relevant information and advice to support improvement, transformation, and sustainability.

6.5 Model the behaviors of continuous improvement and 21st century school transformation.

6.6 Facilitate or influence tough decisions needed to achieve needed changes and breakthroughs.

7. Monitor Accountability and Adoption

7.1 Check purposely (keep an eye on) performance, conditions, and results by observing people's behavior and interim results.

7.2 Apply corrective action or refocus efforts, when needed, to reach the targeted performance and results.

7.3 Address underperformance or lack of progress toward goals and performance targets using data and evidence.

7.4 Recognize and communicate effort, improvement, and achievements.

7.5 Ensure school improvement and transformation are aligned between schools and with the district office or management entity so that schools' efforts support system-wide improvement without undesirable impact on other schools.

8. Demonstrate Organizational Sensitivity

8.1 Establish professional credibility, gain respect, and build trust.

8.2 Follow accepted rules of etiquette, precedence, or conventions appropriate to the context.

8.3 Demonstrate a high level of professionalism through appropriate dress, speech, written communication, and behavior.

8.4 Interact in ways that make people feel their roles, positions, and views are valued.

8.5 Behave in ways that increase the likelihood that people stay engaged and honor their commitments.

9. **Build Capacity**

9.1 Use effective adult learning and performance interventions aligned with the desired outcomes and results.

9.2 Coach and provide feedback against clear criteria.

9.3 Ask questions that cause reflection so that others surface new possibilities and recognize self-imposed barriers.

9.4 Facilitate study, inquiry, and informed action that address complex challenges while working effectively with colleagues.

9.5 Facilitate sharing of learning that leads to improved practices, innovation, and positive change.

9.6 Facilitate adoption of defined and aligned practices in hiring, selection, assignment, development, and formative and summative performance evaluation that support improved performance of teachers, administrators, and staff.

10. **Implement for Sustainability**

10.1 Ensure continuity of interventions, fidelity of execution of plans, and sustainability of gains and improvements.

10.2 Establish and transfer ownership.

10.3 Facilitate and celebrate quick wins to build momentum and confidence of stakeholders.

10.4 Track and manage leading indicators of behavior change and achievement, including adoption of improved practices.

10.5 Allow time and gain support for long-term, sustainable improvement and transformation to meet 21st century needs.

ISPI's Code of Ethics

C

This document includes:

- Statement of Expectations: Overall statement summarizing ethical behavior.
- Principles: Basic concepts that address appropriate conduct for a performance improvement professional.
- Individual Principles with Guidelines: General statements of appropriate behavior.
- Examples: Collection of examples of ethical behaviors.

Statement of Expectations

ISPI's Code of Ethics and Standards are intended to promote ethical practice in the profession of human performance technology.

The objective of the work of a professional is to:

(a) Provide organizations and/or individuals with the skills, knowledge, abilities, and/or attitude necessary to create opportunities for achieving desired and/or required individual, organizational, and societal results,

(b) Assist in the generation of new and valid knowledge that will lead to the attainment of results meeting the performance criteria demanded by individuals, organizations, and society,

(c) Acquire the knowledge through systematic research methods without jeopardizing the success of my client, my client's clients, or society, and

(d) Produce the results required by the client.[1]

---

[1]Paraphrased from the Preliminary Code of Professional Conduct, a section in the article, *A Scientific Dialogue: A Performance Accomplishment Code of Professional Conduct* by Ryan Watkins, Doug Leigh, and Roger Kaufman. Reprinted with permission of the authors.

The Principles

The Code of Ethics is based on the following six principles:

1. Add Value
2. Validated Practice
3. Collaboration
4. Continuous Improvement
5. Integrity
6. Uphold Confidentiality

Add Value Principle

Conduct yourself, and manage your projects and their results, in ways that add value for your clients, their customers, and the global environment.

Guidelines

- Base recommendations and actions on an objective need assessment conducted in partnership with the client.
- Define, justify empirically, and achieve useful results that can be aligned with both the organization's mission, objective, and positive contributions to society.
- Focus on results and consequences of the results. Measure performance based on results, not on procedures performed for the client.
- Set clear expectations about the systematic process you will follow and about the expected outcomes.
- Add value by serving your clients with integrity, competence, and objectivity as you apply human performance technology.
- Respect and contribute to the legitimate and ethical objectives the organization.
- Help the organization move to where it needs to be in the future.
- Prevent problems from occurring rather than solve problems that could have been predicted and avoided.

Validated Practice Principle

Make use of and promote validated practices in performance technology strategies and standards. In the absence of validated practices relevant to the project goals, ethical practice includes sharing information with the client and using practices that are consistent with an existing body of theory, research, and practice knowledge.

Guidelines

- Deliver activities, methods, and procedures that have positive value and worth.
- Promote good performance technology practices by utilizing positive reinforcement.
- Conduct research required to have adequate knowledge of new technologies that may be beneficial to the client.
- Commit to the implementation of socially responsible practices, as well as those that make a positive fiscal impact on the organization.
- Make data based decisions.
- Clarify goals and desired accomplishments.
- Detect and analyze opportunities to improve human performance.
- Objectively evaluate the impact of interventions.

Collaboration Principle

Work collaboratively with clients and users, functioning as a trustworthy strategic partner.

Guidelines

- Integrate the company's needs, constraints, and concerns when devising a solution.
- Meet the interests of all parties involved in an intervention, project, or process, so there is a win-win outcome.
- Anticipate the client's issues; demonstrate empathy for their concerns and issues.
- Cooperate fully with your clients' request to partner with others, even if they represent your own competition.

Continuous Improvement Principle

Continually improve your proficiency in the field of performance technology.

Guidelines

- Evaluate your skills and knowledge of performance improvement on a regular basis.
- Investigate new methods, concepts, tools, strategies, and technologies that may be beneficial to your client.
- Ask your clients how you can improve the effectiveness of your services.
- Promote the application of performance improvement.

Integrity Principle

Be honest and truthful in representations to your client, colleagues, and others with whom you may come in contact with while practicing performance technology.

Guidelines

- Acknowledge any factors that may compromise your objectivity, so your clients can make decisions that represent their best interests.
- Accept only engagements for which you are qualified by experience and competence.
- Exhibit the highest level of professional objectivity in gathering, evaluating, and communicating information about the activity or process being examined, or the results achieved.
- Let clients know when you believe they are going in the wrong direction.
- Give credit for the work of others to whom it is due.
- Do not use information for any personal gain or in any manner that would be contrary to the law or detrimental to the legitimate and ethical objectives of the client's organization.
- Take responsibility and/or credit only for the portion of results that are clearly linked to your efforts. Do not advertise the attainment of results that cannot be clearly linked to your work.

Uphold Confidentiality Principle

Maintain client confidentiality, not allowing for any conflict of interest that would benefit yourself or others.

Guidelines

- Respect the intellectual property of clients, other consulting firms, and sole practitioners and do not use proprietary information or methodologies without permission.
- Respect and value the ownership of information received.
- Do not disclose information without appropriate authority.

Examples of Ethical Behavior

- Recommend interventions that you believe will meet client needs and goals, instead of simply agreeing with clients' assessment of what is needed or what they want to hear.
- Let a client know that you receive a bonus if they choose a particular product that is included in your recommendations.
- Decline a job if you don't have the expertise the client is requesting.
- When possible recommend a colleague who does have the expertise.
- Don't be selective or skew the data to make your intervention look better.
- Scale graphs and visuals to show the situation honestly.
- Don't promise results you can't deliver.
- Even in the face of client resistance, use and promote the ISPI Standards.
- Avoid turf and territory battles.
- Listen objectively to client concerns, constraints, issues, etc.

- Never knowingly mislead or lie to your client.
- Hesitate before recommending solutions you haven't been able to implement for yourself.
- Be responsible for the results of your work.
- Not advertise the attainment of results that cannot be clearly linked to your work.
- Inform the client if at any time you are no longer qualified to complete a process or task, and help obtain a specialist, if appropriate.
- Conduct research; (a) read journals inside and outside the fields of management, training, performance improvement, and educational research, (b) attend conferences and professional meetings, and (c) consult with credible colleagues in the field.

Glossary

Analysis—Process of breaking complex concepts into smaller component aspects in order to increase understanding of underlying issues.

360 Feedback—A multi-source assessment that taps the collective wisdom of those who work with an individual, including supervisors, peers, direct reports, and internal and external customers.

Avatars—Digital representations of computer user characters or images that represent one person in an interactive exchange.

Acquisitions—When one firm acquires more than 50 percent of the voting stock of another firm and, therefore, controls that firm.

Action Learning—Builds opportunities for learning around real problems or opportunities. Members of the group share, question, experience, reflect, make decisions, and take action on an individual or group basis.

Appreciative Inquiry (AI)—A philosophy and a process to determine what is working successfully within an organization. Systematic in approach and brings out the best in people, in the processes that are crucial to their work, and in the dynamic environment in which accomplishment is primary.

Assumption—Something that is taken for granted to be true.

Balanced Scorecard—A management tool that measures and manages an organization's progress toward strategic goals and objectives. Incorporates financial indicators with three other perspectives: customer, internal business processes, and learning and growth.

Balance Sheet—Shows how management invests resources in assets and how assets are financed by liabilities and owners' equity.

Benchmarking—A systematic process of comparing an organization to other organizations for the purposes of identifying better work methods and determining best practices. Helps define customer requirements, establish effective goals and objectives, develop true measures of productivity, and identify education and training needs for current and future employees.

Benefits—The noncash portion of a compensation program intended to improve the quality of work life for an organization's people.

Blended Intervention—A combination of intervention types that are integrated to improve performance, for example, an incentive and reward intervention might also include organizational communication, learning, performance support, and/or motivation interventions.

Blended Learning—Combines more than one format for learning, such as face-to-face instruction and learning with computer-mediated instruction; can be successful at a variety of levels.

Business Case—Framework for making decisions, explanation of benefits and costs, anticipated outcomes, and project factors associated with a performance improvement effort.

Business Plan—The formal planning involved in starting a new business, making an improvement, or pursuing an opportunity. Views the entire picture and describes all the related elements.

Capital—The source of long-term financing (investments and loans) available to an organization. Assets or resources available for use in the production of further wealth. Excess of assets over liabilities.

Capital Investment—Commitment or use of money and other assets made in anticipation of greater financial returns in the future, usually involving large sums of money.

Capital Spending—Involves risk-return tradeoff analysis to secure long-term financial advantage.

Career Development—Attempts to match the person's abilities and interests to the person's position and career plan, with a focus on professional growth and enhancement of the work role.

Career Pathing—A planned sequence of job assignments, usually involving growth-oriented tasks and experiences, which people assume in preparation for future job opportunities.

Case Studies—In-depth accounts of an event or situation presented in story form and designed to seek justifiable answers or solutions to problems or opportunities. Length may vary from one page to several hundred pages. Traditionally, learning tools rather than tools for implementing performance improvement. Participants may analyze the case individually, then discuss and analyze it as a group.

Cash-Flow Analysis—Provides information about inflows and outflows of cash during a specific period of time.

Cash-Flow Forecast—A financial tool used by organizations and banks considering loan applications to analyze cash inflow and outflow cycles.

Cause Analysis—The process of determining the root cause of past, present, and future performance gaps.

Change Management—Involves problem solving in a concerted effort to adapt to changing organizational needs.

Certified Performance Technologist (CPT)—Designation that the person applies performance technology or performance improvement principles and processes and has met the rigorous International Society for Performance Improvement (ISPI) Human Performance Technology (HPT) standards and code of ethics and been judged by highly trained reviewers.

Certified School Improvement Specialist (CSIS)—Designation for a person who has demonstrated adherence to International Society for Performance Improvement (ISPI) school improvement standards and code of ethics. The only proficiency-based credential for professionals engaged in improving student, teacher, and school leader performance.

Classroom Learning—Education or training delivered by a live instructor to a group of learners at a location separated from the actual work site.

Coaching—Assistance that managers give employees by evaluating and guiding on-the-job performance or a more accomplished person provides to a novice to help him or her improve what he or she does or says. Organizational coaching helps employees gain competencies and overcome barriers to improving performance. Involves one-on-one suggestions related to observable workplace situations, usually by a supervisor or manager. Can be formal and planned, or spontaneous and provided on the spot. Builds on the assumption that most employees are eager to do well, please their managers, and achieve positions in an organization.

Cognitive Ergonomics—The study of the impact of the physical/sensory environment on mental (cognitive) aspects of work processes.

Collaboration—Cooperation by working together for an improved quality of work life. Also cooperating with others to achieve a desired output or outcome. Working creatively together toward a common goal.

Communication—The transfer of meaning between sender and receiver.

Communication Networks—The patterns that form when messages move from sender to receiver. Illustrate the relationships and interactions between and among individuals and organizations. Either formal or informal and flow in a variety of directions, for example, top down, bottom up, or horizontally. Influence job performance and job satisfaction.

Communities of Professional Practice—Individuals who join together with a specific and genuine shared interest in a discipline, a field of study, or some other organizing format to think about and share ideas, collaborate with one another, and learn from each other's contributions, successes, and failures.

Compensation—Pay for work and performance, plus disability income; deferred income; health, accident, and liability protection; loss-of-job income; and continuation of spouse's income when there is a loss due to a person's relocation.

Competencies—Those characteristics or capabilities of an individual that result in successful job performance, including knowledge, skills, abilities, behavior, accomplishment, performance outcomes, motivation, determination, and proper attitude for the tasks involved.

Competency Testing—Examines current job knowledge and skills that will be needed for present and future performance. In an employment test are representative of job tasks and equipment that are actually part of the job. Proximity to the real job is critical for the test to be legally sound.

Confirmative Evaluation—Provides information about the continuing competence and effectiveness of people to explain, confirm, or demonstrate the value of the performance intervention over time.

Conflict—A natural condition that evolves when an individual, group, or organization holds and expresses opinions or ideas that do not match those of another individual, group, or organization. Can range from a resolvable difference of opinion to all-out war, depending on the degree of collaboration that is supported by the environment.

Conflict Resolution—Alleviating a disagreement between two or more people who share differing views. Also called dispute resolution.

Content Management System (CMS)—A collaborative space within a secure Internet connection; allows access to digital files from practically anywhere.

Continuous Improvement—The ongoing, organization-wide framework in which stakeholders (employees, customers, and suppliers) are committed to and involved in monitoring and evaluating all aspects of a company's activities (inputs, process, and outputs) to continuously improve them.

Corporate Universities—A strategic learning structure for developing and educating employees, customers, and suppliers in order to accomplish business goals and strategies.

Cost Center—A center charged with managing costs; has neither revenue budget nor obligations to earn revenues.

Cost Targets—The maximum amount an organization can pay for a product or service and still make a profit or remain within budget parameters.

Cultural Intelligence—Global conscientiousness; ability to understand cultural background; accept and adapt to national, ethnic, vocational, and other differences.

Culture—A shared system of values, beliefs, and behaviors that characterize a group of organization.

Culture Audit—An analysis procedure that focuses on the world view, workers, work processes, and workplace, and answers the question "How do we think about things or do things in our organization?"

Dashboards—Business intelligence tools that display performance indicators, present data and information at both summary and detailed levels, and assist decision-makers employing them to act on the information they present.

Decision Making—Making choices, ideally based on structured problem solving.

Design—A plan or outline to accomplish goals and purpose based on evidence and analysis. Degree of detail depends on the situation, such as prototypes and storyboards.

Development—Elaboration or fulfillment of design; creation, organization, and production of techniques and activities, including field and pilot testing.

Dispute Resolution—Alleviating a disagreement between two or more people who share differing views.

Distance Learning—A system for delivering instruction to learners who are separated by time and/or space. Also known as distance education, distance training, and teletraining. Uses a variety of print (yes, print), computer, and telecommunication technologies.

Distributed Learning—A form of distance learning that adapts to and supports the expressed needs of the learner. While the terms distance learning and distributed learning often are used synonymously, there are operational distinctions between the two. For example, distributive learning has a just-in-time, just-for-me orientation.

Diversity—Represents differences in gender, ethnicity, economic background, age, abilities, religion, culture, and sexual orientation. Many are known as "protected categories" in U.S. employment legislation and executive orders.

Documentation (Job Specifications) and Standards—Codify information to preserve it and to make it accessible in the workplace through descriptions, policies, procedures, guidelines, reference manuals, quality assurance plans, bylaws, articles of incorporation, partnership agreements, contracts, and letters of intent.

Economies of Scale—The cost savings that result when goods and services are produced in large volume or purchased and consumed in large volume.

Education—Improves work performance in a focused direction beyond the person's current job. Emphasis on broad knowledge, understanding, comprehension, analysis, synthesis, and evaluation, and on transferring knowledge to future objectives, as well as to immediate job applications. Also preparing youth and others to be productive citizens through traditional and non-traditional academic approaches.

Electronic Performance Support System (EPSS)—A highly sophisticated job aid, offering access to large databases of information designed to coach users via a user-friendly question-and-answer format. Example is the help function in software.

Emotional Intelligence (EI)—The ability to identify, assess, monitor, and control emotions of self to guide thinking and impact effective actions of others.

Employee Development—Acquiring knowledge, skills, and attitudes through employer-sponsored learning opportunities, including (1) traditional instruction, (2) technology-oriented formats, (3) informally by means of mentoring coaching, or on-the-job training, and (4) by team participation.

Employee Selection—Choosing the right person for the job.

Empowerment—Enabling people to work to their highest levels by believing in themselves and establishing processes and systems that support their efforts.

Enterprise Learning—Any system that delivers instruction that is critical to the entire organization and must be disseminated to a large number of people dispersed over a wide geographic area.

Environmental Analysis—The process used to identify and prioritize the realities that support actual performance: organizational environment, world, workplace, work, workers.

Environmental Scanning—A strategic planning technique for monitoring trends in the external environment of an organization. Involves observing, assessing, and documenting economic situations, political events, technical developments and structural changes in similar organizations or industries.

Environment Support Analysis—Seeks to define causes related to information (data, information, and feedback), instrumentation (environmental support, resources, and tool), and motivation (consequences, incentives, and rewards).

Ergonomics—The study of how physical laws of nature affect the worker and the work environment. Primary focus is the design or redesign of machines and tools to match the physical ability of the employee to use and react to the tools or machinery required for a job or task. Assessing and improving user friendliness and environmental factors, such as noise and lighting.

Ethics—Defines good and bad standards of conduct. Culturally based and vary among countries, companies, incidents, and situations.

Evaluation—Systemic and systematic methodology to determine merit, worth, significance, or value based on goals and standards.

Executive Development—Enhances senior management's ability to create vision, values, and business strategies.

Expectations—What the organization and other stakeholders think or perceive will happen as a result of the performance improvement intervention. May or may not match reality.

Expert Systems—Fall under the computer applications category of artificial intelligence. Composed of a knowledge base, an inference system, and a human machine interface.

Explicit Knowledge—Recorded information, for example, a written policy or procedure.

Feasibility—Determine whether effort or project can be successfully accomplished based on consideration of economic, legal, technical, cost-benefit, and scheduling issues, that is, logical and likely to succeed.

Feedback—Information provided by others designed to help people adjust their behavior, continue successful performance, or establish goals.

Financial Forecasting—Anticipating the future needs for money and resources.

Financial Systems—Monetary affairs (income, reserves, expenses, and dividends) of an organization, usually summarized in an annual report that includes an income statement, balance sheet, cash-flow statement, and explanatory notes.

Force Field Analysis—A theory of change developed by Kurt Lewin as a way to see what is happening in an organization by reflecting the forces, driving and restraining, at work at a particular time. Select forces to add or remove in order to create change.

Forecasting—Anticipating the future using quantitative techniques, such as mathematical and statistical rules and analysis of past data to predict the future, plus qualitative techniques, such as expert judgment and opinions to validate or adjust predictions.

Formative Evaluation—Conducted to improve the design, development, and implementation of performance interventions. Begins during the performance analysis, continues through the selection, design, and development of interventions, and may extend into early intervention implementation. Purpose is to improve the inputs, processes, outputs, and outcomes of the phases.

Full-Scope Evaluation—Concept that views evaluation as an integral part of the life cycle of a performance improvement intervention. Includes formative, summative, confirmative, and meta evaluation.

Games—Activities for two or more participants that contain elements of competition and fun. Frequently used in connection with training teams to solve problems and make decisions. May bring an element of familiarity to the training by emulating popular board games or TV game shows.

Gap Analysis—Describes the difference between current results and consequences and desired results and consequences.

Globalization—A means of achieving higher productivity and efficiency by identifying and focusing on an organization's efforts and resources in major world markets.

"Goodness"—A term used by ISD practitioners in the military to describe the quality of a process or product using *bad, good, better, best* as the descriptors.

Green Workplace—Devoted to environmentally-sensitive green business initiatives and practices; creates a climate of environmental awareness.

Grievance Systems—Provide mechanisms for people in unions to dispute a decision that is believed to be in violation of a contract.

Health and Wellness—Programs designed to enhance employee morale and productivity and reduce absentee rates and healthcare costs.

Human Factors—An interdisciplinary approach in which machine and person are consciously linked to produce results. (See Ergonomics.)

Human Performance Technology (HPT)—Analyzes performance problems and their underlying causes and describes exemplary performance and success indicators. Identifies or designs interventions, implements them, and evaluates the results. A systematic process of linking business goals and strategies with the workforce responsible for achieving the goals.

Human Resource Development (HRD)—Organized formal or informal activities within an organization designed to enhance human capital and improve individual or organizational performance or personal growth, such as career development, training, coaching, or mentoring.

Human Resource Development (HRD) Interventions—Conscious, deliberate, planned talent management, individual growth, and organizational growth activities designed to improve organizational and human performance and solve workplace problems.

Human Resource Management—A subcategory of human resources that refers to interventions such as staffing, compensation, retirement planning, health and wellness, and employee development.

Human Resources—The people aspects of organizations.

Implementation—Execution or fulfillment of a plan or design; putting into action.

Incentives—Tangible incentives link pay with a standard for performance, such as salary, differential pay, allowances, time off with pay, deferred income, and so forth. Intangible incentives include promotions, more attractive work assignments, conference participation, committee assignments, or situations such as pizza parties and more.

Inclusion Strategies—Refer to the degree to which the culture respects and values diversity and is open to anyone who can perform a job, regardless of diverse attributes.

Income Statement—Shows all the revenues and costs with net income resulting as revenues minus costs.

Indirect (Support) Functions—Those organizational units that support and enable the direction operations to occur.

Individual Growth—A sub-category of human resources that focuses on the organizational need to encourage and retain high-performance employees.

Information Systems—The varied manual and automated communication mechanisms within an organization that store, process, disseminate, and sometimes even analyze information for those who need it.

In-House—Products or services that are designed and developed for the organization by an individual or team within the organization. May or may not be made available to other organizations after they are developed and implemented.

Inputs—Resources (money, people, time, materials) required to implement a process.

Instructional Performance Support System (PSS)—Helps workers initiate new performance or changes their actual performance until that performance is equal to or better than desired performance. May also support or replace learning interventions.

Interactive Technologies—Provide a channel for interactions between learner and instructor.

Interface Design—The linkage between machinery (mainly computer) and processes to ensure smooth and easy, user-friendly functionality.

Interventions—Conscious, deliberate, planned activities designed to improve organizational performance and human performance and to solve workplace problems. Can be targeted at society, organizations, departments, work groups, and individuals.

Intervention Components—Aspects or parts of an intervention element. Sometimes, the terms *component* and *element* are used interchangeably to refer to the aspects or parts of an intervention category.

Intervention Elements—Aspects or parts of the intervention that must be in place to create a complete intervention.

Job Aids (also known as Performance Support Tools or PST)—Provide just-in-time, on-the-job, and just-enough information to enable a worker to perform a task efficiently and successfully without special training or reliance on memory. May inform, support procedures, or support decisions.

Job Analysis—A formal way of evaluating job requirements by looking at the job itself and at the kind of person needed to complete the job successfully. Collects information about duties, tasks, and responsibilities for specific jobs. Identifies, lists, and describes the tasks (job description) and performances (job specifications) required for successful completion of the job.

Job Analysis Interventions—Include the analysis process itself, plus the outputs of the process: job descriptions, and job specifications.

Job Description—A written statement documenting the tasks and functions of a job. Includes what is done on the job, how it is done, and under what conditions.

Job Design—The process of putting tasks together to form complete jobs. Job designers must consider how tasks are performed, the relationship of the job to organizational work, and employee-related issues such as challenge and empowerment.

Job Enrichment—A job design option that makes a job more rewarding and satisfying by adding tasks (horizontal job enrichment) or responsibilities (vertical job enrichment).

Job Rotation—A form of job enlargement that occurs when employees do numerous and entirely different jobs on a flexible, revolving schedule without disrupting the workflow. Usually involves cross-training.

Job Specifications—A list of the minimum qualifications a person must possess in order to perform a specific job successfully.

Joint Ventures—When two or more organizations join forces for a common purpose, such as exploring new technologies, pursuing new markets, generating new products, and others.

Just-in-Time Learning—A training design that takes place just before or concurrent with the trainee's need to use a specific knowledge or skill; can be real-time or virtual learning.

Key Performance Indicators (KPIs)—Quantitative performance measures that define the critical success factors of an organization, help the organization measure progress toward its goals and objectives, and identify areas for organizational performance and improvement.

Knowledge Capture and Management—The process of acquiring, storing, and managing access to bodies of data, information, knowledge, and organizational experience that assist people in performing their jobs with efficiency and precision.

Labor Relations—The system of continuous relationships that exists between workers and management in regard to employee fair treatment, working conditions, wages, and other issues.

Leadership Development—Prepares employees to cope with changes through prioritizing, overcoming obstacles and assumptions, and initiating action.

Lean Organization—Maximizes customer or shareholder value while minimizing waste, thus creating more value with fewer resources using customary improvement approaches.

Learning Management System (LMS)—Software system used to manage and deliver learning content and resources to learners. Generally web-based and provide any time and anywhere access.

Learning Organization—Values and supports continuous improvement and lifelong learning for all members of the organization and aligns learning with the achievement of business goals. Considered a competitive strategy and a broad, long-term intervention to achieve continuous improvement. The belief and practice that individuals and teams can learn continuously and cooperatively to foster an organization's competitive advantage. Hallmarks: sharing the organizational vision, individual excellence, team learning, creating common mental models, and use of systems thinking.

Learning Technologies—Methods or media that are designed and used to present information to learners: instructor-led classroom and distance learning. Delivery systems use computer technologies and wired or wireless telecommunication technologies to enable and enhance learning.

Localization—The process of customizing and adapting a global application for a particular culture and locale.

Management Development—Prepares managers to support the organization's mission, strategy, goals, and objectives.

Measurement—Systematically determining or estimating dimension, quantity, and capacity in order to assign value.

Mentoring—The offering of experience, emotional support, and guidance by an experienced person to a less experienced person.

Mergers—When two separate organizations combine operations and become one company.

Meta Evaluation—The process of evaluating formative, summative, and confirmative evaluation by literally investigating the evaluation processes, products, and outcomes to take a close look at what happened and why.

Milestones—A project management term to describe points along a timeline when a delay or lag in meeting the milestone deadline would impact other project activities and/or the results of the project. Represent sub-goals or special events along the process of accomplishing the desired outcome.

Motivation—Encourages behavior; the desire to accomplish tasks; can be intrinsic or extrinsic.

Networking—Establishing patterns of interpersonal communication interactions to facilitate the dissemination and collection of information.

Non-Technical Learning—Soft-skills learning designed to change attitudes rather than to gain knowledge or skills. Non-technical also includes general skills not specific to any job, such as leadership, communications, project management, report writing, and so forth.

Off-the-Shelf—Products or services that are prepared by and purchased from external vendors or consultants and are available to a variety of clients. May be customized to suit a specific situation.

Online Learning—A system for delivering instruction to learners using Internet or intranet technology. Also called web-based learning, web-based training, e-learning, or distance learning.

On-the-Job Learning or Training (OJT)—A strategy to train new employees; defined by time, place, resources; can be formal or informal. Occurs on the job with someone experienced teaching the new person or the person being cross-trained how to accomplish the particular job task.

Open Book Management—When everyone in the organization helps the business make money. Financial status fully shared and employees are active participants in financial performance.

Operations—The direct functions that are the lifeblood of the organization.

Operations Management—The direction, coordination, and control of the inputs (raw materials), throughputs (whatever is done to the raw materials), and outputs (whatever is produced).

Organization—A collection of people working together to achieve a common purpose and a specific set of objectives.

Organizational Analysis—Examines the organizational mission, vision, values, goals, strategies, and critical issues.

Organizational Communication—Refers to the transfer of information and knowledge among employees, suppliers, and customers for the purpose of accomplishing efficiency and effectiveness.

Organizational Design and Development—A process that examines the operation and management of an organization and facilitates needed change in an effort to improve efficiency and competitiveness.

Organizational Growth—A sub-category of human resources that addresses the organizational need for long-term success.

Organizational Values—Help people succeed by supporting the "right" decisions, maximizing the significance of employee, supplier, customer, and client, encouraging workers to think globally, and treating people with respect and trust.

Outcomes—The results of a process.

Outputs—The end product of a process.

Outsourcing—The process of contracting out or transferring responsibility for an area of work that had been or often is performed inside the organization.

Overhead—Organizational functions and activities that do not contribute directly to revenue.

Partnerships or Partnering—Working with other involved individuals and groups to accomplish performance improvement efforts.

Performance Analysis—Identifies and clarifies a problem or performance gap by focusing on three areas: desired performance state, actual performance state, and gap between desired and actual performance. Looks at three levels—world (society, culture, social responsibility), workplace (organization, resources, tools, stakeholders, and competition), work (work flow, procedures, responsibilities, and ergonomics) and worker (knowledge, skill, capacity, motivation, and expectations).

Performance Appraisal—A structured process used by managers to provide feedback on an individual's performance to encourage improvement. Also provide information for salary decisions and promotions.

Performance Improvement (PI)—Analyzes performance problems and their underlying causes, looks at opportunities and challenges, and describes exemplary performance and success indicators. Identifies or designs interventions, implements them, and evaluates the results. The systematic process of linking business goals and strategies with the workforce responsible for achieving the goals.

Performance Intervention Package—Includes all the elements and components (processes, media, and materials) required to implement a performance improvement intervention. (See also Elements and Components.)

Performance Objectives—Statements of the desired knowledge, skill, or attitude changes the individual should achieve and be able to apply as a result of the performance improvement intervention. Includes required inputs, process for achieving the change, outputs or proofs that change has occurred, outcomes or results, conditions that affect the process, and the consequences of success or failure.

Performance Standards—Concise statements that serve as a gauge for measuring accomplishment. Set by the organization, the industry, workers, and/or government or other regulatory agencies to guide the performer and evaluate the performance outputs and outcomes.

Performance Support Interventions—Affect the workplace, the work, and worker through planned change efforts based on knowledge and skills transfer. Can be instructional (when the problem is a result of a lack of knowledge) or non-instructional (to improve individual, group, or team performance; improve processes, products, and services; and guide business plans, deliverables, results, and success measures).

Performance Support Systems (PSS)—Integrate learning and doing and technology to help workers obtain the knowledge or skill they need to initiate new performance or improve existing performance. Support the performer on the job and just in time. May replace or enhance training.

Performance Technology—The science and art of improving people, processes, and performance.

Personal Development Interventions—Planned work-related activities that are the employee's personal responsibility. Individuals assume ownership of their success or failure.

Preventive Maintenance—A proactive approach to equipment maintenance to avert breakdowns and failures.

Pro-Action—Thinking ahead, planning for the future with creativity and commitment, and understanding the economic, political, and social climate sufficiently to inspire employee confidence.

Problem Solving—A structured process of defining the problem, gathering data about the situation and causes, considering alternatives, making choices, implementing choices, evaluating the new situation, and making adjustments based on evaluation.

Process—Activities conducted to accomplish a job, activity, or task.

Process Consulting—Results in revising processes and often involves reengineering or restructuring an entire organization.

Profit (Revenue) Center—A center charged with controlling costs and generating revenues; has an expense and a revenue budget.

Quality—The predetermined standard of excellence that may be applied to a product or service to measure how closely the product or service conforms to the standard and satisfies the customer.

Quality Control, Management, and Assurance—The system used to ensure products and services meet customer needs and exceed customer expectations. Also known as Total Quality Management (TQM).

Quality Improvement—Conducting business right the first time and every time.

Realignment—Helping the organization focus on its core competencies.

Reengineering—The radical redesign of processes for the purpose of extensive (not gradual) performance improvements.

Repertory of Behavior Analysis—Examines people-oriented factors that cause performance problems related to information (skills and knowledge), instrumentation (individual capacity), and motivation (motivation and expectation). Term developed by Thomas Gilbert and referred to as individual factors under cause analysis in the Performance Improvement/HPT Model.

Request for Proposal (RFP)—A detailed document sent to vendors early in the procurement process asking them to submit a proposal to supply a given product, program, or service.

Responsibility Center—Units, locations, or areas within an organization where costs occur and where costs are assigned.

Restructuring—Reorganizes the units or departments, usually resulting in a new organizational chart, new responsibilities, and may involve new reporting relationships.

Retention—Encourages employees to remain with an employer due to systematic efforts to create and foster positive policies and practices meeting the diverse needs of the workforce.

Retirement Planning—Helps people prepare for financial and legal issues, housing arrangements, and health and wellness following their working years.

Review-Revise-Approve Cycle—Used to gain feedback and required approval for the elements and components of a performance improvement package.

Rewards—Designed to change or reinforce behavior through techniques such as public recognition, gift certificates, or vacations and travel based on meeting sales quotas. Should be monetary or non-monetary incentives and not only used for quotas.

Safety Engineering—Continually evaluating materials and processes to eliminate or minimize hazards and conditions that cause accidents.

School Improvement—Efforts and outcomes of initiatives and projects that result in increased achievement scores, scholarship, preparation for citizenship, or general well-being and operation of schools. Elements or indicators of success or increase based on such factors as educational settings, curriculum, instruction, or learning environment.

Security Management—Policies, standards, procedures, and guidelines to protect assets, intellectual and physical property, and ensure safety.

Scope—The range of features and functions that categorize a performance improvement intervention.

Selection—Predicting the best candidate for a job. Involves such things as reviewing applications and résumés, interviewing and screening candidates, and making a final offer. (See also Intervention Selection.)

Self-Directed Learning—Learning designed to master material independently and at the person's own pace.

Simulations—Highly interactive experiential learning activities that mirror reality and allow participants to manipulate equipment or situations to practice a task, for example, land a plane, troubleshoot electrical circuits, or decide how to handle a dispute between two employees. Useful when training requires a show-and-do approach and it is impossible to do it in the real world because of excessive costs or safety factors. Range in complexity from paper-based to computer-based simulations; from simple linear video to interactive video; from role plays to sophisticated digital simulators.

Six Sigma—A systematic quality improvement process used on both the production and transactional sides of the business to design, manufacture, and market goods and services that customers may desire to purchase.

Social Intelligence(SI)—The ability to get along with others. Combines sensitivity to the needs and interests of others and practical skills of interacting with them.

Social Learning—Learning from each other. Capacity to observe, analyze, and understand social relationships through awareness, imitation, modeling, and acting wisely.

Social Media—Use of web-based and mobile technology to communicate and share content. Includes the use of tweets, blogs, texting, email, multimedia messages, and a constantly expanding suite of Web 2.0 and higher, plus mobile applications.

Social Responsibility—A genuine interest and concern for the well-being of individuals, to plan, think, do, and act in a socially responsible way, and be a sensitive team member in personal and professional relationships.

Staffing—The human resource management function that anticipates and fills open positions in organizations.

Stakeholders—Individuals or groups who will be affected by the results of a performance improvement intervention.

Standards—The principles or criteria for consistent, ultimate, superior performance outcomes or for how individuals and organizations conduct themselves (ethics). (See also Performance Standards.)

Statement of Cash Flow—Shows sources of all funds the organization acquires and how the funds are used.

Strategic Management—Supports the organizational vision through the day-to-day implementation of the strategic plan.

Strategic Planning—The process by which an organization envisions its future and develops the necessary goals and procedures to achieve that vision.

Succession Planning—A systematic identification and development of employees, usually for senior management positions.

Suggestions Systems—Allow employees to increase workplace responsibility and accountability by offering ideas for improving products or services. Rewards often provided for suggestions that bring positive results to the organization.

Summative Evaluation—Measures the effectiveness, efficiency, impact, and value of the *immediate* reaction, knowledge, skills, attitude change, and/or application of the intervention.

Supervisory Development—Prepares trainers, advisers, mentors, facilitators, coaches, leaders, behavioral specialists, and others in critical competencies of a conceptual, interpersonal, technical, and political nature. Enables front-line managers to establish work standards and enforce organizational policies and procedures primarily for non-management employees.

Sustainability—A situation or object that endures over time. The extent to which an environment or program's legacy is successfully institutionalized.

SWOT Analysis—An analysis process highlighting strengths, weaknesses, opportunities, and threats to an entity.

System—Connecting aspects of a complex whole; interconnectedness; interdependence.

Systemic—Affecting the entire situation as a whole instead of concentrating on the individual components or parts.

Systematic—Methodical or step-by-step procedures; acting according to plan; repeatable.

Synthesis—Combining unique elements or parts in new ways, creating a different coherent whole.

Tacit Knowledge—Knowledge that resides in people's heads. Also referred to as know-how, rules of thumb, or heuristics.

Talent Management—Focuses on core business functions (staffing, employee development, retention of employees, compensation and benefits, health and wellness, retirement planning, and labor relations). Requires a new mindset and a new way of thinking to achieve business success.

Team—A group of people working together as a cohesive unit to accomplish a common goal.

Team Strategies—The methods that people who are in a team experience and work out in advance for accomplishing the objective at hand.

Team Building—Based on the philosophy that people work better and more creatively in groups than they do alone. Focuses on trust, collaboration, openness, and other interpersonal factors.

Technical Learning—Declarative procedural knowledge and problem solving associated with scientific and practical, job-related activities.

Technique—A procedure used to accomplish a job, activity, or task. Include interview, survey, task analysis, pilot testing, and many others.

Tool—A job aid, document, form, or other print or computer-based material used to help the performance improvement practitioner complete a task. For example, an interview guide and report form are tools for performing an interview during the Performance Analysis phase; (See also Performance Support Tool.)

Toolkit—A collection of tools that the performance improvement practitioner can use to analyze, select, design, develop, implement, and/or evaluate performance improvement interventions.

Total Quality Management—A philosophy and a set of principles that set the stage for a continuously improving organization. (See also Quality Control, Management, and Assurance.)

Training—Refers to instructional experiences often provided by employers to help employees achieve changes in knowledge, skills, or attitude.

Value Chain—Composed of all the stakeholders (designers, suppliers, manufacturers, customers, and others) who add value to or receive value from specific products or services.

Vendors—External consultants or others who provide a variety of products or services to organizations.

Virtual Teams—Teams of people who interact electronically, working in geographically different sites to achieve common organizational goals.

Wiki—A collection of web pages that can be easily created and edited by the individuals who use it.

Work—What the worker must do on the job.

Work Design—A blueprint of job tasks structured to improve organizational efficiency and employee satisfaction.

Work Design Interventions—Include job design (rotation, enlargement, enrichment), human factors (ergonomics, safety engineering, PM) and quality improvement (TQM, continuous improvement).

Workplace Learning and Performance (WLP)—Refers to the integration of learning and other performance interventions to improve human performance and align it with individual and organizational needs.

Work Methods—Documents by which an organization defines what work needs to be done and how it will be accomplished.

About the Authors

Darlene M. Van Tiem, Ph.D., CPT, CPLP, is on the faculty of Capella University, primarily mentoring doctoral dissertations and grading comprehensive examinations. Darlene is associate professor emerita and formerly coordinator of the graduate-level Performance Improvement and Instructional Design Program, School of Education, University of Michigan–Dearborn. Previously, she was the human resources training director at AT&T (Ameritech) Yellow Pages (responsible for Michigan, Ohio, Indiana, and Wisconsin); and previously curriculum manager for the General Motors Technical Curriculum, including training General Motors suppliers. Darlene is a past-president of international ISPI and served on the international board of directors from 2006 to 2011. She was lead author, with James Moseley and Joan Dessinger, of two award-winning ISPI companion books: *Fundamentals of Performance Technology: A Guide to Improving People, Process, and Performance* (2nd ed., 2004) and *Performance Improvement Interventions: Enhancing People and Performance Through Performance Technology* (2001). She has published more than fifty journal articles and presented approximately fifty juried presentations for professional associations. She earned an M.S.A. from Central Michigan University; an M.Ed. from Marygrove College; M.A. from Michigan State University; and a Ph.D. from Wayne State University; and Certificate in Integrated Resource Management (Manufacturing and Production Management) from Oakland University, Graduate School of Business. You may reach Darlene at dvt@umich.edu or darlene .vantiem@capella.edu.

James L. Moseley, Ed.D., LPC, CHES, CPT, is an associate professor at Wayne State University's College of Education Instructional Technology Program. He is a licensed professional counselor in the state of Michigan, a certified health education specialist, and a certified performance technologist. He teaches and advises doctoral students in program evaluation, performance improvement, and curriculum development. He is the recipient of honors and awards, including the 2012 Outstanding Graduate Mentor Award in the Social Sciences, Business, and Education and the 2012 Kathleen Reilly Koory Endowed Faculty Development Award from Wayne State University. He has published and presented in our discipline. Moseley was most recently co-editor of the ISPI/Pfeiffer *Handbook of Improving Performance in the Workplace, Volume 3: Measurement and Evaluation.* He has co-authored six other Pfeiffer/ISPI titles, four of them award-winning. He holds six graduate degrees, including M.A., M.S.L.S., M.Ed., M.S.A., Ed.S., and Ed.D., in addition to certificates in high school teaching, health administration, and gerontology, as well as professional business certificates from Oxford and Harvard. Moseley is a member of ISPI and ASTD and presents at local, regional, national, and international conferences. He can be contacted via email at jmosele@comcast.net.

Joan Conway Dessinger, Ed.D, CPT, is the editor of ISPI's *Performance Improvement Journal.* She is also founder and senior consultant with The Lake Group, a performance improvement consulting firm, and an adjunct faculty member in the Wayne State University Instructional Technology Graduate Program. Joan co-authored *Confirmative Evaluation* (2004) and *Training Older Workers and Learners* (2007) and co-edited *Handbook of Improving Performance in the Workplace, Volume Three: Measurement and Evaluation* (2010) with James Moseley. She also co-authored *Fundamentals of Performance Technology* (2000; 2004) and *Performance Improvement Interventions* (2001) with James Moseley and Darlene Van Tiem. *Fundamentals, Interventions, Confirmative Evaluation,* and *Training Older Workers and Learners* won ISPI Awards for Excellence in Instructional Communication. She was also a contributor to *Distance Training* (1998); *Performance Improvement Intervention: Instructional Design and Training* (1998); *Sustaining Distance Training* (2001); the *2007 Pfeiffer Annual: Training;* and the third edition of *Handbook of Human Performance Technology* (2006). Joan has also been invited to present at local, national, and international conferences. She is a "general practitioner" who has applied all the phases of performance improvement in a variety of sectors from nuclear power to healthcare, from manufacturing to education. Joan's email address is jdesssinger@aol.com or joandessinger@ispi.org

Name Index

Subject Index

Page references followed by *fig* indicate an illustrated figure; followed by *t* indicate a table; followed by *e* indicate an exhibit.